The Stages of the Family Life Cycle

Family Life-Cycle Stage	Emotional Process of Transition: Key Principles	Second-Order Changes in Family Status Required to Proceed Developmentally
Leaving home: single young adults	Accepting emotional and financial responsibility for self	a. Differentiation of self in relation to family of origin b. Development of intimate peer relationships c. Establishment of self in respect to work and financial independence
The joining of families through marriage: the new couple	Commitment to new system	a. Formation of marital system b. Realignment of relationships with extended families and friends to include spouse
Families with young children	Accepting new members into the system	a. Adjusting marital system to make space for children b. Joining in childrearing, financial and household tasks c. Realignment of relationships with extended family to include parenting and grandparenting roles
Families with adolescents	Increasing flexibility of family boundaries to permit children's independence and grandparents' frailties	a. Shifting of parent–child relationships to permit adolescent to move into and out of system b. Refocus on midlife marital and career issues c. Beginning shift toward caring for older generation
Launching children and moving on	Accepting a multitude of exits from and entries into the family system	a. Renegotiation of marital system as a dyad b. Development of adult-to-adult relationships c. Realignment of relationships to include in-laws and grandchildren d. Dealing with disabilities and death of parents (grandparents)
Families in later life	Accepting the shifting generational roles	a. Maintaining own and/or couple functioning and interests in face of physiological decline: exploration of new familial and social role options b. Support for more central role of middle generation c. Making room in the system for the wisdom and experience of the elderly, supporting the older generation without overfunctioning for them d. Dealing with loss of spouse, siblings, and other peers and preparation for death

Why Do You Need this New Edition?

- Revised and clarified presentations of basic theoretical concepts that students have had trouble grasping

- Several new case studies

- New summary of major theoretical concepts (Chapter 4)

- Convenient condensation of the basic concepts of the Bowenian theory (Chapter 5)

- New section on working with common forms of family triangles, e.g., "The Wedding Gift Triangle," in which a husband turns over the relationship with his mother to his new wife (Chapter 5)

- The difference between family structure and process (Chapter 7)

- Updated section on techniques of structural family therapy (Chapter 7)

- Guidelines for production problem-solving conversations (Chapter 10)

- New section on Sex and the Internet (Chapter 11)

- New section on Neuroscience and Relationships (Chapter 11)

- A completely new chapter reviewing research and research methods in family therapy (Chapter 16)

Family Therapy

NINTH EDITION

Family Therapy
CONCEPTS AND METHODS

Michael P. Nichols
College of William and Mary

Foreword by
Salvador Minuchin

PEARSON

Boston   Columbus   Indianapolis   New York   San Francisco   Upper Saddle River
Amsterdam   Cape Town   Dubai   London   Madrid   Milan   Munich   Paris   Montreal   Toronto
Delhi   Mexico City   Sao Paulo   Sydney   Hong Kong   Seoul   Singapore   Taipei   Tokyo

Executive Editor: *Ashley Dodge*
Editorial Assistant: *Carly Czech*
Senior Marketing Manager: *Wendy Albert*
Marketing Assistant: *Kyle VanNatter*
Production Editor: *Karen Mason*
Manufacturing Buyer: *Debbie Rossi*
Cover Administrator: *Joel Gendron*
Editorial Production and Composition Service: *Modern Graphics, Inc.*
Photo Researcher: *PoYee Oster*

Credits appear on page 493, which constitutes an extension of the copyright page.

Allyn & Bacon
is an imprint of

ISBN-10: 0-205-78682-0
ISBN-13: 978-0-205-78682-4

Brief Contents

Contents

2   LESSONS FROM THE EARLY MODELS: GROUP PROCESS AND COMMUNICATIONS ANALYSIS   43

3   BASIC TECHNIQUES OF FAMILY THERAPY   57

14 INTEGRATIVE MODELS 369

15 COMPARATIVE ANALYSIS 389

Major Events in the History of Family Therapy

Social and Political Context	Development of Family Therapy
1945 F.D.R. dies, Truman becomes president World War II ends in Europe (May 8) and the Pacific (August 14)	Bertalanffy presents general systems theory
1946 Juan Perón elected president of Argentina	Bowen at Menninger Clinic Whitaker at Emory Macy Conference
1947 India partitioned into India and Pakistan	
1948 Truman reelected U.S. president State of Israel established	Whitaker begins conferences on schizophrenia
1949 Communist People's Republic of China established	Bowlby: "The Study and Reduction of Group Tensions in the Family"
1950 North Korea invades South Korea	Bateson begins work at Palo Alto V.A.
1951 Julius and Ethel Rosenberg sentenced to death for espionage Sen. Estes Kefauver leads Senate probe into organized crime	Ruesch & Bateson: *Communication: The Social Matrix of Society* Bowen residential treatment of mothers and children Lidz at Yale
1952 Eisenhower elected U.S. president	Bateson receives Rockefeller grant to study communication in Palo Alto Wynne at NIMH
1953 Joseph Stalin dies	Whitaker & Malone: *The Roots of Psychotherapy*
1954 Supreme Court rules school segregation unconstitutional	Bateson project research on schizophrenic communication Bowen at NIMH
1955 Rosa Parks refuses to move to the back of the bus; Martin Luther King, Jr., leads boycott in Montgomery, Alabama	Whitaker in private practice, Altanta, Ga.

	Social and Political Context	*Development of Family Therapy*
1956	Nasser elected president of Egypt Soviet troops crush anti-Communist rebellion in Hungary	Bateson, Jackson, Haley, & Weakland: "Toward a Theory of Schizophrenia"
1957	Russians launch *Sputnik I* Eisenhower sends troops to Little Rock, Ark., to protect school integration	Jackson: "The Question of Family Homeostasis" Ackerman opens the Family Mental Health Clinic of Jewish Family Services in New York Boszormenyi-Nagy opens Family Therapy Department at EPPI in Philadelphia
1958	European Common Market established Charles De Gaulle becomes French premier	Ackerman: *The Psychodynamics of Family Life*
1959	Castro becomes premier of Cuba	MRI founded by Don Jackson
1960	Kennedy elected U.S. president	Family Institute founded by Nathan Ackerman (renamed the Ackerman Institute in 1971) Minuchin and colleagues begin doing family therapy at Wiltwyck
1961	Berlin Wall erected	Bell: *Family Group Therapy* *Family Process* founded by Ackerman and Jackson
1962	Cuban Missile Crisis	Bateson's Palo Alto project ends Haley at MRI
1963	Kennedy assassinated	Haley: *Strategies of Psychotherapy*
1964	Johnson elected U.S. president Nobel Peace Prize awarded to Martin Luther King, Jr.	Satir: *Conjoint Family Therapy* Norbert Wiener dies (b. 1894)
1965	Passage of Medicare Malcolm X assassinated	Minuchin becomes director of Philadelphia Child Guidance Clinic Whitaker at University of Wisconsin
1966	Red Guards demonstrate in China Indira Gandhi becomes prime minister of India	Brief Therapy Center at MRI begun under directorship of Richard Fisch Ackerman: *Treating the Troubled Family*
1967	Six-Day War between Israel and Arab states Urban riots in Cleveland, Newark, and Detroit	Watzlawick, Beavin, & Jackson: *Pragmatics of Human Communication* Dicks: *Marital Tensions*

	Social and Political Context	*Development of Family Therapy*
1968	Nixon elected U.S. president Robert Kennedy and Martin Luther King, Jr., assassinated	Don Jackson dies (b. 1920)
1969	Widespread demonstrations against war in Vietnam	Bandura: *Principles of Behavior Modification* Wolpe: *The Practice of Behavior Therapy*
1970	Student protests against Vietnam War result in killing of four students at Kent State	Masters & Johnson: *Human Sexual Inadequacy* Laing & Esterson: *Sanity, Madness and the Family*
1971	Twenty-Sixth Amendment grants right to vote to eighteen-year-olds	Nathan Ackerman dies (b. 1908)
1972	Nixon reelected U.S. president	Bateson: *Steps to an Ecology of Mind* Wynne at University of Rochester
1973	Supreme Court rules that states may not prohibit abortion Energy crisis created by oil shortages	Center for Family Learning founded by Phil Guerin Boszormenyi-Nagy & Spark: *Invisible Loyalties*
1974	Nixon resigns	Minuchin: *Families and Family Therapy* Watzlawick, Weakland, & Fisch: *Change*
1975	Vietnam War ends	Mahler, Pine, & Bergman: *The Psychological Birth of the Human Infant* Stuart: "Behavioral Remedies for Marital Ills"
1976	Carter elected U.S. president	Haley: *Problem-Solving Therapy* Haley to Washington, D.C.
1977	President Carter pardons most Vietnam War draft evaders	Family Institute of Westchester founded by Betty Carter
1978	Camp David Accords between Egypt and Israel	Hare-Mustin: "A Feminist Approach to Family Therapy" Selvini Palazzoli et al.: *Paradox and Counterparadox*
1979	England's Margaret Thatcher becomes West's first woman prime minister Iranian militants seize U.S. Embassy in Tehran and hold hostages	Founding of Brief Therapy Center in Milwaukee Bateson: *Mind and Nature*
1980	Reagan elected U.S. president U.S. boycotts summer Olympics in Moscow	Haley: *Leaving Home* Milton Erickson dies (b. 1901) Gregory Bateson dies (b. 1904)

	Social and Political Context	*Development of Family Therapy*
1981	Sandra Day O'Connor becomes first woman justice of Supreme Court	Hoffman: *The Foundations of Family Therapy* Madanes: *Strategic Family Therapy* Minuchin & Fishman: *Family Therapy Techniques*
1982	Equal Rights Amendment fails ratification Falklands war	Gilligan: *In a Different Voice* Fisch, Weakland, & Segal: *Tactics of Change* *The Family Therapy Networker* founded by Richard Simon
1983	U.S. invades Grenada Terrorist bombing of Marine headquarters in Beirut	Doherty & Baird: *Family Therapy and Family Medicine* Keeney: *Aesthetics of Change*
1984	Reagan reelected U.S. president U.S.S.R. boycotts summer Olympics in Los Angeles	Watzlawick: *The Invented Reality* Madanes: *Behind the One-Way Mirror*
1985	Gorbachev becomes leader of U.S.S.R.	de Shazer: *Keys to Solution in Brief Therapy* Gergen: "The Social Constructionist Movement in Modern Psychology"
1986	Space shuttle *Challenger* explodes	Anderson et al.: *Schizophrenia and the Family* Selvini Palazzoli: "Towards a General Model of Psychotic Family Games"
1987	Congress investigates the Iran–Contra affair	Tom Andersen: "The Reflecting Team" Guerin et al.: *The Evaluation and Treatment of Marital Conflict* Scharff & Scharff: *Object Relations Family Therapy*
1988	George H. W. Bush elected U.S. president	Kerr & Bowen: *Family Evaluation* Virginia Satir dies (b. 1916)
1989	The Berlin Wall comes down	Boyd-Franklin: *Black Families in Therapy*
1990	Iraq invades Kuwait	Murray Bowen dies (b. 1913) White & Epston: *Narrative Means to Therapeutic Ends*
1991	Persian Gulf War against Iraq	Harold Goolishian dies (b. 1924)
1992	Clinton elected U.S. president	Family Institute of New Jersey founded by Monica McGoldrick
1993	Ethnic cleansing in Bosnia Los Angeles police officers convicted in Rodney King beating	Israel Zwerling dies (b. 1917) Minuchin & Nichols: *Family Healing*

	Social and Political Context	Development of Family Therapy
1994	Republicans win majority in Congress Nelson Mandela elected president of South Africa	David and Jill Scharf leave Washington School of Psychiatry to begin the International Institute of Object Relations Therapy
1995	Oklahoma City federal building bombed	Carl Whitaker dies (b. 1912) John Weakland dies (b. 1919) Salvador Minuchin retires Family Studies Inc. renamed The Minuchin Center
1996	Clinton reelected U.S. president	Edwin Friedman dies (b. 1932) Eron & Lund: *Narrative Solutions in Brief Therapy* Freedman & Combs: *Narrative Therapy*
1997	Princess Diana dies in auto accident Hong Kong reverts to China	Michael Goldstein dies (b. 1930)
1998	President Clinton impeached by House of Representatives	Minuchin, Colapinto, & Minuchin: *Working with Families of the Poor*
1999	President Clinton acquitted in impeachment trial	Neil Jacobson dies (b. 1949) John Elderkin Bell dies (b. 1913) Mara Selvini Palazzoli dies (b. 1916)
2000	George W. Bush elected U.S. president	Millennium Conference, Toronto, Canada
2001	September 11 terrorist attacks	James Framo dies (b. 1922)
2002	Sex abuse scandal in Catholic Church Corporate corruption at Enron	Lipchik: *Beyond Techniques in Solution-Focused Therapy*
2003	U.S. invades Iraq	Greenan & Tunnell: *Couple Therapy with Gay Men*
2004	George W. Bush reelected U.S. president	Gianfranco Cecchin dies (b. 1932)
2005	Hurricane Katrina devastates New Orleans	Steve de Shazer dies (b. 1940)
2006	Democrats regain control of U.S. House and Senate	Minuchin, Nichols, & Lee: *Assessing Families and Couples*
2007	Shootings at Virginia Tech	Jay Haley dies (b. 1923) Lyman Wynne dies (b. 1923) Insoo Kim Berg dies (b. 1934) Albert Ellis dies (b. 1913) Thomas Fogarty dies (b. 1927)
2008	Barack Obama elected U.S. President	Michael White dies (b. 1949)
2009	Worldwide Economic Recession	The Family Institute of Cambridge closes

Foreword

In this volume, Mike Nichols tells the story of family therapy—and tells it very well. It's hard to imagine a more readable and informative guide to the field.

Born in the late 1950s, family therapy seemed to spring fully formed out of the heads of a group of seminal thinkers. Over five decades later, both theory and practice show the uncertainties and doubts that define maturity. But in the beginning—as the storytellers say—there was Gregory Bateson on the West Coast, a tall, clean-shaven, angular intellectual, who saw families as systems, carriers of ideas. On the East Coast was Nathan Ackerman, short, bearded, portly, the quintessential charismatic healer, who saw families as collections of individuals struggling to balance feelings, irrationalities, and desires. Bateson and Ackerman complemented each other perfectly, the Don Quixote and Sancho Panza of the family systems revolution.

For all the diversity of the 1960s that saw the new clinical practice called *family therapy* take a variety of names—systemic, strategic, structural, Bowenian, experiential—there was also a remarkable solidarity in the shared beliefs that defined the field.

As family therapy succeeded and expanded, it was extended to encompass different client populations, with specific interventions for various special groups—clients with drug addictions, hospitalized psychiatric patients, the welfare population, violent families, and so on. All posed their own complexities. Practitioners re-sponded to this expanded family therapy with an array of new approaches, some of which even questioned the fundamental allegiance to systems thinking.

The challenges to systems theory (the official science of the time) took two forms. One was purely theoretical: a challenge to the assumption that systemic thinking was a universal framework, applicable to the functioning of all human collectives. A major broadside came from feminists who questioned the absence of concepts of gender and power in systems thinking and pointed to the distorting consequences of genderless theory when focusing on family violence. The other challenge concerned the connection between theory and practice: a challenge to the imposition of systems theory as the basis for therapeutic practice. The very techniques that once defined the field were called into question. Inevitably, the field began to re-open for examination its old taboos: the individual, intrapsychic life, emotions, biology, the past, and the particular place of the family in culture and society.

As is always characteristic of an official science, the field tried to preserve established concepts while a pragmatic attention to specific cases was demanding new and specific responses. As a result, today we have an official family therapy that claims direct descendence from Bateson and a multitude of excellent practitioners doing sensitive and effective work that is frequently quite different from what systems theory prescribes.

I see the therapeutic process as an encounter between distinct interpersonal cultures. Real respect for clients and their integrity can allow therapists to be other than fearfully cautious, can encourage them to be direct and authentic—respectful and compassionate—but also at times honest and challenging.

This conception of the therapist as an active knower—of himself or herself *and* of the different family members—is very different from the neutral therapist of the constructivists. But, of course, these two prototypes are entirely too simplified. Most practitioners fall somewhere between these two poles of neutrality and decisiveness.

The choice between action and interventionism, on the one hand, and meaning and conversation, on the other, is but one of the questions the field is grappling with today; there are many others. Are the norms of human behavior universal, or are they culturally constructed products of political and ideological constraint? How do we become experts? How do we know what we know? Can we influence people? Can we not influence them? How do we know that we are not simply agents of social control? How do we know that we are accomplishing anything at all?

These questions and the rich history and contemporary practice of family therapy are explored in *Family Therapy: Concepts and Methods*. It is a thorough and thoughtful, fair and balanced guide to the ideas and techniques that make family therapy such an exciting enterprise. Dr. Nichols has managed to be comprehensive without becoming tedious. Perhaps the secret is the engaging style of his writing, or perhaps it is how he avoids getting lost in abstraction while keeping a clear focus on clinical practice. In any case, this superb book has long set the standard of excellence as the best introduction and guide to the practice of family therapy.

Salvador Minuchin, M.D.
Boca Raton, Florida

Preface

One thing that tends to get lost in academic discussions of family therapy is the feeling of accomplishment that comes from sitting down with an unhappy family and being able to help them. Beginning therapists are understandably anxious and not sure they'll know how to proceed. ("How do you get *all of them* to come in?") Veterans often speak in abstractions. They have opinions and discuss big issues—postmodernism, managed care, second-order cybernetics. While it's tempting to use this space to say Important Things, I prefer to be a little more personal. Treating troubled families has given me the greatest satisfaction imaginable, and I hope that the same is or will be true for you.

In this ninth edition of *Family Therapy: Concepts and Methods*, I've tried to describe the full scope of family therapy—its rich history, the classic schools, the latest developments—but with increasing emphasis on practical issues. There are a lot of changes in this edition:

- A new section on sex and the Internet
- A new section on the neuroscience of family relationships
- A new chapter on the role of research in understanding what works best in family therapy

- Revised and clarified presentation of basic theoretical concepts that students have had trouble grasping
- An updated section on the techniques of structural family therapy
- Guidelines for productive problem-solving conversations
- A new summary of theoretical concepts
- Quite a few more case studies
- More consistent emphasis on clinical technique throughout

Albert Einstein once said, "If you want to learn about physics, pay attention to what physicists do, not what they say they do." When you read about therapy, it can be hard to see past the jargon and political packaging to the essential ideas and practices. So in preparing this edition, I've traveled widely to visit and observe actual sessions of the leading practitioners. I've also invited leading practitioners to share some of their best case studies with you. The result is a more pragmatic, clinical focus. I hope you like it.

Acknowledgments

So many people have contributed to my development as a family therapist and to the writing of this book that it is impossible to thank them all. But I would like to single out a few. To the people who taught me family therapy—Lyman Wynne, Murray Bowen, and Salvador Minuchin—thank you.

Some of the people who went out of their way to help me prepare this ninth edition were Yvonne Dolan, Jerome Price, Deborah Luepnitz, William Madsen, David Waters, Frank Dattilio, Vicki Dickerson, Randy Walton, and Salvador Minuchin. To paraphrase John, Paul, George, and Ringo, I get by with *a lot* of help from my friends—and I thank them one and all. I am especially grateful to Carly Czech at Allyn & Bacon for making a hard job easier.

Finally, I would like to thank my postgraduate instructors in family life: my wife, Melody, and my children, Sandy and Paul. In the brief span of forty years, Melody has seen me grow from a shy young man, totally ignorant of how to be a husband and father, to a shy middle-aged man, still bewildered and still trying. My children never cease to amaze me. If in my wildest dreams I had imagined children to love and be proud of, I wouldn't even have come close to children as fine as Sandy and Paul.

M. P. N.

Family Therapy

Introduction

The Foundations of Family Therapy

Leaving Home

There wasn't much information on the intake sheet. Just a name, Holly Roberts, the fact that she was a senior in college, and her presenting complaint: "trouble making decisions."

The first thing Holly said when she sat down was, "I'm not sure I need to be here. You probably have a lot of people who need help more than I do." Then she started to cry.

It was springtime. The tulips were up, the trees were turning leafy green, and purple clumps of lilacs perfumed the air. Life and all its possibilities stretched out before her, but Holly was naggingly, unaccountably depressed.

The decision Holly was having trouble making was what to do after graduation. The more she tried to figure it out, the less able she was to concentrate. She started sleeping late, missing classes. Finally, her roommate talked her into going to the Health Service. "I wouldn't have come," Holly said. "I can take care of my own problems."

I was into cathartic therapy back then. Most people have stories to tell and tears to shed. Some of the stories, I suspected, were dramatized to elicit sympathy. We seem to give ourselves permission to cry only with some acceptable excuse. Of all the human emotions we're ashamed of, feeling sorry for ourselves tops the list.

I didn't know what was behind Holly's depression, but I was sure I could help. I felt comfortable with depressed people. Ever since my senior year in high school when my friend Alex died, I'd been a little depressed myself.

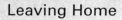

After Alex died, the rest of the summer was a dark blur. I cried a lot—and got mad whenever anybody suggested that life goes on. Alex's minister said that his death wasn't really a tragedy, because now "Alex was with God in heaven." I wanted to scream but I numbed myself instead. In the fall, I went off to college, and, even though it seemed disloyal to Alex, life did go on. I still cried from time to time, but with the tears came a painful discovery. My grief wasn't all for Alex. Yes, I loved him. Yes, I missed him, but his death also provided me the justification to cry about the everyday sorrows in my own life. Maybe grief is always like that. At the time, it struck me as a betrayal. I was using Alex's death to feel sorry for myself.

✧

What, I wondered, was making Holly so sad? In fact, Holly didn't have a dramatic story. Her feelings weren't focused. After those first moments in my office, she rarely cried. When she did, it was more an involuntary tearing up than a sobbing release. She talked about the future and not knowing what she wanted to do with her life. She talked about not having a boyfriend—in fact, she rarely had any dates. She didn't say much about her family. If the truth be told, I wasn't much interested. Back then, I thought home was the place you left in order to grow up.

Holly was suffering and needed someone to lean on, but something made her hold back, as though she didn't feel safe, didn't quite trust me. It was frustrating. I wanted to help.

A month went by and Holly's depression got worse. I started seeing her three times a week, but we weren't getting anywhere. One Friday afternoon, Holly was feeling so despondent that I didn't think she should go back to her dorm alone. I asked her instead to lie down on the couch in my office and, with her permission, I called her parents.

Mrs. Roberts answered the phone. I told her that I thought she and her husband should come to Rochester and meet with me and Holly to discuss the advisability of Holly taking a med-ical leave of absence and going home. Unsure as I was of my authority back then, I steeled myself for an argument. Mrs. Roberts surprised me by agreeing to come at once.

The first thing that struck me about Holly's parents was the disparity in their ages. Mrs. Roberts looked like a slightly older version of Holly; she couldn't have been much over thirty-five. Her husband looked sixty. It turned out that he was Holly's stepfather. They had married when Holly was sixteen.

Looking back, I don't remember much that was said in that first meeting. Both parents were very worried about Holly. "We'll do whatever you think best," Mrs. Roberts said. Mr. Morgan (Holly's stepfather) said they could arrange for a good psychiatrist "to help Holly over this crisis." But, Holly said she didn't want to go home, and she said this with more energy than I'd heard from her in a long time. That was on Saturday. I said that there was no need to rush into a decision, so we arranged to meet again on Monday.

When Holly and her parents sat down in my office on Monday morning, it was obvious that something had happened. Mrs. Roberts's eyes were red from crying. Holly glowered at her and looked away. Mr. Morgan turned to me. "We've been fighting all weekend. Holly heaps abuse on me, and when I try to respond, Lena takes her side. That's the way it's been since day one of this marriage."

The story that came out was one of those sad histories of jealousy and resentment that turn ordinary love into bitter, injured feelings and, all too often, tear families apart. Lena Roberts was thirty-four when she met Tom Morgan. He was a robust fifty-six. The second obvious difference between them was money. He was a stockbroker who'd retired to run a horse farm. She was waitressing to support herself and her daughter. It was a second marriage for both of them.

Lena thought Tom could be the missing father figure in Holly's life. Unfortunately, Lena couldn't accept all the rules Tom felt invited to enforce, and so Tom became the wicked step-father. He made the mistake of trying to take over and, when the predictable arguments ensued, Lena sided with her daughter. There were tears and midnight shouting matches. Twice Holly ran away to a friend's house for a few days. This triangle nearly proved the marriage's undoing, but things calmed down when Holly left for college.

Holly expected to leave home and not look back. She would make new friends. She would study hard and choose a career. She would never depend on a man to support her. Unfortunately, she left home with unfinished business. She hated Tom for the way he picked on her and for the way he treated her mother. He was always demanding to know where her mother was going, who she was going with, and when she would be back. If she was the least bit late, there would be a scene. Why did her mother put up with it?

Blaming Tom was simple and satisfying, but another set of feelings, harder to face, was eating at Holly. She hated her mother for marrying Tom and for letting him be so mean to her. What had her mother seen in him? Had she sold out for a big house and a fancy car? Holly didn't have an answer to these questions; she didn't even allow them into full awareness. Unfortunately, repression doesn't work like locking something in a closet and forgetting about it. It takes a lot of energy to keep unwelcome emotions at bay.

Holly found excuses not to go home much during college. It didn't feel like her home anymore. She buried herself in her studies, but rage and bitterness gnawed at her until, in her senior year, facing an uncertain future, knowing only that she couldn't go home again, she gave in to hopelessness. No wonder she was depressed.

I found the whole story sad. Not knowing about family dynamics and never having lived in a stepfamily, I wondered why they couldn't just try to get along. Why did they have so little sym-pathy for each other? Why couldn't Holly accept her mother's right to find love a second time around? Why couldn't Tom respect the priority of his wife's relationship with her daughter? And why couldn't Lena listen to her daughter's adolescent anger without getting so defensive?

That session with Holly and her parents was my first lesson in family therapy. Family members in therapy talk not about actual experiences but about reconstructed memories that resemble the original experiences only in certain ways. Holly's memories resembled her mother's memories very little, and her stepfather's not at all. In the gaps between their truths, there was little room for reason and no desire to pursue it.

Although that meeting may not have been terribly productive, it did put Holly's unhappiness in perspective. No longer did I think of her as a tragic young woman, all alone in the world. She was that, of course, but she was also a daughter torn between running away from a home she no longer felt part of and being afraid to leave her mother alone with a man she didn't trust. I think that's when I became a family therapist.

To say that I didn't know much about families, much less about techniques for helping them, would be an understatement. But family therapy isn't just a new set of techniques; it's a whole new approach to understanding human behavior—as fundamentally shaped by its social context.

 THE MYTH OF THE HERO

Ours is a culture that celebrates the uniqueness of the individual and the search for an autonomous self. Holly's story could be told as a coming-of-age drama: a young person's struggle to break away from childhood and provincialism, to take hold of adulthood and promise and the future. If she fails, we're tempted to look inside the young adult, the failed hero.

While the unbounded individualism of the hero may be encouraged more for men than women, as a cultural ideal it casts its shadow on us all. Even if Holly cared about connection as much as autonomy, she may be judged by the prevailing image of accomplishment.

We were raised on the myth of the hero: the Lone Ranger, Robin Hood, Wonder Woman. When we got older, we searched out real-life heroes: Eleanor Roosevelt, Martin Luther King, Nelson Mandela. These men and women stood for something. If only we could be a little more like these larger-than-life individuals who seemed to rise above their circumstances.

Only later did we realize that the circumstances we wanted to rise above were part of the human condition—our inescapable connection to our families. The romantic image of the hero is based on the illusion that authentic selfhood can be achieved as an autonomous individual. We do many things alone, including some of our most heroic acts, but we are defined and sustained by a network of human relationships. Our need to worship heroes is partly a need to rise above littleness and self-doubt, but perhaps equally a product of imagining a life unfettered by all those pesky relationships that somehow never quite go the way you want them to.

When we do think about families, it's often in negative terms—as burdens holding us back or as destructive elements in the lives of our patients. What catches our attention are differences and discord. The harmonies of family life—loyalty, tolerance, mutual aid, and assistance—often slide by unnoticed, part of the taken-for-granted background of life. If we would be heroes, then we must have villains.

These days there's a lot of talk about dysfunctional families. Unfortunately, much of this amounts to little more than parent bashing. People suffer because of what their parents did: Their mother's drinking, their father's unreasonable expectations—these are the cause of individuals' unhappiness. Perhaps this is an advance on stewing in guilt and shame, but it's a long way from understanding what really goes on in families.

One reason for blaming family sorrows on the personal failings of parents is that it's hard for the average person to see past individual personalities to the structural patterns that make them a family—a system of interconnected lives governed by strict but unspoken rules.

People feel controlled and helpless not because they are victims of parental folly and deceit but because they don't understand the forces that tie husbands and wives and parents and children together. Plagued by anxiety and depression, or merely troubled and uncertain, some people turn to psychotherapy for help. In the process, they turn away from the irritants that propel them into therapy. Chief among these are unhappy relationships—with friends and lovers and with the family. Our disorders are private ailments. When we retreat to the safety of a synthetic relationship, the last thing we want is to take our families with us. Is it any wonder, then, that when Freud ventured to explore the dark forces of the mind, he locked the family outside the consulting room?

 PSYCHOTHERAPEUTIC SANCTUARY

Psychotherapy was once a private enterprise. The consulting room was a place of healing, yes, but it was equally a sanctuary, a refuge from a troubled and troubling world.

Buffeted about in love and work, unable to find solace elsewhere, adults came to therapy to find satisfaction and meaning. Parents, worried about their children's misbehavior, shyness, or lack of achievement, sent them for guidance and direction. In many ways, psychotherapy displaced the family's role in solving the problems of everyday life.

It's tempting to look back on the days before family therapy and see those who insisted on segregating patients from their families as exponents of a fossilized view of mental disorder, according to which psychiatric maladies were firmly embedded in the heads of individuals.

Considering that clinicians didn't begin treating families together until the mid 1950s, it's tempting to ask "What took them so long?" In fact, there were good reasons for conducting therapy in private.

The two most influential approaches to psychotherapy in the twentieth century, Freud's psychoanalysis and Rogers's client-centered therapy, were both predicated on the assumption that psychological problems arose from unhealthy interactions with others and could best be alleviated in a private relationship between therapist and patient.

Freud's discoveries indicted the family, first as a breeding ground of childhood seduction and later as the agent of cultural repression. If people grew up a little bit neurotic—afraid of their own natural instincts—who should we blame but their parents?

Given that neurotic conflicts were spawned in the family, it seemed natural to assume that the best way to undo the family's influence was to isolate relatives from treatment, to bar their contaminating influence from the psychoanalytic operating room.

Freud discovered that the less he revealed of himself, the more his patients reacted as though he were a significant figure from their families. At first, these *transference* reactions seemed a hindrance, but Freud soon realized that they provided an invaluable glimpse into the past. Thereafter, analyzing transference became the cornerstone of psychoanalytic treatment. This meant that since the analyst was interested in the patient's memories and fantasies, the family's presence would only obscure the subjective truth of the past. Freud wasn't interested in the living family; he was interested in the family-as-remembered.

By conducting treatment in private, Freud safeguarded patients' trust in the sanctity of the therapeutic relationship and thus maximized the likelihood that they would repeat, in relation to the analyst, the understandings and misunderstandings of childhood.

Carl Rogers also believed that psychological problems stemmed from destructive early interactions. Each of us, Rogers said, is born with an innate tendency toward *self-actualization*. Left to our own devices, we tend to follow our own best interests. Because we are curious and intelligent, we explore and learn; because we have strong bodies, we play sports and games; and because being with others brings us joy, we are outgoing, loving, and affectionate.

Unhappily, said Rogers, our instinct for actualization gets subverted by our craving for approval. We learn to do what we think others want, even though it may not be what's best for us.

Gradually, this conflict between self-fulfillment and need for approval leads to denial and distortion of our inner promptings—and even the feelings that signal them. We swallow our anger, stifle our exuberance, and bury our lives under a mountain of expectations.

The therapy Rogers developed was designed to help patients uncover their real feelings. His image of the therapist was that of a midwife—passive but supportive. The Rogerian therapist didn't *do* anything for patients but offered support to help them discover what they needed to do, by providing *unconditional positive regard*. The therapist listened sympathetically, offering understanding and respect. In the presence of such an accepting listener, patients gradually got in touch with their own feelings and inner promptings.

Freud excluded the family from psychoanalysis to help patients feel safe to explore the full range of their thoughts and feelings.

Like the psychoanalyst, the client-centered therapist maintained absolute privacy in the therapeutic relationship to avoid any possibility that patients' feelings might be subverted to win approval. Only an objective outsider could be counted on to provide the unconditional acceptance to help patients rediscover their real selves. That's why family members had no place in the process of client-centered therapy.

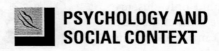

FAMILY VERSUS INDIVIDUAL THERAPY

As you can see, there are valid reasons for conducting psychotherapy in private. Although a strong claim can be made for individual psychotherapy, equally strong claims can be made for family therapy.

Individual psychotherapy and family therapy each offer two things: an approach to treatment and a way of understanding human behavior. Both have their virtues. Individual therapy provides the concentrated focus to help people face their fears and learn to become more fully themselves. Individual therapists have always recognized the importance of family life in shaping personality, but they have assumed that these influences are internalized and that intrapsychic dynamics become the dominant forces controlling behavior. Treatment can and should, therefore, be directed at the person and his or her personal makeup. Family therapists, on the other hand, believe that the dominant forces in our lives are located externally, in the family. Therapy based on this framework is directed at changing the organization of the family. When family organization is transformed, the life of every family member is altered accordingly.

This last point—that changing a family changes the life of each of its members—is important enough to elaborate. Family therapy isn't predicated merely on changing the individual patient in context. Family therapy exerts change on the entire family; therefore, improvement can be lasting because each family member is changed *and* continues to exert synchronous change on each other.

Almost any human difficulty can be treated with either individual or family therapy, but certain problems are especially suited to a family approach, among them problems with children (who must, regardless of what happens in therapy, return home to their parents), complaints about a marriage or other intimate relationship, family feuds, and symptoms that develop in an individual at the time of a major family transition.

If problems that arise around family transitions make a therapist think first about the role of the family, individual therapy may be especially useful when people identify something about themselves that they've tried in vain to change while their social environment remains stable. Thus, if a woman gets depressed during her first year at college, a therapist might wonder if her sadness is related to leaving home and leaving her parents alone with each other. But if the same woman were to get depressed in her thirties, during a long period of stability in her life, we might wonder if there's something about her approach to life that hasn't worked for her. Examining her life in private—away from troubled relationships—doesn't, however, mean that she should believe she can fulfill herself in isolation from other people in her life.

The view of persons as separate entities, with families acting on them, is consistent with the way we experience ourselves. We recognize the influence of other people—especially as obligation and constraint—but it's hard to see that we are embedded in a network of relationships, that we are part of something larger than ourselves.

PSYCHOLOGY AND SOCIAL CONTEXT

Family therapy flourished not only because of its clinical effectiveness but also because we have rediscovered the interconnectedness that characterizes our human community. Ordinarily, the question of individual versus family therapy is posed as a technical one: Which approach works best with a given problem? But the choice also reflects a philosophical understanding of human nature. Although psychotherapy can succeed by focusing on either the psychology of the individual or the organization of the family, both perspectives—psychology and social context—are indispensable for a full understanding of people and their problems.

Family therapists taught us that the family is more than a collection of separate individuals; it is a system, an organic whole whose parts function in a way that transcends their separate characteristics. But even as members of family systems, we don't cease being individuals, with hearts and minds, and wills of our own. Although it isn't possible to understand people without taking into account their social context, notably the family, it is misleading to limit the focus to the surface of interactions—to social behavior divorced from inner experience.

Working with the whole system means not only considering all the members of the family but also the personal dimensions of their experience. Consider a father who smiles despite himself during a discussion of his son's delinquent behavior. Perhaps the smile reveals the father's secret pleasure at the boy's rebelling in a way the father is afraid to. Or take the case of a husband who complains that his wife won't let him spend time with his friends. The wife may indeed voice objections, but the fact that the husband surrenders without a fight suggests that he may be conflicted about having fun. Will negotiating with his wife clear up this man's inner anxieties about doing things on his own? Probably not. If he resolves his own inner constraints, will his wife suddenly start encouraging him to go out and have a good time? Not likely. These impasses, like most human problems, exist in the psychology of individuals and are played out in their interactions. The point is this: To provide effective and lasting psychological help, a therapist needs to understand and motivate individuals *and* influence their interactions.

THINKING IN LINES, THINKING IN CIRCLES

Mental illness has traditionally been explained in linear terms, either medical or psychological. Both paradigms treat emotional distress as a symptom of internal dysfunction with historical causes.

Linear explanations take the form of *A* causes *B*. This type of thinking works fine in some situations. If you're driving along and your car suddenly sputters to a stop, go ahead and look for a simple explanation. Maybe you're out of gas. If so, there's a simple solution. Human problems are usually a bit more complicated.

When things go wrong in relationships, most people generously credit the other person. Because we look at the world from inside our own skins, it's easier to see other people's contributions to our mutual problems. Blaming is only natural. The illusion of unilateral influence tempts therapists too, especially when they hear only one side of a story. But once they understand that reciprocity is the governing principle of relationship, therapists can help people get past thinking in terms of villains and victims.

Suppose, for example, that a father complains about his teenage son's behavior.

Father: It's my son. He's rude and defiant.
Therapist: Who taught him that?

Instead of accepting the father's perspective that he's a victim of his son's villainy, the therapist's provocative question invites him to look for patterns of mutual influence. The point isn't to shift blame from one person to another but to get away from blame altogether. As long as he sees the problem as his son's doing, the father has little choice but to hope that the boy will change. (Waiting for other people to change is like planning your future around winning the lottery.) Learning to think in circles rather than lines empowers the father to look at the half of the equation he can control.

THE POWER OF FAMILY THERAPY

The power of family therapy derives from bringing parents and children together to transform their interactions. Instead of isolating individuals from the emotional origins of their conflict, problems are addressed at their source.

What keeps people stuck is their inability to see their own participation in the problems that plague them. With eyes fixed firmly on what recalcitrant others are doing, it's hard for most people to see the patterns that bind them together. The family therapist's job is to give them a wake-up call. When a husband complains that his wife nags, and the therapist asks how he contributes to her doing that, the therapist is challenging the husband to see the hyphenated him-and-her of their interactions.

When Bob and Shirley came for help with marital problems, her complaint was that he never shared his feelings; his was that she always criticized him. This is a classic trading of complaints that keeps couples stuck as long as they fail to see the reciprocal pattern in which each partner provokes in the other precisely the behavior he or she can't stand. So the therapist said to Bob, "If you were a frog, what would you be like if Shirley changed you into a prince?" When Bob countered that he doesn't talk with her because she's so critical, it seemed to the couple like the same old argument—but the

therapist saw this as the beginning of change— Bob starting to speak up. One way to create an opening for change in rigid families is to support the blamed person and help bring him back into the fray.

When Shirley criticized Bob for complaining, he tried to retreat, but the therapist said, "No, continue. You are still a frog."

Bob tried to shift responsibility back to Shirley. "Doesn't she have to kiss me first?"

"No," the therapist said. "In real life, that comes afterward. You have to earn it."

In the opening of *Anna Karenina*, Tolstoy wrote: "All happy families resemble one another; each unhappy family is unhappy in its own way." Every unhappy family may be unhappy in its own way, but everyone stumbles over the same familiar challenges of family life. It's no secret what these challenges are—learning to live together, dealing with difficult relatives, chasing after children, coping with adolescence, and so on. What not everyone realizes, however, is that, once understood, a relatively small number of systems dynamics illuminate these challenges and enable families to move successfully through the predictable dilemmas of life. Like all healers, family therapists sometimes deal with bizarre and baffling cases, but much of their work is with ordinary human beings learning life's painful lessons. Their stories, and the stories of the men and women of family therapy who have undertaken to help them, are the inspiration for this book.

RECOMMENDED READINGS

Minuchin, S. 1974. *Families and family therapy.* Cambridge, MA: Harvard University Press.

Nichols, M. P. 1987. *The self in the system.* New York: Brunner/Mazel.

Nichols, M. P. 2008. *Inside family therapy,* 2nd ed. Boston: Allyn & Bacon.

The Evolution of Family Therapy

1

A Revolutionary Shift in Perspective

In this chapter, we explore the antecedents and early years of family therapy. There are two fascinating stories here, one of personalities, one of ideas. You will read about the pioneers—visionary iconoclasts who broke the mold of seeing life and its problems as a function of individuals and their psychology. Make no mistake: The shift from an individual to a systemic perspective was a revolutionary one, providing those who grasped it with a powerful tool for understanding and resolving human problems.

The second story in the evolution of family therapy is one of ideas. The restless curiosity of the first family therapists led them to ingenious new ways of conceptualizing the joys and sorrows of family life.

As you read this history, stay open to surprises. Be ready to reexamine easy assumptions—including the assumption that family therapy began as a benevolent effort to support the institution of the family. The truth is, therapists first encountered the family system as an adversary.

 ## THE UNDECLARED WAR

Although we came to think of asylums as places of cruelty and detention, they were originally built to rescue the insane from being locked away in family attics. Accordingly, except for purposes of footing the bill, hospital psychiatrists have long kept families at arm's length. In the 1950s, however, two puzzling developments forced therapists to recognize the family's power to alter the course of treatment.

Therapists began to notice that often when a patient got better, someone else in the family got worse, almost as though the family *needed* a symptomatic member. As in the game of hide-and-seek, it didn't seem to matter who was "It" as long as someone played the part. In one case, Don Jackson (1954) was treating a woman for depression. When she began to improve, her husband complained that she was getting worse. When she continued to improve, her husband lost his job. Eventually, when the woman was completely well, her husband killed himself. Apparently this man's stability was predicated on having a sick wife.

In another of Jackson's cases, a husband urged his wife to seek treatment for "frigidity." When, after several months of therapy, she grew sexually responsive, he became impotent.

Another strange story of shifting disturbance was that patients frequently improved in the hospital only to get worse when they went home. In a bizarre case of Oedipus revisited, Salvador Minuchin treated a young man hospitalized several times for trying to scratch out his own eyes. The man functioned normally in Bellevue but returned to self-mutilation each time he went home. He could be sane, it seemed, only in an insane world.

It turned out that the young man was extremely close to his mother, a bond that grew even tighter during the seven years of his father's mysterious absence. The father was a compulsive gambler who disappeared shortly after being declared legally incompetent. The rumor was that the Mafia kidnapped him. When, just as mysteriously, the father returned, his son began his bizarre attempts at self-mutilation. Perhaps he wanted to blind himself so as not to see his obsession with his mother and hatred of his father.

But this family was neither ancient nor Greek, and Minuchin was more pragmatist than poet. So he challenged the father to protect his son by

beginning to deal directly with his wife, and then he challenged the man's demeaning attitude toward her, which made her seek her son's proximity and protection. The therapy was a challenge to the family's structure and, in Bellevue, working with the psychiatric staff toward easing the young man back into the family, into the lion's den.

Minuchin confronted the father, saying, "As a father of a child in danger, what you're doing isn't enough."

"What should I do?" asked the man.

"I don't know," Minuchin replied. "Ask your son." Then, for the first time in years, father and son began talking to each other. Just as they were about to run out of things to say, Dr. Minuchin commented to the parents: "In a strange way, he's telling you that he prefers to be treated like a young child. When he was in the hospital he was twenty-three. Now that he's returned home again, he's six."

What this case dramatizes is how parents sometimes use their children—as a buffer to protect them from intimacy—*and* how some children accept that role.

To the would-be Oedipus, Minuchin said, "You're scratching your eyes for your mother, so that she'll have something to worry about. You're a good boy. Good children sacrifice themselves for their parents."

What these cases demonstrated was that families are made of strange glue—they stretch but never let go. Few blamed the family for outright malevolence, yet there was an invidious undercurrent to these observations. The official story of family therapy is one of respect for the family, but maybe none of us ever quite gets over the adolescent idea that families are the enemy of freedom.

The impact of a patient's improvement on the family isn't always negative. Fisher and Mendell (1958) reported a spread of positive changes from patients to other family members. Whether the influence patients and their families have on each other is benign or malignant isn't the point. The point is, change in one person changes the system.

 ## SMALL GROUP DYNAMICS

Those who first sought to understand and treat families found a ready parallel in small groups. **Group dynamics** are relevant to family therapy because group life is a complex blend of individual personalities and superordinate properties of the group.

During the 1920s, social scientists began studying natural groups in society in the hope of learning to solve political problems by understanding social interaction in organized groups. In 1920, the pioneering social psychologist William McDougall published *The Group Mind*,

in which he described how a group's continuity depends on the group being an important idea in the minds of its members; on the need for boundaries and structures in which differentiation of function could occur; and on the importance of customs and habits, so that relationships could be fixed and defined. A more scientific approach to group dynamics was ushered in during the 1940s by Kurt Lewin, whose *field theory* (Lewin, 1951) guided a generation of researchers, industrial psychologists, group therapists, and agents of social change.

Drawing on the Gestalt school of perceptual psychology, Lewin developed the notion that the group is more than the sum of its parts. This transcendent property of groups has obvious relevance to family therapists, who must work not only with individuals but also with family systems—and with their famous resistance to change.

Analyzing what he called *quasi-stationary social equilibrium*, Lewin pointed out that change in

The first people to practice family therapy turned to group therapy for a model.

group behavior requires "unfreezing." Only after something shakes up a group's beliefs will its members be prepared to accept change. In individual therapy this process is initiated by the disquieting experiences that lead a person to seek help. Once an individual decides to meet with a therapist, that person has already begun to unfreeze old habits. When families come for treatment, it's a different story.

Many family members aren't sufficiently unsettled by the symptomatic member's predicament to think about changing their own ways. Furthermore, family members bring their primary reference group with them, with its traditions, mores, and habits. Consequently, more effort is required to unfreeze, or shake up, families before real change can take place. The need for unfreezing foreshadowed early family therapists' concern about disrupting family *homeostasis*, a notion that dominated family therapy for decades.

Wilfred Bion was another major student of group dynamics who emphasized the group as a whole, with its own dynamics and structure. According to Bion (1948), most groups become diverted from their primary tasks by engaging in patterns of *fight–flight*, *dependency*, or *pairing*. Bion's basic assumptions are easily extrapolated to family therapy: Some families are so afraid of conflict that they skirt around hot issues like a cat circling a snake. Others use therapy to bicker endlessly, never really contemplating compromise, much less change. Dependency masquerades as therapy when families allow a therapist to subvert their autonomy in the name of problem solving. Pairing is seen in families when one parent colludes with the children to mock and undermine the other parent.

The distinction between **process** and **content** in group dynamics had a major impact on family treatment. Experienced therapists learn to attend as much to *how* families talk as to the content of their discussions. For example, a mother might tell her daughter that she shouldn't play with Barbie dolls because she shouldn't aspire to an image of bubble-headed beauty. The *content* of the mother's message is, Respect yourself as a person, not an ornament. But, if the mother expresses her point of view by disparaging the daughter's wishes, then the *process* of her message is, Your feelings don't count.

Unfortunately, the content of some discussions is so compelling that therapists get sidetracked from the process. Suppose, for example, that a therapist invites a teenager to talk with his mother about wanting to drop out of school. Say the boy mumbles something about school being stupid, and his mother responds with a lecture about the importance of education. A therapist who gets drawn in to support the mother's position may be making a mistake. In terms of content, the mother might be right; a high school diploma can come in handy. But maybe it's more important at the moment to help the boy learn to speak up for himself—and for his mother to learn to listen.

Role theory, explored in the literatures of psychoanalysis and group dynamics, had important applications to the study of families. The expectations that roles carry bring regularity to complex social situations.

We often describe family members in terms of a single role (wife or husband), but we need to remember that a wife may also be a mother, a friend, a daughter, and a career woman. Even roles that aren't currently being performed are potential and therefore important. When members of unhappy families get bogged down in few and rigid roles, they develop interpersonal arthritis, a disease that leads to family rigidity and the atrophy of unused life.

While a narrowing of roles shrinks the possibilities of group (and family) life, group members required to play too many roles are subject to overload (Sherif, 1948). Among the potential roles in a family, for example, are parent, housekeeper, breadwinner, cook, and chauffeur. These roles can be divided—one partner is the breadwinner, the other cooks and cleans—or shared—both work outside the home and divide the other chores. But a person is caught in a role conflict if she's forced to choose between staying late for a staff meeting and going home to cook dinner and drive the kids to soccer practice—because, even though she has a partner, he doesn't play those roles.

Roles tend to be stereotyped in most groups, and so there are characteristic behavior patterns of group members. Virginia Satir (1972) described family roles such as "the placator" and "the disagreeable one" in her book *Peoplemaking*. You may realize that you played a fairly predictable role in your family. Perhaps you were "the helpful child," "the moody one," "the rebel," or "the successful child." The trouble is that such roles can be hard to put aside. Dutifully doing what you're told and patiently waiting for recognition may work for "the good child," but it may not work in a professional career, where assertive action is sometimes called for.

One thing that makes role theory so useful in understanding families is that roles tend to be reciprocal and complementary. Say, for example, that a woman is slightly more anxious to spend time with her boyfriend than he is. Maybe, left to his own devices, he'd call twice a week. But if she calls three times a week, he may never get around to picking up the phone. If their relationship progresses and this pattern is played out, she may always be the pursuer and he the distancer. Or take the case of two parents, both of whom like their children to behave at the dinner table. The father has a slightly shorter fuse—he tells them to quiet down five seconds after they start getting rowdy, whereas his wife would wait half a minute. But if he's always first to speak up, she'll never get a chance. Eventually these parents may become polarized into complementary roles of strictness and leniency. What makes such reciprocity resistant to change is that the roles reinforce each other—and each person waits for the other to change.

Psychoanalytic group therapists regarded the group as a re-creation of the family, with the therapist as parent figure and group members as siblings. Thus, ironically, analytic group therapy, which became one of the prototypes for family treatment, began by treating the group as an ersatz family.

In the group dynamics approach, developed by Foulkes, Bion, Ezriel, and Anthony in Great Britain, the focus shifted from individuals to the group itself, seen as a transcendent entity with its own inherent laws. These therapists studied group interactions not only for what they revealed about individual personalities but also to discover themes or dynamics common to all group members. This *group process* was considered a fundamental characteristic of social interaction and a major vehicle for change.

Experiential group therapy, inspired by existential psychiatrists Ludwig Binswanger, Medard Boss, and Rollo May in Europe and by Carl Rogers, Carl Whitaker, and Thomas Malone in the United States, emphasized deep personal involvement with patients as opposed to the constaints of analytic neutrality. Phenomenology took the place of analysis, and immediate experience, especially emotional experience, was seen as the royal road to personal growth.

Moreno's psychodrama, in which patients act out their conflicts instead of discussing them, was one of the earliest approaches to group treatment (Moreno, 1945). Psychodramas are role-played enactments from the lives of participants, using techniques to stimulate emotional expression and clarify conflicts. Because the focus is on interpersonal action, psychodrama is a powerful vehicle for exploring relationships and resolving family problems. Although psychodrama remained tangential to the mainstream of group therapy, Moreno's role-playing techniques were widely adopted by group leaders and family therapists.

Fritz Perls's Gestalt therapy aims to enhance awareness to increase spontaneity, creativity, and personal responsibility. Although frequently used in groups, Gestalt therapy discourages group members from interacting while one person at a time works with the therapist. Although more widely used in individual treatment, Gestalt techniques have been borrowed by family therapists to stimulate emotional interaction (e.g., Kempler, 1974; Schwartz, 1995).

Given the extensive and diverse procedures for exploring interpersonal relationships developed by group therapists, it was natural that some family therapists would apply group treatment models to working with families. It was a short step from observing a patient's reactions to other members of a group—some of whom might be similar to siblings or parents—to observing interactions in real families. What are families, after all, but collective groups of individuals?

From a technical viewpoint, group and family therapies are similar: Both are complex and dynamic, more like everyday social reality than individual therapy. In groups and families, patients must react to a number of people, not just a therapist, and therapeutic use of this interaction is the definitive mechanism of change in both settings. Consequently, many group and family therapists endeavor to remain relatively decentralized so that patients will interact with each other.

On closer examination, however, we can see that the differences between families and groups are so significant that the group therapy model has only limited applicability to family treatment. Family members have a long history and, more importantly, a future together. Revealing yourself to strangers is safer than exposing yourself to members of your own family. In fact, serious harm can be done by therapists who are so naive as to push family members to always be completely honest and open with each other. There's no taking back rash disclosures that might better have remained private—the affair, long since over, or the admission that a woman *does* care more about her career than about her children. Continuity, commitment, and shared distortions all make family therapy very different from group therapy.

In one of the few small group studies using families, Strodtbeck (1954) tested a variety of propositions derived from groups of strangers and found major differences, which he ascribed to the enduring relationship of family members. Strodtbeck (1958) later substantiated the opinion that family interactions, unlike those in ad hoc groups, can be understood only in terms of the history of the family group.

Therapy groups are designed to provide an atmosphere of warmth and support. This feeling of safety among sympathetic strangers cannot be part of family therapy, because instead of separating treatment from a stressful environment, the stressful environment is brought into treatment. Furthermore, in group therapy, patients can have equal power and status, whereas democratic equality isn't appropriate in families. Someone has to be in charge. Furthermore, the official patient in the family is likely to feel isolated and stigmatized. After all, he or she is "the problem." The sense of protection in being part of a therapeutic group of strangers, who won't have to be faced across the dinner table, doesn't exist in family therapy.

Although group therapy was used as a model for family therapy by some early practitioners, only the process/content distinction and role theory had any lasting impact on the field. One application of group methods that has persisted in family therapy are couples groups, and we will examine this form of treatment in later chapters.

THE CHILD GUIDANCE MOVEMENT

It was Freud who introduced the idea that psychological disorders were the consequence of unsolved problems of childhood. Alfred Adler was the first of Freud's followers to pursue the implication that treating the growing child might be the most effective way to prevent adult neuroses. To that end, Adler organized child guidance clinics in Vienna, where not only children, but also families and teachers were counseled. Adler offered support and encouragement to help alleviate children's feelings of inferiority so they could work out a healthy lifestyle, achieving confidence and success through social usefulness.

In 1909, William Healy founded the Juvenile Psychopathic Institute (later known as the Institute for Juvenile Research) in Chicago, a forerunner among child guidance clinics. In 1917, Healy moved to Boston and established the Judge Baker Guidance Center, devoted to evaluation and treatment of delinquent children.

When the child guidance movement expanded in the 1920s, under a grant from the Commonwealth Fund (Ginsburg, 1955), Rudolph Dreikurs, one of Adler's students, was one of its most effective proponents. In 1924, the American Orthopsychiatric Association was organized to work toward the prevention of emotional disorders in children. Although child guidance clinics remained few in number until after World War II, they now exist in every city in the United States, providing for the study and treatment of childhood problems and the complex social and family forces contributing to them.

Gradually, child guidance workers concluded that the real problem wasn't the obvious one, the child's symptoms, but rather the tensions in the family that were the source of those symptoms. At first there was a tendency to blame the parents, especially the mother.

The chief cause of childhood psychological problems, according to David Levy (1943), was *maternal overprotectiveness*. Mothers who had themselves been deprived of love growing up became overprotective of their children. Some were domineering, others overindulgent. Children of domineering mothers were submissive at home but had difficulty making friends; children with indulgent mothers were disobedient at home but well behaved at school.

During this period, Frieda Fromm-Reichmann (1948) coined one of the most damning phrases in the history of psychiatry, the **schizophrenogenic mother**. These domineering, aggressive, and rejecting women, especially when they were married to passive men, were thought to provide the pathological parenting that produces schizophrenia.

The tendency to blame parents, especially mothers, for problems in the family was an evolutionary misdirection that continues to haunt the field. Nevertheless, by paying attention to what went on between parents and children, Levy and Fromm-Reichmann helped pave the way for family therapy.

Although the importance of the family was recognized, mothers and children were still treated separately, and discussion between therapists was discouraged on the grounds that it might compromise the individual therapeutic relationships. The usual arrangement was for a psychiatrist to treat the child while a social worker saw the mother. Counseling the mother was an adjunct to the primary goal of treating the child. In this model, the family was viewed as an extension of the child, rather than the other way around.

Eventually, the emphasis in the child guidance movement changed from seeing parents as pathogenic to the view that pathology was inherent in the relationships among patients, parents, and significant others. This shift had profound consequences. No longer was psychopathology isolated in individuals; no longer were parents villains and patients victims. Now their interaction was the problem.

John Bowlby's work at the Tavistock Clinic exemplified the transition to a family approach. Bowlby (1949) was treating a teenager and making slow progress. Feeling frustrated, he decided to see the boy and his parents together. During the first half of a two-hour session, the child and parents took turns complaining, each blaming the other. During the second half of the session, Bowlby interpreted to each of them what he thought their contributions to the problem were. Eventually, by working together, all three members of the family developed some sympathy for each other's point of view.

Although he was intrigued by the usefulness of this conjoint interview, Bowlby remained wedded to the one-to-one format. Family meetings might be a useful catalyst but only as a supplement to the *real* treatment, individual psychoanalytic therapy.

What Bowlby began as an experiment, Nathan Ackerman saw to fruition—family therapy as the primary form of treatment. As early as 1938, Ackerman advocated viewing the family as a unit when dealing with disturbance in any of its members (Ackerman, 1938). Subsequently he recommended studying the family as a means of understanding the child—instead of the other way around (Ackerman & Sobel, 1950). Once he saw the need to understand the family in order to diagnose problems, Ackerman soon took the next step—family treatment. Before we get to that, however, let us examine parallel developments in social work and research on schizophrenia that led to the birth of family therapy.

THE INFLUENCE OF SOCIAL WORK

No history of family therapy would be complete without mentioning the enormous contribution of social workers and their tradition of public service. Since the beginning of the profession, social workers have been concerned with the family, both as the critical social unit and as the focus of intervention (Ackerman, Beatman, & Sherman, 1961). Indeed, the core paradigm of social work—treating the person-in-the-environment—anticipated family therapy's ecological approach long before systems theory was introduced.

The field of social work grew out of the charity movements in Great Britain and the United States in the late nineteenth century. Then as now, social workers were dedicated to improving the condition of society's poor and underprivileged. In addition to ministering to clients' basic needs for food, clothing, and shelter, social workers sought to relieve emotional distress and to redress the social forces responsible for extremes of poverty and privilege.

The *friendly visitor* was a caseworker who visited families in their homes to assess their needs and offer help. By bringing helpers out of their offices and into the homes of their clients, these visits helped break down the artificiality of the doctor–patient model. (Family therapists these days are relearning the value of getting out of the office and meeting clients where they live.)

These turn-of-the-century caseworkers understood something it took psychiatry fifty more years to discover—that families must be considered as units. Mary Richmond (1917), in her classic text, *Social Diagnosis*, prescribed treatment of the whole family and warned against isolating family members from their natural context. Richmond's concept of *family cohesion* had a strikingly modern ring, anticipating as it did later work on role theory, group dynamics, and structural family theory. According to Richmond, emotional bonding between family members was critical to their ability to survive and flourish.

Richmond also anticipated something that family therapy became concerned with in the 1980s by viewing families as systems within systems. As Bardhill and Saunders (1988) pointed out,

> She recognized that families are not isolated wholes (closed systems), but exist in a particular social context, which interactively influences and is influenced by their functioning (i.e., they are open). She graphically depicted this situation using a set of concentric circles to represent various systemic levels from the individual to the cultural. Her approach to practice was to consider the potential effect of all interventions on every systemic level, and to understand and to use the reciprocal interaction of the systemic hierarchy for therapeutic purposes. She truly took a systemic view of human distress. (p. 319)

When the family therapy movement was launched, social workers were among the most important contributors. Among the leaders who came into family therapy through social work training were Virginia Satir, Ray Bardhill, Peggy Papp, Lynn Hoffman, Froma Walsh, Insoo Berg, Jay Lappin, Richard Stuart, Harry Aponte, Michael White, Doug Breunlin, Olga Silverstein, Lois Braverman, Steve de Shazer, Peggy Penn, Betty Carter, Braulio Montalvo, and Monica McGoldrick. (Incidentally, even starting such a list is difficult because unless it went on for pages, it would have to omit a host of important names.)

RESEARCH ON FAMILY DYNAMICS AND THE ETIOLOGY OF SCHIZOPHRENIA

Families with schizophrenic members proved to be an especially fertile area for research because their strange patterns of interaction were so dramatic. The fact that family therapy emerged from research on schizophrenia led to the hope that family therapy might be the way to cure this baffling form of madness.

Family therapists didn't discover the role of the family in schizophrenia, but by actually observing families interacting, they witnessed patterns that their predecessors had only speculated about. Family influences on schizophrenia had been recognized at least as early as Freud's famous account (1911) of Dr. Schreber. In this first psychoanalytic formulation of psychosis, Freud suggested how the patient's bizarre relationship with his father played a role in his fantastic delusions.

Harry Stack Sullivan focused on interpersonal relations in his brilliant work with schizophrenics. Beginning in 1927, he emphasized the importance of the "hospital family"—physicians, nurses, and aides—as a benevolent substitute for the patient's real family. Sullivan did not, however, take his ideas a step further and directly involve families in treatment. Frieda Fromm-Reichmann also believed that families played a part in the dynamics of schizophrenia and considered the hospital family crucial in the resolution of schizophrenic episodes. Although these interpersonal psychiatrists recognized the importance of family life in schizophrenia, they continued to treat the family as a toxic environment from which patients should be removed.

In the 1940s and 1950s, research on the link between family life and schizophrenia led to the pioneering work of the first family therapists.

Gregory Bateson—Palo Alto

One of the groups with the strongest claim to originating family therapy was Gregory Bateson's schizophrenia project in Palo Alto, California. A scientist in the classic mold, Bateson studied animal behavior, learning theory, evolution, and ecology, as well as psychiatry. He worked with Margaret Mead in Bali and New Guinea; then, becoming interested in cybernetics, he wrote *Naven* and worked on synthesizing cybernetic ideas with anthropological data.[1] He entered the psychiatric field when, together with Jurgen Ruesch at the Langley Porter Clinic, he wrote *Communication: The Social Matrix of Psychiatry*. In 1962 Bateson shifted to studying communication among animals and from 1963 until his death in 1980 worked at the Oceanographic Institute in Hawaii.

The Palo Alto project began in the fall of 1952 when Bateson received a grant from the Rockefeller Foundation to study the nature of

---

[1]Norbert Wiener (1948) coined the term *cybernetics* for the emerging body of knowledge about how feedback controls information-processing systems. Applied to families, the cybernetic metaphor focused on how families become stuck in repetitive loops of unproductive behavior.

communication in terms of levels. All communications, Bateson (1951) had written, have two different levels or functions—*report* and *command*. Every message has a stated content, for instance, "Wash your hands, it's time for dinner"; but in addition, the message carries how it is to be taken. In this case, the second message is that the speaker is in charge. This second message—**metacommunication**—is covert and often unnoticed. If a wife scolds her husband for running the dishwasher when it's only half full, and he says OK but turns around and does exactly the same thing two days later, she may be annoyed that he doesn't listen to her. She means the message—but maybe he didn't like the metamessage. Maybe he doesn't like her telling him what to do as though she were his mother.

Bateson was joined in 1953 by Jay Haley and John Weakland. Haley was primarily interested in social and psychological analysis of fantasy; Weakland was a chemical engineer who'd become interested in cultural anthropology. Later that same year, a psychiatrist, William Fry, joined them; his major interest was the study of humor. This group of eclectic talents and catholic interests studied otters at play, the training of guide dogs, the meaning and uses of humor, the social and psychological significance of popular movies, and the utterances of schizophrenic patients.

In 1954, Bateson received a two-year grant from the Macy Foundation to study schizophrenic communication. Shortly thereafter, the group was joined by Don Jackson, a brilliant psychiatrist who served as clinical consultant and supervisor of psychotherapy.

Bateson and his colleagues hypothesized that family stability is achieved by feedback that regulates the behavior of the family and its members. Whenever a family system is threatened—that is, disturbed—it endeavors to maintain stability, or **homeostasis**. Thus, apparently puzzling behavior might become understandable if it were seen as a homeostatic mechanism. For example, if whenever two parents argue, one of the children exhibits symptomatic behavior, the symptoms may be a way to interrupt the fighting by uniting the parents in concern. Thus symptomatic behavior can serve the cybernetic function of preserving the family's equilibrium.

In 1956, Bateson and his colleagues published their famous report "Toward a Theory of Schizophrenia," in which they introduced the concept of the **double bind**. They assumed that psychotic behavior might make sense in the context of pathological family communication. Patients weren't crazy in some autonomous way; they were an extension of a crazy family environment. Consider someone in an important relationship in which escape isn't feasible and response is necessary. If he or she receives two related but contradictory messages on different levels but finds it difficult to detect or comment on the inconsistency (Bateson, Jackson, Haley, & Weakland, 1956), that person is in a double bind.

Because this difficult concept is often misused as a synonym for paradox or simply contradiction, it's worth reviewing each feature of the double bind as the authors listed them:

1. Two or more persons in an important relationship.
2. Repeated experience.
3. A primary negative injunction, such as "Don't do *X* or I will punish you."
4. A second injunction at a more abstract level conflicting with the first, also enforced by punishment or perceived threat.
5. A tertiary negative injunction prohibiting escape and demanding a response. Without this restriction the victim won't feel bound.
6. Finally, the complete set of ingredients is no longer necessary once the victim is conditioned to perceive the world in terms of double binds; any part of the sequence becomes sufficient to trigger panic or rage.

Most examples of double binds in the literature are inadequate because they don't include all the critical features. Robin Skynner, for instance, cited (1976): "Boys must stand up for themselves and not be sissies"; but "Don't be rough . . . don't be rude to your mother." Confusing? Yes. Conflict? Maybe. But these two messages don't constitute a double bind; they're merely a contradiction. Faced with two such statements, a child is free to obey either one, alternate, or even complain about the contradiction. This and many similar examples neglect the specification that the two messages are conveyed on different levels.

A better example is one given in the original article by Bateson, Jackson, Haley, and Weakland (1956). A young man recovering in the hospital from a schizophrenic episode was visited by his mother. When he put his arm around her, she stiffened. But when he withdrew, she asked, "Don't you love me anymore?" He blushed, and she said, "Dear, you must not be so easily embarrassed and afraid of your feelings." Following this exchange, the patient became upset; after the visit was over, he assaulted an aide and had to be put in seclusion.

Notice that all six features of the double bind were present in this exchange and also that the young man was obviously caught. There is no bind if the subject is not bound. The concept is interactional.

Another example of a double bind would be a teacher who urges his students to participate in class but gets impatient if one of them actually interrupts with a question or comment. Then a baffling thing happens. For some strange reason that scientists have yet to decipher, students tend not to speak up in classes where their comments are disparaged. When the professor finally does get around to asking for questions and no one responds, he gets angry. ("Students are so passive!") If any of the students has the temerity to comment on the professor's lack of receptivity, he'll probably get even angrier. Thus the students will be pun-ished for accurately perceiving that the teacher really wants only his own ideas to be heard and admired. (This example is, of course, purely hypothetical.)

We're all caught in occasional double binds, but the schizophrenic has to deal with them continually—and the effect is maddening. Unable to comment on the dilemma, the schizophrenic responds defensively, perhaps by being concrete and literal, perhaps by speaking in metaphors. Eventually the schizophrenic may come to assume that behind every statement lies a concealed meaning.

The discovery that schizophrenic symptoms made sense in the context of some families may have been a scientific advance, but it also had moral and political overtones. Not only did these investigators see themselves as avenging knights bent on rescuing **identified patients (IPs)** by slaying family dragons, but they were also crusaders in a holy war against the psychiatric establishment. Outnumbered and surrounded by hostile critics, the champions of family therapy challenged the orthodox assumption that schizophrenia was a biological disease. Psychological healers everywhere cheered. Unfortunately, they were wrong.

The observation that schizophrenic behavior seems to *fit* in some families doesn't mean that families *cause* schizophrenia. In logic, this kind of inference is called "Jumping to Conclusions." Sadly, families of schizophrenic members suffered for years under the assumption that they were to blame for the tragedy of their children's psychoses.

After the publication of the double-bind paper, members of the project began interviewing parents together with their schizophrenic offspring. These meetings were exploratory rather than therapeutic, but they did represent a major advance: actually observing family interactions rather than merely speculating about them. These conjoint family sessions helped launch the family therapy movement, and we'll see what they revealed in the next section.

All the discoveries of the Bateson group were united on one point: the centrality of communication to the organization of families. What makes families toxic, they concluded, was pathological communication. What they disagreed about was the underlying motivation for the disordered messages they observed. Haley believed that a covert struggle for control was the motivating force for double binding; Bateson and Weakland thought it was the urge to conceal unacceptable feelings. But they all agreed that unhealthy behavior may be adaptive in the family context. The two great discoveries of this talented team's output were (1) multiple levels of communication, and (2) that destructive patterns of relationship are maintained by self-regulating interactions of the family group.

Theodore Lidz—Yale

Theodore Lidz challenged the belief that maternal rejection was the major distinguishing feature of schizophrenic families. Frequently, the more destructive influence was that of fathers. In a landmark paper entitled "Intrafamilial Environment of the Schizophrenic Patient, I: The Father" (Lidz, Cornelison, Fleck, & Terry, 1957a), Lidz and his colleagues described five patterns of pathological fathering in families of schizophrenics.

The first group was domineering and in constant conflict with their wives. The second group was hostile toward their children rather than toward their wives. These men rivaled their children for the mother's attention and affection, behaving more like jealous siblings than parents. The third group of fathers were aloof and distant. The fourth group were failures in life and nonentities in their homes. Children in these families grew up as though fatherless. The fifth group were submissive men who acted more like children than parents. These passive fathers failed to counterbalance the domineering influence of their wives. Lidz concluded that it might be better to grow up without a father than with one who is too aloof or weak to serve as a healthy model for identification.

After describing some of the pathological characteristics of fathers in schizophrenic families, Lidz turned his attention to deficits in the marital relationships. The theme underlying his findings was an absence of *role reciprocity*. In a successful relationship, it's not enough to fulfill your own role—to be an effective person; it's also necessary to balance your role with your partner's—to be an effective pair. In the schizophrenic families Lidz studied, the spouses were inadequate to fulfill their own role and disinclined to support those of their mates.

In focusing on the failure to arrive at cooperative roles, Lidz identified two general types of marital discord (Lidz, Cornelison, Fleck, & Terry, 1957b). In the first, **marital schism**, there was a failure to accommodate to each other or to achieve role reciprocity. These husbands and wives chronically undercut each other's worth and competed openly for their children's affection. Their marriages were combat zones. The second pattern, **marital skew**, involves serious psychopathology in one partner who dominates the other. Thus one parent becomes extremely dependent while the other appears to be a strong parent figure but is, in fact, a pathological bully. The weaker spouse—in Lidz's cases, usually the father—goes along with the pathological distortions of the dominant one. In all these families, unhappy children were torn by conflicting loyalties and weighed down with the pressure to balance their parents' precarious marriages.

Lyman Wynne—National Institute of Mental Health

Like others before him, Lyman Wynne examined the effects of communication and family roles. What distinguished his work was his focus on how pathological thinking is transmitted in families.

Wynne's studies of schizophrenic families began in 1954 when he started seeing the parents of his hospitalized patients in twice-weekly therapy sessions. What struck Wynne about disturbed families were the strangely unreal qualities of both positive and negative emotions, which he labeled *pseudomutuality* and *pseudohostility*, and the nature of the boundaries around them—*rubber fences*—apparently flexible but actually impervious to outside influence (especially from therapists).

Pseudomutuality (Wynne, Ryckoff, Day, & Hirsch, 1958) is a facade of togetherness that masks conflict and blocks intimacy. Pseudomutual families are so preoccupied with togetherness that there's no room for separate identities or divergent self-interests. These families cannot tolerate either deeper, more honest relationships or independence.

Pseudohostility is a different guise for a similar collusion to obscure *alignments* and *splits* (Wynne, 1961). Although noisy and intense, it signals only a superficial split. Pseudohostility is more like the bickering and sparring of situation-comedy families than it is real animosity. Like pseudomutuality, it blurs intimacy and affection as well as deeper hostility; pseudohostility distorts communication and impairs rational thinking about relationships.

The **rubber fence** is an invisible barrier that stretches to permit obligatory extrafamilial involvement, such as going to school, but springs back if that involvement goes too far. The family's rigid role structure is thus protected by its social isolation. The most damaging feature of the rubber fence is that those who most need outside contact to correct family distortions are the ones allowed it least. Instead of being a subsystem of society (Parsons & Bales, 1955), the schizophrenic family becomes a sick little society unto itself.

Lyman Wynne's studies linked *communication deviance* in families to thought disorder in schizophrenic patients.

Wynne linked the new concept of *communication deviance* with the older notion of *thought disorder*. He saw communication as the vehicle for transmitting thought disorder, which is the defining characteristic of schizophrenia. Communication deviance is a more interactional concept than thought disorder, and more readily observable than double binds. By 1978, Wynne had studied over 600 families and gathered incontrovertible evidence that disordered styles of communication are a distinguishing feature of families with young adult schizophrenics. Similar disorders also appear in families of borderlines, neurotics, and normals but are progressively less severe (Singer, Wynne, & Toohey, 1978). This observation—that communication deviance isn't confined solely to schizophrenic families but exists on a continuum (greater deviance with more severe pathology)—is consistent with other studies that describe a "spectrum of schizophrenic disorders."

Role Theorists

The founders of family therapy gained momentum for their fledgling discipline by concentrating on verbal communication. Doing so may have been adaptive at the time, but focusing exclusively on this one aspect of family life neglected both individual intersubjectivity and broader social influences.

Role theorists, such as John Spiegel, described how individuals were differentiated into social roles within family systems. This important fact was obscured by oversimplified versions of systems theory, according to which individuals were treated like cogs in a machine. As early as 1954, Spiegel pointed out that the system in therapy includes the therapist as well as the family (an idea reintroduced later as "second-order cybernetics"). He also made a valuable distinction between "interactions" and "transactions." Billiard balls *interact*—they collide and alter each other's course but remain essentially unchanged. People *transact*—they come together in ways that not only alter each other's course, but also affect internal changes.

Ironically for a field in which circular causality was to become a favorite concept, the unfortunate evolutionary misdirection of describing negative influences in families as linear—blaming parents for rejecting or overprotecting or double binding their children—was not only unfair but also did lasting damage to the reputation of family therapy. Families of mentally ill persons had reason to resent being blamed for the misfortunes of their children.

In 1951, the Group for the Advancement of Psychiatry (GAP) decided that families had been neglected in psychiatry and therefore appointed a committee, chaired by John Spiegel, to survey the field and report their findings. The GAP committee's report (Kluckhohn & Spiegel, 1954) emphasized roles as the primary structural components of families. They concluded that healthy families contained relatively few and stable roles and that this pattern was essential to teach children a sense of status and identity.

Family roles don't exist independently of each other; every role is circumscribed by reciprocal roles. You can't have a domineering partner, for example, without a submissive mate. Role behavior of two or more people involved in a reciprocal transaction defines and regulates their interchange. A common example is that in many families one parent is stricter than the other. Their differences may be slight at first, but the stricter one parent is, the more lenient the other is likely to become. The GAP committee explained roles as a function both of external social influences and of inner needs and drives. Thus role theory served as a link between *intra*personal and *inter*personal structures.

Spiegel went on to Harvard Medical School in 1953, where he pursued his interests in role theory and family pathology. He observed that symptomatic children tend to be involved in their parents' conflicts; nonsymptomatic children may also have parents in conflict, but these children don't get directly involved. Spiegel (1957) described his observations in psychoanalytic terms: The child identifies with the unconscious wishes of the parents and acts out their emotional conflict. The child's acting out serves as a defense for the parents, who are thereby able to avoid facing their own conflicts—and each other.

R. D. Laing's analysis of family dynamics was more polemical than scholarly, but his observations helped popularize the family's role in psychopathology. Laing (1965) borrowed Karl Marx's concept of **mystification** (class exploitation) and applied it to the "politics of families." Mystification refers to the process of distorting children's experience by denying or relabeling it. One example of this is a parent telling a child who's feeling sad, "You must be tired" (*Go to bed and leave me alone*). Similarly, the idea that good children are always quiet breeds compliant, but spiritless, children.

The prime function of mystification is to maintain the status quo. Mystification contradicts perceptions and feelings and, more ominously, reality. When parents continually mystify a child's experience, the child's existence becomes inauthentic. Because their feelings aren't accepted, these children project a *false self* while keeping the *real self* private. In mild instances, this produces a lack of authenticity, but if the real self/false self split is carried to extremes, the result is madness (Laing, 1960).

 MARRIAGE COUNSELING

For many years, there was no apparent need for a separate profession of marriage counselors. People with marital problems were more likely to discuss them with their doctors, clergy, lawyers, and teachers than to seek out mental health professionals.

The first professional centers for marriage counseling were established around 1930. Paul Popenoe opened the American Institute of Family Relations in Los Angeles, and Abraham and Hannah Stone opened a similar clinic in New York. A third center was the Marriage Council of Philadelphia, begun in 1932 by Emily Hartshorne Mudd (Broderick & Schrader, 1981). Members of this new profession started meeting annually in 1942 and formed the American Association of Marriage Counselors in 1945.

While these developments were taking place, a parallel trend among some psychoanalysts led to conjoint marital therapy. Although the majority of psychoanalysts have always followed Freud's prohibition against contact with the patient's family, a few have broken the rules and experimented with **concurrent** and **conjoint therapy** for married partners.

The first report on the psychoanalysis of married couples was made by Clarence Oberndorf (1938) at the American Psychiatric Association's 1931 convention. Oberndorf advanced the theory that married couples have interlocking neuroses and are best treated in concert. This was to be the underlying point of agreement among those in the analytic community who became interested in treating couples. "Because of the continuous and intimate nature of marriage, every neurosis in a married person is strongly anchored in the marital relationship. It is a useful and at times indispensable therapeutic measure to concentrate the analytic discussions on the complementary patterns and, if necessary, to have both mates treated" (Mittleman, 1944, p. 491).

In 1948, Bela Mittleman of the New York Psychoanalytic Institute published the first account of concurrent marital therapy in the United States. Mittleman (1948) suggested that husbands and wives could be treated by the same

analyst and that by seeing both it was possible to reexamine their irrational perceptions of each other. This was a revolutionary point of view from an analyst: that the reality of object relationships may be at least as important as their intrapsychic representations.

Meanwhile in Great Britain, where **object relations theory** was the central concern of psychoanalysts, Henry Dicks and his associates at the Tavistock Clinic established a family psychiatric unit. Here couples referred by the divorce courts were helped to reconcile their differences (Dicks, 1964). Subsequently, the Balints affiliated their Family Discussion Bureau with the Tavistock Clinic, adding the clinic's prestige to their marital casework agency and indirectly to the entire field of marriage counseling.

In 1956, Mittleman wrote a more extensive description of his views on marital disorders and their treatment. He described a number of complementary marital patterns, including aggressive/submissive and detached/demanding. These odd matches are made, according to Mittleman, because courting couples distort each other's personalities through the eyes of their illusions: She sees his independence as strength; he sees her dependency as adoration. Mittleman also pointed out that a couple's reactions to each other are shaped by their relationship with their parents. Without insight, unconscious motivation may dominate marital behavior, leading to reciprocal neurotic actions and reactions. For treatment, Mittleman believed that 20 percent of the time one therapist could handle all members of the family, but in other cases separate therapists for each member would perhaps be better.

At about this time Don Jackson and Jay Haley were also writing about marital therapy within the framework of communications analysis. As their ideas gained prominence among marital therapists, the field of marital therapy was absorbed into the larger family therapy movement.

Many writers don't distinguish between marital and family therapy. Therapy for couples, according to this way of thinking, is just family therapy applied to a particular subsystem. We tend to agree with this way of thinking and therefore you will find our description of various approaches to couples and their problems embedded in the discussions of the models considered in this book. There is, however, a case to be made for considering couples therapy a distinct enterprise (Gurman, 2008).

Historically, many of the influential approaches to couples therapy came before their family therapy counterparts. Among these are cognitive-behavioral marital therapy, object relations marital therapy, emotionally focused couples therapy, and many of the integrative approaches considered in Chapter 14. Beyond the question of which came first, couples therapy differs in practice from family therapy in allowing for more in-depth focus on the experience of individuals. Sessions with the whole family tend to be noisy affairs. While it's possible in this context to spend time talking with family members about their feelings, wishes, and fears, it isn't possible to spend much time exploring the psychology of any one individual—much less two. Doing therapy with couples, on the other hand, permits a much closer focus on both dyadic exchanges and on the underlying experience of intimate relationships.

FROM RESEARCH TO TREATMENT: THE PIONEERS OF FAMILY THERAPY

We have seen how family therapy was anticipated by developments in hospital psychiatry, group dynamics, interpersonal psychiatry, the child guidance movement, research on schizophrenia, and marriage counseling. But who actually started family therapy? Although there are rival claims to this honor, the distinction should probably be shared by John Elderkin Bell, Don Jackson, Nathan Ackerman, and Murray Bowen. In addition to these founders of family therapy, Jay Haley, Virginia Satir, Carl Whitaker,

Lyman Wynne, Ivan Boszormenyi-Nagy, Christian Midelfort, and Salvador Minuchin were also significant pioneers.

John Bell

John Elderkin Bell, a psychologist at Clark University in Worcester, Massachusetts, who began treating families in 1951, occupies a unique position in the history of family therapy. He may have been the first family therapist but is mentioned only tangentially in two of the most important historical accounts of the movement (Guerin, 1976; Kaslow, 1980), because although he began seeing families in the 1950s, he didn't publish his ideas until a decade later. Moreover, unlike the other parents of family therapy, he had few offspring. He didn't establish an important clinical center, develop a training program, or train well-known students.

Bell's approach (Bell, 1961, 1962) was taken directly from group therapy. *Family group therapy* relied primarily on stimulating an open discussion to help families solve their problems. Like a group therapist, Bell intervened to encourage silent participants to speak up, and he interpreted the reasons for their defensiveness.

Bell believed that family group therapy goes through predictable phases just as do groups of strangers. In his early work (Bell, 1961), he carefully structured treatment in a series of stages, each of which concentrated on a particular segment of the family. Later, he became less directive and allowed families to evolve through a naturally unfolding sequence. For a more complete description of family group therapy, see Chapter 2.

Palo Alto

The Bateson group stumbled onto family therapy more or less by accident. Once they began to meet with schizophrenic families in 1954, hoping to decipher their patterns of communication, project members found themselves drawn into helping roles by the pain of these unhappy people (Jackson & Weakland, 1961). While Bateson was the scientific leader of the group, Don Jackson and Jay Haley were most influential in developing family therapy.

Jackson rejected the psychodynamic concepts he learned in training and focused instead on the dynamics of interchange between persons. Analysis of communication was his primary instrument.

By 1954, Jackson had developed a rudimentary family therapy, which he reported in "The Question of Family Homeostasis," a paper delivered to the American Psychiatric Association convention in St. Louis. Borrowing from biology and systems theory, Jackson described families as homeostatic units.

Jackson's concept of **family homeostasis**—families as units that resist change—was to become the defining metaphor of family therapy's early years. In hindsight, we can say that the emphasis on homeostasis overestimated the conservative properties of families and underestimated their flexibility. At the time, however, the recognition that families resist change was enormously productive for understanding what keeps people stuck.

In "Schizophrenic Symptoms and Family Interaction" (Jackson & Weakland, 1959), Jackson illustrated how patients' symptoms preserve stability in their families. In one case, a young woman diagnosed as a catatonic schizophrenic had as her most prominent symptom a profound indecisiveness. When she did behave decisively, however, her parents fell apart. Her mother became helpless and dependent; her father became literally impotent. In one family meeting, her parents failed to notice when the patient made a simple decision. Only after listening to a taped replay of the session *three* times did the parents finally hear their daughter's statement. The patient's indecision was neither crazy nor senseless; rather it protected her parents from facing their own difficulties. This case is one of the earliest published examples of how psychotic symptoms can be meaningful in the family context. This paper also contains the shrewd observation that children's symptoms are often an exaggerated version of their parents' problems.

In moving away from mentalistic inference to behavioral observation of sequences of communication, Jackson found that he needed a new language of interaction. His basic assumption was that all people in continuing relationships develop set patterns of interaction. He called this patterning *behavioral redundancy* (Jackson, 1965).

The term *redundancy* not only captures an important feature of family behavior but also reflects Jackson's phenomenological stance. Traditional psychiatric terms like *projection*, *defense*, and *regression* imply far more about inner states of motivation than the simple descriptive language of early family therapists. Even when using concepts that imply prescription, Jackson remained committed to description. Thus, his *rules hypothesis* was simply a means of summarizing the observation that within any committed unit (dyad, triad, or larger group), there are redundant behavior patterns. Rules (as any student of philosophy learns when studying determinism) can describe regularity, rather than regulation. A second part of the rules hypothesis was that family members use only some of the full range of behavior available to them. This seemingly innocent fact is precisely what makes family therapy so useful.

Don Jackson described problematic patterns of communication in ways that are still useful today.

Families who come to therapy can be seen as stuck in a narrow range of options or unnecessarily rigid rules. Since the rules in most families aren't spelled out, no one ratifies them, and they're hard to change. The therapist, however, as an outsider can help families see—and reexamine—the rules they live by.

Jackson's therapeutic strategies were based on the premise that psychiatric problems resulted from the way people behave with each other in a given context. He sought first to distinguish interactions (*redundant behavior patterns*) that were functional from those that were dysfunctional (*problem maintaining*). To do so, he observed when problems occurred and in what context, who was present, and how people responded to the problem. Given the assumption that symptoms are homeostatic mechanisms, Jackson often inquired how a family might be worse off if the problem got better. The individual might want to get better, but the family may need someone to play the sick role. Even positive change can be a threat to the defensive order of things.

A father's drinking, for example, might keep him from making demands on his wife or from enforcing discipline on his children. Unfortunately, some family therapists jumped from the observation that symptoms may serve a purpose to the assumption that some families *need* a sick member, which, in turn, led to a view of parents victimizing *scapegoated* children. Despite the fancy language, this was part of the time-honored tradition of blaming parents for the failings of their children. If a six-year-old boy misbehaves around the house, perhaps we should look to his parents. But a husband's drinking isn't necessarily his family's fault, and certainly it wasn't fair to imply that families were responsible for the psychotic symptoms of their schizophrenic members.

Looking back, we can see how the cybernetic metaphor of family as machine led to a view of the therapist as more mechanic than healer. In their zeal to rescue "family scapegoats" from the clutches of their "pathological" families, early family therapists may have provoked some of the resistance they complained of. Therapists who see themselves as rescuing innocent victims from their families and who take up an adversarial stance are not unlike the person who whacks a turtle on the back and then complains that the creature won't come out of its shell.

Another construct important to Jackson's thinking was the dichotomy between *complementary* relationships and *symmetrical* ones. (Like so many of the seminal ideas of family therapy, this one was first articulated by Bateson.) In **complementary relationships**, people are different in ways that fit together: If one is logical, the other is emotional; if one is weak, the other is strong. **Symmetrical relationships** are based on equality and similarity. Marriages between two people who both have careers and share housekeeping chores are symmetrical.

Most of Jackson's concepts (*complementary/symmetrical*, *double bind*) describe relationships between two people. Although his intent was to develop a descriptive language of family interaction, Jackson's major success was in describing relationships between husbands and wives. This narrow focus on the marital dyad has always been one of the limits of the Palo Alto group. Their interest in communication led to an adult-centered bias, and they tended to neglect children as well as the various triads that make up families.

The great discovery of the Bateson group was that there's no such thing as a simple communication; every message is qualified by a different message on another level. In *Strategies of Psychotherapy*, Jay Haley (1963) explored how covert messages are used in the struggle for control that characterizes many relationships. Symptoms, he argued, represent an incongruence between levels of communication. The symptomatic person does something, such as touching a doorknob six times before turning it, while at the same time denying that he's *really* doing it. He can't help it; it's his condition. Meanwhile, the person's symptoms—over which he has no control—have consequences. A person who has a compulsion of such proportions can hardly be expected to get himself out of the house in the morning, can he?

Because symptomatic behavior wasn't reasonable, Haley didn't rely on reasoning with patients to help them. Instead, therapy became a strategic game of cat and mouse.

Haley (1963) defined his therapy as a directive form of treatment and acknowledged his debt to Milton Erickson, with whom he studied hypnosis from 1954 to 1960. In what he called *brief therapy*, Haley zeroed in on the context and possible function of the patient's symptoms. His first moves were often designed to gain control of the therapeutic relationship. Haley cited Erickson's device of advising patients that in the first interview there will be things they may be willing to say and other things they'll want to withhold and that these, of course, should be withheld. Here, of course, the therapist is directing patients to do precisely what they would do anyway and thus subtly gaining the upper hand.

The decisive technique in brief therapy was the use of *directives*. As Haley put it, it isn't enough to explain problems to patients; what counts is getting them to *do* something about them.

One of Haley's patients was a freelance photographer who compulsively made silly blunders that ruined every picture. Eventually the patient became so preoccupied with avoiding mistakes that he was too nervous to take pictures at all. Haley instructed the man to go out and take three pictures, making one deliberate error in each. The obvious paradox is that you can't make a mistake accidentally if you're doing so deliberately.

In another famous case, Haley told an insomniac that if he woke up in the middle of the night he should get out of bed and wax the kitchen floor. Instant cure! The cybernetic principle illustrated here is: People will do almost anything to get out of housework.

Most of the ideas that came out of the Palo Alto group—double bind, complementarity—focused on dyads, but Haley also became interested in triads or, as he called them, **coalitions**. Coalitions are distinct from alliances—cooperative arrangements between two parties, not formed at the expense of a third. In the symptomatic families that Haley observed, most coalitions were cross-generational, one parent ganging up with a child against the other parent.

In "Toward a Theory of Pathological Systems," Haley described what he called "perverse triangles," which may lead to violence, psychopathology, or the breakup of a system. A *perverse triangle* is a hidden coalition that undermines generational hierarchies. Examples include a child running to her grandmother every time her mother tries to punish her, or one parent complaining about the other to the children. Perverse triangles also occur in organizations when, for example, a supervisor joins with one subordinate against another or when a professor complains to her students about the department chair. In looking beyond cybernetics and dyads to triads and hierarchies, Haley was to become a bridging figure between strategic and structural approaches to family therapy.

Another member of the Palo Alto group who played a leading role in family therapy's first decade was Virginia Satir, one of the great charismatic healers. Known more for her clinical artistry than for theoretical contributions, Satir's impact was most vivid to those lucky enough to see her in action. Like her confreres, Satir was interested in communication, but she added a dimension of feeling that helped counterbalance what was otherwise a relatively cool and calculated approach.

Satir saw troubled family members as trapped in narrow family roles, such as *victim, placator, defiant one*, or *rescuer*, that constrained relationships and sapped self-esteem. Her concern with identifying such life-constricting roles and freeing family members from their grip was consistent with her major focus, which was always on the individual. Thus, Satir was a humanizing force in the early days of family therapy, when many were so enamored of the systems metaphor that they neglected the emotional life of families.

Satir concentrated on clarifying communication, expressing feelings, and fostering a climate of mutual acceptance and warmth. Her great strength was to connect with families, not in terms of anger and resentment, but in terms of hopes and fears, yearnings, and disappointments. A therapist who can bring out the loneliness and longing behind an angry outburst is a therapist who can bring people together.

Satir was justly famous for her ability to turn negatives into positives. In one case, cited by Lynn Hoffman (1981), Satir interviewed the family of an adolescent boy, son of the local minister, who had gotten two of his classmates pregnant. On one side of the room sat the boy's parents and siblings. The boy sat in the opposite corner with his head down. Satir introduced herself and said to the boy, "Well, your father has told me a lot about the situation on the phone, and I just want to say before we begin that we know one thing for sure: We know you have good seed." The boy looked up in amazement as Satir turned to the boy's mother and asked brightly, "Could you start by telling us your perception?"

The 1964 publication of Satir's book *Conjoint Family Therapy* did much to popularize the family therapy movement. This book, along with *Pragmatics of Human Communication* (Watzlawick, Beavin, & Jackson, 1967), helped make the Palo Alto group's brand of systemic thinking the leading model of the 1960s.

Murray Bowen

Like many of the founders of family therapy, Murray Bowen was a psychiatrist who special-ized in schizophrenia. Unlike others, however, he emphasized theory in his work, and to this day Bowen's theory is the most fertile system of ideas family therapy has produced.

Bowen began his clinical work at the Menninger Clinic in 1946, where he studied mothers and their schizophrenic children. His major interest at the time was mother–child symbiosis, which led to his concept of **differentiation of self** (autonomy from others and separation of thought from feeling). From Menninger, Bowen moved to NIMH, where he developed a project to hospitalize whole families with schizophrenic members. This project expanded the concept of mother–child symbiosis to include the role of fathers, and led to the concept of *triangles* (diverting conflict between two people by involving a third). In 1959, Bowen left NIMH for Georgetown Medical School, where he was a professor of psychiatry and director of his own training program until his death in 1990.

In the first year of the NIMH project (1954), Bowen provided separate therapists for individual family members. He discovered, however, that these efforts tended to fractionate families. Instead of trying to work out their mutual problems together, family members had a tendency to think, "I'll take up my problems with *my* therapist" (Bowen, 1976). (Of course this never happens when nice people like you and me go to *our* individual therapists.) After a year, concluding that the family was the unit of disorder, Bowen began treating the families together. Thus, in 1955, Bowen became one of the first to invent family therapy.

Beginning in 1955, Bowen began holding large group therapy sessions for the entire project staff and all the families. In this early form of network therapy, Bowen assumed that togetherness and open communication would be therapeutic—for problems within families and between families and staff.

At first Bowen employed four therapists to manage these multifamily meetings, but he became dissatisfied when he noticed that the therapists tended to pull in different directions, so he put one therapist in charge and consigned the others to supporting roles. However, just as multiple therapists tended to pull in different directions, so did multiple families. As soon as a hot topic was broached in one family, someone from another family would become anxious and change the subject. Finally, Bowen decided that families had to take turns—one family became the focus for each session, with the others as silent auditors.

At first Bowen's approach to single families was the same one he used in the large meetings. He did what most new family therapists do: brought family members together and tried to get them talking. He reasoned that families would improve simply by coming together and discussing mutual concerns. He soon rejected this idea. Unstructured family chats are about as productive for therapy as an unrefereed boxing match between several combatants of various sizes.

When Bowen brought family members together to discuss their problems, he was struck by their **emotional reactivity**. Feelings overwhelmed thinking and drowned out individuality in the chaos of the group. Bowen felt the family's tendency to pull him into the center of this **undifferentiated family ego mass**, and he had to make a concerted effort to remain objective (Bowen, 1961). The ability to remain neutral and attentive to the process, rather than the content, of family discussions is what distinguishes a therapist from a participant in a family's drama.

To control the level of emotion, Bowen encouraged family members to talk to him, not to each other. He found that it was easier for people to listen without becoming reactive when family members spoke to the therapist instead of to each other.

Bowen discovered that therapists weren't immune to being sucked into family conflicts. This awareness led to his greatest insight: Whenever two people are struggling with a conflict they can't resolve, there is an automatic tendency to involve a third party. In fact, as Bowen

came to believe, the **triangle** is the smallest stable unit of relationship.

A husband who can't stand his wife's habitual lateness, but who also can't stand up and tell her so, may start complaining to his children. His complaining may relieve some of his tension, but the very process of complaining to a third party makes him less likely to address the problem at its source. We all complain about other people from time to time, but Bowen realized that this "triangling" process is destructive when it becomes a regular feature of a relationship.

Another thing Bowen discovered about triangles is that they spread out. In the following case, a family had become entangled in a whole labyrinth of triangles.

One Sunday morning "Mrs. McNeil," who was anxious to get the family to church on time, yelled at her nine-year-old son to hurry up. When he told her to "quit bitching," she slapped him. At that point, her fourteen-year-old daughter, Megan, grabbed her, and the two of them started wrestling. Then Megan ran next door to her friend's house. When the friend's parents noticed that Megan had a cut lip and she told them what had happened, they called the police. By the time the family came to therapy, several triangles were in place. Mrs. McNeil, who'd been ordered out of the house by the family court judge, was allied with her lawyer against the judge; she also had an individual therapist who joined her in thinking she was being hounded unfairly by the child protective workers. The nine-year-old was still mad at his mother, and his father supported him in blaming her for flying off the handle. Mr. McNeil, who was a recovering alcoholic, formed an alliance with his sponsor, who felt that Mr. McNeil was on his way to a breakdown unless his wife started being more supportive. Meanwhile, Megan had formed a triangle with the neighbors, who thought her parents shouldn't be allowed to have children. In short, everyone had an advocate—everyone, that is, except the family unit.

In 1966, an emotional crisis in Bowen's family led him to initiate a personal voyage of discovery that turned out to be as significant for Bowen's theory as Freud's self-analysis was for psycho-analysis. As an adult, Bowen, the oldest of five children from a tightly knit rural family, kept his distance from his parents and the rest of his extended family. Like many of us, he mistook avoidance for emancipation. But as he later realized, unfinished emotional business stays with us, making us vulnerable to repeat conflicts we never got around to working out with our families.

Bowen's most important achievement was detriangling himself from his parents, who'd been accustomed to complaining to him about each other. Most of us are flattered to receive such confidences, but Bowen came to recognize this triangulation for what it was, and when his mother complained about his father, he told his father: "Your wife told me a story about you; I wonder why she told me instead of you." Naturally, his father discussed this with his mother, and naturally, she was annoyed.

Although his efforts generated the kind of emotional upheaval that comes of breaking family rules, Bowen's maneuver was effective in keeping his parents from trying to get him to take sides—and made it harder for them to avoid discussing things between themselves. Repeating what someone says to you about someone else is one way to stop triangling in its tracks.

Through his efforts in his own family Bowen discovered that *differentiation of self* is best accomplished by developing a person-to-person relationship with each parent and with as many members of the extended family as possible. If visiting is difficult, letters and phone calls can help reestablish relationships, particularly if they're personal and intimate. Differentiating one's self from the family is completed when these relationships are maintained without becoming emotionally reactive or taking part in triangles.

Nathan Ackerman

Nathan Ackerman was a child psychiatrist whose pioneering work with families remained faithful to his psychoanalytic roots. Although his focus on intrapsychic conflict may have seemed less innovative than the Palo Alto group's attention to communication as feedback, he had a keen sense of the overall organization of families. Families, Ackerman said, may give the appearance of unity, but underneath they are emotionally split into competing factions. This you may recognize as similar to the psychoanalytic model of individuals who, despite apparent unity of personality, are actually minds in conflict, driven by warring drives and defenses.

Ackerman joined the staff at the Menninger Clinic and in 1937 became chief psychiatrist of the Child Guidance Clinic. At first, he followed the child guidance model of having a psychiatrist treat the child and a social worker see the mother. However, by the mid-1940s, he began to experiment with having the same therapist see both. Unlike Bowlby, Ackerman did more than use these conjoint sessions as a temporary expedient; instead, he began to see the family as the basic unit for diagnosis and treatment.

In 1955, Ackerman organized the first session on family diagnosis at a meeting of the American Orthopsychiatric Association. There Jackson, Bowen, Wynne, and Ackerman learned about each other's work and joined in a sense of common purpose. Two years later, Ackerman opened the Family Mental Health Clinic of Jewish Family Services in New York City and began teaching at Columbia University. In 1960, he founded the Family Institute, which was renamed the Ackerman Institute following his death in 1971.

In addition to his clinical innovations, Ackerman also published several important articles and books. As early as 1938, he wrote "The Unity of the Family," and some consider his article "Family Diagnosis: An Approach to the Preschool Child" (Ackerman & Sobel, 1950) as the beginning of the family therapy movement (Kaslow, 1980). In 1962, Ackerman, with Don Jackson, cofounded the field's first journal, *Family Process.*

While other family therapists downplayed the psychology of individuals, Ackerman was always concerned with what goes on inside people, as well as between them. He never lost sight of feelings, hopes, and desires. In fact, Ackerman's model of the family was like the psychoanalytic model of individuals writ large; instead of conscious and unconscious issues, Ackerman talked about how families confront some issues while avoiding others, particularly those involving sex and aggression. He saw his job as a therapist as stirring things up, bringing family secrets into the open.

In *Treating the Troubled Family*, Ackerman (1966) illustrated his irreverence for politeness and pretense with a clinical vignette. A family of four came for treatment when the fighting between the eleven-year-old daughter and sixteen-year-old son started getting out of hand. The girl had recently threatened her brother with a butcher knife. The father sighed as he sat down. Ackerman asked him why he was sighing and refused to be put off by the father's excuse that he was tired, suggesting that perhaps he had another reason to sigh. Then his wife broke in to announce that she'd been keeping a journal of everyone's misdeeds during the week. Her stridency perfectly complemented her husband's mild-mannered evasiveness. Ackerman's bemused response was: "You come armed with a notebook. Fire away!"

As the mother began to read out her bill of particulars, Ackerman, who sensed that this was just business as usual, commented on the father's nonverbal behavior. "You're picking your fingers." This triggered a discussion about who does what, which the mother gradually took over and turned into an indictment of the father's many nervous habits. At this point, the son broke in with an accusation. Pointing to his mother, he said, "She belches!" The mother acknowledged this little embarrassment and then tried to change the subject, but Ackerman wasn't about to let her off the hook.

It turned out that the mother's belching occurred mostly in bed. The father said he was upset by her belching in his face, but he was interrupted by the children, who started bicker-

ing. Ackerman said, "Isn't it interesting that this interruption occurs just as you two are about to talk about your love life?" The father then described how it felt when he wanted to kiss his wife and she belched in his face. "You need a gas mask," he said. The daughter tried to interrupt, but Ackerman asked her to move her seat so that her parents could talk.

A few minutes later, the children left the session and Ackerman reopened the door to the parents' bedroom. At first the couple played out their familiar pattern: She complained and he withdrew. They were a perfectly matched pair: She was up, he was down. But Ackerman unbalanced them by playfully teasing the wife and provoking the husband to stand up for himself.

Although there's always room in after-the-fact descriptions to accuse a therapist of taking sides, it's worth noting that in this instance the wife didn't seem to feel criticized or put down by Ackerman—nor did the husband seem to get the idea that Ackerman was trying to elevate him over his wife. Rather, by the end of the session, this grim, angry couple were beginning to laugh and appreciate each other. They saw how they'd drifted apart and allowed their children to distract them. Thus, although Ackerman's work has been described as essentially psychoanalytic, we see here beginning efforts to reorganize the structure of families.

To promote honest emotional interchange, Ackerman "tickled the defenses" of family members—his phrase for provoking people to open up and say what's really on their minds. To encourage families to relax their restraint, Ackerman himself was unrestrained. He freely sided first with one part of the family and later with another. He didn't think it was necessary—or possible—to always be neutral; instead, he believed that an impartial balance was achieved in the long run by moving back and forth, giving support now to one, later to another family member. At times, he was unabashedly blunt. If he thought someone was lying, he said so. To critics who suggested this directness might generate too much anxiety, Ackerman replied that people get more reassurance from honesty than from pious politeness.

While it's impossible to neatly summarize Ackerman's freewheeling approach, there were consistent themes. One was the necessity for depth of therapeutic commitment and involvement. Ackerman became emotionally involved with families, in contrast, for example, to Murray Bowen, who cautioned therapists to remain somewhat distant to avoid being triangulated. Depth also characterized the issues on which Ackerman focused—family analogues of the kinds of conflicts that lie buried in the individual unconscious. His psychoanalytic orientation sensitized him to hidden themes in the interpersonal unconscious of the family, and his provocative style enabled him to help families bring these themes into the open.

Ackerman was one of the first to envision whole family treatment, *and* he had the inventiveness and energy to actually carry it out. Ackerman's major impact was as a peerless artist of therapeutic technique. He was one of the great geniuses of the movement. Those who observed him at work all attest to his clinical wizardry. Among those fortunate enough to study with him was Salvador Minuchin, who acknowledges his debt to Ackerman's genius.

Ackerman urged therapists to become emotionally engaged with families and to bring dormant conflicts into the open. How does a therapist encourage candid disclosure? Ackerman did it by challenging avoidance and emotional dishonesty ("tickling the defenses"). Perhaps his most enduring contribution was his consistent respect for individual persons *and* whole families; he never lost sight of the self in the system.

Carl Whitaker

Even among the iconoclastic founders of family therapy, Carl Whitaker stood out as the most irreverent. His view of psychologically troubled people was that they are alienated from feeling and frozen into devitalized routines (Whitaker & Malone, 1953). Whitaker turned up the emotional temperature. His "Psychotherapy of the Absurd" (Whitaker, 1975) was a blend of warm support and emotional goading, designed to loosen people up and help them get in touch with their experience in a deeper, more personal way.

Given his innovative approach to therapy, it wasn't surprising that Whitaker became one of the first to experiment with family treatment. In 1943, he and John Warkentin, working in Oak Ridge, Tennessee, began including spouses and children in their patients' treatment. Whitaker also pioneered the use of cotherapy, in the belief that a supportive partner helped free therapists to react spontaneously without fear of unchecked countertransference.

Whereas Jackson, Haley, and Bowen developed theoretical concepts that were intriguing and easy to grasp, Whitaker eschewed theory in favor of spontaneity. His work has therefore been less accessible to students than that of his colleagues. Nevertheless, he had the respect of his peers. Those who really understood what went on in families could see that there was always method to his madness.

Whitaker created tension by teasing and confronting families because he believed that stress is necessary for change. He never seemed to have an obvious strategy, nor did he use predictable techniques, preferring, as he said, to let his unconscious run the therapy (Whitaker, 1976). Although his work seemed totally spontaneous, even outrageous at times, there was a consistent theme. All of his interventions promoted flexibility. He didn't so much push families to change in a particular direction as he challenged and cajoled them to open up—to become more fully themselves and more fully together.

In 1946, Whitaker became chairman of the department of psychiatry at Emory University, where he continued to experiment with family treatment with a special interest in schizophrenics and their families. During this period, Whitaker organized a series of conferences that eventually led to the first meeting of the family therapy movement. Beginning in 1946, Whitaker and his colleagues began twice-yearly conferences during which they observed and discussed each other's work with families. The group found these sessions enormously helpful; and mutual observation, using one-way vision screens, has since become one of the hallmarks of family therapy.

Whitaker resigned from Emory in 1955 and entered private practice with Warkentin, Thomas Malone, and Richard Felder. He and his partners at the Atlanta Psychiatric Clinic developed an "experiential" form of psychotherapy, using a number of provocative techniques, combined with the force of their own personalities, in the treatment of families, individuals, groups, and couples (Whitaker, 1958).

During the late 1970s, Whitaker seemed to mellow and added a greater understanding of family dynamics to his shoot-from-the-hip interventions. In the process, the former wild man of family therapy became one of its elder statesmen. Whitaker's death in April 1995 left the field with a piece of its heart missing.

Ivan Boszormenyi-Nagy

Ivan Boszormenyi-Nagy, who came to family therapy from psychoanalysis, was one of the seminal thinkers in the movement. In 1957, he founded the Eastern Pennsylvania Psychiatric Institute (EPPI) in Philadelphia, where he was able to attract a host of highly talented colleagues. Among these were James Framo, one of the few psychologists in the early family therapy movement; David Rubenstein, a psychiatrist who later launched a separate family therapy training program; and Geraldine Spark, a social worker who worked with Boszormenyi-Nagy as cotherapist and coauthor of *Invisible Loyalties* (Boszormenyi-Nagy & Spark, 1973).

This group was joined by Ross Speck, who developed, along with Carolyn Attneave, *network*

therapy, which broadened the context of treatment beyond the nuclear family. In this approach, as many people as possible who are connected to the patient are invited to attend therapy sessions. Often as many as fifty people, including extended family, friends, neighbors, and teachers, are brought together to discuss ways to support and help the patient change (Speck & Attneave, 1973).

Boszormenyi-Nagy went from being an analyst, prizing secrecy and confidentiality, to a family therapist, fighting the forces of pathology on an open battlefield. One of his most important contributions was to add ethical accountability to therapeutic goals and techniques. According to Boszormenyi-Nagy, neither pleasure nor expediency is a sufficient guide to human behavior. Instead, he believed that family members have to base their relationships on trust and loyalty and that they must balance the ledger of entitlement and indebtedness. He died in 2008.

Salvador Minuchin

When Minuchin first burst onto the scene, it was the drama of his clinical interviews that people found so captivating. This compelling man with the elegant Latin accent would seduce, provoke, bully, or bewilder families into changing—as the situation required. But even Minuchin's legendary flair didn't have the same galvanizing impact of the practical simplicity of his structural model.

Minuchin began his career as a family therapist in the early 1960s when he discovered two patterns common to troubled families: Some are **enmeshed**—chaotic and tightly interconnected; others are **disengaged**—isolated and seemingly unrelated. Both types lack clear lines of authority. Enmeshed parents are too entangled with their children to exercise leadership; disengaged parents are too distant to provide effective support.

Family problems are tenacious and resistant to change because they're embedded in powerful but unseen structures. Take, for example, a mother futilely remonstrating with a willful child.

The mother can scold, punish, reward, or try leniency, but as long as she's enmeshed (overly involved) with the child, her efforts will lack force because she lacks authority. Moreover, because the behavior of one family member is always related to that of others, the mother will have trouble stepping back as long as her husband remains disengaged.

Once a social system such as a family becomes structured, attempts to change the rules constitute what family therapists call *first-order change*—change within a system that itself remains invariant. For the mother in the previous example to start practicing stricter discipline would be first-order change. The enmeshed mother is caught in an illusion of alternatives. She can be strict or lenient; the result is the same because she remains trapped in a triangle. What's needed is *second-order change*—a change in the system itself.

Minuchin worked out his ideas while struggling with the problems of juvenile delinquency at the Wiltwyck School for Boys in New York. Family therapy with urban slum families was a new development, and publication of his discoveries (Minuchin, Montalvo, Guerney, Rosman, & Schumer, 1967) led to his being invited to become the director of the Philadelphia Child Guidance Clinic in 1965. Minuchin brought Braulio Montalvo and Bernice Rosman with him, and they were joined in 1967 by Jay Haley. Together they transformed a traditional child guidance clinic into one of the great centers of the family therapy movement.

Minuchin's first notable achievement at the Philadelphia Child Guidance Clinic was a unique program for training members of the local black community as paraprofessional family therapists. In 1969, Minuchin received a training grant to launch an intensive two-year program in which Minuchin, Haley, Montalvo, and Rosman developed a highly successful approach to training as well as one of the most important systems of family therapy. According to Haley, one of the advantages to training people with no previous experience as clinicians is that they have less to unlearn and therefore are less resistant to thinking in terms of systems.

The techniques of *structural family therapy* fall into two general strategies. First, the therapist must accommodate to the family in order to "join" them. To begin by challenging a family's preferred mode of relating is almost guaranteed to provoke resistance. If, instead, the therapist starts by trying to understand and accept the family, they'll be more likely to accept treatment. (No one is eager to accept advice from someone who doesn't understand them.) Once this initial *joining* is accomplished, the structural therapist begins to use *restructuring* techniques. These are active maneuvers designed to disrupt dysfunctional structures by strengthening diffuse boundaries and loosening rigid ones (Minuchin & Fishman, 1981).

In 1981, Minuchin moved to New York and established what is now known as the Minuchin Center for the Family, where he pursued his dedication to teaching family therapists from all over the world and his commitment to social justice by working with the foster care system. He also continued to turn out a steady stream of the most influential books in the field. His 1974 *Families and Family Therapy* is deservedly the most popular book in the history of family therapy, and his 1993 *Family Healing* contains some of the most moving descriptions of family therapy ever written.

Other Early Centers of Family Therapy

In New York, Israel Zwerling (who had been analyzed by Nathan Ackerman) and Marilyn Mendelsohn (who was analyzed by Don Jackson) organized the Family Studies Section at Albert Einstein College of Medicine and Bronx State Hospital. Andrew Ferber was named director in 1964, and later Philip Guerin, a protégé of Murray Bowen's, joined the section. Nathan Ackerman served as a consultant, and the group assembled an impressive array of family therapists with diverse orientations. These included Chris Beels, Betty Carter, Monica McGoldrick, Peggy Papp, and Thomas Fogarty.

Philip Guerin became director of training of the Family Studies Section in 1970 and in 1972 established an extramural training program in Westchester. Shortly thereafter, in 1973, he founded the Center for Family Learning, where he developed one of the finest family therapy training programs in the nation.

In Galveston, Texas, Robert MacGregor and his colleagues developed *multiple impact therapy* (MacGregor, 1967). It was a case of necessity being the mother of invention. MacGregor's clinic served a population scattered widely over southeastern Texas, and many of his clients had to travel hundreds of miles. Because they had to come such distances, most of these people were unable to return for weekly sessions. Therefore, to have maximum impact in a short time, MacGregor assembled a large team of professionals who worked intensively with the families for two full days. Although few family therapists have used such marathon sessions, the team approach continues to be one of the hallmarks of the field.

In Boston, the two most significant early contributions to family therapy were both in the experiential wing of the movement. Norman Paul developed an *operational mourning* approach designed to uncover and express unresolved grief. According to Paul, this cathartic approach is useful in almost all families, not just those who've suffered an obvious recent loss.

Also in Boston, Fred and Bunny Duhl set up the Boston Family Institute, where they developed *integrative family therapy*. Along with David Kantor and Sandy Watanabe, the Duhls combined ideas from several family theories and added a number of expressive techniques, including *family sculpting*.

In Chicago, the Family Institute of Chicago and the Institute for Juvenile Research were important centers of the early scene in family therapy. At the Family Institute, Charles and Jan Kramer developed a clinical training program, which was later affiliated with Northwestern University Medical School. The Institute for Juvenile Research also mounted a training program under the leadership of Irv Borstein, with the consultation of Carl Whitaker.

The work of Nathan Epstein and his colleagues, first formulated in the department of psychiatry at McMaster University in Hamilton, Ontario, was a problem-centered approach (Epstein, Bishop, & Baldarin, 1981). The McMaster model goes step by step—elucidating the problem, gathering data, considering alternatives for resolution, and assessing the learning process—to help families understand their own interaction and build on their newly acquired coping skills. Epstein later relocated to Brown University in Providence, Rhode Island.

Important developments in family therapy also occurred outside the United States: Robin Skynner's (1976) use of psychodynamic family therapy at the Institute of Family Therapy in London; British psychiatrist John Howells's (1971) system of family diagnosis as a necessary step for planning therapeutic intervention; and West German Helm Stierlin's (1972) integrative efforts, bringing together psychodynamic and systemic ideas to bear on understanding and treating troubled adolescents. In Rome, Maurizio Andolfi worked with families early in the 1970s and founded, in 1974, the Italian Society for Family Therapy; Mara Selvini Palazzoli and her colleagues founded the Institute for Family Studies in Milan in 1967.

This section concludes with the contributions of Christian Midelfort. Even more than was the case with John Bell, Midelfort's pioneering work in family therapy was slow to gain recognition. He began treating families of hospitalized patients in the early 1950s, delivered what was probably the first paper on family therapy at a professional meeting in 1952 at the American Psychiatric Association Convention, and published one of the first complete books on family therapy in 1957. Nevertheless, as a staff psychiatrist in LaCrosse, Wisconsin, he remained isolated from the rest of the family therapy movement. Midelfort's method of treating families combined psychoanalytic insights with techniques of support and encouragement. At first his concern was to counsel family members on the best ways to help the identified patient, but gradually he evolved a systems viewpoint and conceived of the family as the patient. His technique was to encourage family members to give each other the love and support that was initially provided by the therapist.

Now that you've seen how family therapy emerged in several different places at once, we hope you haven't lost sight of one thing: There is a tremendous excitement to seeing how people's behavior makes sense in the context of their families. Meeting with a family for the first time is like turning on a light in a dark room.

THE GOLDEN AGE OF FAMILY THERAPY

In their first decade, family therapists had all the bravado of new kids on the block. "Look at this!" Haley and Jackson and Bowen seemed to say when they discovered how the whole family was implicated in the symptoms of individual patients.

While they were struggling for legitimacy, family clinicians emphasized their common beliefs and downplayed their differences. Troubles, they agreed, came in families. But, if the watchword of the 1960s was "Look at this!"—emphasizing the leap of understanding made possible by seeing whole families together—the

rallying cry of the 1970s was "Look what I can do!" as the new kids flexed their muscles and carved out their own turf.

The period from 1970 to 1985 saw the flowering of the famous schools of family therapy as the pioneers established training centers and worked out the implications of their models. The leading approach to family therapy in the 1960s was the communications model developed in Palo Alto. The book of the decade was *Pragmatics of Human Communication*, the text that introduced the systemic version of family therapy. The model of the 1980s was strategic therapy, and the books of the decade described its three most vital approaches: *Change* by Watzlawick, Weakland, and Fisch[2]; *Problem-Solving Therapy* by Jay Haley; and *Paradox and Counterparadox* by Mara Selvini Palazzoli and her Milan associates. The 1970s belonged to Salvador Minuchin. His *Families and Family Therapy* and the simple yet compelling model of family structure it described dominated the decade.

Structural theory seemed to offer just what the would-be family therapist was looking for: a simple yet meaningful way of describing family organization and a set of easy-to-follow steps to treatment. In hindsight, we might ask whether the impressive power of Minuchin's approach was a product of the method or the man. (The answer is, probably a little of both.) But in the 1970s the widely shared belief that structural family therapy could be easily learned drew people from all over the world to study at what for a decade was the mecca of family therapy: the Philadelphia Child Guidance Clinic.

The strategic therapy that flourished in the 1980s was centered in three unique and creative groups: MRI's brief therapy group, including John Weakland, Paul Watzlawick, and Richard

---

[2]Although actually published in 1974, this book and its sequel, *The Tactics of Change*, were most widely read and taught in the 1980s.

Fisch; Jay Haley and Cloe Madanes, codirectors of the Family Therapy Institute of Washington, DC; and Mara Selvini Palazzoli and her colleagues in Milan. But, the leading influence on the decade of strategic therapy was exerted by Milton Erickson, albeit from beyond the grave.

Erickson's genius was much admired and much imitated. Family therapists came to idolize Erickson the way children idolized Captain Marvel. We may have been little and the world big, but we could dream of being heroes—strong enough to overpower or clever enough to outwit all that we were afraid of. We'd come home from Saturday matinees all pumped up, get out our toy swords, put on our magic capes—and presto! *We* were superheroes. We were just kids and so we didn't bother translating our heroes' mythic powers into our own terms. Unfortunately, many of those who were starstruck by Erickson's legendary therapeutic tales did the same thing. Instead of grasping the principles on which they were predicated, many therapists simply tried to imitate his "uncommon techniques." To be any kind of competent therapist, you must keep your psychological distance from the supreme artists—the Minuchins, the Milton Ericksons, the Michael Whites; otherwise, you end up aping the magic of their style, rather than grasping the substance of their ideas.

Part of what made Haley's strategic directives so attractive was that they were a wonderful way to gain control over people—for their own good—without the usual frustration of trying to convince them to do the right thing. (Most people already know what's good for them. The hard part is getting them to *do* it.) So, for example, in the case of a bulimic, a strategic directive might be for the bulimic's family to set out a mess of fried chicken, french fries, cookies, and ice cream. Then, with the family watching, the bulimic would mash up all the food with her hands, symbolizing what goes on in her stomach. After the food was reduced to a soggy mess, she would stuff it into the toilet. Then when the toilet clogged, she would have to ask the family

member she resented most to unclog it. This task would symbolize not only what the bulimic does to herself, but also what she puts the family through (Madanes, 1981).

So compelling were such clever interventions that they were much imitated, unfortunately often with little appreciation of the principles underlying them. People were so taken by the creative directives that they often lost sight of Haley's developmental framework and emphasis on hierarchical structure.

What the strategic camp added to Erickson's creative approach to problem solving was a simple framework for understanding how families got stuck in their problems. According to the MRI model, problems develop from mismanagement of ordinary life difficulties. The original difficulty becomes a problem when mishandling leads people to get stuck in more-of-the-same solutions. It was a perverse twist on the old adage "If at first you don't succeed, try, try again."

The Milan group built on the ideas pioneered at MRI, especially the use of the therapeutic double bind, or what they referred to as "counterparadox." Here's an example from *Paradox and Counterparadox* (Selvini Palazzoli, Boscolo, Cecchin, & Prata, 1978). The authors describe a counterparadoxical approach to a six-year-old boy and his family. At the end of the session, young Bruno was praised for acting crazy to protect his father. By occupying his mother's time with fights and tantrums, the boy generously allowed his father more time for work and relaxation. Bruno was encouraged to continue doing what he was already doing, lest this comfortable arrangement be disrupted.

The appeal of the strategic approach was pragmatism. Making use of the cybernetic metaphor, strategic therapists zeroed in on how family systems were regulated by negative feedback. They achieved remarkable results simply by disrupting the interactions that surrounded and maintained symptoms. What eventually turned therapists off to these approaches was their gamesmanship. Their interventions were transparently manipulative. The result was like watching a clumsy magician—you could see him stacking the deck.

Meanwhile, as structural and strategic approaches rose and fell in popularity, four other models of family therapy flourished quietly.

Though they never took center stage, experiential, psychoanalytic, behavioral, and Bowenian models grew and prospered. Although these schools never achieved the cachet of family therapy's latest fads, each of them produced solid clinical approaches, which will be examined at length in subsequent chapters.

SUMMARY

Family therapy has a short history but a long past. For many years, therapists resisted the idea of seeing members of a patient's family, to safeguard the privacy of the patient-therapist relationship. Freudians excluded the real family to uncover the unconscious, introjected family; Rogerians kept the family away to provide unconditional positive regard; and hospital psychiatrists discouraged family visits because they might disrupt the benign milieu of the hospital.

Several converging developments in the 1950s led to a new view of the family as a living system, an organic whole. Hospital psychiatrists noticed that often when patients improved, someone else in the family got worse. Thus it became clear that change in any one person changes the whole system. Eventually it became apparent that changing the family might be the most effective way to change the individual.

Although practicing clinicians in hospitals and child guidance clinics prepared the way for family therapy, the most important breakthroughs were achieved in the 1950s by workers who were scientists first, healers second. In Palo Alto, Gregory Bateson, Jay Haley, Don Jackson, and John Weakland discovered that schizophrenia made sense in the context of pathological family communication. Schizophrenics weren't crazy in some meaningless way; their apparently senseless behavior made sense in their families. At Yale, Theodore Lidz found a striking pattern of instability and conflict in the families of schizophrenics. *Marital schism* (open conflict) and *marital skew* (pathological balance) had pro-

found effects on the development of children. Murray Bowen's observation of how mothers and their schizophrenic offspring go through cycles of closeness and distances was the forerunner of the *pursuer–distancer* dynamic. By hospitalizing whole families for observation and treatment, Bowen implicitly located the problem of schizophrenia in an *undifferentiated family ego mass* and even extended it beyond the nuclear family to three generations. Lyman Wynne linked schizophrenia to the family by demonstrating how *communication deviance* contributes to thought disorder.

These observations launched the family therapy movement, but the excitement they generated blurred the distinction between what the researchers observed and what they concluded. What they observed was that the behavior of schizophrenics *fit* with their families; what they concluded was that the family must be the *cause* of schizophrenia. A second conclusion was even more influential. Family dynamics—double binds, pseudomutuality, undifferentiated family ego mass—began to be seen as products of a system, rather than features of persons who share certain qualities because they live together. Thus was born a new creature, *the family system.*

Who was the first to practice family therapy? This turns out to be a difficult question. As in every field, there were visionaries who anticipated the recognized development of family therapy. Freud, for example, treated "Little Hans" by working with his father as early as 1909. However, such experiments weren't sufficient to challenge the hegemony of individual therapy until the climate of the times was receptive. In the early 1950s, family therapy was begun independently in four different places: by John Bell at Clark University, Murray Bowen at the Menninger Clinic and later at NIMH, Nathan Ackerman in New York, and Don Jackson and Jay Haley in Palo Alto.

These pioneers had distinctly different backgrounds. Not surprisingly, the approaches they developed were also quite different. This diversity still characterizes the field today. Had family therapy been started by a single person, as was psychoanalysis, it's unlikely that there would have been so much creative competition.

In addition to those just mentioned, others who made significant contributions to the founding of family therapy include Lyman Wynne, Theodore Lidz, Virginia Satir, Carl Whitaker, Ivan Boszormenyi-Nagy, Christian Midelfort, Robert MacGregor, and Salvador Minuchin.

What we've called family therapy's golden age—the flowering of the schools in the 1970s and 1980s—was the high-water mark of our self-confidence. Armed with Haley's or Minuchin's latest text, therapists pledged allegiance to one school or another and set off with a sense of mission. What drew them to activist approaches was certainty and charisma. What soured them was hubris. To some, structural family therapy—at least as they had seen it demonstrated at workshops—began to seem like bullying. Others saw the shrewdness of the strategic approach as manipulative. The tactics were clever but cold. Families were described as stubborn; they couldn't be reasoned with. You don't tell a cybernetic machine what you really believe. Therapists got tired of that way of thinking.

In the early years, family therapists were animated by a tremendous sense of enthusiasm and conviction. Today, in the wake of postmodern critiques, managed care, and a resurgence of biological psychiatry, we're less sure of ourselves. In subsequent chapters we'll see how today's family therapists have managed to synthesize creative new ideas with some of the best of the earlier models. But as we explore each of the famous models in depth, we'll also see how some good ideas have been unwisely neglected.

All the complexity of the family field should not, however, obscure its basic premise: The family is the context of human problems. Like all human groups, the family has emergent properties—the whole is greater than the sum of its parts. Moreover, no matter how many and varied the explanations of these emergent properties, they all fall into two categories: *structure* and *process*. The structure of families includes *triangles*, *subsystems*, and *boundaries*. Among the processes that describe family interaction—*emotional reactivity*, *dysfunctional communication*, and so on—the central concept is circularity. Rather than worry about who started what, family therapists understand and treat human problems as a series of moves and countermoves in repeating cycles.

RECOMMENDED READINGS

Ackerman, N. W. 1958. *The psychodynamics of family life.* New York: Basic Books.

Bowen, M. 1960. A family concept of schizophrenia. In *The etiology of schizophrenia*, D. D. Jackson, ed. New York: Basic Books.

Greenberg, G. S. 1977. The family interactional perspective: A study and examination of the work of Don D. Jackson. *Family Process. 16*:385–412.

Haley, J., and Hoffman, L., eds. 1968. *Techniques of family therapy.* New York: Basic Books.

Jackson, D. D. 1957. The question of family homeostasis. *The Psychiatric Quarterly Supplement. 31*:79–90.

Jackson, D. D. 1965. Family rules: Marital quid pro quo. *Archives of General Psychiatry. 12*:589–594.

Lidz, T., Cornelison, A., Fleck, S., and Terry, D.

1957. Intrafamilial environment of schizophrenic patients. II: Marital schism and marital skew. *American Journal of Psychiatry. 114*:241–248.

Vogel, E. F., and Bell, N. W. 1960. The emotionally disturbed child as the family scapegoat. In *The family*, N. W. Bell and E. F. Vogel, eds. Glencoe, IL: Free Press.

Weakland, J. H. 1960. The "double-bind" hypothesis of schizophrenia and three-party interaction. In *The etiology of schizophrenia*, D. D. Jackson, ed. New York: Basic Books.

Wynne, L. C., Ryckoff, I., Day, J., and Hirsch, S. I. 1958. Pseudo-mutuality in the family relationships of schizophrenics. *Psychiatry. 21*:205–220.

REFERENCES

Ackerman, N. W. 1938. The unity of the family. *Archives of Pediatrics. 55*:51–62.

Ackerman, N. W. 1966. *Treating the troubled family.* New York: Basic Books.

Ackerman, N. W., Beatman, F., and Sherman, S. N., eds. 1961. *Exploring the base for family therapy.* New York: Family Service Assn. of America.

Ackerman, N. W., and Sobel, R. 1950. Family diagnosis: An approach to the preschool child. *American Journal of Orthopsychiatry. 20*:744–753.

Bardhill, D. R., and Saunders, B. E. 1988. In *Handbook of family therapy training and supervision*, H. A. Liddle, D. C. Breunlin, and R. C. Schwartz, eds. New York: Guilford Press.

Bateson, G. 1951. Information and codification: A philosophical approach. In *Communication: The social matrix of psychiatry*, J. Ruesch and G. Bateson, eds. New York: Norton.

Bateson, G., Jackson, D. D., Haley, J., and Weakland, J. 1956. Toward a theory of schizophrenia. *Behavioral Sciences. 1*:251–264.

Bell, J. E. 1961. *Family group therapy.* Public Health Monograph No. 64. Washington, DC: U.S. Government Printing Office.

Bell, J. E. 1962. Recent advances in family group therapy. *Journal of Child Psychology and Psychiatry. 3*:1–15.

Bion, W. R. 1948. Experience in groups. *Human Relations. 1*:314–329.

Boszormenyi-Nagy, I., and Spark, G. L. 1973. *Invisible loyalties: Reciprocity in intergenerational family therapy.* New York: Harper & Row.

Bowen, M. 1961. Family psychotherapy. *American Journal of Orthopsychiatry. 31*:40–60.

Bowen, M. 1976. Principles and techniques of multiple family therapy. In *Family therapy: Theory and practice*, P. J. Guerin, ed. New York: Gardner Press.

Bowlby, J. P. 1949. The study and reduction of group tensions in the family. *Human Relations. 2*:123–138.

Broderick, C. B., and Schrader, S. S. 1981. The history of professional marriage and family therapy. In *Handbook of family therapy*, A. S. Gurman and D. P. Kniskern, eds. New York: Brunner/Mazel.

Broderick, C. B. 1991. The history of professional marriage and family therapy. In *Handbook of family therapy*, Vol. II, A. S. Gurman and D. P. Kniskern, eds. New York: Brunner/Mazel.

Dicks, H. V. 1964. Concepts of marital diagnosis and therapy as developed at the Tavistock Family Psychiatric Clinic, London, England. In *Marriage counseling in medical practice*, E. M. Nash, L. Jessner, and D. W. Abse, eds. Chapel Hill: University of North Carolina Press.

Epstein, N. B., Bishop, D. S., and Baldarin, L. M. 1981. McMaster Model of Family Functioning. In *Normal family problems*, F. Walsh, ed. New York: Guilford Press.

Fisher, S., and Mendell, D. 1958. The spread of psychotherapeutic effects from the patient to his family group. *Psychiatry. 21*:133–140.

Freud, S. 1911. Psycho-analytical notes on an autobiographical case of paranoia. *Standard Edition. 12*:3–84. London: Hogarth Press.

Fromm-Reichmann, F. 1948. Notes on the development of treatment of schizophrenics by psychoanalytic psychotherapy. *Psychiatry. 11*:263–274.

Ginsburg, S. W. 1955. The mental health movement and its theoretical assumptions. In *Community programs for mental health*, R. Kotinsky and H. Witmer, eds. Cambridge, MA: Harvard University Press.

Guerin, P. J. 1976. Family therapy: The first twenty-five years. In *Family therapy: Theory and practice*, P. J. Guerin, ed. New York: Gardner Press.

Gurman, A. S. 2008. *Clinical handbook of couple therapy*, 4th ed. New York: Guilford Press.

Haley, J. 1963. *Strategies of psychotherapy*. New York: Grune & Stratton.

Hoffman, L. 1981. *Foundations of family therapy*. New York: Basic Books.

Howells, J. G. 1971. *Theory and practice of family psychiatry*. New York: Brunner/Mazel.

Jackson, D. D. 1954. Suicide. *Scientific American. 191*:88–96.

Jackson, D. D. 1965. Family rules: Marital quid pro quo. *Archives of General Psychiatry. 12*:589–594.

Jackson, D. D., and Weakland, J. H. 1959. Schizophrenic symptoms and family interaction. *Archives of General Psychiatry. 1*:618–621.

Jackson, D. D., and Weakland, J. H. 1961. Conjoint family therapy, some considerations on theory, technique, and results. *Psychiatry. 24*:30–45.

Kaslow, F. W. 1980. History of family therapy in the United States: A kaleidoscopic overview. *Marriage and Family Review. 3*:77–111.

Kempler, W. 1974. *Principles of Gestalt family therapy*. Salt Lake City, UT: Desert Press.

Kluckhohn, F. R., and Spiegel, J. P. 1954. *Integration and conflict in family behavior*. Group for the Advancement of Psychiatry, Report No. 27. Topeka, Kansas.

Laing, R. D. 1960. *The divided self*. London: Tavistock.

Laing, R. D. 1965. Mystification, confusion and conflict. In *Intensive family therapy*, I. Boszormenyi-Nagy and J. L. Framo, eds. New York: Harper & Row.

Levy, D. 1943. *Maternal overprotection*. New York: Columbia University Press.

Lewin, K. 1951. *Field theory in social science*. New York: Harper.

Lidz, T., Cornelison, A., Fleck, S., and Terry, D. 1957a. Intrafamilial environment of the schizophrenic patient. I: The father. *Psychiatry. 20*:329–342.

Lidz, T., Cornelison, A., Fleck, S., and Terry, D. 1957b. Intrafamilial environment of the schizophrenic patient: II. Marital schism and marital schew. *American Journal of Psychiatry. 114*: 241–248.

MacGregor, R. 1967. Progress in multiple impact theory. In *Expanding theory and practice in family therapy*, N. W. Ackerman, F. L. Bateman, and S. N. Sherman, eds. New York: Family Services Association.

Madanes, C. 1981. *Strategic family therapy*. San Francisco: Jossey-Bass.

Minuchin, S. 1974. *Families and family therapy*. Cambridge, MA: Harvard University Press.

Minuchin, S., and Fishman, H. C. 1981. *Family therapy techniques*. Cambridge, MA: Harvard University Press.

Minuchin, S., Montalvo, B., Guerney, B. G., Rosman, B. L., and Schumer, F. 1967. *Families of the slums*. New York: Basic Books.

Minuchin, S., and Nichols, M. P. 1993. *Family healing*. New York: Free Press.

Mittleman, B. 1944. Complementary neurotic reactions in intimate relationships. *Psychoanalytic Quarterly. 13*:474–491.

Mittleman, B. 1948. The concurrent analysis of married couples. *Psychoanalytic Quarterly. 17*: 182–197.

Moreno, J. L. 1945. *Psychodrama*. New York: Beacon House.

Oberndorf, C. P. 1938. Psychoanalysis of married people. *Psychoanalytic Review. 25*:453–475.

Parsons, T., and Bales, R. F. 1955. *Family, socialization and interaction process*. Glencoe, IL: Free Press.

Richmond, M. E. 1917. *Social diagnosis*. New York: Russell Sage.

Satir, V. 1964. *Conjoint family therapy*. Palo Alto, CA: Science and Behavior Books.

Satir, V. 1972. *Peoplemaking*. Palo Alto, CA: Science and Behavior Books.

Schwartz, R. 1995. *Internal family systems therapy*. New York: Guilford Press.

Selvini Palazzoli, M., Boscolo, L., Cecchin, G., and Prata, G. 1978. *Paradox and counterparadox*. New York: Jason Aronson.

Sherif, M. 1948. *An outline of social psychology*. New York: Harper & Brothers.

Singer, M. T., Wynne, L. C., and Toohey, M. L. 1978. Communication disorders and the families of schizophrenics. In *The nature of schizophrenia*, L. C. Wynne, R. L. Cromwell, and S. Matthysse, eds. New York: Wiley.

Skynner, A. C. R. 1976. *Systems of family and marital psychotherapy.* New York: Brunner/Mazel.

Speck, R., and Attneave, C. 1973. *Family networks: Rehabilitation and healing.* New York: Pantheon.

Spiegel, J. P. 1957. The resolution of role conflict within the family. *Psychiatry. 20*:1–16.

Stierlin, H. 1972. *Separating parents and adolescents.* New York: Quadrangle/New York Times Books.

Strodtbeck, F. L. 1954. The family as a three-person group. *American Sociological Review. 19*:23–29.

Strodtbeck, F. L. 1958. Family interaction, values, and achievement. In *Talent and society,* D. C. McClelland, A. L. Baldwin, A. Bronfenbrenner, and F. L. Strodtbeck, eds. Princeton, NJ: Van Nostrand.

Watzlawick, P. A., Beavin, J. H., and Jackson, D. D. 1967. *Pragmatics of human communication.* New York: Norton.

Whitaker, C. A. 1958. Psychotherapy with couples. *American Journal of Psychotherapy. 12*:18–23.

Whitaker, C. A. 1975. Psychotherapy of the absurd: With a special emphasis on the psychotherapy of aggression. *Family Process. 14*:1–16.

Whitaker, C. A. 1976. A family is a four-dimensional relationship. In *Family therapy: Theory and practice,* P. J. Guerin, ed. New York: Gardner Press.

Whitaker, C. A., and Malone, T. P. 1953. *The roots of psychotherapy.* New York: Balkiston.

Wiener, N. 1948. *Cybernetics, or control and communication in the animal and the machine.* New York: Wiley.

Wynne, L. C. 1961. The study of intrafamilial alignments and splits in exploratory family therapy. In *Exploring the base for family therapy,* N. W. Ackerman, F. L. Beatman, and S. N. Sherman, eds. New York: Family Services Association.

Wynne, L. C., Ryckoff, I., Day, J., and Hirsch, S. I. 1958. Pseudomutuality in the family relationships of schizophrenics. *Psychiatry. 21*:205–220.

Lessons from the Early Models

GROUP PROCESS AND COMMUNICATIONS ANALYSIS

2

A Very Special Kind of Group

Most people who practiced family therapy in the early years used some combination of group therapy and the communications theory that came out of Bateson's schizophrenia project. In this chapter, we will explore those two models and see how they had to be modified to fit the unique challenges of treating troubled families.

Those of us who practiced family therapy in the 1960s could often be seen engaged in a strange ritual. When a family filed in for their first session, all anxious and uncertain, the therapist, all smiles, would kneel in front of one of the children. "Hi! What's your name?" Then, "Do you know why you're here?" meanwhile ignoring the parents. The most common answers to this question were "Mommy said we were going to the doctor's," in a frightened voice, or, confused, "Daddy said we were going for a ride." Then the therapist, trying not to sound scornful, would turn to the parents and say, "Perhaps you could explain to Johnny why you *are* here."

The reason for this little charade was that before they understood how families were structured, therapists treated the family as a group, in which the youngest members were presumed to be the most vulnerable and, therefore, in need of expert help to express themselves—as though the parents weren't in charge, as though everybody's opinion were equal.

Another common scene was therapists making solemn comments about patterns of communication: "I notice that when I ask Suzie a question, she turns to Mom to see if it's okay to answer." Very clever. Not only did we expect families to be impressed by such bright remarks, we imagined that they'd somehow instantly start communicating according to some ideal model in *our* heads—"I-statements" and all the rest.

Are we being a little condescending here? Absolutely. The first family therapists turned to models from group therapy and communications analysis because there were no other models available.

SKETCHES OF LEADING FIGURES

Not only did early family therapists turn to the group therapy literature for guidance in treating families, but many of the pioneers of family therapy were themselves products of group therapy training. By far, the most influential of these was John Elderkin Bell.

Bell (1975) credited his start as a family therapist to a fortunate misunderstanding. When he was in London in 1951, Bell heard that Dr. John Bowlby of the Tavistock Clinic was experimenting with group therapy for families. This inspired Bell to try this approach as a means of dealing with behavior problems in children. As Bell later put it, if so eminent an authority as John Bowlby was using family therapy, it must be a good idea. It turned out that Bowlby had only interviewed one family as an adjunct to treating a troubled child, but Bell didn't learn this until years later.

Communications therapy was one of the earliest and most influential approaches to family therapy. The leading characters who developed the communications model were the members of Bateson's schizophrenia project and the Mental Research Institute in Palo Alto, most notably Don Jackson and Jay Haley.

Virginia Satir was also a prominent member of the Mental Research Institute group, but because her emphasis shifted to emotional experiencing, we will consider her in Chapter 8.

THEORETICAL FORMULATIONS

Although he's better known for studying the psychology of individuals, Freud was also interested in interpersonal relations, and many would consider his *Group Psychology and the Analysis of the Ego* (Freud, 1921) the first great text on the psychology of the group. According to Freud, the major requirement for transforming a collection of individuals into a group is the emergence of a leader. In addition to manifest tasks of organization and direction, the leader serves as a parent figure on whom the members become more or less dependent. Members *identify* with the leader as a parent surrogate and with other group members as siblings. *Transference* occurs in groups when members repeat unconscious attitudes formed in the process of growing up.

Freud's concept of *resistance* in individual therapy also applies to groups, because group members—seeking to ward off anxiety—may oppose the progress of treatment by being silent or hostile, missing sessions, or avoiding painful topics. Family groups resist treatment by scapegoating, superficial chatting, prolonged dependency on the therapist, refusing to follow therapeutic suggestions, and allowing difficult family members to stay home.

Like Freud, Wilfred Bion (1961) attempted to develop a group psychology of the unconscious and described groups as functioning on *manifest* and *latent* levels. The group's official task is on the manifest level, but people also join groups to fulfill powerful, but unconscious, primal needs. At the latent level, groups seek a leader who will permit them to gratify their needs for *dependence*, *pairing*, and *fight-flight*.

According to Kurt Lewin's (1951) *field theory*, conflict is an inevitable feature of group life, as members vie with one another for adequate *life space*. Just as animals need their own territory, people seem to need their own "space," and for this reason there is an inherent tension between the needs of the individual and those of the group. The level of conflict generated by this tension depends on the amount of restriction imposed by the group compared with the amount of support it gives in exchange. (People who give up a lot for their families expect a lot in return.)

What distinguished Lewin's model of group tensions from earlier theories is that it was *ahistorical*. Instead of worrying about who did what to whom in the past, Lewin concentrated on what was going on in the *here and now*. This focus on *process* (how people talk), rather than *content* (what they talk about), is one of the keys to understanding the way a group (or family) functions.

❧

Communications therapists adopted the **black box concept** from telecommunications and applied it to the individuals within the family. This model disregards the internal complexities of individuals and concentrates on their input and output; that is, communication. It isn't that these clinicians denied the phenomena of mind—thinking and feeling; they just found it useful to ignore them.

Communications theorists also disregarded the past, leaving that to psychoanalysts, while they searched for patterns with which to understand behavior in the present. They considered it unimportant to determine cause and effect, preferring to use a model of circular causality in which chains of behavior are seen as effect-effect-effect.

Relationships between communicants can be described as either complementary or symmetrical. *Complementary* relationships are based on differences that fit together. A common complementary pattern is where one person is assertive and the other submissive, with each reinforcing the other's position. It's important to understand that these are descriptive, not evaluative, terms. Moreover, it's a mistake to assume that one person's position *causes* the other's, or that one is weaker than the other. As Sartre (1964) pointed out, it is the masochist as well as the sadist who creates a sadomasochistic relationship.

Symmetrical relationships are based on equality; the behavior of one mirrors that of the other. Symmetrical relationships between husbands and wives, where both pursue careers and share housekeeping and childrearing, are often thought of as ideal by today's standards. However, from a communications analysis, there's no reason to assume that such a relationship would be any more stable or functional for the system than a traditional complementary one.

Symmetrical relationships offer the promise of equality, but in them lurks the danger of competitiveness. Equality always seems most reassuring to the person who manages to be a little more equal. Complementary relationships can be mutually supportive, but they carry the danger of domination and unfairness.

Another aspect of communication is that it can be *punctuated* in various ways (Bateson & Jackson, 1964). An outside observer might hear a dialogue as an uninterrupted flow of communication, but each participant may believe that what he or she says is caused by what the other says. Couples therapists are familiar with the stalemate created by the wife who says she only nags because her husband withdraws, while he insists that he only withdraws because she nags. Another example is the wife who says she'd be in the mood for sex more often if her husband were more affectionate, to which he counters that he'd be more affectionate if she'd have sex more often.

As long as couples punctuate their interactions in this fashion, there is little likelihood of change. Each insists that the other causes the problem, and each waits for the other to change.

Communications theory doesn't accept linear causality or look for underlying motives; instead, this model assumes circular causality and analyzes interactions occurring at the present time. Considerations of underlying causality are treated as conceptual noise. The behavior that communications theorists observe is a pattern of communication linked in additive chains of stimulus and response. This model of sequential causality enables therapists to treat behavioral chains as *feedback loops*. When the response to one family member's problematic behavior exacerbates the problem, that chain is seen as a *positive feedback loop*. The advantage of this formulation is that it focuses on interactions that perpetuate problems, which can be changed, instead of inferring underlying causes, which aren't observable and often not subject to change.

NORMAL FAMILY DEVELOPMENT

Now that we have rich literatures on child development and the family life cycle, it may not seem worthwhile to turn to the group dynamics literature to help us understand normal family development. Nevertheless, in the early days of family therapy, therapists borrowed concepts of group development and applied them to families. Among the most well known of these was Talcott Parsons's idea (1950) that groups need an **instrumental leader** to take charge and an **expressive leader** to look after the *social-emotional* needs of the group. Guess who was elected to which roles.

As systems purists, communications therapists treated behavior as ahistorical. Their focus was on the here and now, with very little interest in development. Families were described as systems, which, like all living organisms, depend on two important processes (Maruyama, 1968). First, they must maintain integrity in the face of environmental disturbances. This is accomplished through *negative feedback*, illustrated by

the example of the thermostat in a home heating unit. When the heat drops below a set point, the thermostat activates the furnace until the room returns to the desired temperature.

No living system can survive without structure, but too rigid a structure leaves a system ill-equipped to adapt to changing circumstances. This is why normal families also have mechanisms of *positive feedback*. Negative feedback minimizes change to maintain a steady state; positive feedback alters the system to accommodate to novel inputs. For example, as children grow older, they change the nature of their input to the family system. The most obvious instance of this is adolescence, at which time children demand more independence. A family system limited to negative feedback can only resist such changes. Normal families, on the other hand, also have positive feedback mechanisms and can respond to new information by modifying their structure.

Normal families become periodically unbalanced (Hoffman, 1971) during transition points in the family life cycle. No family passes through these changes unperturbed; all experience stress, resist change, and develop vicious cycles. But flexible families aren't trapped in these cycles; they're able to engage in positive feedback to modify themselves. Dysfunctional families remain stuck, using a symptomatic member to avoid change.

Concepts from general systems theory, such as positive feedback, have the virtues of wide applicability and theoretical elegance, but often seem a little abstract. When we recognize that the channel for positive feedback is communication, it's possible to state the case more plainly. Healthy families are able to change because they communicate clearly and are flexible. When their children say they want to grow up, healthy parents listen.

DEVELOPMENT OF BEHAVIOR DISORDERS

From a group theory perspective, symptoms were considered products of disturbed and disturbing group processes—but groups weren't thought to *cause* disturbance in their members; rather, the behavior of the members was part of the disturbance of the group. Thus group researchers and therapists rejected linear causality in favor of a form of circular causality they called *group dynamics*. Family group therapists were less concerned with the origins of psychopathology than with the conditions that perpetuate it. These include stereotyped roles, breakdowns in communication, and blocked channels for giving and receiving support.

Rigidity of roles forces group interactions to occur within a narrow, stereotyped range. When options are reduced for individuals, the flexibility of the group is constrained. Groups with inflexible roles and rigid structures tend to malfunction when confronted with changed circumstances. Moreover, if flexibility is threatening, such groups don't risk communicating about unmet needs; the result is often frustration and sometimes symptomatic disturbance in one of the group's members. If the needs that generate acute disturbance continue to go unmet, symptoms may be perpetuated as a role, and the group organizes itself around a sick member.

According to communications therapists, the function of symptoms is to maintain the homeostatic equilibrium of family systems. (As we will see, the notion that symptoms are functional—implying that families *need* their problems—was to become controversial.) Pathological families were seen as trapped in maladaptive patterns of communication (Jackson & Weakland, 1961). These families respond to a need for change as negative feedback; that is, change is treated not as an opportunity for growth but as a threat and a signal to change back.

In their theoretical papers, communications theorists maintained that pathology inheres in the system as a whole (Hoffman, 1971; Jackson, 1967; Watzlawick, Beavin, & Jackson, 1967). The *identified patient* was considered a role with

complementary counterroles, all of which contributed to the maintenance of the system. The identified patient might be the victim, but in this framework *victim* and *victimizer* were seen as mutually determined roles—neither is good or bad, and neither causes the other. Although this circular causality was stressed in their theorizing, communications therapists often lapsed into demonizing parents.

 GOALS OF THERAPY

The goal of treating family groups was the same as treating stranger groups: individuation of group members and improved relationships. Individual growth is promoted when unmet needs are verbalized and confining roles are explored and expanded. Notice the difference in emphasis between this—considering families as groups of individuals, each of whom must be helped to develop—and the systemic view of the family as a unit. Treating families as though they were like any other group failed to appreciate the need for hierarchy and structure.

The goal of communications family therapy was "to alter poorly functioning patterns of interaction . . ." (Watzlawick, Beavin, & Jackson, 1967, p. 145). Because *patterns of interaction* are synonymous with *communication*, this meant changing patterns of communication. In the early days of family therapy, especially in Virginia Satir's work, this translated into a generic goal of improving communication in the family. Later, the goal was narrowed to altering specific patterns of communication that maintained problems. By 1974, Weakland wrote that the goal of therapy was resolving symptoms, not reorganizing families: "We see the resolution of problems as primarily requiring a substitution of behavior patterns so as to interrupt the vicious, positive feedback circles" (Weakland, Fisch, Watzlawick, & Bodin, 1974, p. 149).

CONDITIONS FOR BEHAVIOR CHANGE

Group family therapists thought the way to help troubled families was simply to have them sit down and talk to each other. The therapist encourages them to talk openly, supports those who seem reticent, and then critiques the process of their interaction. The therapist's support helps family members open up where they once held back, and this in turn often shows them in a new light, which enables others in the family to relate to them in new ways. For example, children who aren't accustomed to being listened to tend to make themselves heard by disruptive behavior, but if a therapist demonstrates a willingness to listen, the children may learn to express their feelings in words rather than actions.

Group-oriented therapists promoted communication by concentrating on *process* rather than *content* (Bell, 1975; Bion, 1961; Yalom, 1985). This is an important point. The minute a therapist gets caught up in the details of solving a family's problems, he or she loses the opportunity to discover what family members are doing that prevents them from working out their own solutions.

According to the communications theorists, all actions have communicative properties: Symptoms were considered covert messages about relationships (Jackson, 1961). Even a headache that develops from tension in the occipital muscles is a message, because it is a report on how the person feels and a command to be responded to. If a symptom is a covert message, then making the message overt eliminates the need for the symptom. Therefore, one of the important ways to change behavior is to bring hidden messages into the open.

As we have pointed out, an essential ingredient of the double bind is that it is impossible to escape—but no change can be generated from within: It can only come from outside the pattern. The therapist is an outsider who supplies what the relationship cannot: a change in the rules.

A therapist can either point out problematic sequences or simply manipulate them to produce therapeutic change. The first strategy relies on the power of insight and depends on a willingness to change; the second does not. It's an attempt to beat families at their own games.

The first strategy, simply pointing out communicational problems, was represented in Virginia Satir's work and widely practiced by those new to family therapy. The second, less-direct approach was characteristic of Haley and Jackson and eventually became the predominant strategy.

Jackson and Haley's early work with families was influenced by the hypnotherapy they learned from Milton Erickson. The hypnotherapist works by giving instructions whose purpose is often obscure. However, before patients will follow directions, the therapist must gain control of the relationship. Haley (1961) recommended asking uncooperative patients to do something in order to provoke a rebellious response, which served to make them concede that they were relating to the therapist. He mentions, as an example, directing a schizophrenic patient to hear voices. If the patient hears voices, then he is complying with the therapist's request; if he doesn't hear voices, then he can no longer claim to be crazy.

TECHNIQUES

The techniques of family group therapy were similar to those of group therapy. The model of the family was a democratic group. The therapist saw them as people with something to say, often in need of help saying it. There was little concern with structure or reinforcing the parents' hierarchical position. If anything, there was a tendency to give extra support to children and encourage them to assume a more equal role in family interactions.

John Bell's approach (1961) was orchestrated in a series of stages. First was a *child-centered phase*, in which children were helped to express their wishes and concerns. Bell was so anxious to help children participate that he held preliminary meetings with parents to encourage them to go along with some of the children's requests as a means of gaining their cooperation.

After the children spoke up and were rewarded with some additional privileges, it was the parents' turn. In the *parent-centered stage*, parents usually began by complaining about their children's behavior. During this phase, Bell was careful to soften the harshest parental criticisms and to focus on problem solving. In the final, or *family-centered*, stage, the therapist equalized support for the entire family while they continued to improve their communication and work out solutions to their problems. The following vignette illustrates Bell's (1975) directive style of intervening:

> After remaining silent for a few sessions, one father came in with a great tirade against his son, daughter, and wife. I noticed how each individual in his own way, within a few minutes, was withdrawing from the conference. Then I said, "Now I think we should hear what Jim has to say about this, and Nancy should have her say, and perhaps we should also hear what your wife feels about it." This restored family participation without closing out the father. (p. 136)

Three specialized applications of group methods to family treatment were *multiple family group therapy*, *multiple impact therapy*, and *network therapy*.

Peter Laqueur began **multiple family group therapy** in 1950 at Creedmore State Hospital in New York and refined this approach at Vermont State Hospital (Laqueur, 1966, 1976). Multiple family group therapy involved treating four to six families together for weekly sessions of ninety minutes. Laqueur and his cotherapists conducted multiple family groups like traditional therapy groups with the addition of encounter-group and psychodrama techniques. Structured exercises were used to increase the level of interaction and intensity of feeling; families were used as cotherapists to help confront members of other families from a more personal position than therapists could take.

Although multiple family therapy lost its most creative force with Peter Laqueur's untimely death, it is still occasionally used, especially in hospital settings, both inpatient (McFarlane, 1982) and outpatient (Gritzer & Okum, 1983).

Robert MacGregor and his colleagues at the University of Texas Medical Branch in Galveston developed **multiple impact therapy** as a way to have maximum impact on families who came from all over Texas to spend several days with a team of professionals (MacGregor, 1967, 1972; MacGregor, Richie, Serrano, Schuster, McDonald, & Goolishian, 1964). Team members met with various combinations of family members and then assembled in a large group to make recommendations. Although multiple impact therapy is no longer practiced, its intense but infrequent meetings prefigured later developments in experiential therapy (Chapter 8) and the Milan model (Chapter 6).

Network therapy was developed by Ross Speck and Carolyn Attneave for assisting families in crisis by assembling their entire social network—family, friends, neighbors—in gatherings of as many as fifty people. Teams of therapists were used, and their emphasis was on breaking destructive patterns of relationship and mobilizing support (Ruevini, 1975; Speck & Attneave, 1973).

Therapeutic teams meet with networks in meetings lasting from two to four hours; groups typically meet three to six times. Encounter group techniques are used to alleviate defensiveness and foster a climate of warm involvement. After the initial enthusiasm wears off, network groups often become discouraged as members realize just how entrenched certain problems are. Uri Ruevini (1975) described one case in which a period of depression set in and the problem family felt isolated and abandoned by the network. Ruevini broke through this impasse by prescribing a cathartic group exercise, "the death ceremony." Family members were asked to close their eyes and imagine themselves dead. The rest of the network were asked to share their feelings about the family: their strengths, their weaknesses, and what each of them meant to their friends. This dramatic device produced an outpouring of feeling that roused the network out of depression.

Speck and Attneave (1973) described breaking the network into problem-solving subgroups, using action instead of affect to move beyond despair. In one case, they assigned a group of friends to watch over an adolescent who was abusing drugs and another group to arrange for him to move out of his parents' house. Breakthrough is achieved when the network's energies are unleashed and directed toward active resolution of problems. Network sessions often produce what Speck and Attneave called "the network effect": a feeling of connectedness and the satisfaction of solving problems once thought to be overwhelming. Once a network has been activated, there's always someone to call when the need arises.

Most of the techniques of communications family therapy consisted of teaching rules of clear communication, analyzing and interpreting communication patterns, and manipulating interactions through a variety of strategic maneuvers. The progression of these strategies from straightforward to strategic reflected the growing awareness of how family systems resist change.

In their early work (Jackson & Weakland, 1961), communications therapists opened by indicating their belief that the whole family was involved in the presenting problem. They explained that all families develop habitual patterns of communication, including some that are problematical. This attempt to convert clients from seeing the identified patient as the problem to accepting mutual responsibility underestimated families' resistance to change. Later, these therapists were more likely to begin by accepting a family's own definition of their problems (Haley, 1976).

After therapists made their opening remarks, they asked family members, usually one at a time, to discuss their problems. The therapist listened but concentrated on the process of communication. When someone in a family spoke in a confused or confusing way, the therapist would point this out and insist on rules of clear communication.

When he began treating families of schizophrenics, Don Jackson thought he needed to protect patients from their families (Jackson & Weakland, 1961), but he came to realize that parents and children were bound together in mutually destructive games. Even now, those new to family therapy, especially if they haven't yet become parents themselves, tend to identify with children and see parents as the bad guys. Not only is this wrong, as Jackson later realized, but it alienates parents and drives them out of treatment. Young therapists often begin "knowing" that parents are to blame for their children's problems. Only later, when they become parents themselves, do they achieve a more balanced perspective—namely, that family problems are all the children's fault.

Jackson began first sessions by saying, "We are here to work together on better understanding one another so that you all can get more out of your family life" (Jackson & Weakland, 1961, p. 37). Not only does this remark structure the meeting, but it also conveys the idea that all members of the family are to become the focus of discussion. Furthermore, it reveals the therapist's intentions and may therefore precipitate a struggle with parents who may resent the implication that they are part of the problem. Thus, we see that Jackson was an active therapist who set the rules at the outset and explained openly what he was doing, to anticipate and disarm resistance.

Today, most family therapists find it more effective not to make speeches or announce their intentions. Many would suggest that it isn't necessary to describe their work as "family therapy" but simply get to work talking about the presenting problem and getting everyone involved in the discussion.

According to Jay Haley, the mere presence of a third person, the therapist, helps couples solve their problems. By dealing fairly with each partner and not taking sides, the therapist disarms the usual blaming maneuvers; in other words, the therapist acts as a referee. In addition to being a referee, the communications therapist relabeled the activity of family members with each other. One strategy was to redefine what family members say, stressing the positive aspects of their relationship. "For example," Haley (1963) said, "if a husband is protesting his wife's constant nagging, the therapist might comment that the wife seems to be trying to reach her husband and achieve more closeness with him. If the wife protests that her husband constantly withdraws from her, the husband might be defined as one who wants to avoid discord and seeks an amiable relationship" (p. 139). This technique, later called *reframing*, became a central feature of strategic therapy.

One of Haley's strategies was to point out the rules that govern family relationships. Dysfunctional rules made explicit become more difficult to follow. For example, some people berate their mates for not expressing themselves, but these people complain and criticize so much that the mates hardly have a chance. If a therapist points this out, it becomes more difficult to follow the implicit rule that the mate should not talk.

Haley's directives were of two sorts: suggestions to behave differently and suggestions to continue to behave the same. Haley's suggestion that family members continue to behave in the same way was a therapeutic paradox. When a rebellious teenager is instructed to "continue to rebel," he is caught in a paradoxical position. Continuing to rebel means following the direction of an authority figure (and admitting that you are rebellious). Only by giving up this behavior can the teenager maintain the illusion of freedom. Sometimes it's effective to have one family member suggest that another continue symptomatic behavior. This may produce a significant shift because it alters who defines the nature of the relationship.

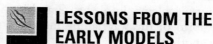

LESSONS FROM THE EARLY MODELS

The most important contribution from group studies was the idea that all groups, including families, have emergent properties. When people join together in a group, relational processes emerge that reflect the individuals involved *and* their collective patterns of interaction. Among the most important **group dynamics** that family therapists identified are triangulation, scapegoating, alignments, coalitions, and splits.

Group theorists also taught us the importance of *roles*, official and unofficial, and how roles organize behavior in groups. Family therapists draw on role theory when they support parents in their role as leaders or point out how covert roles can detract from group functioning, such as how a father who constantly plays the role of jokester distracts the family from discussing problems. Therapists also help family members realize how rigid roles trap them in narrow and inflexible performances, such as when teenagers are so busy *not* being their parents that they never figure out how to be themselves.

The distinction between **process** and **content** was profoundly important to family therapists. When families seek treatment, they expect help solving their problems. They might want to know how to help a shy youngster make friends or how to get a defiant teenager to show respect.

But what a family therapist tries to figure out is: Why hasn't the family been able to solve their own problems? What about the way they've been going about it isn't working? Therefore, when a family discusses their problems, the therapist listens as much to the process of the discussion—who speaks to whom and in what way—as to the content of what they're saying.

The shift from attending to what people say to how they say it—openly or defensively, cooperatively or competitively—is one of the critical strategies in all forms of therapy. Stated another way, most family therapists focus on the here and now, bringing problems into the consulting room in the form of the way family members relate to one another.

The primary group therapy technique—promoting free and open discussion—helped therapists encourage dialogue in families. But although helping families talk over their problems may enable them to resolve a minor crisis, conversation alone is rarely sufficient to solve more difficult problems. Moreover, the model of a democratic group on which this technique is predicated overlooks the unique structural properties of families. Unlike therapy groups, families are *not* made up of equals. Every member of a family may have an equal right to his or her feelings, but someone has to be in charge. Therapists who encourage everyone to have an equal say fail to respect the family's need for leadership and hierarchy.

Group family therapists were directive to the extent of encouraging people to speak up when they appeared to have something to say; otherwise, they were relatively passive. In therapy groups, with contrasting defenses and personality styles, therapists can act as catalysts to prompt members to confront and challenge each other. Families, however, often share defenses and unproductive attitudes, and therapists can't rely on other group members to challenge family norms. That's why contemporary family therapists, who treat families more actively, confront family patterns of interaction (rather than individual reticence) and look for ways to circumvent defenses that are more powerful in families than in groups of strangers.

Both multiple impact therapy and network therapy brought tremendous resources to bear on families in crisis. Although family therapists in clinics often work in teams, today we usually rely on one therapist to treat a family. Perhaps there are times when it makes sense to launch the all-out effort that multiple impact therapy represented. The additional advantage of network therapy was that it mobilized the natural resources of a family's community. Perhaps this model is still useful: It uses community resources that remain available after treatment is over, and it's a useful antidote to the isolation of many families.

Communications therapy was one of the first and most influential forms of family treatment. Its theoretical development was tied to general systems theory, and the therapy that emerged was a systems approach par excellence. Communication was the detectable input and output therapists used to analyze interpersonal systems. Communication was described as *feedback*, as a tactic in interpersonal power struggles, and as a symptom. In fact, all behavior was considered communication. The trouble is, when all actions are treated as communication, communications analysis may be taken to mean everything and therefore nothing. Human relations aren't all a matter of communication: Communication may be the matrix in which interactions are embedded, but human interactions have other attributes as well—motivation, emotion, cognition, conflict.

The Bateson group may be best remembered for the concept of the double bind, but their enduring contribution was applying communications analysis to a wide range of behavior, including family dynamics. In fact, the idea of metacommunication is a more useful concept than the double bind, and it has been incorporated not only by family therapists but also by the general public. Whether they are familiar with the term *metacommunication*, most people understand that all messages have both report and command functions.

Another of the most significant ideas of communications therapy is that families are rule-governed systems, maintained by *negative feedback* mechanisms. Negative feedback accounts for the stability of normal families and the inflexibility of dysfunctional ones. Families without adequate positive feedback mechanisms are unable to adjust to changing circumstances.

Communications theorists borrowed the *open systems* model from general systems theory, but their clinical interventions were based on the *closed systems* paradigm of cybernetics. Therapy was conceived as a power struggle in which the therapist takes control to outwit the forces of symptom maintenance.

When communication takes place in a closed system—an individual's fantasies or a family's private conversations—there's little opportunity for adjusting the system. Only when someone outside the system provides input can correction occur. This is the premise on which communications therapy was based. Because the rules of family functioning are largely unknown to the family, the best way to examine and correct them is to consult an expert.

While there were major differences among the therapeutic strategies of Haley, Jackson, Satir, and Watzlawick, they were all committed to altering dysfunctional patterns of communication. They pursued this goal by direct and indirect means. The direct approach, favored by Satir, sought change by teaching clear communication. This approach included such tactics as telling people to speak for themselves and pointing out nonverbal messages.

The trouble is, as Haley noted, "One of the difficulties involved in telling patients to do something is the fact that psychiatric patients are noted for their hesitation about doing what they are told." For this reason, communications therapists came to rely on more indirect strategies,

designed to provoke change rather than foster awareness.

Resistance was treated with a variety of paradoxical directives, known as *therapeutic double binds*. Milton Erickson's technique of prescribing resistance was used as a lever to gain control—for example, as when a therapist tells family members not to reveal everything in the first session. The same ploy was used to prescribe symptoms, an action that made unrecognized rules explicit, implied that such behavior was voluntary, and put the therapist in control.

Today, the theories of communications therapy have been absorbed into the mainstream of family therapy and the symptom-focused interventions became the basis of the strategic and solution-focused models.

 ## SYSTEMS ANXIETY

Therapists first encountered the family as an adversary. Freud's discoveries indicted families as seducers of innocent children and later as agents of cultural repression, the source of all guilt and anxiety. Hospital psychiatrists saw patients as victims of their families and, except for purposes of footing the bill, kept the family at arm's length.

Communications therapists rescued schizophrenics from psychiatric invalidation by demonstrating that their crazy conversation made sense as a desperate solution to desperate family situations. It wasn't the patient but the **family system** that was deranged.

The Bateson group's observations were meant to be scientific, yet their language for describing family systems was combative, often suggesting not just resistance but willful opposition to change. The idea that families were oppositional put family therapists in an adversarial stance. Because families were seen as mindless systems, at once rigid (holding fast to their own ways) and slippery (hard to pin down), interviewing them became a struggle.

The shift from working with individuals to families was discontinuous and required new ways of thinking. Cybernetics and general systems theory provided useful metaphors to help clinicians organize the patterned interactions of family life.

The great advance of systemic thinking was the recognition that people's lives are linked such that behavior in families becomes a product of mutual influence. The danger of forgetting that systems metaphors are just that is the danger of overestimating their influence—and of dehumanizing individual family members. One myth of the system is that it is determinative rather than influential. Thus, for example, an overinvolved mother who steps back, makes room for her husband to become more involved, but this shift in the system doesn't *make* him get involved. By the same token, although it may be difficult for a disengaged parent to spend more time with children enmeshed with the other parent, it isn't impossible.

Much of what we do may be automatic and channeled by patterns of interaction, but although we don't always reflect and act rationally, we sometimes do. We aren't simply links in a circular chain of events; we are people with names who experience ourselves as centers of initiative. Certainly, we are linked to others. Much of what we do is with other people in mind, some of what we do is with others, and once in a while for others, but the *we* who are the authors of the doing are individuals, with hearts and minds and wills of our own.

Early family therapists treated the family as a *cybernetic system* that governs itself through feedback. Perhaps they overemphasized negative feedback, which makes families resist change, in part because they were studying schizophrenic families, who tend to be particularly rigid. Nevertheless, as we came to realize, although systems thinking alerts us to our interconnections, the metaphor of an inanimate system is not an adequate model for human systems. When we think systemically, we realize that individuals are systems within systems and that although they respond to forces outside themselves, they are also initiators, with imagination, memory, reason, and desire.

RECOMMENDED READINGS

Bell, J. E. 1961. *Family group therapy.* Public Health Monograph No. 64. Washington, DC: U.S. Government Printing Office.

Bell, J. E. 1975. *Family therapy.* New York: Jason Aronson.

Haley, J. 1963. *Strategies of psychotherapy.* New York: Grune & Stratton.

Hoffman, L. 1971. Deviation-amplifying processes in natural groups. In *Changing families,* J. Haley, ed. New York: Grune & Stratton.

Jackson, D. D. 1961. Interactional psychotherapy. In *Contemporary psychotherapies,* M. T. Stein, ed. New York: Free Press.

Jackson, D. D. 1967. *Therapy, communication and change.* Palo Alto, CA: Science and Behavior Books.

Lederer, W., and Jackson, D. D. 1968. *Mirages of marriage.* New York: Norton.

MacGregor, R., Richie, A. M., Serrano, A. C., Schuster, F. P., McDonald, E. C., and Goolishian, H. A. 1964. *Multiple impact therapy with families.* New York: McGraw-Hill.

Satir, V. 1964. *Conjoint family therapy.* Palo Alto, CA: Science and Behavior Books.

Sluzki, C. E. 1978. Marital therapy from a systems theory perspective. In *Marriage and marital therapy,* T. J. Paolino and B. S. McCrady, eds. New York: Brunner/Mazel.

Speck, R. V., and Attneave, C. A. 1971. Social network intervention. In *Changing families,* J. Haley, ed. New York: Grune & Stratton.

Watzlawick, P., Beavin, J. H., and Jackson, D. D. 1967. *Pragmatics of human communication.* New York: Norton.

REFERENCES

Bateson, G., and Jackson, D. D. 1964. Some varieties of pathogenic organization. *Disorders of Communication.* 42:270–283.

Bell, J. E. 1961. *Family group therapy.* Public Health Monograph No. 64. Washington, DC: U.S. Government Printing Office.

Bell, J. E. 1975. *Family group therapy.* New York: Jason Aronson.

Bion, W. R. 1961. *Experiences in groups.* New York: Tavistock Publications.

Freud, S. 1921. *Group psychology and the analysis of the ego.* Standard Edition. Vol. 18. London: Hogarth Press, 1955.

Gritzer, P. H., and Okum, H. S. 1983. Multiple family group therapy: A model for all families. In *Handbook of family and marital therapy,* B. B. Wolman and G. Stricker, eds. New York: Plenum Press.

Haley, J. 1961. Control in psychotherapy with schizophrenics. *Archives of General Psychiatry.* 5: 340–353.

Haley, J. 1963. *Strategies of psychotherapy.* New York: Grune & Stratton.

Haley, J. 1976. *Problem-solving therapy.* San Francisco: Jossey-Bass.

Hoffman, L. 1971. Deviation-amplifying processes in natural groups. In *Changing families,* J. Haley, ed. New York: Grune & Stratton.

Jackson, D. D. 1961. Interactional psychotherapy. In *Contemporary psychotherapies,* M. T. Stein, ed. New York: Free Press.

Jackson, D. D. 1967. Aspects of conjoint family therapy. In *Family therapy and disturbed families,* G. H. Zuk and I. Boszormenyi-Nagy, eds. Palo Alto, CA: Science and Behavior Books.

Jackson, D. D., and Weakland, J. H. 1961. Conjoint family therapy: Some considerations on theory, technique, and results. *Psychiatry.* 24:30–45.

Laqueur, H. P. 1966. General systems theory and multiple family therapy. In *Handbook of psychiatric therapies,* J. Masserman, ed. New York: Grune & Stratton.

Laqueur, H. P. 1976. Multiple family therapy. In *Family therapy: Theory and practice,* P. J. Guerin, ed. New York: Gardner Press.

Lewin, K. 1951. *Field theory in social science.* New York: Harper.

MacGregor, R. 1967. Progress in multiple impact theory. In *Expanding theory and practice in family therapy,* N. W. Ackerman, F. L. Beatman, and S. N. Sherman, eds. New York: Family Service Association.

MacGregor, R. 1972. Multiple impact psychotherapy with families. In *Family therapy: An introduction to theory and technique,* G. D. Erickson and T. P. Hogan, eds. Monterey, CA: Brooks/Cole.

MacGregor, R., Richie, A. M., Serrano, A. C., Schuster, F. P., McDonald, E. C., and Goolishian, H. A. 1964. *Multiple impact therapy with families.* New York: McGraw-Hill.

Marayuma, M. 1968. The second cybernetics: Deviation-amplifying mutual causal processes. In *Modern systems research for the behavioral scientist,* W. Buckley, ed. Chicago: Aldine.

McFarlane, W. R. 1982. Multiple-family therapy in the psychiatric hospital. In *The psychiatric hospital and the family,* H. T. Harbin, ed. New York: Spectrum.

Parsons, T. 1950. Psychoanalysis and the social structure. *Psychoanalytic Quarterly.* 19:371–380.

Ruevini, U. 1975. Network intervention with a family in crisis. *Family Process.* 14:193–203.

Sartre, J. P. 1964. *Being and nothingness.* New York: Citadel Press.

Speck, R. V., and Attneave, C. A. 1973. *Family networks.* New York: Pantheon.

Watzlawick, P., Reavin, J. H., and Jackson, D. D. 1967. *Pragmatics of human communication.* New York: Norton.

Weakland, J., Fisch, R., Watzlawick, P., and Bodin, A. M. 1974. Brief therapy focused problem resolution. *Family Process.* 13:141–168.

Yalom, I. D. 1985. *The theory and practice of group psychotherapy,* 3rd ed. New York: Basic Books.

Basic Techniques of Family Therapy

3

From Symptom to System

 GETTING STARTED

The Initial Telephone Call

The goal of the initial contact is to get an overview of the presenting problem and arrange for the family to come in for a consultation. Listen to the caller's description of the problem and identify all members of the household as well as others who might be involved (including the referral source and other agencies). Although the initial phone call should be brief, it's important to establish a connection with the caller as a basis for engagement. Then, schedule the first interview, specifying who should attend (usually everyone in the household) and the time and place.

Although there are things you can learn to say to encourage the whole family to attend, the most important consideration is attitudinal. First, understand and respect that the worried mother who wants you to treat her child individually or the unhappy husband who wants to talk to you alone has a perfectly legitimate point of view, even if it doesn't happen to coincide with your own. But if you expect to meet with the entire family, at least for an initial assessment, a matter-of-fact statement such as "That's how I work" will get most families to agree to a consultation.

When the caller presents the problem as limited to one person, a useful way to broaden the focus is to ask how the problem is affecting other members of the family. If the caller balks at the idea of bringing in the family or says that a particular member won't attend, say that you'll need to hear from everyone, at least initially, in order to get as much information as possible. Most people accept the need to give their point of view; what they resist is the implication that they're to blame.

The initial phone contact should be relatively brief to avoid developing an alliance with just one family member.

When a child is the identified patient, parents may be reluctant to bring along siblings they don't see as part of the problem. Like the uninvolved husband who is "too busy" to attend, nonsymptomatic brothers and sisters may be important to help broaden the focus from the identified patient's failings to relationship issues in the family. It isn't necessary to suggest that everyone is involved in the problem. (It may help to mention that you're not implying that.)

What is important is getting everyone to work together toward a solution.[1]

Finally, because most families are reluctant to come in and face their conflicts, a reminder call before the first session helps cut down on the no-show rate.

The First Interview

The goals of the first interview are to build an alliance with the family and develop a hypothesis about what's maintaining the presenting problem. It's a good idea to come up with a tentative hypothesis (in technical terms, a hunch) after the initial phone call and then test it in the first interview. (Remain open to refuting, not just confirming, your initial hypothesis.) The point isn't to jump to conclusions but to start actively thinking. In addition to developing a hypothesis about what may be constraining a family from solving their problems, it's also important to think about what things they are already doing, or have done in the past, that support them in moving forward in their lives.

The primary objectives of a consultation are to establish rapport and gather information. Introduce yourself to the contact person and then to the other adults. Ask parents to introduce their children. Shake hands with everyone. Orient the family to the room (observation mirrors, videotaping, toys for children) and to the format of the session (length and purpose). Repeat briefly what the caller told you over the phone (so as not to leave others wondering), and then ask for elaboration. Once you've acknowledged that person's point of view ("So what

---

[1]Not all therapists routinely meet with the entire family. Some find that they have more room to maneuver by meeting first with individuals or subgroups and then gradually involving others. Others attempt to work with the *problem-determined system*, those people directly involved. Still others try to determine who are the "cus-

tomers," those who seem most concerned. If a therapist suspects violence or abuse, individual sessions may enable family members to reveal what they might not discuss in front of the whole family. The point to remember is that family therapy is more a way of looking at things than a technique that requires seeing the whole family together.

you're saying is . . ."), ask the other family members for their viewpoint.

One of the things beginning therapists worry about is that bringing in an entire family may lead to a shouting match that will escalate out of control. Some clients respond to being asked what's wrong by trading accusations in an increasingly emotional manner. The antidote to arguing is insisting that family members speak one at a time and that others not interrupt. Giving everyone a chance to talk and be heard is a good idea in every case; with emotionally reactive families, it's imperative.

Most families aren't so reactive that they will break into arguments in the first session. Speaking to them one at a time is easy. The more volatile the clients, the more firmly the therapist will have to insist that they not interrupt each other. If you know that you won't tolerate interruptions (because they can lead to things getting out of control), it's relatively easy to say so firmly, to raise your voice if need be, and even to stand up and use hand gestures if absolutely necessary. Interrupting people to prevent arguments isn't impolite; it's therapeutic.

As therapists gain experience, they learn when to relax the rule against interruptions. They are more tolerant of arguments because they have confidence that they can cut off disputes that start to get out of hand. Making sure that everyone gets a chance to express his or her point of view is an essential part of the alliance-building process. Reticent family members may need to be drawn out; at the very least, they should not be ignored.

Most families are anxious and uncertain about therapy. They're not sure what to expect. They may be uncomfortable discussing their concerns with the entire family present. Above all, most people are afraid that someone is going to blame them for family problems or expect them to change in ways they aren't prepared to. For these reasons, it's imperative to establish and maintain a bond of sympathy and understanding with every member of the family.

Early in your first contact with a family, it's useful to ask each person "How did *you* feel about coming in?" This encourages honesty and helps establish the therapist as someone willing to listen. If, for example, a child says "I didn't want to come" or "I think it's stupid," you can say "Thanks for being honest."

Beginning therapists may be so anxious to avoid upsetting clients that they spend too much time making small talk. Later, this same anxiety may manifest itself in a reluctance to challenge detrimental ways of interacting. There is nothing passive about good therapy. Change often requires active intervention. By the same token, there's nothing passive about maintaining a therapeutic alliance; it requires an active effort to listen and understand. Most people will accept challenges or new ways of looking at things; what they won't accept is a lack of respect for their ideas.

While most of the first session should be taken up with a discussion of the presenting problem, this problem-centered focus can have a disheartening effect. Spending some time exploring family members' interests and accomplishments is never wasted and sometimes dramatically changes the emotional energy of sessions. People need to be seen as more than just problems (the distant father, the rebellious teenager); they need to be seen as three-dimensional human beings.

Bringing in the whole family means including young children. The inclusion of children allows you to see how their parents relate to them. Are the parents able to get the children to play quietly in the corner if you ask them to? Do they overmanage minor squabbles between siblings? Do both parents interact with the children or only the mother? Children of about five and under should be provided with toys so they can play and feel comfortable. The inhibited child who is fearful of the family's disapproval will sit quietly on a chair and may be afraid to play. The aggressive child will attack the toys and play violent games. The anxious child will flit around the room, unable to settle on any one thing. The enmeshed child will continue to intrude him- or herself into the parents' conversation with the therapist.

In gathering information, some therapists find it useful to take a family history, and many use **genograms** to diagram the extended family network (see Chapter 5). Others believe that whatever history is essential will emerge in the natural course of events; they prefer to concentrate on the family's presenting complaint and the circumstances surrounding it.

Family therapists develop hypotheses about how family members might be involved in the presenting problem by asking what they've done to try to solve it and by watching how they interact. Ideas are as important as actions, so it's useful to notice unhelpful explanations as well as unproductive interactions.

Two kinds of information that are particularly important are *solutions that don't work* and *transitions in the life cycle*. If whatever the family has been doing to resolve their difficulties hasn't worked, it may be that those attempts are part of the problem. A typical example is overinvolved parents trying to help a shy child make friends by coaxing and criticizing. Sometimes, family members will say they've "tried everything." Their mistake may be inconsistency. They give up too quickly.

Despite the natural tendency to focus on problems and what causes them, it is a family's strengths, not their weaknesses, that are most important in successful therapy. Therefore, the therapist should search for resilience (Walsh, 1998). What have these people done well? How have they handled problems successfully in the past? What would a hopeful future look like? What is each person's greatest success? Even the most disheartened families have been successful at times, but those positive episodes may be obscured by the frustration they feel over their current difficulties. Clients appreciate a therapist who is as interested in their best moments as in their worst.

Although it isn't always apparent to families, most seek treatment because they have failed to adjust to changing circumstances. If a husband or a wife develops problems within a few months

The challenge of first interviews is to develop an alliance without accepting at face value the family's description of one person as the problem.

after a baby's birth, it may be because they haven't shifted effectively from being a unit of two to a unit of three. A young mother may be depressed because she doesn't have enough support. A young father may be jealous of the attention his wife now lavishes on the baby.

Even though the strain of having a new baby may seem obvious, you'd be amazed at how often depressed young mothers are treated as though there were something wrong with them—"unresolved dependency needs," "inability to cope," or perhaps a Prozac deficiency. The same is true when families develop problems around the time a child starts school, enters adolescence, or reaches any other developmental milestone. The transitional demands on the family are obvious, *if* you think about them.

Young therapists may have no experience with some of the challenges their clients are struggling with. This underscores the need for therapists to remain curious and respectful of families' predicaments rather than jumping to conclusions. For example, a young married therapist couldn't understand why so many clients with young children rarely went out together as a couple. He assumed that they were avoiding being alone together. Later, with small children of his own, he began to wonder how those couples got out at all!

Family therapists explore the process of family interaction by asking questions about how family members relate to each other and by inviting them to discuss their problems with one another in the session. The first strategy, asking *process* or *circular* questions, is favored by Bowenians, and the second, by structural therapists. In either case, the question is "What's keeping the family stuck?"

Once the therapist has met with a family, learned about the problem that brings them to treatment, made an effort to understand the family's context, and formulated a hypothesis about what needs to be done to resolve the problem, he or she should make a recommendation to the family. This might include consulting another professional (a learning disability expert, a physician, a lawyer) or even suggesting that the family doesn't need—or doesn't seem ready for—treatment. Most often, however, the recommendation will be for further meetings. Although many therapists try to make recommendations at the end of the first interview, doing so may be hasty. If you need two or three sessions to form a bond with the family, understand their situation, and find out if you can work with them, then take two or three sessions.

If you think you can help the family with their problems, offer them a *treatment contract*. Acknowledge why they came in, say that it was a good idea, and say that you think you can help. Then establish a meeting time, the frequency and length of sessions, who will attend, the presence of observers or use of videotape, the fee, and how insurance will be handled. Remember that resistance doesn't magically disappear after the first (or fourteenth) session. Stress the importance of keeping appointments, the need for everyone to attend, and your willingness to hear about dissatisfactions with you or the therapy. Finally, don't forget to emphasize the family's goals and the strengths you have observed to meet them.

First Session Checklist

1. Make contact with each member of the family, and acknowledge his or her point of view about the problem and feelings about coming to therapy.
2. Establish leadership by controlling the structure and pace of the interview.
3. Develop a working alliance with the family by balancing warmth and professionalism.
4. Compliment clients on positive actions and family strengths.
5. Maintain empathy with individuals and respect for the family's way of doing things.
6. Focus on specific problems and attempted solutions.

7. Develop hypotheses about unhelpful interactions around the presenting problem. Be curious about why these have persisted. Also notice helpful interactions that can support the family in moving forward.
8. Don't overlook the possible involvement of family members, friends, or helpers who aren't present.
9. Negotiate a treatment contract that acknowledges the family's goals and specifies the therapist's framework for structuring treatment.
10. Invite questions.

The Early Phase of Treatment

The early phase of treatment is devoted to refining the initial hypothesis into a formulation about what's maintaining the problem and then beginning to work on resolving it. The strategy shifts from building an alliance to challenging actions and assumptions. Most therapists are able to figure out what needs to change; what sets good therapists apart is their willingness to push for those changes.

Pushing for change may suggest a confrontational style, but what's required to help people risk change isn't any particular way of working; rather, it is a relentless commitment to helping make things better. This commitment is evident in Michael White's dogged questioning of problem-saturated stories, Phil Guerin's calm insistence that family members stop blaming each other and start looking at themselves, and Virginia Goldner's determined insistence that violent men take responsibility for their behavior.

No matter what techniques a therapist uses to push for change, it's important to maintain a strong therapeutic alliance. Although the term *therapeutic alliance* may sound like jargon, there's nothing abstract about it. It means listening to and acknowledging the client's point of view. It is this empathic understanding that makes family members feel respected—and that makes them open to accepting challenges.

Regardless of what model they follow, effective therapists are persistent in their pursuit of change. This doesn't just mean perseverance. It means being willing to intervene, at times energetically. Some therapists prefer to avoid confrontation and find it more effective to use gentle questions or persistent encouragement. Regardless of whether they work directly (and at times use confrontation) or indirectly (and avoid it), good therapists are finishers. Strategies and techniques vary, but what sets the best therapists apart is their commitment to doing what it takes to see families through to successful resolution of their problems.

Effective family therapy addresses interpersonal conflict, and the first step in doing so is to bring it into the consulting room and locate it between family members. Often this isn't a problem. Couples in conflict or parents arguing with their children will usually speak right up about their disagreements. If the family only came because someone sent them (the court, the school, the Department of Protective Services), then the therapist should begin by addressing the family's problem with these agencies. How must the family change to resolve their conflict with these authorities?

When one person is presented as the problem, the therapist challenges linearity by asking how others are involved or affected. What role did others play in creating or managing the problem? How have they responded to it? For example, a parent might say, "The problem is Malik. He's disobedient." The therapist might follow up by asking "How does he get away with that?" or "How do you respond when he's disobedient?" A less-confrontational therapist might ask "When do you notice this?" or "What does he do that seems disobedient?" or "How does this disobedience affect you?"

In response to a family member who says "It's me, I'm depressed," the therapist might ask "Who in the family is contributing to your depression?"

An answer such as "No one" would draw the question "Then who's helping you with it?"

Challenges can be blunt or gentle, depending on the therapist's style and assessment of the family. The point, incidentally, isn't to switch from blaming one person (say, a disobedient child) to another (a parent who doesn't discipline effectively) but to broaden the problem to an interactional one—to see the problem as shared and comaintained. Maybe Mother is too lenient with Malik because she finds Father too strict; moreover, she may be overinvested in the boy because of emotional distance in the marriage.

The best way to challenge unhelpful interactions is to point out patterns that seem to be keeping people stuck. A useful formula is "The more you do *X*, the more he does *Y*—and the more you do *Y*, the more she does *X*." (For *X* and *Y*, try substituting *nag* and *withdraw* or *control* and *rebel*.) Incidentally, when you point out what people are doing that isn't working, it's a mistake to then tell them what they *should* be doing. Once you shift from pointing out something to giving advice, the clients' attention shifts from their behavior to your advice. Consider this exchange:

> *Therapist:* When you ignore your wife's complaints, she feels hurt and angry. You may have trouble accepting the anger, but she doesn't feel supported.
> *Client:* What should I do?
> *Therapist:* I don't know. Ask your wife.

Refusing to make suggestions, especially when asked, creates tension that encourages family members to draw on their own resources. A solution-focused alternative to challenging unhelpful actions is to ask about successful efforts and then to encourage more of these.

Even though family therapists sometimes challenge assumptions or actions, they continue to listen to people's feelings and points of view. *Listening* is a silent activity—rare at times, even among therapists. Family members seldom listen to each other for long without becoming defensive. Unfortunately, therapists don't always listen, either—especially when they're eager to jump in with advice. But remember that people aren't likely to reconsider their assumptions until they feel they've been heard and understood.

Homework can be used to test flexibility (simply seeing if it's carried out measures willingness to change), to make family members more aware of their role in problems (telling people just to notice something, without trying to change it, is often instructive), and to suggest new ways of relating. Typical homework assignments include suggesting that overinvolved parents hire a babysitter and go out together, having argumentative partners take turns talking about their feelings and listening to one another without saying anything (but noticing tendencies to become reactive), and having dependent family members practice spending time alone (or with someone outside the family) and doing more things for themselves. Homework assignments that are likely to generate conflict, such as negotiating house rules with teenagers, should be avoided. Difficult discussions should be saved for when the therapist can act as referee.

The point of homework isn't necessarily to solve problems but to get people to try something different:

> *Therapist:* So, are you ever nice to your sister?
> *Client:* Not much.
> *Therapist:* Could you be if you wanted to? Could you try something nice with her this week and surprise her?

Early Phase Checklist

1. Identify major conflicts and bring them into the consulting room.
2. Develop a hypothesis and refine it into a formulation about what the family is doing to perpetuate (or fail to resolve) the presenting problem. A formulation should consider process and structure, family rules, triangles, and boundaries.
3. Keep the focus on primary problems and the interpersonal conditions supporting

them, but do not fail to support constructive interactions.

4. Assign homework that addresses problems and the underlying structure and dynamics perpetuating them.
5. Challenge family members to see their own roles in the problems that trouble them.
6. Push for change during the session and between sessions at home.
7. Make use of supervision to test the validity of formulations and effectiveness of interventions.

The Middle Phase of Treatment

When therapy is anything other than brief and problem focused, much of the middle phase is devoted to helping family members deal more constructively with each other in sessions. If a therapist is too active in this process—filtering all conversation through him- or herself—family members won't learn to deal with each other and will continue to manage only as long as they remain in therapy. For this reason, in the middle phase, the therapist takes a less active role and encourages family members to interact more with each other. As they do so, the therapist steps back and observes the process. When dialogue bogs down, the therapist either points out what went wrong or simply encourages them to keep talking—but with less interruption and criticism.

When family members address their conflicts directly, they tend to become reactive. Anxiety is the enemy of listening. Some therapists (Bowenians, for example) attempt to control anxiety by having family members talk only to them. Others prefer to let family members deal with their own anxiety by helping them learn to talk with each other less defensively (by saying how they feel and acknowledging what others say). However, even therapists who work primarily with family dialogue need to interrupt when anxiety escalates and conversations become destructive.

Thus, in the middle phase of treatment, the therapist takes a less-directive role and encourages family members to begin to rely on their own resources. The level of anxiety is regulated by alternating between having family members talk with each other or with the therapist. In either case, the therapist encourages family members to get beyond trading blame to talking directly about what they feel and what they want—and to learn to see their own part in unproductive interactions.

What enables therapists to push for change without provoking undue resistance is an empathic bond with clients. We mentioned the importance of the working alliance in our discussion of the opening session, but it's such an important subject that we would like to re-emphasize it. Although there is no formula for developing a good relationship with clients, four attitudes are important in maintaining an effective therapeutic alliance: *calmness, curiosity, empathy,* and *respect*.

Calmness on the part of the therapist is an essential antidote to the anxiety that keeps families from seeing their dilemmas in a broader perspective. Two things that enable a therapist to remain reassuringly composed are (1) not taking responsibility for solving a family's problems and (2) knowing where to look for the constraints that are keeping them from doing so. Letting go of the illusion that anyone but the clients can solve their problems allows the therapist to concentrate on the job at hand, which is helping clients *in the session* to discover something new and useful. Calmness conveys confidence that problems, however difficult, can be solved.

Being curious implies that you don't know all the answers. The curious therapist says, in effect, "I don't understand, but I'd like to. Please tell me about how it is with you."

Empathy and respect have been reduced to the status of clichés, but since we think both are essential, let us be clear about what we mean. People resist efforts to change them by therapists they feel don't understand them. That makes it difficult for therapists to get anywhere if they can't put themselves in their clients' shoes and get a sense of what the world looks like to them. Some therapists are all too ready to say "I understand" when they don't. You can't fake empathy.

Instead of telling an overprotective mother that you understand her worrying about her children, be honest enough to ask "How did you learn to be a worrier?" or "Where did you learn to look at the negatives?" Or say "I've never been a single mom. Tell me what it is that scares you."

If you're trying to develop an honest relationship with a man who hit his wife during an argument, you might say that you can understand getting angry, and you can even understand banging the wall or throwing a glass on the floor, but a man hitting his wife you don't pretend to understand. "How come you do that?" you might ask, "Where did you learn that that was okay?"

Finally, respect. What passes for respect in therapists isn't always sincere. Showing respect doesn't mean treating people with kid gloves, nor does it mean accepting their version of events as the only possible way to look at the situation. Respect means treating clients as equals, not patronizing them or deferring to them because you're afraid to risk making them angry. Treating clients with respect means being honest with them, respecting their ability to handle the truth, and respecting your right to say what you think and their right to do the same. Respecting people also means believing in their capacity for change. You demonstrate respect for a problem child by speaking to her as a reasonable person worth talking to and worth showing an interest in. You show respect for the parents of such a child by being honest enough to explore what they might be doing ineffectively to deal with the child's problems in a way that does not feel blaming or belittling.

Middle Phase Checklist

1. Use intensity to challenge family members, ingenuity to get around resistance, and empathy to get underneath defensiveness.

2. Avoid being so directive that the family doesn't learn to improve their own ways of relating to each other.
3. Foster individual responsibility and mutual understanding.
4. Make certain that efforts to improve relationships are having a positive effect on the presenting complaint.
5. If you meet with subgroups, don't lose sight of the whole-family picture, and don't neglect any individuals or relationships—especially those contentious ones that are so tempting to avoid.
6. Does the therapist take too active a role in choosing what to talk about? Have the therapist and family developed a social relationship that has become more important than addressing conflicts? Has the therapist assumed a regular role in the family (an empathic listener to the spouses or a firm parent figure to the children), substituting for a missing function in the family? When therapists find themselves drawn to taking an active response to family members' needs, they should ask themselves who in the family should be taking that role and then encourage that person to do so.

Termination

Termination comes for brief therapists as soon as the presenting problem is resolved. For psychoanalytic therapists, therapy is a long-term learning process and may continue for years. For most of us, termination comes somewhere between these two extremes and has to do both with the family feeling that they've achieved what they came for and our sense that treatment has reached the point of diminishing returns. One clue that it may be time to terminate is when the family comes in with nothing but small talk (assuming, of course, that they aren't avoiding conflict) and no real work is getting done.

In individual therapy, where the relationship to the therapist is often the primary vehicle of change, termination focuses on reviewing the relationship and saying good-bye. In family therapy, the focus is more on what the family has been doing. Termination is therefore a good time to review what they've accomplished. Although some strategic therapists are content to manipulate change without concern that the family understands it, most family therapy has a kind of teaching function, and termination is the time to make sure the family has learned something about how to get along.

It can be helpful to ask clients to anticipate upcoming challenges that might cause setbacks and to discuss how they will handle those difficulties: "How will you know when things are heading backward, and what will you do?" Families can be reminded that their present harmony can't be maintained indefinitely and that people have a tendency to overreact to the first sign of relapse, which can trigger a vicious cycle. To paraphrase Zorba the Greek, life *is* trouble. To be alive is to confront difficulties. The real test is how you handle them.

Finally, although in the business of therapy no news is usually good news, it might be a good idea to check in with the family a few weeks after termination to see how they're doing. This can be done with a letter, phone call, or brief follow-up session. The family will appreciate the therapist's interest, and the therapist will feel a sense of closure. A therapeutic relationship is of necessity somewhat artificial or at least constrained. But there's no reason to make it less than human—or to forget about families once you've terminated with them.

Termination Checklist

1. Has the presenting problem improved?
2. Is the family satisfied that they have achieved what they came for, or are they interested in continuing to learn about themselves and improve their relationships?
3. Does the family understand what they were doing that wasn't working and how to avoid similar problems in the future?
4. Do minor recurrences of problems reflect the lack of resolution of some underlying dynamic or merely that the family has to readjust to function without the therapist?
5. Have family members developed and improved relationships outside the immediate family context as well as within it?

 FAMILY ASSESSMENT

Although the topic of assessment logically belongs in the previous section on getting started in family therapy, we've chosen to put it here in order to go into it in more detail. Assessment turns out to be more complicated and more important than most beginning therapists realize.

Family therapists vary widely in the extent to which they make formal assessments. Bowenians complete elaborate three-generational genograms, psychoanalysts take thorough personal histories, and behaviorists employ a variety of questionnaires and checklists. At the other extreme, solution-focused and narrative therapists do little in the way of formal evaluation. But regardless of their model's official posture on assessment, most therapists spend too little time making careful evaluations before launching into treatment.

Rather than attempt an exhaustive comparison of assessment procedures, we will instead describe some of the dimensions of family functioning that therapists should consider before embarking on a course of treatment.

The Presenting Problem

Every first session presents the fundamental challenge of being a therapist: A group of unhappy strangers walks in and hands you their most urgent problem—and expects you to solve it.

"My fifteen-year-old is failing tenth grade.
  What should I do?"
"We never talk anymore. What's happened
  to our marriage?"
"It's me. I'm depressed. Can you help me?"

There are land mines in these opening presentations: "What should we do?" "What's wrong with Johnny?" These people have been asking themselves these questions for some time, maybe years—and they usually have fixed ideas about what the answers are, even if they don't always agree. Furthermore, they typically have evolved a strategy to deal with their problems, which they insist on repeating even if it hasn't worked. In this, they are like a car stuck in the mud, with wheels spinning, sinking deeper and deeper into the mire.

The stress that accompanies life's troubles makes for anxiety, and anxiety makes for rigid thinking. And so families who come for therapy tend to hold tenaciously to their assumptions: "He (or she) is hyperactive, depressed, bipolar, insensitive, selfish, rebellious . . ." or some other negative attribute that resides inside the complicated machinery of the stubborn human psyche. Even when the complaint is phrased in the form of "*We* don't communicate," there's usually an assumption of where the responsibility lies—and that somewhere is usually elsewhere.

The first step in helping families move from a sense of helplessness to an awareness of how by working together they can overcome their problems is to explore the presenting symptom. It may seem obvious that the first consideration should be the presenting complaint. Nevertheless, it's worth emphasizing that inquiry into the presenting problem should be detailed and empathic. The minute some therapists hear that a family's problem is, say, misbehavior or poor communication, they're ready to jump into action. Their training has prepared them to deal with misbehaving children and communication problems, and they're raring to go. They know what needs to be done—but before they get

started, they should realize that they're *not* dealing with misbehaving children or communication problems. Rather, they're dealing with a unique instance of one of these difficulties.

Exploring the presenting problem begins with hearing the family's account. Each member of the family should have a chance to express his or her viewpoint, and individual perspectives and feelings should be acknowledged. This open-ended inquiry should be followed by detailed questions to find out more about the precise nature of the problem. If a child misbehaves, what exactly does she do? How often? Under what circumstances? Does she misbehave at school or at home or both?

In exploring the presenting complaint, the challenge for a systemic therapist is to reexamine the family's settled certainty about who has the problem and why. When a family seeks therapy for a problem they've been unable to solve, the psychotherapeutic approach is to try to discover *why* they've been unable to do so and then help them reorganize so that they can solve this problem and others like it in the future. In short, it's not the problem that's the problem; it's the family's inability to solve it. Jay Haley used to say, "Family therapy is not about solving the problem; it's about repairing the problem-solving mechanism."

Therefore, the first challenge for a family therapist is to move families from linear ("It's Zack") and medical model thinking ("He's hyperactive") to an interactional perspective. To initiate this shift, a therapist begins by asking about the presenting problem. However, these inquiries are intended not merely to get details about the condition as described but to open up the family's entrenched beliefs about what is the problem and who has it.

As we've tried to demonstrate, the first step in effective family therapy is opening up fixed character explanations in order to explore family members' actions and interactions. The movement is from intrapsychic to interpersonal. A therapist accomplishes this first step by asking questions. Here are some useful tactics at this stage:

1. Explore the scope of the presenting problem, looking for alternative possibilities.
2. Give every family member a chance to express his or her feelings and tell his or her story.
3. Explore the strengths as well as deficits of the identified patient.
4. Explore how other people respond to the identified patient and his or her symptoms.

A therapist must allow all family members to tell their stories and express their opinions in order to make them feel understood and gain their trust. On the other hand, a therapist should not simply accept a family's description of the problem as located entirely in one person. Questions that are limited to exploring the presenting symptom and its history may only serve to confirm linear notions about a family's problems.

Helpful questions convey respect for family members' feelings but skepticism about accepting the identified patient as the only problem in the family. Helpful questions continue to explore and open things up. Helpful questions invite new ways of seeing the problem or the family generally. Unhelpful questions accept things as they are described and concentrate only on the identified patient. To be effective in this first stage, a therapist's attitude must always be "I don't quite understand, but I'm interested. I know about families, but I'm curious about the particular way you organize your life." A therapist who is too ready to ingratiate him- or herself by saying "Oh, yes, I understand" closes off exploration.

The next thing to explore is the family's attempts to deal with the problem. What have they tried? What's been helpful? What hasn't worked? Has anyone other than those present been involved in trying to help with or hinder these difficulties? This exploration makes room

to discover how family members may be responding in ways that perpetuate the presenting problem. This isn't a matter of shifting blame—say, from a misbehaving child to an indulgent parent. It's always worth remembering that even actions that perpetuate problems usually have benign intentions. Most people are doing the best they can—and we aren't suggesting that family problems are typically caused by how people treat the identified patient. In fact, what family therapists call *circular causality* is a misnomer. The shift from linear to circular thinking not only expands the focus from individuals to patterns of interaction, but it also moves away from cause-and-effect explanations. Instead of joining families in a logical but unproductive search for who started what, circular thinking suggests that problems are sustained by an ongoing series of actions and reactions. Who started it? It rarely matters.

By helping family members see how their actions may be inadvertently maintaining the problems that plague them, a therapist empowers them to become their own agents of change. A woman who recognizes that scolding her husband to spend more time with her only drives him away is in a position to consider more effective ways of getting the affection she longs for. Similarly, a father who can be helped to see that continuing to nag his son to wake up in the morning prevents the boy from taking responsibility for himself can stop acting as his son's alarm clock.[2]

Talking with family members about how they may be contributing to the presenting problem involves overcoming a natural resistance to being blamed. No one wants to be told that they

---

[2]This may lead to a new problem: The son doesn't get up and misses school. Regardless, the issue will be clarified: Either the son is responsible, or the father enables him not to be.

are responsible for their mate's neglect or their child's irresponsibility. Although there is no formula to avoid making people defensive, it may help to keep in mind that circular thinking isn't designed to spread blame for causing problems; it's designed to expand people's options and discover who's in a position to resolve them.

Understanding the Referral Route

It's important to understand who referred your clients and why. What were their expectations? What expectations did they communicate to the family?

It's important to know whether a family's participation is voluntary or coerced, whether all or only some of them recognize the need for treatment, and whether other agencies will have continuing involvement with the case.

When individual therapists make a family referral, they often have a particular agenda in mind. A college student's counselor once referred him and his family for treatment. The young man had uncovered a repressed memory of sexual abuse and assumed that it must have been his father. The family therapist was somehow supposed to mediate between the young man, who couldn't imagine who else might have been responsible for this vaguely remembered incident, and his parents, who vehemently denied that any such thing ever happened. Did the individual therapist expect confrontation, confession, atonement? Some sort of negotiated agreement? What about the boy himself? It's best to find out.

It's also important to learn if clients have been in treatment elsewhere. If so, what happened? What did they learn about themselves or their family? What expectations or concerns did the previous therapy generate? It's even more important to find out if anyone in the family is currently in treatment. Few things are more likely to cause a stalemate than two therapists pulling in different directions.

Identifying the Systemic Context

Regardless of whom a therapist elects to work with, it's imperative to have a clear understanding of the interpersonal context of the problem. Who is in the family? Are there important figures in the life of the problem who aren't present, such as a live-in boyfriend or a grandmother who lives next door? Are other agencies involved? If so, what's the nature of their input? Does the family see them as helpful?

Remember that family therapy is an approach to people *in context*. The most relevant context may be the immediate family, but no family exists in a vacuum. It may be important to meet with the teachers and counselors of a child who's having trouble at school. There are even times when the nuclear family isn't the most important context. Sometimes, for example, a college student's depression has more to do with what's going on in the classroom or dormitory than with what's happening back home.

Stage of the Life Cycle

A family's context has temporal as well as interpersonal dimensions. Most families come to treatment not because there's something inherently wrong with them but because they've gotten stuck in a life cycle transition (Chapter 4). Sometimes this will be apparent. Parents may complain, for example, that they don't know what's gotten into Janey. She used to be such a good girl, but now that she's fourteen, she's become sullen and argumentative. (One reason parenting remains an amateur sport is that just when you think you've got the hang of it, the kids get a little older and throw you a whole new set of curves.) Adolescence is that stage in the life cycle when young parents have to grow up and relax their grip on their children.

Sometimes it isn't obvious that a family is having trouble adjusting to a new stage in the life cycle. Couples who marry after living together for years may not anticipate how matrimony stirs up unconscious expectations about what it means to be a family. More than one couple has been surprised to discover a sharp falling off in their sex life after tying the knot. At other times, significant life cycle changes occur in the grandparents' generation, and you won't always learn of these influences unless you ask.

Always consider life cycle issues in formulating a case. One of the best questions a therapist can ask is "Why now? Why is the problem happening or being addressed at this point?"

Family Structure

The simplest systemic context for a problem is an interactional dynamic between two parties. She nags and he withdraws. Harsh control provokes adolescent rebellion and vice versa, but sometimes a dyadic perspective doesn't take in the whole picture.

Family problems become entrenched because they're embedded in powerful but unseen structures. Regardless of what approach a therapist takes, it's wise to understand something about a family's **structure**. What are the **subsystems** and the nature of the **boundaries** between them? What is the status of the boundary around the couple or the family? What **triangles** are present? Who plays what roles in the family? Are individuals and subsystems protected by boundaries that allow them to operate without undue interference—but with access to support?

In enmeshed families, parents may intrude into sibling conflicts so regularly that brothers and sisters never learn to negotiate their differences or to settle their own fights with people outside the family. In disengaged families, parents may not only refrain from interrupting sibling quarrels but also fail to offer sympathy and support for a child who feels bad about his or her sibling's treatment.

Here, too, there is a temporal dimension. If a wife goes back to work after years of staying home with the children, the parental subsystem is challenged to shift from a complementary to a symmetrical form. Whether family members complain directly about these strains, they're likely to be relevant.

Communication

Although some couples come to therapy saying they have "communication problems" (usually meaning that one person won't do what the other one wants), working on communication has become a cliché in family therapy. Because communication is the vehicle of relationship, all therapists deal with it.

Conflict doesn't magically disappear when family members start to listen to each other, but it's unlikely that conflicts will get solved *before* people start to listen to each other (Nichols, 2009). If after a session or two (and the therapist's encouragement) family members still seem unable to listen to each other, talk therapy will likely be an uphill battle.

Family members who learn to listen to each other with understanding often discover that they don't need to change each other (Jacobson & Christensen, 1996). Many problems can be solved, but the problem of living with other people who don't always see things the way you do isn't one of them.

Drug and Alcohol Abuse

The most common mistake novice therapists make regarding substance abuse is to overlook it. Substance abuse is especially common with people who are depressed or anxious. It's also associated with violence, abuse, and accidents. Although it may not be necessary to ask every client about drug and alcohol consumption, it's critical to inquire carefully if there is any suspicion that this may be a problem. Don't be too polite. Ask straightforward and specific questions.

Questions that may help to uncover problem drinking (Kitchens, 1994) include the following:

- Do you feel you are a normal drinker?
- How many drinks a day do you have?
- How often do you have six or more drinks?
- Have you ever awakened after a bout of drinking and been unable to remember part of the day or evening before?
- Does anyone in your family worry or complain about your drinking?
- Can you stop easily after one or two drinks? Do you?
- Has drinking ever created problems between you and your partner?
- Have you ever gotten into trouble at work because of your drinking?
- Do you ever drink before noon?

These same questions can be asked about substances other than alcohol. If a member of a family who's seeking couples or family therapy is abusing drugs or alcohol, think twice about assuming that talk therapy will be the answer to the family's problems.

Domestic Violence and Child Abuse

If there is any hint of domestic violence or child abuse, the therapist should look into it. The process of questioning can start with the family present, but when there is a suspicion of abuse or neglect, it may be wise to meet with family members individually, which will allow them to talk more openly.

Most states require therapists and other professionals who work with children to report any suspicion of child abuse. Reporting suspected child abuse can jeopardize a therapeutic alliance, but sometimes therapy needs to take second place to safety. Any clinician who considers not reporting suspected child abuse should consider the possible consequences of making a mistake.

Perpetrators and victims of childhood sexual maltreatment don't usually volunteer this information. Detection is up to the clinician, who may have to rely on indirect clues. Further exploration may be indicated if a child shows any of the following symptoms: sleep disturbance, encopresis or enuresis, abdominal pain, an exaggerated startle response, appetite disturbance, sudden unexplained changes in behavior, overly sexualized behavior, regressive behavior, suicidal thoughts, or running away (Edwards & Gil, 1986).

Interviewing suspected child abuse victims requires specialized training and experience. If child abuse is suspected, novice therapists should immediately inform their supervisors. A therapist who is experienced in cases of child abuse may continue to explore this issue or refer the child to a specialist, usually through a child protective agency. We will explore specialized treatment approaches to child abuse later in this chapter.

Extramarital Involvements

The discovery of an affair is a crisis that will strike many couples some time in their relationship. Infidelity is common, but it's still a crisis. It can destroy a marriage. Extramarital involvements that don't involve sexual intimacy may be less obvious, but they can still sabotage treatment if one or both partners regularly turn to third parties to deal with issues that should be worked out by the couple. (One clue that an outside relationship is part of a triangle is that it isn't talked about.) Would-be helpful third parties may include family members, friends, and therapists.

A couple once came to therapy complaining that the intimacy had gone out of their relationship. It wasn't so much a matter of conflict; they just never seemed to spend any time together. After a few weeks of slow progress, the wife revealed that she'd been seeing an individual therapist. When the couples therapist asked why, she replied that she needed someone to talk to. When he asked why she hadn't told him, she said, "You didn't ask."

Gender Issues

Unrecognized gender inequalities contribute to family problems in a variety of ways. A wife's dissatisfaction may have deeper roots than the family's current problems. A husband's reluctance to become more involved in the family may be as much a product of cultural expectations as of any flaw in his personality.

Every therapist must work out for him- or herself how to avoid the extremes of naively ignoring gender inequality or imposing his or her personal point of view on clients. One way to strike a balance is to raise questions but allow clients to find their own answers. You can raise moral questions without being moralistic. It is, however, not reasonable to assume that both partners enter marriage with equal power or that complementarity between spouses is the only dynamic operating in their relationship.

Conflict over gender expectations, whether discussed openly or not, is especially common given the enormous shifts in cultural expectations over recent decades. Is it still considered a woman's duty to follow her husband's career, moving whenever necessary for his advancement? Is it still true that women should be strong, self-supporting, and the primary (which often turns out to be a euphemism for *only*) caregivers for infants and young children?

Regardless of the therapist's values, do the gender roles established in a couple seem to work for them—or do unresolved differences, conflict, or confusion appear to be sources of stress? Perhaps the single most useful question to ask about gender inequality is "How does each partner experience the fairness of give-and-take in the relationship?"

It's not uncommon for differences in gender socialization to contribute to conflict in couples (Patterson, Williams, Grauf-Grounds, & Chamow, 1998), as the following example illustrates.

Case Study

Kevin complained that Courtney was always checking up on him, which made him feel that she didn't trust him. Courtney insisted that she only asked about what Kevin was doing in order to be part of his life. She expected the same interest in her life from him. She wasn't checking up on him; she just wanted them to share things.

When Courtney asked Kevin too many questions, he got angry and withdrew, which made her feel shut out. Happy not to be interrogated any further, Kevin didn't notice how hurt and angry Courtney was until finally she exploded in tearful recrimination. Kevin felt helpless in the face of Courtney's crying, and so he did his best to placate her. When he reassured her that he loved her and promised to tell her more about what was going on in his life, she calmed down and peace was restored. Until the next time.

For couples like Courtney and Kevin, gender socialization contributes to the pursuer–distancer dynamic. Men are typically socialized to value independence and to resist anything they see as an effort to control them. Thus, Kevin interpreted Courtney's questions about his activities as attempts to restrict his freedom. Courtney, on the other hand, was socialized to value caring and connection. Naturally, she wanted to know what was going on in Kevin's life. She couldn't understand why he got so defensive about her wanting them to check in with each other.

Although it's a mistake to ignore gender socialization in favor of family dynamics, it's also a mistake to assume that gender socialization isn't influenced by family dynamics. In the previous example, the enmeshed family that Courtney grew up in reinforced the notion that family members should share everything and that being involved in independent activities was disloyal. Kevin's reluctance to tell his wife everything he was doing was partly a residue of his coming from a family with two bossy and controlling parents.

Gender issues underlie many relationship difficulties. Here are three more examples:

- Blair, a partner in a prestigious law firm, sought therapy after years of escaping from a stagnant marriage by having a series of affairs. When asked to consider couples therapy, Blair responded, "What good is talking going to do?"
- Sandy complained, "The only time I ever really get to talk about my feelings is with my friends. Pat takes everything I say literally and either gets defensive or gives advice. All I really want is to be listened to."
- Sam explained, "When I come home at the end of the day, I need time to decompress, but Chris always wants to talk and won't even give me fifteen minutes to unwind. Sure, I want to talk, but not the minute I get in the door."

These are familiar skirmishes in the war between the sexes. So familiar, in fact, that they call up a set of assumptions about gender that may preclude looking more closely at the particular men and women involved. Most troubled couples have one partner pressing for more closeness and the other pulling away—and while the pursuer is often the woman, it's sometimes the other way around. Let's return to the three examples, but first a confession: I deliberately chose examples from my practice that did not conform to gender stereotypes.

Not long ago, a high-powered attorney sought counsel for dealing with a pattern of extramarital affairs resulting from (or was it resulting in?) an emotionally sterile marriage. Blair was the emotional distancer and sexual pursuer for years until, weary of emotional demands and sexual frustration, she finally gave up and took refuge in the arms of a series of lovers. This was a twenty-first–century version of a familiar stereotype— the high-powered professional who comes home too tired to give much emotionally but expecting to be soothed and excited—only with the roles reversed. That didn't make much difference, however, in the pursuer–distancer dynamic that drove a stake through the heart of this marriage.

Sandy complained that his wife Pat was always responding to him literally and made no attempt to understand his feelings. And Sam, the wife in the third example, complained that her husband Chris was always pressuring her to talk about the relationship and wouldn't give her time to unwind at the end of the day.

Perhaps there are general patterns of differences between men and women. Maybe systems-oriented family therapists are more eager than most not to see these patterns—not to accept gender differences as fixed and given. Maybe that's why I remembered these examples, which are after all exceptions to the rule. Besides, if men are dominant, aggressive, and insensitive, where does that leave male therapists, most of whom have no wish to see these traits in themselves?

Even so, the notion that people are more alike than different has its own invidious implications. Seeing society as open and fair to all reinforces the status quo. And if the status quo is one in which the dominant group derives unfair advantage from a history of privilege, then women will continue to be underrepresented in positions of public power and overrepresented in the nursery.

Cultural Factors[3]

In assessing a family for treatment, a therapist should consider the unique subculture of the family (McGoldrick, Pearce, & Giordano, 2005) as well as the effect of unquestioned assumptions from the larger culture that may affect their problems (Doherty, 1991).

In working with minority families, it may be more important to develop *cultural sensitivity* than to actually share the same background as the clients. A family may come to trust a therapist who has taken the time to learn about their particular culture as much as one who happens to be of the same race or nationality. One way to develop cultural sensitivity is to make connections after working hours. For example, if you happen to be white, you could attend an African American church service in the community where your clients live, go to a Latino dance, or visit an Asian community center. Such efforts don't make you an expert, but they may help client families feel that you care enough to respect their ways. It's also important to take a *one-down position* in regard to cultural and ethnic diversity; that is, to ask your clients to teach you about their experience and traditions.

The challenge for the practitioner is twofold: learning to respect diversity and developing sensitivity to some of the issues faced by members of other cultures. A host of books are available describing the characteristics and values of various ethnic groups, many of which are listed in the section on multiculturalism in Chapter 11 of this volume. In addition to these academic books, novels such as *Love in the Time of Cholera*, *Beloved*, *The Scent of Green Papaya*, and *The Mambo Kings Play Songs of Love*, often bring other cultures more vividly to life.

In working with clients from other cultures, it's more important to be respectful of differences and curious about other ways of doing things

than to attempt to become an expert on ethnicity. Yet while it's important to respect other people's differences, it can be a problem to accept uncritically statements to the effect that "We do these (counterproductive) things because of our culture." Unfortunately, it's difficult for a therapist from another culture to assess the validity of such claims. Perhaps the best advice is to be curious. Stay open, but ask questions.

Even when working with clients from your own culture, it's important to consider the impact of cultural assumptions. How do cultural expectations affect the family you're working with? One patient recently complained that his wife expected family life to be like *The Brady Bunch*. His wife's reply was "It doesn't always have to be *The Jerry Springer Show*, either."

Among the cultural assumptions you may want to be alert for are that getting married means living happily ever after, that sexual satisfaction is something that just comes naturally, that adolescence is necessarily a time of turmoil, and that teenagers only want freedom and no longer need their parents' love and understanding.

THE ETHICAL DIMENSION

Most therapists are aware of the ethical responsibilities of their profession:

- Therapy should be for the client's benefit, not to work out unresolved issues for the therapist.
- Clients are entitled to confidentiality and so limits on privacy imposed by requirements to report to probation officers, parents, or managed care companies should be made clear from the outset.
- Therapists should avoid exploiting the trust of their clients and students and therefore must make every effort to avoid dual relationships.

---

[3]Issues of culture, as well as race, ethnicity, and social class, will be examined throughout this book. In this section, we merely wish to offer some preliminary considerations to help novice therapists get through their first few family sessions.

- Professionals are obligated to provide the best possible treatment; if they aren't qualified by training or experience to meet the needs of a particular client, they should refer the case to someone who is.

Whenever there is any question or doubt regarding ethical issues, it's a good idea to consult with a colleague or supervisor.

Although most therapists are aware of their own responsibilities, many think less than they might about the ethical dimensions of their clients' behavior. This is an area where there are no hard-and-fast rules. However, a complete and conscientious assessment of every family should include some consideration of family members' entitlements and obligations: What obligations of loyalty do members of a family have?; Are invisible loyalties constraining their behavior? (Boszormenyi-Nagy & Spark, 1973). If so, are these loyalties just and equitable? What is the nature of the partners' commitment to each other? Are these commitments clear and balanced? What obligations do family members have with regard to fidelity and trustworthiness? Are these obligations being met?

A good place to start in understanding the ethical responsibilities of clinical practice is with the guidelines of your profession. The ethics code of the American Psychological Association (APA), for example, outlines principles such as these:

- Psychologists offer services only within the areas of their competence based on their education, training, supervision, and professional experience.
- When understanding age, gender, race, ethnicity, culture, national origin, religion, sexual orientation, disability, language, or socioeconomic status is essential for the effective delivery of services, psychologists will have or seek out training and supervision in these areas or make the appropriate referrals.
- When psychologists become aware of personal problems that might interfere

with their professional duties, they take appropriate measures, such as obtaining professional assistance and determining whether they should limit, suspend, or terminate their work-related duties.

The code of ethics for the National Association of Social Workers (NASW) mandates the following:

- Social workers should not engage in dual relationships with clients or former clients.
- Social workers should not solicit private information from clients unless it is essential to providing services.
- Social workers should not disclose confidential information to third-party payers unless clients have authorized such disclosure.
- Social workers should terminate services to clients when such services are no longer required.

While some of these principles may seem obvious, they provide fairly strict guidelines within which practitioners should operate. When it comes to working with couples and families, however, complications arise that create a host of unique ethical dilemmas. When, for example, should a family therapist share with parents information learned in sessions with a child? If a twelve-year-old starts drinking, should the therapist tell her parents?

Recently, professional codes of conduct have added guidelines to address issues involved in treating couples and families. For example, the APA specifies that when a psychologist provides services to several people who have a relationship (such as spouses or parents and children), he or she must clarify at the outset which individuals are clients and what relationship he or she will have with each person. In addition, if it becomes apparent that a psychologist may be called on to perform potentially conflicting roles (such as family therapist and then witness for one party in divorce proceedings), he or she must attempt to clarify and modify those rules or withdraw from them appropriately.

Similarly, the NASW states that when social workers provide services to couples or family members, they should clarify with all parties the nature of their professional obligations to the various individuals receiving services. When social workers provide counseling to families, they should seek agreement among the parties concerning each individual's right to confidentiality.

The American Association for Marriage and Family Therapy (AAMFT, 1991) publishes its own code of ethics, which covers many of the same points as the codes of the APA and NASW. The AAMFT does, however, directly address complications with respect to confidentiality when a therapist sees more than one person in a family. Without a written waiver, a family therapist should not disclose information received from any family member, presumably not even to other family members.

Still, as with many things, it may be easier to expound ethical principles in the classroom than to apply them in the crucible of clinical practice. Consider the following:

*I*t's clear that therapists must protect their clients' right to confidentiality. But what if a woman reveals she's having an extramarital affair and isn't sure whether to end it? When she goes on to say that her marriage has been stale for years, the therapist recommends a course of couples therapy to see if the marriage can be improved. The woman agrees. But when the therapist then suggests that she either break off the affair or tell her husband about it, the woman adamantly refuses. What should the therapist do?

Can a therapist offer effective couples treatment while one of the partners is carrying on an extramarital relationship? How much pressure should a therapist exert on a client to do something he or she doesn't want to do? How much pressure should a therapist apply to urge a family member to reveal a secret that might have dangerous consequences? When does a therapist have the right to discontinue treatment of a client who wants to continue because the client refuses to accept the therapist's recommendation?

One way to resolve ambiguous ethical dilemmas is to use your own best judgment. In the case of the woman who wanted to work on her marriage but wasn't willing to end her affair or inform her husband, a therapist might decline to offer therapy under circumstances that would make it unlikely to be effective. In that case, the therapist would be obligated to refer the client to another therapist.

Subprinciple 1.6 of the AAMFT's Code of Ethical Principles (1991) states that "Marriage and family therapists assist persons in obtaining other therapeutic services if a marriage and family therapist is unable or unwilling, for appropriate reasons, to see a person who has requested professional help." Subprinciple 1.7 states that "Marriage and family therapists do not abandon or neglect clients in treatment without making reasonable arrangements for the continuation of such treatment."

Given the same set of circumstances, another therapist might decide that even though the woman refuses to end her affair, treating the couple might make it possible for the woman to break off the affair later or talk to her husband about it. In this scenario, the therapist would be bound by the principle of confidentiality not to reveal what the woman discussed in private.

While the outlines of ethical professional conduct are clear, the pressures on practitioners are often powerful and subtle. When dealing with clients who are having affairs or considering divorce—or marriage, for that matter—therapists may be influenced by their own unconscious attitudes as well as clients' projections. What would you assume, for example, about a therapist whose depressed, married clients all tended to get divorced after their individual therapy? What might you speculate about the level of satisfaction in that therapist's own marriage?

The risk involved in trusting your own judgment in ambiguous ethical situations lays in imposing your own values on what should be a professional decision. The principles of sound ethical practice are more broad and may be more strict than our own private morality and good intentions. When in doubt, clinicians should ask themselves two questions: First, what would happen if the client or important others found out about your actions? Thus, for example, strategically telling two siblings in separate conversations that each is the only one mature enough to end the fighting between them violates the "what-if" principle, because it's entirely possible that one or both might brag to the other about what the therapist said. (Trust me!)

The second question to ask in ethical decision making is "Can you talk to someone you respect about what you're doing or considering?" If you're afraid to discuss with a supervisor or a colleague that you are treating two married couples in which the wife of one is having an affair with the husband of the other or that you're considering lending a client money, you may be guilty of the arrogance of assuming that you are above the rules that govern your profession. Feeling compelled to keep something secret suggests that it may be wrong. The road to hell is paved with the assumption that this situation is special, that this client is special, or that you are special.

The following "red flags" should signal potentially unethical practices:

- *Specialness*—Something about this situation is special; the ordinary rules don't apply.
- *Attraction*—Intense attraction of any kind, not only romantic but also being impressed with the status of the client.
- *Alterations in the therapeutic frame*—Longer or more frequent sessions, exces-

sive self-disclosure, being unable to say no to the client, and so on may signal a potential violation of professional boundaries.
- *Violating clinical norms*—Not referring someone in a troubled marriage for couples therapy, accepting personal counseling from a supervisor, and so on.
- *Professional isolation*—Not being willing to discuss your decisions with professional colleagues.

In reading over the topics for family assessment, you may have noticed that there is no section on *individual dynamics*. This is deliberate. The distinction between individual and systemic levels of experience is artificial. Regardless of whether you're treating individuals or family groups, as a competent therapist, you should keep in mind that there are both interactional and personal dimensions to all human experience (Nichols, 1987).

An individual therapist who fails to consider the impact of the therapeutic relationship (as well as relationships outside the office) on a patient's material is missing a most important contribution. Therapists are never blank screens. By the same token, a family therapist who fails to consider the psychology of family members' behavior is dealing with only half a deck. Families were never black boxes. Sometimes when family interactions get stuck, it's important to consider the contributions of individual psychopathology, psychodynamics, and just plain failures of resolve.

FAMILY THERAPY WITH SPECIFIC PRESENTING PROBLEMS

Once, most family therapists assumed that their approach could be applied to almost any problem.

Today, this one-size-fits-all notion is no longer valid, and it has become increasingly common to develop specific techniques for particular populations and problems.

The following are a sample of special treatment approaches for two frequently encountered clinical problems: marital violence and sexual abuse of children. While we hope these suggestions will provide some ideas for dealing with these difficult situations, remember that responsible therapists recognize the limits of their expertise and refer cases they aren't equipped to handle to more experienced practitioners.

Marital Violence

The question of how to treat people engaged in marital violence polarizes the field like no other. The prevailing paradigm is to separate couples and assign the offender to an anger management or batterer intervention program while referring his partner for treatment in a battered women's group (Edleson & Tolman, 1992; Gondolf, 1995). Traditional couples therapy is seen as dangerous, because placing a violent man and his abused partner in close quarters and inviting them to address contentious issues puts the woman in danger and provides the offender with a platform for self-justification (Avis, 1992; Bograd, 1984, 1992; Hansen, 1993). Treating the partners together implies that they share responsibility for the violence and confers a sense of legitimacy on a relationship that may be malignant.

The argument for seeing violent couples together is that violence is the outcome of mutual provocation—an escalation, albeit unacceptable, of the emotionally destructive behavior that characterizes many relationships (Goldner, 1992; Minuchin & Nichols, 1993). When couples are treated together, violent men can learn to recognize the emotional triggers that set them off and to take responsibility for controlling their actions. Their partners can learn to recog-

nize the same danger signals and to take responsibility for ensuring their own safety.

Because few systemic therapists advocate treating couples together when the violence has gone beyond pushing and shoving, some of the debate between advocates of a systemic versus an offender-and-victim model is between apples and oranges. Michael Johnson (1995) argues that there are two types of partner violence in families. The first type is *patriarchal terrorism*, which is part of a pattern in which violence is used to exercise control over the partner. Patriarchal terrorism is frequent and severe and tends to escalate over time. The second pattern is *common couple violence* and doesn't involve a pattern of power and control. This violence erupts as a response to a particular conflict, is more likely to be mutual, tends to occur infrequently, and tends

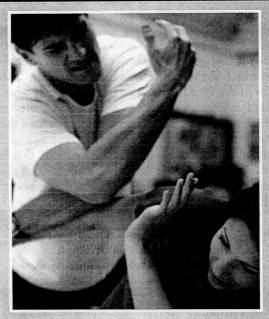

In cases of domestic violence, couples therapy may be inadvisable unless the man's violence is infrequent, not physically injurious, not psychologically intimidating, and not fear producing for his partner.

not to escalate. Nevertheless, many feminist thinkers remain opposed to couples therapy when any form of violence is present (Avis, 1992; Bograd, 1984; Hansen, 1993).

In the absence of empirical evidence showing gender-specific group treatment to be safer or more effective than couples therapy (Brown & O'Leary, 1995; Feldman & Ridley, 1995), clinicians remain split into two camps when it comes to the treatment of marital violence. Rather than choose between attempting to resolve the relationship issues that lead to violence or concentrating on providing safety and protection for the victims, it's possible to combine elements of both approaches—not, however, by doing traditional couples therapy.[4]

In working with violent couples, there must be no compromise on the issue of safety. A therapist doesn't have to choose between maintaining therapeutic neutrality (and focusing on relationship issues) or advocating on behalf of the victim (and focusing on safety) but rather can follow both agendas. Relationship issues can be construed as mutual, but the perpetrator must be held responsible for the crime of violence. As Pamela Anderson said when her husband Tommy Lee was arrested for domestic battery "It takes two people to start an argument, but it only takes one to break the other one's nose."

In the initial consultation with a couple in which there is a suspicion of violence, it's useful to meet with the partners together and then separately. Seeing the couple together permits you to see them in action, while speaking with the woman privately allows you to inquire whether she has left out information about the level of violence or other forms of intimidation to which she has been subjected.

Violent men and battered women trigger strong reactions in anyone who tries to help them. When such couples seek therapy, they are often polarized between love and hate, blaming and feeling ashamed, wanting to escape and remaining obsessed with each other. Thus, it's not surprising that professional helpers tend to react in extremes: siding with one against the other, refusing ever to take sides, exaggerating or minimizing danger, treating the partners like children or like monsters—in other words, splitting into good and bad, just like the dynamics of the couples themselves. In order to form an alliance with both partners, it's important to convey respect for them as persons, even if you can't condone all of their actions.

To assess the level of violence, it's important to ask direct questions: "How often do conflicts between the two of you end in some kind of violence?" "When did this happen most recently?" "What's the worst thing that's ever happened?" It's important to determine if any incidents have resulted in injuries, if weapons have been used, and if the woman is currently afraid.

If the woman has been violent as well as the man, the therapist can make it clear that violence in any form is unacceptable, but it's useful to point out that unless a woman uses a weapon, her aggression is not as dangerous as the man's because she is not as physically powerful. This point can be emphasized by asking the man if he actually feels physically afraid of his partner during an argument (which is her experience of him).

The more that violence is used to intimidate and the more there is a pattern of violence, the more dangerous the man. This is especially true of violence outside the home. A man who gets into fights with other men is far more explosive than a man who is only violent with someone who can't really fight back. It's also useful to inquire about drinking and drug use, because they loosen inhibitions. Therapy must emphasize restraint.

Occasionally, a man may act violently, not as an explosive response to emotional upset but rather as a cold-blooded, manipulative action.

---

[4]The following guidelines draw heavily from the work of Virginia Goldner and Gillian Walker, codirectors of the Gender and Violence Project at the Ackerman Institute.

Such men seldom come voluntarily, and whether they do or not, couples therapy is not indicated.

In addition to assessing the level of violence, a therapist must also evaluate the partners' ability to work constructively in therapy. Is the man willing to accept responsibility for his behavior? Is he argumentative or defensive toward his partner? Toward the therapist? Is the woman willing to take responsibility for her own protection, making her physical safety the first priority? Is the couple able to talk together and take turns, or are they so emotionally reactive that the therapist must constantly interrupt to control them?

If a therapist decides to treat the couple together, it's essential to establish zero tolerance for violence. One way of doing this is to make therapy contingent on no further episodes of physical aggression. Virginia Goldner and Gillian Walker define the first couple of sessions as a consultation to determine whether it's possible to create a "therapeutic safety zone," where issues can be confronted without putting the woman in harm's way. They use these initial sessions to focus on the risk of violence and the question of safety, while reserving the right to terminate the consultation and propose other treatment alternatives if they feel the case is too dangerous for couples therapy (Goldner, 1998).

With most couples, it's useful to encourage dialogue as a way of exploring how the partners communicate. Violent couples, however, tend to be emotionally reactive, and when that's the case, it's better to have them take turns talking to the therapist. In the early stages of work with a volatile couple, the therapist should do everything possible to slow them down and make them think.

One of the best antidotes to emotionality is to ask for specific, concrete details. A good place to start is with the most recent violent incident. Ask each partner for a detailed, moment-to-moment description of what happened. Be alert for linguistic evasions. A violent man may describe his actions as the result of his partner's "provocation" or of "built-up pressures." Thus, it isn't he who hits his wife; it's the pressures that are the culprit. A more subtle form of evasion is for the violent partner to describe the problem as his impulsivity. When arguments escalate, he starts to "lose it." In this formulation, the man's impulsive actions are not a choice he makes but an unavoidable consequence of emotions welling up inside of him.

*T*o this kind of evasion a therapist might respond, "When you say you start to 'lose it,' let's think about what you mean. What happened inside of you at that moment that you felt justified in breaking your promise never to hit her again?" The therapeutic task is to hold the man accountable for his violence, while also trying to understand him in complex and sympathetic terms. This double agenda is in contrast to either shaming the man, which will only exacerbate his rage or trying to understand the couple's dynamics without also holding the man responsible for his actions.

Once both partners have begun to take responsibility for their actions—he for choosing to control his violent impulses and she for taking steps to ensure her safety—it becomes possible to explore the relationship issues that lead to escalating emotional reactivity (Holtzworth-Munroe, Meehan, Rehman, & Marshall, 2002). This does *not*, however, mean that at a certain point a violent couple can be treated just like any other couple. Exploring the interactional processes that both partners participate in should never be allowed to imply that both are equally *responsible* for acts of violence.

When the couple is ready to explore relationship issues, it should be possible to encourage dialogue so that the therapist and couple can understand what transpires when they try to talk with each other. This brings the relationship into the consulting room. It's one thing to tell a man that he should leave before he gets too angry. It's another thing to actually observe the beginnings of emotional escalation and ask him if he's aware that he's starting to get upset and interrupt his partner. It then becomes possible to say, "*This* is the moment when you should leave." At this same point, his partner can be asked if she has begun to feel the first signs of tension and fear.

Taking time-out is an almost universally employed strategy in marital violence programs. Recognizing the cues of escalating anger (racing heart, growing agitation, standing up, pacing) and removing oneself from the situation before violence occurs is encouraged as a way to head off destructive actions that the partners will later regret. Saying "I'm feeling angry (or scared), and I'm going to take a time-out" helps distinguish this safety device from simply refusing to talk. Each person must be responsible for his or her own time-outs. Telling the other person to take a time-out is not allowed nor is trying to stop the other from leaving.

Although eliminating the escalating aggressive interactions must be the first priority, couples should also learn more constructive methods of addressing their differences. Here, there is a paradox: Violent men must learn to control their behavior, but it is counterproductive to stifle their resentments and complaints. In fact, it is precisely this kind of suppression that leads to the emotional buildups that result in violent explosions. Moreover, a man who resorts to violence with his partner is usually a weak man—weak in the sense of not knowing how to articulate his feelings in a way that his partner can hear. Thus, in helping couples learn to negotiate their differences, it is essential to ensure that both partners learn to speak up and to listen to each other.

Sexual Abuse of Children

When treating a family in which a child has been sexually abused, the primary goals are first to ensure that the abuse doesn't recur and second to reduce the long-term effects of the trauma (Trepper & Barrett, 1989). As with treatment of marital violence, treatment of sexual abuse tends to fall into one of two categories: (1) a *child protective approach*, which can undermine the integrity of the family or (2) a *family systems approach*, which can fail to protect the child. We recommend supporting the family while at the same time protecting the child. When these goals seem incompatible—for example, when a father has raped his daughter—protection of the child should take precedence.

Assessment of sexual abuse is often complicated by conflicting stories about what happened (Herman, 1992). A father may say that touching his daughter's labia was accidental, whereas the daughter may report that this has happened repeatedly. A grandfather may claim that his caressing of his grandson is perfectly innocent, while the child experiences it as abusive. A child protective worker may believe that a mother is tacitly supporting her husband's abuse of her child, while a family therapist may see a mother who is doing her best to save her marriage. Such discrepancies must be resolved by social and legal agencies.

The first priority is restricting unsupervised access to children for the offender. Next, a careful assessment should be made to uncover other possible incidents of abuse or patterns of inappropriate sexual expression (Furniss, 1991). The offender must take responsibility for his or her behavior and receive appropriate treatment for his or her actions (which may include legal punishment). Often, these measures will have already been taken by a child protective agency before the family is referred for therapy.

One of the goals of therapy should be to establish a support system to break through the isolation that facilitates abuse and inhibits disclosure. For this reason, many programs favor a multimodal approach that includes individual, group, and family sessions (Bentovim, Elton, Hildebrand, Tranter, & Vizard, 1988; Trepper &

Barrett, 1989). Family sessions should be geared toward increasing support for the victimized child, which may entail strengthening the parental unit.

When a child is the victim of sexual abuse, social control agents may have to step in to protect the child, which can involve taking over what might be considered parental responsibilities. In the long run, however, it is the family who will be responsible for the child. Therefore, supporting the parents in developing appropriate ways of carrying out their responsibilities, rather than taking over for them, is usually in the best interests of the child.

In cases where a father or stepfather is sent to jail for sexual crimes against his children, part of a therapist's job is to help the family draw a boundary that excludes the offender. The same is true if the children are taken out of the home and sent to live with relatives or foster parents. Subsequently, however, if reunion is planned, therapy involves gradually reopening this boundary through visits and phone calls, which gives the family and therapist the opportunity to work together to improve the family's functioning.

One of the keys to helping resolve the trauma of abuse is to give the child a safe forum to explore his or her complex and often ambivalent feelings about what happened. In addition to feeling violated and angry, the child may feel guilty about getting an adult in trouble. Often, a child will secretly blame the other parent, usually the mother, for not preventing the abuse. Finally, the child may fear that his or her mother's dependence on the abuser might result in his return, leaving the child again vulnerable to abuse.

A combination of individual and conjoint sessions helps make it safe to talk about feelings. Meeting first with the nonoffending parent (or parents) allows the mother (or parents) to describe what happened and to express feelings about the abuse without having to edit what she says because the child is present. Among the mother's complex feelings will surely be rage and

a sense of betrayal, but a part of her may still love the abuser and miss him if he's been sentenced. She may also feel guilty for not having protected her child. It's important to make it safe for her to share all of these feelings.[5]

When first meeting with the mother and abused daughter, it's reassuring to say that although they will probably eventually want to talk about the abuse, it's up to them to choose where to start. It's also helpful to give parents and children the choice of how much to talk about the abuse and whether to do so first in an individual session or conjointly. If children choose to discuss their feelings privately, they should be reassured that it's up to them to decide what they later want to share with their parents.

When meeting with abused children, it's helpful to explain that the more they talk about what happened, the less troubling their feelings are likely to be. However, it's essential to let *them* decide when and how much to open up. Remember that abused children need to recover a sense of control over their lives (Sheinberg, True, & Fraenkel, 1994).

When family members talk about their feelings, it's wise to keep in mind that feelings don't come in *either/or* categories. One way to help make it safe for them to talk about complex and even contradictory emotions is to use the metaphor of parts of the self (Schwartz, 1995). Thus, an abused child might be asked "Does part of you think your mother should have figured out what was happening?" Likewise, the mother might be asked "Does part of you miss him?"

One problem with meeting privately with a child is that doing so creates secrets. At the end of a private session, it's helpful to ask the child what she wants to share with her family and how she wants to do it. Some children ask the therapist to take the lead in opening up some of what

---

[5]For the sake of simplicity, the following discussion will assume the common instance of a stepfather as abuser and a mother and her abused daughter as clients.

they want their mothers to understand but find it hard to talk about. Finally, although it's important to help children voice any thoughts they may have about feeling guilty for what happened, after exploring these feelings, abused children need to hear over and over that what happened was not their fault.

WORKING WITH MANAGED CARE

Rarely has a profession undergone such upheaval as mental health providers have experienced with the advent of **managed care**. Practitioners who have been used to making decisions based on their own clinical judgment are now told by the managed care industry which patients they can see, which treatments to apply, what they can charge, and how many sessions they should offer. Professionals taught to maintain confidentiality in their dealings with patients now find themselves negotiating with anonymous strangers over the telephone.

The managed care industry itself has been slow to get its act together. Some of the horror stories about treatment being disallowed or abruptly terminated come from the early days of managed care, when the industry tended to manage by fiat rather than mediation. Given the mandate to stem the flow of hemorrhaging health care costs, when asked to approve any but the most limited forms of treatment, the industry's first impulse was to just say no.

Now twenty-five years into its existence, the managed care industry is coming to terms with two important facts. First, while their mandate is still to contain costs, their ultimate responsibility is to see that patients receive effective treatment. Second, despite what seems to be a built-in adversarial relationship with practitioners, industry case managers are discovering something that clinicians should also come to terms with: that both sides profit when they begin to work in partnership. In fact, increased competition among managed care companies has increased the pressure to build trust and loyalty among providers and to reduce internal costs by spending less administrative time micromanaging providers.

The key to succeeding in a managed care environment is to get over the sense that the case manager is your enemy. Actually, for those who learn to collaborate with managed care, case managers can be the best source of referrals.

For students, learning to work with managed care should begin as early as planning their education. Most managed care companies accept licensed practitioners with graduate degrees in nursing, social work, psychology, and psychiatry. Some, but by no means most, accept other degrees, although not usually on their preferred provider lists. So, just as it's prudent to take state licensing requirements into account when planning a postgraduate education, it's also wise to consider the requirements of the major managed care companies. Moreover, because most companies require at least three years of postdegree experience, it's a good idea to plan on beginning your career in a supervised agency. Working in a public agency almost invariably includes regular internal and external oversight and the opportunity not only to refine clinical practices but also effective ways to document them.

In areas with a high concentration of mental health providers, it may be necessary to market your skills in order to be selected as a managed care provider. Case managers are always looking for practitioners who can make their jobs easier. Showing willingness to accept crisis referrals and work with difficult cases (e.g., borderlines, chronic and multiproblem clients), being accessible, and having specialized expertise help make therapists attractive to managed care companies.

Once you have the opportunity to become a provider, remember to work *with* case managers, not against them. Managed care companies maintain databases that include information such as the average number of sessions a professional provides to each client. Outliers who use a significantly greater number of sessions per client are warned and referrals often decrease. Treatment plans that include clear, measurable objectives are probably the most helpful but most often poorly executed component of clinical documentation. The paperwork can be frustrating, but keep in mind that case managers have feelings, too—and they have memories. They're just trying to do the job they were hired to do. The biggest mistake a practitioner can make is to butt heads with a case manager.

Case managers appreciate getting succinct and informative reports. When challenged, many therapists eventually fall back on justifying their requests by saying "It's my clinical opinion." Being asked to justify their conclusions makes some practitioners angry. They feel they are doing the best they can for their patients. They are practicing efficiently—but they're not used to having someone looking over their shoulder. Get used to it. If you use sound clinical judgment, you should be able to provide reasons for your recommendations.

If you can't reach agreement with a case manager, don't lose your temper. If you can't be friendly, don't be hostile. Follow the grievance procedure. Do the required paperwork, and submit it on time. Write concise, well-defined treatment plans. Return phone calls promptly. Make arrangements with a colleague to provide backup if you're out of town or unable to accept a referral.

In addition to maintaining a positive attitude, being successful in the current health care climate means developing a results-oriented mindset. If you're trained in solution-focused therapy, by all means say so, but don't try to pass yourself off as something you're not. Calling yourself "eclectic" is more likely to sound fuzzy than flexible. Your goal is to establish a reputation for working within established time limits—and getting results.

SUMMARY

Getting the whole family to come in; developing a systemic hypothesis, pushing for change; knowing when to terminate; being sensitive to ethnicity, gender, and social class; working with managed care—there's a lot to learn, isn't there? Yes, and it takes time—but there are some things you can't learn, at least not from books.

Personal qualities, such as having respect for other people and being dedicated to making a difference, are also important. Techniques may be the tools, but human qualities are what distinguish the best therapists. You can't be an effective therapist without learning how to intervene, but without compassion and respect for people and their ways of doing things, therapy will remain a technical operation, not a creative human endeavor.

RECOMMENDED READINGS

Anderson, C., and Stewart, S. 1983. *Mastering resistance: A practical guide to family therapy.* New York: Guilford Press.

Madsen, W. C. 2007. *Collaborative therapy with multi-stressed families*, 2nd ed. New York: Guilford Press.

Minuchin, S., and Fishman, H. C. 1981. *Family therapy techniques.* Cambridge, MA: Harvard University Press.

Minuchin, S., Nichols, M. P., and Lee, W-Y. 2006. *Assessing families and couples: From symptom to system.* Boston: Allyn & Bacon.

Patterson, J. E., Williams, L., Grauf-Grounds, C., and Chamow, L. 1998. *Essential skills in family therapy.* New York: Guilford Press.

Sheinberg, M., True, F., and Fraenkel, P. 1994. Treating the sexually abused child: A recursive, multimodel program. *Family Process. 33*:263–276.

Taibbi, R. 1996. *Doing family therapy: Craft and creativity in clinical practice.* New York: Guilford Press.

Trepper, T. S., and Barrett, M. J. 1989. *Systemic treatment of incest: A therapeutic handbook.* New York: Brunner/Mazel.

Walsh, F. 1998. *Strengthening family resilience.* New York: Guilford Press.

REFERENCES

AAMFT. 1991. Code of ethical principles. Washington, DC: American Association for Marriage and Family Therapy.

Avis, J. M. 1992. Where are all the family therapists? Abuse and violence within families and family therapy's response. *Journal of Marital and Family Therapy. 18*:223–233.

Bentovim, A., Elton, A., Hildebrand, J., Tranter, M., and Vizard, E., eds. 1988. *Child sexual abuse within the family.* London: Wright.

Bograd, M. 1984. Family systems approaches to wife battering: A feminist critique. *American Journal of Orthopsychiatry. 54*:558–568.

Bograd, M. 1992. Values in conflict: Challenges to family therapists' thinking. *Journal of Marital and Family Therapy. 18*:243–257.

Boszormenyi-Nagy, I., and Spark, G. 1973. *Invisible loyalties: Reciprocity in intergenerational family therapy.* New York: Harper & Row.

Brown, P. D., and O'Leary, K. D. July 1995. Marital treatment for wife abuse: A review and evaluation. Paper presented at the Fourth International Family Violence Research Conference, Durham, NC.

Doherty, W. 1991. Family therapy goes postmodern. *Family Therapy Networker. 15*(5):36–42.

Edelson, E., and Tolman, R. 1992. *Intervention for men who batter.* Newbury Park, CA: Sage.

Edwards, D. L., and Gil, E. 1986. *Breaking the cycle: Assessment and treatment of child abuse and neglect.* Los Angeles: Association for Advanced Training in Behavioral Science.

Feldman, C. M., and Ridley, C. A. 1995. The etiology and treatment of domestic violence between adult partners. *Clinical Psychology: Science and Practice. 2*:317–348.

Furniss, T. 1991. *The multiprofessional handbook of child sexual abuse: Integrated management, therapy, and legal intervention.* London: Routledge.

Goldner, V. 1992. Making room for both/and. *The Family Therapy Networker. 16*(2):55–61.

Goldner, V. 1998. The treatment of violence and victimization in intimate relationships. *Family Process. 37*:263–286.

Gondolf, E. W. 1995. Gains and process in state batterer programs and standards. *Family Violence and Sexual Assault Bulletin. 11*:27–28.

Hansen, M. 1993. Feminism and family therapy: A review of feminist critiques of approaches to family violence (pp. 69–82). In *Battering and family therapy: A feminist perspective*, M. Hansen and M. Harway, eds. Newbury Park, CA: Sage.

Herman, J. L. 1992. *Trauma and recovery.* New York: Basic Books.

Holtzworth-Munroe, A., Meehan, J. C., Rehman, U., and Marshall, A. D. 2002. Intimate partner violence: An introduction for couple therapists. In *Clinical handbook of couple therapy*, 3rd ed., A. Gurman and N. Jacobson, eds. New York: Guilford Press.

Jacobson, N. S., and Christensen, A. 1996. *Integrative couple therapy.* New York: Guilford Press.

Johnson, M. P. 1995. Patriarchal terrorism and common couple violence: Two forms of violence against women. *Journal of Marriage and the Family, 57*:283–294.

Kitchens, J. M. 1994. Does this patient have an alcohol problem? *Journal of the American Medical Association. 272*:1782–1787.

McGoldrick, M., Pearce, J., and Giordano, J. 2005. *Ethnicity and family therapy*, 3rd ed. New York: Guilford Press.

Meyer, J. P., and Pepper, S. 1977. Need compatibility and marital adjustment among young married couples. *Journal of Personality and Social Psychology.* 35:331–342.

Minuchin, S., and Nichols, M. P. 1993. *Family healing: Tales of hope and renewal from family therapy.* New York: Free Press.

Morris, C. W. 1938. Foundations on the theory of signs. In *International encyclopedia of united science,* O. Neurath, R. Carnap, and C. O. Morris, eds. Chicago: University of Chicago Press.

Nichols, M. P. 1987. *The self in the system.* New York: Brunner/Mazel.

Nichols, M. P. 2009. *The lost art of listening,* 2nd ed. New York: Guilford Press.

Patterson, J. E., William ps, L., Grauf-Grounds, L., and Chamow, L. 1998. *Essential skills in family therapy: From the first interview to termination.* New York: Guilford Press.

Schwartz, R. C. 1995. *Internal family systems therapy.* New York: Guilford Press.

Sheinberg, M., True, F., and Fraenkel, P. 1994. Treating the sexually abused child: A recursive, multimodal program. *Family Process.* 33:263–276.

Trepper, T. S., and Barrett, M. J. 1989. *Systemic treatment of incest: A therapeutic handbook.* New York: Brunner/Mazel.

Walsh, F. 1998. *Strengthening family resilience.* New York: Guilford Press.

Winch, R. F. 1955. The theory of complementary needs in mate selection: A test of one kind of complementariness. *American Sociological Review.* 20:52–56.

The Fundamental Concepts of Family Therapy

4

A Whole New Way of Thinking about Human Behavior

Family therapy is often misunderstood as just another variation of psychotherapy, one in which the whole family is brought into treatment. It is that, of course, but it also involves a whole new way of thinking about human behavior—that is, as fundamentally organized by interpersonal context.

Prior to the advent of family therapy, the individual was regarded as the locus of psychological problems and the target for treatment. If a mother called to complain that her fifteen-year-old son was depressed, a clinician would meet with the boy to find out what was wrong with him. A Rogerian might look for low self-esteem, a Freudian for repressed anger, and a behaviorist for a lack of reinforcing activities. But all would assume that the forces shaping the boy's mood were located within him and that therapy, therefore, required only the presence of the patient and a therapist.

Family therapy changed all that. Today, if a mother were to seek help for a depressed teenager, most therapists would meet with the boy and his parents together. If a fifteen-year-old is depressed, it's not unreasonable to assume that something might be going on in the family. Perhaps the boy's parents don't get along and he's worried that they might get divorced. Maybe he's having a hard time living up to the expectations created by a successful older sister.

Suppose you are the therapist. You meet with the boy and his family and discover that he's not worried about his parents or jealous of his sister. In fact, "everything is fine" at home. He's just depressed. Now what?

That *now-what* feeling is a common experience when you start seeing families. Even when there *is* something obviously wrong—the boy is worried about his parents, or everybody is shouting and no one is listening—it's often hard to know where to start. You could start by trying to solve the family's problems for them—but then you wouldn't be helping them deal with *why* they're having problems.

To address what's making it hard for a family to cope with their problems, you have to know where to look. For that, you need some way of understanding what makes families tick. You need a theory.

When they first began to observe families discussing their problems, therapists could see immediately that everyone was involved. In the clamor of noisy quarrels, however, it's hard to see beyond personalities—the sullen adolescent, the controlling mother, the distant to notice the patterns that connect them. Instead of concentrating on individuals and their personalities, family therapists consider how problems may be, at least in part, a product of the relationships surrounding them. How to understand those relationships is the subject of this chapter.

CYBERNETICS

The first and perhaps most influential model of how families operate was **cybernetics**, the study of feedback mechanisms in self-regulating systems. What the family shares with other cybernetic systems is a tendency to maintain stability by using information about its performance as feedback.

At the core of cybernetics is the **feedback loop**, the process by which a system gets the information necessary to maintain a steady course. This feedback includes information about the system's performance relative to its external environment as well as the relationship among the system's parts. Feedback loops can be negative or positive. This distinction refers to the effect they have on deviations from a homeostatic state, not to whether they are beneficial.

Negative feedback indicates how far off the mark a system is straying and the corrections needed to get it back on course. It signals the system to restore the status quo. Thus, negative

feedback is not such a negative thing. Its error-correcting information gives order and self-control to automatic machines, to the body and the brain, and to people in their daily lives. **Positive feedback** is information that confirms and reinforces the direction a system is taking.

A familiar example of negative feedback occurs in a home heating system. When the temperature drops below a certain point, the thermostat triggers the furnace to heat the house back to the pre-established range. It is this self-correcting feedback loop that makes the system cybernetic, and it is the system's response to change as a signal to restore its previous state that illustrates negative feedback.

Figure 4.1 shows the basic circularity involved in a feedback loop. Each element has an effect on the next, until the last element "feeds back" the cumulative effect into the first part of the cycle. Thus A affects B, which in turn affects C, which feeds back to A, and so on.

In the example of a home heating system, A might be the room temperature, B the thermostat, and C the furnace. Figure 4.2 shows a similar cybernetic feedback loop for a couple. In this case, Jan's housecleaning efforts (output) affect how much housework gets done, which subsequently affects how much housecleaning Billie has to do, which then feeds back (input) to how much housecleaning Jan thinks still needs to be done, and so on.

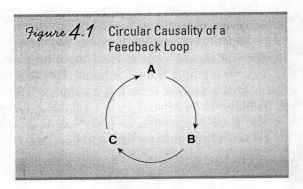

Figure **4.1**   Circular Causality of a Feedback Loop

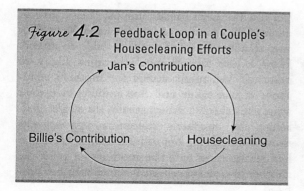

Figure **4.2** Feedback Loop in a Couple's Housecleaning Efforts

Jan's Contribution

Billie's Contribution   Housecleaning

The cybernetic system turned out to be a particularly useful metaphor for describing how families maintain stability (Jackson, 1959). Sometimes this is a good thing, as for example, when a family continues to function as a cohesive unit despite being threatened by conflict or stress. Sometimes, however, resisting change is not such a good thing, as when a family fails to accommodate to the growth of one of its members. More about this later.

As with negative feedback, positive feedback can have desirable or undesirable consequences. If left unchecked, the reinforcing effects of positive feedback tend to compound a system's errors, leading to runaway processes. The hapless driver on an icy road who sends positive feedback to his automobile engine by stepping on the accelerator can spiral out of control because his brakes are useless to provide the negative feedback to stop the car. Similarly, malignant worry, phobic avoidance, and other forms of neurotic behavior may start out with a relatively trivial concern and escalate into an out-of-control process.

Consider, for example, how a panic attack may start out as a relatively harmless instance of being out of breath, but a panicky response to breathlessness may spiral into a terrifying experience. Or, for a slightly more complex example, take the workings of the federal government. Because presidents generally surround themselves with advisers who share their viewpoint

CYBERNETICS was the brainchild of MIT mathematician Norbert Wiener (1948), who developed what was to become the first model of family dynamics in an unlikely setting. During World War II, Wiener was asked to work on the problem of how to get antiaircraft guns to hit German planes moving so fast that it was impossible to calibrate settings rapidly enough for gunnery batteries to hit their targets. His solution was to incorporate a system of internal feedback rather than rely on observers to readjust the guns after every miss.

Gregory Bateson came into contact with cybernetics at a remarkable series of interdisciplinary meetings called the Macy conferences, beginning in 1942 (Heims, 1991). Bateson and Wiener immediately hit it off at these meetings, and their dialogues were to have a profound impact on Bateson's application of systems theory to family therapy.

Because cybernetics emerged from the study of machines, where positive feedback loops led to destructive "runaways," causing the machinery to break down, the emphasis was on negative feedback and the maintenance of homeostasis. The system's environment would change—the temperature would go up or down—and this change would trigger negative feedback mechanisms to bring the system back to homeostasis—the heat would go on or off. Negative feedback loops control everything from endocrine systems to ecosystems. Animal species are balanced by starvation and predators when they overpopulate and by increases in birthrates when their numbers are depleted. Blood sugar levels are balanced by increases in insulin output when they get too high and increases in appetite when they get too low.

and are eager to maintain access, these counselors have a tendency to support whatever position the president takes. This positive feedback can result in taking a bad policy and running with it—such as Lyndon Johnson's escalation of the Vietnam War. Fortunately, however, the checks and balances provided by the legislative and judicial branches usually provide the negative feedback to keep administrations from going too far in unwise directions. To survive and adapt to the world around them, all communication systems—including families—need a balance of negative and positive feedback. As we will see, however, early family therapists tended to overemphasize negative feedback and resistance to change.

As applied to families, cybernetics focused attention on: (1) **family rules**, which govern the range of behavior a family system can tolerate (the family's homeostatic range); (2) *negative feedback* mechanisms that families use to enforce those rules (guilt, punishment, symptoms); (3) *sequences of family interaction* around a problem that characterize a system's reaction to it (the feedback loops around a deviation); and (4) what happens when a system's accustomed negative feedback is ineffective, triggering *positive feedback loops*.

Examples of positive feedback loops are vicious cycles, in which the actions taken only make things worse. The well-known *self-fulfilling prophecy* is one such positive feedback loop; one's apprehensions lead to actions that precipitate the feared situation, which in turn justifies one's fears, and so on. Another example of positive feedback is the *bandwagon effect*—the tendency of a cause to gain support simply because of its growing number of adherents. You can probably think of some fads and more than a few pop music groups that owe much of their popularity to the bandwagon effect.

As an example of a self-fulfilling prophesy, let's consider a young therapist who expects men to be uninvolved in family life. She believes that fathers *should* play an active role in the lives of their children, but her own experience has taught her not to expect much. Suppose she's trying to arrange for a family consultation, and the mother says that her husband won't be able to attend. How is our hypothetical therapist likely to respond? She might accept the mother's statement at face value and thus collude to ensure what she expected. Alternatively, she might challenge the mother's statement aggressively, thereby displacing her attitude toward men into her relationship with the mother—or push the mother into an oppositional stance with her husband.

To shift to a family example, in a family with a low threshold for the expression of anger, Marcus, the adolescent son, blows up at his parents over their insistence that he not stay out past midnight. Mother is shocked by his outburst and begins to cry. Father responds by grounding Marcus for a month. Rather than reducing Marcus's deviation—bringing his anger back within homeostatic limits—this negative feedback produces the opposite effect: Marcus explodes and challenges their authority. The parents respond with more crying and punishing, which further increases Marcus's anger, and so on. In this way, the intended negative feedback (crying and punishing) becomes positive feedback. It amplifies rather than diminishes Marcus's deviation. The family is caught in a positive-feedback "runaway," otherwise known as a vicious cycle, which escalates until Marcus runs away from home.

Later, cyberneticians like Walter Buckley and Ross Ashby recognized that positive feedback loops aren't always bad; if they don't get out of hand, they can help systems adjust to changed circumstances. Marcus's family might need to recalibrate their rules to accommodate an adolescent's increased assertiveness. The crisis that this positive feedback loop produced could lead to a reexamination of the family's rules—if the family could step out of the loop long enough to get some perspective. In so doing, they would be **metacommunicating**, communicating about their ways of communicating, a process that can lead to a change in a system's rules (Bateson, 1956).

Family cyberneticians focused on the feedback loops within families, otherwise known as patterns of communication, as the fundamental source of family dysfunction. Hence, the family theorists most influenced by cybernetics came to be known as the *communications school* (see Chapters 2 and 6). Poor communication results in inaccurate feedback, so the system cannot self-correct (change its rules) and consequently overreacts or underreacts to change.

 ## SYSTEMS THEORY

The greatest challenge facing anyone who treats families is to see past personalities to the patterns of influence that shape family members' behavior. We're so used to seeing what happens in families as a product of personal qualities, like selfishness, tolerance, rebelliousness, submissiveness, and so on, that learning to see patterns of relationship requires a radical shift in perspective.

Experience teaches that what shows up as one person's behavior may be a product of relationship. The same individual may be submissive in one relationship, dominant in another. Like so many qualities we attribute to individuals, submissiveness is only half of a two-part equation. In fact, family therapists use a host of concepts to describe how two people in a relationship contribute to what goes on between them, including *pursuer–distancer, overfunctioning–underfunctioning, control-and-rebel cycles,* and so on. The advantage of such concepts is that either party can change his or her part in the pattern. But while it's relatively easy to discover themes in two-person relationships, it's more difficult to see patterns of interaction in larger groups like families. That's why family therapists found systems theory so useful.

Systems theory had its origins in mathematics, physics, and engineering in the 1940s, when theoreticians began to construct models of the structure and functioning of mechanical and biological units. What these theorists discovered was that things as diverse as jet engines, amoebas, and the human brain share the attributes of a system—that is, an organized assemblage of parts forming a complex whole. Bateson and his colleagues found systems theory to be a perfect vehicle for illuminating the ways in which families functioned as units.

According to systems theory, the essential properties of an organism, or living system, are properties of the whole, which none of the parts have. They arise from the interactions and relationships among the parts. These properties are lost when the system is reduced to isolated elements. The whole is always greater than the sum of its parts. Thus, from a systems perspective, it would make little sense to try to understand a child's behavior by interviewing him without the rest of his family.

While some people use terms like *systemic* and *systems theory* to mean little more than considering families as units, systems actually have a number of specific and interesting properties. To begin with, the shift from looking at the individual to considering the family as a system means shifting the focus from individuals to the patterns of their relationship.

Let's take a simple example. If a father scolds his son, his wife tells him not to be so harsh, and the boy continues to misbehave, a systemic analysis would concentrate on this sequence. For it is this *sequence of interaction* that reveals how the system functions. In order to focus on inputs and outputs, a systems analysis avoids asking *why* individuals do what they do. The most radical expression of this systemic perspective was the "black box" metaphor:

The impossibility of seeing the mind "at work" has in recent years led to the adoption of the Black Box concept from telecommunication . . . applied to the fact that electronic hardware is by now so complex that it is sometimes more expedient to disregard the internal structure of a device and concentrate on the study of its specific input–output relations. . . . This concept, if applied to psychological and psychiatric problems, has the heuristic advantage that no ultimately unverifiable intrapsychic hypotheses need be invoked, and that one can limit oneself to observable input–output relations, that is, to communication. (Watzlawick, Beavin, & Jackson, 1967, pp. 43–44)

Viewing people as black boxes may seem like the ultimate expression of mechanistic thinking, but this metaphor had the advantage of simplifying the field of study by eliminating speculation about motivations and intentions in order to concentrate on people's input and output (communication, behavior).

Among the features of systems seized on by early family therapists, few were more influential—or later more controversial—than **homeostasis**, the self-regulation that keeps systems in a state of dynamic balance. Don Jackson's notion of **family homeostasis** emphasized that dysfunctional families' tendency to resist change went a long way toward explaining why, despite heroic efforts to improve, so many patients remain stuck (Jackson, 1959). Today we look back on this emphasis on homeostasis as exaggerating the conservative properties of families and underestimating their resourcefulness.

Thus, although many of the cybernetic concepts used to describe machines could be extended by analogy to human systems like the family, living systems, it turns out, cannot be adequately described by the same principles as mechanical systems.

General Systems Theory

During the 1940s, an Austrian biologist, Ludwig von Bertalanffy, attempted to combine concepts from systems thinking and biology into a universal theory of living systems—from the human mind to the global ecosphere. Starting with his investigations of the endocrine system, he began extrapolating to more complex social systems, and he developed a model that came to be called **general systems theory**.

Mark Davidson (1983), in his fascinating biography *Uncommon Sense*, summarized Bertalanffy's definition of a system as

any entity maintained by the mutual interaction of its parts, from atom to cosmos, and including such mundane examples as telephone, postal, and rapid transit systems. A Bertalanffian system can be physical like a television set, biological like a cocker spaniel, psychological like a personality, sociological like a labor union, or symbolic like a set of laws. . . . A system can be composed of smaller systems and can also be part of a larger system, just as a state or province is composed of smaller jurisdictions and also is part of a nation. (p. 26)

The last point is important. Every system is a subsystem of larger systems. But family therapists tended to forget this spreading network of influence when they adopted the systems perspective. They treated the family as a system while largely ignoring the larger systems of community, culture, and politics in which families are embedded.

Bertalanffy pioneered the idea that a system is more than the sum of its parts, just as a watch is more than a collection of cogs and springs. There's nothing mystical about this; simply that when things are organized into a system, something new emerges, the way water comes from the interaction of hydrogen and oxygen. Applied to family therapy, these ideas—that a family system is more than just a collection of individuals, and that therapists should focus on interactions rather than on personalities—became central tenets of the field.

Bertalanffy used the metaphor of an organism for social groups but an organism that was an **open system**, continuously interacting with its environment. Open systems, as opposed to closed systems (e.g., machines), sustain themselves by exchanging resources with their environment; for example, taking in oxygen and expelling carbon dioxide. Another property of living systems that mechanists forgot was that they don't just react to stimuli; they actively initiate efforts to flourish.

Bertalanffy was a lifelong crusader against the mechanistic view of living systems, particularly those living systems called people. He believed that, unlike machines, living organisms demonstrate **equifinality**, the ability to reach a final goal in a variety of ways.

With a mechanical system, there is a direct cause-and-effect relationship between the initial conditions and the final state. But, in a biological or social system, like the family, the results may be achieved with different initial conditions and in different ways. Thus, there is never only one way to achieve a family's objectives.

Living organisms are active and creative. They work to sustain their organization, but they aren't motivated solely to preserve the status quo. In open systems, feedback mechanisms operate so that the system receives information from the environment that helps it adjust. For example, the cooling of the blood from a drop in environmental temperature stimulates certain centers of the brain to activate heat-producing mechanisms of the body so that temperature is maintained at a steady level. Family therapists picked up on the concept of homeostasis, but according to Bertalanffy, an overemphasis on this conservative aspect of the organism reduced it to the level of a machine: "If [this] principle of homeostatic maintenance is taken as a rule of behavior, the so-called well-adjusted individual will be [defined as] a well-oiled robot" (quoted in Davidson, 1983, p. 104).

While homeostasis remains an important concept in family therapy, its limited ability to account for human creativity has been repeatedly acknowledged by family therapists in ways that echo Bertalanffy's concerns (Dell, 1982; Hoffman, 1981; Speer, 1970).

Early systems models of the family were based on closed systems and emphasized the role of negative feedback in maintaining homeostatic equi-librium. Families are more aptly described, in Walter Buckley's (1968) terms, as *complex adaptive systems*. Such systems are open and susceptible to significant changes in the nature of the components themselves with important consequences for the system as a whole. Their feedback loops make possible not only self-regulation (as in homeostatic systems) but also self-direction, such that the system may modify its structure in order to evolve. Unlike mechanical systems, which strive only to maintain a fixed structure, family systems seek not only to remain stable but also to change when necessary to adapt to new circumstances. Buckley coined the term **morphogenesis** to describe this plastic quality of adaptive systems.

To summarize, Bertalanffy brought up many of the issues that have shaped family therapy:

- A system as more than the sum of its parts
- Emphasis on interaction within and among systems versus reductionism
- Human systems as ecological organisms versus mechanism
- Concept of equifinality
- Homeostatic reactivity versus spontaneous activity

Many of these issues will reappear throughout this book.

SOCIAL CONSTRUCTIONISM

Systems theory taught us to see how people's lives are shaped by their interchanges with those around them. But in focusing on patterns of interaction, systems theory left something out—actually, two things: how family members' beliefs affect their actions and how cultural forces shape those beliefs.

Constructivism

Constructivism captured the imagination of family therapists in the 1980s when studies of brain function showed that we can never know the world as it exists out there; all we can know is our subjective experience of it. Research on neural nets (von Foerster, 1981) and experiments on the vision of frogs (Maturana & Varela, 1980) indicated that the brain doesn't process images literally, like a camera, but rather registers experience in patterns organized by the nervous system.[1] Nothing is perceived directly. Everything is filtered through the mind of the observer.

When this new perspective on knowing was reported to the family field by Paul Watzlawick (1984), Paul Dell (1985), and Lynn Hoffman (1988), the effect was a wake-up call—alerting us to the importance of cognition in family life.

Constructivism is the modern expression of a philosophical tradition that goes back at least as far as the eighteenth century. Immanuel Kant (1724–1804), one of the pillars of Western philosophy, regarded knowledge as a product of the way our imaginations are organized. The outside world doesn't simply impress itself onto the *tabula rasa* (blank slate) of our minds, as British Empiricist John Locke (1632–1704) believed. In fact, as Kant argued, our minds are anything but blank. They are active filters through which we process and interpret the world.

Constructivism first found its way into psychotherapy in the *personal construct theory* of George Kelly (1955). According to Kelly, we make sense of the world by creating our own constructs of the environment. We interpret and organize events, and we make predictions that guide our actions on the basis of these constructs. You might compare this way of interpreting experience to seeing the world through a pair of eyeglasses. Because we may need to alter or discard constructs, therapy became a matter of revising old constructs and developing new ones—trying on different lenses to see which ones enable a person to navigate the world in more satisfying ways.

The first example of constructivism in family therapy was the technique of **reframing**—relabeling behavior to shift how family members respond to it. Clients will respond very differently to a child seen as "hyperactive" than to one perceived as "misbehaving." Likewise, the parents of a rebellious ten-year-old will feel better about themselves if they become convinced that, rather than being "ineffectual disciplinarians," they have an "oppositional child." The first diagnosis suggests that the parents should get tough but also that they probably won't succeed. The second suggests that coping with a difficult child may require strategizing. The point isn't that one description is more valid than the other but rather that if whatever label a family applies to its problems leads to ineffective coping strategies, then perhaps a new label will alter their viewpoint sufficiently to elicit a more effective response.

When constructivism took hold of family therapy in the mid-1980s, it triggered a fundamental shift in emphasis. Systems metaphors focused on action; constructivism shifted the focus to the assumptions people have about their problems. Meaning itself became the target. The goal of therapy changed from interrupting problematic patterns of behavior to helping clients find new perspectives in their lives.

In the vanguard of this movement were Harry Goolishian and Harlene Anderson, whose *collaborative language-based systems* approach was defined less by what therapists do than by what they don't do. In this model therapists *don't* adopt the role of expert, *don't* assume that they know how families should change, and *don't* push them in any particular direction. The role of the therapist isn't to change people but to open doors for them to explore new meanings in their lives.

---

[1] The eye of the frog, for example, doesn't register much but lateral movement—which may be all you really need to know if your main interest in life is catching flies with your tongue.

The therapist does not control the interview by influencing the conversation toward a particular direction in the sense of content or outcome, nor is the therapist responsible for the direction of change. The therapist is only responsible for creating a space in which dialogical conversation can occur. (Anderson & Goolishian, 1988, p. 385)

Constructivism teaches us to look beyond behavior to the ways we interpret our experience. In a world where all truth is relative, the perspective of the therapist has no more claim to objectivity than that of the clients. Thus constructivism undermined the status of the therapist as an objective authority with privileged knowledge of cause and cure.

Acknowledging that how we perceive and understand reality is a construction doesn't mean that there is nothing real out there to perceive. Sticks and stones *can* break your bones. Moreover, even the most ardent constructivists (e.g., Efran, Lukens, & Lukens, 1990) remind us that some constructions are more useful than others.

Constructivism was a revolt against an authoritarian model of therapy, against the image of the therapist as bully. Anderson and Goolishian (1988) favored what they called an attitude of "not-knowing," in which they make room for the clients' ideas to come forward. Instead of approaching families with preconceived notions about structure and functioning, they brought only curiosity. It is probably well to remember that even our most cherished metaphors for family life—*system*, *enmeshment*, *dirty games*, *triangles*, and so on—are just that: metaphors. They don't exist in some objective reality; they are constructions, some more useful than others.

In emphasizing the idiosyncratic perspective of the individual, constructivists were accused by some (e.g., Minuchin, 1991) of ignoring the social context. Once that solipsistic streak was pointed out, leading constructivists clarified their position: When they said that reality was constructed, they meant *socially* constructed.

The Social Construction of Reality

Social constructionism expands on constructivism much as family therapy expanded on individual psychology. Constructivism says that we relate to the world on the basis of our own interpretations. **Social constructionism** points out that those interpretations are shaped by the social context in which we live.

If a fourteen-year-old consistently disobeys his parents, a constructivist might point out that the boy may not think they deserve his respect. In other words, the boy's actions are not simply a product of the parents' disciplinary efforts but also of the boy's construction of their authority. A social constructionist would add that an adolescent's attitudes about parental authority are shaped by the culture at large.

At school or work, at lunch, in phone conversations, at the movies and from television, we absorb attitudes and opinions that we carry into our families. Television, to pick one very potent influence on the average fourteen-year-old, has made today's children more sophisticated and more cynical. As communications scholar Joshua Meyrowitz (1985) argues in *No Sense of Place*, today's children are exposed to the "backstage" of the adult world, to otherwise hidden doubts and conflicts, foolishness and failures of adult types they see on TV. This demystification undermines adolescent trust in traditional authority structures. It's hard to maintain an ideal of adult wisdom when your image of a parent figure is Homer Simpson.

Both constructivism and social constructionism focus on interpretation of experience as a mediator of behavior. But while constructivists emphasized the subjective mind of the individual, social constructionists place more emphasis on the intersubjective influence of language and culture. According to constructivism, people have problems not merely because of the objective conditions of their lives but also because of their interpretation of those conditions. What social constructionism adds is a recognition of how such meanings emerge in the process of talking with other people.

Therapy then becomes a process of **deconstruction**—of freeing clients from the tyranny of entrenched beliefs. How this plays out in practice is illustrated in the two most influential new versions of family therapy: the solution-focused model and narrative therapy.

Inherent in most forms of therapy is the idea that before you can solve a problem, you must figure out what's wrong. This notion seems self-evident, but it is a construction—only one way of looking at things. **Solution-focused therapy** turns this assumption on its head, using a totally different construction; namely, that the best way to solve problems is to discover what people do when they're *not* having the problem.

Suppose, for example, that a woman's complaint is that her husband never talks to her. Instead of trying to figure out what's wrong, a solution-focused therapist might ask the woman if she can remember **exceptions** to this complaint. Perhaps she and her husband do have reasonably good conversations when they go for walks or out to dinner. In that case, the therapist might simply suggest that they do more of that. We'll see how solution-focused therapy builds on the insights of constructivism in Chapter 12.

Like their solution-focused colleagues, practitioners of **narrative therapy** create a shift in their clients' experience by helping them reexamine how they look at things. But, whereas solution-focused therapy shifts attention from current failures to past successes in order to mobilize behavioral solutions, narrative therapy's aim is broader and more attitudinal. The decisive technique in this approach—**externalization**—involves the truly radical reconstruction of defining problems not as properties of the persons who suffer them but as alien oppressors. Thus, for example, while the parents of a girl who doesn't keep up with her homework might define her as lazy or a procrastinator, a narrative therapist would talk instead about

times when "procrastination" gets the better of her—and times when "it" doesn't.

Notice how the former construction—"The girl is a procrastinator"—is relatively deterministic, while the latter—"Procrastination sometimes gets the better of her"—frees the girl from a negative identity and turns therapy into a struggle for liberation. We'll talk more about narrative therapy in Chapter 13.

Both solution-focused and narrative therapy are founded on the premise that we develop our ideas about the world in conversation with other people (Gergen, 1985). If some of those ideas bog us down in our problems, then new and more productive perspectives can usefully evolve within a cradle of narrative reconstruction. If problems are stories that people have learned to tell themselves, then deconstructing these stories can be an effective way to help people master their problems.

Critics, ourselves among them (Nichols & Schwartz, 2001), have pointed out that by emphasizing the cognitive dimension of individuals and their experience, social constructionists have turned their backs on some of the defining insights of family therapy—namely, that families operate as complex units and that psychological symptoms are often the result of conflicts within the family. Our experience and our identities are partly linguistic constructions—but only partly. But if social constructionists have tended to ignore the insights of systems theory and to downplay family conflict, there is nothing inherent in social constructionism that makes this necessary. The kinds of polarized interactions that Bateson, Jackson, and Haley first described fifty years ago—in terms like *complementary* and *symmetrical*—can be understood as reflecting behavioral interactions *and* social constructions, rather than either one or the other.

Italian psychiatrist Valeria Ugazio (1999) describes how family members differentiate themselves not merely by their actions but by the way they talk about themselves in semantic polarities. Thus, for example, in a family whose talk about themselves and others can be characterized by the polarity dependence/independence, conversations will tend to be organized around fear and courage, the need for protection, and the desire for exploration. As a result of these conversations, members of such a family will grow to define themselves as shy and cautious or bold and adventurous.

ATTACHMENT THEORY

As the field matured, family therapists showed a renewed interest in the inner life of the individuals who make up the family. Now, in addition to theories about the broad, systemic influences on family members' behavior, *attachment theory* has emerged as a leading tool for describing the deeper roots of close relationships.

Attachment theory has been especially fruitful in couples therapy (e.g., Johnson, 2002), where it helps explain how even healthy adults need to depend on each other. In the early years of family therapy, couples treatment was a therapy without a theory. Most therapists treated couples with the same models designed for families (e.g., Bowen, 1978; Haley, 1976; Minuchin, 1974). The exception was behaviorists, who implied that intimacy was a product of reinforcement. Nobody talked much about love or longing. Dependency might be okay for children, but in adults, we were told, it was a sign of *enmeshment.*

In emotionally focused couples therapy, Susan Johnson uses attachment theory to deconstruct the familiar dynamic in which one partner criticizes and complains while the other gets defensive and withdraws. What attachment theory suggests is that the criticism and complaining are protests against disruption of the attachment bond—in other words, the nagging partner may be more insecure than angry.

The notion that how couples deal with each other reflects their attachment history can be traced to the pioneering studies of John Bowlby and Mary Ainsworth. When Bowlby graduated from Cambridge in the 1940s, it was assumed that infants became attached to their mothers as a consequence of being fed. But Konrad Lorenz (1935) showed that baby geese become attached to parents who don't feed them, and Harry Harlow (1958) observed that, under stress, infant monkeys prefer, not the wire-mesh "mothers" that provided food, but the cloth-covered "mothers" who provided contact comfort. Human babies, too, become attached to people who do not feed them (Ainsworth, 1967).

In the 1940s and 1950s, a number of studies found that young children who were separated from their mothers go through a series of reactions that can be described as *protest, despair,* and finally *detachment* (e.g., Burlingham & Freud, 1944; Robertson, 1953). In attempting to understand these reactions, Bowlby (1958) concluded that the bond between infants and their parents was based on a biological drive for proximity that evolved through the process of natural selection. When danger threatens, infants who stay close to their parents are less likely to be killed by predators.

Attachment means seeking closeness in the face of stress. (You can hug your blankie, but it doesn't hug back.) Attachment can be seen in cuddling up to mother's warm body and being cuddled in return; looking into her eyes and being looked at fondly; and holding on to her and being held. These experiences are profoundly comforting.

According to Mary Ainsworth (1967), infants use their attachment figure (usually the mother) as a *secure base* for exploration. When an infant feels threatened, he or she will turn to the caregiver for protection and comfort. Variations in this pattern are evident in two insecure strategies of attachment. In the *avoidant* strategy, the infant tends to inhibit attachment seeking; in the *resistant* strategy, the infant clings to mother and avoids exploration.

Security in the relationship with an attachment figure indicates that an infant is able to rely on that caregiver as a source of comfort and protection. When threats arise, infants in secure relationships are able to direct *attachment behavior* (approaching, crying, reaching out) to their caregivers and take comfort in their reassurance. Infants with secure attachments are confident in the availability of their caregivers and, consequently, confident in their interactions in the world.

This confidence is not evident in infants who have anxious attachment relationships. Bids for attention may have been met with indifference or rebuff (Ainsworth, Blehar, Walters, & Wall, 1978; Bowlby, 1973). As a result, such infants remain anxious about the availability of caregivers. Moreover, Bowlby argued that because attachment relationships are internalized, these early experiences shape expectations for later relationships of friendship, parenting, and romantic love.

One of the things that distinguishes attachment theory is that it has been extensively studied. What is clear is that it is a stable and influential trait throughout childhood. The type of attachment shown at twelve months predicts (1) type of attachment at eighteen months (Main & Weston, 1981; Waters, 1978); (2) frustratability, persistence, cooperativeness, and task enthusiasm at eighteen months (Main, 1977; Matas, Arend, & Sroufe, 1978); (3) social competence of preschoolers (Easterbrook & Lamb, 1979; Lieberman, 1977; Waters, Wippman, & Sroufe, 1979); and (4) self-esteem, empathy, and classroom deportment (Sroufe, 1979). The quality of relationship at one year is an excellent predictor of quality of relating up through five years, with the advantage to the securely attached infant compared with the resistantly or avoidantly attached infant.

What is less clearly supported by research is the proposition that styles of attachment in childhood are correlated with attachment styles in adult relationships. Nevertheless, the idea that romantic love can be conceptualized as an attachment process (Hazan & Shaver, 1987) remains a compelling if as yet unproven proposition. What the research has established is that individuals who are anxious over relationships report more relationship conflict, suggesting that some of this conflict is driven by basic insecurities over love, loss, and abandonment. Those who are anxious about their relationships often engage in coercive and distrusting ways of dealing with conflict, which are likely to bring about the very outcomes they fear most (Feeney, 1995).

Researchers are now suggesting that attachment issues are especially acute in abusive and violent relationships (Dutton, 1998; Fonagy, 1999; West & George, 1999). Like children with reactive attachment disorders, men often refuse to recognize women as independent centers of subjectivity in order to deny the reality of their profound dependence on them. There is also strong evidence that violent men were typically abused as boys by violent fathers who also abused their mothers (Feldman & Ridley, 1995). Violent men can be distinguished from other men by their very high scores on measures of insecure attachment (Dutton, 1998). Women who end up in violent relationships are more likely to have been neglected than actively abused. Such women often grow up with the message that being loved is contingent on self-abnegation. Violent and abusive couples cycle between violent quarrels and romantic reconciliations. The battered woman's most positive image of herself is brought forth when her partner begs her forgiveness for what he has done by telling her how much he adores her.

Attachment theory is applied to clinical treatment by linking symptomatic expressions of fear and anger to disturbances in attachment relationships. Parents can be helped to understand some of their children's disruptive behavior as stemming from the child's anxiety about the parents' availability and responsiveness. Couples can be helped to understand the attachment fears and vulnerabilities behind angry and defensive interactions (Gottman, 1994; Johnson, 1996).

Therapists can use attachment theory to illuminate current relationships by showing how a child's misbehavior might reflect an insecure attachment, or how a husband's avoidance may be due to ambivalent attachment, or how a wife's animosity may be an expression of anxious attachment. When family therapists feel drawn in to play a role in the family's script, they can not only avoid taking over a role that's missing in the family, but they can also use attachment theory to point out family members' needs for being securely cared for. Instead of being recruited to soothe an anxious child or comfort a distressed spouse, the therapist can hand back responsibility to the parents or the partner and encourage them to become less defensive and more sympathetic and supportive.

 ## CONCLUSIONS

After reading this chronology of how theories in family therapy have evolved, the reader may feel overwhelmed by the number of paradigm shifts in the field. It may help to point out a pattern in this apparent discontinuity.

The focus of therapy has expanded toward ever-wider levels of context. This process started when therapists looked beyond individuals to their families. Suddenly, unexplainable behavior began to make sense. Early family therapists concentrated on assessing and altering the behavioral interactions surrounding problems. Next, it was recognized that those interactions were manifestations of a family's underlying structure, and structure became the target of change. Then a family's structure was seen to be a product of multigenerational processes that were governed by belief systems, and therapists aimed their interventions at those underlying beliefs. More recently it dawned on therapists that these belief systems did not arise in a vacuum, hence the current interest in cultural influences.

Family therapists, naturalists on the human scene, discovered how behavior is shaped by trans-

actions we don't always see. Systems concepts—feedback, circularity, and so on—helped make complex interactions predictable. In keeping with our emphasis on how ideas are actually applied in clinical practice, we will now consider the fundamental working concepts of family therapy.

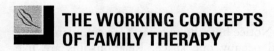 # THE WORKING CONCEPTS OF FAMILY THERAPY

Interpersonal Context

The fundamental premise of family therapy is that people are products of their **context**. Because few people are closer to us than our parents and partners, this notion can be translated into saying that a person's behavior is powerfully influenced by interactions with other family members. Thus the importance of context can be reduced to the importance of family. It can be, but it shouldn't be.

Although the immediate family is often the most relevant context for understanding behavior, it isn't always. A depressed college student, for example, might be more unhappy about what's going on in the dormitory than about what's happening at home.

The clinical significance of context is that attempts to treat individuals by talking to them once a week for fifty minutes may have less influence than their interactions with other people during the remaining 167 hours of the week. Or to put this positively, often the most effective way to help people resolve their problems is to meet with them *and* important others in their lives.

Complementarity

Complementarity refers to the reciprocity that is the defining feature of every relationship. In any relationship one person's behavior is yoked to the other's. Remember the symbol for yin and yang, the masculine and feminine forces in the universe?

Notice how the two parts are complementary and occupy one space. Relationships are like that. If one person changes, the relationship changes. If John starts doing more grocery shopping, Mary will likely do less.

Family therapists should think of complementarity whenever they hear one person complaining about another. Take, for example, a husband who says that his wife nags. "She's always complaining." From the perspective of complementarity, a family therapist would assume that the wife's complaining is only half of a pattern of mutual influence. Whenever a person is perceived as nagging, it probably means that she hasn't received a fair hearing for her concerns. Not being listened to makes her feel angry and unsupported. No wonder she comes across as nagging.

If instead of waiting for her to complain, John starts asking her how she feels, Mary will feel like he cares about her—or at least she is likely to feel that way. Complementarity doesn't mean that people in relationships control each other; it means that they influence each other.

A therapist can help family members get past blaming—and the powerlessness that goes with it—by pointing out the complementarity of their actions. "The more you nag, the more he ignores you. *And* the more you ignore her, the more she nags."

Circular Causality

Before the advent of family therapy, explanations of psychopathology were based on linear models: medical, psychodynamic, and behavioral. Etiology was conceived in terms of prior events—disease, emotional conflict, or learning history. With the concept of *circularity*, Bateson helped change the way we think about psychopathology, from something caused by events in the past to something that is part of ongoing, circular feedback loops.

The notion of **linear causality** is based on the Newtonian model, in which the universe is like a billiard table where the balls act unidirectionally on each other. Bateson believed that while linear causality is useful for describing the world of objects, it's a poor model for the world of living things, because it neglects to account for communication and relationships.

To illustrate this difference, Bateson (1979) used the example of a man kicking a stone. The effect of kicking a stone can be predicted by measuring the force and angle of the kick and the weight of the stone. If the man kicks a dog, on the other hand, the effect would be less predictable. The dog might respond to a kick in any number of ways—cringing, running a way, biting, or trying to play—depending on the temperament of the dog and how it interpreted the kick. In response to the dog's reaction, the man might modify his behavior and so on, so that the number of possible outcomes is unlimited.

The dog's actions (biting, for example) loop back and affect the man's next moves (taking the Lord's name in vain, for example), which in turn affect the dog, and so on. The original action prompts a circular sequence in which each subsequent action recursively affects the others. Linear cause and effect is lost in a circle of mutual influence.

This idea of mutual or **circular causality** is enormously useful for therapists because so many families come in looking to find the cause of their problems and determine who is responsible. Instead of joining the family in a logical but unproductive search for who started what, circular causality suggests that problems are sustained by an ongoing series of actions and reactions. Who started it? It rarely matters.

Triangles

Most clients express their concerns in linear terms. It might be a four-year-old who is "unmanageable" or perhaps an ex-wife who "refuses to cooperate" about visitation rights. Even though such complaints suggest that the problem resides in a single individual, most therapists would think to look for relationship issues. "Unmanageable" four-year-olds often turn out to have parents who are ineffective disciplinarians; and ex-wives who are "unreasonable" probably have their own sides of those stories. So a therapist, certainly a family therapist, would probably want to see the four-year-old together with her parents and to meet with both the angry father and his ex-wife.

Let's suppose that the therapist who meets with the four-year-old and her parents sees that indeed the real problem is a lack of discipline. The mother complains that the girl never does what she's told, the father nods in agreement, and the child runs around the room ignoring her mother's requests to sit still. Maybe the parents could use some advice about setting limits. Perhaps. But experience teaches that a child who misbehaves is often standing on one parent's shoulders. When children are disobedient, it usually means that their parents have some conflict about the rules or how to enforce them.

Perhaps the father is a strict disciplinarian. If so, his wife might feel that she needs to protect her daughter from her husband's harshness, and so she becomes more of a friend and ally to her child than a parent-in-charge. Some parents are so angry with each other that their disagreements are plain to see. Many, however, are less open. Their conflicts are painful, so they keep them private. Maybe they think that their relationship is none of the therapist's business, or perhaps the father has decided that if his wife doesn't like how he does things, "Then she can damn well do them herself!" The point is this: Relationship problems often turn out to be triangular (Bowen, 1978), even though it may not always be apparent.

A less obvious example of triangular complications often occurs in the case of divorced parents who fight over visitation rights. Most divorces generate enough hurt and anger to make a certain amount of animosity between the exes inevitable. Add to that a healthy dose of parental guilt (felt and projected), and you would seem to have a formula for arguments about who gets the kids for holidays, whose turn it is to buy new sneakers, and who was late picking them up or dropping them off last weekend. Meeting with the embattled exes may do little to disconfirm the assumption that the problem is between the two of them. Yet even two people who are very angry at each other will eventually find a way to work things out—unless third parties mix in.

What do you suppose happens when a divorced father complains to his girlfriend about his ex's "unreasonableness"? The same thing that usually happens when one person complains about another. The girlfriend sympathizes with him and, often as not, urges him to get tough with his ex. Meanwhile the mother is equally likely to have a friend encouraging her to become more aggressive. Thus, instead of two people left to work things out between them, one or both of them is egged on to escalate their conflict.

Do all relationship problems involve third parties? No, but most do.

Process/Content

Focusing on the **process** of communication (*how* people talk), rather than on its **content** (*what* they talk about), may be the single most productive shift a family therapist can make. Imagine, for example, that a therapist encourages a moody freshman to talk to her parents. Imagine further that the young woman rarely expresses herself in words but rather in passive-aggressive protest and that her parents are, in contrast, all too good at putting their opinions into words. Suppose that the young woman finally begins to express her feeling that college is a waste of time, and her parents counter with an argument about the importance of staying in school. A therapist made anxious by the idea that the young woman might actually drop out of college who intervenes to support the *content* of the parents' position will miss an opportunity to support the *process* whereby the young woman learns to put her feelings into words, rather than into self-destructive actions.

Families who come for treatment are usually focused on content. A husband wants a divorce, a child refuses to go to school, a wife is depressed, and so on. The family therapist talks with the family about the content of their problems but thinks about the process by which they try to resolve them. While the family discusses what to do about the child's refusal to go to school, the therapist notices whether the parents seem to be in charge and whether they support each other. A therapist who tells the parents how to solve the problem (by making the child go to school) is working with content, not process. The child may start going to school, but the parents won't have improved their decision-making process.

Sometimes, of course, content is important. If a wife is drinking to drown her worries or a husband is molesting his daughter, something needs to be done. But to the extent that therapists focus exclusively on content, they're unlikely to help families become better functioning systems.

Family Structure

Family interactions are predictable—some might say stubborn—because they are embedded in powerful but unseen structures. Dynamic patterns, like pursuer/distancer, describe the **process** of interaction; **structure** defines the organization within which those interactions take place. Initially, interactions shape structure, but once established, structure shapes interactions.

Families, like other groups, have many options for relating. Soon, however, interactions that were once free to vary become regular and predictable. Once these patterns are established, family members use only a fraction of the full range of alternatives available to them (Minu-

chin & Nichols, 1993). Families are structured in **subsystems**—determined by generation, gender, and function—which are demarcated by interpersonal **boundaries**, invisible barriers that regulate the amount of contact with others (Minuchin, 1974).

Like the membranes of living cells, boundaries safeguard the separateness and autonomy of the family and its subsystems. By spending time alone together and excluding friends and family from some of their activities, a couple establishes a boundary that protects their relationship from intrusion. Later, if they marry and have children, that boundary is preserved by making time to be alone together without the children. If, on the other hand, the couple includes their children in all of their activities, the boundary separating the generations wears thin and the couple's relationship is sacrificed to parenting. Moreover, if their parents are involved in all of their activities, children won't develop autonomy or initiative.

Psychoanalytic theory also emphasizes the need for interpersonal boundaries. Beginning with "the psychological birth of the human infant" (Mahler, Pine, & Bergman, 1975), psychoanalysts describe the progressive separation and individuation that culminates in the resolution of oedipal attachments and eventually in leaving home. But this is a one-sided emphasis on poorly defined boundaries.

Psychoanalysts pay insufficient attention to the problems of emotional isolation stemming from rigid boundaries. This belief in separation as the model and measure of maturity may be an example of male psychology overgeneralized and unquestioned. The danger of people losing themselves in relationships is no more real than the danger of isolating themselves from intimacy.

What family therapists discovered is that problems result when boundaries are either too rigid or too diffuse. Rigid boundaries permit little contact with outside systems, resulting in **disengagement**. Disengagement leaves people independent but isolated; it fosters autonomy but limits affection and nurture. **Enmeshed** subsystems have diffuse boundaries: They offer access to support but at the expense of independence and autonomy. Enmeshed parents are loving and attentive; however, their children tend to be dependent and may have trouble relating to people outside their family. Enmeshed parents respond too quickly to their children; disengaged parents respond too slowly.

Another important point about boundaries is that they are reciprocal. A mother's enmeshment with her children is related to the emotional distance between her and her husband. The less she gets from her husband, the more she needs from her children—and the more preoccupied she is with her children, the less time she has for her husband.

It should not go unnoticed that these arrangements are gendered. This doesn't make them any more right or wrong, but it should make us cautious about blaming mothers for cultural expectations that perpetuate their role as primary caretakers of children (Luepnitz, 1988). A therapist who recognizes the normative nature of the enmeshed-mother/disengaged-father syndrome but puts the burden on the mother to let go should ask himself why it doesn't occur to him to challenge the father to take hold.

The Meaning (Function) of Symptoms

When family therapists discovered that an identified patient's symptoms often had a stabilizing effect on the family, they spoke of this homeostatic influence as the **function of the symptom** (Jackson, 1957). In a seminal paper, "The Emotionally Disturbed Child as a Family Scapegoat," Ezra Vogel and Norman Bell (1960) observed that emotionally disturbed children are almost invariably involved in the tensions between their parents. By detouring their conflicts onto one of their children, the parents are able to maintain a reasonably stable relationship, though the cost to the child may be great.

The idea that a family member's symptoms may serve a homeostatic function alerted therapists to look beyond presenting complaints for latent conflicts that might lie behind them. If a

child is a behavior problem, for example, it's often the case that her parents will be in conflict about how to deal with her. However, this is not the same thing as saying that the child's misbehavior *benefits* the family. The parents' conflict may be a result rather than the cause of the child's problems. Notice, incidentally, that the term *scapegoat* is one-sided and judgmental.

The worst consequence of assuming that symptoms serve the family's purposes was setting up an adversarial relationship between families and therapists. This antagonism is often fueled by a tendency to sympathize with children and see parents as oppressors. (Isn't that how a lot of us felt growing up?) It's hard being a parent. Having a difficult child doesn't make it any easier. If parents have to deal with a therapist who assumes that they somehow profit from their child's problems, who could blame them for resisting?

The idea that symptoms serve a function in families has been discredited, and most schools of therapy now call for a collaborative relationship with clients. However, although it is a mistake to assume that symptoms necessarily serve a homeostatic function, it is worth considering the possibility that in some cases a mother's depression or a child's refusal to attend school *might* serve a protective function for the family.

Family Life Cycle

When we think of the life cycle, we tend to think of individuals moving through time, mastering the challenges of one period, then moving on to the next. The cycle of human life may be orderly, but it's not a steady, continuous process. We progress in stages with plateaus and developmental hurdles that demand change. Periods of growth and change are followed by periods of relative stability during which changes are consolidated.

The idea of a **family life cycle** adds two things to our understanding of individual development: First, families must reorganize to accommodate to the growth and change of their members; second, developments in any of the family's generations may have an impact on one or all of the family's members. When a son or daughter heads off to kindergarten or reaches puberty, not only must the child learn to cope with a new set of circumstances, but the whole family must readjust. Moreover, the developmental transitions that affect children aren't merely their own but their parents' as well—in some cases, even their grandparents'. The strain on a fourteen-year-old's relationship with his parents may be due as much to his father's midlife crisis or his mother's worrying about her own father's retirement as anything the boy himself is going through.

Monica McGoldrick's work reminds therapists that families often have trouble coping with changes in the family life cycle.

Changes in one generation complicate adjustments in another. A middle-aged father may become disenchanted with his career and decide to become more involved with his family just as his children are growing up and pulling away. His wish to get closer may frustrate their need to be on their own. Or to cite another example becoming more and more familiar, just as a man and woman begin to do more for themselves after launching their children, they may find the children back in the house (after dropping out of school, being unable to afford housing, or recovering from an early divorce) and therefore be faced with an awkward version of second parenthood.

One property that families share with other complex systems is that they don't change in a smooth, gradual process, but rather in discontinuous leaps. Falling in love and political revolutions are examples of such leaps. Having a baby is like falling in love and undergoing a revolution at the same time.

Sociologists Evelyn Duvall and Reuben Hill applied a developmental framework to families in the 1940s by dividing family life into discrete stages with tasks to be performed at each stage (Duvall, 1957; Hill & Rodgers, 1964). Family therapists Betty Carter and Monica McGoldrick (1980, 1999) enriched this framework by adding a *multigenerational* point of view, recognizing culturally diverse patterns and considering stages of divorce and remarriage (Table 4.1).

It's important to recognize that there is no universal version of the family life cycle. Not only do families come in a variety of forms—single-parent families, same-sexed couples, stepfamilies—but various religious, cultural, and ethnic groups may have different norms for various stages. The real value of the life-cycle concept isn't so much learning what's normal or expected at particular stages but recognizing that families often develop problems at transitions in the life cycle.

Problems develop when a family encounters a challenge—environmental or developmental—and is unable to accommodate to the changed circumstances. Thus problems are usually assumed to be a sign not of a dysfunctional family but simply of one that's failed to readjust at one of life's turning points.

Resistance

Because families often fear what might happen if their conflicts were brought into the open, they may resist focusing on their most sensitive problems. Early family therapists misinterpreted *resistance—fear* might be a better word—as stubbornness or opposition to change (homeostasis). More recently, therapists have recognized that all human systems are reluctant to make changes they perceive as risky.

Families *should* resist change—even change that to outsiders may seem beneficial—until it's clear that the consequences of those changes are

Table 4.1 The Stages of the Family Life Cycle

Family Life-Cycle Stage	Emotional Process of Transition: Key Principles	Second-Order Changes in Family Status Required to Proceed Developmentally
Leaving home: single young adults	Accepting emotional and financial responsibility for self	a. Differentiation of self in relation to family of origin b. Development of intimate peer relationships c. Establishment of self in respect to work and financial independence
The joining of families through marriage: the new couple	Commitment to the new system	a. Formation of marital system b. Realignment of relationships with extended families and friends to include spouse
Families with young children	Accepting new members into the system	a. Adjusting marital system to make space for children b. Joining in childrearing, financial and household tasks c. Realignment of relationships with extended family to include parenting and grandparenting roles
Families with adolescents	Increasing flexibility of family boundaries to support children's independence and grandparents' frailties	a. Shifting of parent–child relationships to permit adolescent to move into and out of system b. Refocus on midlife marital and career issues c. Beginning shift toward caring for older generation
Launching children and moving on	Accepting a multitude of exits from and entries into the family system	a. Renegotiation of marital system as a dyad b. Development of adult-to-adult relationships c. Realignment of relationships to include in-laws and grandchildren d. Dealing with disabilities and death of parents (grandparents)
Families in later life	Accepting the shifting generational roles	a. Maintaining own and/or couple functioning and interests in face of physiological decline: exploration of new familial and social role options b. Support for more central role of middle generation c. Making room in the system for the wisdom and experience of the elderly, supporting the older generation without overfunctioning for them d. Dealing with loss of spouse, siblings, and other peers and preparation for death

safe and the therapist is trustworthy. Thus it's possible to see resistance as prudent, rather than bullheaded. Therapists who recognize the protective function of resistance realize that it's better to make families feel secure enough to lower their walls than to sneak around them or batter them down. They try to create a warm, nonblaming therapeutic environment that engenders hope that healing of even the most threatening issues is possible.

Case Study

Emily was a single mother whose attempts to discipline her son were undermined by his grandmother's protectiveness. Emily avoided taking on her mother because she didn't believe it would do any good. She was afraid that if challenged, her mother would become even less supportive and make her feel more depressed. These fears weren't unrealistic. In the past, when Emily had said anything critical of her mother, that's just what had happened. Other people's defenses look unreasonable only because we can't see their memories.

For Emily to be convinced to try again to let her mother know about her feelings, the therapist needed to build up her trust that working with him would improve things with her mother. To achieve this credibility, the therapist had to respect Emily's pace and recognize her fears, rather than confront or manipulate her resistance. Therapists encounter far less resistance when they approach families as partners, trying to help them identify what constrains them from relating the way they want, rather than as experts who point out their flaws and give advice.

As you imagine doing family therapy, you may wonder how as a nice, respectful therapist you can keep angry family members from screaming at one another or glaring in stony silence as the minutes tick by. Creating a safe atmosphere involves more than just being empathic. A therapist must also show that he or she can prevent family members from hurting each other, so they know that they can drop their guard without fear of attack.

In family therapy's early years, it was thought that goading family members into emotional confrontations was necessary to unfreeze their homeostatic patterns. Over time, however, therapists learned that, while conflict is real and shouldn't be feared, change is still possible when family members interact in respectful and compassionate ways. It's in those moments that they feel safe enough to be real with each other.

One of family therapy's distinguishing features is its optimistic view of people. It's assumed that behind people's defensive displays of anger or anxiety lies a healthy core self that can be reasonable, tolerant, and willing to change. When family members interact in this state, they often find that they can solve their problems themselves. It's their protective emotions that produce impasses. Regardless of the therapist's technique, the key to generating productive interactions even in acrimonious sessions is the belief that this constructive potential exists in everyone.

Family Narratives

The first family therapists looked beyond individuals to their relationships to explain how problems were perpetuated. Actions, it turned out, were embedded in interactions—and, of course, the most obvious interactions are behavioral. Double binds, problem-maintaining sequences, aversive control, triangles—these concepts all focused on behavior. But in addition to being actors in each other's lives, family members are also storytellers.

By reconstructing the events of their lives in coherent narratives, family members are able to make sense of their experience (White & Epston, 1990). Thus it is not only actions and interactions that shape a family's life but also the stories they construct. The parents of a two-year-old who tell themselves that he's "defiant" will respond very differently than parents who tell themselves that their little one is "spunky."

Family narratives organize and make sense of experience. They emphasize certain events that reinforce the plot line and filter out events that don't fit. The parents who see their two-year-old as defiant are more likely to remember the times she said no than the times she said yes. The family's interactions and their narrative of events are related in circular fashion: Behavioral events are perceived and organized in narrative form; this narrative in turn shapes expectations that influence future behavior, and so on.

Interest in family narrative has become identified with one particular school, Michael White's narrative therapy, which emphasizes the fact that families with problems come to therapy with defeatist narratives that tend to keep them from acting effectively. But a sensitivity to the importance of personal narrative is a useful part of any therapist's work. However much a therapist may be interested in the process of interaction or the structure of family relationships, he or she must also learn to respect the influence of how they experience events—including the therapist's input.

Gender

When family therapists first applied the systems metaphor—an organization of parts plus the way they function together—they paid more attention to the way families functioned than to their parts. Families were understood in terms of abstractions like *boundaries*, *triangles*, and *parental subsystems*, while family members were sometimes treated as cogs in a machine. The parts of a family system never cease being individual human beings, but the preoccupation with the way families were organized tended to obscure the personhood of the individuals who made up the family, including their psychodynamics, psychopathology, personal responsibility—and gender.

Common sense tells us that gender is a fact of life (though no one should underestimate social scientists' ability to transcend common sense). As long as society expects the primary parenting to be done by mothers, girls will shape their identities in relation to someone they expect to be like, while boys will respond to their difference as a motive for separating from their mothers. The result is what Nancy Chodorow (1978) called "the reproduction of mothering."

Traditionally, women have been raised to have more permeable psychological boundaries, to develop their identities in terms of connection, to cultivate their capacity for empathy, and to be at greater risk for losing themselves in relationships. Men, on the other hand, tend to emerge with more rigid psychological boundaries and disown their dependency needs, fear being engulfed, and often have greater difficulty empathizing with others. We all know men who are nurturing and women who are not, but these are exceptions to the rule.

Awareness of gender and gender inequity have long since penetrated not only family therapy but our entire culture. Translating this awareness into concrete clinical practice, however, is complicated.

There is room for disagreement between those who strive to maintain clinical neutrality and those who believe that failing to raise gender issues in treatment—money, power, child care, fairness, and so on—runs the risk of reinforcing traditional roles and social arrangements (Walters, Carter, Papp, & Silverstein, 1988). However, it is not possible to be a fair and effective therapist without being sensitive to how gender issues pervade the life of the family. A therapist who ignores gender may inadvertently show less interest in a woman's career, assume that a child's problems are primarily the mother's responsibility, have a double standard for extramarital affairs, and expect—or at least tolerate—a father's nonparticipation in the family's treatment.

If patriarchy begins in the home, a gender-sensitive therapist must recognize the enduring significance of early experience and of unconscious fantasies. How children respond to their parents has significance not only for how they get along but also for the men and women they will become. When a girl speaks derisively about her "bitchy" mother, she may inadvertently be disparaging the female in herself. In addition to identification with the same-sex parent, the child's relationship with the other parent is part of what programs future experience with the opposite sex.

A gender-sensitive therapist must also avoid potential inequities in some of the basic assumptions of family therapy. The notion of *circular causality*, for example, which points to repetitive patterns of mutually reinforcing behavior, when applied to problems such as battering, incest, or alcoholism, tends to bypass questions of responsibility and makes it hard to consider influences external to the interaction, such as cultural beliefs about appropriate gender behavior. The concept of *neutrality* suggests that all parts of the system contribute equally to its problems and thus renders invisible differences in power and influence. The same is true of *complementarity*, which suggests that in traditional relationships between men and women, the roles are equal though different. Reconciling these contradictions is not always easy, but ignoring them isn't the answer.

Culture

Among the influences shaping family behavior few are more powerful than the cultural context. A family from Puerto Rico, for example, may have very different expectations of loyalty and obligation from their adult children than, say, a white middle-class family from Minnesota. One reason for therapists to be sensitive to cultural diversity is to avoid imposing majority values and assumptions on minority groups. There are now a host of excellent books and articles designed to familiarize therapists with families from a variety of backgrounds, including African American (Boyd-Franklin, 1989), Latino (Falicov, 1998), Haitian (Bibb & Casimir, 1996), Asian American (Lee, 1996), and urban poverty (Minuchin, Colapinto, & Minuchin, 2007), to mention just a few. These texts serve as guides for therapists who are about to venture into relatively unknown territory, although the best way to develop an understanding of people from other cultures is to spend time with them.

Although they are sometimes used interchangeably, there is a difference between culture and ethnicity. **Culture** refers to common patterns of behavior and experience derived from the settings in which people live. **Ethnicity** refers to the common ancestry through which individuals have evolved shared values and customs—especially among groups that are not white Anglo-Saxon Protestants. *Culture* is the more generic term, and we have chosen it here to emphasize that cultural context is always relevant, even with a family who comes from a background similar to the therapist's.

Although cultural influences may be most obvious with families from foreign backgrounds, it is a mistake to assume that members of the same culture necessarily share values and assumptions. A young Jewish therapist might, for example, be surprised at the unsympathetic attitudes of a middle-aged Jewish couple about their children's decision to adopt a black baby. Just because a therapist is African American or Italian or Irish doesn't mean that he or she shares the same experiences or attitudes as families from a similar background. Every family is unique.

Appreciating the cultural context of families is complicated by the fact that most families are influenced by multiple contexts, which makes generalization difficult. For example, as noted by Nancy Boyd-Franklin (1989), middle-class African American families stand astride three cultures. There are cultural elements that may be traced to African roots, those that are part of the dominant U.S. culture, and finally the adaptations that people of color have to make to racism in the dominant culture. Moreover, the cultural context may vary among family members. In immigrant families, for example, it's not uncommon to see conflicts between parents who retain a strong sense of ethnic identity and children who are more eager to assimilate the ways of the host country. First-generation parents may blame their children for abandoning the old ways and dishonoring the family, while the children may accuse their parents of being stuck in the past. Later, the children's children may develop a renewed appreciation for their cultural traditions.

The first mistake a therapist can make in working with clients from different backgrounds is to pathologize cultural differences. Although a lack of boundaries between a family and their neighbors and kin might seem problematic to a middle-class white therapist, more inclusive family networks are not atypical for African American families. The second mistake is to think that a therapist's job is to become an expert on the various cultures with which he or she works. While it may be useful for therapists to familiarize themselves with the customs and values of the major groups in their catchment area, an attitude of respect and curiosity about other people's cultures may be more useful than imposing ethnic stereotypes or assuming an understanding of other people. It's important to acknowledge what you do not know.

The third mistake therapists make in working with families from other cultures is to accept everything assumed to be a cultural norm as functional. An effective therapist must be respectful of other people's ways of doing things without giving up the right to question what appears to be counterproductive. Although fluid boundaries may be typical among urban poor families, that doesn't mean it's inevitable for poor families to be dependent on various social services or for agency staff to presume that a family's need entitles work-

Among Latino families, family loyalty is often a paramount virtue.

ers to enter, unannounced and uninvited, into the family's space, physically or psychologically (Minuchin, Lee, & Simon, 1996).

SUMMARY

We've covered a lot of ground in this chapter—theories from cybernetics to social constructionism, and working concepts from complementarity to culture. Some of these ideas may be familiar, while some may be new to you. Here's a brief summary.

Cybernetics is the study of how feedback is used to regulate mechanical systems. Applied to families, cybernetics teaches that when a family functions like a closed system the response to a problem may actually perpetuate it. To employ this concept clinically, therapists simply identify how family members have been responding to their problems and then get them to try something different.

According to *systems theory*, it's impossible to understand the behavior of individual family members without considering how the family system as a whole operates. To do so it may be necessary to look at *process* (how family mem-

bers interact), and *structure* (how the family is organized).

Constructivism reintroduced cognition to family therapists. Family systems may be regulated by interpersonal interactions, but those interactions are shaped by how family members interpret each other's behavior. *Social constructionism* reminds us that families are open systems—our interpretations are heavily influenced by assumptions we absorb from the culture.

The trajectory of these concepts broadened our focus beyond the individual to relationships, to the family as a whole, and finally to society at large. *Attachment theory* can be seen as part of an effort to restore our grounding in psychology. Attachment theory emphasizes the basic need for security in close relationships, both in childrearing and intimate partnership.

In the section on "The Working Concepts of Family Therapy," we tried to show how therapists can apply the insights of these various theories in clinical practice. Beyond the specifics, what we'd hope to get across is that families are more than a collection of individuals; they have superordinate properties that may not always be apparent. It may be obvious, for example, that there are always two parties to a relationship—and that problems, as well as solutions, are a function of both parties. But even this reality can get lost in the heat of emo-

tion. This is as true for therapists as for the people involved. Each of the various other working concepts offers its own particular insights into understanding family joys and sorrows.

In the following sections, we'll see how the various schools of family therapy approach the task of understanding and treating family problems. But even as the models get specific, it's always a good idea to keep in mind the general principles of family functioning explained in this chapter.

RECOMMENDED READINGS

Bateson, G. 1971. *Steps to an ecology of mind.* New York: Ballantine.

Bateson, G. 1979. *Mind and nature.* New York: Dutton.

Bertalanffy, L. von. 1950. An outline of General System Theory. *British Journal of the Philosophy of Science. 1:*134–165.

Bertalanffy, L. von. 1967. *Robots, men and minds.* New York: Braziller.

Bowlby, J. 1988. *A secure base: Clinical application of attachment theory.* London: Routledge.

Carter, E., and McGoldrick, M., eds. 1999. *The expanded family life cycle: A framework for family therapy,* 3rd ed. Boston: Allyn & Bacon.

Davidson, M. 1983. *Uncommon sense: The life and thought of Ludwig von Bertalanffy.* Los Angeles: Tarcher.

Dell, P. F. 1982. Beyond homeostasis: Toward a concept of coherence. *Family Process. 21:*21–42.

Haley, J. 1985. Conversations with Erickson. *Family Therapy Networker. 9*(2):30–43.

Hoffman, L. 1981. *Foundations of family therapy.* New York: Basic Books.

Wiener, N. 1948. *Cybernetics or control and communication in the animal and the machine.* Cambridge, MA: Technology Press.

REFERENCES

Ainsworth, M. D. S. 1967. *Infancy in Uganda: Infant care and the growth of attachment.* Baltimore: Johns Hopkins University Press.

Ainsworth, M. D. S., Blehar, M. C., Walters, E., and Wall, S. 1978. *Patterns of attachment: A psychological study of the strange situation.* Hillsdale, NJ: Erlbaum.

Anderson, H., and Goolishian, H. A. 1988. Human systems as linguistic systems: Evolving ideas about the implications of theory and practice. *Family Process. 27:*371–393.

Bateson, G. 1956. *Naven.* Stanford, CA: Stanford University Press.

Bateson, G. 1979. *Mind and nature.* New York: Dutton.

Bernard, C. 1859. *Leçons sur les proprietes physiologiques et les alterations pathologiques des liquides de l'organsime.* Paris: Balliere.

Bertalanffy, L. von. 1968. *General systems theory.* New York: Braziller.

Bibb, A., and Casimir, G. J. 1996. Hatian families. In *Ethnicity and family therapy,* M. McGoldrick, J. Giordano, and J. K. Pearce, eds. New York: Guilford Press.

Bowen, M. 1978. *Family therapy in clinical practice.* New York: Jason Aronson.

Bowlby, J. 1958. The nature of the child's tie to his mother. *International Journal of Psycho-Analysis. 41:*350–373.

Bowlby, J. 1973. *Attachment and loss: Vol. 2. Separation.* New York: Basic Books.

Boyd-Franklin, N. 1989. *Black families in therapy: A multisystems approach.* New York: Guilford Press.

Buckley, W. 1968. Society as a complex adaptive system. In *Modern systems research for the behavioral scientist: A sourcebook*, W. Buckley, ed. Chicago: Aldine.

Burlingham, D., and Freud, A. 1944. *Infants without families.* London: Allen & Unwin.

Carter, E., and McGoldrick, M., eds. 1980. *The family life cycle: A framework for family therapy.* New York: Gardner Press.

Carter, E., and McGoldrick, M., eds. 1999. *The expanded family life cycle.* 3rd ed. Boston: Allyn & Bacon.

Chodorow, N. 1978. *The reproduction of mothering.* Berkeley: University of California Press.

Davidson, M. 1983. *Uncommon sense.* Los Angeles: Tarcher.

Dell, P. F. 1982. Beyond homeostasis: Toward a concept of coherence. *Family Process.* 21(1):21–42.

Dell, P. F. 1985. Understanding Bateson and Maturana: Toward a biological foundation for the social sciences. *Journal of Marital and Family Therapy.* 11:1–20.

Dutton, D. 1998. *The abusive personality.* New York: Guilford Press.

Duvall, E. 1957. *Family development.* Philadelphia: Lippincott.

Easterbrook, M. A., and Lamb, M. E. 1979. The relationship between quality of infant–mother attachment and infant competence in initial encounters with peers. *Child Development.* 50:380–387.

Efran, J. S., Lukens, M. D., and Lukens, R. J. 1990. *Language, structure and change: Frameworks of meaning in psychotherapy.* New York: Norton.

Falicov, C. J. 1998. *Latino families in therapy.* New York: Guilford Press.

Feeney, J. A. 1995. Adult attachment and emotional control. *Personal Relationships.* 2:143–159.

Feldman, C., and Ridley, C. 1995. The etiology and treatment of domestic violence between adult partners. *Clinical Psychology in Scientific Practice.* 2:317–348.

Foerster, H. von. 1981. *Observing systems.* Seaside, CA: Intersystems.

Fonagy, P. 1999. Male perpetrators of violence against women: An attachment theory perspective. *Journal of Applied Psychoanalytic Studies.* 1:7–27.

Gergen, K. J. 1985. The social constructionist movement in modern psychology. *American Psychologist.* 40:266–275.

Gottman, J. 1994. *What predicts divorce.* Hillsdale, NJ: Erlbaum.

Haley, J. 1976. *Problem-solving therapy.* San Francisco: Jossey-Bass.

Harlow, H. 1958. The nature of love. *American Psychologist.* 13:673–685.

Hazan, C., and Shaver, P. R. 1987. Romantic love conceptualized as an attachment process. *Journal of Personality and Social Psychology.* 52:511–524.

Heims, S. 1991. *The cybernetics group.* Cambridge, MA: MIT Press.

Hill, R., and Rodgers, R. 1964. The developmental approach. In *Handbook of marriage and the family*, H. T. Christiansen, ed. Chicago: Rand McNally.

Hoffman, L. 1981. *Foundations of family therapy.* New York: Basic Books.

Hoffman, L. 1988. A constructivist position for family therapy. *The Irish Journal of Psychology.* 9: 110–129.

Jackson, D. D. 1957. The question of family homeostasis. *Psychiatric Quarterly Supplement.* 31:79–90.

Jackson, D. D. 1959. Family interaction, family homeostasis, and some implications for conjoint family therapy. In *Individual and family dynamics*, J. Masserman, ed. New York: Grune & Stratton.

Johnson, S. 1996. *Creating connection: The practice of emotionally focused marital therapy.* New York: Brunner/Mazel.

Johnson, S. 2002. *Emotionally focused couple therapy with trauma survivors: Strengthening attachment bonds.* New York: Guilford Press.

Kelly, G. A. 1955. *The psychology of personal constructs.* New York: Norton.

Lee, E. 1996. Asian American families: An overview. In *Ethnicity and family therapy*, M. McGoldrick, J. Giordano, and J. K. Pearce, eds. New York: Guilford Press.

Lieberman, A. F. 1977. Preschoolers' competence with a peer: Relations with attachment and peer experience. *Child Development.* 48:1277–1287.

Lorenz, K. E. 1935. Der Kumpan in der Umvelt des Vogels. In *Instinctive behavior*, C. H. Schiller, ed. New York: International Universities Press.

Luepnitz, D. A. 1988. *The family interpreted: Feminist theory in clinical practice.* New York: Basic Books.

Mahler, M., Pine, F., and Bergman, A. 1975. *The psychological birth of the human infant.* New York: Basic Books.

Main, M. 1977. Sicherheit und wissen. In *Entwicklung der Lernfahigkeit in der sozialen umwelt*, K. E. Grossman, ed. Munich: Kinder Verlag.

Main, M., and Weston, D. 1981. The quality of the toddler's relationships to mother and father: Related to conflict behavior and readiness to establish new relationships. *Child Development.* 52:932–940.

Matas, L., Arend, R., and Sroufe, L. A. 1978. Continuity of adaptation in the second year: The relationship between quality of attachment and later competence. *Child Development.* 49:547–556.

Maturana, H. R., and Varela, F. J. eds. 1980. *Autopoiesis and cognition: The realization of the living.* Boston: Reidel.

Meyrowitz, J. 1985. *No sense of place.* New York: Oxford University Press.

Minuchin, P., Colapinto, J., and Minuchin, S. 2007. *Working with families of the poor*, 2nd ed. New York: Guilford Press.

Minuchin, S. 1974. *Families and family therapy.* Cambridge, MA: Harvard University Press.

Minuchin, S. 1991. The seductions of constructivism. *Family Therapy Networker.* 15(5):47–50.

Minuchin, S., and Nichols, M. P. 1993. *Family healing: Tales of hope and renewal from family therapy.* New York: Free Press.

Minuchin, S., Lee, W-Y., and Simon, G. M. 1996. *Mastering family therapy: Journeys of growth and transformation.* New York: Wiley.

Nichols, M. P., and Schwartz, R. C. 2001. *Family therapy: Concepts and methods*, 5th ed. Boston: Allyn & Bacon.

Robertson, J. 1953. *A two-year-old goes to hospital.* [Film]. London: Tavistock Child Development Research Unit.

Speer, D. C. 1970. Family systems: Morphostasis and morphogenesis, or "Is homeostasis enough?" *Family Process.* 9(3):259–278.

Sroufe, L. A. 1979. The coherence of individual development: Early care, attachment and subsequent developmental issues. *American Psychologist.* 34:834–841.

Ugazio, V. 1999. *Storie permesses, storie proibite: Polarita semantiche familiari e psicopatologie.* Turin, Italy: Bollati Boringhieri.

Vogel, E. F., and Bell, N. W. 1960. The emotionally disturbed child as a family scapegoat. In *The family*, N. W. Bell and E. F. Vogel, eds. Glencoe, IL: Free Press.

Walters, M., Carter, B., Papp, P., and Silverstein, O. 1988. *The invisible web: Gender patterns in family relationships.* New York: Guilford Press.

Waters, E. 1978. The reliability and stability of individual differences in infant–mother attachment. *Child Development.* 49:483–494.

Waters, E., Wippman, J., and Sroufe, L. A. 1979. Attachment, positive affect and competence in the peer group: Two studies of construct validation. *Child Development.* 51:208–216.

Watzlawick, P., ed. 1984. *The invented reality.* New York: Norton.

Watzlawick, P., Beavin, J. H., and Jackson, D. D. 1967. *Pragmatics of human communication.* New York: Norton.

West, M., and George, C. 1999. Abuse and violence in intimate adult relationships: New perspectives from attachment theory. *Attachment and Human Development.* 1:137–156.

White, M., and Epston, D. 1990. *Narrative means to therapeutic ends.* New York: Norton.

Wiener, N. 1948. *Cybernetics or control and communication in the animal and the machine.* Cambridge, MA: MIT Press.

Bowen Family Systems Therapy

5

An Intergenerational Approach to Family Therapy

The pioneers of family therapy recognized that people are products of their context but limited their focus to the nuclear family. Yes, our actions are influenced by what goes on in our families, but what are the forces—past and present—that mold those influences? What makes a husband distance himself from family life? What makes a wife neglect her own development to manage her children's lives? Murray Bowen sought answers to such questions in the larger network of family relationships.

According to Bowen, human relationships are driven by two counterbalancing life forces: *individuality* and *togetherness*. Each of us needs companionship and a degree of independence. What makes life interesting—and maddening—is the tendency for our needs to polarize us. When one partner presses for more connection, the other may feel crowded and pull away. As time goes by, the pursuit of one and withdrawal of the other drives the pair through cycles of closeness and distance.

How successfully people reconcile these two polarities of human nature depends on the extent to which they have learned to manage emotionality, or to use Bowen's term, on their *differentiation of self*. More about this later.

While no one doubts the formative influence of the family, many people imagine that once they leave home, they are grown-up, independent adults, free at last of their parents' influence. Some people prize individuality and take it as a sign of growth to separate from their parents. Others wish they could be closer to their families but find visits too painful, and so they stay away to protect themselves from disappointment and hurt. Once out of range of the immediate conflict, they forget and deny the discord. But, as Bowen discovered, the family remains with us wherever we go. As we will see, unresolved emotional reactivity to our parents is the most important unfinished business of our lives.

SKETCHES OF LEADING FIGURES

Murray Bowen's professional interest in the family began when he was a psychiatrist at the Menninger Clinic from 1946 to 1954. Turning his attention to the enigma of schizophrenia, Bowen was struck by the exquisite emotional sensitivity between patients and their mothers. Others called this reactivity *symbiosis*, as though it were some kind of parasitic mutation. Bowen saw it simply as an exaggeration of a natural process, a more intense version of the tendency to react emotionally to one another that exists in all relationships.

In 1954, Bowen moved to the National Institute of Mental Health (NIMH), where he initiated a project of hospitalizing entire families containing a schizophrenic member. What he found was that the intense emotional tie between mothers and their emotionally disturbed offspring inevitably involved the whole family. At the heart of the problem was *anxious attachment*, a pathological form of closeness driven by anxiety. In these troubled families, people were emotional prisoners of the way the others behaved. The hallmark of these emotionally stuck-together, or *fused*, relationships was a lack of personal autonomy.

When the NIMH project ended in 1959 and Bowen moved to Georgetown University, he began working with families whose problems were less severe. What he discovered, to his surprise, were many of the same mechanisms he had observed in psychotic families. This convinced him that there is no discontinuity between normal and disturbed families but that all families vary along a continuum from emotional fusion to differentiation.

During his thirty-one years at Georgetown, Bowen developed a comprehensive theory of family therapy, inspired an entire generation of students, and became an internationally renowned leader of the family therapy movement. He died after a long illness in October 1990.

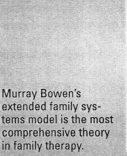

Murray Bowen's extended family systems model is the most comprehensive theory in family therapy.

Among the most prominent of Bowen's students are Philip Guerin and Thomas Fogarty, who joined in 1973 to form the Center for Family Learning in New Rochelle, New York. Under Guerin's leadership, the Center for Family Learning became one of the major centers of family therapy training. Guerin is a laid-back, virtuoso therapist and teacher, and two of his books, *The Evaluation and Treatment of Marital Conflict* and *Working with Relationship Triangles*, are among the most useful in all the family therapy literature.

Betty Carter and Monica McGoldrick are best known for their exposition of the family life cycle (Carter & McGoldrick, 1999) and for championing feminism in family therapy. Michael Kerr, M.D., was a long-time student

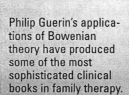

Philip Guerin's applications of Bowenian theory have produced some of the most sophisticated clinical books in family therapy.

and colleague of Bowen's and since 1977 has been the director of training at the Georgetown Family Center. Kerr is perhaps the most faithful advocate of all Bowen's students, as his brilliant account of Bowenian theory in the book *Family Evaluation* (Kerr & Bowen, 1988) richly demonstrates.

THEORETICAL FORMULATIONS

Most of family therapy's pioneers were *pragmatists*, more concerned with action than insight, more interested in technique than theory. Bowen was the exception. He was always more committed to systems theory as a way of thinking than as a set of interventions.

According to Bowen, we have less autonomy in our emotional lives than we assume. Most of us are more dependent and reactive to one another than we like to think. Bowen's theory describes how the family, as a multigenerational network of relationships, shapes the interplay of individuality and togetherness using six interlocking concepts (Bowen, 1966): *differentiation of self, triangles, nuclear family emotional process, family projection process, multigenerational transmission process*, and *sibling position*. In the 1970s, Bowen added two additional concepts: *emotional cutoff* and *societal emotional process* (1976). Because three of the original six concepts (*nuclear family emotional process, family projection process*, and *multigenerational transmission process*) all refer to how family problems are passed down through the generations, we have collapsed these three concepts into one, which we'll call *multigenerational emotional processes*.

Differentiation of Self

The cornerstone of Bowen's theory is both an intrapsychic and an interpersonal concept. Roughly analogous to *ego strength*, **differentiation of self** is the capacity to think and reflect, to not respond automatically to emotional pressures, internal or external (Kerr & Bowen, 1988). It is the ability to be flexible and act wisely, even in the face of anxiety.

Undifferentiated people are easily moved to emotionality. Their lives are driven by reactivity to those around them. The differentiated person is able to balance thinking and feeling: capable of strong emotion and spontaneity but also possessing the self-restraint that comes with the ability to resist the pull of emotional impulses.

In contrast, undifferentiated people tend to react impetuously—with submissiveness or defiance—toward other people. They find it difficult to maintain their own autonomy, especially around anxious issues. Asked what they think, they say what they feel; asked what they believe, they echo what they've heard. They either agree with whatever you say or argue with everything. In contrast, differentiated people are able to take stands on issues because they're able to think things through, decide what they believe, and then act on those beliefs.

Emotional Triangles

Take a minute to think about the most troublesome current relationship in your life. That relationship almost certainly involves one or more third persons. Virtually all relationships are shadowed by third parties—relatives, friends, even memories.

The major influence on the activity of triangles is *anxiety* (Guerin, Fogarty, Fay, & Kautto, 1996). As anxiety increases, people experience a greater need for emotional closeness—or, in reaction to pressures from others, a greater need for distance. The more people are driven by anxiety, the less tolerant they are of one another and the more they are polarized by differences.

When two people have problems they are unable to resolve, they get to the point where it's hard to talk about certain things. Why go through all that aggravation when it only leads to hurt and anger? Eventually, one or both partners will turn to someone else for sympathy or the conflict will draw in a third person to try to help. If the third party's involvement is only temporary or pushes the two people to work out their differences, the triangle doesn't become fixed. If the third person stays involved, however, as often happens, the triangle becomes a part of the relationship.

The involvement of a third person decreases anxiety in the twosome by spreading it through three relationships. Thus, for example, a wife upset with her husband's distance may increase her involvement with one of the children. What makes this a triangle is diverting energy that might otherwise go into the marriage. Spending time with her daughter may take pressure off the wife's husband to do things he doesn't care to. However, it also decreases the likelihood that husband and wife will learn to develop interests they can share—and it undermines the daughter's independence.

A group of three isn't necessarily a triangle. In a viable threesome, each twosome can interact one on one; each person has options for his or her behavior; and each can take "I-positions" without trying to change the other two. In a triangle, on the other hand, each twosome's interaction is tied to the behavior of the third person; each person is driven by reactive forms of behavior, none of them can take a position without feeling the need to change the other two; and each person gets involved in the relationship between the other two. Picture a rubber band around three people who cannot allow it to drop. It constrains their movement such that if two people get closer the third must move farther away.

Some triangles seem so innocent that we hardly notice them. Most parents can't resist complaining to their children about their mates. "Your mother's *always* late!" "Your father *never* lets anyone else drive!" These interchanges seem harmless enough. What makes triangles problematic is that they have a tendency to become habitual and to corrupt the original relationship.

Triangulation lets off steam but freezes conflict in place. It isn't that complaining or seeking solace is wrong, but rather that triangles become diversions that undermine relationships.

Most family problems are triangular, which is why working only on a twosome may have limited results. Teaching a mother better techniques for disciplining her son won't resolve the problem if she is overinvolved with the boy as a result of her husband's distance.

Multigenerational Transmission Processes

These are the emotional forces in families that operate over the years in interconnected patterns. Bowen originally used the term *undifferentiated family ego mass* to describe an excess of emotional reactivity, or **fusion**, in families. If you know someone who rarely responds calmly to what you're trying to say because he or she is given to emotional outbursts, then you know how frustrating it can be to deal with emotionally reactive people.

Lack of differentiation in the family of origin produces emotionally reactive children, which may be manifest either as emotional overinvolvement or *emotional cutoff* from the parents, which in turn lead to fusion in marriage—because people with limited emotional resources typically project all their needs onto each other. Because this new fusion is unstable, it tends to produce one or more of the following: (1) emotional distance between the partners; (2) physical or emotional dysfunction in one partner; (3) marital conflict; or (4) projection of problems onto the children. The intensity of these problems is related to the degree of undifferentiation, extent of emotional cutoff from families of origin, and level of stress in the system.

Emotional fusion in a couple creates tension that leads to conflict, emotional distance, or reciprocal over- and underfunctioning. A common case is when a husband who is emotionally reactive to his family keeps his emotional distance from his wife. This predisposes her to focus on the kids. Kept at arm's length by her husband, she becomes anxiously attached to the children, usually with greatest intensity toward one child. This might be the oldest son or daughter, the youngest, or perhaps the child most like one of the parents. This connection is different from caring concern; it's anxious, enmeshed concern. Because it relieves his own anxiety, the husband accepts his wife's overinvolvement with the children, reinforcing their entanglement and his distance.

The object of this projection process—the child the mother lives through most—achieves the least differentiation of self and becomes the most vulnerable to psychological problems. This doesn't mean that patterns of emotional functioning *cause* psychiatric disturbance; it means that these emotional processes in the family are a major influence on an individual's ability to adapt to other factors that precipitate dysfunction. The more a mother focuses her anxiety on a child, the more that child's functioning is stunted. This underdevelopment encourages the mother to hover over the child, distracting her from her own anxieties but crippling the child emotionally.

The more anxiety that's focused on one of the children, the less that child will be able to regulate his or her own emotionality and grow up a mature and happy person. In every generation, the child most involved in the family's fusion moves toward a lower level of differentiation of self (and chronic anxiety), while the least-involved child moves toward a higher level of differentiation (and less anxiety).

Parents who anxiously intrude their concerns on their children leave them little choice but to conform or rebel. Instead of learning to think for themselves, such children function in reaction to others. When these children leave home, they expect to become authors of their own lives. They're not going to turn out like their parents! Unfortunately, although we may fight against our inheritance, it usually catches up with us.

Sibling Position

Bowen believed that children develop personality characteristics based on their position in the family (Toman, 1969). So many variables are involved that prediction is complex, but knowledge of general characteristics plus specific knowledge of a particular family is helpful in predicting what part a child will play in the family emotional process.

Bowen's theory offers an interesting perspective with which to reconsider the familiar notion of sibling rivalry. Say that a mother is anxious to make sure that her children feel equally loved (as though the truth might be otherwise). Her anxiety is translated into treating them exactly alike—an attempt at perfect fairness that betrays the apprehension behind it. Each child then becomes highly sensitive to the amount of attention he or she receives in relation to siblings. This can result in fighting and resentment—just what the mother sought to prevent. Moreover, because the mother is anxious to control how the children feel, she may step in to settle their fights, thus depriving them of the opportunity to do so themselves—and giving them additional reason to feel unequally treated. ("How come *I* have to go to my room? *He* started it!")

Thus sibling conflict, often explained as an outcome of inevitable rivalry (as though rivalrousness were the only natural relationship between brothers and sisters), may be just one side of a triangle. (Of course the intensity of a mother's preoccupation with her children is related to other triangles—including her relationships with friends, her career, and her husband.)

The importance of birth order was documented in *Born to Rebel*, by Frank Sulloway (1996). Culling biographical data from five hundred years of history, Sulloway's conclusions were supported by a multivariate analysis of more than a million biographical data points. Personality, he argues, is the repertoire of strategies that siblings use to compete with one another to secure a place in the family.

Firstborns have a tendency to identify with power and authority: They employ their size and strength to defend their status and try to minimize the cost of having siblings by dominating them. (Alfred Adler suggested that firstborns become "power-hungry conservatives" as they struggle to restore their lost primacy within the family.) Winston Churchill, George Washington, Ayn Rand, and Rush Limbaugh are examples.

As underdogs in the family, laterborns are more inclined to identify with the oppressed and to question the status quo. They're more open to experience because this openness aids them, as latecomers to the family, in finding an unoccupied niche. From their ranks have come the bold explorers, iconoclasts, and heretics of history. Joan of Arc, Marx, Lenin, Jefferson, Rousseau, Virginia Woolf, Mary Wollstonecraft, and Bill Gates are representative laterborns.

What developmentalists once thought of as a shared family context turns out not to be shared at all. Every family is a multiplicity of microenvironments, a collection of niches, consisting of distinct vantage points from which siblings experience the same events in very different ways.

Emotional Cutoff

Emotional cutoff describes the way people manage anxiety between generations. The greater the emotional fusion between parents and children, the greater the likelihood of cutoff. Some people seek distance by moving away; others do so emotionally, by avoiding personal conversations or insulating themselves with the presence of third parties.

Michael Nichols (1986) describes how some people mistake emotional cutoff for maturity:

> We take it as a sign of growth to separate from our parents, and we measure our maturity by independence of family ties. Yet many of us still respond to our families as though they were radioactive and capable of inflicting great pain. Only one thing robs Superman of his extra-

Betty Carter is a highly respected Bowenian therapist and a forceful advocate for gender equality.

ordinary power: kryptonite, a piece of his home planet. A surprising number of adult men and women are similarly rendered helpless by even a brief visit to or from their parents. (p. 190)

Societal Emotional Process

Bowen anticipated the contemporary concern about social influence on how families function. Kerr and Bowen (1988) cite the example of the high-crime rate that results in communities with great social pressure. Bowen agreed that sexism and class and ethnic prejudice are toxic social emotional processes, but he believed that individuals and families with higher levels of differentiation were better able to resist these destructive social influences.

To the theoretical concerns of Bowenian therapists, Monica McGoldrick and Betty Carter added gender and ethnicity. These feminist Bowenians believe that it isn't possible to ignore gender inequalities without ignoring some of the primary forces that keep men and women trapped in inflexible roles. Moreover, they might point out that the previous sentence is inaccurate in implying that men and women alike are victims of gender bias. Women live with constraining social conditions *and* with men who perpetuate them—men who may not feel powerful with their wives and mothers but who live with, and take for granted, social advantages that make it easier for men to get ahead in the world.

McGoldrick has also been a leader in calling attention to ethnic differences among families. Her book *Ethnicity and Family Therapy* (McGoldrick, Pearce, & Giordano, 1982) was a landmark in family therapy's developing sensitivity to this issue. Without understanding how cultural values differ from one ethnic group to the next, the danger is of therapists imposing their own ways of looking at things on families whose perspectives aren't dysfunctional but legitimately different.

NORMAL FAMILY DEVELOPMENT

Optimal development is thought to take place when family members are differentiated, anxiety is low, and partners are in good emotional contact with their own families. Most people leave home in the midst of transforming relationships with their parents from an adolescent to an adult basis. Thus the transformation is usually incomplete, and most of us, even as adults, continue to react with adolescent sensitivity to our parents—or anyone else who pushes the same buttons.

Normally, but not optimally, people reduce contact with their parents and siblings to avoid the anxiety of dealing with them. Once out of the house and on their own, people tend to assume that they've put the old difficulties behind them. However, we all carry unfinished business in the form of unresolved sensitivities that flare up in intense relationships wherever we go. Having learned to ignore their role in family conflicts, most people are unable to prevent recurrences in new relationships.

Another heritage from the past is that the emotional attachment between intimate partners comes to resemble that which each had in their families of origin. People from undifferentiated families will continue to be undifferentiated when they form new families. Those who handled anxiety by distance and withdrawal will tend to do the same in their marriages. Therefore, Bowen was convinced that differentiation of autonomous personalities, accomplished primarily in the family of origin, was both a description of normal development and a prescription for therapeutic improvement.

Carter and McGoldrick (1999) describe the **family life cycle** as a process of expansion, contraction, and realignment of the relationship system to support the entry, exit, and development of family members.

In the *leaving home stage*, the primary task for young adults is to separate from their families without cutting off or fleeing to an emotional substitute. This is the time to develop an autonomous self before pairing off to form a new union.

In the *joining of families through marriage stage*, the primary task is commitment to the new couple—but this is not simply a joining of two individuals; it is a transformation of two entire systems. While problems in this stage may seem to be primarily between the partners, they may reflect a failure to separate from families of origin or cutoffs that put too much pressure on a couple. The formation of an intimate partnership requires the partners to shift their primary emotional attachment from their parents and friends to the relationship with their mates. Making wedding plans, choosing a place to live, buying a car, having a baby, and choosing a school are all times when this struggle may become explicit.

Families with young children must make space for the new additions, cooperate in childrearing, keep the marriage from being submerged in parenting, and realign relationships with the extended family. Young mothers and fathers must fulfill their children's needs for nurture and control—and work together as a team. This is an extremely stressful time, especially for new mothers, and it is the stage with the highest divorce rate.

The reward for parents who survive the preceding stages is to have their children turn into adolescents. *Adolescence* is a time when children no longer want to be like Mommy and Daddy; they want to be themselves. They struggle to become autonomous individuals and to open family boundaries—and they struggle however hard they must. Parents with satisfying lives of their own welcome (or at least tolerate) the fresh air (pun intended) that blows through the house at this time. Those who insist on controlling their teenagers as though they were still little ones may provoke painful escalations of the rebelliousness that's normal for this period.

In the *launching of children and moving on stage*, parents must let their children go and take hold of their own lives. This can be liberating or it can be a time of *midlife crisis* (Nichols, 1986). Parents must not only deal with changes in their children's and their own lives but also with changes in their relationships with aging parents who may need increasing support—or at least don't want to act like parents anymore.

Families in later life must adjust to retirement, which not only means a loss of vocation but also a sudden increase in proximity for the couple. With both partners home all day, the house may seem a lot smaller. Later-in-life families must cope with declining health, illness, and then death, the great equalizer.

One variation in the life cycle that can no longer be considered abnormal is *divorce*. With the divorce rate at 50 percent and the rate of redivorce at 61 percent (Kreider & Fields, 2002), divorce now strikes the majority of U.S. families. The primary tasks of a divorcing couple are to end the marriage but maintain cooperation as parents. Some postdivorce families become single-parent families—consisting in the main of mothers and children and in the vast majority of those cases staggering under the weight of financial strain. The alternative is remarriage and the formation of stepfamilies, in which, often, loneliness is swapped for conflict.

DEVELOPMENT OF BEHAVIOR DISORDERS

Symptoms result from stress that exceeds a person's ability to manage it. The ability to handle stress is a function of differentiation: The more well-differentiated the person, the more resilient he or she will be, and the more flexible and sus-

taining his or her relationships. The less well-differentiated the person, the less stress it takes to produce symptoms.

If *differentiation* were reduced to *maturity*, the Bowenian formula wouldn't add much to the familiar diathesis-stress model, which says that illness develops when an individual's vulnerability is taxed. The difference is that differentiation isn't just a quality of individuals but also of relationships. A person's basic level of differentiation is largely determined by the degree of autonomy achieved in his or her family, but the *functional level of differentiation* is influenced by the quality of current relationships. Thus a somewhat immature person who manages to develop healthy relationships will be at less risk than an equally immature person who's alone or in unhealthy relationships. Symptoms develop when the level of anxiety exceeds the *system's* ability to handle it.

The most vulnerable individual (in terms of isolation and lack of differentiation) is most likely to absorb the anxiety in a system and develop symptoms. For example, a child of ten with a conduct disorder is likely to be the most triangled child in the family and thereby the one most emotionally caught up in the conflict between the parents or most affected by one of the parent's tensions.

According to Bowen, the underlying factor in the genesis of psychological problems is *emotional fusion*, passed down from one generation to the next. The greater the fusion, the more one is programmed by primitive emotional forces, and the more vulnerable to the emotionality of others. Although it isn't always apparent, people tend to choose mates with similar levels of undifferentiation.

Emotional fusion is based on anxious attachment, which may be manifest either as dependency or isolation. Both the overly dependent and the emotionally isolated person respond with emotional reactivity to stress. The following clinical vignette illustrates how emotional fusion in the **family of origin** is transmitted.

Case Study

Janet and Warren Langdon requested help for their fifteen-year-old son Martin after Mrs. Langdon found marijuana in a plastic bag at the bottom of his underwear drawer. Mr. and Mrs. Langdon didn't object when the therapist said she'd like to meet with the three of them in order to get as much information as possible. It turned out that the discovery of marijuana was just the latest incident in a long series of battles between Mrs. Langdon and her son. Lots of fifteen-year-olds experiment with marijuana; not all of them leave the evidence around for their mothers to find.

After meeting with the family and then talking with the boy and his parents separately, the therapist concluded that Martin did not appear to have a serious drug problem. Of greater concern, however, were the intensity of his shouting matches with his mother and his poor social adjustment at school. What she told the family was that she was concerned not only about the marijuana but also about these other signs of unhappy adjustment and that she'd like to extend the evaluation by having a couple of additional meetings with Martin and his parents separately. Mr. and Mrs. Langdon agreed without enthusiasm. Martin didn't protest as much as might have been expected.

After his father died, Mr. Langdon and his older sister were raised by their mother. They were all she had left, and she increasingly devoted all her energy to shaping their lives. She was demanding and critical and resentful of anything they wanted to do outside the family. By late adolescence, Warren could no longer tolerate his domineering mother. His sister was never able to break free; she remained single and lived at home with her mother. Warren, however, was determined to become independent. Finally, in his mid-twenties, he left home and turned his back on his mother.

Janet Langdon came from a close-knit family. She and her four sisters were very much attached to each other and remained best friends. After graduating from high school, Janet an-

nounced that she wanted to go to college. This was contrary to the family norm that daughters stay at home and prepare to be wives and mothers. Hence, a major battle ensued between Janet and her parents; they were struggling to hold on, and she was struggling to break free. Finally she left for college, but she was ever after estranged from her parents.

Janet and Warren were immediately drawn to one another. Both were lonely and cut off from their families. After a brief, passionate courtship, they married. The honeymoon didn't last long. Never having really differentiated himself from his dictatorial mother, Warren was exquisitely sensitive to criticism and control. He became furious at Janet's slightest attempt to change his habits. Janet, on the other hand, sought to reestablish in her marriage the closeness she'd had in her family. In order to be close, she and Warren would have to share interests and activities. But when she moved toward him, suggesting that they do something together, Warren got angry and resentful, feeling that she was impinging on his individuality. After several months of conflict, the two settled into a period of relative equilibrium. Warren put most of his energy into his work, leaving Janet to adjust to the distance between them. A year later, Martin was born.

Both of them were delighted to have a baby, but what was for Warren a pleasant addition to the family was for Janet a way to fulfill a desperate need for closeness. The baby meant everything to her. While he was an infant, she was the perfect mother, loving him tenderly and caring for his every need. When Warren tried to become involved with his infant son, Janet hovered about making sure he didn't "do anything wrong." This infuriated Warren, and after a few bitter blowups, he left Martin to his wife's care.

As Martin learned to walk and talk, he got into mischief, as all children do. He grabbed things, refused to stay in his playpen, and fussed whenever he didn't get his way. His crying was unbearable to Janet, and she found herself unable to set limits on her precious child.

Martin grew up with a doting mother, thinking he was the center of the universe. Whenever he didn't get what he wanted, he threw a tantrum. Bad as things got, at least the family existed in a kind of equilibrium. Warren was cut off from his wife and son, but he had his work. Janet was alienated from her husband, but she had her baby.

Martin's difficulties began when he went off to school. Used to getting his own way, he found it impossible to get along with other children. His tantrums did nothing to endear him to his schoolmates or teachers. Other children avoided him, and he grew up having few friends. With teachers, he acted out his father's battle against any effort to control him. When Janet heard complaints about Martin's behavior, she sided with her son: "Those people don't know how to deal with a creative child!"

Martin grew up with a terrible pattern of adjustment to school and friends but retained his extremely close relationship with his mother. The crisis came with adolescence. Like his father before him, Martin tried to develop independent interests outside the home. However, he was far less capable of separating than his father had been, and his mother was incapable of letting go. The result was the beginning of chronic conflicts between Martin and his mother. Even as they argued and fought, they remained centered on each other. Martin spent more time battling his mother than doing anything else with his life.

Martin's history illustrates Bowen's theory of behavior disorder. Symptoms break out when the *vertical* problems of anxiety and toxic family issues intersect with the *horizontal* stresses of transition points in the life cycle. Thus Martin's greatest vulnerability came when the unresolved fusion he inherited from his mother intersected with the stress of his adolescent urge for independence.

Even emotionally fused children reach a point when they try to break away—but breaking away in such instances tends to be accomplished by emotional cutoff, rather than mature resolution of family ties. In childhood, we relate as children to our parents. We depend on them to take care of us, we uncritically accept most of their attitudes and beliefs, and we behave in ways that are generally effective in getting our way. This usually means some combination of being good, patiently waiting to be rewarded, and being upset and demanding. Most of this childish behavior doesn't work in the adult world. However, most of us leave home before changing to an adult-to-adult pattern with our parents. We—and they—only begin to change before it's time to leave.

The daughter who didn't get past the good-little-girl stage with her parents will probably adopt a similar stance outside the home. When it doesn't work, she may react with temper. Those who cut themselves off from their parents to minimize tension carry their childish ways with them.

According to Bowen, people tend to choose mates with similar levels of undifferentiation. When conflict develops, each partner will be aware of the emotional immaturity—in the other one. Each will be prepared for change—in the other one. He will discover that her treating him like a father entails not only clinging dependence but also tirades and temper tantrums. She will discover that he withdraws the closeness she found so attractive in courtship as soon as she makes any demands. He fled from his parents because he needs closeness but can't handle it. Faced with conflict, he again withdraws. Sadly, what turned them on to each other carries the switch that turns them off.

What follows is marital conflict, dysfunction in one of the spouses, overconcern with one of the children, or a combination of all three. When families come for help, they may present with any one of these problems. Whatever the presenting problem, however, the dynamics are similar; undifferentiation in families of origin is transmitted to marital problems, which are projected onto a symptomatic spouse or child. Thus the problems of the past are visited on the future.

GOALS OF THERAPY

Bowenians don't try to change people; nor are they much interested in solving problems. Instead, they see therapy as an opportunity for people to learn more about themselves and their relationships, so that they can assume responsibility for their own problems. This is not to say, however, that therapists sit back and allow families to sort out their own issues. On the contrary, Bowenian therapy is a process of active inquiry, in which the therapist, guided by the most comprehensive theory in family therapy, helps family members get past blaming in order to explore their own roles in family problems.

Tracing the pattern of family problems means paying attention to **process** and **structure**. *Process* refers to patterns of emotional reactivity; *structure*, to the interlocking network of triangles.

In order to change a system, modification must take place in the most important triangle in the family—the one involving the marital couple. To accomplish this, the therapist creates a new triangle, a therapeutic one. If the therapist stays in contact with the partners while remaining emotionally neutral, they can begin the process of **detriangulation** and differentiation that will profoundly change the entire family system.

The clinical methodology tied to this formulation calls for (1) increasing the parents' ability to manage their own anxiety, and thereby becoming better able to handle their children's behavior, and (2) fortifying the couple's emotional functioning by increasing their ability to operate with less anxiety in their families of origin.

In the modification of these goals taken by Guerin and Fogarty, more emphasis is put on establishing a relationship with the symptomatic child and working with reactive emotional processes in the nuclear family triangles. Extended family work is put off unless it's directly linked to symptom formation. In other words, where Bowen generally went straight for the family of origin, second-generation Bowenians pay more attention to the **nuclear family** and

are likely to wait to institute work on the family of origin as a way to reinforce gains and to enhance individual and family functioning.

 ## CONDITIONS FOR BEHAVIOR CHANGE

Increasing the ability to distinguish between thinking and feeling and learning to use that ability to resolve relationship problems is the guiding principle of Bowenian therapy. Lowering anxiety and increasing self-focus—the ability to see one's own role in interpersonal processes —is the primary mechanism of change.

Understanding, not action, is the vehicle of cure. Therefore, two of the most important elements in Bowenian therapy may not be apparent to anyone who thinks primarily about techniques. The atmosphere of sessions and the therapist's stance are designed to minimize emotionality. Therapists ask questions to foster self-reflection and direct them at individuals one at a time, rather than encourage family dialogues— which have an unfortunate tendency to get overheated. Because clients aren't the only ones to respond emotionally to family dramas, Bowenian therapists strive to control their own reactivity and avoid triangulation. This, of course, is easier said than done. The keys to staying detriangled are to avoid taking sides and to nudge each party toward accepting more responsibility for making things better.

Bowen differed from most systems therapists in believing that meaningful change does not require the presence of the entire family.[1] Instead he believed that change is initiated by individuals or couples who are capable of affecting the rest of the family.

Therapy may not require the presence of the entire family, but it *does* require an awareness of

---

[1] Although willingness to see individuals has become commonplace among solution-focused and narrative therapists, these therapists don't always take a systemic perspective.

the entire family. "A family therapist may treat two parents and their schizophrenic son, but not attach much importance to the fact that the parents are emotionally cut off from their families of origin. The parents' cutoff from the past undermines their ability to stop focusing on their son's problems; once again, the therapy will be ineffective" (Kerr & Bowen, 1988, p. vii).

Part of the process of differentiating a self is to develop a personal relationship with everyone in the **extended family**. The power of these connections may seem mysterious—particularly for people who don't think of their well-being as dependent on family ties. A little reflection reveals that increasing the number of relationships will enable an individual to spread out his or her emotional energy. Instead of concentrating one's investment in one or two family relationships, it's diffused into several.

Freud had a similar notion on an intrapsychic level. In "The Project for a Scientific Psychology," Freud described his neurological model of the mind. The immature mind has few outlets (*cathexes*) for channeling psychic energy and hence little flexibility or capacity to delay responding. The mature mind, on the other hand, has many channels of response, which permits greater flexibility. Bowen's notion of increasing the emotional family network is like Freud's model, writ large.

Therapy with couples is based on the premise that tension in the dyad will dissipate if they remain in contact with a third person (in a stable triangle)—*if* that person remains neutral and objective rather than emotionally entangled. Thus a therapeutic triangle can reverse the insidious process of problem-maintaining triangulation. Furthermore, change in any one triangle will change the entire family system.

THERAPY

The major techniques in Bowenian therapy include genograms, process questions, relationship experiments, detriangling, coaching, taking "I-positions," and displacement stories. Because seeing one's own role in family problems as well as how those problems are embedded in the history of the extended family are so important in Bowenian therapy, assessment is more critical in this approach than almost any other.

Assessment

Assessment begins with a history of the presenting problem. Exact dates are noted and later checked for their relationship to events in the extended family. Next comes a history of the nuclear family, including information about when the parents met, their courtship, their marriage, and childrearing. Particular attention is paid to where the family lived and when they moved, especially in relation to the location of the extended families. The next part of the evaluation is devoted to the history of both spouses' births, sibling positions, significant facts about their childhoods, and about the past and current functioning of their parents. All of this information is recorded on a *genogram*, covering at least three generations.

Genograms are schematic diagrams listing family members and their relationships to one another. Included are ages, dates of marriage, deaths, and geographical locations. Men are represented by squares and women by circles, with their ages inside the figures. Horizontal lines indicate marriages, with the date of the marriage written on the line; vertical lines connect parents and children (Figure 5.1)[2]

What makes a genogram more than a static portrait of a family's history is the inclusion of relationship conflicts, cutoffs, and triangles. The fact that Uncle Fred was an alcoholic or that Great-Grandmother Sophie migrated from Russia is relatively meaningless without some understanding of the patterns of emotional reactivity passed down through the generations.

_____
[2]For more detailed suggestions, see McGoldrick & Gerson, 1985.

Figure **5.1** Basic Symbols Used in Genograms	*Figure* **5.2** Genogram Symbols for Relationship Dynamics

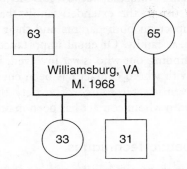

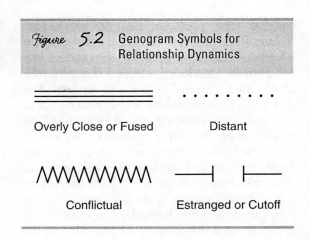

Certain triangles occur most commonly in different developmental stages. In early marriage, in-law triangles are common—raising issues of primacy of attachment and influence. When children are born and when they reach adolescence, parent–child triangles are so common as to be the norm.

Dates of important events, such as deaths, marriages, and divorces, deserve careful study. These events send emotional shock waves throughout the family, which may open lines of communication, or these issues may get buried and family members progressively more cut off. Another significant piece of information on the genogram is the location of various segments of the family. Dates, relationships, and localities provide the framework to explore emotional boundaries, fusion, cutoffs, critical conflicts, amount of openness, and the number of current and potential relationships in the family. Figure 5.2 shows symbols that can be used to describe the relationship dynamics among family members.

If three parallel lines are used to indicate overly close (or fused) relationships, a zigzag line to indicate conflict, a dotted line to indicate emotional distance, and a broken line to indicate estrangement (or cutoff), triangular patterns across three generations often become vividly clear—as shown in an abbreviated diagram of Sigmund Freud's family (Figure 5.3).

The history of the nuclear family begins with the courtship of the parents: What attracted them to each other? What was the early period of their relationship like? Were there any serious problems during that period? When were the children born, and how did the parents adapt to the new additions?

If a therapist fails to take a careful history, associations that can help people gain perspec-

Figure **5.3** Genogram of Sigmund Freud's Family

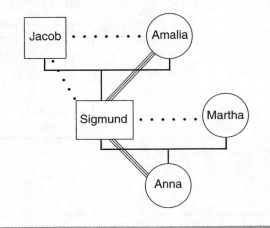

tive on their problems may be overlooked. Things like moves and important events, such as a husband's cancer surgery two years earlier, may not even be mentioned, unless a therapist asks. One woman who had been seeing an individual therapist didn't consider it important enough to mention. "What does my seeing a therapist have to do with my daughter's problems?" she said.

Of particular interest are the stresses the family has endured and how they have adapted. This information helps to evaluate the intensity of chronic anxiety in the family and whether it is linked more to an overload of difficult life events or to a low level of adaptiveness in the family.

As Figure 5.4 shows, the bare facts of a nuclear family genogram only provide a skeleton on which to flesh out information about the Langdon family. The decision to extend the assessment beyond the nuclear family depends on the extent of crisis and degree of anxiety the immediate family is in. In the case of the Langdons, both parents seemed eager to discuss their family backgrounds.

In gathering information about extended families, a therapist should ascertain which members of the clan are most involved with the family being evaluated, because it is the nature of ongoing ties to the extended family that has a great impact on both parents and their role in the nuclear family. Of equal importance, however, is finding out who is *not* involved, because people with whom contact has been cut off can be an even greater source of anxiety than the people with whom contact has been maintained.

Therapeutic Techniques

Bowenian therapists believe that understanding how family systems operate is more important than this or that procedure. Bowen himself spoke of *technique* with disdain, and he was distressed to see therapists relying on formulaic interventions.

If there were a magic bullet in Bowenian therapy—one essential technique—it would be the process question. *Process questions* are queries designed to explore what's going on inside peo-

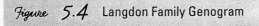

Figure 5.4   Langdon Family Genogram

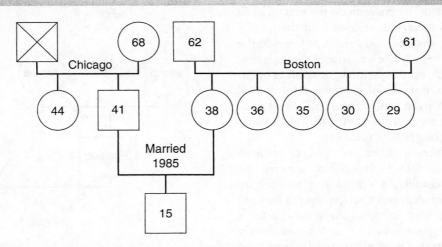

ple and between them: "When your boyfriend neglects you, how do you deal with it?" "What about your wife's criticism upsets you most?" "When your daughter goes on dates, what goes on inside you?" Process questions are designed to slow people down, diminish reactive anxiety, and start them thinking—not just about how others are upsetting them but about how they participate in interpersonal problems.

Case Study

In interviewing a couple in which the husband was a recovering alcoholic with a history of abuse, the therapist asked, "Where are you with the thoughts about the damage you've done to your wife and kids with your alcoholism?"

When the man acknowledged responsibility for his abusive behavior and seemed genuinely remorseful, the therapist asked about his progress toward recovery, using process questions to focus on rational planning and personal responsibility. For example:

"What makes that step so hard?"
"Pride."
"How does that manifest itself?"
"I get nasty."

Notice how this line of questioning explores not only the man's personal progress but also how his problems affect others in the family. Relationships take place in a systemic web of connections, but individuals are responsible for their own behavior.

Then the therapist shifted to open a discussion of the wife's role in the couple's difficulties. "So, you're getting better at taking responsibility for the drinking and the behavior connected with it? Do you think your wife appreciates what you're doing and the progress you're making?" And then a few minutes later: "Has your wife ever been able to talk to you about the things she's contributed to the relationship going sour?"

When the therapist asked the wife about her thinking, she reiterated all the annoying things her husband was doing—pressuring her to forgive him and get back together. Although he would eventually like her to consider her own role in the process, the therapist tried to empathize with her upset. "So, he's just bugging you by trying to get you to change your mind?" Then after a few minutes, the therapist tried to shift the wife to thinking more and feeling less. "Can you give me a summary of your thinking—how you came to that conclusion?" When the wife again got angry and blamed her husband, the therapist just listened. A moment later he asked, "What do you do in the face of that abuse?"

"I get upset."
"Do you understand what it is about you that sets him off?"
"No."
"Has he ever been able to tell you?"

Notice how the therapist attempts to explore the process of the couple's relationship, asking both partners to think about what's going on between them, increase their awareness of their own contributions, and consider what they're planning to do to take responsibility to make things better.

Those who follow Bowen still ask questions, but they also move in occasionally to challenge, confront, and explain. Betty Carter, for example, asks questions designed to help couples understand their situation, but she then tries to intensify the process and speed it up by explaining what works or doesn't work and by assigning tasks calculated to move people out of triangles. She might, for example, encourage a wife to visit her mother-in-law or a husband to begin calling his mother on the phone. Another favorite device of Carter's is to encourage people to write letters, addressing unresolved issues in the family. One way to prevent such letter writing from degenerating into telling people off is to help clients edit out the anger and emotional reactivity.

Guerin, perhaps more than any other Bowenian, has developed clinical models that feature specific techniques for specific situations. His categorizing marital conflict into four stages of severity with detailed suggestions for treating each stage (Guerin, Fay, Burden, & Kautto, 1987) is the most elaborate demonstration of his well-worked-out technique.

The second major technique in Bowenian therapy is the *relationship experiment*. Process questions are designed to help family members realize that it isn't just what other people do, but how they respond to what other people do that perpetuates their problems. Relationship experiments are designed to help clients experience what it's like to act counter to their usual emotionally driven responses. Some of these experiments may help clients resolve their problems, but their primary purpose is to help people discover their ability to move against the ways their emotions are driving them.

Case Study

The Kennedys came to therapy because sixteen-year-old David was doing badly in school. David was on the verge of flunking out of an exclusive private school partly because he was a poor student but partly because his evenings with friends included heavy drinking and marijuana smoking. His father had gotten after him to study harder and had suspended his driving privileges after he came home one school night quite drunk. Unfortunately, these efforts hadn't been very effective, because David didn't respect his father, who was an alcoholic and frequently falling down drunk around the house. David's stepmother, who'd been living with them for only two years, had little ability to control him, and she knew enough not to try.

I told the parents that I wouldn't see them in family therapy because David didn't respect the father who was drunk every night and who, I added, didn't show any signs of being ready to do anything about his drinking. I did agree, however, to see David to try to help him finish the school year with passing grades.

David was able to pass the eleventh grade, and I continued to see him into the following year, not entirely comfortable in my role as substitute father figure. Although I maintained my resolve not to do therapy with a family that included a member who was actively abusing alcohol, I did meet with the family during three or four crises. The first three crises occurred when Mr. Kennedy's drinking (and, it turned out, cocaine abuse) got way out of control and his father and wife insisted that he reenter treatment.

The most prominent triangle in this case was that Mr. Kennedy's wife and father got together to pressure him to quit drinking. He had gone to rehab several times, but even the few times he'd actually finished a program, he soon returned to drinking. The only reason he ever sought help was as a result of ultimatums from his wife and father. His wife threatened to leave him, and his father threatened to cut him off from the family estate. This case would go nowhere until this triangle could be modified.

I encouraged Mr. Kennedy's wife and father to work on being less reactive while separating from each other around the issue of Mr. Kennedy's drinking. Mr. Kennedy needed to take a stand for himself, rather than comply with his wife's and his father's wishes. In fact, I wondered aloud with him if taking an honest stance with his family wouldn't mean telling them that he didn't intend to quit drinking. What he decided to tell them was that while he was willing to work on controlling his drinking and use of cocaine, he didn't intend to quit.

I encouraged Mr. Kennedy's father to back off and let the other two battle it out. Reluctantly, he agreed to do so. I then got Mrs. Kennedy to make a clear statement about how she felt about her husband's drinking but to discontinue her fruitless efforts to make him stop. I encouraged her to maintain her connection with her father-in-law but without talking about her husband all the time. Two months later, Mr. Kennedy decided to stop drinking and using cocaine.

This time he successfully completed a twenty-eight-day rehab program and entered AA and NA. Six weeks later, he once again relapsed. Over the following eight months, Mr. Kennedy's drinking and cocaine abuse got much worse. Finally, after a serious altercation with a Jamaican drug dealer, Mr. Kennedy made a serious decision to get sober. This time, instead of going to the respected local rehabilitation center that his father had recommended, he did some research on his own and decided to enter a famous drug treatment center in California. As of this writing, Mr. Kennedy has been sober for six years.

Bowenian Therapy with Couples. The essence of couples therapy is to stay connected with both partners without letting them triangle you. In practice, Bowen would connect with each person, one at a time, often beginning with the overfunctioning or more motivated partner. He would ask nonconfrontational questions, verify facts, and hear feelings, but he would frame each question to stimulate thinking rather than encourage expression of feelings. His objective was to explore the perceptions and opinions of each partner, without siding emotionally with either one. It's taking sides that keeps people from learning to deal with each other.

When things are calm, feelings can be dealt with more objectively and partners can talk rationally with each other. However, when feeling outruns thinking, it's best to ask questions that get couples to think more and feel less—and to talk to the therapist rather than to each other.

Couples who've argued for years about the same old issues are often amazed to discover that the first time they really hear each other is when they listen to their partners talking to a therapist. It's easier to hear when you aren't busy planning your own response. If all else fails to cool things down, Fogarty (1976) recommends seeing spouses in separate sessions.

Guerin (1971) recommends the *displacement story* as a device for helping family members achieve sufficient distance to see their own roles in the family system. The displacement story is about other families with similar problems. For example, a couple too busy attacking each other to listen might be told "It must be frustrating not getting through to each other. Last year I saw a couple who just couldn't stop arguing long enough to listen to each other. Only after I split them up and they blew off steam for a few sessions individually did they seem to have any capacity to listen to what the other was saying."

Displacement can also be used to frame process questions to avoid provoking defensive responses. Instead of asking someone in the throes of upset and anger when he or she might get over those feelings in order to start working to change things—which might provoke them to think that their feelings are being denied, a therapist might ask, "Do you think anyone ever gets over all that anger and upset?" Or if asking why someone hasn't been able to accomplish something might make him or her defensive, a therapist might ask, "What do you think makes that step so hard for people?"

Armed with a knowledge of triangles, the therapist endeavors to remain neutral and objective. This requires an optimal level of emotional distance, which Bowen (1975) said is the point where a therapist can see both the tragic and comic aspects of a couple's interactions. Although other people's problems are nothing to laugh at, a sense of irony may be preferable to the unctuous earnestness so popular in some quarters.[3]

---

[3]It's easier for therapists to remain calm and objective when they concentrate on doing their job in the session without feeling responsible for what the clients do outside.

Bowenian couples therapy is designed to reduce anxiety and foster self-focus.

Staying detriangled requires a calm tone of voice and talking about facts more than about feelings. This calm objectivity on the part of Bowen systems therapists is expressed and enhanced by the use of process questions—questions aimed to cut through emotional reactivity and make contact with family members' reasonableness.

As partners talk, the therapist concentrates on the *process* of their interaction, not on the details under discussion. Concentrating on the content of a discussion is a sign that the therapist is emotionally entangled in a couple's problems. It may be hard to avoid being drawn in by hot topics like money, sex, or discipline, but a therapist's job isn't to settle disputes; it's to help couples do so. The aim is to get clients to express ideas, thoughts, and opinions to the therapist in the presence of their partners. Should one break down in tears, the therapist remains calm and inquires about the thoughts that touched off the tears. If a couple begins arguing, the therapist becomes more active, calmly questioning one, then the other, focusing on their respective thoughts. Asking for detailed descriptions of

events is one of the best ways to cool overheated emotion and make room for reason.

Metaphors of complementarity are helpful for highlighting the process underlying the content of family interactions. Fogarty (1976), for example, described the *pursuer-distancer* dynamic. The more one presses for communication and togetherness, the more the other distances —watches TV, works late, or goes off with the kids. Frequently, partners pursue and distance in different areas. Men commonly distance themselves emotionally but pursue sexually. The trick, according to Fogarty, is "Never pursue a distancer." Instead, help the pursuer explore his or her own inner emptiness: "What's in your life other than the other person?"

To underscore the need for objectivity, Bowen spoke of the therapist as a "coach" or "consultant." He didn't mean to imply indifference but rather to emphasize the neutrality required to avoid triangulation. In traditional terms, this is known as *managing countertransference*. Just as analysts are analyzed themselves so they can recognize countertransference, Bowen considered differentiating a self in one's own family the best way to avoid being emotionally triangled by couples.

To help partners define positions as differentiated selves, it's useful for a therapist to take an "I-position" (Guerin, 1971). The more a therapist takes an autonomous position in relation to the family, the easier it is for family members to define themselves to each other. Gradually, family members learn to calmly state their own beliefs and convictions and to act on them without attacking others or becoming overly upset by their responses.

After sufficient harmony had been won with progress toward self-differentiation, Bowen taught couples how emotional systems operate and encouraged them to explore those webs of relationship in their own families (Bowen, 1971). For example, a woman locked into the role of emotional pursuer might be asked to describe her relationship with her father and then compare it to her current relationships. If lessening her preoccupation with her husband and children seems advisable, the therapist might encourage her to connect with the most emotionally distant member of her family, often her father. The idea wouldn't be to shift her attachment from one set of relationships to another but to help her understand that the intensity of her need is due in part to unfinished business.

Kerr (1971) suggests that when relationship problems in the nuclear family are being discussed, therapists should occasionally ask questions about similar patterns in the family of origin. If family members see that they are repeating earlier patterns, they are more likely to recognize their own emotional reactivity. Recently, this author saw a couple unable to decide what to do with their mentally ill teenage daughter. Although the daughter was virtually uncontrollable, her mother found it difficult to consider hospitalization. When asked what her own mother would have done, without hesitating she replied that her long-suffering mother would have been too guilt ridden even to consider placement—"no matter how much she and

the rest of the family might suffer." Little more needed to be said.

More didactic teaching occurs in the transition from brief to long-term therapy. Knowledge of family systems theory helps people trace the patterns that have a hold on them, so they can unlock themselves. Such information is useful when tensions have abated, but trying to impart it can be risky during periods of conflict and anxiety. At such times, battling couples are liable to distort any statements about how families function as support for one or the other of their opposing positions. So primed are warring mates to make the other wrong in order for themselves to be right, that they hear much of what a therapist says as either for or against them. But when calm, they can get past the idea that for one to be right, the other must be wrong, and they can profit from didactic sessions. As they learn about systems theory, both partners are sent home for visits to continue the process of differentiation in their extended families.

Bowenian Therapy with One Person. Bowen's own success at differentiating from his family convinced him that a single highly motivated individual can be the fulcrum for changing an entire family system (Anonymous, 1972). Subsequently, he made family therapy with one person a major part of his practice. He used this method with one partner when the other refused to participate and with single adults who lived far from their parents. Aside from these cases in which Bowen made a virtue of necessity, he used this approach extensively with mental health professionals. Extended family work with each partner is also the focus of couples treatment after the presenting anxiety and symptoms subside.

The goals of working with individuals are the same as when working with larger units: developing person-to-person relationships, seeing family members as people rather than emotionally charged images, learning to observe one's self in triangles, and, finally, detriangling oneself (Bowen, 1974).

The extent of unresolved emotional attachment to parents defines the level of undifferentiation. More intense levels of undifferentiation go hand in hand with more extreme efforts to achieve emotional distance, either through defense mechanisms or physical distance. A person might handle mild anxiety with parents by avoiding personal discussions, but when anxiety rises, he or she may find it necessary to walk out of the room or even leave town. However, the person who runs away is as emotionally attached as the one who stays home and uses psychological distancing mechanisms to control the attachment. People who shrink from contact need closeness but can't handle it. When tension mounts in other intimate relationships, they will again withdraw.

Two sure signs of emotional cutoff are denial of the importance of the family and an exaggerated facade of independence. Cutoff people boast of their emancipation and infrequent contact with their parents. The opposite of emotional cutoff is an open relationship system, in which family members have genuine, but not confining, emotional contact.

The person who embarks on a quest of learning more about his or her family usually knows where to look. Most families have one or two members who know who's who and what's what—perhaps a maiden aunt, a patriarch, or a cousin who's very family centered. Phone calls, letters, or, better yet, visits to these family archivists will yield much information, some of which may produce surprises.

Gathering information about the family is an excellent vehicle for the second step toward differentiation, establishing person-to-person relationships with as many family members as possible. This means getting in touch and speaking personally with them, not about other people or impersonal topics. If this sounds easy, try it. Few of us can spend more than a few minutes talking personally with certain family members without getting anxious. When this happens,

we're tempted to withdraw, physically or emotionally, or triangle in another person. Gradually, extending the time of personal conversation will improve the relationship and help differentiate a self.

There are profound benefits to be derived from developing person-to-person relationships with members of the extended family, but they have to be experienced to be appreciated. In the process of opening and deepening personal relationships, you will learn about the emotional forces in the family. Some family triangles will immediately become apparent; others will emerge only after careful examination. Usually, we notice only the most obvious triangles because we're too emotionally engaged to be good observers. Few people can be objective about their parents. They're either comfortably fused or uncomfortably reactive. Making frequent short visits helps control emotional reactiveness so that you can become a better observer.

Many of our habitual emotional responses to the family impede our ability to understand and accept others; worse, they make it impossible for us to understand and govern ourselves. It's natural to get angry and blame people when things go wrong. The differentiated person, however, is capable of stepping back, controlling emotional responsiveness, and reflecting on how to improve things. Bowen (1974) called this "getting beyond blaming and anger" and said that, once learned in the family, this ability is useful for handling emotional snarls throughout life.

Ultimately, differentiating yourself requires that you identify interpersonal triangles you participate in and detriangle from them. The goal is to relate to people without gossiping or taking sides and without counterattacking or defending yourself.

Triangles can be identified by asking who or what people go to when they distance from someone with whom they have been close. One sign of a triangle is its repetitive structure. The process that goes on in a triangle is predictable because it's reactive and automatic. The symptomatic expression of a triangle usually takes the form of relationship conflict (or cutoff) or dysfunction in one of the individuals, such as anxiety, depression, or physical illness. Typically, a third person moves into the role of peacemaker or supporter for the one perceived as the victim.

A common triangle starts with one parent and a child. Suppose that every time you talk to your mother, she starts complaining about your father. Maybe it feels good to be confided in. Maybe you have fantasies about rescuing your parents—or at least your mother. In fact, this triangle is destructive to all three relationships: you and Dad, Dad and Mom, and, yes, you and Mom. In triangles, one pair is close and two are distant (Figure 5.5). Sympathizing with Mom alienates Dad. It also makes it less likely that she'll work out her complaints with him.

Once you recognize a triangle for what it is, you can plan to stop participating in it. The idea is to do something to get the other two people to work out their own relationship. The simplest and most direct approach is to suggest that they do so. In the example just given, you might suggest that your mother discuss her concerns with your father, *and* you can refuse to listen to more complaints. Less direct but more powerful is to

tell Dad that his wife has been complaining about him and you don't know why she doesn't tell him about it. She'll be annoyed but not forever. A more devious ploy is to overagree with Mom's complaints. When she says he's messy, you say he's a complete slob; when she says he's not very thoughtful, you say he's an ogre. Pretty soon she'll begin to defend him. Maybe she'll decide to work out her complaints with him—or maybe she won't, but either way you'll have removed yourself from the triangle.

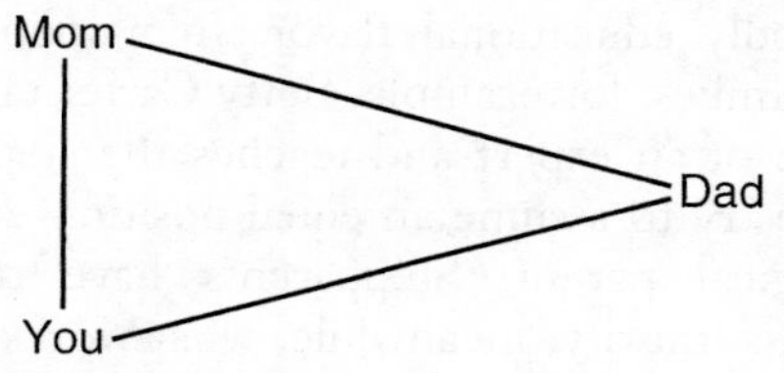

Once you look for them, you'll find triangles everywhere. Common examples include griping with colleagues about the boss; telling someone that your partner doesn't understand you; undercutting your spouse with the kids; and watching television to avoid talking to your family. Breaking free of triangles may not be easy, but the rewards are great. The payoff comes not only from enriching those relationships but also from enhancing your ability to relate to anyone—friends, colleagues, clients, and your spouse and children. Furthermore, if you can remain in emotional contact but change the part you play in your family—and maintain the change despite pressures to change back, the family will have to adjust to accommodate to your change.

Useful guidelines to help families avoid falling back into unproductive but familiar patterns have been enumerated by Carter and Orfanidis (1976), Guerin and Fogarty (1972), and Herz (1991). You can also read about how to work on family tensions by resolving your own emotional sensitivities in two marvelous books by Harriet Lerner: *The Dance of Anger* (1985) and *The Dance of Intimacy* (1989).

Reentry into the family of origin is necessary to open the closed system. Sometimes all that's required is visiting. Other times, buried issues must be raised. Returning to the previous example, if you can't move directly toward your father without his withdrawing, move toward other people with whom he is close.

Figure **5.5** Cross-Generational Triangle

In reentry, it's advisable to begin by opening closed relationships before trying to change conflictual ones. Don't start by trying to resolve the warfare between yourself and your mother. Deal with personal issues, but avoid stalemated conflicts. If your contacts with some sections of the family are routine and predictable, make them more creative. Those who continue working on their family relationships beyond the resolution of a crisis, or beyond the first flush of enthusiasm for a new academic interest, can achieve profound changes in themselves, in their family systems, and in their own clinical work.

EVALUATING THERAPY THEORY AND RESULTS

What makes Bowen's theory so useful is that it explains the emotional forces that regulate how we relate to other people. The single greatest impediment to understanding one another is our tendency to become emotionally reactive. Like all things about relationships, emotionality is a two-way street: Some people express themselves with such emotionalism that others react to that pressure rather than hear what the person is trying to say. Bowenian theory locates the origin of this reactivity in the lack of differentiation of self and explains how to reduce emotionalism and move toward mature self-control—by cultivating relationships widely in the family and learning to listen without becoming defensive or untrue to one's own beliefs.

In Bowenian theory, *anxiety* is the underlying explanation for why people are dependent or avoidant and why they become emotionally reactive, reminiscent of Freudian conflict theory (which explains all symptoms as the result of anxiety over sex and aggression). The second pivotal concept in the Bowenian system is *differentiation*. Because differentiation is roughly synonymous with *maturity*, students might ask: To what extent is the proposition that more dif-ferentiated people function better a circular argument? In respect to the Bowenian tradition of asking questions rather than imposing opinions, we'll let this stand as an open issue for your consideration.

A possible shortcoming of the Bowenian approach is that in concentrating on individuals and their extended family relationships, it may neglect the power of working directly with the nuclear family. In many cases, the most direct way to resolve family problems is to bring together everyone in the same household and encourage them to face each other and talk about their conflicts. These discussions may turn heated and contentious, but a skilled therapist can help family members realize what they're doing and guide them toward understanding.

There are times when families are so belligerent that their dialogues must be interrupted to help individuals get beyond defensiveness to the hurt feelings underneath. At such times, it's useful, perhaps imperative, to block family members from arguing with each other. But an approach, such as Bowen's, that encourages therapists to always speak to individual family members one at a time underutilizes the power of working directly with families in action.

Phil Guerin and Tom Fogarty have made notable contributions not only in promulgating Bowenian theory but also in refining techniques of therapy. Both are master therapists. Betty Carter and Monica McGoldrick have made more of a contribution in studying how families work: the normal family life cycle, ethnic diversity, and the pervasive role of gender inequality. Because they are students of the family as well as therapists, some of their interventions have a decidedly educational flavor. In working with stepfamilies, for example, Betty Carter takes the stance of an expert and teaches the stepparent not to try to assume an equal position with the biological parent. Stepparents have to earn moral authority; meanwhile, what works best is supporting the role of the biological parent. Just as Bowen's approach is influenced by his personal experience, it seems that both Carter and McGoldrick infuse their work as family therapists with their experience as career women and their convictions about the price of inequality.

Recent reviews of the clinical outcome literature have failed to find any controlled outcome studies that tested the effectiveness of Bowenian therapy (Johnson & Lebow, 2000; Miller, Johnson, Sandberg, Stringer-Seibold, & Gfeller-Strouts, 2000). This, of course, is not surprising, considering that research is usually conducted by academics, most of whom are more interested in behavioral models than in traditional approaches such as psychoanalysis and Bowen systems theory.

There have, however, been attempts to test the empirical validity of some of the propositions of Bowen's theory. Three psychometrically sound measures of differentiation of self have been developed. Haber's (1993) Level of Differentiation of Self Scale contains twenty-four items that focus on emotional maturity, such as "I make decisions based on my own set of values and beliefs" and "When I have a problem that upsets me, I am still able to consider different options for solving the problem." This scale significantly correlates (negatively) with chronic anxiety and psychological distress, which is consistent with Bowen theory. Skowron's Differentiation of Self Inventory (DSI) (Skowron & Friedlander, 1998) contains four subscales: Emotional Cutoff ("I need to distance myself when people get too close to me," "I would never consider turning to any of my family members for emotional support"); "I"-Position ("I do not change my behavior simply to please another person"); Emotional Reactivity ("At times my feelings get the best of me and I have trouble thinking clearly"); and Fusion with Others ("It has been said of me that I am still very attached to my parents"). As Bowen theory predicts, the DSI correlates significantly with chronic anxiety, psychological distress, and marital satisfaction.

Chabot's Emotional Differentiation (CED) Scale was designed to measure Bowen's intrapsychic aspect of differentiation—the ability to think rationally in emotionally charged situations (Licht & Chabot, 2006). The CED asks subjects to respond to seventeen questions that assess integration of thinking and feeling in nonstressful periods and periods of prolonged stress, as well as when relationships are going well and when there are difficulties in relationships.

Research has supported Bowen's notion that differentiation is related to trait anxiety (negatively) (Griffin & Apostal, 1993; Haber, 1993; Skowron & Friedlander, 1998), psychological and physical health problems (negatively) (Bohlander, 1995; Davis & Jones, 1992; Elieson & Rubin, 2001; Haber, 1993; Skowron & Friedlander, 1998), and marital satisfaction (positively) (Haber, 1984; Richards, 1989; Skowron & Friedlander, 1998; Skowron, 2000). Several studies have shown a significant relationship between triangulation and marital distress (Gehring & Marti, 1993; Vuchinich, Emery, & Cassidy, 1988; Wood, Watkins, Boyle, Nogueira, Zimand, & Carroll, 1989) as well as problems in intimate relationships (Protinsky & Gilkey, 1996; West, Zarski, & Harvill, 1986). Finally, consistent with Bowen's belief in the multigenerational transmission of emotional process, researchers have found that parents' and children's beliefs are highly correlated (e.g., Troll & Bengston, 1979) and that violence (e.g., Alexander, Moore, & Alexander, 1991), divorce (e.g., Amato, 1996), marital quality (e.g., Feng, Giarrusso, Bengston, & Fry, 1999), eating disorders (e.g., Whitehouse & Harris, 1998), depression (Whitbeck et al., 1992), and alcoholism (e.g., Sher, Gershuny, Peterson, & Raskin, 1997) are transmitted from one generation to the next.

Ultimately, the status of extended family systems therapy rests not on empirical research but on the elegance of Murray Bowen's theory, clinical experiences with this approach, and the personal experiences of those who have worked at differentiating themselves in their families of origin. Bowen himself was decidedly cool to empirical research (Bowen, 1976), preferring instead to refine and integrate theory and prac-tice. Like psychoanalysis, Bowen systems theory is probably best judged not as true or false but as useful or not useful. On balance, it seems emi-nently useful.

SUMMARY

Bowen's conceptual lens was wider than that of most family therapists', but his actual unit of treatment was smaller. His concern was always with the multigenerational family system, even though he usually met with individuals or couples. Since first introducing the **three-generational hypothesis of schizophrenia**, he was aware of how interlocking triangles connect one generation to the next—like threads inter-woven in a total family fabric. Although Bowen-ian therapists are unique in sending patients home to repair their relationships with parents, the idea of intergenerational connections has been very influential in the field.

According to Bowen, the major problem in families is *emotional fusion*; the major goal is *dif-ferentiation*. Emotional fusion grows out of an instinctual need for others but is an unhealthy exaggeration of this need. Some people manifest fusion directly as a need for togetherness; others mask it with a pseudoindependent facade. The person with a differentiated self need not be iso-lated but can stay in contact with others and maintain his or her own integrity. Similarly, the healthy family is one that remains in viable emo-tional contact from one generation to another.

In Bowenian theory, the *triangle* is the univer-sal unit of analysis—in principle and in practice. Like Freud, Bowen stressed the pivotal impor-tance of early family relations. The relationship between the self and parents is described as a tri-angle and considered the most important in life. Bowen's understanding of triangles is one of the seminal ideas in family therapy.

Bowen discouraged therapists from trying to fix relationships and instead encouraged them to remain neutral while exploring conflictual rela-tionships with process questions. Bowenian therapists rarely give advice. They just keep ask-ing questions. The goal isn't to solve people's problems but to help them learn to see their own role in how their family systems operate. This self-discovery is more than a matter of intro-spection, because understanding is seen as a tool for repairing relationships and enhancing one's own autonomous functioning.

Six techniques are prominent in the practice of Bowenian family systems therapy:

1. *Genogram.* From his earliest NIMH days, Bowen used what he termed a *family dia-gram* to collect and organize important data con-cerning the multigenerational family system. In 1972, Guerin renamed the family diagram the *genogram*. The main function of the genogram is to organize data during the evaluation phase and to track relationship processes and key triangles over the course of therapy. The most compre-hensive guide to working with genograms is Monica McGoldrick and Randy Gerson's book *Genograms in Family Assessment* (McGoldrick & Gerson, 1985).

2. *Neutralizing Triangles.* This technique is based on the theoretical assumption that conflict-ual relationship processes within the family have activated key symptom-related triangles in an attempt to reestablish stability. The family will automatically attempt to include the therapist in the triangling process. If they succeed, therapy will be stalemated. On the other hand, if the ther-apist can remain free of reactive emotional entan-glements—in other words, stay detriangled—the family system and its members will calm down to the point where they can begin to work out their dilemmas.

3. *Relationship Experiments.* Relationship experiments are carried out around structural alterations in key triangles. The goal is to help family members become aware of systems processes—and learn to recognize their own role in them. Among the best such experiments are those developed by Fogarty for use with emotional pursuers and distancers. Pursuers are encouraged to restrain their pursuit, stop making demands, and decrease pressure for emotional connection—and see what happens, in themselves and in the relationship. This exercise isn't designed to be a magic cure (as some people hope) but to help clarify the emotional processes involved. Distancers are encouraged to move toward their partners and communicate personal thoughts and feelings; in other words, to find an alternative to either avoiding or capitulating to the other person's demands.

4. *Coaching.* Coaching is the Bowenian alternative to the more emotionally involved role common to most other forms of therapy. By acting as coach, the Bowenian therapist hopes to avoid taking over for patients or becoming embroiled in family triangles. Coaching doesn't mean telling people what to do. It means asking questions designed to help clients figure out family emotional processes and their role in them.

5. The "*I-Position.*" Taking a personal stance—saying what you feel, instead of what others are doing—is one of the most direct ways to break cycles of emotional reactivity. It's the difference between saying "You're lazy" and "I wish you would help me more" or between "You're always spoiling the children" and "I think we should be stricter with them." It's a big difference.

Bowenian therapists not only encourage clients to take "I-positions," but they also do so

themselves. An example would be when after a family session the mother pulls the therapist aside and confides that her husband has terminal cancer, but she doesn't want the children to know. What to do? Take an "I-position": Say to the mother, "I believe your children have a right to know about this." What she does, of course, is still up to her.

Another assumption in Bowenian therapy is that confrontation increases anxiety and decreases the ability to think clearly and see options. Therefore, displacing the focus, making it less personal and less threatening, is an excellent way to increase objectivity. This forms the basis for two related techniques: multiple family therapy and displacement stories.

6. *Process Questions.* Process questions are used to invite clients to reduce their reactive anxiety and become more aware of how they are responding to the stresses that drive that anxiety. Process questions work by decreasing anxiety and enabling people to think more clearly. This clarity enables them to discover options for managing their problems. In addition, they become more open to experimenting with modified patterns of relating that are suggested by the therapist.

Finally, although students of family therapy are likely to evaluate different approaches according to how much sense they make and how useful they promise to be, Bowen himself considered his most important contribution to be showing the way to make human behavior a science. Far more important than developing methods and techniques of family therapy, Murray Bowen made profound contributions to our understanding of how we function as individuals, how we get along with our families, and how these are related.

RECOMMENDED READINGS

Anonymous. 1972. Differentiation of self in one's family. In *Family interaction*, J. Framo, ed. New York: Springer.

Bowen, M. 1978. *Family therapy in clinical practice.* New York: Jason Aronson.

Carter, E., and Orfanidis, M. M. 1976. Family therapy with one person and the family therapist's own family. In *Family therapy: Theory and practice*, P. J. Guerin, ed. New York: Gardner Press.

Fogarty, T. F. 1976. Marital crisis. In *Family therapy: Theory and practice*, P. J. Guerin, ed. New York: Gardner Press.

Fogarty, T. F. 1976. Systems concepts and dimensions of self. In *Family therapy: Theory and practice*, P. J. Guerin, ed. New York: Gardner Press.

Guerin, P. J., and Pendagast, E. G. 1976. Evaluation of family system and geogram. In *Family therapy: Theory and practice*, P. J. Guerin, ed. New York: Gardner Press.

Guerin, P. J., Fay, L., Burden, S., and Kautto, J. 1987. *The evaluation and treatment of marital conflict: A four-stage approach*. New York: Basic Books.

Guerin, P. J., Fogarty, T. F., Fay, L. F., and Kautto, J. G. 1996. *Working with relationship triangles: The one-two-three of psychotherapy*. New York: Guilford Press.

Kerr, M. E., and Bowen, M. 1988. *Family evaluation*. New York: Norton.

REFERENCES

Alexander, P. C., Moore, S., and Alexander, E. R. 1991. Intergenerational transmission of violence. *Journal of Marriage and the Family*. 53:657–667.

Amato, P. R. 1996. Explaining the intergenerational transmission of divorce. *Journal of Marriage and the Family*. 58:628–640.

Anonymous. 1972. Differentiation of self in one's family. In *Family interaction*, J. Framo, ed. New York: Springer.

Bohlander, J. R. 1995. *Differentiation of self, need-fulfillment, and psychological well-being in married women*. Unpublished doctoral dissertation, New York University.

Bowen, M. 1966. The use of family theory in clinical practice. *Comprehensive Psychiatry*. 7:345–374.

Bowen, M. 1971. Family therapy and family group therapy. In *Comprehensive group psychotherapy*, H. Kaplan and B. Sadock, eds. Baltimore, MD: Williams & Wilkins.

Bowen, M. 1974. Toward the differentiation of self in one's family. In *Georgetown Family Symposium*, Vol. 1, F. Andres and J. Lorio, eds. Washington, DC: Department of Psychiatry, Georgetown University Medical Center.

Bowen, M. 1975. Family therapy after twenty years. In *American handbook of psychiatry*, Vol. 5, S. Arieti, ed. New York: Basic Books.

Bowen, M. 1976. Theory in the practice of psychotherapy. In *Family therapy: Theory and practice*, P. J. Guerin, ed. New York: Gardner Press.

Carter, B., and McGoldrick, M. 1999. *The expanded family life cycle*, 3rd ed. Boston: Allyn & Bacon.

Carter, E., and Orfanidis, M. M. 1976. Family therapy with one person and the family therapist's own family. In *Family therapy: Theory and practice*, P. J. Guerin, ed. New York: Gardner Press.

Davis, B., and Jones, L. C. 1992. Differentiation of self and attachment among adult daughters. *Issues in Mental Health Nursing*. 13:321–331.

Elieson, M. V., and Rubin, L. J. 2001. Differentiation of self and major depressive disorders: A test of Bowen theory among clinical, tradition, and internet groups. *Family Therapy*. 29:125–142.

Feng, D., Giarrusso, R., Bengston, V. L., and Frye, N. 1999. Intergenerational transmission of marital quality and marital instability. *Journal of Marriage and the Family*. 61:451–463.

Fogarty, T. F. 1976. Marital crisis. In *Family therapy: Theory and practice*, P. J. Guerin, ed. New York: Gardner Press.

Gehring, T. M., and Marti, D. 1993. The family system test: Differences in perception of family structures between nonclinical and clinical children. *Journal of Child Psychology and Psychiatry*. 34:363–377.

Griffin, J. M., and Apostal, R. A. 1993. The influence of Relationship Enhancement training on differentiation of self. *Journal of Marital and Family Therapy*. 19:267–272.

Guerin, P. J., Fay, L., Burden, S., and Kautto, J. 1987. *The evaluation and treatment of marital conflict: A four-stage approach*. New York: Basic Books.

Guerin, P. J. 1971. A family affair. *Georgetown Family Symposium*, Vol. 1, Washington, DC.

Guerin, P. J., and Fogarty, T. F. 1972. Study your own family. In *The book of family therapy*, A. Ferber, M. Mendelsohn, and A. Napier, eds. New York: Science House.

Guerin, P. J., Fogarty, T. F., Fay, L. F., and Kautto, J. G. 1996. *Working with relationship triangles: The one-two-three of psychotherapy.* New York: Guilford Press.

Haber, J. E. 1984. *An investigation of the relationship between differentiation of self, complementary psychological need patterns, and marital conflict.* Unpublished doctoral dissertation, New York University.

Haber, J. E. 1993. A construct validity study of a differentiation of self scale. *Scholarly Inquiry for Nursing Practice.* 7:165–178.

Herz, F., ed. 1991. *Reweaving the family tapestry.* New York: Norton.

Johnson, S., and Lebow, J. 2000. The "coming of age" of couple therapy: A decade review. *Journal of Marital and Family Therapy.* 26:23–38.

Kerr, M. 1971. The importance of the extended family. *Georgetown Family Symposium*, Vol. 1, Washington, DC.

Kerr, M., and Bowen, M. 1988. *Family evaluation.* New York: Norton.

Kreider, R. M., and Fields, J. M. 2002. *Number, timing, and duration of marriages and divorces.* Washington, DC: U.S. Census Bureau.

Lerner, H. G. 1985. *The dance of anger: A woman's guide to changing patterns of intimate relationships.* New York: Harper & Row.

Lerner, H. G. 1989. *The dance of intimacy: A woman's guide to courageous acts of change in key relationships.* New York: Harper & Row.

Licht, C., and Chabot, D. 2006. The Chabot emotional differentiation scale: A theoretically and psychometrically sound instrument for measuring Bowen's intrapsychic aspect of differentiation. *Journal of Marital and Family Therapy.* 32:167–180.

McGoldrick, M., and Gerson, R. 1985. *Genograms in family assessment.* New York: Norton.

McGoldrick, M., Pearce, J., and Giordano, J. 1982. *Ethnicity in family therapy.* New York: Guilford Press.

Miller, R. B., Johnson, L. N., Sandberg, J. G., Stringer-Seibold, T. A., and Gfeller-Strouts, L. 2000. An addendum to the 1997 outcome research chart. *American Journal of Family Therapy.* 28:347–354.

Nichols, M. P. 1986. *Turning forty in the eighties.* New York: Norton.

Protinsky, H., and Gilkey, J. K. 1996. An empirical investigation of the construct of personality authority in late adolescent women and their level of college adjustment. *Adolescence.* 31:291–296.

Richards, E. R. 1989. Self reports of differentiation of self and marital compatibility as related to family functioning in the third and fourth stages of the family life cycle. *Scholarly Inquiry for Nursing Practice.* 3:163–175.

Sher, K. J., Gershuny, B. S., Peterson, L., and Raskin, G. 1979. The role of childhood stressors in the intergenerational transmission of alcohol use disorders. *Journal of Studies on Alcohol.* 58:414–427.

Skowron, E. A. 2000. The role of differentiation of self in marital adjustment. *Journal of Counseling Psychology.* 47:229–237.

Skowron, E. A., and Friedlander, M. L. 1998. The differentiation of self inventory: Development and initial validation. *Journal of Counseling Psychology.* 45:235–246.

Sulloway, F. 1996. *Born to rebel.* New York: Pantheon.

Toman, W. 1969. *Family constellation.* New York: Springer.

Troll, L., and Bengston, V. L. 1979. Generations in the family. In *Contemporary theories about the family*, Vol. 1. W. R. Burr, R. Hill, F. I. Nye, and I. L. Reiss, eds. New York: Free Press.

Vuchinich, S., Emery, R. E., and Cassidy, J. 1988. Family members as third parties in dyadic family conflict: Strategies, alliances, and outcomes. *Child Development.* 59:1296–1302.

West, J. D., Zarski, J. J., and Harvill, R. 1986. The influence of the family triangle on intimacy. *American Mental Health Counselors Association Journal.* 8:166–174.

Whitbeck, L., Hoyt, D., Simons, R., Conger, R., Elder, G., Lorenz, F., and Huck, S. 1992. Intergenerational continuity of parental rejection and depressed affect. *Journal of Personality and Social Psychology.* 63:1036–1045.

Whitehouse, P. J., and Harris, G. 1998. The intergenerational transmission of eating disorders. *European Eating Disorders Review.* 6:238–254.

Wood, B., Watkins, J. B., Boyle, J. T., Nogueira, J., Zimand, E., and Carroll, L. 1989. The "psychosomatic family" model: An empirical and theoretical analysis. *Family Process.* 28:399–417.

Strategic Family Therapy

6

Problem-Solving Therapy

With their compelling application of cybernetics and systems theory, strategic approaches once captivated family therapy. Part of their appeal was a pragmatic, problem-solving focus, but there was also a fascination with strategies to outwit resistance and provoke families into changing, with or without their cooperation. It was this manipulative aspect that eventually turned many people against strategic therapy.

The dominant approaches of the twenty-first century elevated cognition over behavior and encouraged therapists to be collaborative rather than manipulative. Instead of trying to solve problems and provoke change, therapists began to reinforce solutions and inspire change. As a consequence, the once celebrated voices of strategic therapy—Jay Haley, John Weakland, Mara Selvini Palazzoli—have been virtually forgotten. Too bad, because their strategic approaches introduced two of the most powerful insights in all of family therapy: that families often perpetuate problems by their own actions and that directives tailored to the needs of a particular family can sometimes bring about sudden and decisive change.

 ## SKETCHES OF LEADING FIGURES

Strategic therapy grew out of the **communications theory** developed in Bateson's schizophrenia project, which evolved into three distinct models: *MRI's brief therapy, Haley and Madanes's strategic therapy*, and the *Milan systemic model*. The birthplace of all three was the Mental Research Institute (MRI), where strategic therapy was inspired by Gregory Bateson and Milton Erickson, the anthropologist and the alienist.[1]

---

[1]See Chapter 2 for a review of the communications model.

In 1952, funded by a Rockefeller Foundation grant to study paradox in communication, Bateson invited Jay Haley, John Weakland, Don Jackson, and William Fry to join him in Palo Alto. Their seminal project, which can be considered the intellectual birthplace of family therapy, led to the conclusion that the exchange of multilayered messages between people defined their relationships.

Under Bateson's influence, the orientation was anthropological. Their goal was to observe families; they stumbled into family therapy more or less by accident. Given Bateson's disinclination to manipulate people, it's ironic that it was he who introduced project members to Milton Erickson. At a time when therapy was considered a laborious, long-term proposition, Erickson's experience as a hypnotherapist convinced him that people could change suddenly, and he made therapy as brief as possible.

Many of what have been called *paradoxical techniques* came out of Erickson's application of hypnotherapeutic principles to turn resistance to advantage (Haley, 1981). For example, to induce a trance a hypnotist learns not to point out that a person is fighting going under but might instead tell the person to keep his or her eyes open "until they become unbearably heavy."

Don Jackson founded the Mental Research Institute in 1959 and assembled an energetic and creative staff, including Jules Riskin, Virginia Satir, Jay Haley, John Weakland, Paul Watzlawick, Arthur Bodin, and Janet Beavin. After a few years, several of the staff members became fascinated with the pragmatic, problem-solving approach of Milton Erickson. This led Jackson to establish the Brief Therapy Project under the direction of Richard Fisch. The original group included Arthur Bodin, Jay Haley, Paul Watzlawick, and John Weakland. What emerged was an elegantly brief approach based on identifying and interrupting vicious cycles that occur when attempts to solve problems only make them worse. However, unlike today's therapies, which are brief by default, the Palo Alto approach was

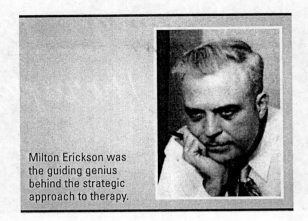

Milton Erickson was the guiding genius behind the strategic approach to therapy.

brief by design. This approach, known as the MRI model, was described by Watzlawick, Weakland, and Fisch (1974) in *Change: Principles of Problem Formation and Problem Resolution*, and in a follow-up volume *The Tactics of Change: Doing Therapy Briefly* (Fisch, Weakland, & Segal, 1982), which remains the most comprehensive statement of the MRI model.

When Jackson died in 1968 at the age of forty-eight, he left a legacy of seminal papers, the leading journal in the field, *Family Process* (which he cofounded with Nathan Ackerman in 1962), and a great sadness at the passing of such a creative talent. The MRI group and the whole field suffered another painful loss in 1995 when John Weakland died of Lou Gehrig's disease.

Jay Haley was always something of an outsider. He entered the field without clinical credentials and established his reputation as a gadfly and critic. His initial impact came from his writing, in which he infused sarcasm with incisive analysis. In "The Art of Psychoanalysis" (Haley, 1963), Haley redefined psychoanalysis as a game of one-upmanship:

> By placing the patient on a couch, the analyst gives the patient the feeling of having his feet up in the air and the knowledge that the analyst has both feet on the ground. Not only is the patient disconcerted by having to lie down while talking, but he finds himself literally below the analyst and so his one-down position

is geographically emphasized. In addition, the analyst seats himself behind the couch where he can watch the patient but the patient cannot watch him. This gives the patient the kind of disconcerted feeling a person has when sparring with an opponent while blindfolded. Unable to see what response his ploys provoke, he is unsure when he is one-up and when one-down. Some patients try to solve this problem by saying something like, "I slept with my sister last night," and then whirling around to see how the analyst is responding. These "shocker" ploys usually fail in their effect. The analyst may twitch, but he has time to recover before the patient can whirl fully around and see him. Most analysts have developed ways of handling the whirling patient. As the patient turns, they are gazing off into space, or doodling with a pencil, or braiding belts, or staring at tropical fish. It is essential that the rare patient who gets an opportunity to observe the analyst see only an impassive demeanor. (pp. 193–194)

After the Bateson project disbanded in 1962, Haley moved to MRI until 1967, when he joined Salvador Minuchin at the Philadelphia Child Guidance Clinic. It was there that he became interested in training and supervision, areas in which he made his greatest contribution (Haley, 1996). In 1976, Haley moved to Washington, D.C., where with Cloe Madanes he founded the Family Therapy Institute. Madanes, known as one of the most creative therapists in the field, had previously worked at MRI and the Philadelphia Child Guidance Clinic. In 1995, Haley moved back to California. He died on February 13, 2007.

Haley and Madanes are such towering figures that their names often overshadow those who followed in their footsteps. James Keim in California, who developed an innovative way of working with oppositional children, is ably carrying on the Haley–Madanes tradition. Other prominent practitioners of this model include Neil Schiff in Washington, D.C., Scott Sells at the Savannah Family Institute, and Jerome Price in Michigan, who specializes in difficult adolescents.

The MRI model had a major impact on the Milan Associates, Mara Selvini Palazzoli, Luigi Boscolo, Gianfranco Cecchin, and Guiliana Prata. Selvini Palazzoli was a prominent Italian psychoanalyst, specializing in eating disorders, when, out of frustration with the psychoanalytic model (Selvini Palazzoli, 1981), she began to develop her own approach to families. In 1967, she led a group of eight psychiatrists who turned to the ideas of Bateson, Haley, and Watzlawick and formed the Center for the Study of the Family in Milan, where they developed the Milan systemic model.

The Ackerman Institute has promulgated both the strategic and Milan models. Prominent contributors from the Ackerman faculty include Peggy Papp (1980, 1983), a creative force in the strategic school; Joel Bergman (1985), who developed original strategies for dealing with difficult families; Peggy Penn (1982, 1985), who elaborated on the Milan innovation of circular questioning; and Olga Silverstein, known for her clinical artistry.

Karl Tomm (1984a, 1984b, 1987a, 1987b), a Canadian psychiatrist in Calgary, Alberta, was a prominent interpreter of the Milan model, but recently, with the influence of Michael White's work (see Chapter 13), Tomm has been developing his own ideas about the impact of the therapist on families. Joseph Eron and Thomas Lund (1993, 1996), in Kingston, New York, have tried to bring strategic therapy up-to-date by integrating it with narrative approaches, based on constructionist principles. Finally, Richard Rabkin (1977), a literate and eclectic social psychiatrist practicing in New York City, was influenced by all the developers of strategic therapy and in turn influenced them.

THEORETICAL FORMULATIONS

In *Pragmatics of Human Communication*, Watzlawick, Beavin, and Jackson (1967) sought to develop a calculus of human communication, which they stated in a series of axioms. The first of these axioms is that *people are always communicating*. Because all behavior is communicative and because one cannot *not* behave, then it follows that one cannot *not* communicate. Consider the following example.

Mrs. Rodriguez began by saying, "I don't know what to do with Ramon. He's not doing well in school and he doesn't help out around the house. All he wants to do is hang with those awful friends of his. But the worst thing is that he refuses to communicate with us."

The therapist turned to Ramon and said, "Well, what do you have to say about all of this?" Ramon said nothing. He just sat there slouched in the corner with a sullen look on his face.

Ramon isn't *not* communicating. He's communicating that he's angry and refuses to talk about it. Communication also takes place when it isn't intentional, conscious, or successful—that is, in the absence of mutual understanding.

The second axiom is that all messages have *report* and *command* functions (Ruesch & Bateson, 1951). The report (or content) of a message conveys information, while the command is a statement about the definition of the relationship. For example, the message "Mommy, Sandy hit me!" conveys information but also implies a command—*Do something about it*. Notice, however, that the implicit command is ambiguous. The reason for this is that the printed word omits facial and contextual clues. This statement shrieked by a child in tears would have very different implications than if it were uttered by a giggling child.

In families, command messages are patterned as *rules* (Jackson, 1965), which can be deduced from observed redundancies in interaction. Jackson used the term **family rules** as a description of regularity, not regulation. Nobody lays down the rules. In fact, families are generally unaware of them.

The rules, or regularities, of family interaction operate to preserve **family homeostasis**

(Jackson, 1965, 1967). Homeostatic mechanisms bring families back to equilibrium in the face of disruption and thus serve to resist change. Jackson's notion of family homeostasis describes the conservative aspect of family systems and is similar to the cybernetic concept of **negative feedback**. According to communications analysis, families operate as goal-directed, rule-governed systems.

Communications theorists didn't look for underlying motives; instead, they assumed circular causality and analyzed patterns of communications linked together in additive chains of stimulus and response as *feedback loops*. When the response to a family member's problematic behavior exacerbates the problem, that chain is seen as a *positive feedback loop*. The advantage of this formulation is that it focuses on interactions that perpetuate problems, which can be changed, instead of inferring underlying causes, which are often not subject to change.

✍

Strategic therapists took the concept of the positive feedback loop and made it the centerpiece of their models. For the MRI group, this translated into a simple yet powerful principle of problem formation: Families encounter many difficulties over the course of their lives, but whether a difficulty becomes a problem depends on how family members respond to it (Watzlawick, Weakland, & Fisch, 1974). That is, families often make commonsensical but misguided attempts to solve their difficulties and, on finding that the problem persists, apply more-of-the-same attempted solutions. This only produces an escalation of the problem, which provokes more of the same, and so on—in a vicious cycle.

For example, if Jamal feels threatened by the arrival of a baby sister, he may become temperamental. If so, his father might think he's being defiant and try to get him to act his age by punishing him—but his father's harshness only confirms Jamal's belief that his parents love his sister more than him, and so he acts even younger. Father, in turn, becomes more critical and punitive, and Jamal becomes increasingly alienated. This is an escalating positive feedback loop: The family system is reacting to a deviation in the behavior of one of its members with feedback designed to dampen that deviation (*negative feedback*), but it has the effect of amplifying the deviation (*positive feedback*).

What's needed is for Father to reverse his solution. If he could comfort rather than criticize Jamal and help him see that he isn't being displaced, then Jamal might calm down. The system is governed, however, by unspoken rules that allow only one interpretation of Jamal's behavior—as disrespectful. For Father to alter his solution, this rule would have to be revised.

In most families, unspoken rules govern all sorts of behavior. Where a rule promotes the kind of rigid attempted solutions described previously, it isn't just the behavior but the rule that needs to change. When only a specific behavior within a system changes, this is **first-order change**, as opposed to **second-order change**, which occurs when the rules of the system change (Watzlawick et al., 1974). How does one change the rules? One way is through **reframing**; that is, changing father's interpretation of Jamal's behavior from disrespect to fear of displacement, from bad to sad.

Thus, the MRI approach to problems is elegantly simple: First, identify the positive feedback loops that maintain problems; second, determine the rules that support those interactions; and third, find a way to change the rules in order to interrupt the problem maintaining behavior.

Jay Haley added a functionalist emphasis to the cybernetic interpretation, with his interest in the interpersonal payoff of behavior. Later, he incorporated structural concepts developed during the years he spent with Minuchin in Philadelphia. For example, Haley might notice that whenever Jamal and Father quarrel, Jamal's

mother protects him by criticizing Father for being so harsh. Haley might also see Jamal becoming more agitated when Mother criticizes Father, trying to get his parents' attention off their conflicts and onto him.

Haley believed that the rules around the **hierarchical structure** of the family were crucial and found inadequate parental hierarchies lurking behind most problems. Indeed, Haley (1976) suggested that "an individual is more disturbed in direct proportion to the number of malfunctioning hierarchies in which he is embedded" (p. 117).

To counter a problem's payoff, Haley borrowed Erickson's technique of prescribing **ordeals**, so that the price for keeping a symptom outweighed that of giving it up. To illustrate, consider Erickson's famous maneuver of prescribing that an insomniac set his alarm every night to wake up and wax the kitchen floor. Haley tried to explain all therapy as based on ordeals, suggesting that people will change to avoid the many ordeals inherent in being a client (Haley, 1984).

Cloe Madanes (1981, 1984) also emphasized the functional aspect of problems, particularly the rescuing operations involved when children use their symptoms to engage their parents. For example, when a daughter sees her mother looking depressed, the daughter can provoke a fight that prods the mother into taking charge. Much of Madanes's approach involves finding ways for symptomatic children to help their parents openly, so that they won't have to resort to symptoms as sacrificial offerings.

Like Haley, Mara Selvini Palazzoli and her associates (1978b) focused on the power games in the family and on the protective function symptoms served for the whole family. They explored families' histories over several generations, searching for evidence to confirm their hypotheses about how the children's symptoms came to be necessary. These hypotheses often involved elaborate networks of family alliances and coalitions. They frequently concluded that the patient developed symptoms to protect one or more other family members so as to maintain the delicate network of extended family alliances.

NORMAL FAMILY DEVELOPMENT

According to **general systems theory**, normal families, like all living systems, depend on two vital processes (Maruyama, 1968). First, they maintain integrity in the face of environmental challenges through *negative feedback*. No living system can survive without a coherent structure. On the other hand, too rigid a structure leaves a system ill equipped to adapt to changing circumstances. That's why normal families also have mechanisms of *positive feedback*. Negative feedback resists disruptions to maintain a steady state; positive feedback amplifies innovations to accommodate to changed circumstances. Recognizing that the channel for positive feedback is communication makes it possible to state the case more plainly: Healthy families are able to adapt because they communicate clearly and are adaptable.

The MRI group resolutely opposed standards of normality: "As therapists, we do not regard any particular way of functioning, relating, or living as a problem if the client is not expressing discontent with it" (Fisch, 1978). Thus, by limiting their task to eliminating problems presented to them, the MRI group avoided taking any position regarding how families *should* behave.

The Milan Associates strove to maintain an attitude of *neutrality* (Selvini Palazzoli, Boscolo, Cecchin, & Prata, 1980). They didn't apply preconceived goals or normative models to their client families. Instead, by raising questions that helped families examine themselves and that exposed hidden power games, they trusted that families would reorganize on their own.

In contrast to the relativism of these two approaches, Haley's assessments *were* based on assumptions about sound family functioning. His therapy was designed to help families reorganize into more functional structures, with clear boundaries and generational hierarchies (Haley, 1976).

DEVELOPMENT OF BEHAVIOR DISORDERS

According to communications theory, the essential function of symptoms is to maintain the homeostatic equilibrium of family systems.[2] Symptomatic families were seen as trapped in dysfunctional, homeostatic patterns of communication (Jackson & Weakland, 1961). These families cling to their rigid ways and respond to signs of change as negative feedback. That is, change is treated not as an opportunity for growth but as a threat, as the following example illustrates.

Laban was a quiet boy, the only child of Orthodox Jewish parents from Eastern Europe. His parents left their small farming community to come to the United States where they both found factory work in a large city. Although they were now safe from religious persecution, the couple felt alien and out of synch with their new neighbors. They kept to themselves and took pleasure in raising Laban.

Laban was a frail child with a number of peculiar mannerisms, but to his parents he was perfect. Then he started school. Laban began to make friends with other children and, eager to be accepted, picked up a number of American habits. He chewed gum, watched cartoons, and

_____

[2]The notion of symptoms as functional—implying that families *need* their problems—was to become controversial.

rode his bicycle all over the neighborhood. His parents were annoyed by the gum chewing and by Laban's fondness for television, but they were genuinely distressed by his eagerness to play with gentile children. They may have come to the United States to escape persecution but not to embrace pluralism, much less assimilation. As far as they were concerned, Laban was rejecting their values—"Something must be wrong with him." By the time they called the child guidance clinic, they were convinced that Laban was disturbed, and they asked for help to "make Laban normal again."

In strategic models, there are three explanations of how problems develop. The first is cybernetic: Difficulties are turned into chronic problems by misguided solutions, forming *positive-feedback escalations*. The second is structural: Problems are the result of *incongruous hierarchies*. The third is functional: Problems result when people try to protect or control one another covertly, so that their *symptoms serve a function for the system*. The MRI group limited itself to the first explanation, while Haley and the Milan associates embraced all three.

To clarify these differences, consider the following example: Sixteen-year-old Juwan recently began refusing to leave the house. An MRI therapist might ask his parents how they had tried to get him to venture out. The focus would be on the parents' attempted solution, on the assumption that this was likely to be maintaining Juwan's refusal, and on their explanation, or *frame*, for Juwan's behavior, believing that their framing of the problem might be driving their false solution.

A Haley-style therapist might be interested in the parents' attempted solutions but would also inquire about their marriage, the ways in which Juwan was involved in struggles between them or other family members, and the possible protective nature of Juwan's problem. This therapist

would be acting on the assumption that Juwan's behavior might be part of a dysfunctional triangle. The therapist might further assume that this triangular pattern was fueled by unresolved conflicts between the parents. Madanes would also be interested in this triangle but, in addition, would be curious about how Juwan's behavior might be protecting his parents from having to face some threatening issue.

A Milan systemic therapist wouldn't focus so much on attempted solutions but instead would ask about past and present relationships in the family. In so doing, the therapist would be trying to uncover a network of power alliances, often continuing across generations, that constituted the family's "game." Some such game left Juwan in the position of having to use his symptoms to protect other family members. The family might reveal, for example, that if Juwan were to grow up and leave home, his mother would be drawn back into a power struggle between her parents, which she had avoided by having a symptomatic child. Also, by not succeeding in life, Juwan might be protecting his father from the shame of having a child who exceeded him in accomplishment, just as he had done with his father.

The essential insight of the strategic model was that problems are often maintained by self-defeating patterns of behavior. By adding a structural perspective to this largely behavioral position, Haley pointed out that such self-defeating patterns may be embedded in dysfunctional family organizations. Not only must families have effective hierarchal arrangements—with parents firmly in charge—but families must also modify their structure to accommodate changes in the lives of family members.

 GOALS OF THERAPY

The MRI group is proudly minimalistic. Once the presenting problem is resolved, therapy is concluded. Even when other problems are apparent, if the family doesn't ask for help with those problems, they aren't targeted. MRI therapists justify this parsimonious position by asserting that because they view people who have problems as stuck rather than sick, their job is simply to help them get moving again.

MRI therapists help families define clear and reachable goals so that everyone knows when treatment has been successful. They often find that much of the therapy takes place simply in the process of pushing clients to set concrete behavioral goals, because in doing so clients are forced to clarify vague dissatisfactions. Also, in getting clients to define achievable goals, MRI therapists help people let go of utopian aspirations, which are bound to lead to disappointment.

The MRI model is behavioral, both in its goals and its focus on observable patterns of interaction, while scrupulously avoiding speculation about intrapsychic intentions. In trying to achieve the goal of problem resolution, the immediate aim is to change the behavioral responses of people to their problems. More specifically, as described earlier, MRI therapists try to interrupt (often to reverse) more-of-the-same vicious feedback loops. To achieve this behavioral change, they may try to reframe the problem and, in that sense, introduce a cognitive element. But any cognitive consideration is only in the service of the primary goal of behavior change.

Haley's approach is also behavioral and, even more than that of the MRI group, downplays the importance of insight. He was scornful of therapies that helped clients understand why they did things but failed to get them to do something different. Haley's ultimate goal is often a structural reorganization of the family, particularly its hierarchy and generational boundaries. Unlike in structural family therapy, however, these structural goals are always directly related to the presenting problem. For example, to improve the relationship between the polarized parents of a rebellious teenager, a structural therapist might get the parents to talk about their marital problems, where Haley would have them talk only about their difficulty working together to deal with their son.

The early work of the Milan group (Selvini Palazzoli, Boscolo, Cecchin, & Prata, 1978b) was heavily influenced by the MRI and Haley models. The Milan associates expanded the network of people involved in maintaining the problem but were still primarily interested in finding ways to interrupt destructive family games. The techniques they developed differed from other strategic schools in that they were less behavioral and instead were designed to expose covert collusions and reframe motives for strange behavior. Although less problem focused and more interested in changing families' beliefs than other strategic therapists, the original Milan approach was no less manipulative: The responsibility for change rested on the therapist whose job it was to outwit resistance.

When the Milan associates split into two groups in the early 1980s, this strategic emphasis remained with Selvini Palazzoli and the groups she subsequently formed. Later, she abandoned brief, strategic models altogether and now does long-term therapy with more focus on insight for the individual patient (Selvini, 1993).

After the breakup of the Milan group, Luigi Boscolo and Gianfranco Cecchin moved away from strategically manipulating families and toward collaborating with them to form systemic hypotheses about their problems. Therapy became more of a research expedition that the therapist entered without specific goals or strategies, trusting that the process of self-examination would allow families to choose to change rather than continuing their unproductive patterns. The therapist was released from responsibility for any certain outcome and adopted an attitude of curiosity (Cecchin, 1987) toward families, rather than the interventive attitude of strategic therapists.

By moving in this direction, Boscolo and Cecchin took a position opposite to that of their strategic predecessors. This collaborative philosophy became the bridge over which many strategic and Milan therapists crossed over to the narrative approaches of the 1990s.

CONDITIONS FOR BEHAVIOR CHANGE

In the early days of family therapy the goal was simply to improve communication. Later, the goal was refined to altering specific patterns of communication that maintained problems. A therapist can either point out problematic sequences or simply manipulate them to effect therapeutic change. The first strategy relies on insight and depends on a willingness to change. The second does not; it's an attempt to beat families at their own games, with or without their cooperation.

For the MRI school, the way to resolve problems is to change the behavior associated with them. It's believed that through seeing the results of altering rigid behavioral responses, clients will become more flexible in their problem-solving strategies. When this happens, clients achieve a second-order change—a change in the rules governing their response to problems.

For example, Maria argues with her father about her curfew and her father grounds her. She then runs away and stays with a friend. A first-order intervention at this point might be to help Maria's father find a more effective punishment to tame his out-of-control child. A second-order strategic intervention might be to direct the father to act disappointed and sad around his daughter, implying that he has given up trying to control her. This shifts Maria from feeling trapped by her father to feeling concerned about him, and she becomes more reasonable. Her father learns that when attempted solutions aren't working, try something different. This change is second order in that it alters the rules governing the way father and daughter interact.

Haley (1976) believed that telling people what they're doing wrong only mobilizes resistance. He believed that changes in behavior alter perceptions, rather than the other way around. The Milan group turned this behaviorism on its head. They were more interested in getting families to see things differently (through a reframing technique called *positive connotation* to be discussed later) than in getting family members to *behave* differently. This shift from behavior to meaning set the stage for the constructivist and narrative movements (see Chapters 4 and 13).

THERAPY

Assessment

The goals of an MRI assessment are to (1) define a resolvable complaint, (2) identify attempted solutions that maintain the complaint, and (3) understand the clients' unique language for describing the problem. The first two goals show where to intervene; the third suggests how.

The first step is to get a very specific, behavioral picture of the complaint, who sees it as a problem, and why it's a problem now. When a therapist asks "What is the problem that brings you here today," many clients reply ambiguously, "We don't communicate," "We think our fourteen-year-old is depressed," or "Clarence seems to be hyperactive." The MRI therapist then inquires about exactly what these complaints mean. "We don't communicate" might mean "My son argues with everything I say" or "My husband hides behind the newspaper and never talks to me." "Depressed" might mean sad and withdrawn or sullen and disagreeable; "hyperactive" might mean disobedient or unable to concentrate. A useful device is to ask "If we had a videotape of this, what would it look like?"

Once the problem has been defined, the therapist tries to determine who has tried to solve it and how. Sometimes the attempted solution seems obviously to have made things worse. For example, the wife who nags her husband to spend more time with her is likely to succeed only in driving him away. Likewise, the parents who punish their son for fighting with his sister might convince him that they favor her. Or the husband who does everything his wife asks in order to keep the peace may become so resentful that he starts to hate her.

From this inquiry emerges a formulation of the problem-solution loop and the specific behavior that will be the focus of intervention. Typically, the strategic objective will be a 180-degree reversal of what the clients have been doing. Although interventions typically involve prescribing some alternative behavior, the key is to stop the performance of the problem-maintaining solution (Weakland & Fisch, 1992).

Grasping the clients' unique language and ways of seeing their dilemmas is important to framing suggestions in ways they will accept. For example, a devoutly religious wife might be amenable to the suggestion that she pray for her husband to become more involved with the family rather than continue to criticize his failings. In another case, cited by Shoham and Rohrbaugh (2002), a young woman was seen as perpetuating her boyfriend's jealous accusations by trying to reassure him. Unfortunately, these efforts to reason with the boyfriend only ended up in arguments, which were painful enough to threaten the relationship. Because the woman was a devotee of "mindfulness meditation," the therapist suggested that the next time the boyfriend asked a jealous question and she felt like defending herself, she should tell him that she was feeling stressed and needed to meditate.

Haley's assessment begins with a careful definition of the problem, expressed from the point of view of every member of the family. However, unlike the MRI group, Haley also observes how family members interact in the session to explore the possibility that structural arrangements in the family may be contributing to their problems—especially pathological triangles, or *cross-generational coalitions*. As Haley said, "Problem children tend to determine what happens in families, which makes for hierarchical difficulties" (Haley, 1996, p. 96).

In addition to structural problems, Haley and Madanes also consider the interpersonal payoff of problem behavior. According to Haley, the apparent helplessness of a patient often turns out to be a source of power in relation to others whose lives are dominated by the demands and fears of the symptomatic person. A schizophrenic who refuses to take his medication might, for example, avoid having to go to work. While it isn't necessary to decide what is or isn't a real illness, Haley tends to assume that all symptomatic behavior is voluntary. Sometimes this is a crucial distinction—as, for example, in cases of drug addiction or losing one's temper.

In the Milan model, assessment begins with a preliminary hypothesis, which is confirmed or disconfirmed in the initial session. These hypotheses are generally based on the assumption that the identified patient's problems serve a protective function for the family. Therefore, assessment of the presenting problem and the family's response to it is based on questions designed to explore the family as a set of interconnected relationships. For example, the reply to a question like "Who has been more worried about this problem, you or your wife?" will suggest a hypothesis about the closeness and distance of family members. The ultimate goal of assessment is to achieve a systemic perspective on the problem.

Therapeutic Techniques

Although strategic therapists shared a belief in the need for indirect methods to induce change in families, they developed distinctly different techniques for doing so.

The MRI Approach. The MRI model follows a six-step treatment procedure:

1. Introduction to the treatment setup
2. Inquiry and definition of the problem
3. Estimation of the behavior maintaining the problem
4. Setting goals for treatment
5. Selecting and making behavioral interventions
6. Termination

Once the preliminaries have been concluded, the therapist asks for a clear definition of the major problem. If a problem is stated in vague terms, such as "We just don't seem to get along," or in terms of presumptive causes, such as "Dad's job is making him depressed," the therapist helps translate it into a clear and concrete goal, asking questions like "What will be the first small sign that things are getting better?"

After the problem and goals are defined, MRI therapists inquire about attempted solutions, which might be maintaining the problem. In general, the solutions that tend to perpetuate problems fall into one of three categories:

1. The solution is to deny that a problem exists; action is necessary but not taken. For instance, parents do nothing despite growing evidence that their teenage son is using drugs.
2. The solution is an effort to solve something that isn't really a problem; action is taken when it shouldn't be. For example, parents punish a child for masturbating.
3. The solution is an effort to solve a problem within a framework that makes a solution impossible; action is taken but at the wrong level. For instance, a husband buys increasingly expensive gifts for his unhappy wife, when what she wants is affection.

Once the therapist conceives a strategy for changing the problem-maintaining sequence, clients must be convinced to follow this strategy.

To sell their directives, MRI therapists *reframe* problems to increase the likelihood of compliance. Thus, a therapist might tell an angry teenager that when his father punishes him, it's the only way his father knows how to show his love.

To interrupt problem-maintaining sequences, strategic therapists may try to get family members to do something that runs counter to common sense. Such counterintuitive techniques have been called *paradoxical interventions* (Haley, 1973; Watzlawick et al., 1974).

For example, Watzlawick and his colleagues (1974) described a young couple who were bothered by their parents' tendency to treat them like children by doing everything for them. Despite the husband's adequate salary, the parents continued to send money and lavish gifts on them, refused to let them pay even part of a restaurant check, and so on. The strategic team helped the couple solve their difficulty with their doting parents by having them become *less* rather than more competent. Instead of trying to show the parents that they didn't need help, the couple was told to act helpless and dependent, so much so that the parents got disgusted and finally backed off.

The techniques most commonly thought of as paradoxical are symptom prescriptions in which a family is told to continue or embellish the behavior they complain about. In some contexts, such a prescription might be made with the hope that the family will comply with it and thereby reverse their attempted solution. If Jorge, who is sad, is told to try to become depressed several times a day and his family is asked to encourage him to be sad, then they will no longer try ineffectively to cheer him up, and he won't feel guilty for not being happy.

At other times, a therapist might prescribe the symptom while secretly hoping the clients will rebel against this directive. The therapist might encourage Jorge to continue to be depressed because, in doing so, he's helping his brother (with whom Jorge is competitive) feel superior.

Sometimes a therapist might prescribe the symptom with the hope that in doing so the network of relationships that maintain the problem will be exposed. The therapist says that Jorge should remain depressed because that way he can continue to occupy his mother's attention, which will keep her from looking to Father for affection, since Father is still overinvolved with his own mother, and so on.

To preclude power struggles, MRI therapists avoid taking a directive posture. Their *one-down stance* implies equality and invites clients to reduce anxiety and resistance. Although some strategists adopt a one-down position disingenuously, a modest approach was consistent with the late John Weakland's own unassuming character. While sitting clouded in the smoke of his pipe, Weakland discouraged families from trying to change too fast, warning them to go slow and worrying out loud about the possibility of relapse when improvements did occur. This **restraining** technique reinforced the therapist's one-down position.

The Haley and Madanes Approach. Jay Haley's approach is harder to describe because it's tailored to address the unique requirements of each case. If *strategic* implies *systematic*, as in the MRI approach, it also implies *artful*, which is especially true of Haley's therapy. As with other strategic approaches, the definitive technique is the use of **directives**—but Haley's directives aren't simply ploys to outwit families or reverse what they're doing; rather, they are thoughtful suggestions targeted to the specific requirements of the case.

Haley (1976) believed that if therapy is to end well, it must begin properly. Therefore, he devoted a good deal of atten-

Jay Haley tailored directives to fit the needs of specific clients and their problems.

tion to the opening moves of treatment. Regardless of who is presented as the official patient, Haley began by interviewing the entire family. His approach to this initial interview followed four stages: a *social stage*, a *problem stage*, an *interaction stage*, and finally a *goal-setting stage*.

Families are often defensive when they come to therapy. Family members don't know what to expect, and they may be afraid that the therapist will blame them for their problems. Therefore, Haley used the initial minutes of a first session to help everyone relax. He made a point of greeting each family member and making sure they were comfortable. Like a good host, he wanted his guests to feel welcome.

After the *social stage*, Haley got down to business in the *problem stage*, asking each person for his or her perspective. Because mothers are usually more central than fathers, Haley recommended speaking first to the father to increase his involvement. This suggestion illustrates Haley's strategic maneuvering, which characterized his whole approach to families.

Haley listened carefully to the way each family member describes the problem, making sure that no one interrupted until each has had a turn. During this phase, Haley looked for clues about triangles and hierarchy, but he avoided making any comments about these observations because this might make the family defensive.

Once everyone had a chance to speak, Haley encouraged them to discuss their points of view among themselves. In this, the *interactional stage*, the therapist can observe, rather than just hear about, the interchanges that surround the problem. As they talk, Haley looked for *coalitions* between family members against others. How functional is the *hierarchy*? Do the parents work well together, or do they undercut each other?

Sometimes Haley ended the first session by giving the family a task. In subsequent sessions, directives played a central role. Effective directives don't usually take the form of simple advice, which is rarely helpful because problems usually persist for a reason. According to Haley, the effective therapist isn't one who tells people what to do but one who gets them to do it.

The following two tasks are taken from Haley's *problem-solving therapy*. One couple, who were out of the habit of being affectionate with each other, were told to behave affectionately "to teach their child how to show affection." In another case, a mother who was unable to control her twelve-year-old son had decided to send him away to military school. Haley suggested that since the boy had no idea how tough life would be at military school, it would be a good idea for the mother to help prepare him. They both agreed. Haley directed her to teach the boy how to stand at attention, be polite, and wake up early every morning to make his bed. The two of them followed these instructions as if playing a game, with the mother as sergeant and the son as private. After two weeks, the son was behaving so well that his mother no longer felt it necessary to send him away.

One thing that remains unique about Haley's approach was his focus on the interpersonal payoff of psychiatric symptoms. The idea that people get something out of their symptoms has been rejected by most schools of family therapy because it is seen as a version of blaming the victim. Haley's point wasn't that people become anxious or depressed in order to manipulate others but that such problems, once they develop, may come to play a role in interpersonal struggles in the family. It is this covert function of symptoms that Haley explored. Although MRI therapists speculate about what may be maintaining the symptoms, they emphasize other people's misguided solutions and don't consider the interpersonal payoff of the symptoms themselves. The primary goal of hypothesizing in Haley's approach is to understand the heart of the family drama that the symptoms revolve around. Haley believed that people's struggles have meaning and therefore suggests that reasonable solutions can be found. The answer is to help families find new ways to solve their problems.

Case Study

In a case treated by Jerome Price, a thirteen-year-old girl was referred to juvenile court because of chronic truancy. She had repeatedly failed to show up at school, and both her parents and school officials had tried a range of threats and punishments—all to no avail. The judge referred the girl to therapy. Price began by asking questions designed to find out *why* the girl was skipping school. The most obvious question was "Where do you go when you don't go to school?" To the therapist's surprise, the girl said that she went to the home of her ninety-two-year-old grandmother. The girl's parents assumed that she was taking advantage of her grandmother. However, when Price asked "Why there?," he learned that the grandmother lived alone and was in constant fear of falling. Her children rarely visited and didn't address her concerns directly, so the granddaughter had taken it upon herself to see that her grandmother was safe.

Price's directives addressed both the purpose of the girl's truancy and the hierarchical imbalance that it reflected in the family. He encouraged the parents to visit the grandmother more often, hire a caregiver to be there during the day, and arrange activities at a local senior center. Knowing that her grandmother was safe—and that her parents were now taking charge—the girl returned to school.

Unlike many contemporary family therapists, Haley openly addressed the issue of interpersonal power in families. Early in his career, Haley (1963) recognized that communication always had an impact on how family members relate to one another in a way that either increased or decreased their influence. This was not meant as a judgment but merely a description of the way things work. Haley devoted much of his early effort to observing how power was used and misused in families, with the idea that therapists can either ignore power struggles or recognize and help families resolve them.

Case Study

When a man beats a woman, people have no trouble seeing this as an issue of power and its misuse. But when sixteen-year-old Brad (Price, 1996) verbally harassed his mother to get the use of her car, his individual therapist didn't see this as Brad's misuse of power. When Brad proceeded to push his mother to the ground and rip the keys out of her hand, the therapist still insisted on exploring Brad's reasons for being angry at his mother.

When Brad's mother got fed up with this approach and sought treatment from a strategic practitioner, the new therapy focused on how Brad had become so powerful and what it would take for his mother to regain leadership. Most of the sessions included the mother and Brad's uncle, who cared very much about him and was therefore more than willing to help discuss and carry out decisions. When Brad was faced with a united front of two adults, who met with him and a therapist and also held meetings at his school, the reformulation of the power balance began calming him down and simplifying his life to the point where he could return to acting like a sixteen-year-old, rather than an abusive husband.

As is often the case, the underlying dynamics in this family didn't emerge until *after* the presenting problem improved. Once Brad started behaving respectfully and performing better in school, his mother's depression became more apparent. In a way, Brad had kept his mother emotionally occupied by reenacting her struggles with his father, which made it unnecessary for her to make new friends, date, and move forward in her life. With Brad improving and no crises to deal with, his mother became conscious of what was missing in her life, and the therapist was able to help her address her own future. Haley would see Brad as trying to help his mother by giving her a problem that distracted her from her own. In some cases, this helpfulness is conscious; in other cases, it isn't.

Metaphor is another recurrent theme in Haley's approach. In the previous case, Brad's misbehavior, which mimicked that of his parents' previous abusive relationship, could be seen as a metaphor for his mother not having resolved her emotional struggle over past abuse. According to this approach, the symptom anyone carries is often a metaphor for the underlying problem. Thus, a school problem in a child may mirror a work problem of a parent. An underachieving child may be a reflection of an underfunctioning parent. An addicted child may point to someone else in the family secretly acting in self-destructive ways.

Such was the case in which thirty-seven-year-old Margery asked for help with her three-year-old daughter. Whenever the two entered a store, the little girl would steal something, such as a pack of gum or candy. Upon further exploration, the therapist learned that Margery was having an affair with her best friend's husband. The metaphor of stealing thus proved apt.

Cloe Madanes (1981) describes how one relationship may metaphorically replicate another. As was the case with Brad and his mother, parents can fight with their children about things they should be addressing between themselves. Two children can fight with each other in the same way their parents would be fighting if they weren't distracted by the children. One child can struggle with parents in a way that deflects the scrutiny that otherwise might be directed at a sibling. This is often the case when there is a young adult at home who is not working or going to school and is generally stuck on the launching pad. A younger sibling may become symptomatic and start failing at school in a way that serves as metaphor to force the parents to deal with the issue of needing to be productive.

Madanes (1984) also addresses power balancing in couples and its role in a wide range of symptoms. She looks at the areas of couples' lives in which power is regulated, including money, education, control of children, coalitions with in-laws, religion, and sex. It often turns out that the partner with the least power develops the most emotional problems. Symptoms such as depression, headaches, substance abuse, eating disorders, phobias, and so on certainly burden the person who suffers them, but they also burden other family members, especially partners. Others in the family often try desperately to do something about such symptoms, but the symptomatic person may refuse to allow him- or herself to be helped, thereby maintaining a perverse sort of power by holding onto troublesome symptoms. Again, this process is typically unconscious, and this way of thinking about it is not offered as some objective truth but rather as one possibly useful clinical hypothesis. Looking at such struggles in the light of power balancing, a therapist is able to have a more flexible view of the drama a couple is embroiled in. Is the abuser someone who actually needs more of a role in his children's lives? Does a partner need an avocation that can help him or her feel more successful?

This dynamic was the case with Mark and Brianna. Mark became more and more depressed and refused to seek a job after being laid off. Six months had passed, and he had done little. He spent money as if his income were still coming in, while Brianna stayed home with the children despite being in demand as a registered nurse. Brianna berated Mark about his lack of action, shouting at him at times and generally exacerbating his general sense of failure. *She* was the expert on the children. *She* took them to church.

Case Study

She had a master's degree, while he had only two years of college.

As Mark became more depressed and did increasingly less, Brianna was forced to go back to work and give up staying home with the children. By what he didn't do—"because he was depressed"—Mark dominated the family that had previously dominated him. He now took care of the children (albeit not to Brianna's satisfaction) and stayed home while she worked, and no one went to church because Brianna had to work the graveyard shift on Saturday nights. Mark's depression had equalized the power imbalance that developed when he lost his job and began to feel like a failure. Brianna's emotional control over their lives had previously been offset by the fact that Mark was the breadwinner. When he lost that role, the couple went into imbalance and Mark had to find another form of power to replace his income. Ironically, the helplessness of depression provided that power.

The artful commonsense component of Haley's strategic therapy can be understood by looking at high-conflict divorce. Rather than think of a high-conflict couple as being pathological, Haley would look at this problem developmentally and in terms of the family life cycle (Haley, 1973; Haley & Richeport-Haley, 2007). This approach attempts to find benevolent hypotheses that describe clients in the best possible light. Rather than see the ex-spouses as personality disordered, a Haley-style therapist would more likely see them as still in need of an emotional divorce (Gaulier, Margerum, Price, & Windell, 2007). Such a conceptualization offers the therapist ideas about what needs to be done to resolve problems.

Rob and Melissa continued to argue over every aspect of their seventeen-year-old daughter Marta's existence. When the therapist asked Marta if these

Case Study

arguments looked like the arguments her parents had when they were married, she sighed and said that the arguments "were identical." The therapist asked the parents whether they were really willing to let go of each other, once and for all. Both resisted the idea that they were still emotionally married, but the therapist challenged them to prove that they were not.

Cloe Madanes's "pretend techniques" are a clever way to help break control-and-rebel cycles.

The therapist asked both parents to collect memorabilia and write accounts of events from their marriage that they would like to leave behind. The therapist led them through a ritual over about a month, in which they brought in the items and accounts, described them to each other and said why they no longer wanted the effects of these things in their lives, and then ritually burned them in the therapist's presence. Rob and Melissa were directed to collect the ashes in a jar and sent on a weekend trip to northern Michigan, where they stopped in a virgin pine forest and ritually buried the ashes. At the therapist's suggestion, they took a boat trip and, at a specific time and in a specific way, threw their wedding rings (which they had kept) into the depths of Lake Superior.

James Keim and Jay Lappin (2002) describe a strategic approach to a case with a nagging wife and withdrawing husband. First, they reframe the problem as a "breakdown in the negotiation process." A *negotiation*, the couple is told, is a conversation in which one party makes a request and the other names a price. This reframing allows the wife to make requests without thinking of herself as a nag—and the husband to see himself as having something to gain in negotiations, rather than as a brow-beaten man who is asked to give in to his wife.

Keim and Lappin recommend introducing couples to the negotiation process as experimenting with a fun exercise designed to get them back on track with reaching agreements. Then the couple is given a handout with elaborate instructions for negotiating in a constructive fashion and asked to progress from negotiating easy issues in the session to doing so at home and then tackling more difficult issues, first in the session and then at home. Finally, the couple is cautioned that even after negotiating some exchanges, they may choose not to accept the quid pro quo terms. Sometimes it's preferable to endure certain problems rather than pay the price of trying to change them.

Madanes (1981) used the observation that people will often do something they wouldn't ordinarily do if it's framed as play to develop a whole range of **pretend techniques**. One such strategy is to ask a symptomatic child to pretend to have the symptom and encourage the parents to pretend to help. The child can give up the actual symptom now that pretending to have it is serving the same family function. The following two cases, summarized from Madanes (1981), illustrate the pretend technique.

Case Study

In the first case, a mother sought therapy because her ten-year-old son had night terrors. Madanes suspected that the boy was concerned about his mother, who was poor, spoke little English, and had lost two husbands. Since the boy had night terrors, the therapist asked all the members of the family to describe their dreams. Only the mother and the son had nightmares. In the mother's nightmare, someone was breaking into the house. In the boy's, he was being attacked by a witch. When Madanes asked what the mother did when the boy had nightmares, she said that she took him into her bed and told him to pray to God. She explained that she thought his nightmares were the work of the devil.

Madanes's conjecture was that the boy's night terrors were both a metaphorical expression of the mother's fears and an attempt to help her. As long as the boy was afraid, his mother had to be strong. Unfortunately, while trying to protect him, she frightened him further by talking about God and the devil. Thus, both mother and child were helping each other in unproductive ways.

The family members were told to pretend that they were home and mother was afraid that someone might break in. The son was asked to protect his mother. In this way, the mother had to pretend to need the child's help instead of really needing it. At first, the family had difficulty playing the scene because the mother would attack the make-believe thief before the son could help. Thus she communicated that she was capable of taking care of herself and didn't need the son's protection. After the scene was performed correctly, with the son attacking the thief, they all discussed the performance. The mother explained that it was difficult to play her part because she was a competent person who could defend herself.

Madanes sent the family home with the task of repeating this dramatization every evening for a week. If the son started screaming during his sleep, his mother was to wake him up and replay the scene. They were told that this was important to do no matter how late it was or how tired they were. The son's night terrors soon disappeared.

In the second case, a mother sought treatment for her five-year-old because he had uncontrollable temper tantrums. After talking with the family for a few minutes Madanes asked the boy to show

Case Study

her what his tantrums were like by pretending to have one. "Okay," he said, "I'm the Incredible Hulk!" He puffed out his chest, flexed his muscles, made a monster face, and started screaming and kicking the furniture. Madanes asked the mother to do what she usually did in such circumstances. The mother responded by telling her son, in a weak and ineffective way, to calm down. She pretended to send him to another room as she tried to do at home. Next, Madanes asked the mother if the boy was doing a good job of pretending. She said he was.

Madanes asked the boy to repeat the scene. This time, he was Frankenstein's monster and his tantrum was performed with a rigid posture and a grimacing face. Then Madanes talked with the boy about the Incredible Hulk and Frankenstein's monster and congratulated the mother for raising such an imaginative child.

Following this discussion, mother and son were told to pretend that he was having a tantrum while she was walking him to his room. The boy was told to act like the Incredible Hulk and to make lots of noise. Then they were told to pretend to close the door and hug and kiss. Next Madanes instructed the mother to pretend that *she* was having a tantrum, and the boy was to hug and kiss her. Madanes instructed mother and son to perform both scenes every morning before school and every afternoon when the boy came home. After every performance, the mother was to give the boy milk and cookies, if he did a good job. Thus the mother was moved from a helpless position to one of authority, in which she was in charge of rewarding her son's make-believe performance. The next week, the mother called to say that they didn't need to come for therapy because the boy was behaving very well and his tantrums had ceased.

Haley (1984) returned to his Ericksonian roots in a book called *Ordeal Therapy*, a collection of case studies in which **ordeals** were prescribed to make symptoms more trouble than they're worth: "If one makes it more difficult for a person to have a symptom than to give it up, the person will give up the symptom" (p. 5). For example, a standard ordeal is for a client to have to get up in the middle of the night and exercise strenuously whenever he or she had symptoms during that day. Another example might be for the client to have to give a present to someone with whom he or she has a poor relationship—for example, a mother-in-law or ex-spouse—each time the symptoms occur.

Haley also used ordeals to restructure families. For example, a sixteen-year-old boy put a variety of items up his behind and then expelled them, leaving his stepmother to clean up the mess. Haley (1984) arranged that after each such episode, the father had to take his son to their backyard and have the boy dig a hole three feet deep and three feet wide, in which he was to bury all the things he was putting up his rear end. After a few weeks of this, Haley reported that the symptom stopped, the father became more involved with his son, and the stepmother became closer to the father.

The current form of Haley/Madanes therapy, called *strategic humanism*, still involves giving directives, but the directives are now more oriented toward increasing family members' abilities to soothe and love than to gain control over one another. This represents a major shift and is in synch with family therapy's movement away from the power elements of hierarchy and toward finding ways to increase harmony.

An excellent example of strategic humanism's combination of compassion and technology is James Keim's work with oppositional children (Keim, 1998). Keim begins by reassuring anxious parents that they aren't to blame for their children's oppositionalism. Next, he explains that there are two sides of parental authority: discipline and nurture. To reinforce the parents' authority while avoiding power struggles, Keim encourages them to concentrate on being sympathetic and supportive for a while. The parent who soothes a child with the forgotten language of understanding is every bit as much in charge as one who tries to tell the child what to do. After progress has been made in calming the child down—especially in breaking the pattern by which oppositional children control the mood in the family by arguing with everything their parents say—Keim coaches the parents to post rules and enforce consequences. This strategy puts parents back in charge of unruly children without the high-intensity melodrama that usually attends work with this population.

The Milan Model. The original Milan model was highly scripted. Families were treated by male–female cotherapists and observed by other members of a therapy team. The standard format had five parts: the *presession*, the *session*, the *intersession*, the *intervention*, and the *postsession discussion*. As Boscolo, Cecchin, Hoffman, and Penn (1987) describe:

> During the presession the team came up with an initial hypothesis about the family's presenting problem. . . . During the session itself, the team members would validate, modify, or change the hypothesis. After about forty minutes, the entire team would meet alone to discuss the hypothesis and arrive at an intervention. The treating therapists would then go back to deliver the intervention to the family, either by positively connoting the problem situation or by a ritual to be done by the family that commented on the problem situation and was designed to introduce change. . . . Finally, the team would meet for a postsession discussion to analyze the family's reactions and to plan for the next session. (p. 4)

As indicated in this description, the primary intervention was either a *ritual* or a *positive connotation*.

The **positive connotation** was the most distinctive innovation to emerge from the Milan model. Derived from the MRI technique of reframing symptoms as serving a protective function—for example, Carlo needs to continue to be depressed to distract his parents from their marital issues—the positive connotation avoided the implication that family members benefited from the patient's symptoms. This implication made for resistance that the Milan team found could be circumvented if the patient's behavior was construed not as protecting specific people but as preserving the family's overall harmony. Indeed, every family member's behavior was often connoted in this system-serving way.

The treatment team would hypothesize about how the patient's symptom fit into the family system and, after a mid-session break, the therapists would deliver this hypothesis to the family, along with the injunction that they should not try to change. Carlo should continue to sacrifice himself by remaining depressed as a way to reassure the family that he will not become an abusive man like his grandfather. Mother should maintain her overinvolvement with Carlo as a way to make him feel valued while he sacrifices himself. Father should continue to criticize Mother and Carlo's relationship so that Mother will not be tempted to abandon Carlo and become a wife to her husband.

Rituals were used to engage families in a series of actions that ran counter to or exaggerated rigid family rules and myths. For example, one family that was enmeshed with their large extended family was told to hold family discussions behind locked doors every other night after dinner during which each family member was to speak for fifteen minutes about the family. Meanwhile, they were to redouble their courtesy to the other members of the clan. By exaggerating the family's loyalty to the extended family while simultaneously breaking that loyalty's rule by meeting apart from the clan and talking about it, the family could examine and break the rule that perpetuated their dysfunctional system.

Rituals were also used to dramatize positive connotations. For example, each family member might have to express his or her gratitude each night to the patient for having the problem (Boscolo et al., 1987). The Milan group also devised a set of rituals based on an odd-and-even-days format (Selvini Palazzoli, Boscolo, Cecchin, & Prata, 1978a). For example, a family in which the parents were deadlocked over parental control might be told that on even days of the week Father should be in charge of the patient's behavior and Mother should act as if she weren't there. On odd days, Mother's in charge and Father is to stay out of the way. Here, again, the family's rigid sequences are interrupted, and they must react differently to each other.

Positive connotations and rituals were powerful and provocative interventions. To keep families engaged while using such methods, the therapist–family relationship became crucial. Unfortunately, the Milan team originally portrayed therapy as a power struggle between therapists and families. Their main advice to therapists was to remain neutral in the sense of avoiding the appearance of taking sides. This **neutrality** was often manifest as distance, so that therapists delivered their dramatic pronouncements while acting aloof; not surprisingly, families often became angry and didn't return.

In the early 1980s, the original Milan team split around the nature of therapy. Selvini Palazzoli maintained the model's strategic and adversarial bent, although she stopped using paradoxical interventions. Instead, she and Guiliana Prata experimented with a specific ritual called the **invariant prescription**, which they assigned to every family they treated.

Selvini Palazzoli (1986) believed that psychotic and anorexic patients are caught up in a "dirty game," a power struggle originally between their parents that these patients are pulled into and ultimately wind up using their symptoms in an attempt to defeat one parent for the sake of the other. In the invariant prescription, parents were directed to tell their children they had a secret. They were to go out together for varying periods of time and to do so mysteriously, without warning other family members. Therapy continued this way until the patient's symptoms abated.

In the 1990s, Selvini Palazzoli reinvented her therapy once more, this time abandoning short-term, strategic therapy (invariant prescription included) for long-term therapy with patients and their families (Selvini, 1993). Thus, she came full circle, beginning with a psychodynamic approach, then focusing on family patterns, and finally returning to a long-term therapy that emphasizes insight and focuses again on the individual. This new therapy revolves around understanding the denial of family secrets and suffering over generations. In this way, it is linked conceptually, if not technically, to her former models.

Boscolo and Cecchin also moved away from strategic intervening, but they moved toward a collaborative style of therapy. This approach grew from their conclusion that the value in the Milan model wasn't so much in the directives (positive connotations and rituals), which had been the model's centerpiece, but in the interview process itself. Their therapy came to center around **circular questioning**, a clinical translation of Bateson's notion of double description. Circular questions are designed to decenter clients by orienting them toward seeing themselves in a relational context and seeing that context from the perspective of other family members. For example, a therapist might ask "How might your father have characterized your mother's relationship with your sister, if he had felt free to speak with you about it?" Such questions are structured so that one has to give a relational description in answer.

By asking about relationship patterns like this, the circular nature of problems becomes apparent. Circular questions have been further refined and cataloged by Peggy Penn (1982, 1985) and Karl Tomm (1987a, 1987b). Boscolo (Boscolo & Bertrando, 1992) remains intrigued with their potential. As an example, let's return to Carlo's family and imagine the following conversation (adapted from Hoffman, 1983):

Q: Who is most upset by Carlo's depression?
A: Mother.
Q: How does Mother try to help Carlo?

A: She talks to him for hours and tries to do things for him.
Q: Who agrees most with Mother's way of trying to help Carlo?
A: The psychiatrist who prescribes his medication.
Q: Who disagrees?
A: Father. He thinks Carlo shouldn't be allowed to do what he wants.
Q: Who agrees with Father?
A: We all think Carlo is babied too much. And Grandma too. Grandpa would probably agree with Mother but he died.
Q: Did Carlo start to get depressed before or after Grandfather's death?
A: Not long after, I guess.
Q: If Grandfather hadn't died, how would the family be different now?
A: Well, Mother and Grandma probably wouldn't fight so much because Grandma wouldn't be living with us. And Mother wouldn't be so sad all the time.
Q: If Mother and Grandma didn't fight so much and Mother wasn't so sad, how do you think Carlo would be?
A: Well, I guess he might be happier too. But then he'd probably be fighting with Father again.

By asking circular questions, the frame for Carlo's problem gradually shifts from a psychiatric one to being symptomatic of changes in the family structure.

Boscolo and Cecchin became aware that the spirit in which these questions were asked determined their usefulness. If a therapist maintains a strategic mindset—uses the questioning process to strive for a particular outcome—the responses of family members will be constrained by their sense that the therapist is after something. If, on the other hand, the therapist asks circular questions out of genuine curiosity (Cecchin, 1987), as if joining the family in a research expedition regarding their problem, an atmosphere can be created in which the family can arrive at new understandings of their predicament.

Other Contributions. Strategic therapists pioneered the *team approach* to therapy. Originally, the MRI group used teams behind one-way mirrors to help brainstorm strategies, as did the Milan group. Peggy Papp (1980) and her colleagues at the Ackerman Institute brought the team directly into the therapy process by turning the observers into a "Greek chorus" who reacted to events in the session. For example, the team might, for strategic purposes, disagree with the therapist. In witnessing the staged debates between the team and their therapist over what a family should do, family members might feel that both sides of their ambivalence were being represented. Having the team interact openly with the therapist or even with the family during sessions paved the way for later approaches in which the team might enter the treatment room and discuss the family while the family watched (Andersen, 1987).

Jim Alexander was a behaviorist who, out of frustration with the limits of his behavioral orientation, incorporated strategic ideas. The result was *functional family therapy* (Alexander & Parsons, 1982), which, as the name implies, is concerned with the function that family behavior is designed to achieve (see also Chapter 10). Functional family therapists assume that most family behaviors are attempts to become more or less intimate and through *relabeling* (another word for *reframing*) help family members see each other's actions in that benign light. They also help family members set up contingency management programs to help them get the kind of intimacy they want. Functional family therapy represents an interesting blend of strategic and behavioral therapies and, unlike other strategic models, retains the behaviorist ethic of basing interventions on sound research.

EVALUATING THERAPY THEORY AND RESULTS

Communications family therapy wasn't just an application of psychotherapy to families; it was a radically new conceptualization that altered the very nature of imagination. What was new was the focus on the form and impact of communication, rather than the *content*. Communication was described as feedback and a tactic in interpersonal power struggles. In fact, all behavior is communicative.

When communication takes place in a closed system—an individual's fantasies or a family's private conversations—there is little opportunity for objective analysis. Only when someone outside the system provides input can correction occur. Because the rules of family functioning are largely unknown to the family, the best way to examine them is to consult an expert in communication. Today, the precepts of communications theory have been absorbed into the mainstream of family therapy, and its symptom-focused interventions have become the basis of the strategic and solution-focused models.

Strategic therapies reached the height of their popularity in the 1980s. They were clever, prescriptive, and expedient—qualities appreciated by therapists who often felt overwhelmed by the emotionality of families in treatment. Then a backlash set in, and people began criticizing strategic therapy's manipulative aspects. Unfortunately, when communications and strategic therapists were confounded by the anxious inflexibility of some families, they may have exaggerated the irrational power of the family system.

In the 1990s, the strategic approaches described in this chapter were replaced on family therapy's center stage by more collaborative models, but even as the field moves away from an overreliance on technique and manipulation, don't lose sight of valuable aspects of strategic therapy. These include having a clear therapeutic goal, anticipating how families might react to interventions, understanding and tracking sequences of interaction, and the creative use of directives.

Most of the research on the effectiveness of strategic therapy isn't very rigorous. More than any other model in this book, information about strategic therapy is exchanged through the case report format. Nearly all of the articles and books on strategic therapy include at least one description of a successful treatment outcome. Thus, strategic therapy appears to have a great deal of anecdotal support for its efficacy (although people tend not to write about their failed cases).

Some early studies of the outcome of family therapies based on strategic therapy helped fuel its popularity. In their classic study, Langsley, Machotka, and Flomenhaft (1971) found that family crisis therapy, with similarities to the MRI and Haley models, drastically reduced the need for hospitalization. Alexander and Parsons found their functional family therapy to be more effective in treating a group of delinquents than a client-centered family approach, an eclectic-dynamic approach, or a no-treatment control group (Parsons & Alexander, 1973). Stanton, Todd, and associates (1982) demonstrated the effectiveness of combining structural and strategic family therapies for treating heroin addicts. The results were impressive because family therapy resulted in twice as many days of abstinence from heroin than a methadone maintenance program.

In the early 1980s, the Milan associates offered anecdotal case reports of amazing outcomes with anorexia nervosa, schizophrenia, and delinquency (Selvini Palazzoli, Boscolo, Cecchin, & Prata, 1978b, 1980). Later, however, members of the original team expressed reservations about the model and implied that it wasn't

as effective as they originally suggested (Boscolo, 1983; Selvini Palazzoli, 1986; Selvini Palazzoli & Viaro, 1988).

Although the original Milan model appears to have gone the way of the dinosaurs, there are currently two thriving strategic camps: the MRI group on the West Coast and the Washington School started by Haley and Madanes on the East Coast.

What people came to rebel against was the gimmickry of formulaic techniques—but gimmickry wasn't inherent in the strategic models. For example, the MRI's emphasis on reversing attempted solutions that don't work is a sound idea. People *do* stay stuck in ruts as long as they pursue self-defeating strategies. If, in some hands, blocking more-of-the-same solutions resulted in a rote application of reverse psychology, that's not the fault of the cybernetic metaphor but of the way it was applied.

Strategic therapists are currently integrating new ideas and keeping up with the postmodern spirit of the twenty-first century. Haley published a book in which the evolution of his thinking is apparent (Haley, 1996), and a new book on the influence of the MRI on the field was released (Weakland & Ray, 1995). In addition, some authors have integrated MRI strategic concepts with narrative approaches (Eron & Lund, 1993, 1996). It's good to see that strategic thinking is evolving, because even in this era of the nonexpert therapist, there is still room for thoughtful problem-solving strategies and therapeutic direction.

SUMMARY

Communications therapy was one of the first and most influential forms of family treatment. Its theoretical development was based on general systems theory, and the therapy that emerged was a systems approach *par excellence*. Communication was the detectable input and output therapists used to analyze the black box of interpersonal systems.

Another significant idea of communications therapy was that families are rule-governed systems, maintained by homeostatic feedback mechanisms. Negative feedback accounts for the stability of normal families and the inflexibility of dysfunctional ones. Because such families don't have adequate positive feedback mechanisms, they're unable to adjust to changing circumstances.

While there were major differences among the therapeutic strategies of Haley, Jackson, Satir, and Watzlawick, they were all committed to altering destructive patterns of communication. They pursued this goal by direct and indirect means. The direct approach, favored by Satir, sought change by coaching clear communication. This approach could be described as establishing ground rules, or metacommunicational principles, and included such tactics as telling people to speak for themselves and pointing out nonverbal and multilevel channels of communication.

The trouble is, as Haley noted, one of the difficulties of telling patients what to do is that "psychiatric patients are noted for their hesitation about doing what they are told." For this reason, communications therapists began to rely on more indirect strategies, designed to provoke change rather than foster awareness. Telling family members to speak for themselves, for example, may challenge a family rule and therefore meet with resistance. With this realization, communications therapy became a treatment of resistance.

Resistance was treated with a variety of paradoxical directives, known loosely as *therapeutic double binds*. Milton Erickson's technique of prescribing resistance was used as a lever to gain control, as, for example, when a therapist tells family members not to reveal everything in the first session. The same ploy was used to prescribe symptoms, an action that made covert rules explicit, implied that such behavior was voluntary, and put the therapist in control.

Strategic therapy, derived from Ericksonian hypnotherapy and Batesonian cybernetics, developed a body of powerful procedures for treating psychological problems. Strategic approaches vary in the specifics of theory and technique but share a problem-centered, pragmatic focus on changing behavioral sequences, in which therapists take responsibility for solving problems. Insight and understanding are eschewed in favor of directives designed to change the way family members interact.

The MRI model is strictly interactional—observing and intervening into sequences of interaction surrounding a problem rather than speculating about the intentions of the interactants. Haley and Madanes, on the other hand, are interested in motives—Haley mainly in the desire to control others and Madanes in the desire to love and be loved. Unlike the MRI group, Haley and Madanes believe that successful treatment often requires structural change, with an emphasis on improving family hierarchy.

Like Haley, the Milan associates originally saw power in the motives of family members. They tried to understand the elaborate multigenerational games that surrounded symptoms. They designed powerful interventions—positive connotation and rituals—to expose those games and change the meaning of problems. Later, the original group split, with Selvini Palazzoli going through several transformations until her current long-term approach based on family secrets. Cecchin and Boscolo moved away from formulaic interventions, became more interested in the questioning process as a way to help families to new understandings, and in so doing paved the way for family therapy's current interest in conversation and narrative.

RECOMMENDED READINGS

Cecchin, G. 1987. Hypothesizing, circularity and neutrality revisited: An invitation to curiosity. *Family Process.* 26:405–413.

Fisch, R., Weakland, J. H., and Segal, L. 1982. *The tactics of change: Doing therapy briefly.* San Francisco: Jossey-Bass.

Haley, J. 1976. *Problem-solving therapy.* San Francisco: Jossey-Bass.

Haley, J. 1980. *Leaving home.* New York: McGraw-Hill.

Haley, J., and Richeport-Haley, M. 2007. *Directive family therapy.* New York: Haworth Press.

Jackson, D. D. 1961. Interactional psychotherapy. In *Contemporary psychotherapies*, M. T. Stein, ed. New York: Free Press of Glencoe.

Jackson, D. D. 1967. *Therapy, communication and change*. Palo Alto, CA: Science and Behavior Books.

Keim, J. 1998. Strategic therapy. In *Case studies in couple and family therapy*, F. Dattilio, ed. New York: Guilford Press.

Lederer, W., and Jackson, D. D. 1968. *Mirages of marriage*. New York: Norton.

Madanes, C. 1981. *Strategic family therapy*. San Francisco: Jossey-Bass.

Madanes, C. 1984. *Behind the one-way mirror*. San Francisco: Jossey-Bass.

Price, J. 1996. *Power and compassion: Working with difficult adolescents and abused parents*. New York: Guilford Press.

Rabkin, R. 1972. *Strategic psychotherapy*. New York: Basic Books.

Selvini Palazzoli, M., Boscolo, L., Cecchin, G., and Prata, G. 1978. *Paradox and counterparadox*. New York: Jason Aronson.

Tomm, K. 1987. Interventive interviewing: Part 1. Strategizing as a fourth guideline for the therapists. *Family Process*. 26:3–14.

Watzlawick, P., Beavin, J. H., and Jackson, D. D. 1967. *Pragmatics of human communication*. New York: Norton.

Watzlawick, P., Weakland, J., and Fisch, R. 1974. *Change: Principles of problem formation and problem resolution*. New York: Norton.

REFERENCES

Alexander, J., and Parsons, B. 1982. *Functional family therapy*. Monterey, CA: Brooks Cole.

Andersen, T. 1987. The reflecting team: Dialogue and meta-dialogue in clinical work. *Family Process*. 26:415–417.

Bergman, J. 1985. *Fishing for barracuda: Pragmatics of brief systems therapy*. New York: Norton.

Boscolo, L. 1983. Final discussion. In *Psychosocial intervention in schizophrenia: An international view*, H. Stierlin, L. Wynne, and M. Wirsching, eds. Berlin: Springer-Verlag.

Boscolo, L., and Bertrando, P. 1992. The reflexive loop of past, present, and future in systemic therapy and consultation. *Family Process*. 31:119–133.

Boscolo, L., Cecchin, G., Hoffman, L., and Penn, P. 1987. *Milan systemic family therapy*. New York: Basic Books.

Cecchin, G. 1987. Hypothesizing, circularity and neutrality revisited: An invitation to curiosity. *Family Process*. 26:405–413.

Eron, J., and Lund, T. 1993. An approach to how problems evolve and dissolve: Integrating narrative and strategic concepts. *Family Process*. 32:291–309.

Eron, J., and Lund, T. 1996. *Narrative solutions in brief therapy*. New York: Guilford Press.

Fisch, R. 1978. Review of problem-solving therapy, by Jay Haley. *Family Process*. 17:107–110.

Fisch, R., Weakland, J., and Segal, L. 1982. *The tactics of change*. San Francisco: Jossey-Bass.

Gaulier, B., Margerum, J., Price, J. A., and Windell, J. 2007. *Defusing the high-conflict divorce: A treatment guide for working with angry couples*. Atascadero, CA: Impact.

Haley, J. 1963. *Strategies of psychotherapy*. New York: Grune & Stratton.

Haley, J. 1973. *Uncommon therapy*. New York: Norton.

Haley, J. 1976. *Problem-solving therapy*. San Francisco: Jossey-Bass.

Haley, J. 1981. *Reflections on therapy*. Chevy Chase, MD: Family Therapy Institute of Washington, DC.

Haley, J. 1984. *Ordeal therapy*. San Francisco: Jossey-Bass.

Haley, J. 1996. *Learning and teaching therapy*. New York: Guilford Press.

Haley, J., and Richeport-Haley, M. 2007. *Directive family therapy*. New York: Haworth Press. Hoffman, L. 1983. A co-evolutionary framework for systemic family therapy. In *Diagnosis and assessment in family therapy*, J. Hansen and B. Keeney, eds. Rockville, MD: Aspen Systems.

Jackson, D. D. 1965. Family rules: The marital quid pro quo. *Archives of General Psychiatry.* 12:589–594.

Jackson, D. D. 1967. Aspects of conjoint family therapy. In *Family therapy and disturbed families*, G. H. Zuk and I. Boszormenyi-Nagy, eds. Palo Alto, CA: Science and Behavior Books.

Jackson, D. D., and Weakland, J. H. 1961. Conjoint family therapy: Some consideration on theory, technique, and results. *Psychiatry.* 24:30–45.

Keim, J. 1998. Strategic family therapy. In *Case studies in couple and family therapy*, F. Dattilio, ed. New York: Guilford Press.

Keim, J., and Lappin, J. 2002. Structural-strategic marital therapy. In *Clinical handbook of couple therapy*, A. S. Gurman and N. S. Jacobson, eds. New York: Guilford Press.

Langsley, D., Machotka, P., and Flomenhaft, K. 1971. Avoiding mental hospital admission: A follow-up study. *American Journal of Psychiatry.* 127:1391–1394.

Madanes, C. 1981. *Strategic family therapy.* San Francisco: Jossey-Bass.

Madanes, C. 1984. *Behind the one-way mirror.* San Francisco: Jossey-Bass.

Marayuma, M. 1968. The second cybernetics: Deviation-amplifying mutual causal processes. In *Modern systems research for the behavioral scientist*, W. Buckley, ed. Chicago: Aldine.

Papp, P. 1980. The Greek chorus and other techniques of paradoxical therapy. *Family Process.* 19:45–57.

Papp, P. 1983. *The process of change.* New York: Guilford Press.

Parsons, B., and Alexander, J. 1973. Short-term family intervention: A therapy outcome study. *Journal of Consulting and Clinical Psychology.* 41:195–201.

Penn, P. 1982. Circular questioning. *Family Process.* 21:267–280.

Penn, P. 1985. Feed-forward: Further questioning, future maps. *Family Process.* 24:299–310.

Price, J. 1996. *Power and compassion: Working with difficult adolescents and abused parents.* New York: Guilford Press.

Rabkin, R. 1977. *Inner and outer space.* New York: Basic Books.

Ruesch, J., and Bateson, G. 1951. *Communication: The social matrix of psychiatry.* New York: Norton.

Selvini, M. 1993. Major mental disorders, distorted reality and family secrets. Unpublished manuscript.

Selvini Palazzoli, M. 1981. *Self-starvation: From the intrapsychic to the transpersonal approach to anorexia nervosa.* New York: Jason Aronson.

Selvini Palazzoli, M. 1986. Towards a general model of psychotic games. *Journal of Marital and Family Therapy.* 12:339–349.

Selvini Palazzoli, M., and Viaro, M. 1988. The anorectic process in the family: A six-stage model as a guide for individual therapy. *Family Process.* 27:129–148.

Selvini Palazzoli, M., Boscolo, L., Cecchin, G., and Prata, G. 1978a. A ritualized prescription in family therapy: Odd days and even days. *Journal of Marriage and Family Counseling.* 4:3–9.

Selvini Palazzoli, M., Boscolo, L., Cecchin, G., and Prata, G. 1978b. *Paradox and counterparadox.* New York: Jason Aronson.

Selvini Palazzoli, M., Boscolo, L., Cecchin, G., and Prata, G. 1980. Hypothesizing—circularity—neutrality: Three guidelines for the conductor of the session. *Family Process.* 19:3–12.

Shoham, V., and Rohrbaugh, M. J. 2002. Brief strategic couple therapy. In *Clinical handbook of couple therapy*, A. S. Gurman and N. S. Jacobson, eds. New York: Guilford Press.

Stanton, D., Todd, T., and Associates. 1982. *The family therapy of drug abuse and addiction.* New York: Guilford Press.

Tomm, K. 1984a. One perspective on the Milan systemic approach: Part I. Overview of development, theory and practice. *Journal of Martial and Family Therapy.* 10:113–125.

Tomm, K. 1984b. One perspective on the Milan systemic approach: Part II. Description of session format, interviewing style and interventions. *Journal of Marital and Family Therapy.* 10:253–271.

Tomm, K. 1987a. Interventive interviewing: Part I. Strategizing as a fourth guideline for the therapist. *Family Process.* 26:3–13.

Tomm, K. 1987b. Interventive interviewing: Part II. Reflexive questioning as a means to enable self-healing. *Family Process.* 26:167–184.

Watzlawick, P., Beavin, J., and Jackson, D. 1967. *Pragmatics of human communication.* New York: Norton.

Watzlawick, P., Weakland, J., and Fisch, R. 1974. *Change: Principles of problem formation and problem resolution.* New York: Norton.

Weakland, J., and Fisch, R. 1992. Brief therapy—MRI style. In *The first session in brief therapy*, S. H.

Budman, N. F. Hoyt, and S. Friedman, eds. New York: Guilford Press.

Weakland, J., and Ray, W., eds. 1995. *Propagations: Thirty years of influence from the Mental Research Institute.* Binghamton, NY: Haworth Press.

Structural Family Therapy

7

The Organization of Family Life

One of the reasons family therapy can be difficult is that families often appear as collections of individuals who affect each other in powerful but unpredictable ways. Structural family therapy offers a framework that brings order and meaning to those transactions. The consistent patterns of family behavior are what allow us to consider that they have a structure, although, of course, only in a functional sense. The emotional boundaries and coalitions that make up a family's structure are abstractions; nevertheless, using the concept of family structure enables therapists to intervene in a systematic and organized way.

Families who seek help are usually concerned about a specific problem. It might be a child who misbehaves or a couple who doesn't get along. Family therapists typically look beyond the specifics of those problems to the family's attempts to solve them. This leads to the dynamics of interaction. The misbehaving child might have parents who scold but never reward him. The couple may be caught up in a pursuer–distancer dynamic, or they might be unable to talk without arguing.

What structural family therapy adds to the equation is a recognition of the overall organization that supports and maintains those interactions. The "parents who scold" might turn out to be two partners who undermine each other because one is wrapped up in the child while the other is an angry outsider. If so, attempts to encourage effective discipline are likely to fail unless the structural problem is addressed and the parents develop a real partnership. Similarly, a couple who don't get along may not be able to improve their relationship until they create a boundary between themselves and intrusive children or in-laws.

The discovery that families are organized in **subsystems** with **boundaries** regulating the contact family members have with each other turned out to be one of the defining insights of family therapy. Perhaps equally important, though, was the introduction of the technique of **enactment,** in which family members are encouraged to deal directly with each other in sessions, permitting the therapist to observe and modify their interactions.

SKETCHES OF LEADING FIGURES

When he first burst onto the scene, Salvador Minuchin's galvanizing impact was as a master of technique. His most lasting contribution, however, was a theory of family structure and a set of guidelines to organize therapeutic techniques.

Minuchin was born and raised in Argentina. He served as a physician in the Israeli army and then came to the United States, where he trained in child psychiatry with Nathan Ackerman in New York. After completing his studies, Minuchin returned to Israel in 1952 to work with displaced children. He moved back to the United States in 1954 to begin psychoanalytic training at the William Alanson White Institute, where he studied the interpersonal psychiatry of Harry Stack Sullivan. After leaving the White Institute, Minuchin took a job at the Wiltwyck School for delinquent boys, where he suggested to his staff that they start seeing families.

At Wiltwyck, Minuchin and his colleagues—Dick Auerswald, Charlie King, Braulio Montalvo, and Clara Rabinowitz—taught themselves to do family therapy, inventing it as they went along. To do so, they built a one-way mirror and took turns observing each other work. In 1962, Minuchin made a hajj to what was then

the mecca of family therapy, Palo Alto. There, he met Jay Haley and began a friendship that blossomed into an extraordinarily fertile collaboration.

The success of Minuchin's work with families at Wiltwyck led to a groundbreaking book, *Families of the Slums* (1967), which first outlined the structural model. Minuchin's reputation as a virtuoso therapist grew, and he became the director of the Philadelphia Child Guidance Clinic in 1965. The clinic then consisted of less than a dozen staff members. From this modest beginning, Minuchin created one of the largest and most prestigious child guidance clinics in the world.

Among Minuchin's colleagues in Philadelphia were Braulio Montalvo, Jay Haley, Bernice Rosman, Harry Aponte, Carter Umbarger, Marianne Walters, Charles Fishman, Cloe Madanes, and Stephen Greenstein, all of whom had a role in shaping structural family therapy. By the 1970s, structural family therapy had become the most widely practiced of all systems of family therapy.

In 1976, Minuchin stepped down as director of the Philadelphia Child Guidance Clinic but stayed on as head of training until 1981. After leaving Philadelphia, Minuchin started his own center in New York, where he continued to practice and teach until 1996, when he retired and moved to Boston. Although he retired (again) and moved to Boca Raton, Florida, in 2005, Dr. Minuchin still travels and teaches throughout the world.

Like players on a team with a superstar, some of Minuchin's colleagues are not as well known as they might be. Foremost among these is Braulio Montalvo, one of the underrated geniuses of family therapy. Born and raised in Puerto

Salvador Minuchin's structural model is the most influential approach to family therapy throughout the world.

Rico, Montalvo, like Minuchin, has always been committed to treating minority families. Like Minuchin, he is also a brilliant therapist, though he favors a gentler, more supportive approach.

Following Minuchin's retirement, the center in New York was renamed the Minuchin Center for the Family in his honor, and the torch has been passed to a new generation. The staff of leading teachers at the Minuchin Center now includes Amy Begel, Patricia Dowds, Ema Genijovich, David Greenan, Richard Holm, George Simon, and Wai-Yung Lee. Their task is to keep the leading center of structural family therapy in the forefront of the field without the charismatic leadership of its progenitor.

Among Minuchin's other prominent students are Jorge Colapinto, now at the Ackerman Institute in New York; Michael Nichols, who teaches at the College of William and Mary; Jay Lappin, who works with child welfare for the state of Delaware; and Charles Fishman, in private practice in Philadelphia.

THEORETICAL FORMULATIONS

Beginners often get bogged down in the content of family problems because they don't have a blueprint to help them see the patterns of family dynamics. Structural family therapy offers such a blueprint. Three constructs are the essential components of structural family theory: *structure*, *subsystems*, and *boundaries*.

It's easy to understand what's meant by the structure of a house: it's the way the components of the house are organized, how many rooms there are, where the rooms are located, how they are connected, and so on. The family that lives in the house is also organized, but this structure is a little harder to define.

Family structure refers to the way a family is organized into subsystems and how the interaction among those subsystems is regulated by boundaries. The *process* of a family's interaction is like the patterns of conversation at the dinner table. The *structure* of the family is like where family members sit in relation to one another. Who sits next to who makes it easier to interact with some people and less so with others.

To grasp a family's structure you must look beyond their interactions to the organizational framework within which they occur, and you must keep in mind that what goes on in any part of a family is affected by the organization of the whole system. Now let's consider how this organizational structure comes about.

As family transactions are repeated, they foster expectations that establish enduring patterns. Once patterns are established, family members use only a fraction of the full range of behavior available to them. The first time the baby cries or a teenager misses the school bus, it's not clear who will do what. Will the load be shared? Will there be a quarrel? Will one person get stuck with most of the work? Soon, however, patterns are set, roles assigned, and things take on a sameness and predictability. "Who's going to . . . ?" becomes "She'll probably . . ." and then "She always. . . ."

Family structure is reinforced by the expectations that establish rules in a family. For example, a rule such as "Family members should always look out for one another" will be manifest in various ways depending on the context and who is involved. If a boy gets into a fight with another boy in the neighborhood, his mother will go to the neighbors to complain. If a teenager has to wake up early for school, her mother wakes her. If a husband is too hung over to get to work in the morning, his wife calls to say he has the flu. If the parents have an argument, their kids interrupt. The parents are so preoccupied with the doings of their children that it keeps them from spending time alone together. These sequences are *isomorphic*: They're structured. Modifying any of them may not change the basic structure, but altering the underlying structure will have ripple effects on all family transactions.

Family structure is shaped partly by universal and partly by idiosyncratic constraints. For example, all families have some kind of hierarchical structure, with adults and children having different amounts of authority. Family members also tend to have reciprocal and complementary functions. Often these become so ingrained that their origin is forgotten and they are presumed necessary rather than optional. If a young mother, burdened by the demands of her infant, gets upset and complains to her husband, he can respond in various ways. Perhaps he'll move closer and share the demands of childrearing. This creates a united parental team. On the other hand, if he decides that his wife is "depressed," she may end up in psychotherapy to get the emotional support she needs. This creates a structure where the father remains distant from the mother, and she has to turn outside the family for sympathy. Whatever the pattern, it tends to be self-perpetuating. Although alternatives are available, families are unlikely to consider them until changing circumstances produce stress in the system.

Families don't walk in and hand you their structural patterns as if they were bringing an apple to the teacher. What they bring is chaos and confusion. You have to discover the subtext, and you have to be careful that it's accurate, not imposed but discovered. Two things are necessary: a theoretical system that explains structure and seeing the family in action. Knowing that a family is a single-parent family or that the parents are having trouble with a middle child doesn't tell you what their structure is. Structure becomes evident only when you observe the actual interactions of family members.

Consider the following. A mother calls to complain of misbehavior in her fifteen-year-old son. She is asked to bring her husband, son, and their three other children to the first session. When they arrive, the mother begins to describe a series of minor ways in which the son is disobedient. He interrupts to say that she's always on his case; he never gets a break from his mother.

This spontaneous bickering reveals an intense involvement between mother and son—a mutual preoccupation no less intense simply because it's conflictual. This sequence doesn't tell the whole story, however, because it doesn't include the father or the other children. They must be engaged to observe their role in the family structure. If the father sides with his wife but seems unconcerned, then it may be that the mother's preoccupation with her son is related to her husband's lack of involvement. If the younger children tend to agree with their mother and describe their brother as bad, then it becomes clear that all the children are close to the mother—close and obedient up to a point, then close and disobedient.

Families are differentiated into *subsystems* based on generation, gender, and function, which are demarcated by interpersonal *boundaries*, invisible barriers that regulate contact with others. A rule forbidding phone calls at dinnertime establishes a boundary that shields the family from intrusion. If children are permitted to freely interrupt their parents' conversations, the boundary separating the generations is eroded and the couple's relationship is subverted to parenting. Subsystems that aren't adequately protected by boundaries limit the development of relationship skills. If parents always step in to settle arguments between their children, the children won't learn to fight their own battles.

Interpersonal boundaries vary from rigid to diffuse (Figure 7.1). Rigid boundaries are restrictive and permit little contact with outside subsystems, resulting in *disengagement*. Disengaged subsystems are independent but isolated. On the plus side, this fosters autonomy. On the other hand, disengagement limits affection and support. Disengaged families must come under extreme stress before they mobilize assistance.

Enmeshed subsystems offer closeness and support, but at the expense of independent competence. Enmeshed parents spend a lot of time with their kids and do a lot for them; but children enmeshed with their parents become de-

Figure **7.1**   Boundaries

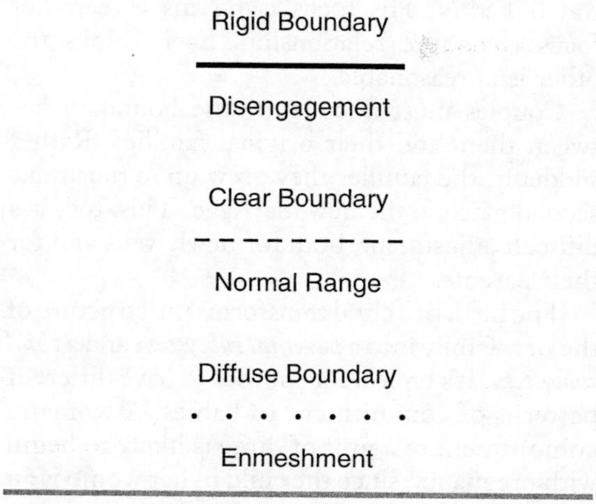

Rigid Boundary

_____

Disengagement

Clear Boundary

- - - - - - - -

Normal Range

Diffuse Boundary

· · · · · · ·

Enmeshment

pendent. They're less comfortable by themselves and may have trouble relating to people outside the family.

Minuchin described some of the features of family subsystems in his most accessible work, *Families and Family Therapy* (Minuchin, 1974). Families begin when two people join together to form a couple. Two people in love agree to share their lives and futures, but a period of often difficult adjustment is required before they can complete the transition from courtship to a functional partnership. They must learn to *accommodate* to each other's needs and styles of interaction. He learns to accommodate her wish to be kissed hello and goodbye. She learns to leave him alone with his morning paper and coffee. These little arrangements, multiplied a thousand times, may be accomplished easily or only after intense struggle.

The couple must also develop complementary patterns of mutual support. Some patterns are transitory and may later change—perhaps, for instance, one works while the other completes school. Other patterns are more lasting. Exaggerated complementary roles can detract from individual growth; moderate complemen-

tarity enables couples to divide functions to support and enrich each other. When one has the flu, the other takes over. One's permissiveness may be balanced by the other's strictness. One's fiery disposition may help to melt the other's reserve. Complementary patterns exist in all couples. They become problematic when they are so rigid that they create a dysfunctional subsystem.

The spouse subsystem must also develop a boundary that separates them from parents, children, and other outsiders. All too often, husband and wife give up the space they need for supporting each other when children are born.

A clear boundary enables children to interact with their parents but excludes them from the spouse subsystem. Parents and children eat together, play together, and share much of each others' lives—but there are some spouse functions that need not be shared. Husband and wife are sustained as a loving couple and enhanced as parents if they have time to be alone together—to talk, to go out to dinner occasionally, to fight, and to make love. Unhappily, the clamorous demands of children often make parents lose sight of their need to maintain a boundary around their relationship.

In addition to maintaining privacy for a couple, a clear boundary supports a **hierarchical structure** in which parents occupy a position of leadership. All too often this hierarchy is disrupted by a child-centered ethos, which influences helping professionals as well as parents. Parents enmeshed with their children argue with them about who's in charge and misguidedly share—or shirk—responsibility for making parental decisions.

In *Institutionalizing Madness* (Elizur & Minuchin, 1989), Minuchin makes a compelling case for a systems view of family problems that extends beyond the family to encompass the entire community. As Minuchin points out, unless therapists learn to look beyond the limited slice of ecology where they work to the larger social structures within which their work is embedded, their efforts may amount to little more than spinning wheels.

NORMAL FAMILY DEVELOPMENT

What distinguishes normal families isn't the absence of problems but a functional structure for dealing with them. All couples must learn to adjust to each other, raise their children, deal with their parents, earn a living, and fit into their communities. The nature of these struggles changes with developmental stages and situational crises.

When two people join to form a couple, the structural requirements for the new union are **accommodation** and **boundary making**. The first priority is mutual accommodation to manage the myriad details of everyday living. Each partner tries to organize the relationship along familiar lines and pressures the other to comply. They must agree on major issues, such as where to live and if and when to have children. Less obvious, but equally important, they must coordinate daily rituals, like what to watch on television, what to eat for supper, when to go to bed, and what to do there.

In accommodating to each other, a couple must also negotiate the nature of the boundary between them as well as the boundary separating them from the outside. A diffuse boundary exists between a couple if they call each other at work frequently, if neither has their own friends or independent activities, and if they come to view themselves only as a pair rather than as two separate personalities. On the other hand, they've established a rigid boundary if they spend little time together, have separate bedrooms, take separate vacations, have different checking accounts, and are more invested in careers or outside relationships than in their relationship.

Each partner tends to be more comfortable with the level of proximity that existed in his or her own family. Because these expectations differ, a struggle ensues that may be the most of the new union. He wants to play golf with the boys; she feels deserted. She wants to talk; he wants to watch ESPN. His focus is on his career; her focus is on the relationship. Each thinks the other is unreasonable.

Couples must also define the boundary between them and their original families. Rather suddenly, the families they grew up in must take second place to the new marriage. This, too, is a difficult adjustment, both for newlyweds and for their parents.

The birth of a child transforms the structure of the new family into a *parental subsystem* and a *child subsystem*. It's typical for spouses to have different patterns of commitment to babies. A woman's commitment to a unit of three is likely to begin with pregnancy, since the child in her womb is an unavoidable reality. Her husband, on the other hand, may only begin to feel like a father when the child is born. Many men don't accept the role of father until their infants are old enough to respond to them. Thus, even in healthy families, children bring great potential for stress and conflict. A mother's life is usually more radically transformed than a father's. She sacrifices a great deal and now needs more support from her husband. The husband, meanwhile, continues his job, and the new baby is far less of a disruption. Though he may try to support his wife, he's likely to resent some of her demands.

Children require different styles of parenting at different ages. Infants primarily need care and feeding. Children need guidance and control, and adolescents need independence and responsibility. Good parenting for a two-year-old may be inappropriate for a five-year-old or a fourteen-year-old.

Minuchin (1974) warns therapists not to mistake growing pains for pathology. Normal families experience anxiety and disruption as their members grow and change. Many families seek help at transitional stages, and therapists should keep in mind that they may simply be in the process of modifying their structure to adjust to new circumstances.

DEVELOPMENT OF BEHAVIOR DISORDERS

Modifications in structure are required when a family or one of its members encounters external pressures (a parent is laid off, the family moves) and when developmental transitions are reached (a child reaches adolescence, parents retire). Healthy families accommodate to changed circumstances; less-adaptive families increase the rigidity of structures that are no longer functional.

In disengaged families, boundaries are rigid and the family fails to mobilize support when it's needed. Disengaged parents may be unaware that a child is depressed or experiencing difficulties at school until the problem is advanced.

A single mother recently brought her twelve-year-old son to the clinic after discovering that he had missed two weeks of school. *Two weeks!* thought the therapist; that's a long time not to know your child's been skipping school. A structural perspective would make two important points. First, the obvious disengagement between this mother and child is no more significant than the disengagement between the mother and school authorities. Second, a structural analysis might help to get past blaming this woman for failing to know what was going on in her son's life. If she's disengaged from her son, what is occupying her elsewhere? Maybe the financial burden of single parenthood is overwhelming. Maybe she's still grief stricken over the death of her husband. The point to remember is that if someone is disengaged in one relationship, she is likely to be preoccupied elsewhere.

In enmeshed families, boundaries are diffuse and family members become dependent on one another. Intrusive parents create difficulties by stunting the development of their children and interfering with their ability to solve their own problems.

In their book of case studies, *Family Healing*, Minuchin and Nichols (1993) describe a common example of enmeshment as a father jumps in to settle minor arguments between his two boys—"as though the siblings were Cain and Abel, and fraternal jealousy might lead to murder" (p. 149). The problem, of course, is that if parents always interrupt their children's quarrels, the children won't learn to fight their own battles.

Although we may speak of enmeshed and disengaged families, it's more accurate to describe particular subsystems as being enmeshed or disengaged. In fact, enmeshment and disengagement tend to be reciprocal, so that a father who's overly involved with his work is likely to be less involved with his family. A frequently encountered pattern is the enmeshed mother/disengaged father syndrome—"the signature arrangement of the troubled middle-class family" (Minuchin & Nichols, 1993, p. 121).

Feminists have criticized the notion of an enmeshed mother/disengaged father syndrome because they reject the stereotypical division of labor (instrumental role for the father, expressive role for the mother) and because they worry about blaming mothers for an arrangement that is culturally sanctioned. Both concerns are valid. But stereotyping and blame are due to insensitive application of these ideas, not to the ideas themselves. Skewed relationships, whatever the reasons for them, can be problematic, though no one individual should be expected to do all the changing.

Hierarchies can be rigid and unfair or weak and ineffective. In the first case, children may find themselves unprotected because of a lack of guidance; in the second, their growth as individuals may be impaired and power struggles may ensue. Just as a functional hierarchy is necessary for a family's stability, flexibility is necessary for it to adapt to change.

The most common expression of fear of change is *conflict avoidance*, when family members shy away from addressing their disagreements. Disengaged people avoid conflict by minimizing contact; enmeshed people avoid conflict by denying differences or by constant bickering, which allows them to vent feelings without resolving issues.

Structural therapists use a few simple symbols to diagram structural problems, and these diagrams suggest what changes may be needed. Figure 7.2 shows some of the symbols used to diagram family structure.

One problem often seen by family therapists arises when parents who are unable to resolve conflicts between them divert the focus of concern onto a child. Instead of worrying themselves, they worry about the child (Figure 7.3). Although this reduces the strain on father (F) and mother (M), it victimizes the child (C).

An equally common pattern is for the parents to argue through the children. Father says Mother is too permissive; she says he's too strict. He may withdraw, causing her to criticize his lack of concern, which in turn makes him with-

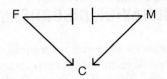

Figure **7.3**   Scapegoating as a Means of Detouring Conflict

draw further. The enmeshed mother responds to children's needs with excessive concern. The disengaged father may not respond at all. Both may be critical of the other's way, but both perpetuate the other's behavior with their own. The result is a **cross-generational coalition** between mother and child (Figure 7.4).

Some families function well when the children are young but are unable to adjust to an older child's need for discipline and control. Young children in enmeshed families (Figure 7.5) receive wonderful care: Their parents give them lots of attention. Although such parents may be too tired from caring for the children to have much time for each other, the system may be moderately successful.

If, however, these doting parents don't teach their children to obey rules and respect authority, the children may be unprepared to negotiate their entrance into school. Used to getting their own way, they may be resistant to authority. Several possible consequences of this situation may bring the family into treatment. The children

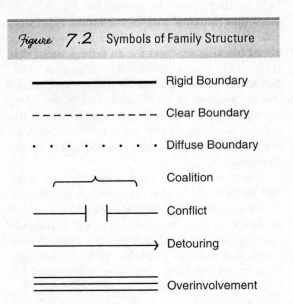

Figure **7.2**   Symbols of Family Structure

——————————— Rigid Boundary

– – – – – – – – – – Clear Boundary

· · · · · · · · · Diffuse Boundary

Coalition

——— | | ——— Conflict

————————→ Detouring

Overinvolvement

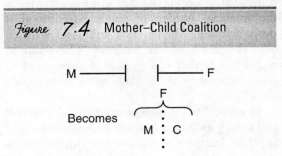

Figure **7.4**   Mother–Child Coalition

M ——— | | ——— F

Becomes

Figure 7.5 Parents Enmeshed with Children

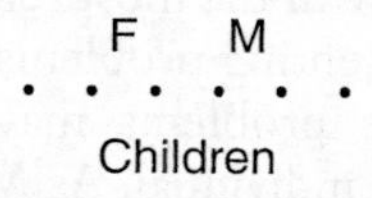

F   M
· · · · ·
Children

may be reluctant to go to school, and their fears may be reinforced by "understanding" parents who permit them to stay at home (Figure 7.6). Such a case may be labeled as school phobia and may become entrenched if the parents permit the children to remain at home for more than a few days.

Alternatively, the children of such a family may go to school, but since they haven't learned to accommodate others, they may be rejected by their schoolmates. In other cases, children enmeshed with their parents become discipline problems at school, in which case school authorities may initiate counseling.

A major upheaval that requires structural adjustment occurs when divorced or widowed spouses remarry. Such *blended families* either readjust their boundaries or soon experience transitional conflicts. When a woman divorces, she and the children must first learn to readjust to a structure that establishes a clear boundary separating the divorced spouses but still permits contact between father and children; then if she remarries, the family must readjust to functioning with a new husband and step-

Figure 7.6 School Phobia

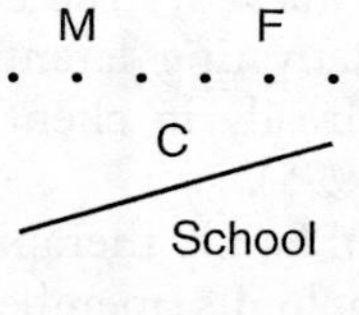

M   F
· · · · ·
C
School

father (Figure 7.7). Sometimes it's hard for a mother and children to allow a stepfather to participate as a partner in the new parental subsystem. Mother and children have long since established transactional rules and learned to accommodate each other. The new parent may be treated as an outsider who's supposed to learn the right way of doing things, rather than as a new partner who will give as well as receive ideas about childrearing (Figure 7.8).

The more the mother and children insist on maintaining their familiar patterns without including the stepfather, the more frustrated and angry he'll become. The result may lead to child abuse or chronic arguing between the parents. The sooner such families enter treatment, the easier it is to help them adjust to the transition.

An important aspect of structural family problems is that symptoms in one member reflect not only that person's interactions but also other relationships in the family. If Johnny, age sixteen, is depressed, it's helpful to know that he's enmeshed with his mother. Discovering that she demands absolute obedience from him and

Figure 7.7 Divorce and Remarriage

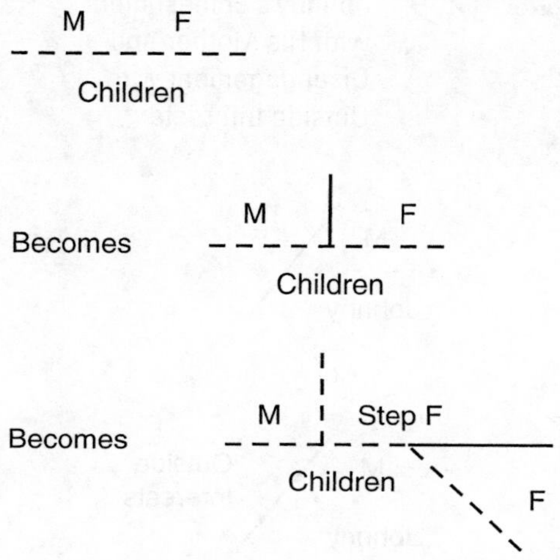

M   F
- - - - - - - -
Children

Becomes

M | F
- - - - | - - - -
Children

Becomes

M | Step F
- - - | - - - - - - -
Children   F

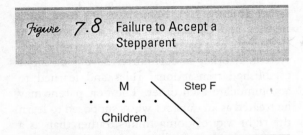

Figure **7.8**   Failure to Accept a Stepparent

refuses to accept independent thinking or outside relationships helps to explain his depression (Figure 7.9). But that's only one segment of the family system.

Why is the mother enmeshed with her son? Perhaps she's disengaged from her husband. Perhaps she's a widow who hasn't made new friends. Helping Johnny resolve his depression may best be accomplished by helping his mother satisfy her need for closeness with other adults in her life.

Because problems are a function of the entire family structure, it's important to include the whole group for assessment, but sometimes even seeing the whole family isn't enough. The family may not always be the complete or most relevant context. A mother's depression might be due

Figure **7.9**   Johnny's Enmeshment with His Mother and Disengagement with Outside Interests

more to her relationships at work than at home. A son's problems at school might be due more to the structural context at school than to the one in the family. In such instances, structural family therapists work with the most relevant context to alleviate the presenting problems.

Finally, some problems may be treated as problems of the individual. As Minuchin (1974) has written, "Pathology may be inside the patient, in his social context, or in the feedback between them" (p. 9). Elsewhere, Minuchin (Minuchin, Rosman, & Baker, 1978) referred to the danger of "denying the individual while enthroning the system" (p. 91). While interviewing a family to see how the parents deal with their children, a careful clinician may notice that one child has a neurological problem or a learning disability. These problems need to be identified and appropriate referrals made. Usually when a child has trouble in school, there's a problem in the family or school setting—usually, but not always.

GOALS OF THERAPY

Structural therapists believe that problems are maintained by dysfunctional family organization. Therefore, therapy is directed at altering family structure so that the family can solve its problems.

The idea that family problems are embedded in dysfunctional family structures has led to the criticism of structural family therapy as pathologizing. Critics see structural maps of dysfunctional organization as portraying a pathological core in client families. This isn't true. Structural problems are viewed as a failure to adjust to changing circumstances. Far from seeing families as inherently flawed, structural therapists see their work as activating latent adaptive structures that are already in client families' repertoires (Simon, 1995).

The structural family therapist joins the family system to help its members change their structure. By altering boundaries and realigning subsystems, the therapist changes the behavior and experience of each family member. The therapist doesn't solve problems; that's the family's job. The therapist helps modify the family's functioning so that family members can solve their own problems.

Although every family is unique, there are common problems and typical structural goals. Most important is the creation of an effective hierarchy. Parents are expected to be in charge, not to relate as equals to their children. Another common goal is to help parents function together as an executive subsystem. When there is only one parent or when there are several children, one or more of the oldest children may be encouraged to become a parental assistant. But these children's needs must not be neglected, either.

With enmeshed families, the goal is to differentiate individuals and subsystems by strengthening the boundaries around them. With disengaged families, the goal is to increase contact by making boundaries more permeable.

CONDITIONS FOR BEHAVIOR CHANGE

Structural therapy changes behavior by opening alternative patterns of interaction that can modify family structure. It's not a matter of creating new structures but of activating dormant ones. When new transactional patterns become regularly repeated and predictably effective, they will stabilize a new and more functional structure.

The therapist produces change by **joining** the family, probing for areas of flexibility, and then activating dormant structural alternatives. Joining gets the therapist into the family; *accommodating* to their style gives him or her leverage; and *restructuring* maneuvers transform the family structure. If the therapist remains an outsider or uses interventions that are too dystonic, the family will reject him or her. If the therapist becomes too much a part of the family

or uses interventions that are too syntonic, the family will assimilate the interventions into previous transactional patterns. In either case, there will be no structural change.

To join a family, the therapist must convey acceptance of family members and respect for their way of doing things. If parents come for help with a child's problems, the therapist doesn't begin by asking for the child's opinion. This would convey a lack of respect for the parents. Only after the therapist has successfully joined with a family is it wise to attempt restructuring—the often dramatic confrontations that challenge families and encourage them to change.

The first task is to understand the family's view of their problems. The therapist does this by tracking their formulations in the words they use to explain them and in the behavior with which they demonstrate them. The family therapist then *reframes* these formulations into one based on an understanding of family structure.

What makes structural family therapy unique is that it uses **enactments** within therapy sessions to bring about the reframing. This is the *sine qua non* of structural family therapy: observing and modifying the structure of family transactions in the immediate context of the session. Structural therapists work with what they see, not what family members describe.

There are two types of in-session interactions on which structural therapy focuses—*enactments* and *spontaneous behavior sequences*. An enactment occurs when the therapist stimulates the family to demonstrate how they handle a particular problem. Enactments commonly begin when the therapist suggests that specific subgroups begin to discuss a particular issue. As they do so, the therapist observes the family process. Working with enactments requires three operations. First, the therapist defines or recognizes a problematic sequence. For example, the therapist observes that when the mother talks to her daughter, they talk as peers, and the little brother gets left out. Second, the therapist directs an enactment. For example, the therapist might say to the mother,

"Talk this over with your kids." Third and most important, the therapist must guide the family to modify the enactment. If the mother talks to her children in such a way that she doesn't take responsibility for major decisions, the therapist must guide her to do so as the family continues the enactment. All the therapist's moves should create new options for the family, options for more productive interactions.

Once an enactment breaks down, the therapist intervenes in one of two ways: commenting on what went wrong or pushing them to keep going. For example, if a father responds to the suggestion to talk with his twelve-year-old daughter about how she's feeling by berating her, the therapist could say to the father, "Congratulations." The father then might ask, "What do you mean?" The therapist could respond, "Congratulations. You win; she loses." Or the therapist could simply nudge the transaction by saying to the father, "Good, keep talking, but help her express her feelings more. She's still a little girl; she needs your help."

In addition to working with enactments,

structural therapists are alert to spontaneous sequences that illustrate family structure. Creating enactments is like directing a play; working with spontaneous sequences is like focusing a spotlight on the action that's already occurring. By observing and modifying such sequences early in therapy, therapists can avoid getting bogged down in a family's usual nonproductive way of doing business.

An experienced therapist develops hunches about family structure even before the first interview. For example, if a family is coming in because of a hyperactive child, it's possible to guess something about the family structure and something about sequences that may occur as the session begins, because hyperactive behavior is often a function of a child's enmeshment with the mother. Mother's relationship with the child may be a product of a lack of hierarchical differentiation within the family; that is, parents and children relate to each other as peers. Furthermore, the mother's overinvolvement with the hyperactive child is likely to be both a result and a cause of emotional distance from her husband.

Structural therapists emphasize the need for parents to maintain a clear hierarchical position of authority.

Knowing that this is a common pattern, the therapist can anticipate that early in the first session, the hyperactive child will begin to misbehave and that the mother will be ineffective in dealing with this misbehavior. Armed with this informed guess the therapist can spotlight such a sequence as soon as it occurs. If the hyperactive child begins to run around the room and the mother protests but does nothing effective, the therapist might say, "I see that your child feels free to ignore you." This challenge may push the mother to behave in a more competent manner. Nonetheless, a hypothesis is only a hypothesis.

THERAPY

Assessment

A structural assessment is based on the assumption that a family's difficulties often reflect problems in the way the family is organized. It is assumed that if the organization shifts, the problem will shift.

Structural therapists make assessments by joining with the family to build an alliance and then setting the family system in motion through the use of enactments, in-session dialogues that permit the therapist to observe how family members interact. Suppose, for example, a young woman complains of obsessional indecisiveness. In responding to the therapist's questions during an initial meeting with the family, the young woman becomes indecisive and glances at her father. He speaks up to clarify what she was having trouble explaining. Now the daughter's indecisiveness can be linked to the father's helpfulness, suggesting a pattern of enmeshment. When the therapist asks the parents to discuss their daughter's problems, they have trouble talking without becoming reactive and the discussion doesn't last long. This suggests disengagement between the parents, which may be related (as cause and effect) to enmeshment between parent and child.

Notice how the structural assessment extends beyond the presenting problem to include the whole family and to the assumption that families with problems may have some kind of underlying structural problem. However, it's important to note that structural therapists make no assumptions about how families *should be* organized. Single-parent families can be perfectly functional, as can families with two mommies or daddies, or indeed any other family variation. It is the fact that a family seeks therapy for a problem they have been unable to solve that gives a therapist license to assume that something about the way they are organized may not be working for them.

Making an assessment is best done by focusing on the presenting problem and then exploring the family's response to it. Consider the case of a thirteen-year-old girl whose parents complain that she lies. The first question might be "Who is she lying to?" Let's say the answer is both parents. The next question would be "How good are the parents at detecting when the daughter is lying?" And then, less innocently "Which parent is better at detecting the daughter's lies?" Perhaps it turns out to be the mother. In fact, let's say the mother is obsessed with detecting the daughter's lies—most of which have to do with seeking independence in ways that raise the mother's anxiety. Thus, a worried mother and a disobedient daughter are locked in struggle over growing up that excludes the father.

To carry this assessment further, a structural therapist would explore the relationship between the parents. The assumption would not, however, be that the child's problems are the result of marital problems but simply that the mother–daughter relationship might be related to the relationship between the parents. Perhaps the parents got along famously until their first child approached adolescence, and then the mother began to worry more than the father. Whatever the case, the assessment would also involve talking with the parents about growing up in their own families in order to explore how their pasts helped shape the way they react to things now.

Dr. Minuchin and his colleagues recently wrote a book in which the process of assessment is organized in four steps (Minuchin, Nichols, & Lee, 2007). The first step is to ask questions about the presenting complaint until family members begin to see that the problem goes beyond the symptom bearer to include the entire family. The second step is to help family members see how their interactions may inadvertently be perpetuating the presenting problem. The third step is a brief exploration of the past, focusing on how the adults in the family came to develop the perspectives that now influence their problematic interactions. The fourth step is to explore options that family members can take to interact in more productive ways that will create a shift in the family structure and help resolve the presenting complaint.

Therapeutic Techniques

In *Families and Family Therapy*, Minuchin (1974) taught family therapists to see what they were looking at. Through the lens of structural family theory, previously puzzling family interactions suddenly swam into focus. This enormously successful book not only taught us to see *enmeshment* and *disengagement* but also let us hope that changing them was just a matter of *joining*, *enactment*, and *unbalancing*. Minuchin made changing families look simple. It isn't.

Like the field itself, structural family therapy has evolved over the years. Today's practitioners still use the patented confrontations ("Who's the sheriff in this family?"), but there is a greater emphasis on helping families understand their organization and less of the combative flavor that sometimes characterized how therapists worked thirty years ago. What's important to keep in mind is that structural family therapy isn't a set of techniques; it's a way of looking at families.

In the remainder of this section, we will present the classic outlines of structural family technique, with the caveat that once therapists master the basics of structural theory, they must learn to translate the approach in a way that suits their own personal style.

In *Families and Family Therapy*, Minuchin (1974) listed three overlapping phases in the process of structural family therapy. The therapist (1) joins the family in a position of leadership; (2) maps their underlying structure; and (3) intervenes to transform this structure. This program is simple, in the sense that it follows a clear plan, but complicated because of the endless variety of family patterns.

If a therapist's interventions are to be effective, they cannot be preplanned or rehearsed. Good therapists are more than technicians. The strategy of therapy, on the other hand, must be organized. In general, structural family therapy follows these steps:

1. Joining and accommodating
2. Enactment
3. Structural mapping
4. Highlighting and modifying interactions
5. Boundary making
6. Unbalancing
7. Challenging unproductive assumptions

Joining and Accommodating. Individual patients generally enter therapy already predisposed to accept the therapist's authority. By seeking treatment, an individual tacitly acknowledges a need for help and willingness to trust the therapist. Not so with families.

The family therapist is an unwelcome outsider. After all, why did he or she insist on seeing the whole family? Family members expect to be told that they're doing something wrong, and they're prepared to defend themselves.

The therapist must first disarm defenses and ease anxiety. This is done by building an alliance of understanding with each member of the family.

Everyone has a story to tell, and in unhappy families almost everyone feels misunderstood. The first step in breaking the cycle of misunderstanding is to offer the empathy family members may be temporarily unable to provide each other. Hearing and acknowledging each person's account of the family's sorrows provides information—and begins to release family members from the resentment of unheard feelings. *Joining*, as this empathic connection is called, opens the way for family members to begin listening to each other and establishes a bond with the therapist that enables them to accept the challenges to come.

These initial conversations convey respect, not only for the individuals in the family but also for the family's structure and organization. The therapist shows respect for parents by honoring their authority. They, not their children, are asked first to describe the problems. If a family elects one person to speak for the others, the therapist notes this but does not initially challenge it.

Children also have special concerns and capacities. They should be greeted gently and asked simple, concrete questions: "Hi, I'm so-and-so; what's your name? Oh, Keisha, that's a nice name. Where do you go to school, Keisha?" Avoid the usual adult platitudes ("And what do *you* want to be when you grow up?"). Try something a little fresher (like "What do you hate most about school?"). Those who wish to remain silent should be allowed to do so. They will anyway. "And what's your view of the problem?" (Grim silence.) "I see, you don't feel like saying anything right now? That's fine; perhaps you'll have something to say later."

It's particularly important to join powerful family members as well as angry ones. Special pains must be taken to accept the point of view of the father who thinks therapy is hooey or the angry teenager who feels like an accused criminal. It's also important to reconnect with such people at frequent intervals, particularly when things begin to heat up.

A useful beginning is to greet the family and then ask for each person's view of the problem. Listen carefully and acknowledge what you hear: "I see, Mrs. Jones, you think Sally must be depressed about something that happened at

school." "So Mr. Jones, you see some of the same things your wife sees, but you're not convinced that it's a serious problem. Is that right?"

Enactment. Family structure is manifest in the way family members interact. It can't always be inferred from their descriptions. Families often describe themselves more as they think they should be than as they are.

Getting family members to talk among themselves runs counter to their expectations. They expect to present their case to an expert and then be told what to do. If asked to discuss something in the session, they'll say "We've already talked about this," or "It won't do any good, he (or she) doesn't listen," or "But *you're* supposed to be the expert."

If the therapist begins by giving each person a chance to speak, usually one will say something about another that can be a springboard for an enactment. When, for example, one parent says that the other is too strict, the therapist can initiate an enactment by saying "She says you're too strict; can you answer her?" Picking a specific issue for response is more effective than vague requests, such as "Why don't you two talk this over?"

Once an enactment is begun, a therapist can discover many things about a family's structure. How long can two people talk without being interrupted—that is, how clear is the boundary? Does one attack, the other defend? Who is central, who peripheral? Do parents bring children into their discussions—that is, are they enmeshed?

Families demonstrate enmeshment by frequently interrupting, speaking for each other, doing things for children that they can do for themselves, or constantly arguing. In disengaged families, one may see a husband sitting impassively while his wife cries, a total absence of conflict, a surprising ignorance of important information about the children, or a lack of concern for each other's interests.

If, as soon as the first session starts, the kids begin running around the room while the parents protest ineffectually, the therapist doesn't need to hear descriptions of what goes on at home to see the executive incompetence. If a mother and daughter rant and rave at each other while the father sits silently in the corner, it isn't necessary to ask how involved he is at home. In fact, asking may yield a less-accurate picture than the one revealed spontaneously.

Structural Mapping. Families usually conceive of problems as located in the identified patient and caused by events in the past. They hope the therapist will change the identified patient—with as little disruption to the family as possible. A structural assessment broadens the problem beyond individuals to the family system and moves the focus from discrete events in the past to ongoing transactions in the present.

Even family therapists often categorize families with constructs that apply more to individuals than to systems. "The problem in this family is that the mother is smothering the kids," or "These kids are defiant," or "He's uninvolved." Structural family therapists try to assess the interrelationship of all family members. Using the concepts of boundaries and subsystems, the structure of the whole system is described in a way that points to desired changes.

Preliminary assessments are based on interactions in the first session. In later sessions, these formulations are refined and revised. Although there is some danger of bending families to fit categories when they're applied too early, the greater danger is waiting too long. Families quickly *induct* therapists into their culture. A family that initially appears to be chaotic and enmeshed soon comes to be just the familiar Jones family. For this reason, it's important to develop structural hypotheses relatively early in the process.

In fact, it's helpful to make some guesses about family structure even before the first session. This starts a process of active thinking and sets the stage for observing the family. For example, suppose you're about to see a family consisting of a mother, a sixteen-year-old daughter, and a stepfather. The mother called to complain

of her daughter's misbehavior. What do you imagine the structure might be, and how would you test your hypothesis? A good guess might be that the mother and daughter are enmeshed, excluding the stepfather. This can be tested by seeing if the mother and daughter talk mostly about each other in the session—whether positively or negatively. The stepfather's disengagement would be confirmed if he and his wife were unable to converse without the daughter's intrusion.

Structural assessments take into account both the problem the family presents and the structure they display—and they include all family members. In this instance, knowing that the mother and daughter are enmeshed isn't enough; you also have to know what role the stepfather plays. If he's reasonably close with his wife but distant from the daughter, finding mutually enjoyable activities for stepfather and stepdaughter will help increase the girl's independence from her mother. On the other hand, if the mother's proximity to her daughter appears to be a function of her distance from her husband, then the marital pair might be the more productive focus.

Without a structural formulation and a plan, a therapist is put in a passive role. Instead of knowing where to go and moving deliberately, the therapist lays back and tries to cope with the family's complaints, put out brush fires, and help them through a succession of incidents. Consistent awareness of the family's structure and focus on one or two structural changes helps the therapist see behind the various content issues that family members bring up.

Highlighting and Modifying Interactions. Once families begin to interact, problematic transactions emerge. Recognizing their structural implications demands focus on process, not content.

Perhaps a wife complains: "We have a communication problem. My husband won't talk to me; he never expresses his feelings." The therapist then initiates an enactment to see what actually does happen: "Your wife says you have a communication problem; can you respond to that? Talk with her." If, when they talk, the wife becomes domineering and critical while the husband grows increasingly silent, then the therapist sees what's wrong: The problem isn't that he doesn't talk (which is a linear explanation), nor is the problem that she nags (also a linear explanation). The problem is that the more she nags, the more he withdraws, and the more he withdraws, the more she nags.

The trick is to modify this pattern. This may require forceful intervening, or what structural therapists call **intensity**.

Intensity isn't a function of personality; it reflects clarity of purpose. Knowledge of family structure and a commitment to help families change make powerful interventions possible.

Structural therapists achieve intensity by selective regulation of affect, repetition, and duration. Tone, volume, pacing, and choice of words can be used to raise the affective intensity of statements. It helps if you know what you want to say. Here's an example of a limp statement: "People are always concerned with themselves, kind of seeing themselves as the center of attention and just looking for whatever they can get. Wouldn't it be nice, for a change, if everybody started thinking about what they could do for others?" Compare that with "Ask not what your country can do for you—ask what you can do for your country." John Kennedy's words had impact because they were brief and to the point. Therapists don't need to make speeches, but they do occasionally have to speak forcefully to get the point across.

Affective intensity isn't simply a matter of clever phrasing. You have to know how and when to be provocative.

ter were enmeshed, while the father was excluded. In this family, the father was the only one to express anger openly, and this was part of the rationale for why he was excluded. His daughter was afraid of his anger, which she freely admitted. What was less clear, however, was that the mother had covertly taught the daughter to avoid him, because she, the mother, couldn't deal with his anger. Consequently, the daughter grew up afraid of her father and of men in general.

At one point, the father described how isolated he felt from his daughter; he said he thought it was because she feared his anger. The daughter agreed, "It's his fault, all right." The therapist asked the mother what she thought, and she replied, "It isn't *his* fault." The therapist said, "You're right."

The mother went on, denying her real feelings to avoid conflict: "It's no one's fault." The therapist answered in a way that got her attention, "That's not true." Startled, she asked what he meant. "It's *your* fault," he said.

This level of intensity was necessary to interrupt a rigid pattern of conflict-avoidance that sustained a destructive coalition between mother and daughter. The content—who really is afraid of anger—was less important than the structural goal: freeing the daughter from her overinvolvement with her mother.

Intensity can also be achieved by extending the duration of a sequence beyond the point where homeostasis is reinstated. A common example is the management of tantrums. Temper tantrums are maintained by parents who give in. Most parents *try* not to give in; they just don't try long enough.

Case Study

Mike Nichols worked with a family in which a twenty-nine-year-old woman with anorexia nervosa was the identified patient. Although the family maintained a facade of togetherness, it was rigidly structured; the mother and her anorexic daugh-

Case Study

A four-year-old girl began to scream bloody murder when her sister left the room. She wanted to go with her sister. Her screaming was almost unbearable, and the parents were ready to back down. However, the therapist urged that they not allow themselves to be defeated and suggested that they hold her until she calmed down. She screamed for twenty minutes! Everyone in the room was frazzled. However, the little girl finally realized that this time she was not going to get her way, and so she calmed down. Subsequently, the parents were able to use the same intensity of duration to break her of this destructive habit.

Sometimes intensity requires repetition of one theme in a variety of contexts. Infantilizing parents may have to be told not to hang up their child's coat, not to speak for her, not to take her to the bathroom, and not to do many other things that she's able to do for herself.

What we're calling *intensity* may strike some as overly aggressive. Although there's no denying that Minuchin and his followers tend to be interventionists, the point of intensity is not to bully people but to push them past the point where they give up on getting through to each other. An alternative strategy for stalemated interactions is the use of **empathy** to help family members get beneath the surface of their defensive wrangling.

If, for example, the parents of a disobedient child are locked in a cycle of unproductive quarreling in which the mother attacks the father for not being involved and he responds with excuses, a therapist could use intensity to push them to come up with a plan for dealing with their child's behavior. Or the therapist could interrupt their squabbling and, using empathy, talk to each of them one at a time about what they're feeling. The wife who shows only anger might be covering up the hurt and longing she feels. The husband who neither gets involved nor fights back when he feels attacked might be too annoyed at his wife's anger to see that she needs him. Once these more genuine emotions are articulated, they can serve as a basis for clients reconnecting with each other in a less defensive manner.

Shaping competence is another method of modifying interactions, and it's a hallmark of structural family therapy. Intensity is used to block the stream of interactions. Shaping competence is like altering the direction of the flow. By highlighting and reinforcing the positive, structural therapists help family members use functional alternatives that are already in their repertoire.

A common mistake made by beginning therapists is to attempt to foster competence only by pointing out mistakes. This focuses on content without regard for process. Telling parents that they're doing something wrong or suggesting they do something different has the effect of criticizing their competence. However well intentioned, it's still criticism. While this kind of intervention cannot be completely avoided, a more effective approach is to point out what they're doing right.

Even when people make a lot of mistakes, it's usually possible to pick out something that they're doing successfully. A sense of timing helps.

In a large chaotic family, the parents were extremely ineffective at controlling their children. At one point, the therapist turned to the mother and said, "It's too noisy in here; would you quiet the kids?" Knowing how much difficulty the woman had with discipline, the therapist was poised to comment on any step in the direction of effective management. The mother had to yell "Quiet!" a couple of times before the children momentarily stopped what they were doing. Quickly—before the children resumed their misbehavior—the therapist complimented the mother for "loving her kids enough to be firm with them." Thus the message was "You're a competent person, you know how to be firm." If the therapist had waited until the chaos resumed before telling the mother she should be more firm, the message would be "You're incompetent."

Case Study

Wherever possible, structural therapists avoid doing things for family members that they're capable of doing themselves. Here, too, the message is "You are competent; you can do it." Some therapists justify taking over family functions by calling it *modeling*. Whatever it's called, it has the impact of treating family members as inadequate.

Recently, a young mother confessed she hadn't known how to tell her children that they were coming to see a family therapist and so had simply said she was taking them for a ride. Thinking to be helpful, the therapist then explained to the children that "Mommy told me there were some problems in the family, so we're all here to talk things over to see if we can improve things." This lovely explanation tells the kids why they came but confirms the mother as incompetent to do so. If instead the therapist had suggested to the mother, "Would you like to tell them now?" Then the mother, not the therapist, would have had to perform as an effective parent.

Boundary Making. In enmeshed families, interventions are designed to strengthen boundaries. Family members are urged to speak for themselves, interruptions are blocked, and dyads are helped to finish conversations without intrusion. A therapist who wishes to support the sibling system and protect it from unnecessary parental intrusion might say, "Susie and Sean, talk this over, and everyone else will listen carefully." If children interrupt their parents, a therapist might challenge the parents to strengthen the hierarchical boundary by saying, "Why don't you get them to butt out so that you two grownups can settle this?".

Although structural therapy is begun with the whole family, subsequent sessions may be held with individuals or subgroups to strengthen their boundaries. An overprotected teenager is supported as an independent person by participating in some individual sessions. Parents so enmeshed with their children that they never have private conversations may begin to learn how if they meet separately with the therapist.

When a forty-year-old woman called the clinic for help with depression, she was asked to come in with the rest of her family. It soon became apparent that this woman was overburdened by her four children and received little support from her husband.

The therapist's strategy was to strengthen the boundary between the mother and children and help the parents move closer to each other. This was done in stages. First, the therapist joined the oldest child, a sixteen-year-old girl, and supported her competence as a potential helper for her mother. Once this was done, the girl was able to assume a good deal of responsibility for her younger siblings, both in sessions and at home.

Freed from their preoccupation with the children, the parents now had the opportunity to talk more with each other. They had little to say, however. This wasn't the result of hidden conflict but instead reflected a marriage of two relatively nonverbal people. After several sessions of trying to get the pair talking, the therapist realized that although talking may be fun for some people, it might not be for others. So to support the bond between the couple, the therapist asked them to plan a special trip together. They chose a boat ride on a nearby lake.

When they returned for the next session, they were beaming. They had a wonderful time. Subsequently, they decided to spend a little time out together each week.

Disengaged families tend to avoid conflict and thus minimize interaction. The structural therapist intervenes to challenge conflict avoidance and to block detouring in order to help disengaged members break down the walls between them.

When beginners see disengagement, they tend to think of ways to increase positive interaction. In fact, disengagement is usually a way of avoiding arguments. Therefore, people isolated from each other typically need to discuss their differences before they can become closer.

Most people underestimate the degree to which their own behavior influences the behavior of those around them. This is particularly true in disengaged families. Problems are usually seen as the result of what someone else is doing, and solutions are thought to require that others change. The following complaints are typical, and typically linear: "We have a communication problem; he won't tell me what he's feeling." "All he cares about is that damn job of his." "Our sex life is lousy—my wife's frigid." "Who can talk to her? All she does is complain about the kids." Each of these statements suggests that the power to change rests with the other person.

Whereas most people see things this way, systemic therapists see the inherent circularity in family interactions. He doesn't tell his wife what he's feeling because she nags and criticizes, *and* she nags and criticizes because he doesn't tell her what he's feeling.

Structural therapists move family discussions from linear to circular perspectives by stressing complementarity. The mother who complains that her son is a troublemaker is taught to consider what she's doing to trigger or maintain his behavior. The person who asks for change must learn to change his or her way of trying to get it. The wife who nags her husband to spend more time with her must learn to make increased involvement more attractive. The husband who complains that his wife never listens to him may have to listen to *her* more, before she's willing to reciprocate.

Structural therapists emphasize complementarity by asking family members to help each other change. When positive changes are reported, they're likely to congratulate others, underscoring family interrelatedness.

Unbalancing.   In boundary making, the therapist aims to realign relationships *between* subsystems. In unbalancing, the goal is to change the relationship *within* a subsystem. What often keeps families stuck in stalemate is that members in conflict are balanced in opposition and, as a result, remain frozen in inaction. In unbalancing, the therapist joins and supports one individual or subsystem.

Taking sides—let's call it what it is—seems like a violation of therapy's sacred canon of neutrality. However, the therapist takes sides to unbalance and realign the system, not because he or she is the arbiter of right and wrong. Ultimately, balance and fairness are achieved because the therapist sides in turn with various members of the family.

Case Study

When the MacLean family sought help for an "unmanageable" child, a terror who'd been expelled from two schools, Dr. Minuchin uncovered a covert split between the parents, held in balance by not being talked about. The ten-year-old boy's misbehavior was dramatically visible; his father had to drag him kicking and screaming into the consulting room. Meanwhile, his little brother sat quietly, smiling engagingly. The good boy.

To broaden the focus from an "impossible child" to issues of parental control and cooperation, Minuchin asked about the little brother, seven-year-old Kevin, who misbehaved invisibly. He peed on the floor in the bathroom. According to his father, Kevin's peeing on the floor was due to "inattentiveness." The mother laughed when Minuchin said, "Nobody could have such poor aim."

Minuchin talked with the boy about how wolves mark their territory and suggested that he expand his territory by peeing in all four corners of the family room.

Minuchin: Do you have a dog?

Kevin: No.

Minuchin: Oh, so you are the family dog?

In the process of discussing the boy who peed—and his parents' response—Minuchin dramatized how the parents polarized and undercut each other.

Minuchin: Why would he do such a thing?
Father: I don't know if he did it on purpose.
Minuchin: Maybe he was in a trance?
Father: No, I think it was carelessness.
Minuchin: His aim must be terrible.

The father described the boy's behavior as accidental; the mother considered it defiant. One reason parents fall under the control of their young children is that they avoid confronting their differences. Differences are normal, but they become detrimental when one parent undermines the other's handling of the children. (It's cowardly revenge for unaddressed grievances.)

Minuchin's gentle but insistent pressure on the couple to talk about how they respond, without switching to focus on how the children behave, led to their bringing up long-held but seldom-voiced resentments.

Mother: Bob makes excuses for the children's behavior because he doesn't want to get in there and help me find a solution for the problem.
Father: Yes, but when I did try to help, you'd always criticize me. So after a while I gave up.

Like a photographic print in a developing tray, the spouses' conflict had become visible. Minuchin protected the parents from embarrassment (and the children from being burdened) by asking the children to leave the room. Without the preoccupation of parenting, the spouses could face each other, man and woman—and talk about their hurts and grievances. It turned out to be a sad story of lonely disengagement.

Minuchin: Do you two have areas of agreement?

He said yes; she said no. He was a minimizer; she was a critic.

Minuchin: When did you divorce Bob and marry the children?

She turned quiet; he looked off into space. She said, softly, "Probably ten years ago."

What followed was a painful but familiar story of how a marriage can drown in parenting. The conflict was never resolved because it never surfaced. And so the rift never healed.

With Minuchin's help, the couple took turns talking about their pain—and learning to listen. By unbalancing, Minuchin brought enormous pressure to bear to help this couple break through their differences, open up to each other, fight for what they want, and finally begin to come together—as husband and wife, and as parents.

Unbalancing is part of a struggle for change that sometimes takes on the appearance of combat. When a therapist says to a father that he's not doing enough or to a mother that she's excluding her husband, it may seem that the combat is between the therapist and the family—that he or she is attacking them. But, the real combat is between them and fear—fear of change.

Challenging Unproductive Assumptions. Although structural family therapy is not primarily a cognitive approach, its practitioners do challenge unproductive assumptions that support structural problems. Changing the way family members interact offers alternative views of their situation. The converse is also true: Changing the way family members view their situation enables them to change the way they interact.

When six-year-old Cassie's parents complain about her behavior, they say she's "hyper," "sensitive," a "nervous child." Such constructions have tremendous power. Is a child's behavior "misbehavior," or is it a symptom of "nervousness?" Is it "naughty," or is it a "cry for help?"

Is the child mad or bad and who is in charge? What's in a name? Plenty.

Sometimes a therapist acts as teacher, offering information and advice, often about structural matters. Doing so is likely to be a restructuring maneuver and must be done in a way that minimizes resistance. A therapist does this by delivering a "*stroke* and a *kick*." If the therapist were dealing with a family in which the mother speaks for her children, he might say to her, "You are very helpful" (stroke). But to the child, "Mommy takes away your voice. Can you speak for yourself?" (kick). Thus mother is defined as helpful but intrusive (a stroke and a kick).

Effective challenges describe what people are doing and its consequences. However, in order for family members to hear what is being pointed out they must not feel attacked. Saying "that's interesting . . ." before pointing something out makes it an object of curiosity rather than an occasion for defensiveness. Moreover, although it's tempting to tell people what they should do, doing so reduces the likelihood of them learning to see what they are doing—and its consequences.

EVALUATING THERAPY THEORY AND RESULTS

In *Families of the Slums*, Minuchin and his colleagues (1967) described the structural characteristics of low-socioeconomic families and demonstrated the effectiveness of family therapy with this population. Prior to treatment, mothers in patient families were found to be either over- or undercontrolling; either way their children were more disruptive than those in control families. After treatment, mothers used less coercive control yet were clearer about their rules and firmer in enforcing them. Seven of eleven families improved significantly after six months to a year of family therapy. Although no control group was used, the authors compared their results favorably to the usual 50 percent rate of successful treatment at Wiltwyck.

(None of the families rated as disengaged improved.)

Some of the strongest empirical support for structural family therapy comes from a series of studies with psychosomatic children and young adult drug addicts. Studies demonstrating the effectiveness of therapy with severely ill psychosomatic children are convincing because of the physiological measures employed and dramatic because of the life-threatening nature of the problems. Minuchin, Rosman, and Baker (1978) reported how family conflict can precipitate ketoacidosis crises in diabetic children. In baseline interviews, parents discussed family problems with children absent. Normal spouses showed the highest levels of confrontation, while psychosomatic spouses exhibited a wide range of conflict-avoidance maneuvers. Next, a therapist pressed the parents to increase the level of their conflict, while their children observed behind a one-way mirror. As the parents argued, only the psychosomatic children got really upset. Moreover, these children's manifest distress was accompanied by dramatic increases in free fatty acid levels, a measure related to ketoacidosis. In the third stage of these interviews, the patients joined their parents. Normal and behavior-disorder parents continued as before, but the psychosomatic parents detoured their conflict, either by drawing their children into their discussions or by switching the subject from themselves to the children. When this happened, the free fatty acid levels of the parents fell, while the children's levels continued to rise. This study provided strong confirmation of the clinical observation that psychosomatic children are involved in the regulation of stress between their parents.

Minuchin, Rosman, and Baker (1978) summarized the results of treating fifty-three cases of anorexia nervosa with structural family therapy. After a course of treatment that included hospitalization followed by outpatient family therapy, forty-three anorexic children were "greatly improved," two were "improved," three showed "no change," two were "worse," and three had dropped out. Although ethical considerations precluded a control treatment with these seriously ill children, the 90 percent improvement rate is impressive, especially compared with the usual 30 percent mortality rate for this disorder. Moreover, the positive results at termination were maintained at follow-up intervals of several years. Structural family therapy has also been shown to be effective in treating psychosomatic asthmatics and psychosomatically complicated cases of diabetes (Minuchin, Baker, Rosman, Liebman, Milman, & Todd, 1975).

Although no body of empirical evidence has established that any one psychotherapeutic approach is consistently better than the others, structural family therapy has proven to be effective in a variety of studies, including many that involved what are usually considered very difficult cases. Duke Stanton showed that structural family therapy can be effective for drug addicts and their families. In a well-controlled study, Stanton and Todd (1979) compared family therapy with a family placebo condition and individual therapy. Symptom reduction was significant with structural family therapy; the level of positive change was more than double that achieved in the other conditions, and these positive effects persisted at follow-up of six and twelve months.

More recently, structural family therapy has been successfully applied to establish more adaptive parenting roles in heroin addicts (Grief & Dreschler, 1993) and as a means to reduce the likelihood that African American and Latino youths would initiate drug use (Santisteban, Coatsworth, Perez-Vidal, Mitrani, Jean-Gilles, & Szapocznik, 1997). Other studies indicate that structural family therapy is equal in effectiveness to communication training and behavioral management training in reducing negative communication, conflicts, and expressed anger between adolescents diagnosed with attention deficit hyperactivity disorder (ADHD) and their parents (Barkley, Guevremont, Anastopoulos, & Fletcher, 1992). Structural family therapy has also been effective for treating adolescent disorders, such as conduct disorders (Chamberlain &

Rosicky, 1995; Santisteban et al., 2003; Szapocznik et al., 1989), and anorexia nervosa (Campbell & Patterson, 1995).

Although structural family therapy is so closely identified with Salvador Minuchin that they were once synonymous, it may be a good idea to differentiate the man from the model. When we think of structural family therapy, we tend to remember the approach as described in *Families and Family Therapy*, published in 1974. That book remains a good introduction to structural theory but emphasizes only the techniques Minuchin favored at the time. Minuchin himself has evolved considerably in the last thirty-five years, from an often blunt young therapist, always ready to challenge families, to a more seasoned clinician, still challenging but far gentler in his approach. If some of the examples in this chapter strike you as overly aggressive, you may be right. Some of these vignettes were taken from the 1970s, when family therapists tended to favor a confrontational style. While the confrontational style may have characterized some practitioners of structural family therapy, it was never an essential feature of this approach.

Minuchin has evolved conceptually as well, from an almost exclusive focus on interpersonal interactions to consider the cognitive perspectives guiding those interactions as well as the past roots of those perspectives (Minuchin, Nichols, & Lee, 2007). But the structural approach he created also exists independently of his work and is embodied in the definitive literature on this model (Minuchin, 1974; Minuchin & Fishman, 1981; Minuchin & Nichols, 1993) as well as in the ongoing work of his students and colleagues.

The structural model directs clinicians to look beyond the content of problems and even beyond the dynamics of interaction to the underlying family organization that supports and constrains those interactions. Much has changed since 1974, but the structural model still stands, and it continues to be the most widely used way of understanding what goes on in troubled families.

SUMMARY

Minuchin may be best known for the artistry of his clinical technique, yet his structural theory has become the most widely used conceptual model in the field. The reason structural theory is so popular is that it's simple, inclusive, and practical. The basic concepts—boundaries, subsystems, alignments, and complementarity—are easily applied. They take into account the individual, family, and social context, and they provide a clear organizing framework for understanding and treating families.

The most important tenet of this approach is that every family has a structure, and this structure is revealed only when the family is in action. According to this view, therapists who fail to consider the entire family's structure, and intervene in only one subsystem, are unlikely to effect lasting change. If a mother's overinvolvement with her son is part of a structure that includes distance from her husband, no amount of therapy for the mother and son is likely to bring about basic change in the family.

Subsystems are units of the family based on function. If the leadership of a family is taken over by a father and daughter, then they, not the husband and wife, are the executive subsystem.

Subsystems are regulated by interpersonal boundaries. In healthy families, boundaries are clear enough to protect independence and permeable enough to allow mutual support. Enmeshed families are characterized by diffuse boundaries; disengaged families by rigid boundaries.

Once they've gained a family's trust, therapists promote family interaction while they assume a decentralized role. From this position, they can observe and make a structural assessment, which includes the problem and the organization that supports it. These assessments are framed in terms of boundaries and subsystems, easily conceptualized as two-dimensional maps used to suggest avenues for change.

Once they have successfully joined and assessed a family, structural therapists proceed to activate dormant structures using techniques that alter alignments and shift power within and between subsystems. These restructuring techniques are concrete and sometimes forceful. However, their success depends as much on effective joining and assessment as on the power of the techniques themselves.

RECOMMENDED READINGS

Colapinto, J. 1991. Structural family therapy. In *Handbook of family therapy*, Vol. II, A. S. Gurman and D. P. Kniskern, eds. New York: Brunner/ Mazel.

Minuchin, S. 1974. *Families and family therapy*. Cambridge, MA: Harvard University Press.

Minuchin, S., and Fishman, H. C. 1981. *Family therapy techniques*. Cambridge, MA: Harvard University Press.

Minuchin, S., Lee, W-Y., and Simon, G. M. 1996. *Mastering family therapy: Journeys of growth and transformation*. New York: Wiley.

Minuchin, S., and Nichols, M. P. 1993. *Family healing: Tales of hope and renewal from family therapy*. New York: Free Press.

Minuchin, S., Nichols, M. P., and Lee, W-Y. 2007. *Assessing families and couples: From symptom to psyche*. Boston: Allyn & Bacon.

Nichols, M. P. *Inside family therapy*. 2000. 2nd ed. Boston: Allyn & Bacon.

Nichols, M. P., and Minuchin, S. 1999. Short-term structural family therapy with couples. In *Short-term couple therapy*, J. M. Donovad, ed. New York: Guilford Press.

REFERENCES

Barkley, R., Guevremont, D., Anastopoulos, A., and Fletcher, K. 1992. A comparison of three family therapy programs for treating family conflicts in adolescents with attention-deficit hyperactivity disorder. *Journal of Consulting and Clinical Psychology. 60:*450–463.

Campbell, T., and Patterson, J. 1995. The effectiveness of family interventions in the treatment of physical illness. *Journal of Marital and Family Therapy. 21:*545–584.

Chamberlain, P., and Rosicky, J. 1995. The effectiveness of family therapy in the treatment of adolescents with conduct disorders and delinquency. *Journal of Marital and Family Therapy. 21:*441–459.

Elizur, J., and Minuchin, S. 1989. *Institutionalizing madness: Families, therapy, and society.* New York: Basic Books.

Grief, G., and Dreschler, L. 1993. Common issues for parents in a methadone maintenance group. *Journal of Substance Abuse Treatment. 10:*335–339.

Minuchin, S. 1974. *Families and family therapy.* Cambridge, MA: Harvard University Press.

Minuchin, S., and Fishman, H. C. 1981. *Family therapy techniques.* Cambridge, MA: Harvard University Press.

Minuchin, S., and Nichols, M. P. 1993. *Family healing: Tales of hope and renewal from family therapy.* New York: Free Press.

Minuchin, S., Nichols, M., P., and Lee, W-Y. 2007. *A four-step model for assessing families and couples: From symptom to psyche.* Boston: Allyn & Bacon.

Minuchin, S., Rosman, B., and Baker, L. 1978. *Psychosomatic families: Anorexia nervosa in context.* Cambridge, MA: Harvard University Press.

Minuchin, S., Montalvo, B., Guerney, B., Rosman, B., and Schumer, F. 1967. *Families of the slums.* New York: Basic Books.

Minuchin, S., Baker, L., Rosman, B., Liebman, R., Milman, L., and Todd, T. C. 1975. A conceptual model of psychosomatic illness in children. *Archives of General Psychiatry. 32:*1031–1038.

Santisteban, D., Coatsworth, J., Perez-Vidal, A., Kurtines, W., Schwartz, S., LaPerriere, A., and Szapocznik, J. 2003. The efficacy of Brief Strategic Family Therapy in modifying Hispanic adolescent behavior problems and substance use. *Journal of Family Psychology. 17*(1):123–133.

Simon, G. M. 1995. A revisionist rendering of structural family therapy. *Journal of Marital and Family Therapy. 21:*17–26.

Stanton, M. D., and Todd, T. C. 1979. Structural family therapy with drug addicts. In *The family therapy of drug and alcohol abuse,* E. Kaufman and P. Kaufmann, eds. New York: Gardner Press.

Szapocznik, J., Rio, A., Murray, E., Cohen, R., Scopetta, M., Rivas-Vazquez, A., Hervis, O., Posada, V., and Kurtines, W. 1989. Structural family versus psychodynamic child therapy for problematic Hispanic boys. *Journal of Consulting and Clinical Psychology. 57:*571–578.

Experiential Family Therapy

8

Family Therapy as an Emotional Encounter

An experiential branch of family therapy emerged from the humanistic wing of psychology that, like the expressive therapies that inspired it, emphasized immediate, **here-and-now experience**. Experiential therapy was popular when family therapy was young, when therapists talked about systems but borrowed their techniques from individual and group therapies. From Gestalt therapy and encounter groups came techniques such as *role-playing* and *emotional confrontation*, while other expressive methods such as *sculpting* and *family drawing* bore the influence of the arts and of psychodrama.

In focusing more on emotional experience than on the dynamics of interaction, experiential therapists seemed out of step with the rest of family therapy. Indeed, by emphasizing individuals and their feelings, experiential treatment may never have been as well suited to family therapy as were approaches that dealt with systems and action. With the passing of the inspirational leaders of this tradition, Virginia Satir and Carl Whitaker, the methods they popularized began to seem a little dated, more a product of the 1960s than of today's world.

Recently, however, experiential approaches have been enjoying a revival and, as we will see, two of the newer models—Greenberg and Johnson's (1985) emotionally focused couples therapy and Schwartz's (1995) internal family systems model—have combined the emotional impact of an experiential focus on the individual with a more sophisticated understanding of family systems.

As the first great cathartic therapist, Sigmund Freud, discovered, getting in touch with painful feelings is not by itself a complete model of psychotherapy. On the other hand, ignoring or rationalizing unhappy emotions may cheat clients out of the opportunity to get to the heart of their problems. Thus, the experiential emphasis on emotional expression continues to be a useful counterweight to the reductionistic emphasis on behavior and cognition common to today's problem-solving approaches.

SKETCHES OF LEADING FIGURES

Two giants stand out in the development of experiential family therapy: Carl Whitaker and Virginia Satir. Whitaker was the leading exponent of a freewheeling, intuitive approach aimed at puncturing pretense and liberating family members to be themselves. He was among the first to do psychotherapy with families, and although he was once considered a maverick, he eventually became one of the most admired therapists in the field. Iconoclastic, even outrageous at times, Whitaker nevertheless retained the respect of the family therapy establishment. He may have been their Puck, but he was one of them.

Whitaker grew up on a dairy farm in upstate New York. Rural isolation bred a certain shyness but also conditioned him to be less bound by social convention. After medical school and a residency in obstetrics and gynecology, Whitaker went into psychiatry, where he became fascinated by the psychotic mind. Unfortunately—or fortunately—back in the 1940s, Whitaker couldn't rely on neuroleptic drugs to blunt the hallucinatory imaginings of his patients; instead he listened and learned to understand thoughts crazy but human, thoughts most of us usually keep buried.

After working at the University of Louisville College of Medicine and the Oakridge Hospital, Whitaker accepted the chair of Emory University's department of psychiatry, where he remained from 1946 to 1955. Then, in the face of mounting pressure to make the department more psychoan-

Carl Whitaker used a freewheeling approach to wake family members up to their own inner longings.

alytic, Whitaker and his entire faculty, including Thomas Malone, John Warkentin, and Richard Felder, resigned to establish the Atlanta Psychiatric Clinic. Experiential psychotherapy was born of this union, and the group produced a number of provocative and challenging papers (Whitaker & Malone, 1953). In 1965, Whitaker moved to the University of Wisconsin Medical School. After his retirement in the late 1980s, he traveled widely to share his wisdom and experience at conventions and workshops. His death in 1995 was a great loss. Among Whitaker's best-known students are Augustus Napier, now in private practice in Atlanta, and David Keith, at the State University of New York in Syracuse.

The other towering figure among experiential family therapists was Virginia Satir. As an early member of the Mental Research Institute (MRI), Satir emphasized communication (see Chapters 2 and 6) as well as emotional experiencing.

Satir began seeing families in private practice in Chicago in 1951. In 1955, she was invited to set up a training program for residents at the Illinois State Psychiatric Institute (where one of her students was Ivan Boszormenyi-Nagy). In 1959, Don Jackson invited her to join him at MRI, where Satir became the first director of training and remained until 1966, when she left to become the director of the Esalen Institute in Big Sur, California.

Satir was the archetypal nurturing therapist in a field enamored with abstract concepts and strategic maneuvers. Her warmth and genuineness gave her tremendous appeal as she traveled the country giving demonstrations and workshops. Her ability to move audiences made her family therapy's most celebrated humanist. Satir died of pancreatic cancer in 1988.

Among the most recent experiential approaches is the emotionally focused couples therapy of Leslie Greenberg and Susan Johnson, which draws on Perls, Satir, and the MRI group (Greenberg & Johnson, 1985, 1986, 1988). Another specialized approach to the inner emotional life of families is Richard Schwartz's (1995) internal family systems therapy, in which clients' conflicting inner voices are personified as "parts" and then reintegrated using a variety of psychodramatic techniques.

THEORETICAL FORMULATIONS

Experiential family therapy is founded on the premise that the root cause of family problems is emotional suppression. Although children must learn that they can't always do whatever they feel like doing, many parents have an unfortunate tendency to confuse the *instrumental* and *expressive* functions of emotion. They try to regulate their children's actions by controlling their feelings. As a result, children learn to blunt their emotional experience to avoid criticism. Although this process is more or less universal, dysfunctional families tend to be less tolerant of unruly emotions than most. Children in such families often grow up estranged from themselves and feeling only the residues of repressed affect: boredom, apathy, and anxiety.

While systemic therapists see the roots of symptomatic behavior in the dance of family interactions, experientialists view those interactions as the result of family members shadow dancing with the projections of each other's defenses. From this perspective, attempts to bring about positive change in families are more likely to be successful if family members first get in touch with their real feelings—their hopes and desires as well as their fears and anxieties. Thus, experiential family therapy works from the inside out, helping individuals uncover their honest emotions, and then forging more genuine family ties out of this enhanced authenticity.

Carl Whitaker summed up the experiential position on theory in a paper entitled "The Hindrance of Theory in Clinical Work" (Whitaker, 1976a). Theory may be useful for beginners, Whitaker said, but his advice was to give up calculation as soon as possible in favor of just being yourself.

Being antitheoretical is, of course, itself a theoretical position. To say that therapy shouldn't be constrained by theories is to say that it should be spontaneous. Despite Whitaker's disdain for theory, however, experiential family therapy is very much a product of the existential-humanistic tradition.

Much of the theorizing of existential psychologists (e.g., Binswanger, 1967; Boss, 1963) was in reaction to perceived mechanism of psychoanalysis and behaviorism. In place of *determinism*, existentialists emphasized freedom and the immediacy of experience. Where psychoanalysts posited a structuralized model of the mind, existentialists treated individuals as whole persons and offered a positive model of humanity in place of what they saw as a pessimistic psychoanalytic model. Instead of settling for a reduction of their neuroses, existentialists believed that people should aim for fulfillment.

Despite their disinclination to theorize, certain basic premises define the experiential position. Whitaker emphasized that self-fulfillment depends on family cohesiveness, and Satir stressed the importance of communication among family members, but the basic commitment was to *individual self-expression*. Although there was some talk about family systems (e.g., Satir, 1972), the experiential model of families was more like a democratic group than a structured organization.

Great emphasis is placed on *flexibility* and *freedom*. Treatment is designed to help individual family members find fulfilling roles for themselves, with less concern for the family as a whole. This is not to say that the needs of the family are denigrated but that they are thought to follow on the heels of individual enhancement.[1]

After reading the previous paragraph, David Keith (in a personal letter) helped put into perspective the experiential position on the claims of the individual versus the claims of the family:

> There is a dialectical tension between the individual and the family—between dependence and independence. To overemphasize either individuality or family connectedness is to distort the human condition.

Theories of families as systems are translated into techniques that promote interaction. The emphasis on altering interactions implies an acceptance of whatever level of individual experience is already present. This is where experiential theory differs from most systems approaches. Here the emphasis is on expanding experience. The assumption is that opening up individuals to their experience is a prerequisite to breaking new ground for the family group.

The underlying premise of experiential therapy is that the way to promote individual growth and family cohesion is to liberate affects and impulses. Efforts to reduce defensiveness and unlock deeper levels of experiencing rest on an assumption of the basic goodness of human nature.

The exception to the experiential deemphasis on theory is Greenberg and Johnson's emotionally focused couples therapy, which draws on attachment theory (Bowlby, 1969). According to

Greenberg and Johnson, emotion organizes attachment responses and serves a communicative function in relationships. When people express their vulnerability directly, they're likely to elicit a compassionate response from their partners. But when an insecurely attached person fears vulnerability and shows anger instead, the response is more likely to be withdrawal. Thus the person most in need of attachment may, by being afraid to expose that need, push away the loved ones he or she longs to get close to. The antidote for this dilemma is what experiential therapy is all about: helping people relax defensive fears so that deeper and more genuine emotions can emerge.

The rediscovery of attachment theory is consistent with a larger effort to reclaim dependency as a natural human proclivity. In Bowlby's (1969) terms, attachment provides a person with a secure base—the ability to regulate emotions and the confidence to explore the world. When attachment is threatened, the first response is likely to be anger and protest, followed by some form of clinging, which eventually gives way to despair. Finally, if attachment figures do not respond, detachment and separation will occur (Bowlby, 1969).

Although attachment may be founded in childhood, Bowlby (1988) believed that every meaningful interaction with others continues to mold beliefs about people's availability and supportiveness. While attachment security may be fairly general, people also develop relationship-specific beliefs based on experiences with particular partners (Collins & Read, 1994). The process is, of course, circular. The more secure and trusting a person, the more likely she is to be open to relationships, and thus the more likely she is to develop relationships that confirm her sense of worth in connection. The converse is, unfortunately, also true: People who are afraid to express their attachment needs may withhold the responsiveness necessary to build secure relationships.

---

[1]Though, at one time, the family was portrayed as the enemy of freedom and authenticity (Laing & Esterson, 1970).

Whether attachment patterns of childhood continue to play a critical role in close relationships in adulthood remains to be demonstrated (see Chapter 4). But as with most clinical hypotheses, the value of attachment theory in the practice of therapy rests more with its usefulness than with empirical proof.

NORMAL FAMILY DEVELOPMENT

Experiential therapists share the humanistic faith in the natural wisdom of honest emotion. Left alone, people tend to flourish, according to this point of view. Problems arise because this innate tendency toward *self-actualization* (Rogers, 1951) runs afoul of social pressures. Society enforces repression to tame people's instincts and make them fit for group living. Unhappily, self-control is achieved at the cost of "surplus repression" (Marcuse, 1955). Families add their own controls to achieve peace and quiet, perpetuating **family myths** (Gehrke & Kirschenbaum, 1967) and relying on **mystification** (Laing, 1967) to alienate children from their experience.

. In the ideal situation, parental control isn't excessive, and children grow up in an atmosphere of support for their feelings and creative impulses. Parents appreciate their children, accept their feelings, and validate their experience. Children are encouraged to experience life fully and to express the full range of human emotions.

Experiential therapists describe the family as a place of sharing experience (Satir, 1972). Functional families are secure enough to support and encourage a wide range of experiencing; dysfunctional families are frightened and bloodless. Neither problem-solving skills nor particular family structures are considered as important as nurturing open, natural, and spontaneous experiencing. In short, the healthy family offers its members the freedom to be themselves.

DEVELOPMENT OF BEHAVIOR DISORDERS

From an experiential perspective, denial of impulses and suppression of feeling are the root of family problems. Dysfunctional families are locked into self-protection and avoidance (Kaplan & Kaplan, 1978). In Harry Stack Sullivan's (1953) terms, they seek *security* rather than *satisfaction*. Their presenting complaints are many, but the basic problem is that they smother emotion and desire.

According to Whitaker (Whitaker & Keith, 1981), there's no such thing as a marriage—only two scapegoats sent out by their families to perpetuate themselves. Together they must work out the inherent conflict in this situation. Couples who remain together eventually reach some kind of accommodation. Whether based on compromise or resignation, reconciling themselves to each other lessens the friction. Dysfunctional families, fearful of conflict, adhere rigidly to the rituals that they work out together. Having experienced the anxiety of uncertainty, they now cling to their routines.

In her portrayal of troubled families, Satir (1972) emphasized the atmosphere of emotional deadness. Such families are cold; they seem to stay together only out of habit or duty. The adults find their children annoying, and the children learn not to respect themselves or care about their parents. In consequence of the lack of warmth in the family, people avoid each other and preoccupy themselves with work and other distractions.

It's important to notice that the dysfunction Satir described isn't the kind found in diagnostic manuals. Like others in the experiential camp, Satir was as concerned with normal people who lead lives of quiet desperation as with the officially recognized patients families usually focus on. As she put it (Satir, 1972):

It is a sad experience for me to be with these families. I see the hopelessness, the helplessness, the loneliness. I see the bravery of people trying to cover up—a bravery that can still bellow or nag or whine at each other. Others no longer care. These people go on year after year, enduring misery themselves or in their desperation, inflicting it on others. (p. 12)

Satir stressed the role of destructive communication in smothering feeling and said that there were four dishonest ways people communicate: *blaming*, *placating*, being *irrelevant*, and being *super reasonable*. What's behind these patterns of inauthentic communication? *Low self-esteem*. If people feel bad about themselves, it's hard to tell the truth about their own feelings—and threatening hear what others feel.

A healthy relationship, according to Susan Johnson, is a secure attachment bond—that is, one characterized by emotional accessibility and responsiveness (Johnson & Denton, 2002). Secure attachment refers both to having grown up with a sense of being loved and to the confidence that comes from having a dependable intimate relationship. But when attachment security is threatened, people typically respond with anger—a protest that, unfortunately, may drive the other person away rather than evoke the desired responsiveness. Recently, Johnson has introduced the notion of *attachment injuries*, traumatic occurrences that damage the bond between partners and, if not resolved, maintain negative cycles and attachment insecurities.

GOALS OF THERAPY

In common with others in the humanistic tradition, experiential therapists believe that the way to emotional health is to uncover deeper levels of experiencing. Virginia Satir (1972) put it this way:

> We attempt to make three changes in the family system. First, each member of the family should be able to report congruently, completely, and honestly on what he sees and hears, feels and thinks, about himself and others, in the presence of others. Second, each

person should be addressed and related to in terms of his uniqueness, so that decisions are made in terms of exploration and negotiation rather than in terms of power. Third, differentness must be openly acknowledged and used for growth. (p. 120)

Experientialists emphasize the feeling side of human nature: creativity, spontaneity, and the ability to play—and, in therapy, the value of experience for its own sake.

New experience for family members is thought to break down rigid expectancies and unblock awareness—all of which promotes individuation (Kaplan & Kaplan, 1978). Bunny and Fred Duhl (1981) speak of their goals as a heightened sense of competence, well-being, and self-esteem. In emphasizing self-esteem, the Duhls echo Virginia Satir (1964), who believed that low self-esteem, and the destructive communication responsible for it, were the main problems in unhappy families. Whitaker (1976a) thought that families come to treatment because they're unable to be close and therefore unable to individuate. By helping family members recover their own potential for experiencing, he believed that he was also helping them recover their ability to care for one another.

CONDITIONS FOR BEHAVIOR CHANGE

Among the misconceptions of those new to family therapy is that families are fragile and therapists must be careful to avoid breaking them. A little experience teaches the opposite: Effective treatment requires powerful interventions—and for experiential family therapists that power comes from emotional experiencing.

Gus Napier (Napier & Whitaker, 1978) wrote in *The Family Crucible*, a nice description of what experiential therapists think causes change. Breakthroughs occur when family members risk being "more separate, divergent, even angrier" as well as "when they risk being closer and more intimate." To help clients take those risks, experiential therapists are alternately provocative and warmly supportive. This permits family members to drop their protective defenses and open up to each other.

Existential encounter is believed to be the essential force in the psychotherapeutic process (Kempler, 1973; Whitaker, 1976a). These encounters must be reciprocal; instead of hiding behind a professional role, the therapist must be a genuine person who catalyzes change using his or her personal impact on families. As Kempler (1968) said:

> In this approach the therapist becomes a family member during the interviews, participating as fully as he is able, hopefully available for appreciation and criticism as well as he is able to dispense it. He laughs, cries and rages. He feels and shares his embarrassments, confusions and helplessness. (p. 97)

For Satir, caring and acceptance were the keys to helping people open up to experience, and to each other:

> Some therapists think people come into therapy not wanting to be changed; I don't think that's true. They don't think they *can* change. Going into some new, unfamiliar place is a scary thing. When I first begin to work with someone, I am not interested in changing them. I am interested in finding their rhythms, being able to join with them, and helping them go inside to those scary places. Resistance is mainly the fear of going somewhere you have not been. (quoted in Simon, 1989, pp. 38–39)

Most approaches aim to help family members tell each other what's on their minds, but this only means that they'll share what they're conscious of feeling. They'll have fewer secrets from each other, but they'll continue to have secrets from themselves in the form of unconscious needs and feelings. Experiential therapists, on the other hand, believe that increasing the experience levels of individual family members will lead to more honest and intimate family interactions. The following example demonstrates this inside-out process.

Case Study

After an initial, information-gathering session, the L. family was discussing ten-year-old Tommy's misbehavior. For several minutes Mrs. L. and Tommy's younger sister took turns cataloging all the "terrible things" Tommy did around the house. As the discussion continued, the therapist noticed how uninvolved Mr. L. seemed to be. Although he dutifully nodded agreement to his wife's complaints, he seemed more apathetic than concerned. When asked what was on his mind, he said very little, and the therapist got the impression that, in fact, very little *was* on his mind—at least consciously. The therapist didn't know the reason for his lack of involvement, but she did know that it annoyed her, and she decided to say so.

Therapist: (To Mr. L.) Are you hearing this? What's going on with you?

Mr. L.: What? (He was shocked; nice people didn't speak that way.)

Therapist: I asked What's going on with you? Here your wife is concerned and upset about Tommy, and you just sit there like a bump on a log. You're about as much a part of this family as that lamp in the corner.

Mr. L.: You have no right to talk to me that way (getting angrier by the minute). I work hard for this family. Who do you think puts bread on the table? I get up six days a week and drive a delivery truck all over town. All day long I have to listen to customers bitching about this and that. Then I come home and what do I get? More bitching. *"Tommy did this, Tommy did that."* I'm sick of it.

Therapist: Say that again, louder.

Mr. L.: I'm sick of it! I'm sick of it!!

This interchange transformed the atmosphere in the session. Suddenly, the reason for Mr. L.'s withdrawal became clear. He was furious at his wife for constantly complaining about Tommy. She, in turn, was displacing much of her disappointment in her husband onto Tommy. In subsequent sessions, as Mr. and Mrs. L. spent more time talking about their relationship, less and less was heard about Tommy's misbehavior.

Following her own instincts, the therapist in this example increased the affective intensity in the session by confronting a member of the family. The anxiety generated as she did so was sufficient to expose a hidden problem. Once the problem was uncovered, it didn't take much pressure to get the family members to fight it out.

Although the reader may be uncomfortable with the idea of a therapist aggressively confronting a family member, it's not unusual in experiential therapy. What makes this move less risky than it may seem is the presence of other family members. When the whole family is there, it seems safer for therapists to be provocative than is true in individual treatment—and as Carl Whitaker (1975) pointed out, families will accept a great deal from a therapist, once they're convinced that he or she genuinely cares about them.

While experiential family therapists emphasize expanded experiencing for individuals as the vehicle for therapeutic change, they are now beginning to advocate inclusion of as many family members as possible in treatment. As experientialists, they believe in immediate personal experiencing; as family therapists, they believe in the interconnectedness of the family.

Carl Whitaker (1976b) liked a crowd in the room when he did therapy. He pushed for at least a couple of meetings with the larger family network, including parents, children, grandparents, and divorced spouses. Inviting these extended family members is an effective way to help them support treatment, instead of undermining it.

THERAPY

Experiential family therapists share the humanistic belief that people are naturally resourceful and, if left to their own devices, will be creative, loving, and productive (Rogers, 1951). The task of therapy is therefore seen as unblocking defenses and releasing people's innate vitality.

Assessment

Because experientialists are less interested in solving problems than in enhancing family functioning, they pay limited attention to the specifics of the presenting problem. Moreover, because they focus on individuals and their experience, they have little interest in the structure of family organization.

The following quotation illustrates the experientialist disdain for evaluation: "Diagnoses are the tombstones of the therapist's frustration, and accusations such as defensive, resistant, and secondary gain, are the flowers placed on the grave of his buried dissatisfaction" (Kempler, 1973, p. 11). The point seems to be that the objective distance necessary for formal assessment fosters a judgmental attitude and isolates therapists from emotional contact with families.

For most experientialists, assessment takes place informally as the therapist gets to know a family. In the process of developing a relationship, the therapist learns what kind of people he or she is dealing with. Whitaker began by asking each family member to describe the family and how it works. In this way, he got a composite picture of individual family members and their perceptions of the family group. This kind of inquiry is about as formal as most experiential therapists get in sizing up families. The majority of what serves as assessment in this approach is an attempt to decode the defenses that emerge in the ongoing course of trying to help family members open up to each other.

Therapeutic Techniques

In experiential therapy, according to Walter Kempler (1968), there are no techniques, only people. This epigram neatly summarizes the faith in the curative power of the therapist's personality. It isn't so much what therapists do that matters, but who they are.

However, this point is at least partly rhetorical. Whoever they *are*, therapists must also *do* something. Even if what they do isn't planned, it can nevertheless be described. Moreover, experiential therapists tend to do a lot; they're highly active and some (including Kempler) use a number of evocative techniques.

Some use structured devices such as *family sculpting* and *choreography*; others like Virginia Satir and Carl Whitaker rely on the spontaneity of just being themselves.

Virginia Satir had a remarkable ability to communicate. Like many great therapists, she was a dynamic personality—but she didn't rely merely on personal warmth. Rather, she worked actively to clarify communication, turned people away from complaining toward finding solutions, supported the self-esteem of every member of the family, pointed out positive intentions (long before *positive connotation* became a strategic device), and showed by example how to be affectionate (Satir & Baldwin, 1983). She was a loving but forceful healer.

One of Satir's hallmarks was the use of touch. Hers was the language of tenderness. She often began by making physical contact with children, as evidenced in her case "Of Rocks and Flowers." Bob, a recovering alcoholic, was the father of two boys, Aaron (four) and Robbie (two), whose mother had abused them repeatedly— pushing them down stairs, burning them with cigarettes, and tying them up under the sink. At the time of the interview, the mother was under psychiatric care and didn't see the children. Bob's new wife, Betty, had been abused by her previous husband, also an alcoholic. She was pregnant and afraid that the boys would abuse the baby. The boys had already been expressing the violence they'd been exposed to— slapping and choking other children. Bob and Betty, acting out of frustration and fear, responded roughly to the boys, which only increased their aggressiveness.

Throughout the session, Satir showed the parents how to touch the children tenderly and how to hold them firmly to stop them from misbehaving. When Bob started to tell Aaron something from a distance, Satir insisted on proximity and touch. She sat Aaron down in front of his father and asked Bob to take the little boy's hands and speak directly to him.

The following fragments from the session are taken from Andreas (1991).

Virginia Satir focused more on helping family members connect than on the psychological and systemic forces that kept them apart.

> Those little hands know a lot of things; they need to be reeducated. OK. Now, there is a lot of energy in both these youngsters, like there is in both of you. And I am going to talk to your therapist about making some room for you to have some respite (from the children). But use every opportunity you can to get this kind of physical contact. And what I would also recommend that you do is that the two of you are clear about what you expect.
>
> And if you (Bob) could learn from Betty how to pay attention (to the kids) more quickly. I would like you to be able to get your message without a "don't" in it, without a

Case Study

"don't"—and that your strength of your arms when you pick them up—I don't know if I can illustrate it to you, but let me have your arm for a minute (reaching for Bob's forearm). Let me show you the difference. Pick up my arm like you were going to grab me. (Bob grabs her arm.) All right. Now when you do that, my muscles all start to tighten, and I want to hit back. (Bob nods.) Now pick up my arm like you wanted to protect me. (Bob holds her arm.) All right. I feel your strength now, but I don't feel like I want to pull back like this. (Bob says, "Yeah.")

And what I'd like you to do is to do *lots* and lots of touching of both of these children. And when things start (to get out of hand), then you go over—don't say anything—go over to them and just take them (demonstrating the protective holding on both of Robbie's forearms) but you have to know in your inside that you're not pulling them (Aaron briefly puts his hands on top of Virginia's and Robbie's arms) like this (demonstrating), but you are taking them in a strong way (stroking Bob's arm with both hands), like you saw the difference. I'll demonstrate it to you (Bob), too. First of all I am going to grab you (demonstrating) like that. (Bob says, "Yeah.") You see you want to pull back. All right. Now, at this time what I am going to do is give you some strength (demonstrating holding his arm with both hands. Robbie pats Virginia's hand). But I am not going to ask you to retaliate. Now this is the most important thing for you to start with.

(Virginia turns to Betty and offers her forearm.) OK. Now I'd like to do the same with you. So, take my arm really tight. . . . (Betty grabs Virginia's arm, and Aaron does, too.) Yeah, that's right, like you really wanted to give me "what for." OK. All right. Now give it to me like you want to give me support, but you also want to give me a boundary. (Aaron reaches toward Betty's hand and Virginia takes Aaron's free hand in her free hand.) It's a little bit tight, a little bit tight.

So the next time you see anything coming, what you do is you go and make that contact (Virginia demonstrates by holding Aaron's upper arm) and then let it go soft. (Virginia takes

Aaron's hands and begins to draw him out of Betty's lap.) Now, Aaron, I'd like you to come up here so I could demonstrate something to your mother for a minute. (Aaron says, "OK.") Now, let's suppose some moment I'm not thinking and I take you like that (grabbing Betty's arms suddenly with both hands). You see what you want to do? (Betty nods.) All right. Now I am going to do it another way. I am giving you the same message (Virginia holds Betty's arm firmly with both hands, looking directly into her eyes, and starts to stand up), but I am doing it like this. And I am looking at you, and I'm giving you a straight message. OK. Now your body at that point is not going to respond negatively to me. It is going to feel stopped, but not negative. And then I will take you like this. (Virginia puts one arm around Betty's back and the other under her upper arm.) Just like this (Virginia puts both arms around Betty and draws her close) and now I will hold you. I will hold you like that for a little bit.

Following this session, Satir commented on her technique:

There had been so many things happening, and the fear was so strong in relation to these children that if you thought of one image it was like they were monsters. So one of the things that I wanted to do was also to see that they had the capacity to respond with a touch, using myself in that regard by having them put their hands on my face—that was a kind of mirror for the family itself, the people in the family. And then allowing them, and encouraging them to do that with their own parents. See, touch, that comes out of the kind of ambience which was there at the time, says things no words can say.

To encourage empathy and bring family members closer together, Satir often used the following exercise (adapted from Satir & Baldwin, 1983):

1. Think of a difficult situation with your child. Perhaps your child has been doing

something that you haven't known how to handle or that drives you up the wall.

2. Run your movie of this situation from your own point of view. Imagine you are going through this situation with your child again. Notice how you feel, what you see, what you hear.

3. Reexperience this situation but this time as your child. Visualize the entire situation slowly and in detail, as you would imagine seeing it through the eyes of your child. Let yourself feel what your child must be feeling. Do you notice any feelings that you weren't aware your child might be having? Do you notice something that your child might need or want that you hadn't been aware of?

4. Reexperience the same situation, this time as an observer. Watch and listen to what's happening, and allow yourself to observe both your child and yourself. Do you notice anything about the way you and your child respond to each other? What do you see more clearly about yourself and your child?

Because Whitaker favored a personal encounter over a calculated approach, it's not surprising that his style was the same with individuals, couples, and groups (Whitaker, 1958). He assiduously avoided directing real-life decisions, preferring instead to open family members up to their feelings and join them in their uncertainty. This may sound trite, but it's an important point. As long as a therapist (or anyone else for that matter) is anxious to change people, it's hard, very hard, to help them feel understood—and even harder to really empathize with them.

A comparison between Whitaker's early (Whitaker, 1967; Whitaker, Warkentin, & Malone, 1959) and later work (Napier & Whitaker, 1978) shows how he changed over the years. He started out as deliberately outlandish. He might fall asleep in sessions and then report his dreams; he wrestled with patients; he talked about his

own sexual fantasies. In later years, he was less provocative. This seems to be what happens to therapists as they mature; they have less need to impose themselves and more willingness to listen.

Because Whitaker's treatment was so intense and personal, he believed it essential that two therapists work together. Having a cotherapist to share the burden keeps therapists from being absorbed in the emotional field of the family. Family therapy tends to activate therapists' own feelings toward certain types of family members. A detached, analytic stance minimizes such feelings; emotional involvement maximizes them.

The trouble with countertransference is that it tends to be unconscious. Therapists are more likely to become aware of such feelings after sessions are over. Easier still is to observe countertransference in others. Consider the example of Dr. Fox, a married man who specializes in individual therapy but occasionally sees married couples in distress. In 75 percent of such cases, Dr. Fox encourages the couple to seek a divorce, and his patients follow his advice at a high rate. Perhaps if Dr. Fox were happier in his own marriage or had the courage to change it, he'd be less impelled to guide his patients where he fears to go.

To minimize countertransference, Whitaker recommended sharing feelings openly with the family. If feelings are openly expressed they're less likely to be acted out.

Whitaker's first sessions (Napier & Whitaker, 1978) were fairly structured, and they included taking a family history. For him, the first contacts with families were opening salvos in "the battle for structure" (Whitaker & Keith, 1981). He wanted the family to know that the therapists were in charge.[2] This began with the first telephone call. Whitaker (1976b) insisted that the largest possible number of family members attend; he believed that three generations were necessary to ensure that grandparents would

[2]We might add that there is a big difference between trying to control the structure of sessions and trying to control people's lives.

support, not oppose, therapy and that their presence would help correct distortions. If significant family members wouldn't attend, Whitaker generally refused to see the family. Why begin with the cards stacked against you?

Along with Virginia Satir, Whitaker was among the foremost exponents of the therapist's use of self as a catalyst for change. But whereas Satir offered a warm, supportive presence, Whitaker was at times blunt, even confrontational. Actually, the provocative interventions of someone like Whitaker only become acceptable to families after the therapist has proven to be an understanding and caring person. Before challenging people, it is first necessary to win their trust.

But whether they are provocative or supportive, experiential therapists are usually quite active. Instead of leaving family members to work out their own issues with each other, they are told "Tell him (or her) what you feel!" or asked "What are you feeling right now?" Just as the best way to get a school teacher's attention is to misbehave, the best way to get an experiential therapist's attention is to show signs of emotion without actually expressing it.

Case Study

Therapist: I see you looking over at Dad whenever you ask Mom a question, what's that about?

Kendra: Oh, nothing. . . .

Therapist: It must mean *something.* Come on, what were you feeling?

Kendra: Nothing!

Therapist: You must have been feeling something. What was it?

Kendra: Well, sometimes when Mom lets me do something, Dad gets mad. But instead of yelling at her, he yells at *me* (crying softly).

Therapist: Tell him.

Kendra: (Angrily, to the therapist) Leave me alone!

Therapist: No, it's important. Tell your Dad how you feel.

Kendra: (Sobbing hard) You're always picking on me! You never let me do anything!

Experiential therapists use a number of expressive techniques in their work, including family sculpting (Duhl, Kantor, & Duhl, 1973),

Experiential therapists use expressive techniques to help families get at underlying feelings.

family puppet interviews (Irwin & Malloy, 1975), family art therapy (Geddes & Medway, 1977), conjoint family drawings (Bing, 1970), and Gestalt therapy techniques (Kempler, 1973). Among the accoutrements of experiential therapists' offices are toys, dollhouses, clay, teddy bears, drawing pens and paper, and batacca bats.

In **family sculpting**, the therapist asks one member of a family to arrange the others in a tableau. This is a graphic means of portraying each person's perceptions of the family and his or her place in it. This was a favorite device of Virginia Satir, who frequently used ropes and blindfolds to dramatize the constricting roles family members trap each other into (Satir & Baldwin, 1983).

The following example of sculpting occurred when a therapist asked Mr. N. to arrange the members of his family into a scene typical of the time when he comes home from work.

Mr. N.: When I come home from work, eh? Okay (to his wife), honey, you'd be by the stove, wouldn't you?

Therapist: No, don't talk. Just move people where you want them to be.

Mr. N.: Okay.

He guided his wife to stand at a spot where the kitchen stove might be and placed his children on the kitchen floor, drawing and playing.

Therapist: Fine, now, still without any dialogue, put them into action.

Mr. N. then instructed his wife to pretend to cook but to turn frequently to see what the kids were up to. He told the children to pretend to play for a while but then to start fighting and complaining to Mommy.

Therapist: And what happens, when you come home?

Mr. N.: Nothing. I try to talk to my wife, but the kids keep pestering her, and she gets mad and says to leave her alone.

Therapist: Okay, act it out.

Mrs. N. acted out trying to cook and referee the children's fights. The children, who thought this a great game, pretended to fight and tried to outdo each other getting Mommy's attention. When Mr. N. "came home," he reached out for his wife, but the children came between them, until Mrs. N. finally pushed all of them away.

Afterwards, Mrs. N. said that she hadn't realized her husband felt ignored. She just thought of him as coming home, saying hello, and then withdrawing into the den with his newspaper and a bottle of beer.

Family sculpting is also used to illuminate scenes from the past. A typical instruction is, "Remember standing in front of your childhood home. Walk in and describe what typically happened." The idea is to make a tableau portraying one's perceptions of family life. It's a device to focus awareness and heighten sensitivity.

Another expressive exercise is *family art therapy*. Kwiatkowska (1967) instructs families to produce a series of drawings, including a "joint family scribble," in which each person makes a quick scribble and then the whole family incorporates the scribble into a unified picture. Elizabeth Bing (1970) describes the conjoint **family drawing** as a means to warm families up and free them to express themselves. In this procedure, families are told to "Draw a picture as you see yourselves as a family." The resulting portraits may disclose perceptions that haven't previously been discussed, or the task may stimulate the person drawing the picture to realize something that he or she had never considered before.

A father drew a picture of the family that showed him off to one side, while his wife and children stood holding hands. Although he was portraying a fact well-known to his wife and himself, they hadn't spoken openly of it. Once he showed his drawing to the therapist, there was no avoiding discussion.

In another case, when the therapist asked each of the family members to draw the family, the teenage daughter was uncertain what to do. She had never thought much about the family or her role in it. When she started to work, her drawing just seemed to emerge. She was surprised to discover that she'd drawn herself closer to her father and sisters than to her mother. This provoked a lively discussion between her and her mother about their relationship. Although the two of them spent time together, the daughter didn't feel close because she thought her mother treated her like a child, never talking about her own concerns, and showing only superficial interest in the daughter's life. For her part, the mother was surprised, and not at all displeased, that her daughter felt ready to establish a relationship on a more mutual, caring basis.

In *family puppet interviews*, Irwin and Malloy (1975) ask one of the family members to make up a story using puppets. This technique, originally used in play therapy, is designed to highlight conflicts and alliances. Puppets also provide a safe avenue for symbolic communication. For example, a child who has used a specific puppet to symbolize his anger (e.g., a dinosaur) may simply reach for the dinosaur whenever he feels threatened.

Diana Arad recently developed the *animal attribution storytelling technique*, which requires family members to choose animals to represent all the members of the family and then tell a story about the animal protagonists. The following case study from Arad (2004) illustrates the application of this technique in a family with an aggressive, acting-out nine-year-old.

Case Study

Sara and Jacob Cohen came to therapy with their daughter Dana (four) and son Roy (nine), who was diagnosed with oppositional defiant disorder. Roy was aggressively rebellious, wet his bed, and alternated between depression and angry outbursts in which he said he wished he were dead. He also showed extreme sibling rivalry with his little sister and frequently punched her during arguments.

Roy entered the office for the first session firmly in his father's grasp. He'd been crying and was determined not to cooperate. The therapist assured him that he wasn't going to be forced to do anything and that he didn't have to participate if he didn't want to.

When the therapist introduced the animal storytelling game, she began by asking Dana, the youngest member of the family, to begin (to prevent her from copying other family members' stories). "If your mother were an animal," the therapist asked Dana, "what animal would she be?"

Dana replied that her mother would be a horse, her father a squirrel, her brother a chicken, and herself a wolf. When asked to make up a story about these animal characters, Dana related the following:

Once upon a time, a horse went to visit his friend the chicken. At the same time, a wolf came to eat the chicken, but the horse saved the chicken. Then the squirrel took the chicken and the horse to visit him under his tree and made the chicken laugh.

What this story revealed was that four-year-old Dana, who was seen as the good child and her brother's victim, saw herself (wolf) as an aggressor to her brother (chicken) and as an outsider to the family interaction (not invited to the fun under the squirrel's tree). Her parents were extremely surprised by this portrayal of the family. When she was asked for an example of acting like a wolf, Dana described how when Roy used the computer, she would watch from the door and then "attack" his mouse-using hand and run to her mother. Roy would chase her, "clucking" like a chicken, but he couldn't retaliate because Dana was protected by mother. Roy usually shouted and raged and then got punished, leaving the computer free for Dana to use.

Here's Roy's story:

Once upon a time, when an elephant (dad) went for a walk in the jungle, he stepped on a cockroach (Dana). The cockroach got squished, but the elephant did not notice and went on his way. A cat (Roy) came, found the squished cockroach, and thought it was a Frisbee. He took it to his friend the dog (mom) in order to play with it. They played Frisbee with it until they were fed up and threw it back to where the cat had found it. The elephant came back, took the squished cockroach, and ate it. The cockroach recovered and ran around inside the elephant. This tickled him so that he burst out laughing, expelling the cockroach through his mouth so hard that it landed in the same place where he was stepped on before. Then one day, the elephant went for a walk again and stepped on it again.

Both children's stories portrayed the father as a disengaged figure—a funny squirrel who appears after the danger is gone and a passing elephant who does damage without even noticing. This picture, which did not match the family's official version of the father as loving and involved, was also reflected in the mother's story, in which the father was represented as a mischievous but unapproachable dolphin. The children's stories helped the parents to see Roy in a different light. They agreed that when Roy started raging, cursing, and throwing things, they would consider it "clucking like a chicken," and they would keep their distance. Moreover, the parents took the children's perspectives into account and stopped blaming Roy for all the fights. They decided to enforce equal consequences when the children fought. They were both sent to time out—"just in case the wolf was at it again." Roy thought this was fair, and sibling rivalry decreased considerably.

Eliana Gil (1994) describes a number of play therapy techniques and explains how they can be used to engage young children in family treatment. In the *typical day interview*, Gil asks children to pick days of the week and select dolls (or puppets) to represent the people in their families. Then the therapist asks the children to use the figures to show where people are and what they do throughout the day. Gil recommends asking specifically about television watching, eating habits, sleeping habits, hygiene, anger, and affection. One ten-year-old who had described everything in his house as fine responded to a question about what he watched on television after school by listing twelve shows, ending with David Letterman. When the therapist asked, "What happens after you watch Letterman?" the boy replied, "I go to sleep." "Who's at home when you go to sleep?" "No one" (Gil, 1994).

Role-playing is another favorite device. Its use is based on the premise that experience, to be real, must be brought to life in the present. Recollection of past events and consideration of hoped-for or feared future developments can be made more immediate by role-playing them in the immediacy of the session. Kempler (1968) encourages parents to fantasize and role-play scenes from childhood. A mother might be asked to role-play what it was like when she was a little girl, or a father might be asked to imagine himself as a boy caught in the same dilemma as his son.

When someone who isn't present is mentioned, therapists may introduce the Gestalt *empty chair technique* (Kempler, 1973). If a child talks about her grandfather, she might be asked to speak to a chair, which is used to personify grandfather. Whitaker (1975) used a similar role-playing technique, which he called "psychotherapy of the absurd." This consists of augmenting the unreasonable quality of a patient's response to the point of absurdity. It often amounts to calling a person's bluff, as the following example illustrates:

Patient: I can't stand my husband!
Therapist: Why don't you get rid of him, or take up a boyfriend?

At times, this takes the form of sarcastic teasing, such as mock fussing in response to a fussy child. The hope is that patients will get objective distance by participating in the therapist's distancing; the danger is that patients will feel hurt at being made fun of.

Susan Johnson's focus on emotional longings can be seen as an antidote to the field's current preoccupation with cognition.

These techniques have proved useful in individual therapy (Nichols & Zax, 1977) to intensify emotional experiencing by bringing memories into focus and acting out suppressed reactions. Whether such devices are necessary in family therapy is open to question. In individual treatment, patients are isolated from the significant figures in their lives, and role-playing may be useful to approximate being with those people. But because family therapy is conducted with significant people present, it seems doubtful that role-playing or other means of fantasy are necessary. If emotional action is wanted, plenty is available simply by opening dialogue between family members.

Two recent emotive approaches to family therapy that represent a more sophisticated understanding of family dynamics are emotionally focused couples therapy and the internal family systems model.

Emotionally Focused Couples Therapy. Emotionally focused couples therapy works on two levels in succession—uncovering the hurt and longing beneath defensive expressions of anger and withdrawal and then helping couples understand how these feelings are played out in their relationship. To begin with, the therapist acknowledges each client's immediate feelings—hurt and anger, say—to make them feel understood (Johnson, 1998).

Case Study

"You're getting angrier and angrier. It's upsetting for you to hear Will picture himself as innocent, isn't it?"

By interrupting a couple's quarrel and reflecting what each of them is feeling, the therapist defuses hostility and helps them focus on their experience, rather than on each other's crimes. Then, to explore the perceptions that underlie the partners' emotional responses to each other, the therapist asks for a description of what happens at home.

"Oh, so part of you believes him, but part of you is suspicious?"
"Part of you is watching and expecting that he'll hurt you?"
"Can you tell me about the part that believes he's being honest?"

Next the therapist points out how the couple's emotions are driving them into cycles of escalating polarization.

The cycle was formulated in terms of Will's protecting himself by staying distant and avoiding Nancy's anger, and Nancy's being vigilant and fighting to avoid being betrayed again. As she became more insecure and distrustful, Will then felt more helpless and distanced himself further. As he distanced, she felt betrayed and became more enraged. Both were framed as victims of the cycle, which I continually framed as a common problem that the partners need to help each other with. (Johnson, 1998, pp. 457–458)

The couple's growing awareness of how their emotional reactivity frustrates their longings sets the stage for uncovering and expressing the deep emotions that lie beneath their sparring. The resulting cathartic expression makes it possible for the couple to deepen their understanding of their destructive pattern with each other, and this circular process continues to be explored in the process of working through.

Attachment theory helps the emotionally focused couples therapist pinpoint the issues that get stirred up when couples talk about their hurts and longings.

"Maybe you feel like no one really loves you?"

"You feel helpless and alone, don't you?"

The impact of this emotional evocation is enhanced by the fact that the partner is present to be addressed in this new and more "feelingful" way.

"So, can you tell her that?"

The ultimate aim of this work is to enable the partners to risk being vulnerable with each other by acknowledging and expressing their attachment needs.

"Only you can face your fear and decide to risk depending on Will. He can't do it, can he? The only one who can drop your defenses and risk trusting him is you, isn't it?"

"What's the worst thing that could happen?"

Again, working together with the couple means that once the partners risk expressing their needs and fears, their mates can be encouraged to respond.

"What happens to you, Will, when you hear this?"

The response to this question will, of course, be very different once the partners let down their guard and begin to talk about what they're afraid of and what they really want from each other.

The therapist frames the couple's experiences in terms of deprivation, isolation, and loss of secure connectedness. This perspective, from attachment theory, helps family members focus on their longings rather than on each other's faults and failings.

The process of therapeutic intervention has been described in nine treatment steps (Johnson, Hunsley, Greenberg, & Schindler, 1999):

1. Assessment, or creating an alliance and explicating the core issues in the couple's conflict using attachment theory
2. Identifying the problematic interaction cycle that maintains attachment insecurity and relationship distress
3. Uncovering the unacknowledged emotions underlying interactional positions
4. Reframing the problem in terms of a problematic cycle with underlying emotions and attachment needs
5. Encouraging acceptance and expression of disowned needs and aspects of the self
6. Encouraging acceptance of the partner's new openness
7. Encouraging the expression of specific needs and wants and creating an intimate, emotional engagement
8. Facilitating new solutions to unresolved relationship issues
9. Consolidating new positions and more honest expression of attachment needs

In all of these steps the therapist moves between helping partners uncover and express their emotional experience and helping them reorganize the pattern of their interactions. For example:

The therapist might, then, first help a withdrawn, guarded spouse formulate his sense of paralyzed helplessness that primes his withdrawal. The therapist will validate this sense of helplessness by placing it within the context of the destructive cycle that has taken over the relationship. The therapist will heighten this experience in the session and then help his partner to hear and accept it, even though it is very different from the way she usually experiences her spouse. Finally, the therapist moves to structuring an interaction around this helplessness, as in, "So can you turn to her and can you tell her, 'I feel so helpless and defeated. I just want to run away and hide.'" This kind of statement, in and of itself, represents a move away from passive withdrawal and is the beginning of active emotional engagement. (Johnson et al., 1999, p. 70)

Internal Family Systems Therapy. In the internal family systems model (Schwartz, 1995), conflicting inner voices are personified as subpersonalities or "parts." What makes this device powerful is that even when client family members are at odds with each other, their conflicts are often based on polarizations of part of what they feel. The truth is that people in conflict with each other are also often in conflict within themselves.

The adolescent's defiance and her parents' distrust are only one aspect of the complex feelings they have for each other—or to choose a different example, a couple caught in a pursuer–distancer pattern may be acting out only those parts of them that are terrified of abandonment and engulfment. By dramatizing the elements of their inner conflicts, internal family systems therapy helps family members sort out their feelings and reconnect with each other in less polarized ways.

To help clients begin to distinguish among their conflicting inner voices, Schwartz begins by introducing the language of parts.

Case Study

"So there's a part of you that gets upset and angry when your son gets down on himself. Do you think that if that part didn't get so stirred up, it would be easier for you to help him?"

"It sounds like part of you agrees with your husband about getting stricter with the kids, but there's another part that says he's being too harsh. What is that second part? What does it say to you? What is it afraid of?"

By listening carefully to what clients are feeling and then construing their reactions as coming from a part of them, the therapist initiates a shift in family polarizations. It's easier for people to acknowledge that "a part of them" feels—angry, helpless, or whatever—than that "they" (as in all of them) feel that way. A parent who has trouble admitting that he's angry at his son

for not doing well in school may find it easier to acknowledge that a part of him gets angry at his son's failures—and, moreover, that the angry part gets in the way of his sympathetic part.

Once the idea is introduced that various parts of family members are reacting to each other, instead of seeing themselves intrinsically at odds, they can begin to see that parts of one are triggering parts of another. The obvious implication is that if their aggravating emotions are contained in only parts of them, they have other feelings and other possibilities for interaction.

Thus: "So that angry part of your father seems to trigger a sad and helpless part of you, is that right?"

And since many such polarizations become triangles, it might be that the father's angry part also triggers a protective part in his wife.

"So when you see your husband's angry part responding to your son that triggers a protective part in you? A part of you feels that you need to fight your husband to protect your son?"

So instead of having a son who is a failure, a father who is unsympathetic, and parents who can't agree, the family discovers that each of them is having trouble with some of their parts. The father is transformed from a tyrant to a parent struggling with a frustrated and angry part of him. His wife ceases to be basically at odds with him and instead is seen as having a protective part that gets triggered by his angry part. And instead of being a failure, the son becomes a boy with a part of him that feels helpless in the face of his father's angry part and his parents' conflict.

Like all experiential models, internal family systems therapy is founded on the belief that underneath people's emotionally reactive parts lays a healthy self at the core of the personality. When the therapist notices various parts taking over, he or she asks the person first to visualize them, and then help them to calm down. If, for example, an angry part were seen as a snarling dog, that person might find that she could calm her anger by approaching the dog and petting it until it felt reassured and settled down—or to use another example (cited by Schwartz, 1998), if a frightened part were imagined as a rag doll, the client might relax her fears by imagining holding and comforting that doll.

Thus, by personifying people's polarizing emotional reactions as parts and then helping them visualize and reassure these reactive parts, internal family systems therapy releases people from the domination of fear and anger, which in turn allows them to work together more effectively to solve personal and family problems.

EVALUATING THERAPY THEORY AND RESULTS

Experiential therapy helps family members get beneath the surface of their interactions to explore the feelings that drive them. At its best, this approach helps people drop their defenses and come together with more immediacy and authenticity. Given family therapy's emphasis on behavior and cognition, the effort to help clients uncover the feeling side of their experience is surely a welcome addition.

Regardless of what approach to family therapy one takes, shifting to individuals and their experience is a good way to break through defensive squabbling. When family members argue, they usually lead with their defenses. Instead of saying "*I'm* hurt," they say "*You* make me mad"; instead of admitting they're afraid, they criticize each other. An effective way to interrupt the unproductive escalation of arguments is to explore the affect of the participants, one at a time. By talking to individuals about what they're feeling—and the roots of such feelings—family members can be helped to get past the defensiveness that keeps them apart and to reconnect on a more genuine level.

However, just as approaches that focus entirely on families and their interactions leave something out, so too does an approach that concentrates too narrowly on individuals and their emotional experience. At the peak of their popularity in the 1970s, experiential therapists approached family therapy as if it were an encounter group for relatives. They put great faith in the value of individual emotional experiencing and had limited appreciation of the role family structure plays in regulating that experience. Not surprisingly, therefore, as family therapy focused more on organization, interaction, and narrative in the 1980s and 1990s, the experiential model fell out of favor.

As we have already suggested, a therapy designed primarily to elicit feelings may be more suited to encounter groups than to family therapy. However, the prevailing behavioral and cognitive models of family therapy could do with a little more attention to people's feelings. If "more attention to people's feelings" sounds a little vague, allow us to make it more concrete. Helping family members get in touch with their feelings accomplishes two things: It helps them as individuals to discover what they really think and feel—what they want and what they're afraid of—and it helps them as a family get beyond defensiveness and begin to relate to each other in a more honest and immediate way.

Two particularly creative approaches to helping individuals get in touch with their inner experience are emotionally focused couples therapy and internal family systems therapy. What sets Johnson and Greenberg's therapy apart is its combination of emotional expressiveness and attention to the dynamics of interaction between couples. Emotionally focused couples therapy begins, as all emotive approaches do, by eliciting and acknowledging the feelings clients come in with—even, or especially, if those feelings are defensive. You don't get beneath the surface of what people are feeling by ignoring it.

The combination of uncovering deeper and more vulnerable emotions and teaching couples about the reactive patterns their feelings drive them through creates a meaningful cognitive experience. As Lieberman, Yalom, and Miles (1973) demonstrated with encounter groups, an emotionally intense therapeutic experience only brings lasting value when paired with an intellectual understanding of the significance of those emotions. The only caveat we might offer is that explanations are most useful following an emotionally significant process of uncovering—which is what distinguishes psychotherapy from a conversation with your Aunt Harriet.

Emotionally focused couples therapy maintains that relationship difficulties generally stem from the disowning of attachment needs, creating defensive interactional cycles and ineffective communication patterns. The model identifies these issues and destructive cycles, helps clients acknowledge the feelings underlying these cycles, encourages empathy for the partner's position, and encourages couples to communicate needs and emotions more effectively in the spirit of generating solutions and solidifying new relationship positions to increase intimacy.

Schwartz's internal family systems approach helps family members come together with more understanding by helping individuals sort out their own conflicted experience. Personifying unruly emotions as "parts" is a powerful device for helping people achieve a clarifying distance from their conflicts. Unlike emotionally focused therapy, internal family systems therapy does not lean heavily on didactic explanations. In this approach, emotional experiencing is clarified but by learning to differentiate among one's own feelings rather than by explanations offered by the therapist.

In addition to anecdotal reports of successful outcomes (Duhl & Duhl, 1981; Napier & Whitaker, 1978) and descriptions of techniques that are effective in catalyzing emotional expression within sessions (Kempler, 1981), emotionally focused couples therapy has received a good deal of empirical support (e.g., Johnson & Greenberg, 1985, 1988; Johnson, Maddeaux, & Blouin, 1998; Johnson et al., 1999).

Recently, researchers seeking to study the effectiveness of experiential techniques have followed Mahrer's (1982) suggestion to focus on the process, rather than the outcome, of therapy. Because he believed that studies of outcome have little impact on practitioners (who already know that what they do works), Mahrer recommended studying *in-therapy outcomes*; that is, what kinds of interventions produce desired results (emotional expression, more open communication) within sessions. Following Mahrer (1982) and others (Pierce, Nichols, & DuBrin, 1983) who looked at such in-therapy outcomes in individual treatment, Leslie Greenberg and Susan Johnson have found that helping an angry and attacking partner to reveal his or her softer feelings characterizes the best session of successful cases (Johnson & Greenberg, 1988) and that intimate self-disclosure leads to more productive sessions (Greenberg, Ford, Alden, & Johnson, 1993).

Once, feeling and expression occupied center stage in psychological therapies; today, that place is held by behavior and cognition. Psychotherapists have discovered that people think and act, but that doesn't mean we should ignore the immediate emotional experience that is the main concern of experiential family therapy.

SUMMARY

Experiential therapy works from the inside out—strengthening families by encouraging individual self-expression, reversing the usual direction of effect in family therapy. Experiential family therapy is also distinguished by a commitment to

emotional well-being as opposed to problem solving. Personal integrity and self-fulfillment are seen as innate human capacities that will emerge spontaneously once defensiveness is overcome. To challenge the familiar and enhance experiencing, therapists use their own lively personalities as well as a host of expressive techniques.

Although the experiential model lost popularity in the 1980s, it is now enjoying something of a resurgence, especially in the innovative work of emotionally focused couples therapy and the internal family systems approach. Once, the idea that families were systems was both novel and controversial; today, it is the new orthodoxy. Now that the pendulum has swung so far in the direction of systems thinking, individuals and their private joys and pains are rarely mentioned. Surely one of the major contributions of experiential family therapy is to remind us not to lose sight of the self in the system.

RECOMMENDED READINGS

Duhl, F. J., Kantor, D., and Duhl, B. S. 1973. Learning, space and action in family therapy: A primer of sculpture. In *Techniques in family therapy*, D. A. Bloch, ed. New York: Grune & Stratton.

Gil, E. 1994. *Play in family therapy*. New York: Guilford Press.

Greenberg, L. S., and Johnson, S. M. 1988. *Emotionally focused therapy for couples*. New York: Guilford Press.

Keith, D. V., and Whitaker, C. A. 1977. The divorce labyrinth. In *Family therapy: Full-length case studies*, P. Papp, ed. New York: Gardner Press.

Napier, A. Y., and Whitaker, C. A. 1978. *The family crucible*. New York: Harper & Row.

Neill, J. R., and Kniskern, D. P., eds. 1982. *From psyche to system: The evolving therapy of Carl Whitaker*. New York: Guilford Press.

Satir, V. M. 1988. *The new peoplemaking*. Palo Alto, CA: Science and Behavior Books.

Satir, V. M., and Baldwin, M. 1983. *Satir step by step: A guide to creating change in families*. Palo Alto, CA: Science and Behavior Books.

Schwartz, R. C. 1995. *Internal family systems therapy*, New York: Guilford Press.

Schwartz, R. C. 1998. Internal family systems therapy. In *Case studies in couple and family therapy*, F. M. Dattilio, ed. New York: Guilford Press.

Whitaker, C. A., and Bumberry, W. M. 1988. *Dancing with the family: A symbolic experiential approach*. New York: Brunner/Mazel.

Whitaker, C. A., and Keith, D. V. 1981. Symbolic-experiential family therapy. In *Handbook of family therapy*, A. S. Gurman and D. P. Kniskern, eds. New York: Brunner/Mazel.

REFERENCES

Andreas, S. 1991. *Virginia Satir: The patterns of her magic*. Palo Alto, CA: Science and Behavior Books.

Arad, D. 2004. If your mother were an animal, what animal would she be? Creating play stories in family therapy: The animal attribution storytelling technique (AASTT). *Family Process*. 43:249–263.

Bing, E. 1970. The conjoint family drawing. *Family Process*. 9:173–194.

Binswanger, L. 1967. Being-in-the-world. In *Selected papers of Ludwig Binswanger*, J. Needleman, ed. New York: HarperTorchbooks.

Boss, M. 1963. *Psychoanalysis and daseinanalysts*. New York: Basic Books.

Bowlby, J. 1969. *Attachment and loss: Vol. 1. Attachment*. New York: Basic Books.

Bowlby, J. 1988. *A secure base*. New York: Basic Books.

Collins, N. L., and Read, S. J. 1994. Cognitive representations of attachment: The structure and function of working models. In *Attachment processes in adulthood*, K. Bartholomew and D. Perlman, eds. London: Jessica Kingsley.

Duhl, B. S., and Duhl, F. J. 1981. Integrative family therapy. In *Handbook of family therapy*, A. S. Gurman and D. P. Kniskern, eds. New York: Brunner/Mazel.

Duhl, F. J., Kantor D., and Duhl, B. S. 1973. Learning, space and action in family therapy: A primer of sculpture. In *Techniques of family psychotherapy*, D. A. Bloch, ed. New York: Grune & Stratton.

Geddes, M., and Medway, J. 1977. The symbolic drawing of family life space. *Family Process.* 16:219–228.

Gehrke, S., and Kirschenbaum, M. 1967. Survival patterns in conjoint family therapy. *Family Process.* 6:67–80.

Gil, E. 1994. *Play in family therapy.* New York: Guilford Press.

Greenberg, L. S., and Johnson, S. M. 1985. Emotionally focused couple therapy: An affective systemic approach. In *Handbook of family and marital therapy*, N. S. Jacobson and A. S. Gurman, eds. New York: Guilford Press.

Greenberg, L. S., and Johnson, S. M. 1986. Affect in marital therapy. *Journal of Marital and Family Therapy.* 12:1–10.

Greenberg, L. S., and Johnson, S. M. 1988. *Emotionally focused therapy for couples.* New York: Guilford Press.

Greenberg, L. S., Ford, C. L., Alden, L., and Johnson, S. M. 1993. In-session change in emotionally focused therapy. *Journal of Consulting and Clinical Psychology.* 61:78–84.

Irwin, E., and Malloy, E. 1975. Family puppet interview. *Family Process.* 14:179–191.

Johnson, S. M. 1998. Emotionally focused couple therapy. In *Case studies in couple and family therapy*, F. M. Dattilio, ed. New York: Guilford Press.

Johnson, S. M., and Denton, W. 2002. Emotionally focused couple therapy: Creating secure connections. In *Clinical handbook of couple therapy*, 3rd ed., A. S. Gurman and N. S. Jacobson, eds. New York: Guilford Press.

Johnson, S. M., and Greenberg, L. S. 1985. Emotionally focused couples therapy: An outcome study. *Journal of Marital and Family Therapy.* 11:313–317.

Johnson, S. M., and Greenberg, L. S. 1988. Relating process to outcome in marital therapy. *Journal of Marital and Family Therapy.* 14:175–183.

Johnson, S. M., Maddeaux, C., and Blouin, J. 1998. Emotionally focused therapy for bulimia: Changing attachment patterns. *Psychotherapy.* 35:238–247.

Johnson, S. M., Hunsley, J., Greenberg, L., and Schindler, D. 1999. Emotionally focused couples therapy: Status and challenges. *Clinical Psychology: Science and Practice.* 6:67–79.

Kaplan, M. L., and Kaplan, N. R. 1978. Individual and family growth: A Gestalt approach. *Family Process.* 17:195–205.

Kempler, W. 1968. Experiential psychotherapy with families. *Family Process.* 7:88–89.

Kempler, W. 1973. *Principles of Gestalt family therapy.* Oslo: Nordahls.

Kempler, W. 1981. *Experiential psychotherapy with families.* New York: Brunner/Mazel.

Kwiatkowska, H. Y. 1967. Family art therapy. *Family Process.* 6:37–55.

Laing, R. D. 1967. *The politics of experience.* New York: Ballantine.

Laing, R. D., and Esterson, A. 1970. *Sanity, madness and the family.* Baltimore, MD: Penguin Books.

Lieberman, M. A., Yalom, I. D., and Miles, M. B. 1973. *Encounter groups: First facts.* New York: Basic Books.

Mahrer, A. R. 1982. *Experiential psychotherapy: Basic practices.* New York: Brunner/Mazel.

Marcuse, H. 1955. *Eros and civilization.* New York: Beacon Press.

Napier, A. Y., and Whitaker, C. A. 1978. *The family crucible.* New York: Harper & Row.

Nichols, M. P., and Zax, M. 1977. *Catharsis in psychotherapy.* New York: Gardner Press.

Pierce, R., Nichols, M. P., and DuBrin, J. 1983. *Emotional expression in psychotherapy.* New York: Gardner Press.

Rogers, C. R. 1951. *Client-centered therapy.* Boston: Houghton Mifflin.

Satir, V. M. 1964. *Conjoint family therapy.* Palo Alto, CA: Science and Behavior Books.

Satir, V. M. 1972. *Peoplemaking.* Palo Alto, CA: Science and Behavior Books.

Satir, V. M., and Baldwin, M. 1983. *Satir step by step: A guide to creating change in families.* Palo Alto, CA: Science and Behavior Books.

Schwartz, R. C. 1995. *Internal family systems therapy.* New York: Guilford Press.

Schwartz, R. C. 1998. Internal family systems therapy. In *Case studies in couple and family therapy*, F. M. Dattilio, ed. New York: Guilford Press.

Simon, R. 1989. Reaching out to life: An interview with Virginia Satir. *The Family Therapy Networker.* 13(1):36–43.

Sullivan, H. S. 1953. *The interpersonal theory of psychiatry.* New York: Norton.

Whitaker, C. A. 1958. Psychotherapy with couples. *American Journal of Psychotherapy.* 12:18–23.

Whitaker, C. A. 1967. The growing edge. In *Techniques of family therapy*, J. Haley and L. Hoffman, eds. New York: Basic Books.

Whitaker, C. A. 1975. Psychotherapy of the absurd: With a special emphasis on the psychotherapy of aggression. *Family Process. 14*:1–16.

Whitaker, C. A. 1976a. The hindrance of theory in clinical work. In *Family therapy: Theory and practice*, P. J. Guerin, ed. New York: Gardner Press.

Whitaker, C. A. 1976b. A family is a four-dimensional relationship. In *Family therapy: Theory and practice*, P. J. Guerin, ed. New York: Gardner Press.

Whitaker, C. A., and Keith, D. V. 1981. Symbolic-experiential family therapy. In *Handbook of family therapy*, A. S. Gurman and D. P. Kniskern, eds. New York: Brunner/Mazel.

Whitaker, C. A., and Malone, T. P. 1953. *The roots of psychotherapy*. New York: Blakiston.

Whitaker, C. A., Warkentin, J., and Malone, T. P. 1959. The involvement of the professional therapist. In *Case studies in counseling and psychotherapy*, A. Burton, ed. Upper Saddle River, NJ: Prentice Hall.

Psychoanalytic Family Therapy

9

Rediscovering Psychodynamics

Many of the pioneers of family therapy, including Nathan Ackerman, Murray Bowen, Ivan Boszormenyi-Nagy, Carl Whitaker, Don Jackson, and Salvador Minuchin, were psychoanalytically trained. But with the eager enthusiasm of converts, they turned away from the old—psychodynamics—and toward the new—systems dynamics. Some, like Jackson and Minuchin, moved far indeed from their psychoanalytic roots. Others, like Bowen and Nagy, retained a distinctly analytic influence in their work.

In the 1960s and 1970s, family therapy followed Jackson and Minuchin in not only ignoring psychoanalytic thinking but denigrating it. Jackson (1967) went so far as to declare the death of the individual, and Minuchin (1989) proclaimed, "We understood that the decontexted individual was a mythical monster, an illusion created by psychodynamic blinders."

Then in the 1980s, a surprising shift occurred: Family therapists took a renewed interest in the psychology of the individual. This revival of interest reflected changes in psychoanalysis—from the individualism of Freudian theory to the more relationship-oriented object relations theories and self psychology—as well as changes in family therapy itself, especially dissatisfaction with the mechanistic elements of the cybernetic model. Among the books calling for a rapprochement with psychoanalysis were *Object Relations: A Dynamic Bridge Between Individual and Family Treatment* (Slipp, 1984), *Object Relations Family Therapy* (Scharff & Scharff, 1987), and *The Self in the System* (Nichols, 1987).

The reason these psychodynamic voices found a receptive audience was that while family therapists discovered profound truths about systemic interactions, many believed they were wrong to turn their backs on depth psychology. Anyone who does not flee from self-awareness knows that the inner life is awash in conflict and confusion, most of it never expressed. While systems therapists focused on the outward expression of this inner

17

life—family interactions—psychoanalytic therapists probed beneath family dialogues to explore individual family members' private fears and longings.

SKETCHES OF LEADING FIGURES

Freud was interested in the family but saw it as old business—the place where people learned neurotic fears, rather than the contemporary context where such fears were maintained. Faced with a phobic Little Hans, Freud (1909) was more interested in analyzing the boy's Oedipus complex than in trying to understand what was going on in his family.

Major advances were achieved in the understanding of family dynamics by child psychiatrists who began to analyze mothers and children concurrently (Burlingham, 1951). One example of the fruits of these studies was Adelaide Johnson's (Johnson & Szurek, 1952) explanation of *superego lacunae*, gaps in personal morality passed on by parents who do things like telling their children to lie about how old they are to save a couple of bucks at the movies.

Subsequently, the concurrent analysis of married couples revealed the family as a group of interlocking, intrapsychic systems (Mittlemann, 1948; Oberndorf, 1938). This notion of interlinked psyches remains an important feature of the psychoanalytic view of families (Sander, 1989).

From the 1930s to the 1950s, psychoanalytic researchers became more interested in the contemporary family. Erik Erikson explored the sociological dimensions of ego psychology. Erich Fromm's observations about the struggle for individuality foreshadowed Bowen's work on differentiation of the self. Harry Stack Sullivan's interpersonal theory emphasized the mother's role in transmitting anxiety to her children.

In the 1950s, American psychoanalysis was dominated by ego psychology (which focuses on intrapsychic structures), while object relations theory (which lends itself to interpersonal analysis) flourished an ocean away in Great Britain. In the 1940s, Henry Dicks (1963) established the Family Psychiatric Unit at the Tavistock Clinic in England, where teams of social workers attempted to reconcile couples referred by the divorce courts. By the 1960s, Dicks (1967) was applying object relations theory to the understanding and treatment of marital conflict. His classic text *Marital Tensions* (Dicks, 1967) is still one of the most insightful books ever written about the inner life of couples.

Meanwhile, the psychoanalysts who helped create family therapy were moving away from psychodynamics, and the analytic influence in their work was deliberately muted. The exception was Nathan Ackerman, who of all the pioneers retained the strongest allegiance to psychoanalysis. Students, among them Salvador Minuchin, flocked to New York to observe this master therapist at work.

Edith Jacobson (1954) and Harry Stack Sullivan (1953) helped bring American psychiatry to an interpersonal point of view. Less well known but more important to the development of family therapy was the work carried out at the National Institute of Mental Health (NIMH). When NIMH opened in 1953, Irving Ryckoff moved from Chestnut Lodge, where he'd been working with schizophrenics, to develop a research project on families of schizophrenics under the leadership of Robert Cohen. This group introduced such concepts as *pseudomutuality* (Wynne, Ryckoff, Day, & Hirsch, 1958), *trading of dissociations* (Wynne, 1965), and *delineations* (Shapiro, 1968). But perhaps their most important contribution was the application of *projective identification* (from Melanie Klein) to family relationships.

In the 1960s, Ryckoff and Wynne inaugurated a course in family dynamics at the Washington School of Psychiatry, which led to a family therapy training program. They were joined by Shapiro, Zinner, and Robert Winer. In 1975, they recruited Jill Savege (now Scharff)

Jill and David Scharff are leading exponents of object relations family therapy.

and David Scharff. By the mid-1980s, the Washington School of Psychiatry, under the directorship of David Scharff, had become a leading center of psychoanalytic family therapy. The Scharffs left in 1994 to form their own institute.

Among others who have incorporated psychoanalytic theory into family therapy are Helm Stierlin (1977), Robin Skynner (1976), William Meissner (1978), Arnon Bentovim and Warren Kinston (1991), Fred Sander (1979, 1989), Samuel Slipp (1984, 1988), Michael Nichols (1987), Nathan Epstein, Henry Grunebaum, and Clifford Sager.

THEORETICAL FORMULATIONS

The essence of psychoanalytic treatment is uncovering and interpreting unconscious impulses and defenses against them. It isn't a question of analyzing individuals instead of family interactions; it's knowing where to look to discover the basic wants and fears that keep those individuals from interacting in a mature way. Consider the case of Carl and Peggy.[1]

_____
[1]This case is taken from *The Self in the System* (Nichols, 1987).

Case Study

Whenever Peggy talked to Carl about their relationship, she got upset and started criticizing. Carl, feeling attacked, was cowed into submission. The more Peggy complained, the quieter Carl became. Only after enduring her tirades for several minutes did Carl get mad and start to shout back at her. As a result, Peggy got the opposite of what she was looking for. Instead of understanding her concerns, Carl felt threatened and withdrew. When that didn't work, he lost his temper. At home, he sometimes slapped her.

The therapist concentrated on interrupting this cycle and then helping the couple see the pattern so that they could prevent its recurrence. Unfortunately, while Carl and Peggy learned to relate more effectively in the therapist's office, at home they forgot. Week after week, it was the same story. They'd manage to listen to each other in their sessions, but at least once a month they'd lose it at home. Eventually, when they got discouraged enough to stop coming, the therapist decided that they just weren't motivated enough to make the necessary changes.

As actors, perhaps we take ourselves too seriously; as observers, we take other selves not seriously enough. As family therapists, we see the actions of our clients as a product of their interactions. Yes, people are connected, but that connectedness should not obscure the fact that the nature of their interactions is partly dictated by psychic organization of unsuspected depth and complexity.

Case Study

Why couldn't (wouldn't) Carl stop hitting his wife? The fact that she provoked him doesn't really explain anything. Not every husband who is provoked hits his wife. Looking back, the therapist remembered how Carl used to say with exaggerated concern, "I must control my temper!" She also remembered how dramatically he described his intimidating outbursts and his wife's cowering—and she remembered that when Peggy talked about Carl's brutality, a smile played around the corner of his mouth. These hints of a willful, motivated quality to Carl's abuse could be described in the jargon of psychodynamics, which, because it is alien, might lead some people to dismiss it as a relic of outmoded thinking. Psychodynamic language might imply that Carl's unconscious was responsible for his abusing his wife; he was helpless in the face of his inner conflicts.

Psychodynamic theory may be useful to understand the self in the system, but it isn't necessary to be highly technical. If we were to write a dramatic narrative about Carl, we could say that he was misrepresenting, even to himself, his feelings and intentions. He fooled his wife, he fooled himself, and he fooled his therapist. Carl, who thinks himself concerned about his temper (his version of nonhuman agency), is actually pleased with his power to intimidate his wife and the manliness it implies. This explanation does not replace the interactional one; it only complicates it. Carl's attacks were triggered by the couple's interactions, but they were propelled by his own unrecognized insecurities. Knowing the motives behind his behavior enables us to help Carl understand that he hits his wife to make up for feeling weak and to help him find some other way to feel more powerful. As long as therapists stay at the simple behavioral level of interaction, they will make little headway with a certain number of their cases.

Recognizing that people are more complicated than billiard balls means that we sometimes have to delve deeper into their experience. Psychoanalytic theory gets so complex when you get into the specifics that it's easy to get lost. Here are the basics.

Freudian Drive Psychology

At the heart of human nature are the drives—sexual and aggressive. Mental conflict arises when children learn and mislearn that acting on these impulses may lead to punishment. The resulting conflict is signaled by unpleasant affect: Anxiety is unpleasure associated with the idea (often unconscious) that one will be punished for acting on a particular impulse—for example, the anger you're tempted to express might make your partner stop loving you. Depression is unpleasure plus the idea (often unconscious) that the feared calamity *has already happened*—for example, your anger at your mother long ago made her stop loving you; in fact, nobody loves you.

The balance of conflict can be shifted in one of two ways: by strengthening the defenses against one's impulses or by relaxing defenses to permit some gratification.

Self Psychology

The essence of **self psychology** (Kohut, 1971, 1977) is that every human being longs to be appreciated. If our parents demonstrate their appreciation, we internalize this acceptance in the form of strong, self-confident personalities. However, to the extent that our parents are flat, unresponsive, or withdrawn, then our craving for appreciation is retained in an archaic manner. As adults, we alternately suppress the desire for attention and then allow it to break through whenever we're in the presence of a receptive audience.

The child lucky enough to grow up with appreciative parents will be secure, able to stand alone as a center of initiative, and able to love. The unhappy child, cheated out of loving affirmation, will move through life forever craving the attention he or she was denied.

Object Relations Theory

Psychoanalysis is the study of individuals and their deepest motives; family therapy is the study of social relationships. The bridge between them is **object relations theory**. While the details of object relations theory can be complicated, its essence is simple: We relate to others on the basis of expectations formed by early experience. The residue of these early relationships leaves **internal objects**—mental images of self and others built up from experience and expectation.

Freud's original focus was on bodily appetites, particularly sex. While these appetites may involve other people, they are primarily biological; relationships are secondary. Sex can't be divorced from object relations, but sexual relations can be more physical than personal.

Melanie Klein combined Freud's psychobiological concepts with her own insights into the mental life of children to develop object-relational thinking. Klein's theory (Segal, 1964) stemmed from her observations of the infant's developing relationship with the first significant object, namely, the mother. According to Klein, an infant doesn't form impressions of mother based solely on real experience but instead sifts experience through a rich fantasy life.

Ronald Fairbairn went even further in the direction of object relations and away from drive psychology. His radical version of object relations theory redefined the ego as object seeking and downplayed the role of instincts—making love more important than sex.

In the late 1930s and 1940s, Fairbairn (1952) elaborated the concept of *splitting*. Freud originally described splitting as a defense mechanism of the ego; he defined it as a lifelong coexistence of two contradictory positions that do not influence each other.

Fairbairn's view of splitting is that the ego is divided into structures that contain (a) part of the ego; (b) part of the object; and (c) the affect associated with the relationship. The external object is experienced in one of three ways: (1) an ideal object, which leads to satisfaction; (2) a rejecting object, which leads to anger; or (3) an exciting object, which leads to longing. As a result of internalizing split objects, the resulting structure of the ego is (1) a *central ego*, conscious, adaptable, satisfied with its ideal object, (2) a *rejecting ego*, unconscious, inflexible, frustrated by its rejecting object, or (3) an *exciting ego*, unconscious, inflexible, forever longing for a tempting but unsatisfying object. To the degree that splitting isn't resolved, object relations retain a kind of "all good" or "all bad" quality.

In their observations of infants and young children, Rene Spitz and John Bowlby emphasized the child's profound need for **attachment** to a single and constant object. If this need is denied, the result is *anaclitic depression* (Spitz & Wolf, 1946), a turning away from the world and withdrawal into apathy. According to Bowlby (1969), attachment isn't simply a secondary phenomenon, resulting from being fed, but a basic need in all creatures. Those who don't have this experience are vulnerable to even the slightest lack of support and may become chronically dependent or isolated. This, in psychoanalytic terms, helps explain the genesis of *enmeshed* and *disengaged* relationships.

Margaret Mahler observed young children and described a process of **separation–individuation**. After an initial period of total merger, the child begins a gradual process of separation from the mother, progressively renouncing symbiotic fusion with her. The result of successful separation and individuation is a well-differentiated self (Mahler, Pine, & Bergman, 1975). Failure to achieve individuation undermines the development of a differentiated identity, resulting in overly intense emotional attachments. Depending on the severity of the failure to separate, crises are liable to develop when a child reaches school age, enters adolescence, or prepares to leave home as an adult.

The shift from drives to object relations can also be seen in the interpersonal psychiatry of Harry Stack Sullivan (1953), who emphasized the importance of early mother–child interactions. When a mother is warm and nurturing, her child

Psychoanalysts see early childhood experience as the key to later problems in relationships.

feels good; when a mother rebuffs or frustrates her child's need for tenderness, the child feels bad; and when the child is exposed to extreme pain or frustration, he dissociates to escape anxiety that would otherwise be intolerable. These experiences create the self-dynamisms: *good me, bad me,* and *not me,* which then become part of the person's response to future interpersonal situations.

The internal world of object relations never corresponds exactly to the actual world of real people. It's an approximation, strongly influenced by the earliest object images, introjections, and identifications. This inner world gradually matures and develops, becoming progressively synthesized and closer to reality. The individual's internal capacity for dealing with conflict and failure is related to the depth and maturity of the internal world of object relations. Trust in one's self and in the goodness of others is based on the confirmation of love from internalized good objects.

NORMAL FAMILY DEVELOPMENT

A child doesn't mature in sublime indifference to the interpersonal world. From the start, we need a facilitating environment in order to thrive.

This environment doesn't have to be ideal; an *average expectable environment* with *good-enough mothering* (Winnicott, 1965a) is sufficient. The parents' capacity to provide security for the baby's developing ego depends on whether they themselves feel secure. To begin with, the mother must be secure enough to channel her energy into caring for her infant. She withdraws interest from herself and her marriage and focuses it on the baby.

The early attachment between mother and child has been shown to be critical for healthy development (Bowlby, 1969). Close physical proximity and attachment to a single maternal object are necessary preconditions for healthy object relations in childhood and adulthood. The infant needs a state of total merging and **identification** with the mother as a foundation for future growth of a strongly formed personal self.

As the baby comes to need less, the mother gradually recovers her self-interest, which allows her to permit the child to become independent (Winnicott, 1965b). If the early relationship with mother is secure and loving, the infant will gradually be able to give her up, while retaining her loving support in the form of a good internal object. In the process, most little children adopt a *transitional object* (Winnicott, 1965b) to ease the loss—a soft toy or blanket that the child clings to when she starts to realize that mother is separate and can go away. The toy that Mommy gives reassures her anxious baby; it's a reminder that stands for her and keeps the image of her alive until she returns. When Mommy says "Goodnight," the child hugs the teddy bear until morning when Mommy reappears.

After passing through the normal autistic and symbiotic phases, the child enters a long *separation-individuation period* at approximately six months (Mahler, Pine, & Bergman, 1975). First efforts at separation are tentative and brief, as symbolized in the game of peekaboo. Soon the child begins to creep and then crawl, first away from and then back to mother. What enables the child to practice separating is the awareness that mother is reliably there for assurance, like a safe harbor.

Recently, Otto Kernberg and Heinz Kohut have brought theories of the self to center stage in psychoanalytic circles. According to Kernberg (1966), the earliest **introjections** occur in the process of separating from mother. If separation is successful and securely negotiated, the child establishes him- or herself as an independent being. A mother must have the capacity to tolerate separation in order to accept her child's growing independence. If the child is excessively dependent and clings in fear of separation, or if the mother is made anxious by the loss of the symbiotic relationship or is excessively rejecting, the process is subverted. The child with a backlog of good object relations matures with the ability to tolerate closeness as well as separateness.

To the very young child, parents are not quite separate individuals; they are, in Kohut's (1971, 1977) term, **selfobjects**, experienced as part of the self. As a selfobject, the mother transmits her love by touch, tone of voice, and gentle words, as though they were the child's own feelings. When she whispers "Mommy loves you," the baby learns that he or she is (a) a person and (b) lovable.

In self psychology, two things are deemed essential for the development of a secure and cohesive self. The first is **mirroring**—understanding plus acceptance. Attentive parents convey a deep appreciation of how their children feel. Their implicit "I see how you feel" validates the child's inner experience. Parents also offer models for **idealization**. The little child who can believe "My mother (or father) is terrific, and I am part of her (or him)" has a firm base of self-esteem. In the best of circumstances, the child, already basically secure in his or her self, draws additional strength from identifying with the power and strength of the parents.

According to Kohut, children begin life with fantasies of a grandiose self and ideal parents. As the child develops, these illusions are revised and integrated into a mature personality. Grandiosity gives way to self-esteem; idealization of parents becomes the basis for personal values. However, if trauma occurs, the most primitive version of the self persists. The grandiose self isn't subdued, and the result is a narcissistic personality.

The narcissistic personality—which Christopher Lasch (1979) described as characteristic of our age—is lonely, craves attention, and is easily angered. The narcissistic person longs to be a hero, but it's hard to live up to such grandiose aspirations. The result, frequently, is rage, turned against the self and sometimes the outside world. Freud took this to be a biologically based eruption of self-preserving instinct. Kohut viewed rage as the response to a narcissistic wound, a blow to the idealized sense of who and what we are.

The most significant recent contribution to the psychoanalytic study of normal family development is the work of Daniel Stern (1985). Stern has painstakingly traced the development of the self through detailed observations of infants and young children. The most revolutionary of Stern's findings is that child development is *not* a gradual process of separation and individuation. Rather, infants differentiate themselves almost from birth and then progress through increasingly complex modes of relatedness. From *attunement* (reading and sharing the child's affective state) to *empathy*, attachment and dependency are needs throughout life.

From a psychoanalytic perspective, the fate of the family is largely determined by the early development of individual personalities that make up the family. If the parents are mature and healthy adults, the family will be happy and harmonious.

Some of the most interesting and productive psychoanalytic ideas are contained in descriptions of the psychodynamics of marriage. In the 1950s, the marital bond was described as a result of unconscious fantasy (Stein, 1956). We marry a blurry blend of real and hoped-for mates. More recently and more interestingly, psychoanalysts have described the overlapping and interlocking of fantasies and projections (Blum, 1987; Sander, 1989). Some authors have described this as *mutual projective identification* (Dicks, 1967; Zinner, 1976), others as *neurotic complementarity* (Ackerman, 1966), *marital collusion* (Dicks, 1967), *mutual adaptation* (Giovacchini, 1958), and *conscious and unconscious contracts* (Sager, 1981).

Among psychodynamic family therapists, few have made more important contributions than Ivan Boszormenyi-Nagy's **contextual therapy**, which emphasizes the ethical dimension of family development. Boszormenyi-Nagy considered relational ethics to be a fundamental force holding families and communities together. In a field that often seeks refuge in the illusion of neutrality, Nagy reminded us of the importance of decency and fairness.

For marital partners, Boszormenyi-Nagy's criterion of health is a balance between rights and responsibilities. Depending on their integrity and the complementarity of their needs, partners can develop a trustworthy give and take (Boszormenyi-Nagy, Grunebaum, & Ulrich, 1991). When needs clash, negotiation and compromise are essential.

DEVELOPMENT OF BEHAVIOR DISORDERS

According to classical psychoanalytic theory, symptoms are attempts to cope with unconscious conflicts over sex and aggression. As psychoanalytic emphasis shifted from instincts to object relations, infantile dependence and incomplete ego development replaced the oedipal complex and repressed instincts as the core problems in development. Fear-dictated flight from object relations, which begins in early childhood, is now considered the deepest root of psychological problems.

One important reason for relationship problems is that children distort their perceptions by attributing the qualities of one person to some-one else. Freud (1905) called this phenomenon **transference** when his patient Dora displaced feelings for her father onto him and terminated treatment abruptly just as it was on the threshold of success. Others have observed similar phenomena and called it *scapegoating* (Vogel & Bell, 1960); *trading of dissociations* (Wynne, 1965); *merging* (Boszormenyi-Nagy, 1967); *irrational role assignments* (Framo, 1970); *delineations* (Shapiro, 1968); *symbiosis* (Mahler, 1952); and *family projection process* (Bowen, 1965).

Regardless of the name, all are variants of Melanie Klein's (1946) concept of **projective identification**, a process whereby the subject perceives an object as if it contained unwelcome elements of the subject's personality *and* evokes responses from the object that conform to those perceptions. Unlike projection, projective identification is interactional. Not only do parents project anxiety-arousing aspects of themselves onto their children, but the children collude by behaving in a way that confirms their parents' fears. By doing so, they may be stigmatized or scapegoated, but they also gratify aggressive impulses (as, for instance, in delinquent behavior) (Jacobson, 1954), realize their own omnipotent fantasies, receive subtle reinforcement from their families, and avoid the terrible fear of rejection for not conforming (Zinner & Shapiro, 1976). Meanwhile, the parents are able to avoid the anxiety associated with certain impulses, experience vicarious gratification, and still punish their children for expressing these impulses. In this way, intrapsychic conflict becomes externalized, with the parent acting as a superego, punishing the child for acting on the dictates of the parental id. That's one reason parents overreact: They're afraid of their own impulses.

Case Study

The J. family sought help controlling fifteen-year-old Paul's delinquent behavior. Arrested several times for vandalism, Paul seemed neither ashamed of nor able to understand his compulsion to strike out against authority. As therapy progressed, it became clear that Paul's father harbored a deep but unexpressed resentment of the social conditions that made him work long hours for low wages in a factory, while the "fat cats didn't do shit, but still drove around in Cadillacs." Once the therapist became aware of Mr. J.'s strong but suppressed hatred of authority, she also began to notice that he smiled slightly whenever Mrs. J. described Paul's latest exploits.

Parents' failure to accept that their children are separate beings can take extreme forms, leading to the most severe psychopathology. Lidz (Lidz, Cornelison, & Fleck, 1965) described a mother of identical twins who, when she was constipated, would give her two sons an enema.

Poorly differentiated children face a crisis in adolescence, when developmental pressures for independence conflict with infantile attachments. The outcome may be a retreat to dependence or a violent rebellion. But the teenager who rebels as a reaction to unresolved dependency needs is ill equipped for mature relationships. Behind their facade of proud self-reliance, such individuals harbor deep longings for dependence. When they marry, they may seek constant approval or automatically reject any influence, or both.

Mr. and Mrs. B.'s complaints were mirror images. He claimed she was "bossy and demanding"; she said that he "had to have everything his own way." Mr. B. was the youngest in a close-knit family of five. He described his mother as warm and loving but said she tried to smother him and that she discouraged all his efforts to be independent. Subjected to these same pressures, his two older sisters knuckled under and still remain unmarried, living with their parents. Mr. B., however, rebelled against his mother's domination and left home to join the Marines at seventeen. As he related his experience in the Marine Corps

and successful business ventures, it was clear that he was fiercely proud of his independence.

Once the story of Mr. B.'s success in breaking away from his domineering mother was brought into the open, both Mr. and Mrs. B. had a clearer understanding of his tendency to overreact to anything he perceived as controlling. Deeper analysis revealed that while Mr. B. staunchly rejected what he called "bossiness," he nevertheless craved approval. He had learned to fear his deep-seated dependency needs and protect himself with a facade of "not needing anything from anybody"; nevertheless, the needs were still there and had in fact been a powerful determinant of his choice of wife.

When it comes to choosing a romantic partner, psychoanalysts assure us, love is blind. Freud (1921) wrote that the overvaluation of the loved object when we fall in love leads us to make poor judgments based on *idealization*. The "fall" of falling in love reflects an overflow of narcissistic libido, so that the object of our love is elevated as a substitute for our own unattained ideals. Our own identity glows in the reflected radiance of an idealized companion.

Further complicating marital choice is that we hide some of our own needs and feelings in order to win approval. Children tend to suppress feelings they fear may lead to rejection. Winnicott (1965a) dubbed this phenomenon the *false self*—children behave as if they were perfect angels, pretending to be what they are not. In its most extreme form, a false self leads to schizoid behavior (Guntrip, 1969); even in less severe manifestations, it affects the choice of a mate. During courtship, most people present themselves in the best possible light. Powerful dependency needs, **narcissism**, and unruly impulses may be submerged before marriage, but once married, spouses relax into themselves, warts and all.

Understanding projective identification is critical to the psychoanalytic perspective on couples and families. Projective identification isn't some mysterious force transmitted from an actor to a recipient, like a ventriloquist and his dummy; rather, it is a way in which interactions between two people in a close relationship can activate latent elements in each other's personalities. In short, it's always mutual. Intimate others have unconscious effects on their partners and share with them both a real and a fantasy relationship.

Gardner was a successful corporate attorney whose second wife, Svetlana, was twenty years younger. The narcissistic man often chooses a mate who is a knockout or a worshipful audience. Svetlana was indeed gorgeous; moreover, as a younger woman who looked up to her powerful husband, she mirrored and validated his uniqueness so that his insecurities could remain underground.

Within weeks after their marriage, Gardner was once again consumed by his career and rarely saw Svetlana except when they went out to entertain clients. She distracted herself by spending the lavish allowance he gave her on expensive clothes and visits to exclusive spas. Gardner encouraged these indulgences because they freed him to devote his energy to his work and because he enjoyed the way Svetlana looked like a trophy on his arm. Gardner didn't confront Svetlana's overspending and not doing more with her life, but he secretly held her in contempt. In this way, Gardner failed to acknowledge his own selfishness and greed and was able to attack these traits in his wife.

Marriage, on the surface, appears to be a contract between two reasonable people; at a deeper level, however, marriage is a transaction between hidden internalized objects. Contracts in marital relations are often described in behavioral terms, but Sager's (1981) treatment of marital contracts also considers unconscious factors. Each contract has three levels of awareness:

1. Verbalized, though not always heard
2. Conscious but not verbalized, usually because of fear of anger or disapproval
3. Unconscious

Each partner acts as though the other should to be aware of the terms of the contract and is angry if he or she doesn't live up to those terms. Every one of us wants our mates to conform to an internalized model, and we are anything but understanding when these unrealistic expectations are disappointed (Dicks, 1963).

Even before they're born, children exist as part of their parents' fantasies (Scharff & Scharff, 1987). The anticipated child may represent, among other things, a more devoted love object than one's mate, someone to succeed where the parent has failed, or a peace offering to reestablish loving relations with grandparents. Zinner and Shapiro (1976) coined the term *delineations* for actions that communicate parental fantasies to children. Pathogenic delineations are based more on parents' defensive needs than on realistic perceptions of the children; moreover, parents are strongly motivated to maintain defensive delineations despite anything the children actually do. Thus, it's not uncommon to see parents who insist on seeing their children as bad, helpless, and sick—or brilliant, handsome, and fearless—regardless of the truth.

Any and all of the children in a family may suffer from such distortions, but usually only one is identified as "the patient" or the "sick one." This child is chosen because of some trait that makes him or her a suitable target for the parents' projected emotions. These children shouldn't, however, be thought of as helpless victims. In fact, they collude in the projected identification in order to cement attachments, assuage unconscious guilt, or preserve their parents' shaky marriages. Often, the presenting symptom is symbolic of the denied parental emotion. A misbehaving child may be acting out her father's repressed anger at his wife; a dependent child may be expressing his mother's fear of leading her own independent life; and a bully may be counterphobically compensating for his father's projected insecurity.

Intrapsychic personality dynamics are obscured by psychological defenses, which mask the true nature of an individual's feelings, both from himself and from others. **Family myths** (Ferreira, 1963) serve the same function in families, simplifying and distorting reality. Stierlin (1977) elaborated on Ferreira's view of family myths and developed the implications for family assessment and therapy. Myths protect family members from facing painful truths and also serve to keep outsiders from learning embarrassing facts. A typical myth is that of family harmony, familiar to family therapists who have worked with conflict-avoiding families. In the extreme, this myth takes the form of the *pseudomutuality* (Wynne, Ryckoff, Day, & Hirsch, 1958) found in schizophrenic families. Often the myth of family harmony is maintained by the use of projective identification; one family member is delegated to be the bad one, and all the others insist that they are well adjusted. This bad seed may be the identified patient or even a deceased relative.

Families as well as individuals experience **fixation** and **regression**. Most families function adequately until they're overtaxed, at which time they become stuck in dysfunctional patterns (Barnhill & Longo, 1978). When faced with too much stress, families tend to decompensate to earlier levels of development. The amount of stress a family can tolerate depends on its level of development and the type of fixations its members have.

Psychiatrists, and especially psychoanalysts, have been criticized (Szasz, 1961) for absolving people of responsibility for their actions. To say that someone acted out repressed sexual urges through an extramarital affair is to suggest that he is not accountable. However, Ivan Boszormenyi-Nagy stressed the idea of ethical accountability in families. Good family relationships include

behaving ethically with other family members and considering each member's welfare and interests.

Boszormenyi-Nagy believed that family members owe one another *loyalty* and that they acquire *merit* by supporting each other. To the degree that parents are fair and responsible, they engender loyalty in their children; however, parents create loyalty conflicts when they ask their children to be loyal to one parent at the expense of the other (Boszormenyi-Nagy & Ulrich, 1981).

Pathological reactions may develop from **invisible loyalties**—unconscious commitments children take on to help their families to the detriment of their own well-being. For example, a child may get sick to unite parents in concern. Invisible loyalties are problematic because they're not subject to rational scrutiny.

GOALS OF THERAPY

The goal of psychoanalytic family therapy is to free family members from **unconscious** constraints so that they'll be able to interact with one another as healthy individuals. Plainly, this is an ambitious task. Couples in crisis are treated with understanding and support to help them through their immediate difficulty. Once the crisis is resolved, the psychoanalytic family therapist hopes to engage the couple in long-term therapy. Some couples accept, but many do not. When a family is motivated only for symptom relief, the therapist should support their decision to terminate.

When psychoanalytic family therapists opt for crisis resolution with symptom reduction as the goal (e.g., Umana, Gross, & McConville, 1980), they function much like other family therapists. They focus more on supporting defenses and clarifying communication than on analyzing defenses and uncovering repressed impulses. In general, however, behavioral changes that in other therapy models would be seen as the object of treatment (e.g., getting a school-phobic child to attend class) are seen by psychodynamic therapists as by-products of the resolution of underlying conflicts.

It's easy to say that the goal of psychoanalytic therapy is personality change, but it is rather more difficult to specify precisely what's meant by that. The most common objective is described as *separation–individuation* (Katz, 1981) or *differentiation* (Skynner, 1981); both terms emphasize autonomy. (Perhaps an additional reason for emphasizing separation–individuation is that enmeshed families are more likely to seek treatment than disengaged families.) Individual therapists often think of individuation in terms of physical separation. Thus, adolescents and young adults may be treated separately from their families in order to help them become more independent. Family therapists, on the other hand, believe that emotional autonomy is best achieved by working through emotional conflicts within the family. Rather than isolate individuals from their families, psychoanalytic therapists convene families to help them learn how to let go of one another in a way that allows individuals to be independent as well as related. The following example illustrates how the goals of psychoanalytic family therapy were implemented with a particular family.

Case Study

Three months after he went away to college, Barry J. had his first psychotic break. A brief hospital stay made it clear that Barry was unable to withstand separation from his family without decompensating; therefore, the hospital staff recommended that he should live apart from his parents in order to help him become more independent. Accordingly, he was discharged to a supportive group home for young adults and seen twice weekly in individual psychotherapy. Unfortunately, he suffered a second breakdown and was rehospitalized.

As the time for discharge from this second hospitalization approached, the ward psychiatrist decided to convene the family in order to discuss plans for Barry's posthospital adjustment. During this meeting, it became painfully obvious that powerful forces within the family were impeding any chance for genuine separation. Barry's parents were pleasant and effective people who separately were most engaging and helpful. Toward each other, however, they displayed an icy disdain. During the few moments in the interview when they spoke to each other, rather than to Barry, their hostility was palpable. Only their concern for Barry prevented their relationship from becoming a battleground—a battleground on which Barry feared one or both of them might be destroyed.

At the staff conference following this interview, two plans for disposition were advanced. One group recommended that Barry be removed as far as possible from his parents and treated in individual therapy. Others on the staff disagreed, arguing that only by treating them conjointly could the collusive bond between Barry and his parents be resolved. After lengthy discussion, the group reached a consensus to try the latter approach.

Most of the early family meetings were dominated by the parents' anxious concern about Barry: about the apartment complex where he lived, his job, his friends, how he was spending his leisure time, his clothes, his grooming—in short, about every detail of his life. Gradually, with the therapist's support, Barry was able to limit how much of his life was open to his parents' scrutiny. As he did so, and as they were less able to preoccupy themselves with him, they began to focus on their own relationship. As Barry became more successful at handling his own affairs, his parents became openly combative with each other.

Following a session during which the parents' relationship was the primary focus, the therapist recommended that the couple come for a few separate sessions. Unable to divert their attention to Barry, the J.s fought viciously, leaving no doubt that theirs was a seriously destructive relationship. Rather than getting better in treatment, their relationship got worse.

After two months of internecine warfare—during which time Barry continued to improve—Mr. and Mrs. J. sought a legal separation. Once they were separated, both parents seemed to become happier, more involved with their friends and careers, and less worried about Barry. As they released their stranglehold on their son, both parents began to develop a warmer and more genuine relationship with him. Even after the parents divorced, they continued to attend family sessions with Barry.

In Boszormenyi-Nagy's contextual therapy, the goal is a balance of fairness in the burdens and benefits of adult life. The well-being of the individual is seen to include giving as well as taking. Family members are helped to overcome irrational, unproductive guilt and to claim their **entitlements**. However, facing realistic guilt—based on actual harm done to others, even inadvertently—is seen as essential to expanding accountability within families. Thus, each person works toward self-fulfillment by asserting his or her rights and by living up to his or her obligations.

 ## CONDITIONS FOR BEHAVIOR CHANGE

Psychoanalytic therapy works through insight; but the idea that insight cures is a myth. Insight may be necessary, but it is not sufficient for successful analytic treatment. In psychoanalytic family therapy, family members expand their insight by learning that their psychological lives are larger than their conscious experience, and by coming to accept repressed parts of their personalities. Whatever insights are achieved, however, must be *worked through* (Greenson, 1967); that is, translated into new and more productive ways of interacting.

Analytic therapists foster insight by looking beyond behavior to hidden motives below. Nat-

urally, families defend against baring their innermost feelings. After all, it's a great deal to ask of anyone to expose old wounds and deep longings. Psychoanalysts deal with this problem by creating a climate of trust and proceeding slowly. Once an atmosphere of security is established, the analytic therapist can begin to identify projective mechanisms and bring them back into the marital relationship. Once they no longer need to rely on projective identification, partners can acknowledge and accept previously split-off parts of their own egos.

The therapist helps couples begin to recognize how their present difficulties emerged from unconscious perpetuation of conflicts from their own families. This work is painful and cannot proceed without the security offered by a supportive therapist. Nichols (1987) emphasizes the need for *empathy* to create a "holding environment" for the whole family.

 ## THERAPY

Assessment

Analysts don't postpone treatment until they've made an exhaustive study of their cases; on the contrary, they may not even arrive at a final formulation until the latter stages of treatment. However, although analytic clinicians may continue to refine their understanding over the course of treatment, effective therapy cannot proceed without at least an initial formulation. Beginning therapists—who lack theory as well as experience—sometimes proceed on the assumption that if they sit back and listen, understanding will emerge. This rarely works in family therapy. The following is an abbreviated sketch of an initial psychoanalytic evaluation of a family.

After two sessions with the family of Sally G., who was suffering from school phobia, the therapist

Case Study

made a preliminary formulation of the family's dynamics. In addition to the usual descriptions of the family members, the presenting problem, and the family history, the formulation included assessments of the parents' object relations and the collusive, unconscious interaction of their marital relationship.

Mr. G. had been initially attracted to his wife as a libidinal object who would fulfill his sexual fantasies, including his voyeuristic propensities. Counterbalancing this was a tendency to idealize his wife. Thus he was deeply conflicted and intensely ambivalent in sexual relations with her.

At another level, Mr. G. had unconscious expectations that his wife would be the same long-suffering, self-sacrificing kind of person that his mother was. Thus, he longed for motherly consolation. However, these dependent longings were threatening to his sense of masculinity, so he behaved outwardly as though he were self-sufficient and needed no one. That he had a dependent inner object inside himself was shown by his tender solicitude toward his wife and children when they were ill—but they had to be in a position of weakness and vulnerability to enable him to overcome his defenses enough for him to gratify his own infantile dependency needs vicariously.

Mrs. G. expected marriage to provide her with an ideal father. Given this unconscious expectation, the very sexuality that attracted men to her was a threat to her wish to be treated like a little girl. Like her husband, she was highly conflicted about sexual relations. Raised as an only child, she expected to come first. She was even jealous of her husband's warmth toward Sally and attempted to maintain distance between father and daughter by her own intense attachment to Sally.

At the level of her early selfobject images, she was a greedy, demanding little girl. Her introjection of her mother provided her with a model of how to treat a father figure. Unfortunately, what worked for her mother didn't work for her.

Thus, at an object-relations level, both spouses felt themselves to be deprived children, each wanting to be taken care of without having to ask. When these magical wishes weren't granted, both seethed with resentment. Eventually, they reacted to trivial provocations with the underlying rage, and horrible quarrels erupted.

When Sally witnessed her parents' violent altercations, she became terrified that her own murderous fantasies might come true. Although her parents hated their own internalized bad-parent figures, they seemed to act them out with each other. Further enmeshing Sally in their conflict was the fact that the ego boundaries between herself and her mother were blurred—almost as though mother and daughter shared one joint personality.

Dynamically, Sally's staying home from school could be seen as a desperate attempt to protect her mother–herself from her father's attacks and to defend both parents against her own, projected, murderous fantasies.

An excellent model for developing a psychodynamic focus is the work of Arnon Bentovim and Warren Kinston in Great Britain (Bentovim & Kinston, 1991), who offer a five-step strategy for formulating a focal hypothesis:

1. How does the family interact around the symptom, and how does the family interaction affect the symptom?
2. What is the function of the current symptom?
3. What disaster is feared in the family that keeps them from facing their conflicts more squarely?
4. How is the current situation linked to past trauma?
5. How would the therapist summarize the focal conflict in a short, memorable statement?

Among the metaphors used to describe psychoanalytic treatment, *depth* and *uncovering* feature prominently. The truth is, all therapies aim to uncover something. Even behaviorists look to uncover unnoticed contingencies of reinforcement. What sets analytic therapy apart is that the process of discovery is protracted and directed not only at conscious thoughts and feelings, but also at fantasies and dreams.[2]

David Scharff (1992) related the following example of the use of dreams in couples treatment.

Case Study

Lila and Clive played the all-too-familiar complementary roles whereby the more she sought closeness, the more he retreated. Unlike a systemic therapist, however, Scharff was interested not merely in the synchronicity of their behavior but in the inner experience underlying it. Because Clive had little awareness of his internal life and few memories of his early years, the therapist was frustrated in his attempts to understand what pushed Clive into retreat. The following dream proved instructive.

Clive dreamed about a baby with a wound on its buttocks. A woman he thought to be the sister was supposed to take care of the baby, but because she wasn't doing much, Clive stepped in and took the baby from her. When asked for his thoughts—"Does anything come to mind in connection with the dream?"—Clive's association was to the prospect of having children and his concern that he might have to take all the responsibility. After acknowledging this worry, Dr. Scharff pointed out that the dream also suggested a fear of something being terribly wrong, so bad that Clive wouldn't be able to fix it. This triggered a memory of a time when Lila was upset and crying. Clive held her and tried to comfort her, but when her crying didn't subside, he got upset and went into the other room. Thus, the dream could also symbolize Clive's fear of taking care of his wife. When she's upset, he may over-estimate the depth of her hurt, and because he feels he's the only one who can take care of her, the responsibility feels overwhelming.

Now Lila spoke up, saying that when she gets upset and Clive tries to comfort her, she ends up having to reassure him that she's okay, that what he's doing *is* enough. Thus, even when she's in need of comfort, she has to take care of him. (As Lila's response demonstrates, dreams in couples therapy not only suggest how the dreamer experiences self and object but also provide additional information about the partners' dynamics in the way dreams are told and related to in the session.)

When asked if she had any other thoughts about Clive's dream, Lila hesitated and then said she wondered if Clive thinks of her as the baby. This led to the interpretation that in addition to Clive's thinking of Lila in some ways as a baby, he also thought of himself as a baby, deeply wounded by childhood hurts.

This insight—that Clive's lifelong fear of female engulfment was superimposed on his own sense of infantile neediness and childhood losses—turned out to be pivotal. Lila began to see Clive's withdrawing less as a rejection of her than as a sign of his own vulnerability. She therefore felt less threatened by abandonment, which she now saw more as her own deep worry than any real possibility. Clive, meanwhile, began to understand his anxiety in the face of his wife's emotional needs not so much as her doing but as something in him, his own vulnerability. As a result of this understanding, he felt less urgency to withdraw from moments of intimacy and emotion.

Therapeutic Techniques

For all the complexity of psychoanalytic theory, psychoanalytic therapy is relatively simple—not easy, but simple. There are four basic techniques: listening, empathy, interpretations, and analytic neutrality. Two of these—listening and

---

[2]Repetitive dreams often represent a trauma that a person has been unable to metabolize.

analytic neutrality—may not sound terribly different from what other therapists do, but they are.

Listening is a strenuous but silent activity, rare in today's culture. Most of the time, we're too busy waiting to get a word in edgewise to listen more than perfunctorily. This is especially true in family therapy where therapists feel a tremendous pressure to do something to help troubled families. This is where the importance of *analytic neutrality* comes in. To establish an analytic atmosphere, it's essential to concentrate on understanding without worrying about solving problems. Change may come about as a by-product of understanding, but the analytic therapist suspends anxious involvement with outcomes. It's impossible to overestimate the importance of this frame of mind in establishing a climate of analytic exploration.

The analytic therapist resists the temptation to reassure, advise, or confront families in favor of a sustained but silent immersion in their experience. When analytic therapists do intervene, they express *empathy* in order to help family members open up, and they make *interpretations* to clarify hidden aspects of experience.

Most psychoanalytic family therapy is done with couples, where conflict between partners is taken as the starting point for exploring interpersonal psychodynamics. Take, for example, a couple who reported having an argument over the breakfast table. A systemic therapist might ask them to talk with each other about what happened, hoping to observe what they do to keep the argument from getting settled. The focus would be on communication and interaction. A psychoanalytic therapist would be more interested in helping the partners understand their emotional reactions. Why did they get so angry? What do they want from each other? What did they expect? Where did these feelings come from? Rather than try to resolve the argument, the analytic therapist would explore the fears and longings that lay underneath it.

The signal of intrapsychic conflict is affect. Instead of focusing on who did what to whom, analytic therapists key in on strong feeling and use it as a starting point for detailed inquiry into its origins. "What were you feeling?" "When have you felt that way before?" "And before that?" "What do you remember?" Rather than stay on the horizontal plane of the couple's current behavior, the therapist looks for openings into the vertical dimension of their internal experience.

To summarize, psychoanalytic couples therapists organize their explorations along four channels: (1) internal experience, (2) the history of that experience, (3) how the partner triggers that experience, and, finally, (4) how the context of the session and therapist's input might contribute to what's going on between the partners. Here's a brief example.

Case Study

Having made great strides in understanding over the course of their first few couples sessions, Andrew and Gwen were all the more upset by their inability to discuss, much less settle, an angry disagreement about buying a new car. It wasn't the car but how to pay for it that set them so infuriatingly at odds. Andrew wanted to take money out of savings for the down payment, to keep the monthly payments low. This made Gwen furious. How could he even consider cutting into their savings! Didn't he understand that their mutual fund paid twice as much interest as they'd have to pay on a car loan?

Unfortunately, they were both too bent on changing the other's mind to make any real effort to understand what was going on inside it. The therapist interrupted their arguing to ask each of them what they were feeling and what they were worried about. He wasn't primarily interested in settling the disagreement—although asking about the feelings underlying an altercation is often an effective opening to understanding and compromise; rather, he felt that the intensity of their reactions indicated that this issue touched key concerns.

Andrew was worried about the burden of monthly expenses. "Don't you see," he implored, "if we don't take out enough to make a substantial down payment, we'll have to worry every month about making the payments?" Gwen was ready to dispute this, but the therapist cut her off. He was more interested in the roots of Andrew's worry than in the couple's trying to convince each other of anything.

It turned out that Andrew had a lifelong fear of not having enough money. Having enough money turned out to mean not a big house or a fancy car but enough to spend on things that might be considered indulgent—nice clothes, going out to dinner, flowers, presents. Andrew connected his urge to reward himself with modest material luxuries to memories of growing up in a spartan household. His parents were children of the Depression who thought that things like going out to dinner and buying clothes except when absolutely necessary were frivolous and wasteful.

At a deeper level, Andrew's memories of austerity were a screen for his never having gotten the attention and affection he craved from his rather reserved mother.[3] Thus, he'd learned to soothe himself with a new shirt or fancy dinner at times when he was feeling low. One of Gwen's chief attractions was her giving and expressive nature. She was openly affectionate and almost always happy to indulge Andrew's wish to buy something for himself.

Gwen connected her anxiety about having a cushion against the unexpected memories of her father as an unreliable breadwinner. Unlike Andrew's parents, hers spent freely. They went out to dinner three or four times a week and

took expensive vacations, and everyone in the family wore nice clothes. But although her father was a free spender, Gwen remembered him as lacking the discipline and foresight to invest wisely or to expand his business beyond its modest success. Although it had never been part of her conscious memories, it seemed that although her father lavished attention and affection on her, he never really took her seriously as a person. He treated her, in the familiar phrase, like "Daddy's little girl," as adorable—and insubstantial—as a kitten. That's why she was so attracted to what she saw as Andrew's serious and self-disciplined nature—and his high regard for her.

How did these two trigger such virulent reactions in each other? Not only did Gwen's anxious need to have money in the bank conflict with Andrew's need to have money to spend, but they each felt betrayed by the other. Part of Gwen's unconscious bargain with Andrew was that she could count on him to be a secure, steady pillar and to build for the future. Part of his unconscious expectations of her were that she would indulge him. No wonder they were so reactive to each other on this issue.

And the therapist's role in all this? On reflection, he realized that he'd been a little too anxious to smooth things over with this couple. Out of his own desire to see marital happiness, he'd controlled the level of conflict in the sessions, intervening actively as a peacemaker. As a result, the couple's progress had come at a price. Deep longings and resentments had been pushed aside rather than explored and resolved. Perhaps, the therapist thought, he'd picked up the couple's fears of facing their own anger.

What use should a therapist make of such countertransferential reactions? Should he disclose his feelings? To say that **countertransference** may contain useful information isn't to say that it's oracular. Perhaps the most useful thing to do is look to countertransference for hypotheses that need confirming

---

[3]In Kohut's terms, Andrew's mother provided an inadequate mirroring selfobject function.

evidence from the patients' side of the experience. In this case, the therapist acknowledged his sense that he'd been trying too hard to smooth things over, and he asked Gwen and Andrew whether they, too, were a little afraid to open up their anger.

Like many descriptions of clinical work, this one may seem a little pat. How did we get from arguing about buying a car to hunger for a mirroring selfobject and someone to idealize? Part of the explanation lies in the inevitably condensed account, but it's also important to recognize that one of the things that enables psychoanalysts to see beneath the surface of things is knowing where to look.

Sessions begin with the therapist inviting family members to discuss current concerns, thoughts, and feelings. In subsequent meetings, the therapist might begin by saying nothing or perhaps "Where would you like to begin today?" The therapist then leans back and lets the family talk. Questions are limited to requests for amplification and clarification: "Could you tell me more about that?"; "Have the two of you discussed how you feel about this?"

When initial associations and spontaneous interactions dry up, the therapist probes gently, eliciting history, people's thoughts and feelings, and their ideas about family members' perspectives: "What does your father think about your problems?; How would he explain them?" This technique underscores the analytic therapist's interest in assumptions and projections. Particular interest is paid to childhood memories. The following vignette shows how transitions are made from the present to the past.

Case Study

Among their major disappointments in each other, Mr. and Mrs. S. both complained that the other one "doesn't take care of me when I'm sick, or listen to my complaints at the end of the day." Not only did they share the perception of the other's lack of "mothering," but they both steadfastly maintained that they were supportive and understanding. Mrs. S.'s complaint was typical: "Yesterday was an absolute nightmare. The baby was sick and fussy, and I had a miserable cold. Everything was twice as hard, and I had twice as much to do. All day long, I was looking forward to John's coming home. But when he finally did, he didn't seem to care about how I felt. He only listened to me for a minute before starting to tell me some dumb story about his office." Mr. S. responded by telling a similar account but with the roles reversed.

At this point, the therapist intervened to ask both spouses to describe their relationships with their mothers. What emerged were two very different but revealing histories.

Mr. S.'s mother was a taciturn woman, for whom self-reliance, personal sacrifice, and unremitting struggle were paramount virtues. Though she loved her children, she withheld indulgence and affection, lest they become "spoiled." Nevertheless, Mr. S. craved his mother's attention and constantly sought it. Naturally, he was often rebuffed. A particularly painful memory was of a time he came home in tears after getting beaten up by a bully in the schoolyard. Instead of the consoling he hoped for, his mother scolded him for "acting like a baby." Over the years, he learned to protect himself from these rebuffs by developing a facade of independence and strength.

With the second significant woman in his life, his wife, Mr. S. maintained his rigid defensiveness. He never talked about his problems, but since he continued to yearn for compassionate understanding, he resented his wife for not drawing him out. His own failure to risk rejection by asking for support served as a self-fulfilling prophecy, confirming his expectation, "She doesn't care about me."

Mrs. S.'s background was quite different from her husband's. Her parents were indulgent and demonstrative. They doted on their only child, communicating their love by expressing constant, anxious concern for her well-being. When she was a little girl, the slightest bump or bruise was an occasion for lavish expressions of concern. She came to marriage used to talking about herself and her problems. At first, Mr. S. was enchanted. "Here is someone who really cares about feelings," he thought. But when he discovered that she didn't ask him to talk about his own concerns, he became resentful and progressively less sympathetic. This convinced her "He doesn't care about me."

After the roots of family conflicts have been uncovered, interpretations are made about how family members continue to reenact past and often distorted images from childhood. The data for such interpretations come from transference reactions to the therapist or to other family members, as well as from actual childhood memories. Psychoanalytic therapists deal less with recollections of the past than with reenactments of its influence in the present.

A therapist explores transference by focusing on clients' emotional reactions to his or her interventions: "You look disappointed. I wonder if you think I don't appreciate what you're saying." When clients feel strong affect, a therapist can explore its roots by asking "Who does this remind you of?" or "How did you feel when I made that last comment?"

Don Catherall (1992) described a very useful process for interpreting projective identification in couples therapy. It's important to understand that projective identification isn't some mysterious process in which quantities of one person's experience are passed to the other completely outside of awareness; rather, the feelings are communicated and provoked by subtle but recognizable signals—though they are usually not focused on. You may have experienced projective identification yourself if you've ever been around someone who was behaving seductively but then acted shocked when you made an advance.

The first step in working with projective identification in couples therapy is to interrupt repetitive squabbling, which is likely to mask any expression of the partners' real feelings. Couples caught up in recurring patterns of conflict and misunderstanding are colluding to avoid feelings of vulnerability. Once a couple's quarreling is blocked, the therapist can explore what the individuals are feeling. Catherall recommends focusing first on what the *recipient* of the projection is feeling. Once that person's feelings are clarified, he or she can be helped to communicate those feelings to the partner. To avoid provoking defensiveness, the recipient describing the formerly disavowed feelings is coached to describe only the feelings themselves, not what the projecting partner did to provoke them. Meanwhile, the *projecting partner* is told just to listen and not comment. When the recipient has finished, the projector is directed to feed back what he or she understood the partner to be saying. This encourages the projecting partner to assume the recipient's point of view and therefore makes it difficult to block identification with those feelings.

The projecting partner is encouraged to empathize with the recipient. Hopefully at this point, the couple can stop trading accusations and start trying to understand how each other feels. Ideally, this sharing of feelings will help bring the partners closer—to understanding, and to each other.

Case Study

Catherall cites the example of David and Sheila. The more anxious David was to have sex with Sheila, the more sensitive he was to any hint of rejection. He would respond to her disinterest by withdrawing, and they would remain distant until Sheila reached out. Sheila ended up feeling the same unloved feelings that David had felt when his mother shut him out. Meanwhile, David felt powerless with Sheila, just as she had felt with an uncle who had molested her. Each, in other words, was experiencing concordant identifications stimulated through a mutual process of projective identification.

The therapist pursued Sheila's feelings by inquiring what it was like for her when David was so distant. Her initial answer was that it made her angry, but the therapist asked what did it make her angry about and what was she feeling prior to getting angry. Sheila was then able to identify feelings of being unloved, uncared for, and generally lonely. These were the feelings that had been stimulated by David's projective identification, and they were feelings that Sheila would normally disavow by becoming angry and cold.

Then the therapist asked Sheila to talk with David about what it was like for her to feel lonely and unloved. The therapist was careful to keep Sheila focused on herself and what she was feeling, not on David and what he may have done to cause those feelings. Now that he was not being blamed, David was able to empathize and identify with the feelings of loneliness that Sheila was describing. When the therapist asked him if he knew what it was like to feel that way, David was finally able to talk more directly about the painful feelings that he had been warding off by projecting them onto Sheila.

Psychoanalytic family therapists emphasize that much of what is hidden in family dialogues is not consciously withheld but rather repressed into unconsciousness. The approach to this material is guarded by resistance often manifest in the form of transference. The following vignette illustrates the interpretation of resistance.

Case Study

Mr. and Mrs. Z. had endured ten years of a loveless relationship in order to preserve the fragile security that being married offered them. Mrs. Z.'s totally unexpected and uncharacteristic affair forced the couple to acknowledge the problems in their relationship, and so they consulted a family therapist.

Although they could no longer deny the existence of conflict, both spouses exhibited major resistance to confronting their problems openly. Their resistance represented a reluctance to acknowledge certain areas of their feelings and collusion to avoid frank discussions of their relational problems.

In the first session, both partners said that married life had been "more or less okay"; that Mrs. Z. had some kind of "midlife crisis"; and that it was she who needed therapy. This request for individual therapy was seen as a resistance to avoid the painful examination of the marriage, and the therapist said so. "It seems, Mr. Z., that you'd rather blame your wife than consider how the two of you might both be contributing to your difficulties. And you, Mrs. Z., seem to prefer accepting all the guilt in order to avoid confronting your husband with your dissatisfaction and anger."

Accepting the therapist's interpretation and agreeing to examine their relationship deprived the couple of one form of resistance, as though an escape hatch had been closed to two reluctant combatants. In the next few sessions, both partners attacked each other vituperatively, but they talked only about her affair and his reactions rather than about problems in the relationship. These arguments weren't productive, because whenever Mr. Z. felt anxious, he attacked his wife, and whenever she felt angry, she became guilty and depressed.

Sensing that their fighting was unproductive, the therapist said, "It's clear that you've put each other through a lot of unhappiness and you're both quite bitter. But unless you get down to talking about specific problems in your marriage, there's little chance that you'll get anywhere."

Thus focused, Mrs. Z. timidly ventured that she'd never enjoyed sex with her husband and wished that he would take more time with foreplay. He snapped back, "Okay, so sex wasn't so great. Is that any reason to throw away ten years of marriage and start whoring around?" At this, Mrs. Z. buried her face in her hands and sobbed uncontrollably. After she regained her composure, the therapist intervened, again confronting the couple with their resistance: "It seems, Mr. Z., that when you get upset, you attack. What makes you so anxious about discussing sex?" Following this, the couple was able to talk about their feelings about sex in their marriage until near the end of the session. At this point, Mr. Z. again lashed out at his wife, calling her a whore and a bitch.

Mrs. Z. began the following session by saying that she'd been depressed and upset, crying off and on all week. "I feel so guilty," she sobbed. "You *should* feel guilty!" retorted her husband. Once again, the therapist intervened. "You use your wife's affair as a club. Are you still afraid to discuss problems in your marriage? And you, Mrs. Z., cover your anger with depression. What is it that you're angry about? What was missing in the marriage? What did you want?"

This pattern continued for several more sessions. The spouses who had avoided discussing or even thinking about their problems for ten years used a variety of resistances to veer away from them in therapy. The therapist persisted in pointing out their resistance and urging them to talk about specific complaints.

Psychoanalytic therapists endeavor to foster insight and understanding; they also urge clients to consider what they're going to do about the problems they discuss. This effort—part of the process of working through—is more prominent in family therapy than in individual therapy. Boszormenyi-Nagy, for example, believed that family members should not only be made aware of their motivations, but also held accountable for their behavior. In contextual therapy, Boszormenyi-Nagy (1987) pointed out that the therapist must help people face the stifling expectations involved in invisible loyalties, and then help them find more positive ways of making loyalty payments in the family ledger. What this boils down to is developing a balance of fairness.

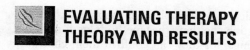

EVALUATING THERAPY THEORY AND RESULTS

Too many family therapists neglect psychology in general and psychoanalytic theory in specific. Regardless of what approach a therapist uses, the writings of psychoanalytically informed clinicians are a rich resource.

Having said this, we also wish to make a cautionary point: Doctrinaire psychoanalytic family therapies are powerful in the hands of trained psychoanalysts. However, many therapists who get discouraged with the usual contentious family dialogues gravitate to psychoanalytic methods as a way to break through the defensive wrangling. Interrupting a family's arguments to explore the individuals' feelings is an excellent way to avoid arguments. However, if therapists make themselves overly central (by directing all conversation through themselves), or if they overemphasize individuals and neglect family interactions, then the power of family therapy—addressing relationship problems directly—may be lost. Interrupting defensive sparring to get to the hopes and fears that lie beneath is all to the good—but unless these interrogatories are followed by unstructured interchanges among family members themselves, these explorations may only produce the illusion of change as long as the therapist is present to act as detective and referee.

Psychoanalytic therapists have generally resisted empirical attempts to evaluate their work. Because symptom reduction isn't the goal, it can't serve as the measure of success—and since the presence or absence of unconscious conflict isn't apparent to outside observers, whether an analysis is successful depends on subjective judgment. Psychoanalytic clinicians consider the therapist's observations a valid means of evaluating theory and treatment. The following quotation from the Blancks (1972) illustrates this point. Speaking of Margaret Mahler's ideas, they wrote:

Clinicians who employ her theories technically question neither the methodology nor the findings, for they can confirm them clinically, a form of validation that meets as closely as possible the experimentalist's insistence upon replication as criterion of the scientific method. (p. 675)

Another example of this point of view can be found in the writing of Robert Langs. "The ultimate test of a therapist's formulation," says Langs (1982), "lies in the use of the therapist's impressions as a basis for intervention" (p. 186). What then determines the validity and effectiveness of these interventions? Langs doesn't hesitate; the patient's reactions, conscious and unconscious, constitute the ultimate litmus test. "True validation involves responses from the patient in both the cognitive and interpersonal spheres."

Is the ultimate test of therapy then the patient's reactions? Yes and no. First, patients' reactions are open to interpretation—especially since validation is sought not only in manifest responses but also in unconsciously encoded derivatives. Moreover, this point of view doesn't take into account the changes in patients' lives that occur outside the consulting room. Occasionally therapists report on the outcome of psychoanalytic family therapy but mostly in uncontrolled case studies. One such report is Dicks's (1967) survey of the outcome of psychoanalytic couples therapy at the Tavistock Clinic, in which he rated as having successfully treated 72.8 percent of a random sample of cases.

SUMMARY

Psychoanalytically trained clinicians were among the first to practice family therapy, but when they began treating families most of them traded in depth psychology for systems theory. Since the mid-1980s, there's been a resurgence of interest in psychodynamics among family therapists, an interest dominated by object relations theory and self psychology. In this chapter, we've sketched the main points of these theories and shown how they're relevant to a psychoanalytic family therapy, integrating depth psychology and systems theory. A few practitioners (e.g., Kirschner & Kirschner, 1986; Nichols, 1987; Slipp, 1984) have combined elements of both; some have developed more frankly psychoanalytic approaches (notably Sander, 1989; Scharff & Scharff, 1987); none has achieved a true synthesis.

Freud's theories were never the last word, any more than Newton's laws of physics were. They both offered valuable observations, but they did not account for all natural phenomena and certainly not those at the edge of chaos. Object relations theory and self psychology joined Freudian drive psychology in offering useful explanations of development, each most applicable to various contemporary pathologies. In the twenty-first century, we see the complexity of cultural context on self and family development, the essential unpredictability of life, and the way in which theories, though useful guides to understanding, will never be more than partial explanations of life's infinite mystery.

In recent years, cognitive and biological perspectives have held center stage in the study of clinical phenomena. Research on attachment theory, theories of affect regulation and neurological development, and trauma theory have added useful insights to our understanding of complex self-organizing systems, but none of them has replaced psychoanalytic theory as the richest source of ideas about people and their problems.

The essential aim of psychoanalytic therapy is to help people understand their basic motives and resolve conflicts over expressing those yearnings. Freudians emphasize sexual and aggressive impulses; self psychologists focus on the longing for appreciation; and object relations therapists concentrate on the need for secure attachment. All, however, are united in the belief that couples and families can be helped to get along better if their individual family members understand and begin to resolve their own personal conflicts.

In practice, psychoanalytic family therapists focus less on the group and their interactions and more on individuals and their feelings. Exploring these feelings is aided by psychoanalytic theory (or theories) that help clinicians understand the basic underlying issues that all people struggle with.

RECOMMENDED READINGS

Ackerman, N. W. 1966. *Treating the troubled family.* New York: Basic Books.

Boszormenyi-Nagy, I. 1972. Loyalty implications of the transference model in psychotherapy. *Archives of General Psychiatry.* 27:374–380.

Boszormenyi-Nagy, I. 1987. *Foundations of contextual therapy.* New York: Brunner/Mazel.

Dicks, H. V. 1967. *Marital tensions.* New York: Basic Books.

Meissner, W. W. 1978. The conceptualization of marriage and family dynamics from a psychoanalytic perspective. In *Marriage and marital therapy,* T. J. Paolino and B. S. McCrady, eds. New York: Brunner/Mazel.

Mitchell, S. A. 1988. *Relational concepts in psychoanalysis.* Cambridge, MA: Harvard University Press.

Nadelson, C. C. 1978. Marital therapy from a psychoanalytic perspective. In *Marriage and marital therapy,* T. J. Paolino and B. S. McCrady, eds. New York: Brunner/Mazel.

Nichols, M. P. 1987. *The self in the system.* New York: Brunner/Mazel.

Sander, F. M. 1989. Marital conflict and psychoanalytic theory in the middle years. In *The middle years: New psychoanalytic perspectives,* J. Oldham and R. Liebert, eds. New Haven, CT: Yale University Press.

Scharff, D., and Scharff, J. S. 1987. *Object relations family therapy.* New York: Jason Aronson.

Stern, M. 1985. *The interpersonal world of the infant.* New York: Basic Books.

Zinner, J., and Shapiro, R. 1976. Projective identification as a mode of perception of behavior in families of adolescents. *International Journal of Psychoanalysts.* 53:523–530.

REFERENCES

Ackerman, N. W. 1966. *Treating the troubled family.* New York: Basic Books.

Barnhill, L. R., and Longo, D. 1978. Fixation and regression in the family life cycle. *Family Process.* 17:469–478.

Bentovim, A., and Kinston, W. 1991. Focal family therapy. In *Handbook of family therapy,* Vol. II, A. S. Gurman and D. P. Kniskern, eds. New York: Brunner/Mazel.

Blanck, G., and Blanck, R. 1972. Toward a psychoanalytic developmental psychology. *Journal of the American Psychoanalytic Association.* 20: 668–710.

Blum, H. P. 1987. Shared fantasy and reciprocal identification: General considerations and gender disorder. In *Unconscious fantasy: Myth and reality,* H. P. Blum et al., eds. New York: International Universities Press.

Boszormenyi-Nagy, I. 1967. Relational modes and meaning. In *Family therapy and disturbed families,* G. H. Zuk and I. Boszormenyi-Nagy, eds. Palo Alto, CA: Science and Behavior Books.

Boszormenyi-Nagy, I. 1987. *Foundations of contextual therapy.* New York: Brunner/Mazel.

Boszormenyi-Nagy, I., and Ulrich, D. N. 1981. Contextual family therapy. In *Handbook of family therapy,* A. S. Gurman and D. P. Kniskern, eds. New York: Brunner/Mazel.

Boszormenyi-Nagy, I., Grunebaum, J., and Ulrich, D. 1991. Contextual therapy. In *Handbook of family therapy,* Vol. II, A. S. Gurman and D. P. Kniskern, eds. New York: Brunner/Mazel.

Bowen, M. 1965. Family psychotherapy with schizophrenia in the hospital and in private practice. In *Intensive family therapy,* I. Boszormenyi-Nagy and J. L. Framo, eds. New York: Harper & Row.

Bowlby, J. 1969. *Attachment and loss.* Vol. 1: *Attachment.* New York: Basic Books.

Burlingham, D. T. 1951. Present trends in handling the mother–child relationship during the therapeutic process. *Psychoanalytic study of the child.* New York: International Universities Press.

Catherall, D. R. 1992. Working with projective identification in couples. *Family Process.* 31:355–367.

Dicks, H. V. 1963. Object relations theory and marital studies. *British Journal of Medical Psychology.* 36:125–129.

Dicks, H. V. 1967. *Marital tensions.* New York: Basic Books.

Fairbairn, W. D. 1952. *An object-relations theory of the personality.* New York: Basic Books.

Ferreira, A. 1963. Family myths and homeostasis. *Archives of General Psychiatry.* 9:457–463.

Framo, J. L. 1970. Symptoms from a family transactional viewpoint. In *Family therapy in transition,* N. W. Ackerman, ed. Boston: Little, Brown.

Freud, S. 1905. Fragment of an analysis of a case of hysteria. *Collected papers.* New York: Basic Books, 1959.

Freud, S. 1909. Analysis of a phobia in a five-year-old boy. *Collected papers, Vol. III.* New York: Basic Books, 1959.

Freud, S. 1921. Group psychology and the analysis of the ego. *Standard edition.* 17:1–22. London: Hogarth Press, 1955.

Giovacchini, P. 1958. Mutual adaptation in various object relations. *International Journal of Psychoanalysis.* 39:547–554.

Greenson, R. R. 1967. *The theory and technique of psychoanalysis.* New York: International Universities Press.

Guntrip, H. 1969. *Schizoid phenomena, object relations theory and the self.* New York: International Universities Press.

Jackson, D. D. 1967. The individual and the larger context. *Family Process.* 6:139–147.

Jacobson, E. 1954. *The self and the object world.* New York: International Universities Press.

Johnson, A., and Szurek, S. 1952. The genesis of antisocial acting out in children and adults. *Psychoanalytic Quarterly.* 21:323–343.

Katz, B. 1981. Separation–individuation and marital therapy. *Psychotherapy: Theory, Research and Practice.* 18:195–203.

Kernberg, O. F. 1966. Structural derivatives of object relationships. *International Journal of Psychoanalysis.* 47:236–253.

Kirschner, D., and Kirschner, S. 1986. *Comprehensive family therapy: An integration of systemic and psychodynamic treatment models.* New York: Brunner/Mazel.

Klein, M. 1946. Notes on some schizoid mechanisms. *International Journal of Psycho-Analysis.* 27:99–110.

Kohut, H. 1971. *The analysis of the self.* New York: International Universities Press.

Kohut, H. 1977. *The restoration of the self.* New York: International Universities Press.

Langs, R. 1982. *Psychotherapy: A basic text.* New York: Jason Aronson.

Lasch, C. 1979. *The culture of narcissism: American life in an age of diminishing expectations.* New York: Basic Books.

Lidz, T., Cornelison, A., and Fleck, S. 1965. *Schizophrenia and the family.* New York: International Universities Press.

Mahler, M. S. 1952. On child psychosis and schizophrenia: Autistic and symbiotic infantile psychoses. *Psychoanalytic Study of the Child.* 7:286–305.

Mahler, M., Pine, F., and Bergman, A. 1975. *The psychological birth of the human infant.* New York: Basic Books.

Meissner, W. W. 1978. The conceptualization of marriage and family dynamics from a psychoanalytic perspective. In *Marriage and marital therapy,* T. J. Paolino and B. S. McCrady, eds. New York: Brunner/Mazel.

Minuchin, S. 1989. Personal communication. Quoted from *Institutionalizing madness,* J. Elizur and S. Minuchin, eds. New York: Basic Books.

Mittlemann, B. 1948. The concurrent analysis of married couples. *Psychoanalytic Quarterly.* 17:182–197.

Nichols, M. P. 1987. *The self in the system.* New York: Brunner/Mazel.

Oberndorf, C. P. 1938. Psychoanalysis of married couples. *Psychoanalytic Review.* 25:453–475.

Sager, C. J. 1981. Couples therapy and marriage contracts. In *Handbook of family therapy*, A. S. Gurman and D. P. Kniskern, eds. New York: Brunner/Mazel.

Sander, F. M. 1979. *Individual and family therapy: Toward an integration.* New York: Jason Aronson.

Sander, F. M. 1989. Marital conflict and psychoanalytic therapy in the middle years. In *The middle years: New psychoanalytic perspectives*, J. Oldham and R. Liebert, eds. New Haven, CT: Yale University Press.

Scharff, D. 1992. *Refining the object and reclaiming the self.* New York: Jason Aronson.

Scharff, D., and Scharff, J. 1987. *Object relations family therapy.* New York: Jason Aronson.

Segal, H. 1964. *Introduction to the work of Melanie Klein.* New York: Basic Books.

Shapiro, R. L. 1968. Action and family interaction in adolescence. In *Modern psychoanalysis*, J. Marmor, ed. New York: Basic Books.

Skynner, A. C. R. 1976. *Systems of family and marital psychotherapy.* New York: Brunner/Mazel.

Skynner, A. C. R. 1981. An open-systems, group analytic approach to family therapy. In *Handbook of family therapy*, A. S. Gurman and D. P. Kniskern, eds. New York: Brunner/Mazel.

Slipp, S. 1984. *Object relations: A dynamic bridge between individual and family treatment.* New York: Jason Aronson.

Slipp, S. 1988. *Technique and practice of object relations family therapy.* New York: Jason Aronson.

Spitz, R., and Wolf, K. 1946. Anaclitic depression: An inquiry into the genesis of psychiatric conditions early in childhood. *Psychoanalytic Study of the Child.* 2:313–342.

Stein, M. 1956. The marriage bond. *Psychoanalytic Quarterly.* 25:238–259.

Stern, D. 1985. *The interpersonal world of the infant.* New York: Basic Books.

Stierlin, H. 1977. *Psychoanalysis and family therapy.* New York: Jason Aronson.

Sullivan, H. S. 1953. *The interpersonal theory of psychiatry.* New York: Norton.

Szasz, T. S. 1961. *The myth of mental illness.* New York: Hoeber-Harper.

Umana, R. F., Gross, S. J., and McConville, M. T. 1980. *Crisis in the family: Three approaches.* New York: Gardner Press.

Vogel, E. F., and Bell, N. W. 1960. The emotionally disturbed as the family scapegoat. In *The family*, N. W. Bell and E. F. Vogel, eds. Glencoe, IL: Free Press.

Winnicott, D. W. 1965a. *The maturational process and the facilitating environment.* New York: International Universities Press.

Winnicott, D. W. 1965b. *The maturational process and the facilitating environment: Studies in the theory of emotional development.* New York: International Universities Press.

Wynne, L. C. 1965. Some indications and contradictions for exploratory family therapy. In *Intensive family therapy*, I. Boszormenyi-Nagy and J. L. Framo, eds. New York: Harper & Row.

Wynne, L., Ryckoff, I., Day, J., and Hirsch, S. 1958. Pseudomutuality in the family relations of schizophrenics. *Psychiatry.* 21:205–220.

Zinner, J. 1976. The implications of projective identification for marital interaction. In *Contemporary marriage: Structure, dynamics, and therapy*, H. Grunebaum and J. Christ, eds. Boston: Little, Brown.

Zinner, J., and Shapiro, R. 1976. Projective identification as a mode of perception and behavior in families of adolescents. *International Journal of Psychoanalysis.* 53:523–530.

Cognitive-Behavioral Family Therapy

10

Beyond Stimulus and Response

When they first began working with families, behavior therapists applied learning theory to train parents in behavior modification and teach couples communication skills. These approaches proved effective with discrete behavioral problems and well-motivated individuals. However, anchored as they were in individual psychology, behavior therapists had little appreciation of the ways in which misbehavior and poor communication were embedded in family systems.

Behaviorists generally worked in academic settings and, despite developing a whole armamentarium of useful techniques, remained relatively isolated from mainstream family therapy. The past ten years, however, have seen sweeping changes in behavioral family therapy, with increasing sophistication of family dynamics and the incorporation of cognitive principles.

 SKETCHES OF LEADING FIGURES

Behavior therapy is a descendant of the investigations of Ivan Pavlov, the Russian physiologist whose work on conditioned reflexes led to the development of **classical conditioning**. In classical conditioning, an *unconditioned stimulus* (UCS), such as food, which leads to an *unconditioned response* (UCR), like salivation, is paired with a *conditioned stimulus* (CS), such as a bell. The result is that the conditioned stimulus begins to evoke the same response (Pavlov, 1932). Subsequently, John B. Watson used classical conditioning to experimentally induce a phobia in "Little Albert" (Watson & Raynor, 1920), while Mary Cover Jones successfully resolved a similar phobia in the case of "Peter" (Jones, 1924).

In 1948, Joseph Wolpe introduced *systematic desensitization*, with which he achieved great success in the treatment of phobias. According to Wolpe (1948), anxiety is a persistent response of the autonomic nervous system acquired through classical conditioning. Systematic desensitization deconditions anxiety through *reciprocal inhibition* by pairing responses incompatible with anxiety to the previously anxiety-arousing stimuli. For example, if Indiana Jones were frightened of snakes, Wolpe would teach Dr. Jones deep-muscle relaxation and then have him imagine approaching a snake in a graded hierarchy of stages. Each time Indy became anxious, he would be told to relax. In this way, the anxiety evoked by imagining snakes would be systematically extinguished.

Systematic desensitization proved to be even more effective when it included actual practice in approaching the feared object or situation (*in vivo desensitization*).

Classical conditioning was applied to family problems primarily in the treatment of anxiety-based disorders, including agoraphobia and sexual dysfunction, pioneered by Wolpe (1958) and later elaborated by Masters and Johnson (1970). Effective behavioral treatments for enuresis were also developed using classical conditioning (Lovibond, 1963).

By far, the greatest influence on behavioral family therapy came from B. F. Skinner's **operant conditioning**. The term *operant* refers to voluntary responses as opposed to involuntary reflexes. The frequency of operant responses is determined by their consequences. Responses that are *positively reinforced* will be repeated more frequently; those that are *punished* or ignored will be *extinguished*.

The operant conditioner carefully observes target behavior and then quantifies its frequency and rate. Then, to complete a **functional analysis of behavior**, the consequences of the behavior are noted to determine the *contingencies of reinforcement*. For example, someone interested in a child's temper tantrums would begin by observing when they occurred and what the consequences were. A typical finding might be that the child throws a tantrum whenever his parents deny his requests and that the parents give in if the tantrums are prolonged. Thus, the parents would be reinforcing the very behavior they least wanted. To eliminate the tantrums, they would be taught to ignore them. Moreover, they would be told that giving in, even occasionally, would maintain the tantrums, because behavior that is *intermittently reinforced* is the most difficult to extinguish. If the child were aware of the contingencies, he might think, "They're not giving in now, but if I keep fussing, they eventually will; if not this time, then the next."

Operant conditioning is particularly effective with children because parents have control over reinforcers and punishments. Boardman (1962) trained parents in effective use of punishment to deal with the aggressive antisocial behavior of their five-year-old. Wolpe (1958) described how to employ parents as cotherapists in anxiety management. Risley and Wolf (1967) trained parents in the operant reinforcement of speech in their autistic children. In technical terms, these parents were trained to eliminate the contingencies that maintained the deviant behavior and to reinforce behavior patterns that were incompatible with the deviant behavior (Falloon, 1991). In plain English, they were taught to ignore inappropriate behavior and reward good behavior.

Although no single figure was responsible for the development of behavioral family therapy, three leaders played a dominant role: a psychologist, Gerald Patterson; a psychiatrist, Robert Liberman; and a social worker, Richard Stuart.

Gerald Patterson, at the University of Oregon, was the most influential figure in developing behavioral parent training. Patterson and his colleagues developed methods for sampling family interactions in the home, trained parents in **social learning theory**, developed programmed workbooks (e.g., Patterson, 1971), and worked out strategies for eliminating undesirable behavior and substituting desirable behavior. Among others prominent in this field are Anthony Graziano, Rex Forehand, Daniel and Susan O'Leary, and Roger McAuley.

The second major figure in the development of behavioral family therapy was Robert Liberman. In his 1970 paper "Behavioral Approaches to Family and Couple Therapy," he outlined the application of an operant learning framework to the family problems of four adult patients with depression, intractable headaches, social inadequacy, and marital discord. In addition to employing contingency management of mutual reinforcers, Liberman introduced the use of **role rehearsal** and **modeling** (Bandura & Walters, 1963) to family therapy.

The third major influence on behavioral family therapy was the **contingency contracting** of Richard Stuart (1969). Rather than focus on how the undesired behavior of one family member could be reduced, Stuart focused on how the exchange of positive behavior could be maximized using **reinforcement reciprocity**.

During the 1970s, behavioral family therapy evolved into three major packages: parent training, behavioral couples therapy, and sex therapy. At present, the leading figures in behavioral couples therapy include Robert Weiss, Richard Stuart, Michael Crowe, Ian Falloon, and Gayola Margolin.

More recently, there has been a rapprochement between stimulus-response models and cognitive theories (e.g., Dattilio, 1998; Epstein, Schlesinger, & Dryden, 1988). **Cognitive-behavioral therapy** refers to those approaches inspired by the work of Albert Ellis (1962) and Aaron Beck (1976) that emphasize the need for attitude change to promote and maintain behavioral modification. Among the leaders in cognitive-behavioral family therapy are Donald Baucom at the University of North Carolina, Norman Epstein at the University of Maryland, and Frank Dattilio at Harvard Medical School and the University of Pennsylvania.

THEORETICAL FORMULATIONS

The basic central premise of behavior therapy is that *behavior is maintained by its consequences*. Consequences that accelerate behavior are called *reinforcers*; those that decelerate behavior are known as *punishers*.

Some responses may not be recognized as operants—something done to get something—because people aren't aware of the reinforcing payoffs. For example, whining is usually reinforced by attention, although the people doing the reinforcing may not realize it. In fact, a variety of undesired behaviors, including nagging and temper tantrums, are often reinforced by attention. Thus, family problems are often maintained under conditions that are counterintuitive.

Extinction occurs when no reinforcement follows a response. Ignoring it is, of course, often the best response to behavior you don't like. The reason some people fail to credit this is because withholding a response rarely leads to *immediate* cessation of unwanted behavior, because most behavior problems have been intermittently reinforced and therefore take time to extinguish.

Despite the mechanistic sound of "schedules of reinforcement" and "controlling behavior," behavior therapists have increasingly become aware that people not only act but also think and feel. This recognition has taken the form of efforts to integrate stimulus-response behaviorism (Skinner, 1953) with cognitive theories (Mahoney, 1977). The central tenet of the cognitive approach is that our interpretation of other people's behavior affects the way we respond to them. Among the most troublesome of *automatic thoughts* are those based on "arbitrary inference," distorted conclusions, shaped by a person's **schemas**, or core beliefs about the world and how it functions. What makes these underlying beliefs problematic is that although they are generally not conscious, they bias how we respond to everything and everyone.

As behavior therapists shifted their attention from individuals to family relationships, they came to rely on Thibaut and Kelley's (1959) **theory of social exchange**, according to which people strive to maximize rewards and minimize costs in relationships. In a successful relationship, partners work to maximize mutual rewards. By contrast, in unsuccessful relationships, the partners are too busy trying to protect themselves from getting hurt to consider ways to make each other happy. According to Thibaut and Kelley, behavior exchanges follow a norm of reciprocity over time, so that aversive or positive stimulation from one person tends to produce reciprocal behavior from the other. Kindness begets kindness, and the opposite is also true.

NORMAL FAMILY DEVELOPMENT

According to the behavior exchange model (Thibaut & Kelley, 1959), a good relationship is one in which giving and getting are balanced— or, in the model's terms, there is a high ratio of benefits to costs. Put as generally as this, little is added to commonsense notions of family satisfaction, but behaviorists have begun to spell out the details of what makes for relationship satisfaction.

For example, Weiss and Isaac (1978) found that affection, communication, and child care are the most important elements in marital satisfaction. Earlier, Wills, Weiss, and Patterson (1974) found that unpleasant behavior reduced marital satisfaction more than positive behavior increased it. A good relationship, then, is one in which there is an exchange of positive responses and, even more important, minimal unpleasantness. Another way of putting this is that good relationships are under *positive reinforcement control*.

Communication skill—the ability to talk, especially about problems—is considered by behaviorists to be the most important feature of good relationships (Gottman, Markman, & Notarius, 1977; Jacobson, Waldron, & Moore, 1980). (It's also the most easily observed feature of relationships.)

In time, all couples run into conflict and, therefore, a critical skill in maintaining family harmony is conflict resolution (Gottman & Krokoff, 1989). Healthy families aren't problem free but have the ability to cope with problems when they arise.

In a good relationship, partners are able to address conflicts. They focus on issues and keep them in perspective, and they discuss specific behaviors of concern to them. They describe their own feelings and request changes in the behavior of others, rather than just criticize and complain. "I've been feeling lonely and I wish you and I could go out and do things more often" is more likely to get a positive response than "You never care what I want! All you care about is yourself!"

Some people assume that good relationships will evolve naturally if people love each other. Behaviorists emphasize the need to develop relationship skills. Good marriages, they believe, aren't made in heaven but are a product of learning effective coping behavior. The late Neil Jacobson (1981) described a good relationship as one in which the partners maintain a high rate of rewards:

Successful couples . . . expand their reinforcement power by frequently acquiring new domains for positive exchange. Spouses who depend on a limited quantity and variety of reinforcers are bound to suffer the ill effects of satiation. As a result, over time their interaction becomes depleted of its prior reinforcement value. Successful couples cope with this inevitable reinforcement erosion by varying their shared activities, developing new common interests, expanding their sexual repertoires, and developing their communication to the point where they continue to interest one another. (p. 561)

DEVELOPMENT OF BEHAVIOR DISORDERS

Behaviorists view symptoms as learned responses. They don't look for underlying motives nor do they posit marital conflict as leading to children's problems. Instead, they concentrate on the symptoms themselves and look for responses that reinforce problem behavior.

At first glance, it might seem puzzling that family members would reinforce undesirable behavior. Why would parents reward temper tantrums? Why would a wife reinforce her husband's distance? The answer lies not in some convoluted motive for suffering but in the simple fact that people often inadvertently reinforce precisely those responses that cause them the most distress.

Parents usually respond to problem behavior by scolding and lecturing. These reactions may seem like punishment, but they might in fact be reinforcing, because attention—even from a critical parent—is a powerful *social reinforcer* (Skinner, 1953). The truth of this is reflected in the sound advice to "Ignore it and it will go away."

The problem is most parents have trouble ignoring misbehavior. Notice, for example, how quickly children learn that certain words get a big reaction.[1] Moreover, even when parents do resolve to ignore misbehavior, they usually don't do so consistently. This can make things even worse, because intermittent reinforcement is the most resistant to extinction (Ferster, 1963). This is why compulsive gambling is so difficult to extinguish.

In addition to behavior problems unwittingly maintained by parental attention, others persist because parents don't know how to make effective use of punishment. They make threats they don't follow through on; they punish too long after the fact; they use punishments so mild as to have no effect; or they use punishments so severe as to generate more anxiety than learning.

Learning, moreover, is not just a one-way street. Consider the behavior of a mother and daughter in the supermarket:

The little girl asks her mother for a candy bar. The mother says no. The child begins crying and complaining. The mother says, "If you think I'm going to buy you candy when you make such a fuss, you have another thing coming, young lady!" But the child escalates her tantrum, getting louder and louder. Finally, exasperated and embarrassed, the mother gives in: "All right, if you'll quiet down, I'll buy you some cookies."

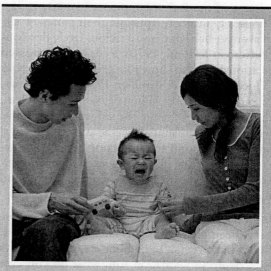

Parents often unintentionally reinforce temper tantrums by giving in or merely by giving extra attention to the child who is throwing the tantrum.

---

[1] Some of these children grow up to become stand-up comedians.

Obviously, the child has been reinforced for throwing a temper tantrum. Not so obviously but also true, the mother has been reinforced for giving in—by the child's calming down. Thus a spiral of undesirable behavior is maintained by *reciprocal reinforcement*.

The reinforcement of undesirable behavior can take even more complex forms in family dynamics. The following is a classic example: A mother, father, and small child are riding in the car. The father speeds up to make it through a yellow light. His wife insists that he slow down and drive more carefully. The father, who hates being told what to do, gets into a silent rage and starts to drive faster. Now his wife shrieks at him to *slow down*. The argument escalates until the child, crying, says, "Don't fight, Mommy and Daddy!" Mother turns to the child and says, "It's okay, honey. Don't cry." Father feels guilty and begins to slow down. Consequently, the child learns at a young age the power and control she has in the family.

The use of **aversive control**—nagging, crying, withdrawing—is often cited as a major determinant of marital unhappiness (Stuart, 1975). Spouses typically reciprocate their partners' use of aversive behavior, and a vicious circle develops (Patterson & Reid, 1970). People in distressed relationships also show *poor problem-solving skills* (Vincent, Weiss, & Birchler, 1975; Weiss, Hops, & Patterson, 1973). When discussing a problem, they frequently change the subject; they phrase wishes and complaints in vague and critical ways; and they respond to complaints with counter-complaints. The following exchange demonstrates sidetracking, cross-complaining, and name-calling, all typical of distressed marriages:

> "I'd like to talk about all the sweets you've been giving the kids lately."
>
> "What sweets! Talk about *me*, you're always stuffing your face. And what do you ever do for the kids? You just come home and complain. Why don't you just stay at the office! The kids and I get along better without you."

Most behavioral analyses point to a lack of reinforcement for positive behavior in distressed families. The old adage "The squeaky wheel gets the grease" seems to apply. Depression, headaches, and temper tantrums tend to elicit concern and therefore more attention than pleasant behavior. Because this process is unwitting, family members are often mystified about their role in reinforcing annoying behavior.

According to cognitive-behaviorists, the schemas that plague relationships are learned in the process of growing up. Some of these dysfunctional beliefs are assumptions about specific family roles, while others are about family life in general. These schemas are the underlying basis of the biased assumptions that poison relationships by distorting family members' responses to each other's actual behavior.

The following eight types of cognitive distortion are taken from Datillio (1998):

1. *Arbitrary inference:* Conclusions are drawn from events in the absence of supporting evidence; for example, a man whose wife is consistently late concludes that she doesn't care about his feelings.
2. *Selective abstraction:* Certain details are highlighted while other important information is ignored; for example, parents of a teenager remember the times she defies them but not the times she goes out of her way to please them.
3. *Overgeneralization:* Isolated incidents are taken as general patterns; for example, a wife rejects her husband's advances twice in a month, and he decides that she isn't interested in sex.
4. *Exaggeration and minimization:* The significance of events is unrealistically magnified or diminished; for example, a husband considers the two times in one month he shops for groceries as fulfilling his share of the household duties, while his wife thinks that he "never does anything."
5. *Personalization:* Events are arbitrarily interpreted in reference to oneself; for

example, a teenager wants to spend more time with his friends, so his father assumes that his son doesn't enjoy his company.

6. *Dichotomous thinking:* Experiences are interpreted as all good or all bad; for example, Jack and Diane have some good times and some bad times, but he remembers only the good times, while she remembers only the bad times.

7. *Labeling:* Behavior is attributed to undesirable personality traits; for example, a woman who avoids talking with her mother about her career because her mother always criticizes is considered "withholding."

8. *Mind reading:* People don't communicate because they assume that they know what others are thinking; for example, a man doesn't ask an attractive classmate out on a date because he assumes that she won't be interested.

 GOALS OF THERAPY

The goal of cognitive-behavioral therapy is to modify specific patterns of behavior to alleviate the presenting problem. This focus on behavior, rather than on the organization of the family or the health of its relationships, gives cognitive-behavioral therapy a more technical flavor than most systemic family therapies.

Behavior therapists tailor treatment to fit the case, but the general intent is to extinguish undesired behavior and reinforce positive alternatives (Azrin, Naster, & Jones, 1973). Thus, for example, parents of a child with temper tantrums might be taught to ignore the tantrums and reward the child for putting her feelings into words.

Sometimes it may be necessary to redefine a family's goal of decreasing negative behavior in terms of increasing incompatible, positive responses (Umana, Gross, & McConville, 1980).

Couples, for example, often state goals of reducing aversive behavior (Weiss, 1978), but the behavioral therapist will also establish a goal of helping them increase satisfaction by accelerating positive behavior.

Behavior therapy also has an educational agenda. In addition to applying learning theory to alleviate specific behavioral problems, behavior therapists also teach communication, problem-solving, and negotiation skills. Similarly, cognitive-behavioral therapists not only help clients reexamine distorted beliefs to solve specific complaints, but also make an effort to teach families how to use cognitive strategies to resolve problems in the future.

CONDITIONS FOR BEHAVIOR CHANGE

The basic premise of behavior therapy is that behavior will change when the contingencies of reinforcement are altered. Behavioral family therapy aims to resolve targeted family problems through identifying behavioral goals, learning theory techniques for achieving these goals, and social reinforcers to facilitate this process.

The hallmarks of behavioral family therapy are (1) careful assessment to determine the baseline frequency of problem behavior, to guide therapy, and to provide feedback about the success of treatment; and (2) strategies designed to modify the contingencies of reinforcement in each unique client family.

The first task of the therapist is to observe the frequency of problem behavior, as well as the stimulus conditions that precede it and the reinforcement that follows it. This enables the therapist to design an individually tailored treatment program.

Moving out of the office and into the home and classroom enabled behaviorists to discover that some of their previous notions about child aggression were erroneous. Contrary to Skinner's assumptions, punishment *does* have long-term effects. The data show that reinforcement of positive behavior, such as cooperation and compliance, doesn't lead to reductions in antisocial behavior. Introducing punishment (time-out, point loss) produces long-term reductions in antisocial behavior (Patterson, 1988).

Furthermore, behavior therapists now realize that the manner in which problems are reinforced in families is often complex (Falloon, 1991). In addition to the reinforcing responses that immediately follow a specific behavior, more remote reinforcers also play a part. These may include tacit approval of aggressive behavior, particularly by men in the family, often accompanied by modeling of this behavior. Spanking children for fighting demonstrates by example the violence a parent may wish to discourage. In addition, behavior that is approved by peers may be difficult to modify at home—especially if the therapist fails to take this wider context into account.

Most behavioral family therapy uses operant conditioning (with the exception of treating sexual dysfunctions), and the focus is on changing dyadic interactions (parent–child or spouse–spouse). This dyadic focus differs from the triadic approach of systems-oriented therapists. Although behavioral family therapists (Dattilio & Epstein, 2004; Falloon & Lillie, 1988; Liberman, 1970) have disputed this distinction, we believe this is a major difference between behavioral and systemic family therapists.

Although behavior change remains the primary focus, more and more behavioral family therapists are recognizing the role of cognitive factors in resolving relationship problems. The cognitive approach first gained attention as a supplement to behavioral couples therapy (Margolin, Christensen, & Weiss, 1975). Interest in cognitive-behavioral approaches to couples therapy eventually led to the recognition that cognition plays a significant role in all family interactions (Alexander & Parsons, 1982).

Barton and Alexander, who call their approach *functional family therapy* (Barton &

Alexander, 1981; Morris, Alexander, & Waldron, 1988), point out that members of unhappy families tend to attribute their problems to negative traits (laziness, irresponsibility, poor impulse control) in other members. Such negative attributions leave family members with a limited sense of control over their lives. After all, what can one person do to change another person's "laziness," "irresponsibility," or "poor impulse control"? Cognitive-behavioral therapists believe that attributional shifts are necessary to make behavior change possible but that, in turn, behavior change is necessary to reinforce new and more productive attributions.

As their experience with families increased in the 1970s and 1980s, behavioral therapists began to incorporate principles from systems theory into their work. Gerald Patterson, for example, studied Minuchin's structural family therapy, and Gary Birchler integrated systems theory and behavioral marital therapy (Birchler & Spinks, 1980; Spinks & Birchler, 1982).

A major tenet of behavioral family treatment is that behavior change is better achieved by accelerating positive behavior than by decelerating negative behavior. Although, as we've seen, there may be a need to introduce punishment to eliminate antisocial behavior in aggressive children, behavior therapists generally try to minimize coercion by aversive control. It's believed that most distressed families use this approach to excess. Therefore only positive reinforcement is widely used in behavioral family therapy.

 THERAPY

Behavioral Parent Training

Most family therapists begin with the assumption that the family, not the individual, is the problem, so that the whole family should be convened to solve it. Behavior therapists, on the other hand, accept the parents' view that the child is the prob-

Behavior therapists teach parents to use positive reinforcement rather than aversive control.

lem and generally meet with one parent (guess which one) and the child, although some behaviorists (Gordon & Davidson, 1981) recommend that both parents and even siblings be included.

The most commonly used approach is operant conditioning, where the reinforcers employed may be tangible or social. In fact, praise and attention have been found to be as effective as money or candy (Bandura, 1969). Operant techniques may be further divided into *shaping, token economies, contingency contracting, contingency management,* and *time-out.*

Shaping (Schwitzgebel & Kolb, 1964) consists of reinforcing change in small steps. **Token economies** (Baer & Sherman, 1969) use points or stars to reward children for good behavior. **Contingency contracting** (Stuart, 1971) involves agreements by parents to make certain changes following changes made by their children. **Contingency management** (Schwitzgebel, 1967) consists of giving and taking away rewards based on the children's behavior. **Time-out** (Rimm & Masters, 1974) is a punishment where children are made to sit in the corner or sent to their rooms.

Assessment. In common with other forms of behavior therapy, parent training begins with a thorough assessment. Although the procedure varies from clinic to clinic, most assessments are based on Kanfer and Phillips's (1970) SORKC model of behavior: S for stimulus, O for the state of the organism, R for the target response, and KC for the nature and contingency of consequences. For example, in the case of parents who complain that their son pesters them for cookies between meals and throws tantrums if they don't give him any, the tantrums would be considered the target behavior, R. O, the state of the organism, might turn out to be hunger or, more likely, boredom. The stimulus, S, might be the sight of cookies in the cookie jar; and the contingency of consequences, KC, might be that the parents give in by feeding the boy cookies occasionally, especially if he makes enough of a fuss.

In simple cases such as this, applying the SORKC model is straightforward, but it quickly becomes more complex with families, in which there are long chains of interrelated behavior. Consider the following.

Mr. and Mrs. J. complain that their two small children whine and fuss at the dinner table. A home observation reveals that when Mr. J. yells at the children for misbehaving, they start to whine and stand by their mother's chair.

Given this sequence it's not difficult to apply the SORKC model. Imagine, however, that this sequence is only part of a more complex picture.

In the morning, Mr. J. makes a sexual overture to his wife, but she, tired from taking care of the children, rolls over and goes back to sleep. Mr. J. is hurt and leaves for work after making some unkind remarks to his wife. She, feeling rejected by her husband, spends the entire day playing with the children for solace.

By the time she has to cook dinner, Mrs. J. is exasperated with the children. Mr. J. comes home after a hard day at the office and tries to make up with his wife by hugging her. She responds but only perfunctorily because she's busy trying to cook. While she's at the stove, the children and Mr. J. vie for her attention, each one wanting to tell her something. Finally, she blows up—at her husband: "Can't you see I'm busy?" He goes into the den and sulks until dinner is ready.

Just as his wife finds it difficult to express her anger at the children and takes it out on him, Mr. J. has trouble directing anger at his wife and so tends to divert it onto the children. At the dinner table, he yells at them for the slightest infraction, at which point they whine and turn to their mother. She lets one sit on her lap while she strokes the other's hair.

In this longer but not atypical sequence, what is stimulus and what is response? Obviously, these definitions become circular, and their application depends on the perspective of the observer.

Assessment in behavioral parent training entails observing and recording the frequency of the behavior to be changed, as well as the events that precede it and those that follow. Interviews,

usually with the mother, are designed to provide a definition of the problem and a list of potential reinforcers. Observations may be conducted behind a one-way mirror or during a home visit. Baseline data may be recorded by therapists or family members. Typically, parents are trained to pinpoint problem behavior, record its occurrence, and note various actions that might serve as stimuli and reinforcers. Checklists and questionnaires provide information that may have been overlooked in interviews. The final product of this stage of the assessment is the selection of target behaviors for modification.

The measurement and functional analysis stage consists of actually observing and recording the target behavior, as well as its antecedents and consequences. This may be done by the parents at home or by therapists in the clinic—and now, more and more, by therapists in the natural setting (Arrington, Sullaway, & Christensen, 1988).

Therapeutic Techniques. Once the assessment is complete, the therapist decides which behaviors should be increased and which decreased. To accelerate behavior, the **Premack principle** (Premack, 1965) is applied; that is, high-probability behavior (particularly pleasant activities) is chosen to reinforce behavior with a low probability of occurrence. Where once it was thought that reinforcers must satisfy some basic drive, such as hunger or thirst, it's now known that any behaviors chosen more frequently (given a wide variety of choices) can serve as reinforcers for those chosen less frequently.

Mrs. G. complained that she couldn't get her five-year-old son Adam to clean up his room in the morning. She went on to say that she tried rewarding him with candy, money, and toys, but "Nothing works!"

A functional analysis of Adam's behavior revealed that, given his choice of things to do, the most probable behaviors were watching television, riding his bicycle, and playing in the mud behind his house. Once these activities were made contingent on tidying his room, he quickly learned to do so.

A variety of material and social reinforcers have been employed to accelerate desired behaviors, but as the Premack principle demonstrates, to be effective, reinforcers must be popular with the child. While money and candy seem like powerful rewards, they may not be as effective for some children as a chance to play in the mud.

Once effective rewards are chosen, parents are taught to **shape** desired behavior by reinforcing successive approximation to the final goal. They are taught to raise the criteria for reinforcement gradually and to present reinforcement immediately contingent on the desired behavior.[2] Once the child is regularly performing the desired response, reinforcement becomes intermittent in order to increase the durability of the new behavior.

The most common technique for decelerating behavior is **time-out**. This means isolating the child after he or she misbehaves. Studies have shown that about five minutes is most effective (Pendergrass, 1971). Children are first warned, giving them a chance to control their own behavior before they are put into time-out. Other techniques used to decelerate behavior include verbal reprimand and ignoring. Simply repeating commands to children has been shown to be the most ineffective way to change their behavior (Forehand, Roberts, Doleys, Hobbs, & Resnick, 1976).

Because of the inconvenience of reinforcing behavior immediately after it occurs, token systems have been popular with parent trainers. Points are earned for desirable behavior and lost for undesirable behavior (Christophersen, Arnold, Hill, & Quilitch, 1972).

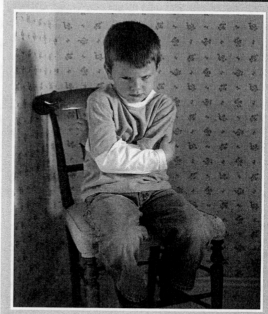

Time-outs are a highly effective form of punishment for young children.

Case Study

Mrs. F. is a mother of two small children who came to the clinic complaining of headaches and crying spells. The intake interviewer found her to be mildly depressed and concluded that the depression was primarily a reaction to difficulty coping with the children. Suzie, age five, was a shy child who had frequent temper tantrums. Robert, who was eight, was more sociable but did poorly in school. The children were a handful, and Mrs. F. felt helpless in dealing with them.

A functional analysis of behavior revealed that Suzie's shyness resulted in extra attention from her anxious mother. Whenever Suzie declined an invitation to play with other children, her mother spent a great deal of time doing things to make her feel better. The therapist selected social behavior (not shyness) as the first target response and instructed Mrs. F. to reinforce all efforts at socializing and to ignore Suzie when she avoided social contact. Thereafter, whenever

---

[2]The importance of immediate proximity is what makes time-out such an effective punishment and grounding second only to lecturing as an ineffective one.

Suzie made any attempt to socialize with other children, Mrs. F. would immediately reinforce her with attention and praise. When Suzie chose to stay home rather than play with other children, her mother ignored her, instead busying herself with her own activities. In three weeks, Mrs. F. reported that Suzie "seemed to have gotten over her shyness."

Following this initial success, the therapist felt it was time to help Mrs. F. tackle the more difficult problem of Suzie's tantrums. Because the tantrums were unlikely to occur while the family was at the clinic or during home visits, the therapist instructed Mrs. F. to make observational notes for a week. These notes revealed that Suzie generally had tantrums when her parents denied her requests for a treat or some special indulgence, such as staying up to watch television. Tantrums were especially likely to occur at the end of the day when Suzie (and her parents) were tired. As for how the parents responded to these maddening outbursts, Mrs. F. reported, "We've tried everything. Sometimes we try to ignore her, but that's impossible; she just screams and shrieks until we can't stand it anymore. Then sometimes we spank her—or give her what she wants, just to shut her up. Sometimes after we spank her, she cries so much that we let her watch television until she calms down. That usually works."

After listening to this description, the therapist explained how Mr. and Mrs. F. had inadvertently been reinforcing the tantrums and told them what they would have to do to stop them. For the next week, the F.s were instructed to ignore fits of temper whenever they occurred. If they occurred at bedtime, Suzie was to be put in bed; if she continued to cry and fuss, she was to be left alone until she stopped. Only when she stopped were her parents to talk with her about what was on her mind.

The following week, Mrs. F. reported that the tantrums had indeed decreased, except for one night when they took on a new and more troubling form. When Suzie was told that she wouldn't

be able to stay up late to watch television, she began to yell and cry as usual. Instead of relenting, Mrs. F. put Suzie in her room and told her to get ready for bed. However, realizing that her parents were going to ignore her, as they had earlier in the week, Suzie began to scream and smash things in her room. "It was awful; she was completely out of control. She even smashed the little dog-shaped lamp I bought her. We didn't know what to do, so just that once we let her stay up." Again, the therapist described the consequences of such behavior and explained to Mrs. F. how, should Suzie again become destructive, both parents should hold her until the tantrum subsided.

At the next session, Mrs. F. described how Suzie did "get out of control again." This time, however, instead of giving in, the parents held her as they had been told. Mrs. F. was amazed at the fury and duration of the resulting tantrum; "But we remembered what you said—there was no way we were going to give in!" It took twenty minutes, but Suzie finally calmed down. This, it turned out, was the last time Suzie ever became violent during a temper tantrum. Nevertheless, she did continue to have occasional flare-ups during the next few weeks.

According to Mrs. F., the few tantrums that did occur seemed to take place in different settings or under different conditions than the usual episodes at home (which Suzie had now learned would not be reinforced). For example, one episode took place in the supermarket when Suzie was told she couldn't have a candy bar. By this time, however, Mrs. F. was thoroughly convinced of the necessity of not reinforcing the tantrums, and so she didn't. Because she was embarrassed at all the noise her daughter was making in public, she did find it necessary to take Suzie out of the store—but she made Suzie sit in the car and took pains not to let it be a pleasant experience. Very few tantrums followed this one.

Next, the therapist turned her attention to Robert's school performance. A careful assessment revealed that Robert usually denied that he had any homework. After checking with Robert's teacher, the therapist discovered that the children generally did have homework and that they were expected to work between thirty minutes and an hour a night. Mrs. F. selected a high-probability behavior, watching television, and made it contingent on Robert's having completed his homework. For the first two weeks of this regimen, Mrs. F. found it necessary to call the teacher every night to verify the assignments, but soon this was no longer necessary. Doing homework fairly quickly became a habit for Robert, and his grades increased from Ds and Cs to Bs and As. At this point, everyone was happier, and Mrs. F. felt the family no longer needed help.

A follow-up session in the fall found things continuing to go well. Suzie was now much more sociable and hadn't had any temper tantrums in months. Robert was doing well in school, although he had begun to neglect some of his more difficult assignments. To address this, the therapist explained to Mrs. F. how to institute a token system, and she was able to use it with excellent results.

The preceding example illustrates a form of behavioral parent training in which the therapist meets with the mother and instructs her in the use of operant conditioning principles. Another format is to observe parent and child interacting behind a one-way mirror in the clinic. In this way, the therapist gets a firsthand look at what actually transpires. With this approach, parents can be taught how to play with their children, as well as how to discipline and negotiate with them. Sometimes, the observing therapist may communicate to the parents through a remote microphone or a "bug in the ear."

Currently, the most widely used approach to behavioral parent training involves teaching prosocial behavior through contingent management with incentive charts. Chores are broken

down into steps, with points given for each step. Rewards include food treats, special time with a parent, household resources (e.g., computer or TV time), privileges, and things that cost money. Rewards are changed regularly to keep things interesting.

Disciplinary techniques are usually introduced after progress has been made in reinforcing positive behavior. For preadolescent children, the most widely used punishment is *time-out*. Time-out usually begins with removal to a boring place for five minutes. (Older children are sent to graduate school.) When a child refuses to go to time-out, the parent is taught to add time, minute by minute, up to a ten-minute maximum. If the child continues to refuse, a privilege is removed. When parents are consistent, children soon learn to go to time-out rather than lose the opportunity to watch TV or use the computer.

Parents of problem children are also taught to monitor their children when they are at school or elsewhere by networking with parents of their children's friends and keeping in touch with teachers as well as leaders of extracurricular activities. Therapists may call parents during the week to check on their progress and encourage their efforts.

As part of the educational component of parent training, parents are taught to make requests in a way that increases the likelihood of compliance. Effective requests are short and simple; are made in the physical proximity of the child; are phrased as statements, not questions; and ask for only one thing at a time. "Please put your dish in the sink," is effective, but "What is your dish doing on the living room rug?" is not.

The techniques that have been described are particularly effective with young children. With teenagers, the use of *contingency contracting* (Alexander & Parsons, 1973; Rinn, 1978) is more widely used. Contracting is introduced as a way for everybody in the family to get something by compromising. Parents and teenagers are asked to specify what behavior they'd like each other to change. These requests form the nucleus of the initial contract. In order to help family members arrive at contracts, the therapist encourages (a) clear communication of content and feelings, (b) clear presentation of requests, leading to (c) negotiation, with each person receiving something in exchange for some concession.

Alexander and Parsons (1973) recommend starting with easy issues while the family is learning the principles of contingency contracting. Success in dealing with minor issues will increase a family's willingness to tackle more difficult problems. Some parents are reluctant to negotiate with their children to do things that they *"should do anyway, without being bribed."* In fact, these parents have a legitimate point, and they should be helped to understand the difference between rules (which are nonnegotiable) and privileges (which can be negotiated).

Behavioral parent training is also conducted in packaged training programs, designed for preventive education. The content of these programs varies from general principles of operant behavior to specific techniques for dealing with specific problems. Many of these programs include instruction in charting the target behavior. Parents are also taught how to state and enforce rules and the importance of consistency. Training in the use of positive reinforcement includes helping parents increase the frequency and variety of reinforcers they apply. In addition to increasing behavior that their children are already engaging in, parents are taught to develop new behaviors through shaping, modeling, instruction, and prompting.

Behavioral Couples Therapy

Assessment. As with parent training, behavioral couples therapy begins with an elaborate, structured assessment. This process usually includes clinical interviews, ratings of specific target behaviors, and marital questionnaires. The most widely used is the Locke-Wallace Marital Adjustment Scale (Locke & Wallace, 1959), a twenty-three-item questionnaire covering various aspects of marital satisfaction, including communication, sex, affection, social activities, and values.

Assessments are designed to reveal strengths and weaknesses of a couple's relationship and the manner in which rewards and punishments are exchanged. Interviews are used to specify and elaborate target behaviors. Some attempt is also made during interviews to understand the etiology of the problems couples describe as well as to observe problems other than those noted by the spouses themselves. In general, however, behavior therapists deemphasize interviews (Jacobson & Margolin, 1979) in favor of written questionnaires and direct observation of couples' interactions. Jacobson (1981) offers an outline for pretreatment assessment (see Table 10.1).

Therapeutic Techniques. After completing an assessment, the behavioral clinician presents the couple with an analysis of their relationship in social learning terms. In doing so, the therapist takes pains to accentuate the positive, striving to maintain optimistic expectancies and a collaborative set (Jacobson, 1981).

Married partners often state their goals negatively: "I wish he wouldn't always argue with me" or "She nags too much." Most have difficulty describing behavior that they want their mates to accelerate. To help them do so, some therapists (Azrin, Naster, & Jones, 1973) ask couples to make a list of pleasing things their partners do during the week. Reviewing these lists in the following session provides an opportunity to emphasize the importance of positive feedback.

Stuart (1975) lists five strategies that summarize the behavioral approach to troubled marriages:

1. Couples are taught to express themselves in clear, behavioral descriptions, rather than in vague complaints.

Table **10.1** Jacobson's Pretreatment Assessment for Marital Therapy

A. Strengths and skills of the relationship

What are the major strengths of this relationship?
What behaviors on the part of each spouse are highly valued by the other?
What shared activities does the couple currently engage in?
What common interests do they share?

B. Presenting problems

What are the major complaints, and how do these complaints translate into explicit behavioral terms?
What are the reinforcers maintaining these behaviors?
What behaviors occur at less than the desired frequency or fail to occur at appropriate times from the standpoint of each spouse?
What are the consequences of these behaviors currently, when they occur?
How did the current problems develop over time?
What kinds of decisions are made collectively as opposed to unilaterally?

C. Sex and affection

Is either spouse currently dissatisfied with rate, quality, or diversity of sex life together?
If sex is currently a problem, was there a time when it was mutually satisfying?
What are the sexual behaviors that seem to be associated with current dissatisfaction?
Are either or both partners dissatisfied with the amount or quality of nonsexual physical affection?
What is the couple's history regarding extramarital affairs?

D. Future prospects

Are the partners seeking therapy to improve their relationship, to separate, or to decide whether the relationship is worth working on?
What are each spouse's reasons for continuing the relationship despite current problems?

E. Assessment of social environment

What are each person's alternatives to the present relationship?
How attractive are these alternatives to each person?
Is the environment (parents, relatives, friends, work associates, children) supportive of either continuance or dissolution of present relationship?

F. Individual functioning of each spouse

Does either spouse exhibit emotional or behavioral problems?
Does either spouse present a psychiatric history of his/her own? Specify.
Have they been in therapy before, either alone or together? What kind of therapy? Outcome?
What is each spouse's past experience with intimate relationships?
How is the present relationship different?

Source: Adapted from Jacobson, N. S. 1981. Behavioral marital therapy. In *Handbook of Family Therapy*, A. S. Gurman and D. P. Kniskern, eds. (pp. 565–566). New York: Brunner/Mazel.

2. Couples are taught new behavior exchange procedures, emphasizing positive control in place of aversive control.
3. Couples are helped to improve their communication.
4. Couples are encouraged to establish clear and effective means of sharing power and making decisions.
5. Couples are taught strategies for solving future problems as a means to maintain and extend gains initiated in therapy.

Behavior exchange procedures are taught to increase the frequency of desired behavior. Couples are advised to express their wishes specifically and behaviorally. A typical device is to ask each partner to list three things he or she would like the other to do more often. While explicitly exchanging "strokes" in this way, couples are implicitly learning ways of influencing each other through positive reinforcement. An alternative tactic is to ask each partner to think of things the other might want, do them, and see what happens. Weiss and his associates direct couples to have "love days," where one partner doubles his or her pleasing behavior toward the other (Weiss & Birchler, 1978). Stuart (1976) has couples alternate "caring days," where one partner demonstrates caring in as many ways as possible.

The following vignette, taken from a video workshop series, illustrates how Richard Stuart concentrates on helping couples learn to make each other happy, rather than try to solve the problems that bring them to therapy.

Case Study

Wesley and Adele are a middle-aged, working-class couple. This is her third marriage and his fourth. Wesley feels rejected because Adele frequently works late; at the same time, she feels that he isn't affectionate with her and that he pulls away whenever she makes a sexual overture. Dr. Stuart begins with a brief family history of each spouse and then explores the history of their relationship. In the second half of the interview, Dr. Stuart offers suggestions for improving the couple's relationship by making an effort to act "as if" things were good and they cared for each other.

When Dr. Stuart tells the couple that they can *choose* to make their marriage work by acting in loving ways toward each other, they seem a little skeptical. When Adele reveals that she doesn't know if Wesley is committed to staying in the relationship, Dr. Stuart suggests that she needs to feel safe in his commitment and, using the example of his own marriage, tells them again that they can accentuate the positive by making a point of expressing their caring for each other.

Later Stuart suggests that Wesley start acting "as if" he felt close to Adele and reassures him that if he acts affectionately, she will respond in kind. Again, Stuart uses his own marriage as an example of how two people can make themselves happy by making a point of acting lovingly toward each other. In fact, he guarantees Wesley that if he acts affectionately, Adele will respond, and Stuart asks Wesley to agree to try doing so as an experiment. Though they still seem a little skeptical, both Wesley and Adele agree to try the idea of acting positively toward each other.

In a carefully designed longitudinal study, Gottman and Krokoff (1989) found that disagreement and angry exchanges, which have often been considered destructive to relationships, may not be harmful in the long run. These patterns were correlated with immediate dissatisfaction but were predictive of improved satisfaction after three years. Defensiveness, stubbornness, and withdrawal from conflict, on the other hand, *did* lead to long-term deterioration in marriages. Passive compliance may create a facade of harmony, but it doesn't work in the long run—as many dominating partners with compliant mates discover when their partners, who "used to be so agreeable," suddenly become "so critical."

Conflict often makes couples uneasy, but it may be an essential prelude to facing and solving problems. The anger that accompanies direct expression of dissatisfaction may be painful, but it may also be healthy. Gottman and Krokoff conclude (1989), "If the wife must introduce and elaborate disagreements in marriages, our data suggest that, for the sake of long-term improvement in marital satisfaction, she may need to do this by getting her husband to confront areas of disagreement and to openly vent disagreement and anger" (p. 51). In other words, confrontation is effective only if it doesn't make the partner defensive. It isn't just honesty that counts but honesty expressed in a way the partner can tolerate.

Training in *communications skills* may be done in a group format (Hickman & Baldwin, 1971; Pierce, 1973) or with individual couples. The training includes instruction, modeling, role-playing, structured exercises, behavior rehearsal, and feedback (Jacobson, 1977; Stuart, 1976). Couples are taught to be specific, phrase requests in positive terms, respond directly to criticism instead of cross-complaining, talk about the present and future rather than the past, listen without interruption, minimize punitive statements, and eliminate questions that sound like declarations.

Once a couple has been taught to communicate in ways that are conducive to problem solving, they are introduced to the principles of *contingency contracting*—agreeing to make changes contingent on the partner making changes. In **quid pro quo** contracts (Knox, 1971), one partner agrees to make a change after a prior change by the other. Each partner specifies desired behavior changes, and with the therapist's help, they negotiate agreements. At the end of the session, a written list is made and both partners sign it. Such a contract might take the following form:

Date _____

This week I agree to:
(1) Come home from work by 6:00 P.M.
(2) Play with the children for half an hour after supper.

_____
Husband's signature

Contingent on the above changes, I agree to:
(1) Go bowling once a week with my husband.
(2) Not serve leftovers for supper on weeknights.

_____
Wife's signature

An alternative form of contracting is the *good faith contract*, in which both partners agree to make changes that aren't contingent on what the other does (Weiss, Hops, & Patterson, 1973). Each partner's independent changes are independently reinforced. In the previous example, the husband who comes home each night by 6:00 P.M. and plays with the children after supper might reward himself by buying a new shirt at the end of the week or be rewarded by his wife with a back rub.

Problem-solving training is used in situations that are too complicated for simple exchange agreements. Negotiations are preceded by a careful definition of problems. Discussions are limited to one problem at a time. Each begins by paraphrasing what the other has said, and they are taught to avoid inferences about motivation—especially inferences of malevolent intent. They're also encouraged to avoid aversive responses. When defining a problem, it's most effective to begin with a positive statement; instead of saying, "You never . . . ," partners are taught to say, "I appreciate the way you . . . and in addition I wish. . . ."

The following guidelines for problem-solving communication are adapted from *The Lost Art of Listening* (Nichols, 2009).

1. Speak for yourself and express your perspective as your own thoughts and feelings, not as absolute truths.
2. Ask for what you want in the form of specific requests, not general complaints.
3. Speak calmly and don't go on and on. Give your partner a chance to respond.
4. Knock to enter: Don't try to talk when your partner is doing something else.
5. Invite your partner to express his or her thoughts and feelings.
6. Listen with the intent to understand, rather than just waiting to respond.
7. Try to understand what the other person is feeling, rather than just reacting to the words.
8. Let your partner know that you understand by acknowledging what he or she has said—and invite him or her to elaborate or correct your impression.
9. When there is major conflict or misunderstanding, devote one entire conversation to drawing out and acknowledging your partner's point of view. Wait until you've demonstrated that you understand him or her before trying to express your side, perhaps in a subsequent conversation.
10. When it comes to discussing solutions, invite your partner's ideas first. Listen to and acknowledge those ideas.
11. When suggesting your own solutions, make sure they address both of your needs.
12. Find a solution that's agreeable to both of you, but plan to implement it on a trial basis, and review the solution at the end of the trial period.

In these early years of the twenty-first century, the most significant advance in behavioral treatment is the increasing use of cognitive-behavioral methods (Dattilio, 1998; Epstein, Schlesinger, & Dryden, 1988). The *cognitive mediation model* (Beck, 1976) posits that emotions and actions are mediated by specific cognitions. Understanding these cognitions (*beliefs*, *attributions*, and *expectancies*) makes it possible to identify factors that trigger and maintain the dysfunctional emotional and behavioral patterns. In practice, this boils down to uncovering negative assumptions that keep people stuck.

The Cognitive-Behavioral Approach to Family Therapy

Cognitive family therapy followed the same progression as cognitive couples therapy—first as a supplement to the behavioral approach, then as a more comprehensive system of intervention. Munson (1993) noted at least eighteen different types of cognitive therapy used by various practitioners, but the focus of this discussion will be limited to those approaches proposed by the rational-emotive (Ellis, 1962) and cognitive-behavior theories (Dattilio, 1994; Teichman, 1984).

The rational-emotive therapist helps family members see how illogical beliefs serve as the foundation for their emotional distress. The *A-B-C theory* is introduced, according to which family members blame their problems on certain activating events in the family (*A*) and are taught to look for irrational beliefs (*B*), which are then challenged (*C*). The goal is to modify beliefs and expectations by putting them on a more rational basis (Ellis, 1978). The therapist's role is to teach the family that emotional problems are caused by unrealistic beliefs and that by revising these self-defeating ideas, they may improve the quality of family life.

With rational-emotive therapy, it's hard to separate the approach from its creator. Ellis didn't merely challenge people's assumptions; he punctured them with fierce and gleeful sarcasm. It isn't necessary to imitate Ellis's acerbic style to take advantage of his insights. It seems fair to say, however, that rational-emotive therapists generally content themselves with lecturing people about generic assumptions rather than probing for more personal and closely held beliefs.

The cognitive-behavior method, which balances the emphasis on cognition and behavior, takes a more expansive and inclusive approach by focusing in greater depth on patterns of family interaction (Epstein, Schlesinger, & Dryden, 1988; Leslie, 1988). Cognitions, emotions, and behavior are viewed as exerting mutual influence on one another, so that a cognitive inference can evoke emotion and behavior, and emotion and behavior can influence cognition.

The cognitive-behavior approach is compatible with systems theory and includes the premise that members of a family simultaneously influence and are influenced by each other. The behavior of one family member triggers behavior, cognitions, and emotions in other members, which in turn elicit reactive cognitions, behavior, and emotions in the original member. As this process plays out, the volatility of family dynamics escalates, rendering the family vulnerable to negative spirals of conflict. Epstein and Schlesinger (1996) cite four means by which family members' cognitions, behavior, and emotions may interact and build to a volatile climax:

1. The individual's own cognitions, behavior, and emotions regarding family interaction (e.g., the person who notices him- or herself withdrawing from the rest of the family)
2. The actions of individual family members toward him or her
3. The combined (and not always consistent) reactions several family members have toward him or her
4. The characteristics of the relationships among other family members (e.g., noticing that two other family members usually are supportive of each other's opinions)

As the number of family members involved increases, so does the complexity of the dynamics, adding momentum to the escalation process.

Cognitive therapy, as set forth by Aaron Beck (1976), emphasizes *schemas*, or "core beliefs," about the world and how it functions (DeRubeis & Beck, 1988). Therapeutic intervention is aimed at distorted assumptions whereby family members interpret and evaluate one another.

Just as individuals maintain core beliefs about themselves, their world, and their future, they also maintain beliefs about their families. Frank Dattilio (2005) suggests that individuals maintain two sets of schemas about family life: (1) a schema related to the parents' experiences growing up in their own families and (2) schemas related to families in general, or personal theories of family life. Both types of schemas influence on how individuals react in the family setting.

For example, a woman raised with the belief that family members should do things together is likely to feel threatened if her husband wants to do certain things on his own. Conflict may be especially pronounced if the husband was brought up to believe that married partners should have their own independent interests.

Beliefs, conscious and unconscious, passed down from the parents' families of origin contribute to jointly held opinions that lead to the development of the current family schema. This set of attitudes is conveyed to and applied to childrearing and, when combined with parents' own individual perceptions of their environment and life experiences, contributes to the further development of the family schema. Here's a case example taken from Frank Dattilio (2005).

Case Study

The family entered treatment because of conflict over the mother's rigid attitudes. Based on her experience with her own fragile and demanding parents, she tended to overreact to any sign of problems in her husband or children. Her anxiety made her intolerant of the children's crying and complaining. The family felt they needed to "walk on eggshells" to avoid making her worry. Thus, the father and children became aligned against the mother, whom they came to regard as a "nut case."

The father's own mother was controlling and overbearing, which led to his developing a schema that women were bossy and unreasonable. His failure to challenge his wife about what he saw as her being unreasonable was thus partly a carryover from his experience with his mother. Instead of confronting his wife, he formed a coalition with his children against her, just as he and his father had joined forces to cope with his own domineering mother.

The therapist used the cognitive technique of the *downward arrow* to identify the mother's core beliefs (see Figure 10.1). This technique was implemented by asking a series of questions to uncover the basic schemas underlying each person's assumptions: "So if that were to occur, what would it mean?"

The children were afraid to be themselves around their mother. They saw her as unreasonable and attributed her unyielding views to hav-

---

Figure **10.1** Downward Arrow Technique

"There's no room for weakness in life."

↓

"If my family members are weak, they'll give in to the overwhelming forces of life."

↓

"That's when people break down, become immobilized, and become a burden to others and a risk to themselves."

↓

"This outcome could easily result in death or suicide."

↓

"If I'm weak, I'll die."

↓

"Hence, we must avoid any signs of weakness."

---

ing grown up with a mother who had attempted suicide and blamed her daughter for not being attentive to her concerns. When the therapist attempted to uncover the children's core beliefs about the situation, one daughter said, "I think my mother is probably on the edge, with all of the stress she's been under her entire life. Therefore, we must go along with her, or something bad might happen to her, and we don't need that—although we often resent having to live this way—all because of my stupid grandmother's problems." The schema adopted by this child was "Children must be cautious with their parents when they have problems."

In addressing the schemas in this family, the therapist followed a series of eight steps to uncover and reexamine them:

1. *Identify family schemas and highlight those areas of conflict that are fueled by them (e.g., "We have to walk on eggshells with Mom. If we show any signs of weakness, she flips out.").* Schemas are uncovered by probing automatic thoughts through techniques such as the downward arrow. Once schemas have been identified, verification should be made by obtaining agreement from other family members.

2. *Trace the origin of family schemas and how they evolved to become an ingrained mechanism in the family process.* This is done by exploring the parents' backgrounds. Similarities and differences between the parents' upbringings should be highlighted to help them understand areas of agreement and conflict. In this case, the father was brought up to believe that it's okay to show vulnerability to those you love, while the mother was taught that it's dangerous to show any sign of weakness.

3. *Point out the need for change, indicating how the restructuring of schemas may facilitate more adaptive and harmonious family interaction.* The therapist stressed to the mother how she was overburdened by her belief that she was always responsible for everyone else in the fam-

ily. The therapist emphasized how much her perceptions had been distorted by her experience with her mother and how she was unintentionally placing a similar burden on her own husband and children.

4. *Elicit acknowledgment of the need to change or modify existing dysfunctional schemas.* This step paves the way for collaborative efforts to change. When family members have different goals, the therapist's job is to help them find common ground.

5. *Assess the family's ability to make changes, and plan strategies for facilitating them.* In this case, the mother was asked what evidence supported her idea that signs of weakness were always a problem. She was helped to consider that this idea might be a distortion based on her own childhood experience. As an experiment, she was asked to see if an occasional display of emotion really was dangerous by allowing herself to cry once in a while in front of her family. The fact that her husband and children seemed relieved to see her show her feelings helped her to think that maybe it's not so terrible to show unhappy emotions at times: "In fact, it felt kind of good," she noted. In a similar process, the husband discovered that if he avoided interfering to protect his wife when she seemed upset, the children were able to be supportive and "nothing terrible happened." The children found out that when they expressed the wish to avoid being put in the middle of their parents' conflicts, they were free to be themselves without worrying about negative consequences.

6. *Implement change.* The therapist encouraged family members to consider modifying some of their beliefs in a collaborative process of brainstorming ideas and weighing their implications. This family considered how they would act with each other if they decided to adopt the belief that "It is important to be tactful in expressing negative feelings to other family members, but family members should have the freedom to share such feelings with each other."

7. *Enact new behaviors.* This step involves trying out changes and seeing how they work. Family members were each asked to select an alternative behavior consistent with the modified schema and to see how acting on it affected the family. Once the children began to see their mother's behavior as her way of expressing love for them in order to protect them from what she went through as a child, they became less defensive and more supportive of her—which, in turn, softened her anxious vigilance.

8. *Solidify changes.* This step involves establishing the new schema and its associated behavior as a permanent pattern in the family. Family members were urged to remain flexible about the possible need for future reevaluations. Although the mother might be seen as the identified patient in this family, the therapist felt it was important for the father and children to recognize their own roles in perpetuating the status quo. They began this process by expressing how they felt, instead of just avoiding the mother. Then, in an effort to challenge their automatic thoughts about the family and see how their own beliefs might be part of the problem, all of the family members were asked to weigh alternative explanations and consider their implications. Dattilio notes that this process is similar to *reframing* but with an important difference: In cognitive-behavior therapy, family members are asked to gather data and weigh the evidence in favor of changing their thinking, rather than merely accept the therapist's alternative explanations.

In some sessions, a cognitive-behavioral therapist will focus primarily on cognitions, while in other sessions the focus will shift to behavior, including all the usual elements in behavior therapy: training in reinforcement reciprocity, communication, problem solving, behavior change agreements, homework assignments, and parenting skills. Cognitive interventions are designed to increase family members' skills at monitoring the validity and appropriateness of their own cognitions.

This is an important point: Cognitive therapy should not be reduced to generic interpretations ("It's a mistake to be dependent on others," "Who says it's disastrous when things go wrong?") nor should the therapist do all the work. Rather, for cognitive intervention to be effective, specific cognitive distortions must be uncovered and clients must learn to test their own assumptions. This exploration is carried out in a Socratic process of asking questions, rather than offering explanations and making suggestions.

A major goal of the cognitive approach is to help family members learn to identify automatic thoughts that flash through their minds. The importance of identifying such automatic thoughts ("She's crying—she must be mad at me") is that they often reflect underlying schemas ("Women usually hold men responsible for their unhappiness") that may be inaccurate.

To improve their skill in identifying automatic thoughts, clients are encouraged to keep a diary and jot down situations that provoke automatic thoughts and the resulting emotional responses. The therapist's role then is to ask a series of questions about these assumptions, rather than to challenge them directly. Here's an example.

Case Study

When thirteen-year-old Frankie's parents caught her walking home from school with a boy she was forbidden to see, they responded by saying "We just can't trust you!" and grounded her for a week. Frankie's automatic thought was "They'll never trust me again," which made her feel, by turns, worried and then angry. This conclusion was followed by the thought "Now I'll *never* have any freedom."

After helping Frankie identify these thoughts, the therapist asked her to test these assumptions and then to consider alternative explanations: "What evidence exists to substantiate this idea?" "Might there be alternative explanations?" "How would you test these assumptions?"

Frankie decided that it was too soon to be sure how her parents would treat her in the future. She decided to test the proposition that if she stopped lying to them they would eventually start to trust her again and that, in this way, she could slowly win back her freedom. Frankie was also asked to examine her defiance and think about the specific connotation it had (anger? emancipation? pride?).

The late 1980s and early 1990s saw the cognitive-behavior approach applied more widely in family therapy. Edited books by Epstein, Schlessinger, and Dryden (1988) and a short text produced by Huber and Baruth (1989) were among the first works to address the cognitive approach to family therapy. This was elaborated in subsequent articles by Schwebel and Fine (1992), Dattilio (1994, 1997), and Teichman (1992). Dattilio (1998) produced a major casebook that discusses the integration of cognitive-behavioral strategies with various modalities of couples and family therapy. This important work discusses the compatibility of cognitive-behavior therapy with a wide array of modalities. The application of cognitive-behavior therapy to couples and families was also featured in the recent addition of the *Handbook of Family Therapy* (Dattilio & Epstein, 2004).

Treatment of Sexual Dysfunction

Wolpe's (1958) introduction of *systematic desensitization* led to major advances in the treatment of sexual dysfunction. According to Wolpe, most sexual problems are the result of conditioned anxiety. His therapy consists of instructing couples to engage in a series of progressively intimate encounters, while avoiding thoughts about erection or orgasm. Another approach that often proved useful was *assertiveness training* (Lazarus, 1965), in which socially and sexually inhibited persons are encouraged to accept and express their needs and feelings.

While these behavioral remedies were often helpful, the real breakthrough came with the publication of Masters and Johnson's (1970) approach. This was followed by others who applied and extended Masters and Johnson's basic procedure (Kaplan, 1974, 1979; Lobitz & LoPiccolo, 1972). More recently, Weekes and Gambescia (2000, 2002) offered a more comprehensive perspective on the topic.

Although the details vary, there is a general approach followed by most sex therapists. As with other behavioral methods, the first step is a thorough assessment, including a complete medical examination and extensive interviews to determine the nature of the dysfunction and establish goals for treatment. In the absence of medical problems, cases involving lack of information, poor technique, and poor communication are most amenable to sexual therapy.

Therapists following Masters and Johnson tended to lump sexual problems into one category—anxiety that interferes with couples' ability to relax into passion. Helen Singer Kaplan (1979) pointed out that there are three stages of the sexual response and hence three types of problems: disorders of desire, arousal disorders, and orgasm disorders. *Disorders of desire* range from low sex drive to sexual aversion. Treatment focuses on (a) deconditioning anxiety and (b) helping clients resist negative thoughts. *Arousal disorders* include decreased emotional arousal and difficulty achieving and maintaining an erection or dilating and lubricating. These problems are often helped with a combination of relaxation and teaching couples to focus on the physical sensations of touching and caressing, rather than worrying about what comes next. *Orgasm disorders* include the timing of orgasm (e.g., premature or delayed), the quality of the

orgasm, or the requirements for orgasm (e.g., some people only have orgasm during masturbation). Premature ejaculation usually responds well to sex therapy; lack of orgasm in women may respond to sex therapy, usually involving teaching the woman to practice on her own and learning to fantasize (Weekes & Gambescia, 2000, 2002).

Although sex therapy must be tailored to specific problems, most treatments are initiated with *sensate focus*, in which couples are taught how to relax and enjoy touching and being touched. They're told to find a time when they're both reasonably relaxed and free from distraction and get in bed together naked, then they take turns gently caressing each other. The person being touched is told to relax and concentrate on the feeling of being touched. Later, the one being touched will let the partner know which touch is most pleasing and which is less so. At first, couples are told not to touch each other in the sensitive breast or genital areas in order to avoid undue anxiety.

After they learn to relax and exchange gentle caressing, couples are encouraged to gradually become more intimate—but to slow down if either should feel anxious. Thus, sensate focus is a form of *in vivo desensitization*. Couples who are highly anxious and fearful of having sex (which some people reduce to a hectic few minutes of poking and panting) learn to overcome their fears through a gradual and progressively intimate experience of mutual caressing. As anxiety decreases and desire mounts, they're encouraged to engage in more intimate exchanges. In the process, couples are taught to communicate what they like and don't like. So, for example, instead of enduring something unpleasant until she finally gets so upset that she snaps at her partner or avoids sex altogether, a woman might be taught how to gently show him "No, not like that; like this."

Once sensate focus exercises have gone smoothly, the therapist introduces techniques to deal with specific problems. Among women, the most common sexual dysfunctions are difficulties with orgasm (Kaplan, 1979). Frequently, these problems are rooted in lack of information. The woman and her partner may be expecting her to have orgasms reliably during intercourse without additional clitoral stimulation. In men, the most common problem is premature ejaculation, for which part of the treatment is the *squeeze technique* (Semans, 1956), in which the woman stimulates the man's penis until he feels the urge to ejaculate. At that point, she squeezes the frenulum (at the base of the head) firmly between her thumb and first two fingers until the urge to ejaculate subsides. Stimulation begins again until another squeeze is necessary.

Techniques to deal with erectile failure are designed to reduce performance anxiety and increase sexual arousal. These include desensitization of the man's anxiety; discussions in which the partners describe their expectations; increasing the variety and duration of foreplay; the *teasing technique* (Masters & Johnson, 1970), in which the woman alternately starts and stops stimulating the man; and beginning intercourse with the woman guiding the man's flaccid penis into her vagina.

Successful sex therapy usually ends with the couple's sex life much improved but not as fantastic as frustrated expectations had led them to imagine—expectations that were part of the problem in the first place. As in any form of directive therapy, it's important for sex therapists to gradually fade out their involvement and control. Therapeutic gains are consolidated and extended by reviewing the changes that have occurred, by anticipating future trouble spots, and by planning in advance to deal with problems according to principles learned in treatment.

EVALUATING THERAPY THEORY AND RESULTS

The distinctive methods of behavioral family therapy are derived from classical and operant conditioning and, increasingly, cognitive theory.

Target behavior is precisely specified in operational terms; operant conditioning, classical conditioning, social learning theory, and cognitive strategies are then used to produce change. As behavior therapists gained experience with family problems, they began to address such traditionally nonbehavioral concerns as the therapeutic alliance, the need for empathy, and the problem of resistance, as well as communication and problem-solving skills. However, even when dealing with such mainstream issues, behaviorists are distinguished by their methodical approach. More than by any technique, behavior therapy is characterized by careful assessment and evaluation.

Behavior therapy was born and bred in a tradition of research, and so it's not surprising that it is the most carefully studied form of family treatment. Two trends emerge from this substantial body of evidence. The first is that both behavioral parent training and behavioral couples therapy have repeatedly been demonstrated to be effective. Among the most well-supported versions of these approaches are Gerald Patterson's parent training therapy (e.g., Patterson & Forgatch, 1995; Patterson, Dishion, & Chamberlain, 1993) and Neil Jacobson's behavioral couples therapy (e.g., Crits-Christoph, Frank, Chambless, Brody, & Karp, 1995).

The second trend in research on behavioral family therapy is that the leading exponents of these approaches have begun to see the need to extend their approaches beyond the basic contingency contracting and operant learning procedures of traditional behavior therapy. As already noted, one form this has taken has been the incorporation of cognitive techniques into more traditional stimulus-response behaviorism (e.g., Baucom & Epstein, 1990; Dattilio & Padesky, 1990).

Cognitive-behavioral therapy still begins with behavior change. There are two general categories of intervention: (1) substituting positive for aversive control and (2) skills training. An example of the former would be to counteract the selective attention to negativity that characterizes many distressed couples, a cognitive-behavioral therapist might ask each partner to write down one positive thing that the other person did each day, to compliment or express appreciation to that individual for this action, and to bring the list to therapy for further discussion (Baucom, Epstein, & LaTaillade, 2002).

The cognitive component of cognitive-behavioral therapy usually comes into play when clients' attitudes and assumptions get in the way of positive behavior changes—for example, when family members notice only negative things about each other. The cognitive-behavioral therapist helps clients explore their assumptions in a process of Socratic questioning. Thus, cognitive-behavioral therapy still focuses on behavior and therapists are still active and directive, but more attention is paid to unhappy emotions and the assumptions underlying them.

The late Neil Jacobson, in partnership with Andrew Christensen, went even further in modifying traditional behavioral couples therapy along the lines of more traditional family therapy approaches. They retained the behavioral change techniques but added novel strategies to bring about increased emotional acceptance in clients. In other words, before they start working with couples to produce changes in the partners' behavior, they endeavor to help them learn to be more accepting of each other. So different, in fact, is the resulting approach that we will consider it more extensively in our chapter on integrative approaches (Chapter 14).

As you are probably aware, cognitive-behavioral therapy is one of the most widely taught approaches to psychological treatment. In a survey conducted by the American Association for Marriage and Family Therapy (Northey, 2002) that asked family therapists to describe their primary treatment approach, the most frequent response (named by 27.3 percent of 292 randomly selected therapists) was cognitive-behavioral therapy.

One reason for this popularity is that cognitive-behavioral couples therapy has been subjected to more controlled outcome studies than any other therapeutic approach. Baucom and associate's (1998) review of outcome studies indicated that cognitive-behavioral couples therapy is effective in reducing relationship distress, especially as an addition to a program that includes communication training, problem-solving training, and behavioral contracts. Less research has been done on the application of cognitive-behavioral therapy in treating individual disorders, such as schizophrenia and child conduct disorders. Outcome studies have demonstrated the effectiveness of behaviorally oriented family interventions with such disorders (Nichols & Schwartz, 2006), but cognitive interventions per se have not been evaluated.

Despite increased public and professional interest in sex therapy, there are few well-controlled studies of its effectiveness. In a careful review, Hogan (1978) found that most of the literature consists of clinical case studies. These reports are little more than "box scores" of successes and failures. Absent are pre- and postmeasures, specification of techniques, points of reference other than the therapists, and follow-up data. Moreover, because most of these reports came from the same handful of therapists, it's impossible to discern what's being evaluated—the techniques of sex therapy or the skill of these particular therapists. This state of the research hadn't changed much by 1990, according to later summary reports (Crowe, 1988; Falloon & Lillie, 1988).

Sex therapy appears to be an effective approach to some very vexing problems. Most observers (Gurman & Kniskern, 1981) agree that it should be considered the treatment of choice when there is an explicit complaint about a couple's sex life.

Three areas of research in family intervention seem ready to move to a more advanced stage of development. These areas are conduct disorders in children (Morris, Alexander, & Waldron, 1988; Patterson, 1986), marital conflict (Follette & Jacobson, 1988), and schizophrenic adults (Falloon, 1985).

SUMMARY

Although behavior therapists have been applying their techniques to family problems for more than thirty years, they have done so for the most part within a linear frame of reference. Family symptoms are treated as learned responses, involuntarily acquired and reinforced. Treatment is generally time limited and symptom focused.

Initially, the behavioral approach to families was based on social learning theory, according to which behavior is learned and maintained by its consequences and can be modified by altering those consequences. This focus has been broadened considerably by the introduction of cognitive interventions to address unhelpful assumptions and distorted perceptions. An essential adjunct to social learning theory is Thibaut and Kelley's theory of social exchange, according to which people strive to maximize interpersonal rewards while minimizing costs. Hence, the general goals of behavioral family therapy are to increase the rate of rewarding exchanges, decrease aversive exchanges, and teach communication and problem-solving skills.

More contemporary approaches to cognitive-behavioral therapy have expanded this approach to include the examination and restructuring of thoughts and perceptions. So, while specific techniques are applied to target behaviors, families are also taught general principles of behavior management along with methods for reevaluating automatic thoughts with an attempt to identify distortions and address misconceptions.

The behaviorists' focus on modifying the consequences of problem behavior accounts for the strengths and weaknesses of this approach. By concentrating on presenting problems, behaviorists have been able to develop an impressive array of effective techniques. Even such relatively intractable problems as delinquent behavior in children and severe sexual dysfunctions have yielded to behavioral technology. Contemporary cognitive-behavioral therapists take the posture, however, that behavior is only part of the human condition, and the problem person is only part of the family. You can't simply teach people to change if unresolved conflict is keeping them stuck.

Unhappiness may center around a behavioral complaint, but resolution of the behavior may not resolve the unhappiness. Treatment may succeed with the symptom but fail the family. Attitudes and feelings *may* change along with changes in behavior but not necessarily—and teaching communication skills may not be sufficient to resolve real conflict. Behavior change alone may not be enough for family members whose ultimate goal is to feel better. "Yes, he's doing his chores now," a parent may agree. "But I don't think he *feels* like helping out. He still isn't really part of our family." Behavior isn't all that family members in distress are concerned about, and to be responsive to all their needs therapists need to deal with cognitive and affective issues as well.

Behaviorists rarely treat whole families. Instead, they see only those subsystems they consider central to the targeted behavior. Unfortunately, failure to include—or at least consider—the entire family in therapy may doom treatment to failure. A therapeutic program to reduce a son's aggressiveness toward his mother can hardly succeed if the father wants an aggressive son or if the father's anger toward his wife isn't addressed. Moreover, if the whole family isn't involved in change, new behavior may not be reinforced and maintained.

Despite these shortcomings, cognitive-behavioral therapy offers impressive techniques for treating problems with children and troubled marriages. Furthermore, its weaknesses can be corrected by broadening the focus of conceptualization and the scope of treatment to include families as systems. Perhaps the greatest strength of behavior therapy is its insistence on observing what happens and then measuring change. Cognitive-behavioralists have developed a wealth of reliable assessment methods and applied them to evaluation, treatment planning, and monitoring progress and outcome. A second important advance has been the gradual movement from eliminating or reinforcing discrete "marker" behaviors to the teaching of general problem-solving, cognitive, and communicational skills. A third major advance in current behavioral family therapy is modular treatment interventions organized to meet the specific and changing needs of the individual and the family. Finally, the shift to address distorted cognitions that may underlie problematic family interactions has added a powerful new dimension to the behavioral approach.

RECOMMENDED READINGS

Barton, C., and Alexander, J. F. 1981. Functional family therapy. In *Handbook of family therapy*, A. S. Gurman and D. P. Kniskern, eds. New York: Brunner/Mazel.

Dattilio, F. M. 1998. *Case studies in couple and family therapy: Systemic and cognitive perspectives.* New York: Guilford Press.

Dattilio, F. M., and Reinecke, M. 1996. *Casebook of cognitive-behavior therapy with children and adolescents.* New York: Guilford Press.

Epstein, N., Schlesinger, S. E., and Dryden, W. 1988. *Cognitive-behavioral therapy with families.* New York: Brunner/Mazel.

Falloon, I. R. H. 1988. *Handbook of behavioral family therapy.* New York: Guilford Press.

Gordon, S. B., and Davidson, N. 1981. Behavioral parent training. In *Handbook of family therapy*, A. S. Gurman and D. P. Kniskern, eds. New York: Brunner/Mazel.

Jacobson, N. S., and Margolin, G. 1979. *Marital therapy: Strategies based on social learning and behavior exchange principles.* New York: Brunner/Mazel.

Kaplan, H. S. 1979. *The new sex therapy: Active treatment of sexual dysfunctions.* New York: Brunner/Mazel.

Masters, W. H., and Johnson, V. E. 1970. *Human sexual inadequacy.* Boston: Little, Brown.

Patterson, G. R. 1971. *Families: Application of social learning theory to family life.* Champaign, IL: Research Press.

Stuart, R. B. 1980. *Helping couples change: A social learning approach to marital therapy.* New York: Guilford Press.

Weiss, R. L. 1978. The conceptualization of marriage from a behavioral perspective. In *Marriage and marital therapy*, T. J. Paolino and B. S. McCrady, eds. New York: Brunner/Mazel.

REFERENCES

Alexander, J. F., and Parsons, B. V. 1973. Short-term behavioral intervention with delinquent families: Impact on family process and recidivism. *Journal of Abnormal Psychology. 51*:219–225.

Alexander, J., and Parsons, B. V. 1982. *Functional family therapy.* Pacific Grove, CA: Brooks/Cole.

Arrington, A., Sullaway, M., and Christensen, A. 1988. Behavioral family assessment. In *Handbook of behavioral family therapy*, I. R. H. Falloon, ed. New York: Guilford Press.

Azrin, N. H., Naster, J. B., and Jones, R. 1973. Reciprocity counseling: A rapid learning-based procedure for marital counseling. *Behavior Research and Therapy. 11*:365–383.

Baer, D. M., and Sherman, J. A. 1969. Reinforcement control of generalized imitation in young children. *Journal of Experimental Child Psychology. 1*:37–49.

Bandura, A. 1969. *Principles of behavior modification.* New York: Holt, Rinehart & Winston.

Bandura, A., and Walters, R. 1963. *Social learning and personality development.* New York: Holt, Rinehart & Winston.

Barton, C., and Alexander, J. F. 1981. Functional family therapy. In *Handbook of family therapy*, A. S.

Gurman and D. P. Kniskern, eds. New York: Brunner/Mazel.

Baucom, D. H., and Epstein, N. 1990. *Cognitive-behavioral marital therapy*. New York: Brunner/Mazel.

Baucom, D. H., Epstein, N. B., and LaTaillade, J. 2002. Cognitive-behavioral couple therapy. In *Clinical handbook of couple therapy*, 3rd ed., A. S. Gurman and N. S. Jacobson, eds. New York: Guilford Press.

Baucom, D. H., Shoham, V., Mueser, K. T., Daiuto, A. D., and Stickle, T. R. 1998. Empirically supported couples and family therapies for adult problems. *Journal of Consulting and Clinical Psychology. 66:*53–88.

Beck, A. T. 1976. *Cognitive therapy and the emotional disorders*. New York: International Universities Press.

Birchler, G. R., and Spinks, S. H. 1980. Behavioral-systems marital therapy: Integration and clinical application. *American Journal of Family Therapy. 8:*6–29.

Boardman, W. K. 1962. Rusty: A brief behavior disorder. *Journal of Consulting Psychology. 26:*293–297.

Christophersen, E. R., Arnold, C. M., Hill, D. W., and Quilitch, H. R. 1972. The home point system: Token reinforcement procedures for application by parents of children with behavioral problems. *Journal of Applied Behavioral Analysis. 5:*485–497.

Crits-Christoph, P., Frank, E., Chambless, D. L., Brody, F., and Karp, J. F. 1995. Training in empirically validated treatments: What are clinical psychology students learning? *Professional Psychology: Research and Practice. 26:*514–522.

Crowe, M. 1988. Indications for family, marital, and sexual therapy. In *Handbook of behavioral family therapy*, I. R. H. Fallon, ed. New York: Guilford Press.

Dattilio, F. M. 1994. Families in crisis. In *Cognitive-behavioral strategies in crisis interventions*, F. M. Dattilio and A. Freeman, eds. New York: Guilford Press.

Dattilio, F. M. 1997. Family therapy. In *Casebook of cognitive therapy*, R. Leahy, ed. Northvale, NJ: Jason Aronson.

Dattilio, F. M. 1998. *Case studies in couple and family therapy: Systemic and cognitive perspectives*. New York: Guilford Press.

Dattilio, F. M. 2005. The restructuring of family schemas: A cognitive-behavioral perspective. *Journal of Marital and Family Therapy, 31:*15–30.

Dattilio, F. M., and Epstein, N. B. 2004. Cognitive-behavioral couple and family therapy. In *The Family Therapy Handbook*, T. L. Sexton, G. R. Weeks, and M. S. Robbins, eds. New York: Routledge.

Dattilio, F. M., and Padesky, C. A. 1990. *Cognitive therapy with couples*. Sarasota, FL: Professional Resource Exchange.

DeRubeis, R. J., and Beck, A. T. 1988. Cognitive therapy. In *Handbook of cognitive-behavioral therapies*, K. S. Dobson, ed. New York: Guilford Press.

Ellis, A. 1962. *Reason and emotion in psychotherapy*. New York: Lyle Stuart.

Ellis, A. 1978. Family therapy: A phenomenological and active-directive approach. *Journal of Marriage and Family Counseling. 4:*43–50.

Epstein, N., and Schlesinger, S. E. 1996. Cognitive-behavioral treatment of family problems. In *Casebook of cognitive-behavior therapy with children and adolescents*, M. Reinecke, F. M. Dattilio, and A. Freeman, eds. New York: Guilford Press.

Epstein, N., Schlesinger, S. E., and Dryden, W., eds. 1988. *Cognitive-behavioral therapy with families*. New York: Brunner/Mazel.

Fallon, I. R. H. 1985. *Family management of schizophrenia: A study of the clinical, social, family and economic benefits*. Baltimore: Johns Hopkins University Press.

Fallon, I. R. H. 1991. Behavioral family therapy. In *Handbook of family therapy*, Vol. II, A. S. Gurman and D. P. Kniskern, eds. New York: Brunner/Mazel.

Fallon, I. R. H., and Lillie, F. J. 1988. Behavioral family therapy: An overview. In *Handbook of behavioral family therapy*, I. R. H. Fallon, ed. New York: Guilford Press.

Ferster, C. B. 1963. Essentials of a science of behavior. In *An introduction to the science of human behavior*, J. I. Nurnberger, C. B. Ferster, and J. P. Brady, eds. New York: Appleton-Century-Crofts.

Follette, W. C., and Jacobson, N. S. 1988. Behavioral marital therapy in the treatment of depressive disorders. In *Handbook of behavioral family therapy*, I. R. H. Fallon, ed. New York: Guilford Press.

Forehand, R., Roberts, M. W., Doleys, D. M., Hobbs, S. A., and Resnick, P. A. 1976. An examination of disciplinary procedures with children. *Journal of Experimental Child Psychology. 21:*109–120.

Gordon, S. B., and Davidson, N. 1981. Behavioral

parent training. In *Handbook of family therapy*, A. S. Gurman and D. P. Kniskern, eds. New York: Brunner/Mazel.

Gottman, J., and Krokoff, L. 1989. Marital interaction and satisfaction: A longitudinal view. *Journal of Consulting and Clinical Psychology.* 57:47–52.

Gottman, J., Markman, H., and Notarius, C. 1977. The topography of marital conflict: A sequential analysis of verbal and nonverbal behavior. *Journal of Marriage and the Family.* 39:461–477.

Gurman, A. S., and Kniskern, D. P. 1981. Family therapy outcome research: Knowns and unknowns. In *Handbook of family therapy*, A. S. Gurman and D. P. Kniskern, eds. New York: Brunner/Mazel.

Hickman, M. E., and Baldwin, B. A. 1971. Use of programmed instruction to improve communication in marriage. *The Family Coordinator.* 20:121–125.

Hogan, D. R. 1978. The effectiveness of sex therapy: A review of the literature. In *Handbook of sex therapy*, J. LoPiccolo and L. LoPiccolo, eds. New York: Plenum Press.

Huber, C. H., and Baruth, L. G. 1989. *Rational-emotive family therapy: A systems perspective.* New York: Springer.

Jacobson, N. S. 1977. Problem solving and contingency contracting in the treatment of marital discord. *Journal of Consulting and Clinical Psychology.* 45:92–100.

Jacobson, N. S. 1978. Specific and nonspecific factors in the effectiveness of a behavioral approach to the treatment of marital discord. *Journal of Consulting and Clinical Psychology.* 46:442–452.

Jacobson, N. S. 1981. Behavioral marital therapy. In *Handbook of family therapy*, A. S. Gurman and D. P. Kniskern, eds. New York: Brunner/Mazel.

Jacobson, N. S., and Margolin, G. 1979. *Marital therapy: Strategies based on social learning and behavior exchange principles.* New York: Brunner/Mazel.

Jacobson, N. S., Waldron, H., and Moore, D. 1980. Toward a behavioral profile of marital distress. *Journal of Consulting and Clinical Psychology.* 48:696–703.

Jones, M. C. 1924. A laboratory study of fear: The case of Peter. *Journal of Geriatric Psychology.* 31:308–315.

Kanfer, F. H., and Phillips, J. S. 1970. *Learning foundations of behavior therapy.* New York: Wiley.

Kaplan, H. S. 1974. *The new sex therapy: Active treatment of sexual dysfunctions.* New York: Brunner/Mazel.

Kaplan, H. S. 1979. *Disorders of sexual desire and other new concepts and techniques in sex therapy.* New York: Brunner/Mazel.

Knox, D. 1971. *Marriage happiness: A behavioral approach to counseling.* Champaign, IL: Research Press.

Lazarus, A. A. 1965. The treatment of a sexually inadequate male. In *Case studies in behavior modification*, L. P. Ullmann and L. Krasner, eds. New York: Holt, Rinehart & Winston.

Leslie, L. A. 1988. Cognitive-behavioral and systems models of family therapy: How compatible are they? In *Cognitive-behavioral therapy with families*, N. Epstein, S. E. Schlesinger, and W. Dryden, eds. New York: Brunner/Mazel.

Liberman, R. P. 1970. Behavioral approaches to family and couple therapy. *American Journal of Orthopsychiatry.* 40:106–118.

Lobitz, N. C., and LoPiccolo, J. 1972. New methods in the behavioral treatment of sexual dysfunction. *Journal of Behavior Therapy and Experimental Psychiatry.* 3:265–271.

Locke, H. J., and Wallace, K. M. 1959. Short-term marital adjustment and prediction tests: Their reliability and validity. *Journal of Marriage and Family Living.* 21:251–255.

Lovibond, S. H. 1963. The mechanism of conditioning treatment of enuresis. *Behavior Research and Therapy.* 1:17–21.

Mahoney, M. J. 1977. Reflections on the cognitive learning trend in psychotherapy. *American Psychologist.* 32:5–13.

Margolin, G., Christensen, A., and Weiss, R. L. 1975. Contracts, cognition and change: A behavioral approach to marriage therapy. *Counseling Psychologist.* 5:15–25.

Masters, W. H., and Johnson, V. E. 1970. *Human sexual inadequacy.* Boston: Little, Brown.

Morris, S. B., Alexander, J. F., and Waldron, H. 1988. Functional family therapy. In *Handbook of behavioral family therapy*, I. R. H. Falloon, ed. New York: Guilford Press.

Munson, C. E. 1993. Cognitive family therapy. In *Cognitive and behavioral treatment: Methods and applications*, D. K. Granvold, ed. Pacific Grove, CA: Brooks/Cole.

Nichols, M. P. 2009. *The lost art of listening*, 2nd ed. New York: Guilford Press.

Nichols, M. P., and Schwartz, R. C. 2006. *Family*

therapy: Concepts and methods, 6th ed. Boston: Allyn & Bacon.

Northey, W. F. 2002. Characteristics and clinical practices of marriage and family therapists: A national survey. *Journal of Marital and Family Therapy*. 28:487–494.

Patterson, G. R. 1971. *Families: Application of social learning theory to family life*. Champaign, IL: Research Press.

Patterson, G. R. 1986. The contribution of siblings to training for fighting: A microsocial analysis. In *Development of antisocial and prosocial behavior: Research, theories, and issues*, D. Olweus, J. Block, and M. Radke-Yarrow, eds. Orlando, FL: Academic Press.

Patterson, G. R. 1988. Foreword. In *Handbook of behavioral family therapy*, I. R. H. Falloon, ed. New York: Guilford Press.

Patterson, G. R., and Forgatch, M. S. 1995. Predicting future clinical adjustment from treatment outcomes and process variables. *Psychological Assessment*. 7:275–285.

Patterson, G. R., and Reid, J. 1970. Reciprocity and coercion; two facets of social systems. In *Behavior modification in clinical psychology*, C. Neuringer and J. Michael, eds. New York: Appleton-Century-Crofts.

Patterson, G. R., Dishion, T. J., and Chamberlain, P. 1993. Outcomes and methodological issues relating to treatment of anti-social children. In *Effective psychotherapy: A handbook of comparative research*, T. R. Giles, ed. New York: Plenum Press.

Pavlov, I. P. 1932. Neuroses in man and animals. *Journal of the American Medical Association*. 99:1012–1013.

Pendergrass, V. E. 1971. Effects of length of timeout from positive reinforcement and schedule of application in suppression of aggressive behavior. *Psychological Record*. 21:75–80.

Pierce, R. M. 1973. Training in interpersonal communication skills with the partners of deteriorated marriages. *The Family Coordinator*. 22:223–227.

Premack, D. 1965. Reinforcement theory. In *Nebraska symposium on motivation*, D. Levine, ed. Lincoln: University of Nebraska Press.

Rimm, D. C., and Masters, J. C. 1974. *Behavior therapy: Techniques and empirical findings*. New York: Wiley.

Rinn, R. C. 1978. Children with behavior disorders. In *Behavior therapy in the psychiatric setting*, M. Hersen and A. S. Bellack, eds. Baltimore: Williams & Wilkins.

Risley, T. R., and Wolf, M. M. 1967. Experimental manipulation of autistic behaviors and generalization into the home. In *Child development: Readings in experimental analysis*, S. W. Bijou and D. M. Baer, eds. New York: Appleton.

Schwebel, A. I., and Fine, M. A. 1992. Cognitive-behavioral family therapy. *Journal of Family Psychotherapy*. 3:73–91.

Schwitzgebel, R. 1967. Short-term operant conditioning of adolescent offenders on socially relevant variables. *Journal of Abnormal Psychology*. 72:134–142.

Schwitzgebel, R., and Kolb, D. A. 1964. Inducing behavior change in adolescent delinquents. *Behaviour Research and Therapy*. 9:233–238.

Semans, J. H. 1956. Premature ejaculation: A new approach. *Southern Medical Journal*. 49:353–357.

Skinner, B. F. 1953. *Science and human behavior*. New York: Macmillan.

Spinks, S. H., and Birchler, G. R. 1982. Behavior systems marital therapy: Dealing with resistance. *Family Process*. 21:169–186.

Stuart, R. B. 1969. An operant-interpersonal treatment for marital discord. *Journal of Consulting and Clinical Psychology*. 33:675–682.

Stuart, R. B. 1971. Behavioral contracting within the families of delinquents. *Journal of Behavior Therapy and Experimental Psychiatry*. 2:1–11.

Stuart, R. B. 1975. Behavioral remedies for marital ills: A guide to the use of operant-interpersonal techniques. In *International symposium on behavior modification*, T. Thompson and W. Docken, eds. New York: Appleton.

Stuart, R. B. 1976. An operant interpersonal program for couples. In *Treating relationships*, D. H. Olson, ed. Lake Mills, IA: Graphic Publishing.

Teichman, Y. 1984. Cognitive family therapy. *British Journal of Cognitive Psychotherapy*. 2:1–10.

Teichman, Y. 1992. Family treatment with an acting-out adolescent. In *Comprehensive casebook of cognitive therapy*, A. Freeman and F. M. Dattilio, eds. New York: Plenum.

Thibaut, J., and Kelley, H. H. 1959. *The social psychology of groups*. New York: Wiley.

Umana, R. F., Gross, S. J., and McConville, M. T. 1980. *Crisis in the family: Three approaches*. New York: Gardner Press.

Vincent, J. P., Weiss, R. L., and Birchler, G. R. 1975.

A behavioral analysis of problem solving in distressed and nondistressed married and stranger dyads. *Behavior Therapy.* 6:475–487.

Watson, J. B., and Raynor, R. 1920. Conditioned emotional reactions. *Journal of Experimental Psychology.* 3:1–14.

Weekes, G. R., and Gambescia, N. 2000. *Erectile dysfunction: Integrating couple therapy, sex therapy and medical treatment.* New York: Norton.

Weekes, G. R., and Gambescia, N. 2002. *Hypoactive sexual desire: Integrating sex and couple therapy.* New York: Norton.

Weiss, R. L. 1978. The conceptualization of marriage from a behavioral perspective. In *Marriage and marital therapy*, T. J. Paolino and B. S. McCrady, eds. New York: Brunner/Mazel.

Weiss, R. L., and Birchler, G. R. 1978. Adults with marital dysfunction. In *Behavior therapy in the psychiatric setting*, M. Hersen and A. S. Bellack, eds. Baltimore: Williams & Wilkins.

Weiss, R. L., and Isaac, J. 1978. Behavior vs. cognitive measures as predictors of marital satisfaction. Paper presented at the Western Psychological Association meeting, Los Angeles, California.

Weiss, R. L., Hops, H., and Patterson, G. R. 1973. A framework for conceptualizing marital conflict, a technology for altering it, some data for evaluating it. In *Behavior change: Methodology, concepts and practice*, L. A. Hamerlynch, L. C. Handy, and E. J. Marsh, eds. Champaign, IL: Research Press.

Wills, T. A., Weiss, R. L., and Patterson, G. R. 1974. A behavioral analysis of the determinants of marital satisfaction. *Journal of Consulting and Clinical Psychology.* 42:802–811.

Wolpe, J. 1948. An approach to the problem of neurosis based on the conditioned response. Unpublished M. D. thesis. University of Witwatersrand, Johannesburg, South Africa.

Wolpe, J. 1958. *Psychotherapy by reciprocal inhibition.* Stanford, CA: Stanford University Press.

Family Therapy in the Twenty-First Century

11

The Shape of Family Therapy Today

From a radical new experiment in the 1960s, family therapy grew into an established force, complete with its own literature, organizations, and legions of practitioners. Unlike approaches organized around a single model (psychoanalysis, behavior therapy), family therapy was always a diverse enterprise, with competing schools and multiple theories. What they shared was a belief that problems run in families. Beyond that, however, each school was a distinct enterprise, with its own leaders, texts, and ways of doing therapy.

Today, all of that has changed. The field is no longer neatly divided into separate schools, and practitioners no longer share a universal adherence to systems theory. As family therapists have always been fond of metaphors, we might say that the field has grown up. No longer cliquish or cocksure, the family therapy movement has been shaken and transformed by a series of challenges—to the idea that any one approach has all the answers, about the nature of men and women, about the shape of the American family, indeed about the possibility of knowing anything with certainty. In this chapter, we'll examine those challenges and see what family therapy looks like in the twenty-first century.

 ## EROSION OF BOUNDARIES

The boundaries between schools of family therapy have gradually blurred to the point where now fewer and fewer therapists would characterize themselves as purely Bowenian or structural or what have you. One reason for this decline in sectarianism was that as they gained experience, practitioners found no reason not to borrow from each other's arsenal of techniques. Suppose, for example, that a card-carrying structural therapist were to read White and Epston's little gem of a book *Narrative Means to Therapeutic Ends* and started spending more time exploring the stories clients tell about their lives. Would this therapist still be a structuralist? A narrative therapist? Or perhaps a little of both?

Suppose our hypothetical therapist were to hear Jim Keim at a conference describing his strategic approach to families with oppositional children and started using it in her own practice. What would we call this therapist now? Structural-narrative-strategic? Eclectic? Or maybe just a family therapist?

In response to this blurring of boundaries, Blow, Sprenkle, and Davis (2007) urged therapists to learn about theories of change rather than concentrate on learning a particular model of therapy. They suggest that therapists become familiar with several models of therapy so that they can apply them judiciously to the needs of particular clients. This may be good advice. We, however, don't agree with those who say that what therapists actually do in therapy is similar across models (e.g., Davis & Piercy, 2007). While there are common elements to most therapies—empathy, encouragement, questioning unproductive assumptions—there are also sharp differences. While Bowenians reason with family members one at a time, structuralists push family members to talk to each other; while most schools carefully explore the presenting complaint, solution-focused therapist suggest that this only reinforces problem-centered thinking. So, while it's clear that family therapists now borrow from each other, there are still distinct conceptual models, each with its own implications for doing therapy. While borrowing techniques can surely be useful, operating without a coherent theoretical model probably isn't.

Another reason for the erosion of orthodoxy was the growing recognition of the need for individualized techniques to deal with specific problems and populations. Once family therapists cherished their models. If a particular family didn't quite fit the paradigm, maybe they just weren't "an appropriate treatment case." Today, one-size-fits-all therapies are no longer seen as viable.

 # POSTMODERNISM

Advances in science at the beginning of the twentieth century gave us a sense that the truth of things could be uncovered through objective observation and measurement. The universe was a mechanism whose laws of operation awaited discovery. Once those laws were known, we could control our environment. This modernist perspective influenced the way family therapy's pioneers approached their clients—as cybernetic systems to be decoded and reprogrammed. The therapist was the expert. Structural and strategic blueprints were used to search for flaws that needed repair, regardless of whether families saw things that way themselves.

Postmodernism was a reaction to this kind of hubris. Not only are we losing faith in the validity of scientific, political, and religious truths, we're also coming to doubt whether absolute truth can ever be known. As Walter Truett Anderson (1990) writes in *Reality Isn't What It Used to Be*, "Most of the conflicts that tore the now-ending modern era were between different belief systems, each of which professed to have the truth: this faith against that one, capitalism against communism, science against religion. On all sides the assumption was that somebody possessed the real item, a truth fixed and beyond mere human conjecture" (p. 2). In family therapy it was structural truth versus psychodynamics, Bowen versus Satir.

Einstein's relativity undermined our faith in certainties. Marx challenged the right of one class to dominate another. In the 1960s we lost trust in the establishment. The feminist movement challenged assumptions about gender that had been considered laws of nature. As the world shrank and we were increasingly exposed to different cultures, we had to reexamine our assumptions about other people's "peculiar" beliefs.

This mounting skepticism became a major force in the 1980s and shook the pillars of every human endeavor. In literature, education, religion, political science, and psychology, accepted practices were **deconstructed**—that is, shown to be social conventions developed by people with their own agendas. Social philosopher Michel Foucault interpreted the accepted principles in many fields as stories perpetuated to protect power structures and silence alternative voices. The first and perhaps most influential of those voices to be raised in family therapy was the feminist critique.

 ## THE FEMINIST CRITIQUE

Feminism prompted family therapy's rudest awakening. In an eye-opening critique heralded by an article of Rachel Hare-Mustin's in 1978, feminist family therapists not only exposed the gender bias inherent in existing models but also advocated a style of therapy that called into question systems theory itself.

Cybernetics encouraged us to view a family system as a flawed machine. Judith Myers Avis (1988) described this family machine as one that

> functions according to special systemic rules and is divorced from its historical, social, economic, and political contexts. By viewing the family out of context, family therapists locate family dysfunction entirely within interpersonal relationships in the family, ignore broader patterns of dysfunction occurring across families, and fail to notice the relationship between social context and family dysfunction. (p. 17)

The Batesonian version of cybernetics had claimed that personal control in systems was impossible because all elements are continually influencing one another in circular feedback loops. If all parts of a system are equally involved in its problems, no one is to blame.

To feminists, however, the notion of equal responsibility for problems looked suspiciously like a sophisticated version of "blaming the victim and rationalizing the status quo" (Goldner, 1985, p. 33). This criticism was particularly germane in crimes against women, such as battering, incest, and rape, for which psychological theories have long been used to imply that women provoke their own abuse (James & MacKinnon, 1990).

The family constellation most commonly cited as contributing to problems was the peripheral father, overinvolved mother, and symptomatic child. For years, psychoanalysts had blamed mothers for their children's symptoms. Family therapy's contribution was to show how the father's lack of involvement contributed to the mother's overinvolvement, and so therapists tried to pry the mother loose by inserting the father in her place. This wasn't the boon for women that it might have seemed, because in too many cases, mothers were viewed no less negatively. Mothers were still "enmeshed," but now a new solution appeared—bringing in good old Dad to the rescue.

What feminists contended that therapists failed to see was that "the archetypal 'family case' of the overinvolved mother and peripheral father is best understood not as a clinical problem, but as the product of an historical process two hundred years in the making" (Goldner, 1985, p. 31). Mothers were overinvolved and insecure not because of some personal flaw but because they were in emotionally isolated, economically dependent, overresponsible positions in families, positions that were crazy-making.

Gender-sensitive therapists sought to help families reorganize so that no one, male or female, remained stuck in such positions. Thus, instead of undermining a mother by replacing her with a peripheral father (who was likely to have been critical of her parenting all along), a feminist family therapist might help the family reexamine the roles that kept mothers down and fathers out. Fathers might be encouraged to become more involved with parenting—not because mothers are incompetent but because it's a father's responsibility (Goodrich, Rampage, Ellman, & Halstead, 1988; Walters, Carter, Papp, & Silverstein, 1988).

Only when we become more gender sensitive will we stop blaming mothers and looking to them to do all of the changing. Only then will we be able to fully counter the unconscious bias toward seeing women as responsible for childrearing and housekeeping, as needing to support their husbands' careers by neglecting their own, and as needing to be married or at least to have a man in their lives (Anderson, 1995). Only then can we stop relying on traditional male traits, such as independence and competitiveness, as the standards of health and stop denigrating or ignoring traits traditionally encouraged in women, like emotionality, nurturance, and relationship focus.

In the following section we'll see how these principles are translated into action.

FEMINIST FAMILY THERAPY

Traditional family therapists focused on interactions within the family while ignoring the social, economic, and material realities that mold those interactions. Feminist therapists extend the level of analysis beyond the family to the social and cultural context and are committed to changing institutions and values that trap women and men in narrow and unequal roles.

Thus, feminist therapy is deliberately political. The aim is to replace patriarchy with a feminist consciousness. This involves helping clients realize that how they define themselves and relate to others is often distorted by gender-role expectations. But having a political agenda imposes a challenge for therapists. There is a fine line between *clinical neutrality*, not taking a position, and *indoctrination*, imposing one's position on clients.

Deborah Luepnitz (1988), whose book *The Family Interpreted* is one of the landmark texts of feminist family therapy, says that the ability to

Peggy Papp, Olga Silverstein, Marianne Walters, and Betty Carter, founding members of the Women's Project in Family

challenge patriarchy in a clinical context has to do with having a feminist *sensibility*, not a feminist *agenda*. Therapy is different from indoctrination. It has to do with creating space for people to examine their assumptions about what it means to live as women and men and to explore greater flexibility in their lives.

Luepnitz's own work exemplifies the feminist sensibility without veering into indoctrination, as illustrated in the following vignette adapted from *The Family Interpreted* (Luepnitz, personal communication, September 25, 2006).

LeRoy Johnson was an African American adolescent who had been in trouble since kindergarten. At fif- teen he had been expelled from a school for delinquents and was on the road to jail. During the assessment for a thirty-day inpatient stay, his mother would hardly look at the consultant as she explained the one-way mirror. The family had had nine bouts of therapy with as many therapists. Dr. Luepnitz had read their reports. They saw Ms. Johnson as "ineffectual," "depressed," "narcissistic," "dependent," "disengaged," and "overinvolved." Attending to the countertransference and realizing that the hopelessness the mother was feeling might be something of the client's that she needed the therapist to experience and contain, Luepnitz tried, as a feminist therapist, to intervene constructively.

Luepnitz: Ms. Johnson, I want to tell you something very important, something I don't think anyone has told you before.
Ms. Johnson: Go ahead.
Luepnitz: LeRoy's problems are not your fault.
Ms. Johnson: (after a long pause): Well, that *is* news.

Ms. Johnson had gotten the message for ten years from schools, guidance counselors, judges, and relatives that she had ruined her child's life and that if he was on his way to prison, that too was her doing. She sat, looking thoughtful.

Ms. Johnson: I have done a lot of things wrong.
Luepnitz: How about the things you've done right?
Ms. Johnson: Such as?
Luepnitz: Who has fed and clothed this child all his life? Who has talked to teachers and therapists and worked two or three jobs?
Ms. Johnson: Any mother does those things if she has to.
Luepnitz: Mothers need help. Who helped you?
Ms. Johnson: I'm self-sufficient.
Luepnitz: Self-sufficient people need loving friends. Who has loved you?
Ms. Johnson: Nobody.

Following this interchange Ms. Johnson and the consultant formed a therapeutic alliance, something this mother had never had before with the more problem-solving, patriarchal clinicians she'd seen. From this base the family was able to work hard and undergo a major transformation. LeRoy was allowed to return home. He went to college and was never in trouble with the law again.

Feminist therapists have also helped women rethink their relationship with their bodies (e.g., Orbach, 1997). By examining the effects of social expectations communicated by the media, women can assign less importance to appearance and focus more on being themselves.

To illustrate the difference between *advocacy* and *indoctrination*, consider how a therapist might raise the issue of cultural conditioning with a young woman struggling with an eating disorder. What are the implications of a therapist saying "Our society is obsessed with thinness" versus asking "Do you know where you got the idea that it was important for a woman to be thin?" The first comment suggests that the therapist knows why the client feels pressured to eat the way she does and invites her to join the therapist in seeing her problem as something imposed on her. The second comment invites the client to join in a mutual search for understanding her problem and empowers her to take an active role in that process.

When it comes to the politics of the family, feminists make a point of exploring the income and work potential of husbands and wives and the implications for the balance of power in their relationship. They help couples clarify the rules by which roles are chosen and rewarded in the family. Useful questions include the following:

Who handles the finances?

Who handles emotional matters?

Who makes social arrangements?

Who decides where the couple is going to live and when they will move?

Who buys and wraps birthday presents?

Who cleans the toilets?

What do the couples believe about appropriate gender roles of a wife and husband?

What gender roles were modeled by their own parents—both positive and negative?

One of the core elements of feminist therapy is *empowerment*. Women are typically brought up to empower others—to respond to the feelings and opinions of others and to foster other people's growth and well-being. If the greatest shame for a man is weakness, then the greatest shame for a woman is selfishness. Underlying the specific conflicts between men and women in families is the cultural programming for men to seek success and the programming for women to nurture and support them, even at the expense of their own development. Feminist therapists aim to redress this imbalance by empowering women to feel competent. Thus, empowerment is in the service of *power to*, not *power over*. *Power to* means having the ability to perform and produce and the freedom and resources to do so. *Power over* refers to having domination and control.

Some men have trouble understanding how women are disempowered, because they don't feel powerful in relationship with their wives and mothers. But the fact that a man may feel powerless in individual circumstances doesn't cancel his membership in the dominant class or eliminate the privileges that go along with that membership (Goodrich, 1991).

Empowerment need not be a zero-sum game. Both people in a relationship can learn to interact in ways that increase connection and enhance personal power for both of them (Miller, 1986; Surrey, 1991). Mutual empowerment means helping women and men differentiate between what they have been taught is socially acceptable and what is actually in their best interests.

In recent years the standard model of marriage has shifted from *complementary* to *symmetrical*. In an egalitarian marriage, mutuality and reciprocity replace hierarchy and control. But the reproduction of patriarchy still appears in the family—from who gets the kids ready for school to who drives the car, from who pleads for conversation to who has the last word, from minor acts of deference to major decisions. Here's an example of one couple's struggle to achieve mutual empowerment.

Case Study

Raised in a generation that takes gender equality for granted, Olivia and Noah found that actually implementing that ideal was easier said than done. Both of them believed that Noah should be as responsible for housework as Olivia, but he had trouble assuming those responsibilities, and she had trouble letting go of them. Olivia expected to be in charge of looking after things, as her mother had been, and she tended to criticize Noah's efforts when he did make them.

Even when a man expresses willingness to assume more responsibility, both he and his partner need to make concessions. Noah insisted on doing the laundry his own way, even if it meant that stains would set and colors would bleed. He wanted to do the grocery shopping when he got around to it, even though that meant that occasionally there would be nothing to pack for school lunches.

A man who wants to share in the responsibility of being part of a family, rather than just "help out," must submit to suggestions. And his partner must let go some. Asking a husband to explain why it's so hard to accept advice from his wife may be a useful way to clear away some of his resentment. Taking suggestions does involve a loss of freedom. You can't just do things your own way if your partner has significant problems with that way.

Family therapists are so used to having women as customers and men as reluctant presences that they tend to ask very little of men. This attitude begins with accepting that Dad can't attend sessions "because he has to work." A therapist who wants to be part of the solution to sexist family arrangements has to stop accepting the nonparticipation of fathers and start insisting that both partners be actively involved in therapy.

Therapists who would challenge men to become more involved with their families must be sensitive to the price a man may have to pay for putting more priority on his family and less on his job. Both partners must be convinced that the therapist is equally committed to their well-being. But the feminist perspective isn't just about sacrificing male prerogatives. It's also about helping men learn to increase their capacity for intimacy, become more involved in the lives of their children, express their emotions, balance their achievement and relationship needs, accept their vulnerabilities, and create collaborative relationships in their work and with significant others that are not based on a power-over model of relating.

The political agenda in feminist therapy has evolved to include not only greater equality in the institution of the family but also in the world outside the home. For career-oriented women the challenge has shifted from access to flexibility. Twenty years ago the gender debate centered on breaking the glass ceiling that kept women out of top management and professional jobs. Today, concerns often revolve around reshaping the climate of the work world to *keep* women involved, including compensating managers for achieving diversity goals and reaching out to women employees with families. Businesses and institutions are beginning to realize that women's needs are often different from those of their male counterparts, and they are making efforts to accommodate the needs of women with families. For their part, women are becoming more aggressive about demanding fulfilling careers and family lives, and many are willing to walk away from organizations that fail to meet those needs.

For poor and working-class women, the challenge is not so much finding a rewarding career as finding someone to watch the kids so they can walk to the bus stop and get to the minimum-wage job that they so need desperately to hang on to. Helping these wives and mothers out of poverty takes more than talk therapy. What's needed are flexible schedules, affordable child care, and greater availability of part-time work.

SOCIAL CONSTRUCTIONISM AND THE NARRATIVE REVOLUTION

Constructivism was the lever that pried family therapy away from its claim to objectivity. Human experience is fundamentally ambiguous; fragments of experience are understood only through a process that organizes it and assigns meaning.

Instead of focusing on patterns of interaction, constructivism shifted the emphasis to exploring the perspectives that people have about their problems. Meaning itself became the primary target.

In the 1980s and 1990s Harlene Anderson and Harry Goolishian translated constructivism into an approach that democratized the therapist–client relationship. Along with Lynn Hoffman and others, these *collaborative therapists* were united in their opposition to the cybernetic model and its mechanistic implications. They sought to move the therapist out of the position of expert into a more egalitarian partnership with clients.

Perhaps the most striking example of this democratization was introduced by the Norwegian psychiatrist Tom Andersen, who leveled the playing field by hiding nothing from his clients. He and his team openly discuss their reactions to what a family says. This **reflecting team** (Andersen, 1991) has become a widely used device in the collaborative model's therapy by consensus. Observers come out from behind the one-way mirror to discuss their impressions with the therapist and family. This process creates an open environment in which the family feels part of a team and the team feels more empathy for the family.

What these collaborative therapists shared was a conviction that too often clients aren't heard because therapists are doing therapy *to* them rather than *with* them. To redress this authoritarian attitude, Harlene Anderson (1993) recommended that therapists adopt a position of not knowing, which leads to genuine conversations with clients in which "both the therapist's and the client's expertise are engaged to dissolve the problem" (p. 325).

This new perspective was in the tradition of an approach to knowledge that emerged from biblical studies called **hermeneutics**, a term derived from the Greek word for *interpretation*. Before it surfaced in family therapy, hermeneutics had already shaken up psychoanalysis. In the 1980s Donald Spence, Roy Schafer, and Paul Ricoeur challenged the Freudian notion that there was one correct interpretation of a patient's symptoms, dreams, and fantasies. The analytic method isn't, they argued, archaeological or reconstructive; it's constructive and synthetic, organizing whatever is there into patterns it imposes (Mitchell, 1993).

From a hermeneutic perspective, what a therapist knows is not simply discovered through a process of free association and analysis—or enactment and circular questioning. It's organized, constructed, and fitted together by the therapist alone or collaboratively with the patient or family. Although there's nothing inherently democratic about hermeneutic exegesis, its challenge to essentialism went hand in hand with the challenge to authoritarianism.

It's hard to give up certainty. A lot is asked of a listener who, in order to be genuinely open to the speaker's story, must put aside his or her own beliefs and, at least temporarily, enter the other's world. In so doing, the listener may find those beliefs challenged. This is more than some therapists are willing to risk.

Constructivism focused on how individuals create their own realities, but family therapy has always emphasized the power of interaction. As a result, another postmodern psychology called **social constructionism** now influences many family therapists.

Social psychologist Kenneth Gergen (1985) emphasized the power of social interaction in generating meaning for people. Gergen challenged the notion that we are autonomous individuals holding independent beliefs and argued instead that our beliefs are fluid and fluctuate with changes in our social context. Gergen (1991) asks, "Are not all the fragments of identity the residues of relationships, and aren't we undergoing continuous transformation as we move from one relationship to another?" (p. 28).

This view has several implications. The first is that no one has a corner on the truth: All truths are social constructions. This idea invites therapists to help clients explore the origins of their beliefs, even those they assumed were laws of nature. The second implication is that therapy is a linguistic exercise; if therapists can lead clients to new constructions about their problems, the problems may open up. Third, therapy should be collaborative. Because neither therapist nor client brings truth to the table, new realities emerge through conversations in which both sides share their opinions and respect each other's perspective.

Social constructionism was welcomed with open arms by those who were trying to shift the focus of therapy from action to cognition, and it became the basis for an approach that took family therapy by storm in the 1990s, *narrative therapy* (Chapter 13). The narrative metaphor focuses on how experience generates expectations and how expectations shape experience through the creation of organizing stories.

The question for the narrative therapist isn't one of truth but of which points of view are useful and lead to preferred outcomes. Problems aren't in persons (as psychoanalysis had it) or in relationships (as systems theory had it); rather, problems are embedded in points of view about individuals and their situations. Narrative therapy helps people reexamine these points of view.

FAMILY VIOLENCE

In the early 1990s family therapy took a look at the dark side of family life. For the first time books and articles on wife battering and sexual abuse began appearing in the mainstream family therapy literature (e.g., Goldner, Penn, Sheinberg, & Walker, 1990; Sheinberg, 1992; Trepper & Barrett, 1989). The field was shaken out of its collective denial regarding the extent of male-to-female abuse in families.

Judith Myers Avis (1992) delivered a barrage of shocking statistics about the number of women who experience sexual abuse before the age of eighteen (37 percent), the percent of abusers who are male (95 percent), the number of women abused each year by the men they live with (one in six), the percent of male college students who had coerced sex from an unwilling partner (25 percent), and those who said they would commit rape if guaranteed immunity from punishment (20 percent). After reiterating the indictment of theories that call for therapist neutrality and that treat the abused as partially responsible for their abuse, she drew this conclusion:

> As long as we train therapists in systemic theories without balancing that training with an understanding of the non-neutrality of power dynamics, we will continue producing family therapists who collude in the maintenance of

male power and are dangerous to the women and children with whom they work. (p. 231)

The systemic view, now under attack, was that family violence was the outcome of cycles of mutual provocation, an escalation, albeit unacceptable, of the emotionally destructive behavior that characterizes many marriages. Advocates for women rejected this point of view. From their perspective, violent men don't lose control, they *take* control—and will stop only when they are held accountable.

While the claim made by some women's advocates that couples therapy has no place in the treatment of violent marriages was controversial, their warnings provided a wake-up call. Domestic violence—let's call it what it is, wife battering and child beating—is a major public health problem, right up there with alcoholism and depression.

MULTICULTURALISM

Family therapy has always billed itself as a treatment of people in context. In the postwar United States of family therapy's birth, this principle was translated into a pragmatic look at the influence of family relationships. Now as we've become a more diverse country enriched by an influx of immigrants from Asia, Central and South America, Africa, and Eastern Europe, family therapy as a profession has shown its willingness to embrace the positiveness of others. Not only are we learning to respect that families from other cultures have their own valid ways of doing things, but our journals and professional organizations are making an effort to become more diverse and inclusive.

Monica McGoldrick and her colleagues (McGoldrick, Pearce, & Giordano, 1982) dealt the first blow to our ethnocentricity with a book describing the characteristic values and structure of a host of different ethnic groups. Following this and a spate of related works (e.g., Boyd-Franklin, 1989; Falicov, 1983, 1998; Fontes,

2008; Ingoldsby & Smith, 1995; McGoldrick, 1998; Mirkin, 1990; Okun, 1996; Saba, Karrer, & Hardy, 1989), we are now more sensitive to the need to know something about the ethnic background of our client families, so we don't assume they're sick just because they're different.

Multiculturalism is certainly an advance over ethnocentrism. Yet in highlighting differences, there is a danger of emphasizing identity politics. Segregation, even in the name of ethnic pride, isolates people and breeds prejudice. Perhaps *pluralism* is a better term than *multiculturalism* because it implies a balance between ethnic identity and connection to the larger group.

As we suggested in Chapter 4, ethnic sensitivity doesn't require becoming an expert—or thinking you're an expert—on every culture you might work with. If you don't know how a rural Mexican family feels about their children leaving home or what Korean parents think about their teenage daughter dating American boys, you can always ask.

RACE

In the early days of family therapy, African American families received some attention (e.g., Minuchin, Montalvo, Guerney, Rosman, & Schumer, 1967), but for many years it seemed that the field, like the rest of the country, tried to ignore people of color and the racism they live with every day. Finally, however, African American family therapists such as Nancy Boyd-Franklin (1993) and Ken Hardy (1993) brought race out of the shadows and forced it into the field's consciousness.

White therapists still have the option to walk away from these issues. People of color don't have that luxury (Hardy, 1993):

> To avoid being seen by whites as troublemakers, we suppress the part of ourselves that feels hurt and outraged by the racism around us, instead developing an "institutional self"—an accommodating facade of calm professionalism calculated to be nonthreatening to whites. . . . Familiar only with our institutional selves, white people don't appreciate the sense of immediate connection and unspoken loyalty that binds black people together. (pp. 52–53)

Laura Markowitz (1993) quotes a black woman's therapy experience:

> I remember being in therapy years ago with a nice white woman who kept focusing me on why I was such an angry person and on my parents as inadequate individuals. . . . We never looked at my father as a poor black man, my mother as a poor black woman and the context in which they survived and raised us. . . . Years later, I saw a therapist of color and the first thing out of her mouth was, "Let's look at what was going on for your parents." It was a joyous moment to be able to see my

Nancy Boyd-Franklin's *Black Families in Therapy* was one of the first—and best—books on treating ethnic minority families.

Ken Hardy advises therapists not to overlook the impact of racism on their clients—or in the therapeutic relationship.

dad not as a terrible person who hated us but as a survivor living under amazingly difficult conditions. (p. 29)

It's hard for whites to realize how many doors are open to them based on their skin color and to understand how burdened by racism non-whites are. African American families not only have to overcome barriers to opportunity and achievement but also the frustration and despair that such obstacles create.

The task of therapists working with nonwhite families is to understand their reluctance to engage in treatment (particularly if the therapist is white) in the context of a history of negative interaction with white people, including many of the social service agents they encounter. In addition, the therapist must recognize the family's strengths and draw from their networks or, if the family is isolated, help them create networks of support.

Finally, therapists must look inside and face their own attitudes about race, class, and poverty. Toward this end, several authors recommend curricula that go beyond lectures to personal encounters—that is, confronting our own demons of racism (Boyd-Franklin, 1989; Green, 1998; Pinderhughes, 1989).

POVERTY AND SOCIAL CLASS

Money and social class are not subjects that helping professionals like to discuss. The shame of economic disadvantage is related to the ethic of self-reliance: that people are responsible for their own success. If you're poor, it must be your own fault.

Despite decreasing fees due to managed care, most therapists are able to maintain a reasonably comfortable lifestyle. They have little appreciation of the obstacles their poor clients face and the psychological impact of those conditions. When poor clients don't show up for appointments or don't comply with directives, some therapists see them as apathetic or irresponsible. This is often the way poor people come to see themselves—and that negative self-image can be an enormous obstacle.

How can we counter this tendency to think that poor people just can't cut it? First, therapists need to educate themselves to the social and political realities of being poor in the United States. Journalist Barbara Ehrenreich (1999) spent a year trying to live like a former welfare recipient coming into the workforce. Living in a

Nonwhite clients may feel that white therapists can't fully understand their experiences.

trailer park and working as a waitress left her with almost nothing after expenses:

> How former welfare recipients and single mothers will (and do) survive in the low-wage workforce, I cannot imagine. Maybe they will figure out how to condense their lives—including child raising, laundry, romance and meals—into the couple of hours between full-time jobs. Maybe they will take up residence in their vehicles [as she found several fellow workers had done], if they have one. All I know is that I couldn't hold two jobs and I couldn't make enough money to live on with one. And I had advantages unthinkable to many of the long-term poor—health, stamina, a working car, and no children to care for or support. . . . The thinking behind welfare reform was that even the humblest jobs are morally uplifting and psychologically buoying. In reality these are likely to be fraught with insult and stress. (p. 52)

The fact is, this isn't the land of equal opportunity. The economy has built-in disparities that make it extremely difficult for anyone to climb out of poverty and that keep nearly one in four children living in privation (Walsh, 1998).

These days, it isn't just families of poverty who live with financial insecurity. As mortgages, energy costs, and college tuitions mount up and corporations lay off employees suddenly and ruthlessly, family life at all but the wealthiest levels is increasingly dominated by economic anxiety. Median family income has declined in the past three decades to the point where young families can't hope to do as well as their parents, even with the two incomes needed to support a very modest standard of living.

Therapists can't pay their clients' rent, but they can help them appreciate that the burdens they live with are not all of their own making. Even when clients don't bring it up, a sensitive therapist should be aware of the role financial pressures play in their lives. Asking how they manage to get by not only puts this issue on the table, but it can also lead to a greater appreciation of the effort and ingenuity that it takes to make ends meet these days.

GAY AND LESBIAN RIGHTS

Family therapy's consciousness was raised about gay and lesbian rights in the same way it was for race. After a long period of neglect and denial, family therapy in the late 1980s began to face the discrimination that a sizable percentage of the population lives with (Carl, 1990; Krestan, 1988; Laird, 1993; Roth & Murphy, 1986; Sanders, 1993). The release in 1996 of a major clinical handbook (Laird & Green, 1996) and the magazine *In the Family* (edited by Laura Markowitz) meant that gay and lesbian issues were finally out of family therapy's closet.

Despite gains in tolerance in some segments of our society, however, gays and lesbians continue to face humiliation, discrimination, and even violence because of their sexuality. After a childhood of shame and confusion, many gays and lesbians are rejected by their families when they come out. Due to the lack of social support, the bonds in gay and lesbian relationships can be strained by the pressures of isolation, generating stress and jealousy.

Parents often feel guilty, in part because they blame themselves for their children's sexual orientation. Parental reactions range from denial, self-reproach, and fear for their child's future to hostility, violence, and disowning (LaSala, 1997). Therapists should remember that a gay or lesbian child may have struggled for years to come to grips with his or her identity, and the child's parents may need time to catch up after the initial shock.

When working with gay, lesbian, bisexual, or transgendered clients, we recommend that therapists get as much information as they can about the unique identity formation and relationship issues that these individuals face. Therapists who aren't well informed about gay and lesbian experience should seek supervision from someone who is or refer these clients to a clinician with more experience. It simply isn't true that individuals and families, regardless of their cultural context, all struggle with the same issues.

We hope the day will come when gay and lesbian families, bisexual and transgendered persons, African Americans, and other marginalized groups are studied by family therapists to learn not only about the problems they face but also about how they survive and thrive against such great odds. For example, gays and lesbians often create "families of choice" out of their friendship networks (Johnson & Keren, 1998). As Joan Laird (1993) suggested, these families have much to teach us "about gender relationships, about parenting, about adaptation to tensions in this society, and especially about strength and resilience" (p. 284). The question is whether we are ready to learn.

ADVANCES IN NEUROSCIENCE

Scientists have come a long way from looking at bumps on the skull for clues to brain functioning. Now, instead of phrenology, we have: *fMRI*—functional magnetic resonance imaging, which measures increases in blood flow to the most active regions of the brain; *PET scan*—positron emission tomography, which provides a sectional view of the brain and its activity; *ERP*—event related potentials, which measure brain activity via electrical signals; and *TMSs*—transcranial magnetic stimulation—magnetic fields administered to the cortex to induce a virtual lesion, if done repeatedly, or pre-activate or interfere with a neural system using single pulses.

These technological advances have produced a growing body of evidence suggesting that people keep doing things they know they shouldn't, and fail to do things they know they should, because their brains are programmed to make decisions for them. Studies of the amygdala, hippocampus, and prefrontal cortex show that the brain becomes conditioned to respond automatically to certain cues by activating neural response circuits that propel people into programmed patterns of thinking and acting (LeDoux, 1996; Siegel, 1999).

These conditioned patterns of responding are similar to what cognitive-behavior therapists refer to as *schemata* (see Chapter 10)—cognitive constructions by which we interpret present experiences on the basis of past experience; but the difference is that many of these schemata are encoded in *implicit memory* and therefore not subject to conscious recall or rational reevaluation.[1]

The evidence from neuroscience is that emotion, not cognition, is the primary organizer of human experience. Thinking counts, but not as much as we have assumed.

There is a good deal of evidence suggesting that the brain gets wired for specific kinds of neural activations at a very young age, and that once these activations are set, they tend to persist throughout a person's life. The discovery of the brain's neural operating systems helps explain why people often persist in self-defeating interactions, even when they know that it would be in their best interests to change. "Emotional responses are, for the most part, generated unconsciously" (LeDoux, 1996, p. 17). It turns out that Freud was right when he described consciousness as the tip of the iceberg.

Emotions do not, as we once thought, emanate strictly from the part of the brain called the limbic system (hypothalamus, hippocampus, and amygdala). Emotion is not limited to some specifically designed circuits of the brain, but rather the subcortical structures of the limbic system appear to have wide-ranging effects on most aspects of brain functioning and mental processes (Watt, 1998).

The amygdala acts like an emotional watchdog, constantly alert for signs of threat. If an experience registers as potentially dangerous, the amygdala broadcasts a distress signal to the entire brain, which sets off a surge of physiological responses, from the release of adrenaline and noradrenaline to speeded-up heart rate to rising

---

[1]Implicit memory is a form of memory based on emotional, behavioral, and perceptual priming, rather than conscious awareness.

blood pressure and muscles mobilized for fight or flight. Within milliseconds, we may explode with rage or freeze in fear well before our conscious minds can assess what's happening, much less persuade us to pause long enough to think about what to do.

When the amygdala tries to assess whether a situation is dangerous, it compares the situation with past emotionally charged events. If any of the key elements of the situation–the tone of voice, a facial expression—are similar, the amygdala sounds its warning siren and sets off an accompanying emotional reaction.

The central role of this hair-trigger brain mechanism in creating marital misery has been thoroughly documented by psychologist John Gottman's research at the University of Washington. What Gottman found was that the brain's atavistic emotional reactions were highly correlated with criticism, contempt, and stonewalling. The gradually emerging portrait of the emotional brain offers an illuminating window on why many clients find it so difficult to contain their reactivity in intimate relationships. It turns out that the trajectory of divorce often originates with frequent, nasty arguments that eventually cause partners to develop a kind of bio-emotional hypersensitivity to each other.

For those who wish people could just learn to get along, the point to remember is that the amygdala often sets off its emotional fireworks before the neocortex ever gets into the act. That's why a clinician can spend hours getting a couple to communicate better only to see the whole thing go up in smoke when one partner says something that feels to the other like an arrow to the heart—or, to put it in the present context, activates a primitive neural circuit.

Exciting as some of these neuroscientific discoveries are, they can lead to unfortunate conclusions. When we describe an individual's actions in human terms—"She flies off the handle," "He doesn't listen," and so on—we tend to hold people responsible. And we believe that therapy can help. But shifting to a biological

explanation may seem to rob people of free will. How can you reason with a pre-programmed neural response circuit? Thus, the current vogue of biological determinism suggests that people do things *because of* what happens in their brain. But this is false.

Biological events don't cause human actions; they occur on a different level of analysis. Understanding that the primitive responses of the amygdala can overwhelm the logical deliberations of the prefrontal cortex sheds light on why it's so difficult to avoid reacting emotionally in certain situations; but we can still hold people accountable for their actions.

If a man punches his wife during an argument, the fact that his amygdala triggered the emotional circuits of his brain doesn't excuse his behavior. It may explain what happened in biological terms, but we still expect the man to learn to resist his aggressive impulses—regardless of what level, biological or behavioral, we describe that process in. In terms of human action, we might say that the man can learn to resist the impulse to hit his wife, even when he gets very upset. In biological terms, affective neuroscientists, such as Richard Davidson (2001, 2003) have found that the prefrontal cortex can moderate emotional reactivity—and that people can learn to activate their prefrontal cortexes and restrain their emotional reactions.

It may be that cognitive intervention only works when clients are calm (Atkinson, 2005)—that is, before their amygdalas have short-circuited their prefrontal cortexes, but isn't this is what Murray Bowen taught us fifty years ago—that family members can't reason together until the therapist has helped them reduce the level of their anxiety?

Neural circuits control the creation of meaning, the regulation of bodily states, the modulation of emotion, the organization of memory, and the capacity for interpersonal communication. But since these same functions are also influenced by relationship experiences, we can see that interpersonal experience and the structure of the brain interact in a circular fashion. In other words, the brain shapes experience and experience shapes the structure and function of the brain.

SPIRITUALITY

Throughout the twentieth century, psychotherapists tried to keep religion out of the consulting room. They also tried to stay out of the moralizing business, striving to remain neutral so that clients could make up their own minds about their lives.

At the turn of the twenty-first century, however, as increasing numbers of people found modern life isolating and empty, spirituality and religion emerged as antidotes to a widespread feeling of alienation—both in the popular press (making covers of both *Time* and *Newsweek*) and in the family therapy literature (Brothers, 1992; Burton, 1992; Doherty, 1996; Prest & Keller, 1993; Walsh, 1999).

Some of a family's most powerful organizing beliefs have to do with how they find meaning in their lives and their ideas about a higher power, yet most therapists never ask about such matters. Is it possible to explore a family's spiritual beliefs without proselytizing or scoffing? More and more therapists believe that it's not only possible but crucial. They believe that people's answers to those larger questions are intimately related to their well-being.

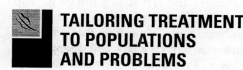

TAILORING TREATMENT TO POPULATIONS AND PROBLEMS

When family therapists came down from the ivory towers of their institutes to grapple with the messy problems of the real world, they found it increasingly necessary to fit their approaches to the needs of their clients, rather than the other way around. The maturing of family therapy is reflected in its literature. Once most of the

writing was about the classic models and how they applied to families in general (e.g., Haley, 1976; Minuchin & Fishman, 1981). Beginning in the 1980s, books no longer tied to any one school began to focus on how to do family therapy with a host of specific types of problems and family constellations.

Books are now available on working with families of people who abuse drugs (Barth, Pietrzak, & Ramier, 1993; Stanton, Todd, & Associates, 1982), alcohol (Elkin, 1990; Steinglass, Bennett, Wolin, & Reiss, 1987; Treadway, 1989), food (Root, Fallon, & Friedrich, 1986; Schwartz, 1995), and each other (Friedrich, 1990; Madanes, 1990; Trepper & Barrett, 1989).

There are books about treating single-parent families (Morawetz & Walker, 1984), stepparent families (Visher & Visher, 1979, 1988), divorcing families (Ahrons & Rogers, 1989; Emery, 1994; Sprenkle, 1985; Wallerstein & Kelley, 1980), blended families (Hansen, 1982; Sager et al., 1983), and families in transition among these states (Falicov, 1988; Pittman, 1987).

There are also books on treating families with young children (Bailey, 1999; Combrinck-Graham, 1989; Freeman, Epston, & Lobovits, 1997; Gil, 1994; Nichols, 2004; Selekman, 1997; Smith & Nylund, 1997; Wachtel, 1994), with troubled adolescents (Micucci, 1998; Price, 1996; Sells, 1998) and young adults (Haley, 1980), and with problems among siblings (Kahn & Lewis, 1988). There are even books on normal families (Walsh, 1982, 1993) and successful families (Beavers & Hampson, 1990).

There are books for working with schizophrenic families (Anderson, Reiss, & Hogarty, 1986), families with bipolar disorder (Miklowitz & Goldstein, 1997), and families with AIDS (Boyd-Franklin, Steiner, & Boland, 1995; Walker, 1991); families who have suffered trauma (Figley, 1985) or chronic illness or disability (McDaniel, Hepworth, & Doherty, 1992; Rolland, 1994); families who are grieving a death (Walsh & McGoldrick, 1991), have a child with a disability (Seligman & Darling, 1996), or have an adopted child (Reitz & Watson, 1992); poor families (Minuchin, Colapinto, & Minuchin, 1998); and families of different ethnicities (Boyd-Franklin, 1989; Falicov, 1998; Lee, 1997; McGoldrick, Pearce, & Giordano, 2007; Okun, 1996). There are also books about treating gay and lesbian families (Greenan & Tunnell, 2003; Laird & Green, 1996).

In addition to these specialized books, the field has extended systems thinking beyond the family to include the impact of larger systems like other helping agents or social agencies and schools (Elizur & Minuchin, 1989; Imber-Black, 1988; Schwartzman, 1985); the importance of family rituals and their use in therapy (Imber-Black, Roberts, & Whiting, 1988), and the sociopolitical context in which families exist (McGoldrick, 1998; Mirkin, 1990).

There are practical guides to family therapy not connected to any one school (Patterson, Williams, Graul-Grounds, & Chamow, 1998; Taibbi, 2007) and edited books that include contributions from all of the schools (Dattilio, 1998; Donovan, 1999). Thus, as opposed to the earlier days of family therapy when followers of a particular model read little outside of what came from that school, the trend toward specialization by content rather than by model has made the field more pluralistic in this postmodern age.

Among the most frequently encountered family constellations with unique challenges are single-parent families, African American families, and gay and lesbian families. The following recommendations are offered as introductions to some of the issues encountered in treating these groups.

Single-Parent Families

The most common structural problem in single-parent families is the same as it is in most two-parent families: an overburdened mother, enmeshed with her children and disengaged from adult relationships. From this perspective, the goal of therapy is to strengthen the mother's hierarchical position in relation to her children and help her become more fulfilled in her own life. However, it's important to keep in mind that single parents rarely have the resources to manage much of a social life on top of working all day and then coming home at night to take care of the kids, cook dinner, wash dishes, and do three loads of laundry.

Before going any further, we should acknowledge that single-parent families come in many varieties (U.S. Census Bureau, 2007). The children may be living with a teenage mother and her parents, a divorced college professor, or a father whose wife died of cancer. Such families may be rich or poor, and they may be isolated or part of a large family network. In the discussion that follows, we will concentrate on the most common variant encountered in clinical situations: a financially burdened mother with children who is going it alone.

In working with single-parent families, therapists should keep in mind that supporting the parent's care of her children and helping her find more satisfaction in her own life are reciprocal achievements. A therapist should enter the system by addressing the presenting complaint, but whether that problem is, say, a mother's depression or a child's school performance, it's important both to help the parent take more effective charge of her children and increase her sources of support.

Effective treatment for a single parent begins with an actively supportive therapeutic relationship. An empathic therapeutic alliance helps shore up a single parent's confidence to make positive changes and serves as a bridge to help her connect with other people in her environment. To begin with, it's well to recognize that single parents are often angry and disappointed over the loss of a relationship, financial hardship, and trying to cope with the demands of work and children.

Poverty may be the most overwhelming burden on single parents and their children (Duncan & Brooks-Gunn, 1997). Therapists should not underestimate the impact of poverty on a mother's depression, self-esteem, independence, and the decisions she makes about putting up with soul-draining jobs and abusive relationships. Many single-parent families live on the edge of crisis, managing most of the time but always aware that any unexpected emergency can push them over the edge. A supportive therapist recognizes the burdens of financial hardship, makes accommodations to the parent's work schedule, and in some cases helps the single parent consider options, like going back to school, that might help her to become more financially stable.

Often one of the most readily available sources of support for the single parent is her own family. Here the therapeutic task is twofold: facilitating supportive connections and reducing conflicts. Sometimes it's easier to develop dormant sources of support than to resolve contentious ones. The sister who lives twenty miles away may be more willing to look after her niece and nephew from time to time than a depressed single mother thinks. A single parent's family can provide financial support, a place to stay, and help with the children. However, since most parents have trouble getting over treating their grown children as children—especially when they ask for help—a therapist may have to meet with the grandparents, develop an alliance, and then help them and their adult children negotiate effective working relationships.

Pointing out these potential sources of assistance for single parents should not be taken to suggest that a family therapist's only or even primary function should be supportive counseling. Most families, single parent or otherwise, seek clinical services because they are stuck in conflict—psychological, interpersonal, or both. In working with single parents, a therapist's most important job is to identify and help resolve the impediments holding clients back from taking advantage of their own personal and interpersonal resources.

Sometimes the most significant conflict for single-mother households isn't visible: It's the potential involvement of the children's father, who is not infrequently described as "out of the

picture." He may be out of the picture, but in most cases he shouldn't be.

Many families of young mothers find it particularly difficult to support the ongoing involvement of the baby's father (Johnson, 2001). They may even consider him an enemy. If their understandable feelings are treated with respect, they can often be helped to support the father's involvement.

Facilitating the continued involvement of teen fathers deserves special attention because it's so challenging (Lehr & MacMillan, 2001). Because it's relatively easy for teen father to abandon their children, it's important to reach out to them, to establish rapport, and to encourage them in becoming responsible parents.

Even invisible fathers may desire more contact and be willing to take on more responsibility for the sake of their children. The therapist should consider contacting the noncustodial father to assess his potential contribution to his children's emotional and financial support.

Here, too, triangles can complicate the picture. In an effort to be sympathetic to their mates (and sometimes from unconscious jealousy), new partners often fan the flames of conflict with the noncustodial parent, which only reinforces the cutoff.

Elana Santos contacted the clinic because her ten-year-old son, Tony, was depressed. "He's having trouble getting over my divorce," she said "I think he misses his father." After two sessions, the therapist determined that Tony was not depressed and, although he did miss his father, it was his mother who hadn't gotten over the divorce. Tony had stopped hanging out with his friends after school; however, it was worrying about his mother, who'd become bitter and withdrawn, rather than depression that was keeping him in the house.

The therapist's formulation was that Mrs. Santos was enmeshed with her son and both were disengaged from contacts outside the family.

The therapist told Mrs. Santos that her son was sad because he worried about her. She didn't seem to be getting on with her life and Tony was sacrificing himself to become her protector. "Do you need your son to be your protector?" the therapist asked.

"No," Mrs. Santos insisted.

"Then I think you need to fire him. Can you convince Tony that he doesn't need to take care of you, that he can spend time with friends and that you'll be alright?"

Mrs. Santos did "fire" her son from the job of being her guardian angel. The therapist then talked about getting Tony more involved in after-school activities where he could meet friends. "Who knows?" the therapist said. "Maybe if Tony starts making friends, you'll have some time to do the same thing."

The only person Mrs. Santos could think of to help look after Tony so that she could have some time for herself was the boy's father, and he was "completely unavailable." Rather than accept this statement at face value, the therapist expressed surprise "that a father would care nothing about his son." When Mrs. Santos insisted that her ex wouldn't be willing to spend any time with Tony, the therapist asked permission to call him herself.

When the therapist told Mr. Santos that she was worried about his son and thought the boy needed his father's involvement in his life, Mr. Santos seemed responsive. But then the therapist heard someone talking in the background, and Mr. Santos started to back off.

What had begun as a problem firmly embedded in one person's head ("It's my son, he's depressed") turned out to involve not just the interaction between the boy and his mother but also a triangular complication in which the father's girlfriend objected to his involvement because she didn't want "that bitch of an ex-wife of his taking advantage" of him. What followed were a series of meetings—with the father and his girlfriend, the father and mother, the father and son, and finally all four of them together—in which the therapist concentrated on helping them clear the air by voicing feelings of resentment that stood in the way of their working cooperatively together.

The father's girlfriend had made the same mistake that a lot of us make when someone we love complains about how someone else is treating them. In response to his complaints about his ex-wife's angry phone calls, she had urged him to have nothing to do with her. In response to these feelings and to Mrs. Santo's own anger and resentment, the therapist helped them to understand an important distinction between two subsystems in a divorce. The first (*the couple*) was dead and should be buried; the second (*the parents*) still needed to find a way to cooperate in the best interests of their child. "Burying" the divorced couple's relationship in this case was facilitated by Mrs. Santo's having an opportunity to ventilate her bitterness and anger at having been abandoned by the man she loved, though most of these discussions took place in individual sessions with the therapist.

Reducing a single parent's disengagement from adult relationships enhances her ability to strengthen the generational boundary between herself and her children. This involves delegating age-appropriate responsibilities to older children, enforcing discipline, and helping the children get involved in activities of their own.

The primary structural goal for the single parent is to assume power as the chief executive in the family system. This task may be particularly difficult for a parent who is demoralized by loss or depression. Therefore some structural goals may not be practical. Setting up charts and token economies to rein in out-of-control children, for example, may require an unrealistic amount of monitoring for an overburdened single parent. When feeling overwhelmed, single parents often lose the ability to set effective limits. Some parents may permit more misbehavior than they think they should to make up for the loss their children have suffered from divorce or lack of father involvement. Chores should be delegated not abdicated—mother is still in charge—and a boy is not "the man of the house" (which implies that he has taken his father's place).

Live-in partners provide additional sources of support and conflict. Many compete with the children for the mother's attention. Some undermine the mother's authority, while others try to enforce their own rules, setting up a triangle in which the mother is forced to side either with her boyfriend or her children. Live-in partners' attempts to enforce discipline are frequently rebuffed, especially by adolescents. Their job isn't that of a parent but that of a backup for the mother as the primary authority over her children.

Children may benefit from increased social contacts to help balance the intensity of the single-parent-and-child connection. Resources to consider include teachers, coaches, Big Brothers and Big Sisters, activity group leaders, community groups (Parents Without Partners and Mother's Day Out), religious congregations, craft classes, and workplace contacts.

Families take many forms; the single-parent family is one of them. Families don't get broken or destroyed, but they do change shapes. Unfortunately, the transition from being together to being apart is a road without maps. No wonder there is so much pain and confusion.

African American Families

Therapists working with African American families should be prepared to expand the definition of family to include an *extended kinship system*. The kinship network remains one of the keys to coping with the pressures of oppression (Billingsley, 1992; Staples, 1994). There may be a number of aunts, uncles, "big mamas," boyfriends, older brothers and sisters, cousins, deacons, preachers, and others who operate in and out of the African American home (White, 1972, p. 45). However, many families who come to the attention of mental health workers have become isolated from their support network. Part of a therapist's task is to search for persons in the family or kin network who represent islands of strength and enlist their support in

helping the family. Asking "Who can you depend on when you need help?" is one way to locate such individuals.

A structural assessment should consider not only those people who are involved with the family but also those who might be called on for support. In the African American community, these potential connections include an extensive kinship network, made up of both family and friends (Billingsley, 1968; McAdoo, 2002).

These extended connections, real and potential, mean that family boundaries and lines of authority can become blurred, as the following example illustrates.

When Juanita Williams entered a residential drug treatment program, she was lucky to have her neighbor and friend, Deena, willing to take in her three children. Six months later Juanita was ready to leave rehab and return home. By that time the Williams children had grown accustomed to living with "Aunt Deena" and her two teenagers.

When the children's case worker arranged a meeting with Juanita and her children and "Aunt Deena," Deena praised Juanita for completing the rehab program and preparing to resume the responsibility for her children. "You know I love them, almost like they was my own," she said to Juanita, who nodded, "but now it's time for them to move back with their rightful mother." However, it appeared to the social worker that Deena had effectively taken over the family and Juanita had lost her position of authority. Deena did most of the talking while Juanita sat quietly, looking down. Martin (fourteen), Jesse (twelve), and Coretta (eleven) said nothing.

The social worker concluded that Deena and the Williams children were enmeshed while Juanita was disengaged, and the worker saw her job as helping Juanita and her children reconnect while Deena stepped back into a supportive but less controlling role. Toward this end, she said that Juanita was lucky to have such a good friend to act as foster mother to her children, but now it was time for her to reclaim her role as head of the family. She then set up an enactment in which she asked Juanita to talk with her children about her plans for the immediate future.

When Juanita began by telling the children how much she had missed them, Deena spoke up to say that the children had missed her, too. Deena's intentions were good, but her interruption was a sign of her overly central role. The therapist complimented Deena for being helpful but said that it was time to show her support by letting Juanita speak for herself. Juanita resumed talking to her children, saying, "I know that I can't promise anything, but every day I will try my hardest to be the right kind of mother to you and not to give in to my disease. And," she went on with tears in her eyes, "I know that with God's help we can be the family that we never were."

Martin looked down, Jesse and Coretta had tears in their eyes. Then Martin turned to the therapist and said, "Can I speak?" "Of course, Martin, you can say whatever you want to your mother."

"I love you, Mommy," he said, "and I hope to God that you don't go back to the drugs. But I will never—*never*—live in a house where I have to watch my mother going into the streets again. When I don't know whether we're going to have any supper that night because you're out getting high. You will never put me through that again."

"Martin—," once again Deena started to interrupt, and once again the social worker blocked her.

Martin went on talking for fifteen minutes about the pain and rage of growing up with a mother who was a drug addict. He held nothing back. Juanita was crying hard. When Martin finished, there was a long, heavy silence.

Then Juanita spoke up. "I know what I put you through, Martin. What I put all my children through. And I know that I can never, ever make up for that. But, as God is my witness, I will do everything in my power never, ever again to let

you down or make you ashamed of me. All I want is another chance."

It was a gut-wrenching exchange. Martin had spoken straight from the heart, and he and his mother had gotten through to each other—with no interference from well-meaning friends, or helpful professionals, anxious to put a good face on things.

The prominence of *religion and spirituality* in African American family life (Hines & Boyd-Franklin, 1982) provides both a real and potential resource. Many African American families have gained strength from church membership and connection to their church community (Billingsley, 1994; Walsh, 1999). Therapists who work with black families can profit from developing a relationship with ministers in the community, who can often help mobilize support for an isolated single mother, an adolescent who is abusing drugs, or a mentally ill adult who is cut off from support following the death of a caregiver (Boyd-Franklin, 2003).

One reason *father-absent households* are so common among African Americans is that there are far fewer men than women in the black community. Among the reasons for the absence of black men are substance abuse, death related to hazardous jobs and delays in seeking health care, military service, homicide, and of course the astonishingly high percentage of black men in prison (U.S. Bureau of the Census, 2003). Not only are there fewer black men, but their participation in family life is often undermined by limited job opportunities and a tendency on the part of mental health professionals to overlook men in the extended family system, including a father's kinship network and a mother's male friends, who may be involved in the children's lives.

Too many therapists resign themselves to the nonparticipation of fathers in family therapy. A father who is regarded as unavailable may agree to attend if contacted directly by the therapist.

Even if the father has trouble getting away from work, he may agree to come to one or two sessions, if he's convinced that he's really needed. Therapists can also use phone calls and letters to keep fathers involved in their family's treatment. Respecting a father's family role decreases the likelihood of his sabotaging treatment (Hines & Boyd-Franklin, 1996), and even limited participation may lead to a structural shift in the family.

Partly as a consequence of absent fathers, many families in the African American community are *three-generational systems*, made up of a mother, her children, and a grandmother. Sometimes grandmothers are asked to take over the job of raising a second set of children. At other times single mothers or fathers and their children may move back in with the grandparents. In some cases teenage mothers will turn their children over to their mothers but later want to take back the responsibility of raising their own children. While none of these family structures is inherently dysfunctional, they all create complications.

Grandmothers who take over may have trouble letting go. They see their young adult children behaving irresponsibly, and they treat them accordingly. Unfortunately, this perpetuates the classic control-and-rebel cycle that so many young people get caught up in with their parents. Therapists can't always remain neutral in this kind of impasse. It may be useful to support the young mother or father in the role of parent, while respecting the grandmother's contribution and availability for advice and support (Minuchin, Nichols, & Lee, 2006).

Even the healthiest families have trouble functioning effectively under the crushing weight of financial hardship. When survival issues—like food, housing, and utilities—are involved, these take precedence over family conflicts. Therapists can act as resources to encourage family members to work with available community and social agents in dealing with housing, job training, employment, and child care (Rojano, 2004).

The combination of racism and poverty has produced a "fierce anger" in many African Americans (Cose, 1993). Service providers must realize that some of this anger may be directed against them. It's important not to get defensive. Nancy Boyd-Franklin (1989) recommends that mental health providers expect a certain amount of distrust and join with their black clients to build trust at the outset of treatment. Communicating respect is key to successfully engaging families.

In working with inner-city African American families, therapists must take into account that they may be enmeshed with a variety of agencies such as schools, hospitals, police courts, juvenile justice systems, welfare, child protective services, and mental health services (Henggeler & Borduin, 1990). Empowering families in this context can be accomplished by (1) setting up meetings with various organizations involved with the family, (2) writing letters in support of the family, and (3) setting up conferences with the supervisors of resistant workers (Boyd-Franklin, 2003). The point is to empower families by encouraging them to take charge of these issues themselves. Therapists can help but shouldn't take over.

Gay and Lesbian Families

Gay and lesbian partners struggle with the same sorrows of conflict and longing as any intimate partners. Every couple must find a way to balance time together with independent interests, choose whether and when to have children, and decide whose family to spend the holidays with. But same-sex couples also face unique challenges, including homophobia in society and their families; resolving relational ambiguities in the areas of commitment, boundaries, and gender-linked behavior; differences about being "out" professionally or socially; and developing networks of social support (Green & Mitchell, 2002). In order to work effectively with gay and lesbian clients, it's important neither to ignore nor exaggerate the unique nature of same-sex pairings.

While it may be reassuring for heterosexual therapists to dissociate themselves from the overt homophobia in our culture, it's a little more difficult to deal with internalized homophobia—in themselves and in their clients. Therapists who aren't comfortable with love and sex between two men or two women may have trouble talking frankly with gay couples or may behave with patronizing deference. A therapist who is overly anxious to convey his or her progressive attitude may find it difficult to push for change or to ask the kinds of tough questions that may be necessary with couples who aren't getting along.

Case Study

Stephen and David sought therapy during a crisis induced by Stephen's wanting to open up their relationship to other partners and David refusing to even discuss this possibility. Their therapist, who was anxious to distance himself from the stereotype that gay men are promiscuous, got caught up in trying to solve the problem of Stephen's inability to commit, rather than exploring the broader problem of the couple's difficulty communicating and making decisions. Had the couple been a man and a wife disagreeing over whether to buy a house or rent an apartment, it's unlikely that the therapist would have so quickly taken sides and reduced therapy to an exercise in problem solving.

Homophobia may also manifest itself in subtle and not so subtle ways in lesbian and gay people themselves (Brown, 1994; Meyer & Dean, 1998). When you grow up in a society in which homosexuality is considered deviant, it's impossible not to absorb at least some of this attitude.

In working with same-sex couples, it's important to probe for subtle manifestations of negative images of homosexuality and same-sex relationships. One stereotype that can be particularly destructive is the cultural expectation that same-sex pairings are inherently unstable. Many people, gay as well as straight, believe that enduring love relationships between same-sex partners (especially gay men) are impossible to achieve.

As with many biases, it's probably more useful for therapists to examine their own assumptions than to imagine themselves to be without bias. Identifying your assumptions makes it easier to hold them in check; pretending that you don't have assumptions allows them to act on you unsuspectingly.

Working with gay and lesbian couples requires sensitivity to the internalization of traditional gender norms. Heterosexual partners have typically been socialized for complementary roles. Women and men may no longer expect to be "Leave-It-to-Beaver" parents, but like it or not, women are still taught to be more caring and to have a less distanced sense of self (Jordan, Kaplan, Miller, Stiver, & Surrey, 1991), while men are brought up to be in control, to be territorial, to tolerate distance, and to thrive on competition. So what happens when same-sex partners get together? Who picks up the towels from the bathroom floor? Who initiates sex?

Many gay and lesbian couples struggle as much as heterosexual couples over whether and when to have children. But unlike their heterosexual counterparts, gays and lesbians have to resolve the issue of who (if either) will be the biological parent.

Case Study

Rachel and Jan had been together for ten years and were considering having a child. Both agreed that they would like to have a biological child. However, both women very much wanted to be the sperm recipient.

Seeing that Rachel and Jan were at an impasse, the therapist suggested that they consider adopting. Worn out and frustrated by their inability to decide which of them would give up the wish to carry their baby, the women jumped at this suggestion. However, their relief turned to anger when they discovered that the state they lived in (which starts with the letter V) did not allow gay and lesbian couples to adopt children. Their experience made them lose confidence in their therapist and they dropped out of treatment.

One of the issues in therapy with same-sex couples is likely to be the need to negotiate clear agreements about commitments and boundaries and roles. Among the questions a therapist might usefully ask are these:

"What are the rules in your relationship about monogamy?"
"What are your agreements about finances, pooling of resources, and joint ownership of property?"
"Who does what tasks in the household, and how is this decided?"

Some of the usual expectations that heterosexuals bring to marriage don't necessarily apply to same-sex couples unless they are discussed and agreed to (Green & Mitchell, 2002). Among these expectations are monogamy, pooled finances, caring for each other through serious illness, moving together for each other's career advancement, caring for each other's families in old age, and mutual inheritance, to name just a few. Because there are no familiar models for being a same-sex couple, partners may have discrepancies in their visions about how these issues will be handled. We suggest that therapists be aware of these issues and prepared to help clients discuss them but not introduce topics that clients don't yet seem ready to deal with.

Some therapists might be surprised to learn that many gay men maintain stable relationships that allow outside sexual activity (Bringle, 1995; Bryant & Demian, 1994). In studying this phenomenon, Michael LaSala (2004a) found no differences on the Dyadic Adjustment Scale between strictly monogamous and openly nonmonogamous gay male couples. However, couples who'd agreed to be monogamous but in which one or both partners engaged in extrarela-

tional sex were less well adjusted. Thus, for some gay men, sexual monogamy may not be a necessary component of a satisfactory committed relationship. LaSala (2004b) found that men in successful open relationships establish guidelines that safeguard their health and affirmed couple primacy. Obviously, therapists need to respect their clients' preferences and help them decide what type of relationship works best for them. But only by being aware of the various options available to male couples can a therapist be expected to help them discover what suits their specific needs.

Heterosexual therapists may underestimate the complexities involved in coming out to family and friends (LaSala, 1997). Here it may be well to remember that therapy isn't about pushing people to go where they're afraid to go but helping them recognize and resolve the fears that hold them back.

Linda Stone Fish and Rebecca Harvey (2005) have written about the tightrope therapists must walk when they suspect that a young client is struggling with his or her sexual orientation. It's important not to confront same-sex attractions before a young person is ready to acknowledge them. But therapists may not want to miss the opportunity to help the young person explore these concerns with a nonjudgmental counselor. Stone Fish and Harvey suggest asking adolescents who may be questioning their sexual orientations but ambivalent about discussing it things like:

"What would you recommend a teenager do when she has a secret about herself and she wants people to get to know her but is afraid if she tells the secret they won't like her?"
"What do you do when you know that you are different, you want to talk to someone about it, and yet you also think that if you talk about it, you will be really hurt—that somebody won't like you or accept you or something even worse?"
"Is it okay if a boy is attracted to other boys?"

"What do you think your parents would do
if they found out someone was a lesbian?"

Another difficulty that heterosexual therapists
may overlook in same-sex relationships is the
prevalence of jealousy on the part of one of the
partners (Green & Mitchell, 2002). This jealousy is based on the belief that others are a
threat because of lack of respect for the couple's
commitment to each other. After all, how can
the relationship be real if the partners aren't
married?

Jim enjoyed the club scene as a
way to socialize with his friends in
the gay community. His partner,
Kyle, preferred to avoid bars and clubs. According to Kyle, his objections weren't so much to
Jim's having a good time, but that he believed
other men in the clubs had little respect for the
fact that Jim was part of a couple. "They don't
care about us if they think they can get good sex
out of hitting on you." Kyle was also concerned
about the prevalence of designer drugs—like
ecstasy, cocaine, crystal meth, and special K—
that were part of the club atmosphere. Jim
insisted that he wasn't interested in other men
and didn't do drugs. He just wanted to hang out
with his friends.

Although some therapists might see Jim's
insistence on going to bars as a failure to accept
that he was no longer single, the therapist in this
case was aware that in fact not going to bars
and clubs can result in a significant disconnect
from much of the gay community. And so, rather
than accept the Hobson's choice the couple presented—either Jim gave in and stayed home or
Kyle gave in and Jim continued to go clubbing—
the therapist wondered out loud if there were
alternative ways for the couple to socialize within
the gay community.

Maybe the best advice for therapists working
with gay and lesbian couples is to have them ask

themselves "What messages am I communicating to this couple about the value of same-sex
relationships?" It isn't just negative messages
that therapists should be alert to but also the
danger of glorifying same-sex relationships.
Denigration and idealization have an equal
potential for harm.

SEX AND THE INTERNET

Few things have transformed the landscape of
the twenty-first century like electronic technology—e-mail, cell phones, pagers, instant messaging, electronic games, and, of course, the
Internet. The Internet facilitates research and
communication: It informs, it helps people connect, and it helps people disconnect—to escape
from active participation in relationships into a
private reverie of solitary pursuits.

Contemporary technologies bring many advantages, but it is important for anyone practicing marriage and family therapy to be aware of a
least one area where technology often creates
problems in family relationships. That area is
cybersex.

A recent survey found that the majority of
marriage and family therapists are seeing clients
presenting with cybersex problems, and the
number of such cases are increasing (Goldberg,
Peterson, Rosen, & Sara, 2008). Therapists who
see families with adolescents may be called on to
deal with issues related to adolescent exposure to
pornography and the dangers of inappropriate
sexual contact. And therapists who work with
couples will almost certainly encounter cases
with problems associated with compulsive consumption of pornography as well as more active
forms of infidelity.

Complicating the clinician's task is the fact
that although problems with cybersex are widespread, they are still shameful and therefore may
not easily be talked about. Consequently, it's
important to know something about these problems in order to know what to look for and what
kinds of questions to ask.

Although there are many areas of the Internet, the World Wide Web is usually the first place teens risk experimenting with online sexual behavior, or becoming the victims of sexual harassment or offense. Social networking sites (MySpace, Facebook, Bebo), video and photo-sharing technologies (MySpace, Google, Video, Photobucket), and online gaming (Gunz, Runescape, World of Warcraft) all present opportunities for inappropriate sexual activities. These activities include posting of sexually provocative photos and videos, and sexual communications via chat rooms, e-mail, or other postings (Gillispie & Gackenbach, 2007).

In addition to understanding the various online venues where teenagers may engage in problematic sexual behavior, it's also important to have a basic grasp of the lingo used online. Two resources that can help educate parents and therapists about online slang are Netlingo (www.netlingo.com) and Noslang (www.noslang.com). Here are some examples:

> Cybering—Engaging in sexual activity with someone online
> POS—Parent over shoulder
> IWSN—I want sex now
> Q2C—Quick to cum
> Lurking—Nonparticipation in a chat room; chat observer
> RUH—Are you horny?
> LMIRL—Let's meet in real life
> TDTM—Talk dirty to me
> P911—Parent alert
> { }—Hugs

When discussing technology with families, it's important to inquire about all forms of Internet access, because cell phones, Blackberries, gaming systems, and iPods all provide access to the Internet and its temptations. It can be hard for parents to supervise their children's computer use because in most families, it is the youngest members who are the most computer savvy. Moreover, the invention of removable storage media (jump drives, USB drives, portable hard drives) allows users to store information from the Internet and other sources onto small devices that can easily be hidden.

There are a variety of software programs designed to screen out sexual content and conversations on a child's computer. But while these programs may be effective with younger children, such programs are easily circumvented by older teens. Although parents may appreciate recommendations about software to prevent problems, these programs should not give a false sense of security about adolescents' Internet use.

Even with the use of blocking software, most teens will be exposed to pornographic pictures, videos, stories, or sexual conversations on the Internet. In fact, 70% of all children from 10 to 17 admit that they have been exposed to some form of pornography on the Internet. The following are some indicators that online behavior problems may be occurring (Delmonico & Griffin, 2008).

- Sacrificing previously enjoyed activities in order to spend more time on the computer.
- Maintaining secrecy about the frequency or types of online activities.
- Signs of depression or anxiety, especially noticeable after Internet use or during times when Internet access is unavailable.
- Taking increased risks with online activity—using computers for pornography at school, meeting people from the Internet without precautions.
- Jeopardizing important activities because of Internet use—missing school or coming late, losing relationships, and so on.

The dangers to which the Internet exposes children include not only pornography but also cyberbullying and cyberharassment and, more ominously, inappropriate sexual contact with people in the real world.

The friend a teenager meets online in a chat room may turn out to be adult predator. As many as 19 percent of American teenagers have been the target of unwanted sexual solicitation.

Girls, older teens, troubled youth, frequent Internet users, chat room participants, and those who communicate online with strangers are at greatest risk. (Mitchell, Finkelhor, & Wolak, 2001). Therapists should be prepared to educate young people about these dangers, including urging them to report such encounters to their parents or other responsible adults.

Here are some suggestions for protecting children from cybersex predators (Weiss & Schneider, 2006).

- Limit computer privacy by placing any computer with Internet access somewhere where it can be easily monitored.
- Monitor the child's Internet use by checking the computer's bookmarks, history of websites accessed, and caches. Consider computer software such as Disk Tracy (www.disktracy.com) that provides a list of every online site accessed by the computer on which it is installed.
- Install blocking software such as Cyber-Patrol (www.cyberpatrol.com) which will deny access to sexually inappropriate sites, including instant messaging.
- Consider using a "family oriented" Internet service provider that blocks sexually inappropriate material from ever reaching your computer.
- Teach children never to reveal to anyone their real name, address, or phone number, or to provide any information (such as the name of their school) that will make it easy to locate them.
- Let children know that it is never acceptable to meet in person someone whom they have met online without parental supervision.
- Talk with children about their Internet activities. Encourage them to discuss any online experiences that make them feel guilty or uncomfortable.
- If you believe a child is being sexually exploited or that someone is attempting

to exploit him or her, consider this a sex crime and report it to the FBI.

Finally, although technology may facilitate problematic sexual behavior, it would be a mistake to think that solving such problems is simply a matter of technology. Although parents may want to install protective software on their children's computers, it's probably more important for therapists to encourage dialogue between parents and teenagers regarding Internet use and sexuality. Moreover, therapists may need to help parents understand that when it comes to protecting teenagers from unhealthy sexual experiences, adult supervision and control isn't the only answer. Once children reach a certain age, parental control—especially if it's perceived as unfair—may produce as much rebellion as compliance. If the issue is curfews or chores, the rebellion may be obvious and take the form of arguments. But when the issue is something as shame-sensitive as sexuality, rebellion may take the form of "silent arguing" (Nichols, 2009)—that is, apparent compliance but with surreptitious acting out. Thus, it's wise to involve teenagers in discussions about limiting computer use, because they are far more likely to accept decisions they have had a chance to contribute to.

When it comes to adults, it can be argued that pornography and other forms of sexual experience are harmless private activities and that they can even enhance the passion in a couple's relationship. But pornography, online relationships, and sexual behavior can become compulsions and are often characterized by secrecy that's detrimental to the trust and intimacy of relationships (Cooper, 2002). As a result, therapists have been seeing more and more cases involving compulsive viewing of pornography and Internet infidelity (Gonyea, 2004). Among the sexually oriented activities that can become problematic are:

- Viewing pornography and masturbating.
- Reading and writing sexually oriented stories and letters.
- Using e-mail to set up meetings.
- Placing ads to meet sexual partners.
- Visiting sexually oriented chat rooms.
- Interactive affairs (including sharing nudity and sexual behavior via webcams).

With the advent of digital video streaming and the relatively modest cost of webcams, images can be captured and sent, and messages returned, all in real time. As the technology of the Internet has advanced, the experience of cybersex has gone beyond photos and recorded videos to live-action images and on-demand sexual responses, or virtual sex. These developments make the experience more compelling and the sense of betrayal in the partner more profound. Given the growing number of cases presenting with cybersex-related issues, therapists should be sufficiently well versed in the ways of technology to know what questions to ask and how to pose them.

The following questions (adapted from Weiss & Schneider, 2006) are designed to explore the nature and extent of a client's online sexual activities.

1. Do you find yourself spending increasing amounts of time online looking at porn or engaged in sexual or romantic intrigue?
2. Have you been involved in romantic or sexual affairs online?
3. Does pornography or online sexual activity violate your marital commitments?
4. Have you been unable to cut back on the frequency of your online sexual activity despite thinking that you should?
5. Have you been unable to stay away from sexual material, sites, or interactions that have made you feel guilty or ashamed of yourself?
6. Does your pornography use interfere with home life, work, or school (including making you tired or late for obligations)?
7. Does pornography use intrude on relationships that are important to you?
8. Do you collect pornography?
9. Do you engage in fantasy acts online or view porn depicting illegal or violent sexual acts, such as rape, bestiality, or child porn?
10. Has the time you spend with friends, family, and loved ones decreased because of your porn use or fantasy involvement?
11. Do you lie or keep secrets about the amount of time you spend viewing porn, the type of porn you choose, or the types of activities you engage in online?
12. Do you have sex—either in fantasy online or in person—with someone other than your spouse or partner?
13. Are you hearing complaints from family or friends about the amount of time you spend online using porn or the type of porn you use?
14. Do you get irritable or angry when asked to give up or reduce porn involvement?
15. Has the primary focus of your sexual or romantic life become increasingly related to images found in magazines, videos, or Internet activity?

Three or more positive answers are grounds for concern.

As with the old-fashioned kind of infidelity, it isn't fair to say that Internet infidelity is caused by problems in relationships. However, from the circular perspective of systems theory, it doesn't matter whether problems in a relationship caused problems with sex on the Internet or the other way around. They feed each other. Instead of worrying about which came first, a clinician can address both fronts simultaneously: encouraging an end to compulsive sexual activity and looking at problems in the relationship that may fuel this activity. For example, anger at one's partner—especially unexpressed or at least unresolved anger—lead some people to feel that they are entitled to seek soothing and excitement outside the relationship.

Like drug and alcohol addiction, sexual obsession affects both men and women. Approximately 25% of people in sex addiction recovery programs are women (Cooper, 2002). While men are more likely to download pornography, women typically prefer chat rooms and personal ads where there is more of a chance to actually get to know the objects of their interest.

Without outside intervention, most compulsive activities tend to escalate over time. This is especially true with highly reinforcing activities like drug taking and sexual behavior. Only when the consequences are severe enough do most people caught up in compulsive self-gratification seek help. When it comes to compulsive sexual behavior, these consequences may include relationship problems, job loss, public shaming, sexually transmitted diseases, arrest, and even imprisonment.

While there are obviously many different approaches to therapy and not all therapists see compulsive sexual behavior as a *sex addiction* or adhere to a twelve-step treatment model, it's important to remember that therapists should not attempt to treat problems outside the range of their expertise. If a therapist doesn't understand pornography abuse and compulsive sexual behavior or have training and experience in treating these problems, he or she should probably refer the case to someone who does. The Society for the Advancement of Sexual Health maintains a website (www.sash.net) that includes a list of professionals knowledgeable about compulsive sexual behavior, organized by country and state.

The problems in couples' relationships that are related—as cause and effect—to outside sexual activity involve communication, boundaries, and commitment. In addressing problems in a couple's communication, a therapist should encourage the partners to talk about their needs and how to meet them. The obvious boundary problem with extramarital affairs that originate with Internet pornography is an inadequate boundary that fails to protect the relationship from one or both partners straying. However, like all boundaries, this one is reciprocal. The complement of a diffuse boundary around a relationship is a rigid boundary (and disengagement) between the partners. And the thing to remember about disengagement is that it exists for a reason. If a couple is disengaged, one or both partners are probably harboring a great deal of unresolved resentment.

If one of the partners goes outside of a relationship to find sexual excitement and intimacy —or just plain attention—there is obviously a problem with commitment. The question for a therapist to explore is why.

HOME-BASED SERVICES

Like traditional family therapy, home-based services target the family as the primary recipient of mental health care (Friesen & Koroloff, 1990). Unlike conventional models, however, the home-based approach focuses more on enhancing family resources than on repairing family dysfunction (Henggeler & Borduin, 1990). While home-based services recognize and address problems in the family system, the primary emphasis is on building relationships between the family and various community resources.

Home-based therapists approach families with a collaborative mind-set and positive expectations. This *strength-based approach*, which assumes that families contain the resources to deal with their own problems, can also be applied to the expectation that competence is inherent in other agencies as well, such as other organizations involved with the family. Consequently, agencies and other influences are viewed not as adversaries but as potential partners in the treatment process.

Home-based services generally include four elements: family support services, therapeutic intervention, case management, and crisis intervention (Lindblad-Goldberg, Dore, & Stern, 1998). *Family support services* include respite care as well as concrete assistance with food, clothing, and shelter. *Therapeutic intervention* may include individual, family, or couples treatment.

The overriding therapeutic goal is strengthening and stabilizing the family unit. Families are empowered by helping them utilize their own strengths and resources for solving problems rather that relying on out-of-home placement of the children. *Case management* involves developing links to community resources, including such things as medical care, welfare, education, job training, and legal services. *Crisis intervention* means making available twenty-four–hour emergency services, either with the home-based agency or by contracting with an outside mental health emergency service.

Visiting a family at home gives a therapist the opportunity to show interest in the things that define their identity—children, pets, religious artifacts, mementos, awards, and so on. Looking through photo albums can be a valuable method in joining with a family and learning about their history and their hopes and dreams. Once a positive relationship has been established—but not before—the therapist can ask the family to reduce such distractions as smoking, loud television playing, or barking dogs. (Barking cats are less often a problem.)

Roles and boundaries that are implicit in an office setting may need to be spelled out. Clarifying roles while in the home begins with defining what the process of treatment entails, the ground rules for sessions, and what the therapist's and family members' roles will be. The following comments illustrate the process of clarifying roles (adapted from Lindblad-Goldberg, Dore, & Stern, 1998).

Case Study

"Before we start, I want to say that I have no intention of coming here and telling you how to run your lives. My job is to help you figure out how you want to deal with your children. I can't solve your problems. Only you can do that.

"In our meetings, it's important for you to say whatever you think and feel. We need to be honest. Tell me what you expect of me, and I'll tell you what I expect of you. I won't act like I have all the answers, because I don't.

"Will Grandmother be coming tonight? If not, that's okay, but I would like her to attend future sessions, because I'm sure she has valuable ideas to contribute.

"Tonight, I'd like to get to know each of you a little bit. After that, I'd like to hear what concerns each of you have about your family life and what you'd like to change."

While family therapists tend to speak glibly about their "eco-systemic" orientation, home-based workers really must coordinate their efforts with other service systems. To do so, it is imperative to understand the concerns of other agencies involved with the family and to develop collaborative relationships with them. Rather than being critical of school personnel or juvenile justice workers who don't seem to support the family and the child, home-based workers must learn to appreciate that these other agencies are equally concerned about the needs of their clients, even though their approaches may differ. A family served by multiple agencies that don't see eye to eye is no different from a child caught in a triangle between parents who can't function together as a team.

While in-home therapy offers a unique opportunity to influence families directly in their natural environment, seeing people in their living rooms also increases the pressures of *induction* into a family's problematic patterns. Working with a cotherapist may help to minimize the tendency to be drawn unwittingly into the family's unproductive way of seeing things. Home-based therapists who don't work with cotherapists must make special efforts to maintain professional boundaries and to avoid being inducted into playing missing roles in the family. For example, if a child needs comforting, it's far better to support the parents in providing it than to take over that function.

The first priority in home-based work should be to demonstrate that the therapist is consistent and genuine. Having a connection with someone who can be counted on may be more important to families with a history of unmet dependency needs than having a worker who is powerful, smart, or controlling.

One of the most damaging things that can happen in any form of psychotherapy is for clients to recreate with their therapists the same unsatisfying kinds of relationships they have with most people. Perhaps the most important thing a therapist can do is to avoid being drawn into the usual pattern. The most dangerous pattern for home-based workers to repeat is moving in too close and then pushing clients to go where they are afraid to go. Rather than start pushing for change right away, it's often more effective to begin by recognizing the obstacles to change.

Beleaguered families fear abandonment; insecure therapists fear not being helpful. The worker who feels a pull to do everything for a client may subsequently feel overwhelmed by the family's needs and back away by setting rigid limits and withholding support. The "rescuer" then becomes another "abandoner." This process reactivates the clients' anxiety and inevitably pushes them away. The lessons for the family are clear: Nothing will ever change—and don't trust anyone.

MEDICAL FAMILY THERAPY AND PSYCHOEDUCATION

Over the past fifteen years a new conception of family therapy has emerged. Rather than solve problems, the goal of this approach is to help families cope with disabilities. This represents a shift from the idea that families cause problems to the idea that problems, like natural disasters, sometimes befall families. **Psychoeducational family therapy** emerged from working with schizophrenic patients and their families, whereas **medical family therapy** developed from helping families struggle with chronic illnesses such as cancer, diabetes, and heart disease.

Psychoeducation and Schizophrenia

The search for a cure for schizophrenia launched the field of family therapy in the 1950s. Ironically, while we now know that schizophrenia is a biologically based illness, family therapy, or at least the psychoeducational model, is once again considered part of the most effective treatment for this baffling disorder.

The psychoeducational model was born of dissatisfaction with both traditional family therapy and psychiatric approaches to schizophrenia. As Carol Anderson, Douglas Reiss, and Gerald Hogarty (1986) lamented,

> We have blamed each other, the patients themselves, their parents and grandparents, public authorities, and society for the cause and for the too often terrible course of these disorders. When hope and money become exhausted, we frequently tear schizophrenic patients from their families, consigning them to the existential terror of human warehouses, single room occupancy hotels, and more recently to the streets and alleys of American cities. (p. vii)

In their attempts to get at the function of the schizophrenic's symptoms, family therapists urged family members to express bottled-up feelings and thus created sessions of highly charged emotion, which often did little more than stir up tension. After noticing the frequent decline in functioning of patients and increased anxiety in their families after such sessions, Anderson and her colleagues (1986) "began to wonder if most 'real' family therapy was in fact antitherapeutic" (p. 2).

Meanwhile, studies began to show that the patients who fared best after hospitalization were those who returned to the least stressful households. A British group, including George Brown, John Wing, Julian Leff, and Christine Vaughn, focused on what they called *expressed emotion (EE)* in the families of schizophrenics—criticism, hostility, and emotional overinvolvement—and found that patients returning to high

EE households had higher rates of relapse (Brown, Birley, & Wing, 1972; Vaughn & Leff, 1976; Vaughn. Snyder, Jones, Freeman, & Falloon, 1984).

Although negativity is one of the most ubiquitous findings in research on troubled family relationships, it appears that young people who are prone to psychotic disorders may be unusually sensitive to arousal dyscontrol and cognitive disruption in the face of critical comments and emotional negativity (Hooley, Gruber, Scott, Hiller, & Yurgelun-Todd, 2005; McFarlane & Cook, 2007). In both schizophrenic and mood disorders, acute episodes have been found to be more frequently in families in which a relative is highly critical of the family member with the disorder. The other family interactional factor consistently associated with schizophrenic and bipolar disorders is communicative deviance (CD), a measure of distracted or vague conversational style (Wynne, 1981).

Research on expressed emotion suggests that schizophrenia is a thought disorder that renders individuals particularly sensitive to criticism and hostility. Intense emotional input makes it difficult for patients to cope with the welter of chaotic thoughts that plague them. When recovering patients return to stressful family settings, where EE is high, intrusive overconcern and critical comments lead to increased emotional arousal, and it is this affective overload that triggers relapse.

Expressed emotion is now the most well-documented factor in the relapse of schizophrenia (Milkowitz, 1995):

> The family, then, is seen as a risk or protective factor that may augment or diminish the likelihood that underlying genetic and/or biological vulnerabilities in a family member will be expressed as symptoms of mental disorder. (p. 194)

The benefits of reducing EE in helping families cope with schizophrenia has been repeatedly demonstrated (Atkinson & Coia, 1995). Lowering EE has also been shown to contribute to reduced relapse rates for major depression and bipolar disorder (Muesser & Glynn, 1995).

With this in mind, three different groups in the late 1970s began experimenting with ways to reduce stress in the most common environments for schizophrenic patients: their parents' homes. Michael Goldstein led a group at UCLA (Goldstein. Rodnick, Evans, May, & Steinberg, 1978) who designed a brief, structured model focused on anticipating the stresses a family was likely to face and reducing conflict around the patient. Following the Goldstein study, groups headed by Ian Falloon at the University of Southern California (whose model is primarily behavioral) and Carol Anderson at the Western Psychiatric Institute in Pittsburgh experimented with psychoeducational models.

Psychoeducators seek to establish a collaborative partnership in which family members feel supported and empowered to deal with the patient. To achieve this kind of partnership, Anderson and her colleagues (1986) find that they must reeducate professionals to give up ideas that the family is somehow responsible for schizophrenia, reinforce family strengths, and share information with the family about this disease. It is this information sharing that constitutes the educational element of psycho*education*. Information about the nature and course of schizophrenia helps family members develop a sense of mastery—a way to understand and anticipate the often chaotic and apparently uncontrollable process.

One of psychoeducation's key interventions is to lower expectations, to reduce pressure on the patient to perform normally. For example, the goals for the first year following an acute episode are primarily the avoidance of a relapse and the gradual taking on of some responsibilities in the home. Family members are to view the patient as someone who's had a serious illness and needs to recuperate. Patients may need a great deal of sleep, solitude, and limited activity for some time following an episode; they may also seem restless and have trouble concentrating. By predicting these developments, psychoeducators try to prevent conflict between the patient and the family.

Anderson's psychoeducational approach looks very much like structural family therapy, except that the family's structural flaws are construed as the *result* of rather than *cause* of the presenting problem. Much of the therapy follows familiar themes: reinforcing generational boundaries, opening up the family to the outside world and developing support networks, urging parents to reinvest in their marriage, and getting family members to not speak or do for the patient.

Anderson and her colleagues begin with a day-long survival skills workshop in which they teach family members about the prevalence and course of schizophrenia, its biological etiology, current modes of pharmacologic and psychosocial treatment, common medications, and prognosis. The patient's needs and the family needs are discussed and family coping skills are introduced. Research findings on expressed emotion are presented and guidelines are offered for keeping EE in check. Families are encouraged not to pressure recovering patients or to urge them to hurry back to normal functioning. Families are also advised to respect boundaries and to allow the recovering family member to withdraw whenever necessary.

The goal for the patient is for symptoms to be reduced rather than cured. Families are encouraged to provide a quiet, stable milieu in which the recovering patient doesn't feel criticized or blamed and told not to expect too much of him or her during recuperation. The goal for the family is to learn coping techniques for the difficult and long-term task of living with a schizophrenic person and preventing or delaying his or her relapse and rehospitalization.

Table 11.1 presents a set of typical psychoeducational guidelines for managing rehabilitation following a schizophrenic episode.

Is the psychoeducational model effective? Yes. For example, consider results of the study by Anderson and colleagues (1986):

Among treatment takers (n = 90), 19% of those receiving family therapy alone experienced a psychotic relapse in the year following hospital discharge. Of those receiving the individual behavioral therapy, 20% relapsed, but *no* patient

Table 11.1   **Psychoeducational Guidelines for Families and Friends of Schizophrenics**

Here is a list of things everyone can do to make things run more smoothly.

1. *Go slow.* Recovery takes time. Rest is important. Things will get better in their own time.
2. *Keep it cool.* Enthusiasm is normal. Tone it down. Disagreement is normal. Tone it down, too.
3. *Give 'em space.* Time out is important for everyone. It's okay to offer. It's okay to refuse.
4. *Set limits.* Everyone needs to know what the rules are. A few good rules keep things calmer.
5. *Ignore what you can't change.* Let some things slide. Don't ignore violence or use of street drugs.
6. *Keep it simple.* Say what you have to say clearly, calmly, and positively.
7. *Follow doctor's orders.* Take medications as they are prescribed. Take only medications that are prescribed.
8. *Carry on business as usual.* Reestablish family routines as quickly as possible. Stay in touch with family and friends.
9. *No street drugs or alcohol.* They make symptoms worse.
10. *Pick up on early signs.* Note changes. Consult with your family physician.
11. *Solve problems step by step.* Make changes gradually. Work on one thing at a time.
12. *Lower expectations, temporarily.* Use a personal yardstick. Compare this month with last month rather than with last year or next year.

Source: McFarlane, 1991, p. 375.

in the treatment cell that received both family therapy and social skills training experienced a relapse. These relapse rates constitute significant effects for both treatments when contrasted to a 41% relapse rate for those receiving only chemotherapy and support. (p. 24)

Other studies have shown equally impressive results (Falloon et al., 1982; Leff, Kuipers, Berkowitz, Eberlein-Vries, & Sturgeion, 1982). There seems to be little question that psychoeducation can delay relapse and readmission to a hospital better than other approaches to schizophrenia.

Medical Family Therapy

If one considers schizophrenia a chronic disease, then psychoeducational family therapy can be seen as a specialized form of medical family therapy. Medical family therapists work with families struggling with illness or disability in much the same way as described previously for families of schizophrenics.

Chronic illness has a devastating impact. It can take over a family's life, ravaging health, hope, and peace of mind. As Peter Steinglass says, it can be like a robber "who has appeared on the doorstep, barged inside the home and demanded everything the family has" (quoted in McDaniel et al., 1992, p. 21).

The demands of the illness interact with the qualities of the family, such as the family's life-cycle stage and the role the stricken family member plays; the family's leadership resources and degree of isolation; and their beliefs about illness and who should help, derived from their ethnicity and history with illness. With an awareness of these factors, therapists can help families prepare to deal with an illness or, if the illness has been with them for years, gain perspective on their resulting polarizations and enmeshments.

In medical family therapy, the system isn't just the sick person's family; it's the family and the physicians and nurses involved in the sick person's care. The goal, therefore, is to foster communication and support not only within the family but also between the family and medical personnel. Illness leaves people feeling helpless and confused. Medical family therapy is designed to combat such feelings by fostering communication and a sense of agency.

Medical family therapists work in collaboration with pediatricians, family practitioners, rehabilitation specialists, and nurses. They advocate that near the time of diagnosis, families should receive a routine consultation to explore their resources relative to the demands of the illness or disability. They cite the growing body of research suggesting a strong relationship between family dynamics and the clinical course of medical conditions (Campbell, 1986) and more recent research showing that family therapy has a positive effect on physical health and health care usage (Law, Crane, & Russell, 2000).

In conclusion, psychoeducational and medical family therapy share many elements with the other models in this chapter, which together represent a significant trend: a move toward a collaborative partnership with families. Therapists are now encouraged to look for a family's strengths rather than deficits and to find ways to lift families out of the guilt and blame that often accompany their problems.

RELATIONSHIP ENRICHMENT PROGRAMS

The psychoeducational method has also been applied to couples and families who wish to acquire skills for coping with everyday relationship problems. Some therapists are skeptical that self-help courses can substitute for the individual attention of a professionally trained therapist, but these programs are enormously popular, not least because participants in *marital enrichment programs* feel little of the stigma that attaches to "being in therapy."

One of the best known of these programs is the Relationship Enhancement system developed by Bernard Guerney, Jr. (1977). Facilitators teach participants to clarify their conflicts and to express what they are feeling, accept each other's feelings, negotiate and work through problems, and learn to achieve satisfaction by becoming emotional partners (Ginsberg, 2000). Both lectures and experiential training take place in each session, and homework assignments are given to practice and extend skills in participants' everyday lives.

Relationship enhancement programs provide couples with training in three sets of core skills (Ginsberg, 2000):

- The *Expressive (Owning) Skill*—gaining awareness of one's own feelings, and taking responsibility for them without projecting them onto others
- The *Empathic Responding (Receptive) Skill*—learning to listen to the other person's feelings and motives
- The *Conversive (Discussion-Negotiation/ Engagement) Skill*—learning to acknowledge the meaning of what was heard; partners may switch positions between listener and speaker

To help couples assess their preparation for marriage, David Olson and his colleagues developed the Premarital Personal and Relationship Inventory (PREPARE). This 165-item questionnaire (Olson, 1996) is designed to help couples understand and discuss their backgrounds, expectations, and areas where they might encounter difficulties. Attitudes and expectations are explored in eleven areas, including marriage expectations, communication, sexual relationship, personality differences, financial management, conflict resolution, childrearing, leisure, family and friends, marital roles, and spiritual beliefs. PREPARE has proven useful for identifying potential conflicts and promoting discussions that may head off problems in the future (Stahmann & Hiebert, 1997).

By far the most popular of the relationship enhancement programs is the *marriage encounter* weekend, first introduced in Barcelona by a Jesuit priest, Father Gabriel Calvo (Chartier, 1986). These weekend retreats, which provide support and enrichment for Catholic couples, were imported into this country in the late 1960s and have since been widely adopted by a variety of church groups (Stahmann & Hiebert, 1997). Thousands of couples have taken advantage of these weekend enrichment programs to work on their communication, problem-solving skills, sexual intimacy, and spiritual issues. Some denominations even require couples to participate in such a program before they can be married in the church.

A more carefully researched relationship enrichment program is the Prevention and Relationship Enhancement Program (PREP), developed by Floyd, Markham, Kelly, Blumberg, and Stanley (1995) at the University of Denver. This social learning approach, developed in the 1980s, teaches communication and conflict resolution skills and explores attitudes and expectations about marriage. The primary goal is to help couples learn to face and resolve conflicts, and thus avoid incorporating unhealthy defensive patterns in their relationship.

PREP sessions come in two formats: weekly meetings over several weeks and marathon sessions held in a hotel over one weekend. Both versions include lectures and experiential exercises focusing on conflict management, communication, and forgiveness, as well as religious practices, recreation, and friendship. Couples learn such things as how and when to bring up conflictual subjects, how to identify hidden issues behind chronic arguments, a structured approach to problem solving, and making time for fun. Outcome results have been encouraging. Short-term gains in relationship satisfaction include improvement in communication, sexual satisfaction, and lower problem intensity. Long-term gains (at follow up to four years) generally show sustained benefits, especially in communication (Silliman, Stanley, Coffin, Markman, & Jordan, 2002).

Table 11.2 offers some guidelines for making relationships work.

Table 11.2   Critical Skills for Effective Functioning as a Couple

A. Structure

1. Accommodation

    Learn to accept and adjust to each other's preferences and expectations, compromising on some issues, but not always giving in, so as not to build up resentment.

    She learned to accept his wish to eat supper early, while he agreed to join her for weekly religious services. But she didn't agree to put her career on a part-time basis; and he continued to take his yearly fishing trip with his brothers despite her hating to be left behind.

2. Boundary Making

    Create a protective boundary around your relationship that reduces but doesn't eliminate contact with outsiders.

    He stopped going out three nights a week with his buddies; she started asking him if it was okay before agreeing to let her parents come for the weekend.

    Demonstrating your commitment to your partner builds a secure base of attachment as well as confidence in the permanence of your relationship. Make sure your partner knows that you care, and that you are committed.

    He stopped defending himself by saying "If you don't like it, why don't you find someone else," because it only made her insecure and angry. She made a point of telling him who she had lunch with, because she knew his jealousy made him worry.

B. Communication

1. Listen to and acknowledge your partner's point of view.

    She discovered that making a sincere effort to say things like "So you like that one better because . . ." before countering with her own opinion made him feel that she respected his point of view. When it came to the most contentious issues, he discovered that asking first how she felt and then listening at length was essential. In some cases it was a good idea not even to express his side of the matter until a later time.

2. Short-circuit escalation in arguments by learning to back off before negative spirals get nasty. Call a time-out and agree to talk at a specific time later.

    "I'm getting upset; let's stop and talk about this tonight after supper, okay?"

3. Avoid invalidation and put-downs.

    "You're so irresponsible" may be obvious but is no more invalidating than *"I think you're overreacting."* Don't criticize your partner's personality or deny what he or she is feeling.

C. Problem Solving

1. Make positive requests, such as "Would you be willing . . . ?" rather than criticisms, such as "You never . . . !"

2. If you ask for something, be prepared to give something in return.

    It was easier to get him to do things with her and the children if she also made a point of suggesting times when he could do some of the things he liked to do by himself. He learned that occasionally

(continued)

Table **11.2**   (continued)

> *volunteering to do the shopping or cook dinner made her feel more like doing things for him—and that volunteering worked better than trying to make deals.*

3. Wait until you're not angry before bringing up a problem to be solved. Raise concerns directly but gently.

    She was furious that he took her father's side against her in an argument. But she decided not to say anything until she calmed down. The following night after supper she began by saying "Honey, I want to talk about something I'm feeling but I'm afraid to because it might make you mad." Emphasizing that it was her feelings and saying that she was concerned about how he might react helped put him in a receptive mood.

4. Think of the two of you as a team working against the problem.

    Instead of battling over his "coldness" and her "dependency," they started talking about how they could adjust for their "different comfort levels." As a result they planned their next vacation so that they could play golf and tennis together, and she could visit friends while he took one day off for fishing.

5. Be sure you understand your partner's concerns before trying to work on a solution.

    He was upset that she wanted to make only a minimal down payment on their new house, because it would result in large mortgage payments. To him it made more sense to put down as much as they could in order to make the monthly payments as low as possible. But instead of continuing to argue he asked her what she was worried about. Her concern turned out to be that without a cushion of savings, they might be wiped out by some unforeseen emergency. Now at least he understood how she felt.

D. Consideration

1. Do pleasing things for your partner and the relationship.

    Spontaneous gestures—like compliments, hugs, little presents, calling in the middle of the day to say "I love you"—reassure your partner that you care and help to maintain a positive feeling about the relationship.

E. Fun

1. Make the effort to spend enjoyable time together, and don't use fun activities as a time to discuss difficult issues or conflicts.

    He got in the habit of inviting her to join him for a movie, a walk in the park, or a visit to the museum and then supper out on Saturdays. She learned that bringing up problems on these trips tended to spoil the mood.

Source: Adapted from Nichols, M. P. 2009. *The Lost Art of Listening*, 2nd ed. New York: Guilford Press.

SUMMARY

Family therapists taught us to see past individual personalities to the patterns that make them a family—an organization of interconnected lives governed by strict but unspoken rules. But in the process they created a mechanistic entity—the family system—and then set about doing battle with it. Most of the challenges that have rocked and reshaped family therapy have been in reaction to this mechanism. But if the systemic revolution went too far in one direction, the same may be true of some of its critics.

The feminist critique was the first and perhaps most influential of the challenges to family therapy's traditions. In taking a stand against mother bashing, feminists challenged the essence of systems thinking by pointing out that concepts like complementarity and circular causality can imply that subjugated women were as much to blame as their oppressors.

Family therapy's bridge to the twenty-first century was social constructionism. Much as was the case when the pioneers shifted their focus from individuals to families, this recent shift from behavior to cognition and from challenging to collaborating is opening up a new world of possibilities. We'll see just how exciting some of those possibilities are in the next few chapters.

The headline story of family therapy's evolution—from first- to second-order cybernetics, from MRI to solution-focused therapy, from Milan systemic to Hoffman and Goolishian, and from constructivism to social constructionism and now narrative—is what's been in the forefront of intellectual discussion. While these front-page developments were taking place, family therapists practicing less trendy approaches (behavioral, psychoanalytic, structural, Bowenian, and experiential) have contin-

ued their work. So it can be a mistake to think that what's new and gets attention is the only or even major thing going on in the field.

The collaborative movement has raised new questions about the therapist's style of leadership. When Harlene Anderson and Harry Goolishian advocated a collaborative approach, what was being rejected was the medical model—an authoritarian role model in which the clinician plays the expert, to whom the patient looks for answers. But being an expert doesn't mean being an ogre. Here the advance is challenging the medical model that, ironically, was perpetuated in such avant garde models of family therapy as the strategic and Milan systemic approaches. No longer do we see the therapist as a technocrat of change, but that doesn't mean therapists shouldn't be experts—leaders in the process of change.

Finally, it should be said that just as family therapy hasn't stood still in recent years, neither has the family. Today's family is evolving and stressed. We've gone from the complementary model of the family in the 1950s to a symmetrical version—though we haven't come to terms with the new model yet. Perhaps it's time to ask this question: As the American family struggles through this stressful time of transition, what concepts does family therapy offer to help us understand and deal with the protean family forms of the twenty-first century?

RECOMMENDED READINGS

Andersen, T. 1991. *The reflecting team.* New York: Norton.

Anderson, C. M., Reiss, D., and Hogarty, B. 1986. *Schizophrenia and the family: A practitioner's guide to psychoeducation and management.* New York: Guilford Press.

Avis, J. M. 1992. Where are all the family therapists? Abuse and violence within families and family therapy's response. *Journal of Marital and Family Therapy.* 18:225–232.

Fontes, L. A. 2008. *Interviewing clients across cultures.* New York: Guilford Press.

Fowers, B., and Richardson, F. 1996. Why is multiculturalism good? *American Psychologist.* 51: 609–621.

Gergen, K. 1985. The social constructionist movement in modern psychology. *American Psychologist.* 40:266–275.

Goldner, V. 1985. Feminism and family therapy. *Family Process.* 24:31–47.

Goodrich, T. J., ed. 1991. *Women and power: Perspectives for family therapy.* New York: Norton.

Greenan, D. E., and Tunnell, G. 2002. *Couples therapy with gay men: A family systems model for healing relationships.* New York: Guilford Press.

Hare-Mustin, R. T., and Marecek, J. 1988. The meaning of difference: Gender theory, postmodernism and psychology. *American Psychologist.* 43:455–464.

Held, B. S. 1995. *Back to reality: A critique of postmodern theory in psychotherapy.* New York: Norton.

Kellner, D. 1991. *Postmodern theory.* New York: Guilford Press.

Krestan, J., and Bepko, C. 1980. The problem of fusion in the lesbian relationship. *Family Process.* 19:277–289.

Laird, J., and Green, R. J. 1996. *Lesbians and gays in couples and families: A handbook for therapists.* San Francisco: Jossey-Bass.

Luepnitz, D. 1988. *The family interpreted: Feminist theory in clinical practice.* New York: Basic Books.

McDaniel, S., Hepworth, J., and Doherty, W. 1992. *Medical family therapy.* New York: Basic Books.

McGoldrick, M., Pearce, J. and Giordano, J. 2007. *Ethnicity and family therapy*, 3rd ed. New York: Guilford Press.

Rolland, J. 1994. *Helping families with chronic and life-threatening disorders.* New York: Basic Books.

Walsh, F., ed. 1993. *Normal family processes*, 2nd ed. New York: Guilford Press.

REFERENCES

Ahrons, C., and Rogers, R. 1989. *Divorced families: Meeting the challenges of divorce and remarriage.* New York: Norton.

Allport, G. 1958. *The nature of prejudice.* Garden City, NJ: Doubleday.

Andersen, T. 1991. *The reflecting team.* New York: Norton.

Anderson, C. M. 1995. *Flying solo.* New York: Norton.

Anderson, C. M., Reiss, D., and Hogarty, G. E. 1986. *Schizophrenia and the family: A practitioner's guide to psychoeducation and management.* New York: Guilford Press.

Anderson, H. 1993. On a roller coaster: A collaborative language systems approach to therapy. In *The new language of change*, S. Friedman, ed. New York: Guilford Press.

Anderson, W. T. 1990. *Reality isn't what it used to be.* San Francisco: Harper & Row.

Aponte, H. 1994. *Bread and spirit: Therapy with the new poor.* New York: Norton Press.

Atkinson, B. J. 2005. *Emotional intelligence in couples therapy: Advances from neurobiology and the science of intimate relationships.* New York: Norton.

Atkinson, J. M., & Coia, D. A. 1995. *Families coping with schizophrenia: A practitioner's guide to family groups.* New York: Wiley.

Avis, J. M. 1988. Deepening awareness: A private study guide to feminism and family therapy. In *Women, feminism, and family therapy*, L. Braverman, ed. New York: Haworth Press.

Avis, J. M. 1992. Where are all the family therapists? Abuse and violence within families and family therapy's response. *Journal of Marital and Family Therapy.* 18:223–230.

Bailey, E. 1999. *Children in therapy: Using the family as a resource.* New York: Norton.

Barth, R., Pietrzak, J., and Ramier, M. 1993. *Families living with drugs and HIV.* New York: Guilford Press.

Beavers, W., and Hampson, R. 1990. *Successful families: Assessment and intervention.* New York: Norton.

Billingsley, A. 1968. *Black families in white America.* Upper Saddle River, NJ: Prentice-Hall.

Billingsley, A. 1992. *Climbing Jacob's ladder: The enduring legacy of African-American families.* New York: Simon & Schuster.

Billingsley, A., ed. 1994. The Black church. *National Journal of Sociology.* 8:(1–2) (double edition).

Blow, A. J., Sprenkle, D. H., and Davis, S. D. 2007. Is who delivers the treatment more important than the treatment itself? The role of the therapist in common factors. *Journal of Marital and Family Therapy.* 33:298–317.

Blumstein, P., and Schwartz, P. 1983. *American couples.* New York: William Morrow.

Bowlby, J. 1988. *A secure base: Parent–child attachment and healthy human development.* New York: Basic Books.

Boyd-Franklin, N. 1989. *Black families in therapy: A multisystems approach.* New York: Guilford Press.

Boyd-Franklin, N. 1993. Race, class, and poverty. In *Normal family processes*, F. Walsh, ed. New York: Guilford Press.

Boyd-Franklin, N. 2003. Race, class and poverty. In *Normal family processes: Growing diversity and complexity*, 3rd ed. F. Walsh, ed. New York: Guilford Press.

Boyd-Franklin, N., Steiner, G., and Boland, M. 1995. *Children, families, and HIV/AIDS*. New York: Guilford Press.

Bringle, R. 1995. Sexual jealousy in the relationships of homosexual and heterosexual men: 1980 and 1994. *Personal Relationships*, 2:313–325.

Brothers, B. J., ed. 1992. *Spirituality and couples: Heart and soul in the therapy process*. New York: Haworth Press.

Brown, G. W., Birley, J. L. T., and Wing, J. K. 1972. The influence of family life on the course of schizophrenic disorders: A replication. *British Journal of Psychology*. 121:241–258.

Brown, L. S. 1994. *Subversive dialogues: Theory in feminist therapy*. New York: Basic Books.

Bryant, A. S., and Demian, S. 1994. Relationship characteristics of American gays and lesbians: Findings from a national survey. *Journal of Gay & Lesbian Social Services*, 1:101–117.

Burton, L. A., ed. 1992. *Religion and the family*. New York: Haworth Press.

Campbell, T. 1986. Family's impact on health: A critical review and annotated bibliography. *Family Systems Medicine*. 4:135–148.

Carl, D. 1990. *Counseling same-sex couples*. New York: Norton.

Carter, B. 1991. Everything I do is for the family. In *Women and power: Perspectives for family therapy*, T. J. Goodrich, ed. New York: Norton.

Chartier, M. R. 1986. Marriage enrichment. In *Psychoeducationalapproaches to family therapy and counseling*, R. F. Levant, ed. New York: Springer.

Combrinck-Graham, L. 1989. *Children in family contexts*. New York: Guilford Press.

Cooper, A. 2002. *Sex and the Internet: A guide for clinicians*. New York: Brunner-Routledge.

Cooper, A., Scherer, C., & Mathy, 2001. Overcoming methodological concerns in the investigation of online sexual activities. *Cyberpsycholgy and Behavior*, 4:437–447.

Corey, G. 2005. *Theory and practice of counseling and psychotherapy*, 7th ed. Belmont, CA: Brooks/Cole.

Cose, E. 1993. *The rage of the privileged class*. New York: HarperCollins.

Dattilio, F., ed. 1998. *Case studies in couple and family therapy*. New York: Guilford Press.

Davidson, R. J. 2001. The neural circuitry of emotion and affective style: Prefrontal cortex and amygdala contributions. *Social Science Information*, 40(1):11–37.

Davidson, R. J. 2003. Seven sins in the study of emotion: Correctives from affective neuroscience. *Brain and Cognition*, 52:129–132.

Davis, S. D., and Piercy, F. P. 2007. What clients of couple therapy model developers and their former students say about change, Part II: Model-independent common factors and integrative framework. *Journal of Marital and Family Therapy*. 33:344–363.

Delmonico, D. and Griffin, E. 2008. Cybersex and the e-teen: What marriage and family therapists should know. *Journal of Marital and Family Therapy*. 34:431–444.

Doherty, W. 1996. *The intentional family*. Reading, MA: Addison-Wesley.

Donovan, J. M., ed. 1999. *Short-term couple therapy*. New York: Guilford Press.

Duncan, G. J., and Brooks-Gunn, J. 1997. *Consequences of growing up poor*. New York: Russell Sage Foundation.

Ehrenreich, B. 1999. Nickel-and-dimed: On (not) getting by in America. *Harpers*. Jan:37–52.

Elizur, J., and Minuchin, S. 1989. *Institutionalizing madness: Families, therapy and society*. New York: Basic Books.

Elkin, M. 1990. *Families under the influence*. New York: Norton.

Emery, R. 1994. *Renegotiating family relationships: Divorce, child custody, and mediation*. New York: Guilford Press.

Falicov, C. 1983. *Cultural perspectives in family therapy*. Rockville, MD: Aspen Systems.

Falicov, C. 1988. *Family transitions: Continuity and change over the life cycle*. New York: Guilford Press.

Falicov, C. 1998. *Latino families in therapy*. New York: Guilford Press.

Falloon, I. J. R., Boyd, J. L., McGill, C. W., Razani, J., Moss, H. B., and Gilderman, A. M. 1982. Family management in the prevention of exacerbations of schizophrenia. *New England Journal of Medicine*. 306:1437–1440.

Figley, C. 1985. *Trauma and its wake: The study and treatment of post-traumatic stress disorder.* New York: Brunner/Mazel.

Floyd, F. J., Markham, H., Kelly, S., Blumberg, S. L., and Stanley, S. M. 1995. Preventive intervention and relationship enhancement. In *Clinical handbook of couples therapy*, N. S. Jacobson and A. S. Garman, eds. New York: Guilford Press.

Fontes, L. A. 2008. *Interviewing clients across cultures.* New York: Guilford Press.

Freeman, J., Epston, D., and Lobovits, D. 1997. *Playful approaches to serious problems.* New York: Norton.

Friedrich, W. 1990. *Psychotherapy of sexually abused children and their families.* New York: Norton.

Friesen, B. J., and Koroloff, N. M. 1990. Family-centered services: Implications for mental health administration and research. *Journal of Mental Health Administration.* 17(1):13–25.

Gergen, K. 1985. The social constructionist movement in modern psychology. *American Psychologist.* 40:266–275.

Gergen, K. 1991. The saturated family. *Family Therapy Networker.* 15:26–35.

Gil, E. 1994. *Play in family therapy.* New York, Guilford Press.

Gillispie, J. and Gackenbach, J. 2007. *Cyber rules: What you really need to know about the Internet.* New York: Norton.

Ginsberg, B. G. 2000. Relationship enhancement couples therapy. In *Comparative treatments of relationship disorders*, F. M. Dattilio and L. J. Bevilacqua, eds. New York: Springer.

Goldberg, P., Peterson, B., Rosen, K., and Sara, M. (2008). Cybersex: The impact of a contemporary problem on the practices of marriage and family therapists. *Journal of Marital and Family Therapy.* 34:469–480.

Goldner, V. 1985. Feminism and family therapy. *Family Process.* 24:31–47.

Goldner, V., Penn, P., Sheinberg, M., and Walker, G. 1990. Love and violence: Gender paradoxes in volatile attachments. *Family Process.* 29:343–364.

Goldstein, M. J., Rodnick, E. H., Evans, J. R., May, P. R., and Steinberg, M. 1978. Drug and family therapy in the aftercare treatment of acute schizophrenia. *Archives of General Psychiatry.* 35:1169–1177.

Gonyea, J. 2004. Internet sexuality: clinical implications for couples. *American Journal of Family Therapy*, 32:375–390.

Goodrich, T. J. 1991. In *Feminist family therapy*, T. J. Goodrich et al., eds. New York: Norton.

Goodrich, T. J., Rampage, C., Ellman, B., and Halstead, K. 1988. *Feminist family therapy: A casebook.* New York: Norton.

Gottman, J. M. 1999. *The marriage clinic: A scientifically based marital therapy.* New York: Norton.

Green, R. J. 1998. Training programs: Guidelines for multicultural transformations. In *Re-visioning family therapy*, M. McGoldrick, ed. New York: Guilford Press.

Green, R. J., and Mitchell, V. 2002. Gay and lesbian couples in therapy: Homophobia, relational ambiguity, and social support. In *Clinical handbook of couple therapy*, 3rd ed. A. S. Gurman and N. S. Jacobson, eds. New York: Guilford Press.

Greenan, D., and Tunnell, G. 2003. *Couple therapy with gay men.* New York: Guilford Press.

Grier, W., and Cobbs, P. 1968. *Black rage.* New York: Basic Books.

Guerney, B. G., Jr., ed. 1977. *Relationship enhancement: Skills training for therapy problem prevention and enrichment.* San Francisco: Jossey-Bass.

Haley, J. 1976. *Problem-solving therapy*, San Francisco: Jossey-Bass.

Haley, J. 1980. *Leaving home.* New York: McGraw-Hill.

Hansen, J. C. 1982. *Therapy with remarried families.* Rockville, MD: Aspen Systems.

Hardy, K. 1993. War of the worlds. *Family Therapy Networker.* 17:50–57.

Hare-Mustin, R. 2001. Family therapy and the future—2001. Plenary address, American Family Therapy Academy Conference of the Americas, Miami, FL, June 27.

Henggeler, S. W., and Borduin, C. M., eds. 1990. *Family therapy and beyond: A multisystemic approach to treating the behavior problems of children and adolescents.* Pacific Grove, CA: Brooks/Cole.

Hill, R. 1999. *The strengths of African American families: Twenty-five years later.* Lanham, MD: University Press of America.

Hines, P. M., and Boyd-Franklin, N. 1982. Black families. In *Ethnicity and family therapy*, M. McGoldrick, J. K. Pierce, and J. Giordano, eds. New York: Guilford Press.

Hines, P. M., and Boyd-Franklin, N. 1996. African American families. In *Ethnicity and family therapy*, 2nd ed. M. McGoldrick, J. K. Pierce, and J. Giordano, eds. New York: Guilford Press.

Activation in dorsolateral prefrontal cortex in response to maternal criticism and praise in recovered depressed and healthy control participants. *Biological Psychiatry, 57*:807–812.

Imber-Black, E. 1988. *Families and larger systems: A family therapist's guide through the labyrinth.* New York: Guilford Press.

Imber-Black, E., Roberts, J., and Whiting, R. 1988. *Rituals in families and family therapy.* New York: Norton.

Ingoldsby, B., and Smith, S. 1995. *Families in multicultural perspective.* New York: Guilford Press.

Isay, R. A. 1989. *Being homosexual: Gay men and their development.* New York: Farrar Straus Giroux.

James, K., and MacKinnon, L. 1990. The "incestuous family" revisited: A critical analysis of family therapy myths. *Journal of Marital and Family Therapy. 16*:71–88.

Johnson, T., and Keren, M. 1998. The families of lesbian women and gay men. In *Re-visioning family therapy*, M. McGoldrick, ed. New York: Guilford Press.

Johnson, W. E. 2001. Paternal involvement among unwed fathers. *Children and Youth Services Review. 23*:513–536.

Jordan, J., Kaplan, A., Miller, J., Stiver, I., and Surrey, J., eds. 1991. *Women's growth in connection: Writings from the Stone Center.* New York: Guilford Press.

Kahn, M., and Lewis, K. G. 1988. *Siblings in therapy.* New York: Norton.

Krestan, J. 1988. Lesbian daughters and lesbian mothers: The crisis of disclosure from a family systems perspective. *Journal of Psychotherapy and the Family. 3*:113–130.

Laird, J. 1993. Lesbian and gay families. In *Normal family processes*, 2nd ed. F. Walsh, ed. New York: Guilford Press.

Laird, J., and Green, R. J. 1996. *Lesbians and gays in couples and families: A handbook for therapists.* San Francisco: Jossey-Bass.

LaSala, M. 1997. The need for thick skin: Coupled gay men and their relationships with their parents and in-laws. *Dissertation Abstracts International. 58*:4444-A.

LaSala, M. 2004a. Extradyadic sex and gay male couples: Comparing monogamous and non-monogamus relationships. *Families in Society: The Journal of Contemporary Social Services. 85*(3): 405–411.

LaSala, M. 2004b. Monogamy of the heart: Extrdyadic sex and gay male couples. *Journal of Gay & Lesbian Social Services, 17*(3).

Law, D., Crane, D., and Russell, D. 2000. The influence of marital and family therapy on health care utilization in a health-maintenance organization. *Journal of Marital and Family Therapy. 26*:281–291.

LeDoux, J. 1996. *The emotional brain.* New York: Simon & Schuster.

Lee, E. 1997. *Working with Asian Americans.* New York: Guilford Press.

Leff, J., and Vaughn, C. 1985. *Expressed emotion in families.* Thousand Oaks, CA: Sage.

Leff, J., Kuipers, L., Berkowitz, R., Eberlein-Vries, R., and Sturgeon, D. 1982. A controlled trial of social intervention in the families of schizophrenic patients. *British Journal of Psychiatry. 141*:121–134.

Lehr, R., and MacMillan, P. 2001. The psychological and emotional impact of divorce: The non-custodial fathers' perspective. *Families in Society. 82*:373–382.

Lindblad-Goldberg, M., Dore, M. M., and Stern, L. 1998. *Creating competence from chaos.* New York: Norton.

Luepnitz, D. 1988. *The family interpreted: Feminist theory in clinical practice.* New York: Basic Books.

Madanes, C. 1990. *Sex, love and violence.* New York: Norton.

Markowitz, L. 1993. Walking the walk. *Family Therapy Networker. 17*:18–24, 27–31.

McAdoo, H., ed. 2002. *Black children: Social, educational and parental environment*, 2nd ed. Thousand Oaks, CA: Sage.

McDaniel, S., Hepworth, J., and Doherty, W. 1992. *Medical family therapy.* New York: Basic Books.

McFarlane, W. R. 1991. Family psychoeducational treatment. In *Handbook of family therapy.* Vol II. A. S. Gurman and D. P. Kniskern, eds. New York: Brunner/Mazel.

McFarlane, W. R., and Cook, W. L. 2007. Family expressed emotion prior to the onset of schizophrenia. *Family Process, 46*:185–197.

McGoldrick, M. 1993. Ethnicity, cultural diversity, and normality. In *Normal family processes*, F. Walsh, ed. New York: Guilford Press.

McGoldrick, M., ed. 1998. *Re-visioning family therapy.* New York: Guilford Press.

McGoldrick, M., Anderson, C., and Walsh, F., eds. 1989. *Women in families: A framework for family therapy.* New York: Norton.

McGoldrick, M., Pearce, J., and Giordano, J. 1982. *Ethnicity and family therapy.* New York: Guilford Press.

McGoldrick, M., Pearce, J., and Giordano, J. 2007. *Ethnicity and family therapy,* 3rd ed. New York: Guilford Press.

McGowen, B. G., and Meezan, W. 1983. *Child welfare: Current dilemmas, future directions.* Itasca, IL: Peacock.

McWhirter, D. P., and Mattison, A. M. 1984. *The male couple: How relationships develop.* New York: Norton.

Meyer, I. H., and Dean, L. 1998. Internalized homophobia, intimacy, and sexual behavior among gay and bisexual men. In *Stigma and sexual orientation: Understanding prejudice against lesbians, gay men, and bisexuals,* G. M. Herek, ed. Thousand Oaks, CA: Sage.

Micucci, J. 1998. *The adolescent in family therapy.* New York: Guilford Press.

Milkowitz, D. J. 1995. The evolution of family-based psychopathology. In *Integrating family therapy: Handbook of family psychology and systems theory,* R. H. Mikesell, D. D. Lusterman, and S. H. McDaniels, eds. Washington, DC: American Psychological Association.

Miklowitz, D., and Goldstein, M. 1997. *Bipolar disorder: A family-focused treatment approach.* New York: Guilford Press.

Miller, J. B. 1986. *Toward a new psychology of women,* 2nd ed. Boston: Beacon.

Minuchin, P., Colapinto, J., and Minuchin, S. 1998. *Working with families of the poor.* New York: Guilford Press.

Minuchin, S., and Fishman, H. C. 1981. *Techniques of family therapy.* Cambridge, MA: Harvard University Press.

Minuchin, S., Nichols, M. P., and Lee, W. Y. 2006. *Assessing families and couples: From symptom to system.* Boston: Allyn & Bacon.

Minuchin, S., Montalvo, B., Guerney, B., Rosman, B., and Schumer, F. 1967. *Families of the slums.* New York: Basic Books.

Mirkin, M. P. 1990. *The social and political contexts of family therapy.* Boston: Allyn & Bacon.

Mitchell, K., Finkelhor, D., and Wolak, J. 2001. Risk factors for and impact of online sexual solicitation of youth. *Journal of the American Medical Association, 285*:3011–3014.

Mitchell, S. 1993. *Hope and dread in psychoanalysis.* New York: Basic Books.

Morawetz, A., and Walker, G. 1984. *Brief therapy with single-parent families.* New York: Brunner/Mazel.

Muesser, K. T., and Glynn, S. M. 1995. *Behavioral family therapy for psychiatric disorders.* Boston: Allyn & Bacon.

Nichols, M. P. 2009. *Stop arguing with your kids.* New York: Guilford Press.

Okun, B. 1996. *Understanding diverse families.* New York: Guilford Press.

Olsen, D. 1996. Predicting marital success for pre-marital couple types based on PREPARE. *Journal of Marital and Family Therapy, 22*:103–119.

Orbach, S. 1997. *Fat is a feminist issue.* Edison, NJ: BBS.

Patterson, J., Williams, L., Graul-Grounds, C., and Chamow, L. 1998. *Essential skills in family therapy.* New York: Guilford Press.

Pinderhughes, E. 1989. *Understanding race, ethnicity and power: The key to efficacy in clinical practice.* New York: Free Press.

Pittman, F. 1987. *Turning points: Treating families in transition and crisis.* New York: Norton.

Pleck, J. H. 1995. The gender role strain paradigm: An update. In *A new psychology of men,* R. F. Levant and W. S. Pollack, eds. New York: Wiley.

Plomin, R. 1990. *Nature and nurture: An introduction to human behavioral genetics.* Pacific Grove, CA: Brooks/Cole.

Pollack, W. S. 1995. No man is an island: Toward a new psychoanalytic psychology of men. In *A new psychology of men,* R. F. Levant and W. S. Pollack, eds. New York: Wiley.

Prest, L., and Keller, J. 1993. Spirituality in family therapy. *Journal of Marital and Family Therapy. 19*:137–148.

Price, J. 1996. *Power and compassion: Working with difficult adolescents and abused parents.* New York: Guilford Press.

Rampage, C. 1998. Feminist couple therapy. In *Case studies in couple and family therapy: Systemic and cognitive perspectives,* F. M. Dattilio, ed. New York: Guilford Press.

Ramsey, R. N. ed. 1989. *Family systems in medicine.* New York: Guilford Press.

Reitz, M., and Watson, K. 1992. *Adoption and the family system.* New York: Guilford Press.

Rojano, R. 2004. The practice of community family therapy. *Family Process. 43*:59–77.

Rolland, J. 1994. *Helping families with chronic and life-threatening disorders.* New York: Basic Books.

Root, M., Fallon, P., and Friedrich, W. 1986. *Bulimia: A systems approach to treatment.* New York: Norton.

Roth, S., and Murphy, B. 1986. Therapeutic work with lesbian clients: A systemic therapy view. In *Women and family therapy*, M. Ault-Riche and J. Hansen, eds. Rockville, MD: Aspen Systems.

Rubin, L. 1994. *Families on the faultline.* New York: HarperCollins.

Saba, G., Karrer, B., and Hardy, K. 1989. *Minorities and family therapy.* New York: Haworth Press.

Sager, C., Brown, H. S., Crohn, H., Engel, T., Rodstein, E., and Walker, L. 1983. *Treating the remarried family.* New York: Brunner/Mazel.

Sanders, G. 1993. The love that dares not speak its name: From secrecy to openness in gay and lesbian affiliations. In *Secrets in families and family therapy*, E. Imber-Black, ed. New York: Norton.

Schwartz, R. C. 1995. *Internal family systems therapy.* New York: Guilford Press.

Schwartzman, J. 1985. *Families and other systems: The macrosystemic context of family therapy.* New York: Guilford Press.

Selekman, M. 1997. *Solution-focused therapy with children.* New York: Guilford Press.

Seligman, M., and Darling, R. B. 1996. *Ordinary families, special children: A systems approach to childhood disability*, 2nd ed. New York: Guilford Press.

Sells, S. 1998. *Treating the tough adolescent.* New York: Guilford Press.

Sheinberg, M. 1992. Navigating treatment impasses at the disclosure of incest: Combining ideas from feminism and social constructionism. *Family Process. 31*:201–216.

Seigel, D. J. 1999. *The developing mind: How relationships and the brain interact to shape who we are.* New York: Guilford Press.

Silliman, B., Stanley, S. M., Coffin, W., Markman, H. J., and Jordan, P. L. 2002. Preventive intervention for couples. In *Family psychology: Science-based interventions*, H. A. Liddle, D. A. Santisban, R. F. Levant, and J. H. Bray, eds. Washington, DC: American Psychological Association.

Smith, C., and Nylund, D. 1997. *Narrative therapies with children and adolescents.* New York: Guilford Press.

Sprenkle, D. 1985. *Divorce therapy.* New York: Haworth Press.

Stahmann, R. F., and Hiebert, W. J. 1997. *Premarital and remarital counseling: The professional's handbook.* San Francisco: Jossey-Bass.

Stanton, M. D., Todd, T., and Associates. 1982. *The family therapy of drug abuse and addiction.* New York: Guilford Press.

Staples, R. 1994. *Black family: Essays and studies*, 5th ed. New York: Van Nostrand Reinhold.

Steinglass, P., Bennett, L., Wolin, S. J., and Reiss, D. 1987. *The alcoholic family.* New York: Basic Books.

Stone Fish, L., and Harvey, R G. 2005. *Nurturing queer youth: Family therapy transformed.* New York: Norton.

Surrey, J. L. 1991. The "self-in-relation": A new theory of women's development. In *Women's growth in connection*, J. V. Jordan, A. G. Kaplan, J. B. Miller, I. P. Stiver, and J. L. Surrey, eds. New York: Guilford Press.

Taibbi, R. 2007. *Doing family therapy*, 2nd ed. New York: Guilford Press.

Treadway, D. 1989. *Before it's too late: Working with substance abuse in the family.* New York: Norton.

Trepper, T. S., and Barrett, M. J. 1989. *Systemic treatment of incest: A therapeutic handbook.* New York: Brunner/Mazel.

U.S. Bureau of the Census. 2003. *Statistical abstract of the United States*, 123rd ed. Washington, DC: U.S. Government Printing Office.

U.S. Bureau of the Census. 2007. *Statistical abstract of the United States*, 127th ed. Washington, DC: U.S. Government Printing Office.

Vaughn, C., and Leff, J. 1976. The measurement of expressed emotion in the families of psychiatric patients. *British Journal of Psychology. 15*:157–165.

Vaughn, C. E., Snyder, K. S., Jones, S., Freeman, W. B., and Falloon, I. R. H. 1984. Family factors in schizophrenic relapse: Replication in California of British research on expressed emotion. *Archives of General Psychiatry. 41*:1169–1177.

Visher, E., and Visher, J. 1979. *Stepfamilies: A guide to working with stepparents and stepchildren.* New York: Brunner/Mazel.

Visher, E., and Visher, J. 1988. *Old loyalties, new ties: Therapeutic strategies with stepfamilies.* New York: Brunner/Mazel.

Wachtel, E. 1994. *Treating troubled children and their families.* New York: Guilford Press.

Walker, G. 1991. *In the midst of winter: Systemic therapy with families, couples, and individuals with AIDS infection.* New York: Norton.

Wallerstein, J., and Kelly J. 1980. *Surviving the breakup: How children and parents cope with divorce.* New York: Basic Books.

Walsh, F. 1982. *Normal family processes.* New York: Guilford Press.

Walsh, F. 1993. *Normal family processes*, 2nd ed. New York: Guilford Press.

Walsh, F. 1998. *Strengthening family resistance.* New York: Guilford Press.

Walsh, F., ed. 1999. *Spiritual resources in family therapy.* New York: Guilford Press.

Walsh, F., and McGoldrick, M., eds. 1991. *Living beyond loss: Death in the family.* New York: Norton.

Walters, M., Carter, B., Papp, P., and Silverstein, O. 1988. *The invisible web: Gender patterns in family relationships.* New York: Guilford Press.

Watt, D. E. 1998. Affect and the limbic system: Some hard problems. *Journal of Neuropsychiatry and Clinical Neurosciences, 10*:113–116.

Weiss, R., and Schneider, J. 2006. *Untangling the web: Sex, porn, and fantasy obsession in the Internet age.* New York: Alyson Books.

White, J. 1972. Towards a black psychology. In *Black psychology*, R. Jones, ed. New York: Harper & Row.

Wynne, L. 1981. Current concepts about schizophrenia and family relationships. *Journal of Nervous and Mental Disease. 1969*:82–89.

Solution-Focused Therapy

12

Accentuate the Positive

Most therapy is based on the premise that when a client presents a problem—depression, say, or perhaps a misbehaving child, the clinician's job is to figure out what's causing the problem so that he or she will know how to solve it. **Solution-focused therapists** take the radical position that it isn't necessary to know what causes problems in order to make things better.

Solution-focused practitioners assume that people who come to therapy are capable of behaving effectively but that their effectiveness has been blunted by a negative mindset. Drawing their attention to forgotten capabilities helps release them from preoccupation with their failures and restores them to their more capable selves. Problems are seen as overwhelming because clients see them as *always* happening. Times when problems aren't happening aren't noticed or dismissed as trivial. The art of solution-focused therapy becomes a matter of helping clients see that their problems have **exceptions**—times when they didn't occur—and that these exceptions are solutions still available to them.

SKETCHES OF LEADING FIGURES

Solution-focused therapy grew out of the work of Steve de Shazer, Insoo Berg, and their colleagues at the Brief Family Therapy Center (BFTC) in Milwaukee. This private training institute was started in 1979 when some of the staff at a community agency who were drawn to the MRI model became dissatisfied with the agency's constraints and broke off to form the BFTC. The initial group included married partners Steve de Shazer and Insoo Berg, Jim Derks, Elaine Nunnally, Marilyn La Court, and Eve Lipchik. Their students included John Walter, Jane Peller, and Michele Weiner-Davis.

The late Steve de Shazer was the primary architect of solution-focused therapy, and his writings are among the most interesting and provocative in this approach (e.g., de Shazer, 1988, 1991b). A scholar as well as a clinician, de Shazer was intrigued by Bateson's theories of communication and Milton Erickson's pragmatic ideas about how to influence change. Early in his career, he worked in Palo Alto and was strongly influenced by the MRI approach. De Shazer died September 11, 2005, in Vienna.

Insoo Kim Berg was, along with Steve de Shazer, one of the primary architects of the solution-focused approach. She trained therapists all over the world and authored a host of books and articles applying the model to a variety of problems and service settings, including alcoholism (Berg & Miller, 1992), marital therapy (Berg, 1994a), and family-based services to the poor (Berg, 1994b). She died in 2007.

After training with de Shazer, Michele Weiner-Davis converted an agency program in Woodstock, Illinois, to the solution-focused model. Weiner-Davis (1992) applied the model to marital problems in her popular book *Divorce-Busting*.

Although Bill O'Hanlon never formally studied at the BFTC, he was trained in brief problem-solving therapy by Milton Erickson, and so the step toward solution-focused therapy was an easy one. O'Hanlon collaborated with Weiner-Davis to write one of the early books on solution-focused therapy (O'Hanlon & Weiner-Davis, 1989) and was thereafter prominently associated with the approach. He is a popular workshop presenter and has written a number of books and articles on his pragmatic approach, which he calls *possibility therapy* (O'Hanlon, 1998).

A student of Berg and de Shazer since the mid 1980s, Yvonne Dolan has applied the solution-focused model to the treatment of trauma and abuse (Dolan, 1991). She has also coauthored an influential volume of case studies (Berg & Dolan, 2001), described the model's application in agency settings (Pichot & Dolan, 2003), and

Steve de Shazer, founder of solution-focused therapy.

presented the state of the art of solution-focused therapy (de Shazer, Dolan, Korman, Trepper, Berg, & McCollum, 2007). Dolan conducts training in solution-focused therapy around the world and is president of the Solution-Focused Brief Therapy Association.

Other well-known solution-focused therapists include Eve Lipchik, Scott Miller, John Walter, and Jane Peller. Lipchik, who worked at the BFTC for eight years until she left in 1988, pioneered the application of the solution-focused model to wife battering (Lipchik & Kubicki, 1996) and recently published one of the most useful books about how to do solution-focused therapy (Lipchik, 2002). Scott Miller worked at the BFTC for three years,

Insoo Kim Berg, a leading practitioner of the solution-focused model.

directing the alcohol and drug treatment services, and has written widely about the model. John Walter and Jane Peller practice together in Chicago. They trained at the BFTC and, after writing a book laying out the steps of the approach (Walter & Peller, 1992), became popular presenters on the workshop circuit.

THEORETICAL FORMULATIONS

One of the defining characteristics of family therapy has always been its focus on the present, where problems are maintained, rather than searching the past for what caused them. Solution-focused therapists prefer to look to the future, where problems can be solved.

Like the MRI group, solution-focused therapists believe that people are constrained by narrow views of their problems into perpetuating rigid patterns of false solutions. As O'Hanlon and Weiner-Davis (1989) put it:

So, the meanings people attribute to behavior limit the range of alternatives they will use to deal with a situation. If the methods used do not produce a satisfactory outcome, the original assumption about the meaning of the behavior is generally not questioned. If it were, new meanings might be considered, which in turn might prompt a different, perhaps more effective, approach. Instead, people often redouble their efforts to solve the problem in an ineffective way, thinking that by doing it more, harder or better (e.g., more punishments, more heart-to-heart talks, and so on) they will finally solve it. (p. 48)

Solution-oriented therapists reject the notion that problems serve ulterior motives or that people somehow *need* their problems. They assume that clients really do want to change. In fact, de Shazer (1984) declared "the death of resistance" by suggesting that when clients don't follow advice, it's their way of telling the practitioner that his or her suggestions don't fit their way of doing things. Imposition breeds opposition.

The MRI model was inspired by Milton Erickson's view of people as containing untapped and often unconscious resources. According to this view, people may only need a slight shift of perspective to release their potential. Part of that shift involves changing the way people talk about their problems.

The language of problems tends to be different from the language of solutions. As Ludwig Wittgenstein put it (1958), "The world of the happy is quite another than that of the unhappy." Usually, "problem talk" is negative, focuses on the past, and often implies the permanence of problems. The language of solutions is more positive, hopeful, and future oriented. Part of the therapist's job is to steer clients from problem talk to solution talk. In the solution-focused model, the future is negotiable.

NORMAL FAMILY DEVELOPMENT

Although family therapists have tended to de-emphasize developmental models in favor of focusing on here-and-now interactions, most therapists have assumptions about what constitutes healthy family life. Normal families are said to have flexible structures, clear boundaries, and well-organized hierarchies, and they use positive reinforcement control, offer secure attachment, and provide mutual need satisfaction—and these objectives serve as goals in helping families recover their potential for happiness.

In the solution-focused model, clients are assumed to be the experts on their own situations. Just as they know what's troubling them, so, too, they know what they need. This philosophy is exemplified by the practice of routinely asking clients "Is there anything else I should have asked you or that you need to tell me?" De Jong and Berg (2002) recommend, "If as a practitioner, you wish to put clients into the position of being experts on their own lives, you will have to know how to set aside your own frame of reference as much as possible and explore those of your clients" (p. 20).

Solution-focused therapists assume that people are resilient and resourceful. The problems they have are not seen as evidence of failure to achieve some adaptive standard but rather as normal life-cycle complications. This optimistic perspective needn't be dismissed as Pollyanna-ish; rather it can be seen as a commitment to the belief that families have the ability to construct solutions that can enhance their lives.

Therapy, then, is highly relativistic. Implicit in this model is an asymptomatic perspective on family normality; that is, a normal family is simply one that has been freed of its presenting problems and thus returned to its own unique functional way of living.

> Solution-oriented therapists don't believe that there is any single "correct" or "valid" way to live one's life. We have come to understand that what is unacceptable behavior in one family or for one person is desirable behavior in another. Therefore, clients, not therapists, identify the goals to be accomplished in treatment. (O'Hanlon & Weiner-Davis, 1989, p. 44)

DEVELOPMENT OF BEHAVIOR DISORDERS

In the solution-focused world, this subject is closed. The very act of categorizing people suggests that they are a certain way all the time. For example, when we say that a couple is *disengaged*, does this mean that there are never times when they are not disengaged? Unfortunately, the act of labeling draws attention from those other times.

Just as solution-focused therapists steer clients away from speculating about problem formation, they also avoid such conjecture themselves. Their conviction is that solutions are often unrelated to the way problems developed and that exploring etiology is engaging in problem talk—exactly what they seek to avoid. Problem talk and the related preoccupation with the problem are the furthest solution-focused therapists go in identifying etiological factors. They believe that problem-focused thinking keeps people from recognizing effective solutions they've already used or could come up with. Problems persist in the way people define situations and in the misdirected actions they persist in taking.

GOALS OF THERAPY

The goal of solution-focused therapy is to resolve presenting complaints as expeditiously as possible. The search for underlying flaws is rejected. As de Shazer (1991b) writes, "Structuralist thought points to the idea that symptoms are the result of some underlying problem, a psychic of structural problem such as incongruent hierarchies, covert parental conflicts, low self-esteem, deviant communication, repressed feelings, 'dirty games,' etc." Solution-focused therapists don't believe that it's necessary to delve into these deeper issues in order to help people resolve their problems.

The solution-focused therapist's goal is never about how families should be structured but only what they want different in their lives. Therefore, goals are defined in the clients' terms and are unique for every family.

The process of goal setting itself is a significant intervention in this approach. Walter and Peller (1992) emphasize the importance of assisting clients in creating well-defined goals that are framed in positive terms, concrete and behavioral, and modest enough to be achievable. Helping people to stop dwelling on their dissatisfactions and envision what they want to be doing instead is seen as the first step in helping them get there. Thus, although clients often come in with complaints stated in negative terms—"I want to be less depressed," "We want

Roger to stop smoking pot"—solution-focused therapists help recast these complaints into positive goals by asking "What will you (or he) be doing instead?" If you've ever tried to lose weight, you've probably discovered that it's a lot more effective to take positive steps, like exercising and eating low-fat meals, than it is to concentrate on *not* eating Big Macs and french fries.

Because success tends to build on itself, solution-focused therapists see modest goals as the beginning of change. Consider, for example, the case of a woman who was unhappy about always being late. Instead of accepting the unrealistic goal of never being late, De Jong and Berg (2002) suggested that it might be more useful to ask "Right now, at this time in your life, for what do you least want to be late?" (p. 80). The woman might have focused on getting to work on time, because although her family and friends may be forgiving, regularly coming late to work might get her fired.

CONDITIONS FOR BEHAVIOR CHANGE

The task of solution-focused therapy is to help clients amplify *exceptions* to their problems—effective solutions already in their repertoire. From Berg and de Shazer's (1993) point of view, what's needed for change is a shift in the way the problem is "languaged":

> Rather than looking behind and beneath the language that clients and therapists use, we think that the language they use is all that we have to go on. . . . What we talk about and how we talk about it makes a difference, and it is these differences that can be used to make a difference (to the client). . . . [W]e have come to see that the meanings arrived at in a therapeutic conversation are developed through a process more like negotiation than the development of understanding or an uncovering of what it is that is "really" going on. (p. 7)

The assumption is that getting people to talk positively will help them think positively and

ultimately to act positively to solve their own problems.

From the Ericksonian perspective that informed de Shazer's thinking, the therapist is to create an atmosphere in therapy in which people's strengths can move out of the shadows and into the foreground. De Shazer (1985, 1986) found these strengths lurking in the spaces between problems—in the "behaviors, perceptions, thoughts, feelings, and expectations that are outside the complaint's constraints. These exceptions . . . can be used as building blocks in the construction of a solution. . . . Solutions involve determining what 'works' so that the client can do more of it" (de Shazer, 1986, p. 48).

Small changes can initiate a positive spiral. For example, a man may believe that the way to improve relationships is to tell other people what they're doing that he doesn't like. Unfortunately, such confrontations make his girlfriend feel bad. His criticisms make her feel rejected. If a therapist suggests that he say what he wants rather than what he doesn't like, the man can change his approach, which may have a beneficial effect on many relationships. What's more, achieving even a small success may encourage the man to believe that he can solve other more difficult problems. According to solution-focused therapists, problems are solved one step at a time.

THERAPY

Assessment

When a therapist asks "How can I be useful to you?," clients usually respond by describing a problem of some sort, while the therapist asks for details. Solution-focused practitioners, however, spend little time talking about problems, and they don't inquire about problems' possible causes. They don't want to get bogged down in negatives or reinforce the expectation that it's important to discover the cause of a problem in order to solve it. Solution-focused therapists listen to problem talk only enough to make clients feel understood; then they turn the conversation toward a search for solutions.

After getting a brief description of the presenting complaint, the therapist moves directly to asking clients how things will be different in their lives when their problems are solved. Then, instead of formulating some kind of intervention plan, the therapist asks about times in the clients' lives when their problems do not happen or are less severe. The following questions (adapted from Lipchik, 2002) suggest the proactive nature of a solution-focused assessment:

"What do you think the problem is now?"
"How will you know when the problem is solved?"
"How will you know you don't have to come here anymore? What will the signs be?"
"What will have to be different for that to happen in terms of your behavior, thoughts, and feelings?"
"What will you notice that is different about others involved in the situation?"
"What is your wildest fantasy about what you want to happen?"

Because they aren't interested in assessing family dynamics, solution-focused practitioners don't feel the need to convene any particular group of people. Instead, they say that anyone who is concerned about the problem should attend sessions. They also need little intake information, because they want to hear clients' constructions of their problems firsthand. Solution-focused therapists ask more about perceptions than about feelings, and they affirm the clients' position. All clients want some indication that their therapists had understood the point of view that guides their actions.

The process of assessment in solution-focused therapy differs radically from problem-solving approaches. The solution-focused therapist doesn't function as an expert in determining what's wrong (enmeshment, triangulation) and planning how to correct it. In this model, clients are the experts in what they want to change (Walter & Peller, 1992). Although solution-focused therapists don't play the role of authority figures who will help clients solve their problems, they do take an active position in moving clients away from worrying about their predicament and toward steps to solution.

The following sorts of questions are asked to lay the groundwork for therapeutic goal development:

"What needs to happen as a result of coming here, so that afterward you will look back and be honestly able to say that it was a good idea?"
"What needs to happen so that this will not have been a waste of your time?"
"Often in our experience, we have found that in between scheduling an appointment and coming in, something happens that contributes to making a problem better. Has anything happened to improve the problem for which you decided to come here today?"

Based on the answers to these questions, the therapist and clients begin to construct a more detailed description of the therapeutic goal. Once this description of the goal has been developed, the therapist asks the clients to assess their current level of progress toward that goal by imagining a scale of 1 to 10, where 1 represents the problem at its worst and 10 is the point at which the problem is gone or the clients are coping with it so well that it's no longer problematic:

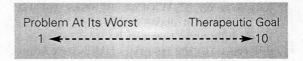

Problem At Its Worst   Therapeutic Goal
1 ◄ - - - - - - - - - - - - - - - - - - ► 10

The clients' rating makes it possible to assess how far they are from the goal. Later, the same scale can be used to determine what specific actions will allow the clients to move toward the goal and to evaluate progress. If clients identify new problems, the therapist makes a new scale to depict desired outcomes and to assess progress toward new solutions.

In an approach as direct as solution-focused therapy, it's important to assess clients' motivation for change. Following de Shazer (1988), practitioners distinguish between *visitors, complainants*, and *customers.*

A visitor is someone who's not really in the market for therapy. Visitors are there at someone else's insistence—a judge, a parent, the school principal—but they don't really have a complaint and don't want to be there. Therapists should not offer any suggestions to these clients or seek to convince them that they really need therapy.

With visitors it's important to pay attention to how they were referred and to consider who the real client is; that is, the person who wants services to be provided. If the people in your office are present only because someone pressured them to be there, a useful strategy is to ask them what they need to do to satisfy the authority that compelled them to seek therapy:

"So, what has to happen to get your mother off your back?"

"What's the minimum we need to accomplish so that you won't have to keep coming for more sessions?"

Complainants do have clear complaints, but they're usually about someone else. Parents often seek therapy because their children are having problems. But while parents of young children may see the need to be involved in the solution, parents of older children often think that it's only the child who has the problems—drugs, depression, shyness—and may not see themselves as part of the solution. Wives seek couples therapy because their "husbands don't communicate," while husbands often show up only to placate their wives.

Complainants don't perceive that they are responsible for the problem or its solution. (One of the great advantages of family therapy is that all the key players are present; one of the disadvantages is that there's always someone else to blame.)

With complainants, it may be useful to suggest noticing exceptions in the problem behavior of the other family member. The solution-focused therapist accepts the complainant's views, gives compliments, and may suggest observing exceptions to the complaint pattern, as the following example illustrates.

Therapist: How can I help you?

Client: It's my daughter. All she does is hang out with her friends. She never does her homework, and she never helps out around the house.

Therapist: So how can I be of help to you?

Client: Nothing I've ever done seems to make a difference. She just doesn't want to grow up and take responsibility for herself.

With such clients, solution-focused therapists try to shift the conversation from problem talk to solution talk.

Therapist: What do you think needs to happen so that your daughter will be a little easier to live with?

Client: She has to start doing her homework. I keep telling her that she won't get anywhere unless she finishes high school.

Therapist: That seems like a big change. But suppose that did happen—suppose she did start doing her homework. What would your daughter be saying about how you are different with her then?

Client: She hates it when I nag her. So she'd probably say that I wasn't nagging as much anymore.

Notice how the therapist at no point challenges the client's notion that the problem is her daughter. Nevertheless, by talking about a solution, the conversation comes around to how the mother might behave differently as part of the solution. This opens the door to her seeing that nagging less may be part of a more productive approach to her daughter.

Some clients who fit the description of a complainant are less flexible than the mother in this example. We've all seen people who steadfastly maintain that everything is someone else's fault. With such clients you can always ask "How were you hoping I might be useful to you?" Then strategize with them about how they can act differently to influence those recalcitrant others.

Customers have clear complaints and are ready to take action. Therapists can be more direct in guiding such clients toward solutions. With a customer, you can move directly to establish goals and then look for solutions. It's much easier to work with people who are ready to make changes.

The point de Shazer makes is that these distinctions—visitor, complainant, and customer—aren't qualities of character but qualities of the therapeutic relationship and therefore fluid. With an apparently unmotivated complainant, the therapist's job is to engage in a solution-focused conversation, compliment the client, and possibly give an assignment to observe exceptions to the problem. By not pushing for change but instead shifting attention away from problems and toward solutions, the relationship may evolve into one in which the client becomes a customer for change.

Therapeutic Techniques

Solution-focused techniques are organized around two fundamental strategies. The first is developing *well-focused goals* within the clients' frame of reference. The second is generating solutions based on *exceptions* (De Jong & Berg, 2002). Therapy is usually brief (three to five sessions on average), and appointments are made one at a time, on the assumption that one more may be enough.

Problem Description. Therapy begins with a description of the clients' problem: "How were you hoping I could help you?" Solution-focused therapists take pains to work within the clients' frame of reference. They ask for the clients' perceptions and are careful to acknowledge them, using the clients' own language as much as possible.

> *Therapist:* So you were saying that you want to do something about being so disorganized?
>
> *Client:* Yes, I can't keep track of half the things I'm supposed to be doing, and I end up scrambling to turn in assignments at the last minute. I hate myself for that! Sometimes I think maybe I just don't want to be doing this job.
>
> *Therapist:* So you think that maybe being disorganized has something to do with not really liking the work you're doing, and you've been feeling discouraged and down on yourself, is that right?

It's a good idea to ask clients what they've already tried to resolve their difficulties. People usually attempt various strategies to deal with their problems, and these efforts may have been more or less successful. Either way, these previous attempts at solution now play an important part in the clients' perception of what works and doesn't work for them.

Goal Setting. After hearing and acknowledging the clients' description of their problems and what they've tried to do about them, the next step is establishing clear and concrete goals. Solution-focused therapists help translate vague or amorphous goals into concrete, behavioral terms by asking questions like these:

"Specifically how will you be doing this?"
"How will the two of you know when you have solved your problems? How will things be different?"
"What specifically will tell you that you've solved your problem (or reached your goal)?"

"What will be the first sign (or smallest step) that will tell you that you're moving in the right direction? What else?"

The clearer the goal, the easier it is to measure progress. If, for example, a woman says that she would like to get along better with her husband, a solution-focused therapist might ask: "Can you tell me more specifically what will be happening when you two are getting along better? What will you be doing differently? What specifically will your husband notice that will tell him that you two are getting along as opposed to not getting along?"

Notice in this example how the therapist asks the woman who wants to have a better relationship "What will you be doing differently?" Part of the process of solution-focused therapy is helping clients think about constructive actions *they* can take, rather than how they can get someone else to change.

Useful goals are specific and include positive actions. They are also modest enough to be achievable. Among the reasons people don't make as many constructive changes as they would like is that they define their goals in overly ambitious terms. For instance, a recently divorced woman who was anxious to get her life back in order wanted to quit smoking, get a job, lose twenty pounds, and start dating. The therapist suggested that she concentrate first on finding a job and postpone trying to lose weight and quit smoking until she had a little less stress in her life.

Once when Insoo Berg was interviewing a woman whose life seemed out of control, she asked the client what needed to happen in order for things to be better. The woman replied that she wasn't sure—she had so many problems. "Maybe only a miracle will help, but I suppose that's too much to expect." Picking up on the client's words, Berg asked, "OK, suppose a miracle happened, and the problem that brought you here is solved. What would be different about your life" (De Jong & Berg, 2002, p. 85).

To Berg's surprise, this woman, who had seemed so overwhelmed and helpless, began to describe a clear and realistic picture of a well-functioning family. Thus was born one of the mainstays of solution-focused therapy: the **miracle question**. Here's how de Shazer (1988) phrases it:

> Now, I want to ask you a strange question. *Suppose* that while you are sleeping tonight and the entire house is quiet, a *miracle* happens. The miracle is that *the problem which brought you here is solved*. However, because you are sleeping, you don't know that the miracle has happened. So, when you wake up tomorrow morning, *what will be different* that will tell you that a miracle has happened and the problem which brought you here is solved? (p. 5)

The miracle question invites clients to envision an unlimited range of possibilities and begins to activate a problem-solving mindset by giving them a mental picture of their goals—perhaps in the same way that visualizing the perfect serve helps a tennis player. The miracle question also helps clients look beyond the problem to see that what they really want may not be the elimination of the problem per se but to be able to do the things that the problem has been obstructing. If the therapist can encourage them to begin doing those things despite the problem, suddenly the problem may not loom as large.

For example, Mary says that if she wasn't bulimic, she'd get closer to people and have more fun. If, with her therapist's encouragement, Mary begins to take interpersonal risks and has more fun, then her bulimia may become less of a problem and less of an obstacle in her life, which might also increase her ability to control it.

The miracle question is most effectively introduced when clients complain in vague terms, as in the following case (based on Friedman & Lipchik, 1999).

A therapist working with a distressed couple tried to shift them away from complaining and toward

Case Study

solutions by asking a series of questions such as "How do you usually solve problems like this?" and "When you're feeling more appreciated by your partner, what is he doing differently?" Although the couple had plenty of complaints about each other, the husband was able to respond positively to the therapist's question "So you both agree, the other feels as bad as you do. Any ideas what the solution might be?"

Husband: "Yeah, the solution would be more acceptance."

Therapist: "On her part? On your part?"

Husband: "Well, for both of us."

Wife: "Well, the only solution I see is similar, but I've lost trust in him."

When the therapist asked her to elaborate on what a solution might look like, the wife kept coming back to her complaints. So the therapist asked a modified form of the miracle question in hopes of shifting her toward a more specific vision of a direction for positive change. "And if by some miracle that trust would be there tomorrow, how would you know? What would the signs be?"

Exploring Exceptions: Probing for exceptions to the problem—times when clients didn't have the problem—invites them to recognize that some potential solutions may already be in their grasp.

The **exception question** may be phrased as follows: "When in the recent past might the problem have happened but didn't (or was less intense or more manageable)? What's different about those times when the problem doesn't happen? How have you let your partner know when he or she does something that makes a positive difference to you?"

Finding exceptions in the recent past is most useful because clients can remember them in greater detail. Also, and since these exceptions just happened, it's more plausible that they could happen again. By exploring these times and what

was different about them, clients find clues to what they can do to expand these exceptions. In addition, when clients recognize that they were able to avoid or overcome the problem before, their outlook toward it may change. It may seem less insurmountable.

For example, Mary, who has bulimia, may remember times the previous week when she had the urge to binge and purge but didn't. She may discover that at those times she was away from her parents and so didn't feel like she was disappointing them. She may decide that it's time to become more independent.

Eve Lipchik (2002) recommends probing for exceptions with some of the following questions:

- Are there times when you don't have this problem?
- What is different at those times?
- How does that make a difference to you? To others?
- What will make it possible for more of that to happen?
- What small changes will you notice?
- What will others notice about you?

Exploring exceptions allows the therapist and client to build on past successes. Failing that, the therapist can ask why things aren't worse—"How did you manage that?"—and then build on that accomplishment. **Coping questions** can help clients recognize that simply by enduring, they are more resourceful than they realize.

"What keeps you going under such difficult circumstances?"

"How come things aren't worse?"

"What have you done to keep them from getting worse?"

If the client provides answers, the therapist can build on them with questions about how that endurance can be maintained and how more of that effort can be brought to bear.

A solution-focused therapist spends most of the session listening attentively for evidence of previous solutions, exceptions, and goals. When these come out, the therapist punctuates them with enthusiasm and support. The therapist, then, works to keep solution talk in the forefront. This requires different skills from those used in traditional problem-focused therapies. Whereas the problem-focused therapist is concerned about missing clues to what caused or is maintaining a problem, the solution-focused therapist is concerned about missing clues to progress and solution. Yvonne Dolan (personal communication) demonstrates this process in the following case vignette.

Case Study

Mother: She comes home and then just ignores me, acts like I'm not there. Comes home from school, just runs into her room. Who knows what she's doing in there? But I have a feeling it's not good.

Daughter: You say we fight all the time, so I just go in my room so we don't fight.

Mother: See? She admits she just tries to avoid me. I don't know why she can't just come home and talk to me a little about school or something, like she used to.

Therapist: Wait a second, when did she "used to"? Cheryl, when did you come home and tell your mom about school?

Daughter: I did that a lot; last semester I did.

Therapist: Can you give me an example of the last time you did that?

Mother: I can tell you. It was last week, actually. She was all excited about her science project getting chosen.

Therapist: Tell me more, what day was that?

Mother: I think last Wednesday.

Therapist: And she came home . . .?

Mother: She came home all excited.

Therapist: What were you doing?

Mother: I think I was getting dinner ready. And she came in all excited, and I asked her what was up, and she told me her science project was chosen for the display at school.

Therapist: Wow, that's quite an honor.

Mother: It is.

Therapist: So then what happened?

Mother: Well, we talked about it, she told me all about it.

Therapist: Cheryl, do you remember this?

Daughter: Sure, it was only last week. I was pretty happy.

Therapist: And would you say that this was a nice talk, a nice talk between you two?

Daughter: Sure. That's what I mean; I don't always go in my room.

Therapist: Was there anything different about that time, last week, that made it easier to talk to each other?

Mother: Well, she was excited.

Daughter: My mom listened. She wasn't doing anything else.

Therapist: Wow, this is a great example. Thank you. Let me ask this: If it were like that more often, where Cheryl talked to you about things that were interesting and important to her, and where Mom, you listened to her completely without doing other things, is that what you two mean by "*better communication?*"

Daughter: Yeah, exactly.

Mother: Yes.

In this example, the therapist used a variety of solution-focused interventions. First, she listened carefully for an exception to the problem—a time when the problem could have happened but didn't. Second, she punctuated that exception by getting more details about it and congratulating the clients on it. Third, she connected the exception to their goal by asking how their goal would be reached if this exception were to occur more often.

Scaling Questions. Scaling questions were introduced to help therapists and clients talk about vague topics such as depression and communication, where it's difficult to identify concrete behavioral changes and goals. Berg and de Shazer (1993) describes the use of scaling questions:

> The therapist asks the depressed client, for example, "On a scale of one to ten, with one being how depressed you felt when you called me and ten being how you feel the day after the miracle, how do you feel right now?"
>
> The client might say two and the therapist might say, "So you feel a little better than when you called. How did you achieve this improvement?" Or the therapist might ask, "What do you think you need to do to achieve a three?" In this way, the therapist and client can recognize and nurture small changes toward the goal rather than being stuck in the "I'm either depressed or I'm not" kind of thinking that typifies such problems.

Scaling questions are also used to get clients to quantify their confidence that they can maintain their resolve: "On a scale of 1 to 10, how confident are you that you will be able to avoid losing your temper this week?" In practice, this device has a kind of "prove-it" implication. The response is followed up by asking clients what they might do to increase the odds of success: "What do you have to do to stick to your guns this time?" Asking scaling questions is a useful way of anticipating and disarming resistance and backsliding and of encouraging commitment to change.

Scaling questions can also be used to reduce goals that seem dauntingly far off to more manageable small steps: "On a scale of 1 to a 100, with 1 being never and 100 being always, what percentage of the time would you say you are experiencing the problem?" Then in response to the answer, ask questions such as these: "How many points would it have to go down for you to feel slightly better?" "What would a step from 75 to 70 look like?" "What would you be doing differently?" "What would others be doing differently?"

Here's an example of the use of scaling questions from a case of a couple who wanted to improve their communication.

Case Study

Therapist: What I want to do now is scale the problem and the goal. Let's say 1 is as bad as the problem ever could be—you never talk, only fight, or avoid all the time. And let's say 10 is where you talk all the time, with perfect communication, never have a fight ever.

Susan: That's pretty unrealistic.

Therapist: That would be the ideal. So where would you two say it was for you at its worst? Maybe right before you came in to see me.

Susan: It was pretty bad. . . . I don't know. . . . I'd say a 2 or a 3.

Jim: Yeah, I'd say a 2.

Therapist: Okay (writing) . . . a 2 or 3 for you and a 2 for you. Now tell me what you would be satisfied with when therapy is over and successful?

Jim: I'd be happy with an 8.

Susan: Well, of course I'd like a 10, but that's unrealistic. Yeah, I agree. An 8 would be good.

Therapist: What would you say it is right now?

Susan: I would say it's a little better, because he's coming here with me, and I see that he's trying. I'd say maybe a 4?

Jim: Well, that's nice to hear. I wouldn't have thought she'd put it that high. I would say it's a 5.

Therapist: Okay, a 4 for you and a 5 for you. And you both want it to be an 8 for therapy to be successful, right?

There are two major components of this intervention. First, it's a solution-focused assessment device; that is, if used each session, the therapist and clients have an ongoing measure of their progress. Second, it's a powerful intervention by itself, because it allows the therapist to focus on previous solutions and exceptions and to punctuate new changes as they occur.

Like the changes made before the first session, there are three things that can happen between each session: (1) things can get better; (2) things can stay the same; or (3) things can get worse. If the scale goes up and things get better from one session to the next, the therapist compliments the clients and then gets details about how they were able to make such changes. This not only supports and solidifies the changes, but it also nudges clients to do more of the same. If things stay the same, the clients can be complimented on maintaining their changes or for not letting things get worse: "How did you keep it from going down?" It's interesting how often that question will lead to a description of changes clients have made, in which case the therapist can again compliment and support and encourage more of that change.

Therapist: Susan, last week you were a 4 on the scale of good communications. I'm wondering where you are this week?

Susan (pause): I'd say a 5.

Therapist: A 5! Wow! Really, in just one week?

Susan: Yes, I think we communicated better this week.

Therapist: How did you communicate?

Susan: Well, I think it was Jim. He seemed to try to listen to me more.

Therapist: That's great. Can you give me an example of when he listened to you more?

Susan: Well, yes, yesterday for example. He usually calls me once a day at work, and—

Therapist: Sorry to interrupt, but did you say he calls you *once a day*?

Susan: Yes.

Therapist: I'm just a little surprised, because not all husbands call their wives every day.

Susan: He's always done that.

Therapist: Is that something you like? That you wouldn't want him to change?

Susan: Yes, for sure.

Therapist: Sorry, go on. You were telling me about yesterday when he called.

Susan: Well, usually it's kind of a quick call. But I told him about some problems I was having, and he listened for a long time, seemed to care, gave me some good ideas. That was nice.

Therapist: So that was an example of how you would like it to be—where you can talk about something, a problem, and he listens and gives good ideas? Support?

Susan: Yes.

Therapist: Jim, did you know that Susan liked your telephoning her at work and listening to her?

Jim: Yeah, I guess so. I've really been trying this week.

Therapist: That's great. What else have you done to try to make the communication better this week?

This example shows how going over the scale with the couple served as a vehicle for tracking their progress. The therapist gathered more and more information about the small changes the clients had made on their own that led to an improvement on the scale. This would naturally lead to suggesting that the couple continue to do the things that are working.

Compliments. Compliments are conveyed with questions that take the form of "How did you do that?" or, to be more accurate, "Wow! How did you do *that?*" Notice that this phrasing calls attention to the fact that the clients have already accomplished something. Rather than ask questions like "Have you ever had a job before," ask "What kinds of jobs have you had before?" Doing so invites clients to describe their successes and thus helps foster self-confidence.

To be effective, compliments should point toward what to do more, not what to eliminate. Most clients know what's wrong but have run out of ideas about how to avoid repeating the same ineffective solutions. Compliments can be used to highlight successful strategies and keep clients focused on those that work.

The following case study from Yvonne Dolan (personal communication) illustrates how compliments can be artfully woven in to support and enhance a client's efforts to make her life better.

Session 1

Case Study

Therapist: What needs to happen as result of coming here in order for you to be able to say when you leave today that it has been useful?

Client: It's my mother. She has Alzheimer's, and she's driving me crazy.

Therapist: That sounds hard.

Client: Oh, you have no idea. She forgets to do things like turn the gas burner off, and sometimes she even leaves the front door open. She forgets to put her clothes on if I don't remind her. I feel so overwhelmed because I have to watch her all the time.

Therapist: So you're with her full time?

Client: Well, I have a woman who comes in a couple of times a week. Then I can get out to the grocery store and, well, you know, do basic things like get my hair cut, do errands, once in a while I get to see a friend. The rest of the time I'm either working or taking care of Mom.

Therapist: Oh, so you work outside the home as well as inside?

Client: Yes. I'm a nail technician. I work part time.

Therapist: I'm impressed that you hold down a job plus being a full-time caregiver. It sounds like an awful lot to do. I can't imagine how you manage it all.

Client: Well, (hesitates) I guess that's why I'm here. It *is* pretty hard.

Therapist: It sounds really like it takes a lot of continuous effort. I think most people would feel overwhelmed by this situation.

Client: Well, that's good to hear. But I've got to do something.

Therapist: Let me see if I understand. Are you saying that you want to find a way to be less overwhelmed, or that you want to change the situation in some way, or it is perhaps something else?

Client: Well, actually, it's all of the above. I mean, my mom isn't going to get better. But I can't go on like this. I just can't (tearfully).

Therapist: Well, there is a strange question that sometimes helps in situations like this. I have to warn you, though, that it's a pretty weird question. Is it okay if I ask you this strange question?

Client: Okay.

Therapist: Well, let's suppose that tonight you go home and you eat dinner, I suppose, perhaps watch some television, things like that—the sorts of things you would normally do on a night like this. (Client nods.) And eventually it gets dark outside, and you do the usual things that you would do to get ready for bed. It gets later, and eventually the house is quiet and your mom is sleeping and eventually you fall asleep, too. And sometime during the night, something really strange happens while you are sleeping: a sort of miracle, but not just any kind of miracle, because in this case, the miracle is that you have found a way to cope with or alter this situation with your mom that really satisfies you. So let's suppose it's now the morning after the miracle, and you wake up and, of course, because you were sleeping, you don't know that the miracle has happened. What would be the very first thing that you would notice that would tell you that something is different—that a miracle has happened and things are better?

Client: Gee, I really don't know. (Long pause while client looks down. Then she stares into the distance and begins speaking.) Well, the first thing is I would be glad to wake up. I would be looking forward to the day.

Therapist: How would that show up?

Client: I would get right up, put on some sort of outfit that had some color in it, and well, I would be able to do that because I would have my laundry done.

Therapist: So you would have an outfit ready, and it would be colorful. Then what?

Client: Well, my mom would still be there, I suppose, but I wouldn't be mad at her. I wouldn't resent her for being in my house. I mean, it isn't her fault that she has Alzheimer's. So I would fix coffee for both of us, and I'd let the dogs out, and maybe she and I would go out and have our breakfast out on the back porch if the weather was nice. You know, a couple of muffins or some fruit, something like that.

Therapist: Sounds kind of nice . . .

Client: Well, actually, it's pretty where I live. We have this really pretty view from the back porch.

Therapist: So what else?

Client: Well, then I wouldn't have to go to work because this is a miracle, right? (laughs)

Therapist: What would you do instead?

Client: I guess I would go take a walk, only I couldn't do this with my mom. I guess, well, I don't want to say that she wouldn't be there, but if she wasn't there, maybe I could take a walk.

Therapist: So you would take a walk—that's part of your miracle. What else?

Client: Well, after the walk, I would call my friend. I haven't talked to my friend for almost a month.

Therapist: You'd call your friend. I wonder what you would talk about.

Client: Well, I wouldn't be complaining about my mother, and I wouldn't be complaining about my weight.

Therapist: I wonder what you would be doing instead.

Client: Well, this is a miracle, so I would have lost the weight the doctor told me to lose.

Therapist: So the extra weight would be gone. And what else?

Client: Well, I would be going out at night sometimes, maybe even a date.

Therapist: Dating?

Client: Yes.

Therapist: Anything else?

Client: Not really. I mean, I suppose I would have lots of money, but other than that. . . . I don't know. (Looks down at floor, sighs.) My life is pretty far from that right now I guess.

Therapist: Let me see if I understand. I want you to imagine a scale. (Picks up a pen and draws a line and numbers on piece of paper.) At one end is a 1, and that represents this problem at its worst, and 10 means that you are coping with it and responding to it the best anyone could ever imagine. In fact, you are managing to live as if this miracle really has happened. Where would you say you are now on the scale? (Therapist hands the pen to the client, who draws a dot slightly to the left of the middle point of the line.)

Client: I would say that I'm at a 4.

Therapist: A 4. How come a 4 and not a 3 or a 2?

Client: Well, I do have somebody coming in twice a week, and I probably could also get my sister to come over or take Mom to her house one of the weekend nights. I mean she has offered. . . .

Therapist: So that's something you might be able to do? Do you think it would make a difference if you were able to do that?

Client: Well, yeah, probably. I would probably go up on the scale if I knew that I could go out on the weekends even one night. Of course, I would have to find someone to go out with. I mean, so many of my friends have kids, or husbands. . . .

Therapist: Assuming you did, that would be something that would make a difference?

Client: Yeah. I guess that would make me . . . something like a 4½.

Therapist: It would make a difference. Hmm, I'm wondering. I know that 10 would be the ideal—you know, the miracle version. What do you think would be the lowest number that would be tolerable—I mean reasonably satisfactory. Would it be 10, or would it be a bit lower do you think?

Client: Are you kidding? I'd be happy with a 7.

Therapist: Really? Tell me what a 7 would look like.

Client: Well, I would have lost ten pounds, my laundry would be done, I would have plans for the weekend and someone to watch Mom, and I would have a cleaning lady one day a week who would also watch Mom, and I would have some plans in place with my sister for what we need to do if we ever get to the point when Mom starts to deteriorate more mentally, if I can't keep her at home.

Therapist: That seems like quite a lot to me. Is that all part of the 7?

Client: Well, I guess it would be an 8.

Therapist: I see . . . I'm going to take a short break to think about everything we talked about, and then I'll come back. But before I do that, is there anything else I should have asked or that you think would be important for me to know?

Client: I don't think so.

Therapist: Okay, I'll be back in 10 minutes.

BREAK

Therapist (re-enters room): Hello again. I spent some time thinking hard about everything you said. I wrote some things down so I wouldn't forget them.

Client: Really? (Looks curious.)

Therapist: Here's what I came up with. May I read it to you?

Client: Of course.

Therapist: Well, the first thing that came to mind was what a remarkable woman you are: managing to hold down a job, caring for an aging mother with Alzheimer's, and then also with two dogs that you also take care of. And the fact that you have friends tells me that other people see something in you, too—perhaps some of the same qualities I see, perhaps different ones. And at the same time, there's something very practical about you. You have this practical quality. You recognized that things at home are hard, that there's a lot of stress, and you decided to come and see someone to try to work out a way to cope in the best way possible. You decided to take action.

Client: Well, actually, I *am* very practical. My mom was always very practical. She had to be. She raised us alone. And I'm kind of like her a little bit that way, I guess, although when I was younger, I didn't ever want to think I was like my mom. God no! But I don't think that's what my friends see. I think they probably see a different side of me. Probably they think I'm really strong and I have a good sense of humor.

Therapist: Oh, you do? Well, I can actually, I can imagine that. . . . I bet they would have a lot to say about what you do that makes them think you are strong.

Client: Oh yeah, I suppose. Well, maybe. (She smiles, looking somewhat embarrassed.)

Therapist: Anyway, I was thinking that perhaps if you wanted to, it might be a good idea in the next week to keep track of anything that you do that helps you move even a little bit in the direction of that 8. What do you think?

Client: Okay. I'll give it a try.

Session 2: One week later

The client said that she had gotten her sister and brother-in-law to care for her mother the previous Saturday night and gone to a movie by herself, because none of her friends were available. She and her mother had enjoyed breakfast on the back porch on two occasions. She had also contacted the local Weight Watchers organization and was thinking of going. When the therapist asked if she'd found anything additional that was helpful, the client answered that it helped to remember all the things that her mother had done for her when she was a little girl, because remembering this made her feel love rather than resentment toward her mother. She rated herself at a 4 1/2. The therapist complimented her and invited her to continue to do what she was doing.

Session 3: Two weeks later

The client said she had joined Weight Watchers. She was frustrated, saying that she had now given up one of her few pleasures: eating chocolate at night while watching television. Her mother had been difficult and angry on two occasions. Nevertheless, the client again rated herself at 4 1/2. The therapist asked how she was managing to cope to the degree she was and maintain the 4 1/2, and the client said that the fact that she was doing something about her weight helped.

Session 4: Two weeks later

The client rated herself at a 5. She had lost three pounds. She was exploring the possibility of adult day care for her mother on the days when the caretaker did not come to the house. She said it had been a "pretty good week." The therapist complimented her on her weight loss and for taking the initiative to find out about adult day care programs.

Session 5: Three weeks later

The client rated herself at a 6 1/2. She ascribed this to losing weight, discussing with her sister long-term care options for her mother, and generally feeling "less alone" with the situation. She was still looking into day-care possibilities. She said she felt less resentful about her situation, although sometimes she did feel sorry for herself. The therapist normalized that this was, in fact, a situation that most people would find challenging. The therapist wondered aloud what might raise the scale even a little bit. The client said she really had no idea, but she would think about it. She said that she felt that things were going "relatively okay" and decided to come back in a month.

Session 6: Four weeks later

The client came in smiling. She was visibly thinner and had a new haircut. She brought a photograph of her mother. Her sister and brother-in-law had cared for her mother the previous weekend, and she had taken a trip to a nearby city with a friend. She rated herself at a 6 3/4. Her sister had agreed to take her mother one weekend a month so that the client could have some respite, and the client said that while it was still a hard situation, she was feeling better. Also, she was going to the local YMCA and swimming after work one day a week, and she thought that had made some difference, too. She was also going to some social activities as part of her church, to which she was able to bring her mother as well. These things together had contributed to her rating herself at 6 3/4. She decided that although she had originally set the goal at 7, in fact, 6 3/4 was good enough and she could terminate therapy for the time being. She said that she would telephone for a follow-up appointment if she began to slip below 5 on the scale.

Update

Three years later, the therapist ran into the client at a local grocery store. After they exchanged a brief greeting, the client told the therapist that she and her sister had eventually had to put her mother in a nursing home but that she was glad she had been able to take care of her at home as long as possible. Looking back on it, even though it had been really hard at times, it had really meant a lot to her to be able to give something back to her mother after all her mother had done for her.

The therapist complimented her saying "I wonder how you got to be such a kind, loving, and generous person?"

The client paused for a moment before she answered with a soft, knowing, half-smile smile, "Probably I got that from my mother." Then while still standing in the grocery store aisle, the client reached out and briefly hugged the therapist, who naturally hugged her back. Then they said good bye.

Taking a Break and Giving Feedback

Solution-focused therapy is often practiced in a team approach, with a therapist in the session and colleagues observing behind the mirror. Whether working with a team or alone, the interviewing therapist usually takes a ten-minute break near the end of the session. During this time, the therapist (with the team or alone) composes a summary message to the clients.

Building on the solution-focused idea that it is the clients who do the real work, Sharry, Madden, Darmody, and Miller (2001) describe how the session break can be used to promote a collaborative mindset:

We're nearing the end of the session and I'd like to take a ten-minute break. This is to give you time to think and reflect about what we have discussed; to pick out any important ideas that came up, or to make decisions or plans. You might also like to think about whether this session has been useful and how you would like us to be further involved, if that would be helpful. While you're thinking, I will consult with my team for their thoughts. We will think together about what you said. When we get back together, I'll be interested to hear what stood out for you today. I'll also share the teams' thoughts with you. Together, then, we can put something together that will be helpful. (pp. 71–72)

When the therapist returns, the first priority is to seek the views of the clients in evaluating the session and constructing a plan of action. At this point, the clients are usually eager to hear what the therapist thinks, and they may be especially receptive to reframing and suggestions.

The goal of the summary message is to provide a more hopeful perspective on the problem and to engender positive expectations. The summary message begins with a recap of what the therapist heard the clients say during the interview, including the problem, its background, the clients' goals, and presession progress and strengths: "What I heard you tell me today, Mr. and Mrs. X, is that . . ." "Did I hear all of you correctly?" "Is there anything of importance that I omitted or that you want to add?"

This recap is followed by a statement reflecting the therapist's reaction, including an expression of empathy ("I'm not surprised you're so depressed!"), a reflection of the emotional impact on the client ("My sense is that you must really be hurting"), compliments on presession changes or strengths ("I was impressed by how many things you've tried to make things better"), and some comment on the clients' shared goals.

The therapist then makes suggestions about building on positives: "I would suggest that you notice what Patrick is doing at school that you want him to continue doing." "Patrick, I would suggest that you try to notice what's happening at school with the kids and your teacher that you like and want to continue to have happen."

Among the suggestions used commonly in solution-focused therapy are the following:

1. *The formula first-session task* (de Shazer, 1985). "Between now and next time we meet, I would like you to observe what happens in your family that you want to continue to have happen."

2. *Do more of what works.* "Since you said that you usually can talk together when you go for a walk, maybe you should try that once or twice and see what happens."

3. *Do something different.* "You mentioned that when you rely on Janine to be responsible for her own homework, she often fails to do it. Maybe you should try something different?" If a client says, "I've said the same thing over and over again until I'm blue in the face," the suggestion to try something different invites the client to discover his or her own solution. The suggestion to do something different can be given as an experiment, as illustrated by Insoo Berg's example of parents who were exasperated by their son's encopresis. When given the suggestion to try something different, they started filling the boy's potty seat with water and a toy boat and telling him that his job was to sink the boat (Berg & Dolan, 2001). It worked!

4. *Go slow.* This suggestion, taken from the MRI model, is designed to help clients overcome fear and resistance to change by asking about possible negative consequences of changing and warning against trying to change too rapidly. "I have what may seem like a strange question: Could there possibly be any advantages to things staying the way they are?"

5. *Do the opposite.* This suggestion, also taken from the MRI model, is based on the notion that many problems are maintained by the attempted solution. Suggesting that clients try the opposite of what they have been doing is especially useful for problems that exist between just two people (one member of a couple or one parent who's having trouble with a child). If scolding a child for being bad isn't working, parents can be encouraged to start praising him or her for being good. If a husband's attempt to avoid conversations with his wife about "the relationship" aren't working, he could try initiating them when he's in the mood.

6. *The prediction task* (de Shazer, 1988). "Before you go to bed tonight, predict whether the problem will be better or the same tomorrow. Tomorrow night rate the day and compare it with your prediction. Think about what may have accounted for the right or wrong prediction. Repeat this every night until we meet again."

As you can see, the compliments and suggestions of the summation message continue the basic thrust of the solution-focused approach, drawing attention to the family's resources and encouraging them to capitalize on their strengths in order to focus on solutions rather than problems.

Later Sessions

Later sessions are devoted to finding, amplifying, and measuring progress. When a family returns for a subsequent session, the solution-focused therapist endeavors to create a cooperative set and then inquires about progress, seeking detailed descriptions of any movement toward the family's goal and the clients' role in attaining it. Then the therapist assists the clients in looking forward to how they will plan their next prosolution steps:

> "What's better?" or "What happened that you liked?"
> "Tell me more. Walk me through how the two of you did that."
> "Wow! That sounds great. What part did you especially enjoy?"
> "And what else is better? So what do you think the next step might be? On a scale of 1 to 10, you say your progress is now at a 5. What would a 6 look like?"

If there was no discernable progress, coping questions may be asked:

> "How did you keep things from getting worse?"
> "What's your idea about what might be helpful?"
> "What do you think the next step should be?"

"Sure, If You Tell Them We Did Most of the Work." To illustrate the process of solution-focused therapy with couples, we will summarize a case reported by Michael Hoyt (2002). Frank, age twenty-nine, and Regina, thirty, had been living together for seven months, and for the last three months since Regina had been pregnant, all they seemed to do was argue.

Case Study

Session 1

The therapist began by saying, "Welcome. The purpose of our meeting is briefly to work together to find a solution to whatever brings you here today. What's up?"

Regina said she was tired of all their arguing. Lately, it seemed as if all she and Frank did was fight.

Frank responded to Regina's complaints by saying, "Everything's all my fault, huh?"

After a few more minutes of bickering, the therapist broke in to say, "Wait a minute! You came here because you want things to be better, don't you?" They nodded. "That's why you're here. You used to get along, so you know *how to*. It seems you came here because you want some help figuring out how to get back to being happy, right?"

They agreed but without much enthusiasm.

The therapist then asked each of them to rate where their relationship was now on a scale from 1 (horrible) to 10 (great). They both gave it a 2.

"Okay," said the therapist. "That gives us some room to work." Then he asked what each of them would have to do to move their level of satisfaction up to a 3 or a 4.

Neither of them had any ideas. So he asked the miracle question: "Suppose tonight, while you're sleeping, a miracle happens . . . and the problems that brought you here are solved! Tomorrow when you wake up, what would be some of the things you'd notice that would tell you that 'Hey, things are better?'"

They both laughed.

Then Regina said, "We'd be getting along, not hassling."

"Yeah," Frank said, "we'd talk, and she wouldn't get so mad at me."

The therapist moved quickly to concretize this goal. "You'd be getting along. What will you be saying and doing?"

In the discussion that followed, the couple described their meeting and courtship, an enjoyable vacation they'd taken, and their hopes for raising a happy child together. When they slipped back into arguing, the therapist redirected them toward their positive experiences. With prompting—"When was the last time you got along okay, even for a few minutes?"—the couple identified some recent moments when things were briefly good between them. The therapist asked numerous questions to expand on those exceptions, and the conversation gradually took on a more optimistic quality.

As the session drew toward a close, the therapist asked whether the meeting had been helpful and, if so, how. The couple agreed that it was helpful to talk without arguing and to be reminded about how they used to get along well. The therapist complimented them for coming in, describing it as an indication of their caring for each other and their desire to make a happy home for their baby. He then asked if they wanted to make another appointment. They did. He offered them a homework assignment to observe whatever they both do to make things better: "It may not be perfect, but try to keep track of whatever positives you or your partner do or attempt to do."

Session 2

In the second session, Frank and Regina said that they'd had a couple of really good days. The therapist complimented them and asked, "How did you do that?" However, they then described an argument that had ensued one evening when Frank came home late from work. The therapist interrupted and said that he had made a mistake. He went on to say that while some therapists try to figure out what people are doing wrong, his approach was to help them figure out what they're doing right and then help them do more of it.

Frank then said that the day after their fight, Regina had called him at work and apologized. "I know I was wrong for being late, but it really hurt my feelings the way she yelled at me."

"She called and apologized?"

"Yeah. I really appreciated it, too."

"You called?"

Thus, even though Frank and Regina were still upset about their argument, the therapist was able to help them focus on how they'd made a constructive effort to get past it. Having helped them recover more positive feelings about each other, he went on to ask them what they appreciated about each other and how they showed it.

Frank acknowledged that when his feelings got hurt, he withdrew, which only served to make Regina more angry. Here, he was moving from a complainant to a customer.

The therapist then asked the couple for their ideas about how to handle tense situations better, and they discussed these and role-played a couple of examples.

At the end of the session, the therapist complimented Regina and Frank again for their efforts and suggested that they keep track of the things that happen that they wanted to continue to happen. When asked when they would like to return, they said three weeks, which would give them time to practice.

Session 3

The couple began the third session by describing a series of positive things each of them had been doing. Regina appreciated Frank's increased help around the house, and he beamed at this praise. They each rated the relationship now as between a 5 and a 6.

The couple did, however, have one significant argument when they were buying things for the new baby's room. Regina was annoyed that Frank wasn't more enthusiastic, and he in turn felt that she didn't appreciate all the compromises and adjustments he was making. Rather than pursue the feelings behind these complaints, the therapist asked for examples of times when the couple had compromised successfully: "What did you do differently during those times you coped constructively with your frustration?" This redirection helped them to think more about how they were able to work together when they didn't let their hurt and anger get the best of them.

The homework assignment this time was to keep track of whatever either of them did that showed they were working together. The therapist also suggested that they each pick a fun outing to do together.

Session 4

The fourth session occurred three weeks later. The couple said it had been the best three weeks since Regina got pregnant. The therapist offered compliments ("Wow!") and asked for details to help them focus on the constructive things they'd done. At this point, Regina rated the relationship a 9, and Frank said 10. The therapist congratulated them on their teamwork, and they scheduled a follow-up session three weeks later.

Session 5

In the fifth session, Regina complained about feeling tired. Frank was also feeling tired from working overtime, but he was able to express sympathy and support for Regina. They agreed that they had continued doing well and had even thought of canceling the session, but they decided to come in to review their progress and talk about how to keep it going. As the couple talked about what they had accomplished, the therapist offered compliments about all the constructive things they reported.

The therapist then asked them how they would remember to work as a team if their problems once again got them down in the future. They replied that they knew they'd have problems in the future but that they'd learned that they can solve their problems. "Now when we start to have an argument, we stop and remember . . . what we've talked about in here—how to use what you called 'solution talk,' how we used to fight, and how we know how to treat each other respectfully, and how to take time out if we need it, and how to listen to each other, and stuff like that."

When the therapist asked whether they wanted to make another appointment, they said not now but that they would call if they needed one.

"I wished them well and asked whether it would be OK for me to write up their story and put it in a book chapter. 'Sure,' they said, 'but only if you promise to tell people that we did most of the work.'"

EVALUATING THERAPY THEORY AND RESULTS

Judging by its popularity, solution-focused therapy may be the treatment for our times. Now one of the most widely used psychotherapy approaches in the world (Trepper, Dolan, McCollum, & Nelson, 2006), its promise of quick solutions has endeared it to the managed care industry, and providers have been eager to identify themselves as solution focused. Its pragmatic focus on coping rather than curing has made it applicable to almost any problem seen by therapists. Its applications include couples therapy (e.g., Hoyt & Berg, 1998; Hudson & O'Hanlon, 1992; Murray & Murray, 2004); family therapy (e.g., Campbell, 1999; McCollum & Trepper, 2001); domestic violence (Lipchik & Kubicki, 1996); sexual abuse (Dolan, 1991); alcoholism

(e.g., Berg & Miller, 1992; de Shazer & Isebaert, 2003); sex therapy (Ford, in press); and schizophrenia (Eakes, Walsh, Markowski, Cain & Swanson, 1997). In addition, there has been a spate of self-help books written from a solution-focused perspective (e.g., Dolan, 1998; O'Hanlon, 1999; Weiner-Davis, 1992). The solution-focused model has also been applied outside of traditional therapeutic practice to include interventions in social service agencies (Pichot & Dolan, 2003); nursing care (Tuyn, 1992); educational settings and model schools (Franklin & Streeter, 2004; Rhodes & Ajmal, 1995); and business systems (Berg & Cauffman, 2002).

What besides its remarkably appealing name has made solution-focused therapy so popular? It is brief and pragmatic, but then so are many other approaches to family therapy. Perhaps the two most powerful ingredients in solution-focused therapy are building on what works and helping people identify what they want rather than what they don't want.

Searching for exceptions turns out to be a simple but powerful intervention. The clients who come to us for help often think of the times when their problems don't occur as unimportant because these occasions seem accidental or inconsistent. Calling attention to past successes and latent abilities helps people rediscover their own best coping strategies. Unlike therapists from other approaches, solution-focused therapists don't teach clients *what to do*; they help them remember *what they already know how to do*.

The miracle question, which can sound like just another gimmick when you first read about it, is also a powerful tool, tapping as it does that wonderful human capacity not just to see things as they are but to imagine things as they might be. One of the great things about the imagination is that with very limited encouragement, people can see themselves as succeeding rather than fumbling and failing (Singer, 1981). What makes this kind of positive thinking more than empty optimism is that in the solution-focused therapist, clients have a coach and guide to help them work toward this brighter future. The problem-solving mindset that helps people move in the direction of their intentions may be especially suited to working in clinic settings with clients who often feel overwhelmed by their circumstances.

To critics, solution-focused therapy has seemed simplistic, and its emphasis on solution talk instead of problem talk has been seen as manipulative. Like any approach in the early stages of evolution, solution-focused therapy has sometimes been presented in a cookbook style, leading some to imagine that treatment can be reduced to a set of formulaic techniques.

Is it true that all you have to do in therapy is ask the miracle question and then talk about times when the problem wasn't a problem? No, of course not. With any new model of therapy, there is a tendency to emphasize what is distinctive—in this case, the miracle question, the search for exceptions, scaling questions, and compliments. The unique features of solution-focused therapy are deceptively easy to describe, but like all therapies, it takes great skill to implement effectively.

A second major criticism of solution-focused therapy is that its insistence on solution talk may cut off clients from empathy and understanding. People want to tell their stories. When they come to therapy, they want someone to understand their problems and be willing to help solve them. Reassuring someone who's worried that there's nothing to worry about isn't very reassuring. It can make you believe that your feelings aren't valid, because you wouldn't have them if you would only look at the bright side of things. Most people aren't very eager to be changed by someone they feel doesn't understand them.

The issue of whether solution-focused therapy is genuinely collaborative has been raised frequently (Efran & Schenker, 1993; Efron & Veendendaal, 1993; Miller, 1994; Nylund & Corsiglia, 1994; O'Hanlon, 1996; Storm, 1991; Wylie, 1990). This approach has even been called "solution-forced therapy" by some people because of the perceived tendency for therapists to pressure clients into discussing only the positive while aggressively disregarding anything negative. As Efran and Schenker (1993) ask, "What assurance is there that clients of solution-focused therapists haven't simply learned to keep their complaints to themselves in the presence of the therapist?"

More recently, solution-focused therapists have stressed the importance of the therapeutic relationship. Eve Lipchik, for example, said, "The speed and success of solution construction depend on the therapist's ability to stay connected with the clients' reality throughout the course of therapy. This is the underpinning for the whole collaborative process, the grease that keeps the axles turning" (Friedman & Lipchik, 1999, p. 329). Like any other therapy, the solution-focused approach won't likely be effective if therapists, in a rush to get to their own agenda, fail to listen to clients and make them feel understood.

Considering the popularity of solution-focused therapy, it's unfortunate that more research hasn't been done to test its effectiveness. Thus far, most of the research has been conducted by solution-focused practitioners themselves. Initial follow-up studies conducted by de Shazer and his colleagues at the Brief Therapy Center in Milwaukee involved surveying clients about their progress and found good success rates (e.g., De Jong & Hopwood, 1996; de Shazer, 1985; de Shazer et al., 1986). More recently, de Shazer and Isebaert (2003) published a follow-up report on male alcoholics who received solution-focused therapy in a hospital setting in Belgium. Of 118 patients contacted by phone four years postdischarge, 84 percent were judged to be improved. When possible, contacts with family members were used to confirm the patients' reports.

In a systematic review of outcome research on solution-focused therapy, Gingerick and

Eisengart (2000) reviewed fifteen controlled outcome studies and judged five of these to be well controlled. Four of these studies found solution-focused therapy better than no treatment controls or treatment as usual, and the fifth found solution-focused therapy equally effective with interpersonal psychotherapy for depression. The less well-controlled studies also generally supported solution-focused therapy. Gingerich and Eisengart concluded by saying that the studies they reviewed provide preliminary support for solution-focused therapy.

SUMMARY

Solution-focused therapy takes the elegance of the MRI model and turns it on its head: While the one aims to help clients do less of what doesn't work, the other promotes more of what does. Both of these pragmatic approaches focus on the presenting complaint and aim to resolve it as quickly as possible. The MRI model does so by looking for failed solutions to eliminate, and the solution-focused approach searches for forgotten solutions to rediscover.

An additional difference between these models is that while the MRI approach focuses on behavior, the solution-focused model emphasizes cognition as well as behavior. MRI therapists urge clients to *do* things differently; solution-focused therapists urge them to *view* things differently (Shoham, Rohrbaugh, & Patterson, 1995). Problems are seen as persisting in the way people define situations and in the misdirected actions they persist in taking. The idea is that people often get stuck in their problems because by trying to get to the bottom of them, they overlook solutions that are right under their noses.

This notion has led to the development of a set of techniques for changing problem talk into solution talk. These techniques include asking exception questions ("Can you think of a time when you didn't have the problem? What were you doing then?"); miracle questions ("Suppose you went to sleep and a miracle happened such that when you awoke, your problem was solved. What would be different?"); scaling questions ("On a scale from 1 to 10, how do you feel now compared to when you called?"); coping questions ("Given how bad that was, how were you able to cope?"); the formula first-session task ("After you leave today, observe what happens that you want to continue during the next week."); and giving compliments ("Wow, you must be very smart to have thought of that!"). These techniques are put into practice as soon as possible to keep the work brief and to discourage clients from dwelling on the negative side of their experience.

More recently, therapists have questioned the emphasis on technique and speculated that qualities of the therapist–client relationship may be at the heart of the model's effectiveness. This has led to a call for greater collaboration with clients so that their feelings are acknowledged and validated before solution-focused techniques are introduced.

Solution-focused therapy continues to have enormous appeal in the world of psychotherapy. Some of its popularity relates to the number of therapists who are struggling to find ways to feel effective while living with managed care's limited number of sessions. In addition, the techniques of solution-focused therapy are relatively easy to learn; the basics can be picked up in a few workshops. The upbeat nature of this approach also makes it more enjoyable for many therapists, yet its easy-to-learn formula leads some therapists to dismiss it as superficial once they get stuck. They don't understand that the techniques only work within the context of the solution-oriented philosophy, which takes time to assimilate.

Critics question whether therapists are really having a respectful conversation with clients when they only praise, search for exceptions, and coaxes optimism. Does such insistently upbeat dialogue have the effect of silencing people's doubts and pain? Can solution-focused therapists find ways to honor client perceptions that don't fit the formula? Can clients trust the feedback of therapists who never challenge or question them? Can clients be honest regarding the outcome of their therapy with therapists who seem to want so much for them to feel better about things?

Other questions highlight the model's strengths. For example, isn't it important for therapists to have clear, concrete guidelines so therapy doesn't become vague and directionless? Isn't it more empowering to help people envision their future goals and focus on their strengths than on their problems and deficits? If people's experience of pain is tied to the way they think or talk about it, then isn't it better to use language that will lead people out of pain rather than to dwell on it?

RECOMMENDED READINGS

de Shazer, S. 1988. *Clues: Investigating solutions in brief therapy.* New York: Norton.

de Shazer, S. 1991. *Putting difference to work.* New York: Norton.

de Shazer, S., Dolan, Y., Korman, H., Trepper, T., Berg, I. K., and McCollum, E. 2007. *More than miracles: The state of the art of solution-focused brief therapy.* Binghamton, NY: Haworth Press.

Dolan, Y. 1991. *Resolving sexual abuse: Solution-focused therapy and Ericksonian hypnosis for adult survivors.* New York: Norton.

Lipchik, E. 2002. *Beyond technique in solution-focused therapy.* New York: Guilford Press.

Miller, S., Hubble, M., and Duncan, B. 1996. *Handbook of solution-focused brief therapy.* San Francisco: Jossey-Bass.

Walter, J., and Peller, J. 1992. *Becoming solution-focused in brief therapy.* New York: Brunner/Mazel.

REFERENCES

Berg, I. K. 1994a. A wolf in disguise is not a grandmother. *Journal of Systemic Therapies.* 13:13–14.

Berg, I. K. 1994b. *Family-based services: A solution-focused approach.* New York: Norton.

Berg, I. K., and Cauffman, L. 2002. Solution focused corporate coaching. *Lernende Organisation.* Janner/Februar: 1–5.

Berg, I. K., and de Shazer, S. 1993. Making numbers talk: Language in therapy. In *The new language of change,* S. Friedman, ed. New York: Guilford Press.

Berg, I. K., and Dolan, Y. 2001. *Tales of solutions: A collection of hope-inspiring stories.* New York: Norton.

Berg, I., and Miller, S. 1992. *Working with the problem drinker: A solution-focused approach.* New York: Norton.

Campbell, J. 1999. Creating the "tap on the shoulder": A compliment template for solution-focused therapy. *American Journal of Family Therapy.* 27:35–47.

De Jong, P., and Berg, I. K. 2002. *Interviewing for solutions,* 2nd ed. Pacific Grove, CA: Brooks/Cole.

De Jong, P., and Hopwood, L. E. 1996. Outcome research on treatment conducted at the Brief Family Therapy Center. In *Handbook of solution-focused brief therapy,* S. D. Miller, M. A. Hubble, and B. L. Duncan, eds. San Francisco: Jossey-Bass.

de Shazer, S. 1984. The death of resistance. *Family Process.* 23:11–21.

de Shazer, S. 1985. *Keys to solutions in brief therapy.* New York: Norton.

de Shazer, S. 1986. An indirect approach to brief therapy. In *Indirect approaches in therapy,* S. de Shazer and R. Kral, eds. Rockville, MD: Aspen Systems.

de Shazer, S. 1988. *Clues: Investigating solutions in brief therapy.* New York: Norton.

de Shazer, S. 1991a. Muddles, bewilderment, and practice theory. *Family Process. 30*:453–458.

de Shazer, S. 1991b. *Putting difference to work.* New York: Norton.

de Shazer, S., and Berg, I. K. 1993. Constructing solutions. *Family Therapy Networker. 12*:42–43.

de Shazer, S., and Isebaert, L. 2003. The Bruges Model: A solution-focused approach to problem drinking. *Journal of Family Psychotherapy. 14*:43–52.

de Shazer, S., Dolan, Y., Korman, H., Trepper, T., Berg, I. K., and McCollum, E. 2007. *More than miracles: The state of the art of solution-focused brief therapy.* Binghamton, NY: Haworth Press.

de Shazer, S., Berg, I. K., Lipchik, E., Nunnally, E., Molnar, A., Gingerich, W., et al. 1986. Brief therapy: Focused solution development. *Family Process. 25*:207–221.

Dolan, Y. 1991. *Resolving sexual abuse: Solution-focused therapy and Ericksonian hypnosis for survivors.* New York: Norton.

Dolan, Y. 1998. *One small step: Moving beyond trauma and therapy to a life of joy.* Watsonville, CA: Papier-Mache Press.

Eakes, G., Walsh, S., Markowski, M., Cain, H., and Swanson, M. 1997. Family-centered brief solution-focused therapy with chronic schizophrenics: A pilot study. *Journal of Family Therapy. 19*:145–158.

Efran, J., and Schenker, M. 1993. A potpourri of solutions: How new and different is solution-focused therapy? *Family Therapy Networker. 17*(3):71–74.

Efron, D., and Veenendaal, K. 1993. Suppose a miracle doesn't happen: The non-miracle option. *Journal of Systemic Therapies. 12*:11–18.

Ford, J. J. In press. Solution-focused sex therapy for erectile dysfunction. *Journal of Couple and Relationship Therapy.*

Franklin, C., and Streeter, C. L. 2004. *Solution-focused alternatives for education: An outcome evaluation of Gaza High School.* Report available from the author at www.utexas.edue/ssw/faculty/franklin.

Friedman, S., and Lipchik, E. 1999. A time-effective, solution-focused approach to couple therapy. In *Short-term couple therapy*, J. M. Donovan, ed. New York: Guilford Press.

Furman, B., and Ahola, T. 1992. *Solution talk: Hosting therapeutic conversations.* New York: Norton.

Gingerich, W. J., and Eisengart, S. 2000. Solution-focused brief therapy: A review of the outcome research. *Family Process. 39*:477–498.

Hoyt, M. F. 2002. Solution-focused couple therapy. In *Clinical handbook of couple therapy*, 3rd ed., A. S. Gurman and N. S. Jacobson, eds. New York: Guilford Press.

Hoyt, M. F., and Berg, I. K. 1998. Solution-focused couple therapy: Helping clients construct self-fulfilling realities. In *Case studies in couple and family therapy: Systemic and cognitive perspectives*, F. M. Dattilio, ed. New York: Guilford Press.

Hudson, P., and O'Hanlon, W. H. 1992. *Rewriting love stories: Brief marital therapy.* New York: Norton.

Lipchik, E. 2002. *Beyond technique in solution-focused therapy.* New York: Guilford Press.

Lipchik, E., and Kubicki, A. 1996. Solution-focused domestic violence views: Bridges toward a new reality in couples therapy. In *Handbook of solution-focused brief therapy*, S. Miller, M. Hubble, and B. Duncan, eds. San Francisco: Jossey-Bass.

McCollum, E. E., and Trepper, T. S. 2001. *Creating family solutions for substance abuse.* New York: Haworth Press.

Miller, S. 1994. The solution-conspiracy: A mystery in three installments. *Journal of Systemic Therapies. 13*:18–37.

Murray, C. E., and Murray, T. L. 2004. Solution-focused premarital counseling: Helping couples build a vision for their marriage. *Journal of Marital and Family Therapy. 30*:349–358.

Nylund, D., and Corsiglia, V. 1994. Becoming solution-focused in brief therapy: Remembering something important we already knew. *Journal of Systemic Therapies. 13*:5–12.

O'Hanlon, W. 1996. Case commentary. *Family Therapy Networker.* January/February:84–85.

O'Hanlon, W. 1998. Possibility therapy: An inclusive, collaborative, solution-based model of psychotherapy. In *The handbook of constructive therapies*, M. H. Hoyt, ed. San Francisco: Jossey-Bass.

O'Hanlon, W. 1999. *Do one thing different: And other uncommonly sensible solutions to life's persistent problems.* New York: Morrow.

O'Hanlon, W., and Weiner-Davis, M. 1989. *In search of solutions: A new direction in psychotherapy.* New York: Norton.

Pichot, T., and Dolan, Y. 2003. *Solution-focused brief therapy: Its effective use in agency settings.* New York: Haworth Press.

Rhodes, J., and Ajmal, Y. 1995. *Solution-focused thinking in schools.* London: BT Press.

Sharry, J., Madden, B., Darmody, M., and Miller, S. D. 2001. Giving our clients the break: Applications of client-directed, outcome-informed clinical work. *Journal of Systemic Therapies. 20:*68–76.

Shoham, V., Rohrbaugh, M., and Patterson, J. 1995. Problem- and solution-focused couple therapies: The MRI and Milwaukee models. In *Clinical handbook of couple therapy*, N. S. Jacobson and A. S. Gurman, eds. New York: Guilford Press.

Singer, J. L. 1981. *Daydreaming and fantasy.* Oxford: Oxford University Press.

Storm, C. 1991. The remaining thread: Matching change and stability signals. *Journal of Strategic and Systemic Therapies. 10:*114–117.

Trepper, T. S., Dolan, Y., McCollum, E. E., and Nelson, T. 2006. Steve de Shazer and the future of solution-focused therapy. *Journal of Marital and Family Therapy. 32:*133–139.

Tuyn, L. K. 1992. Solution-focused therapy and Rogerian nursing science: An integrated approach. *Archives of Psychiatric Nursing. 6:*83–89.

Walter, J., and Peller, J. 1992. *Becoming solution-focused in brief therapy.* New York: Brunner/Mazel.

Weiner-Davis, M. 1992. *Divorce-busting.* New York: Summit Books.

Wittgenstein, L. 1958. *The blue and brown books.* New York: Harper & Row.

Wylie, M. S. 1990. Brief therapy on the couch. *Family Therapy Networker. 14:*26–34, 66.

Narrative Therapy

13

Restorying Lives

The narrative approach is a perfect expression of the postmodern revolution. When all knowledge is regarded as constructed rather than discovered, it's fitting that a leading approach to family therapy is concerned with the ways people construct meaning rather than the ways they behave.

The underlying premise is that personal experience is fundamentally ambiguous. This doesn't mean that experience isn't real or that it's necessarily mysterious or opaque; rather, understanding human experience, including one's own, is never simply a matter of observing it. The elements of experience are understood only through a process that organizes those elements, puts them together, assigns meaning, and prioritizes them. To say that experience is fundamentally ambiguous is to say that its meaning isn't inherent or apparent but instead lends itself to multiple interpretations.

To illustrate how experience is shaped by the language we use to describe it, consider the difference between calling the heart-racing tension most people feel before speaking in public as "stage fright" or "excitement." The first description makes this agitation a problem, something to overcome. The second suggests that it's a natural response to standing up in front of people whose approval you hope to win.

Whether people experience anxiety or excitement depends on how they interpret their arousal. Strategic therapists give clients *reframes*, or new interpretations, for their experience: "The next time you're speaking, think of yourself as excited rather than frightened." Narrative therapists believe that such interpretations won't take unless they fit the stories people construct about themselves. A man whose life story is that he's boring will have trouble seeing his trembling hands as due to excitement, no matter how hard someone tries to convince him. If the same man were helped to construct a new, more positive story about himself, the reframe becomes unnecessary. Once he starts to think well of himself, he will expect people to appreciate what he has to say.

Unlike the cybernetic metaphor, which focused on self-defeating patterns of *behavior*, the narrative metaphor focuses on self-defeating *cognitions*—the stories people tell themselves about their problems. With the cybernetic metaphor, therapy meant blocking maladaptive interactions. The narrative metaphor, on the other hand, focuses on expanding clients' thinking to allow them to consider alternative ways of looking at themselves and their problems.

Stories don't just mirror life; they shape it. That's why people have the interesting habit of becoming the stories they tell about their experience. It's also why therapists in too much of a hurry to impose their own perspectives on clients often fail—and why, by delving into people's stories, narrative therapists are able to understand and influence what makes them act as they do.

SKETCHES OF LEADING FIGURES

Michael White, founder of the narrative movement, lived in Adelaide, Australia. He and Cheryl White were based at the Dulwich Centre, out of which came training, clinical work, and publications related to White's approach. The *International Journal of Narrative Therapy and Community Work*, a quarterly journal, is a major vehicle through which White's ideas are disseminated. In addition, the Dulwich Centre has published several collections of his writings and interviews (available by writing to Dulwich Centre Publications, Hutt Street, P.O. Box 7192, Adelaide, South Australia 5000, or through www.dulwichcentre.com.au).

White initially worked as a mechanical draftsman before realizing that he preferred working

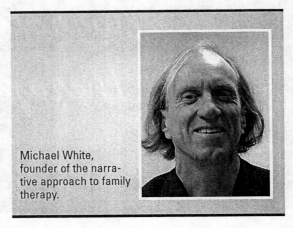

Michael White, founder of the narrative approach to family therapy.

with people to analyzing machines. Not surprisingly, he became staunchly antimechanistic and moved away from systems thinking and cybernetics. Some of his early experiences on inpatient units soured him on traditional approaches to therapy and inspired his interest in the writings of Michel Foucault and Erving Goffman, who criticized the dehumanizing impact of institutions and authoritarian experts.

In the late 1970s, White was drawn to the work of Gregory Bateson but found himself more interested in what Bateson said about how people construe the world than in the behavioral patterns of systems-based models. Under the influence of Bateson and Foucault, White developed his novel ideas about how problems affect people (regarding them as things operating on persons, rather than as things persons are doing). Sadly, Michael White died in 2008.

David Epston, a family therapist from Auckland, New Zealand, is the second most influential leader of the narrative movement. Through his interest in anthropology, Epston encountered the narrative metaphor and convinced White that it was more useful than cybernetics. He'd long had an interest in literature and for years was known as a storyteller, writing the "Story Corner" for the *Australian and New Zealand Journal of Family Therapy*.

Epston has contributed to most aspects of narrative theory and practice but in particular emphasized that for clients to maintain their new narratives, they need supportive communities. He fostered the development of self-help "leagues"—groups of clients battling similar problems, such as the Anti-Anorexia/Anti-Bulimia League of New Zealand. His coauthored book *Biting the Hand That Starves You* (Maisel, Epston, & Borden, 2004) chronicles this work. He also advocates writing letters to clients, pointing out that long after the influence of the therapist's presence has faded, clients can reread letters that bolster their new stories and resolve.

Jill Freedman and Gene Combs direct a training center in Evanston, Illinois. Before joining the narrative camp, they were strategic therapists and social activists, drawn to White's approach in large part by its political emphasis. This combination—strategic therapy and political activism—characterizes the backgrounds of many prominent narrative therapists. Freedman and Combs's book *Narrative Therapy* (1996) is an excellent guide to narrative therapy.

Jeffrey Zimmerman and Vicki Dickerson were cofounders of the Bay Area Family Therapy Training Associates and together with John Neal taught narrative therapy at the Mental Research Institute (MRI) in Palo Alto (1992–1998). These two creative therapists pioneered the use of narrative therapy with difficult adolescents and with couples (Dickerson & Zimmerman, 1992; Zimmerman & Dickerson, 1993) and also contributed *If Problems Talked: Narrative Therapy in Action* (Zimmerman & Dickerson, 1996) to the body of narrative therapy literature.

Stephan Madigan (1994; Madigan & Epston, 1995) in Vancouver, Canada, has also contributed greatly to narrative theory and is the founder of the Vancouver Anti-Anorexia/Anti-Bulimia League, a grassroots organization that provides support and encouragement to resist media images that promote "body guilt." Other prominent narrative therapists include Kaethe Weingarten, Sallyann Roth, and Bill Madsen at the Family Institute of Cambridge and Janet Adams-Wescott in Tulsa, Oklahoma.

Harlene Anderson and the late Harry Goolishian, who developed a collaborative, conversational approach to family therapy (described in Chapter 11), can be seen as forerunners of the narrative model. Their work was based on the premise that problems are maintained in language and subsequently dissolved through conversation. By adopting a "not-knowing" stance, Goolishian and Anderson subsumed their own expertise to allow clients to become the experts on their own lives. The link between this work and the narrative school was the belief that conversation generates meaning and that therapy should be a collaborative enterprise.

THEORETICAL FORMULATIONS

The narrative approach first found its way into psychotherapy in the hermeneutic tradition in psychoanalysis. Following Freud, classical analysts believed there was one correct way to interpret experience. Patients might not understand their dreams or symptoms because their motives were unconscious, but an analyst possessed of the truth of psychoanalytic theory could discover unconscious meaning, much like an archeologist uncovers the buried remains of the past.

Then in the 1980s, revisionists such as Donald Spence, Roy Schafer, and Paul Ricoeur began to argue against this positivistic conception of psychoanalytic reality. The truth of experience, they said, isn't discovered; it's created. The goal of therapy shifted from historical truth to narrative intelligibility. The challenge was to construct truths in the service of self-coherence, not to resurrect a true picture of the past. The therapist became more of an anthropologist or novelist than an archeologist.

Family therapists found this narrative metaphor extremely useful. As they began to ask clients about their stories, therapists came to recognize how much narrative accounts affected people's perceptions. Life stories function as filters that screen out experiences that don't fit the plot line or, if they can't be screened out, distort events until they somehow do fit. Consider the following example.

According to Tim, Kayla was never satisfied. All she did was complain. Their apartment, the furniture, her clothes—nothing was ever good enough. No matter what they had, she wanted more.

Case Study

Kayla had no idea what Tim was talking about. She was perfectly content. Well, except for one thing. Every time she'd see a picture in a magazine of a beautiful sofa or a pretty dress, she'd point it out to Tim. "Wow, look at that," she'd say. "Maybe we should get one of those." She was just dreaming out loud. But to Tim, who was brought up never to ask for anything, Kayla's fantasies felt like complaints. Notice, however, that it wasn't so much what Kayla said that hurt Tim, but how he interpreted it.

Looking deeper, it turned out that Tim was never satisfied with his own accomplishments. Growing up with a mother who wasn't given much to praise, Tim dreamt of someday doing great things. Unfortunately, his own very real achievements never lived up to his fantasies. Sure, other people praised him, but he still secretly dreamed the grand and glorious dreams of childhood.

Until he could begin to accept himself, it was hard for Tim to believe that anyone else could truly appreciate him. Trying to get such a man to change his behavior without addressing his controlling life story would be futile, because no matter how many successes he had, he'd still find ways to dismiss them and continue to dwell on his failures—and his partner's (presumed) dissatisfaction.

Narrative therapists believe that systems thinking encourages therapists to view families from the position of detached observers, as one might study a broken machine, without reference to its history, point of view, or environment. In contrast, narrative theory encourages therapists to see problems as located in dominant cultural narratives that influence people to think of themselves as inadequate. Thus, narrative therapists (1) take a keen interest in their clients' stories; (2) search for times in clients' histories when they saw themselves as more successful; (3) use questions to take a nonimposing, respectful approach to any new story put forth; (4) never label people but treat them as human beings with unique personal histories; and (5) help people separate from the dominant cultural narratives they have internalized so as to open space for alternative life stories (Freedman & Combs, 1996; White, 1995).

Narrative therapists oppose the functionalist elements in family systems and psychoanalytic models, which imply that problems are inherent in individuals (as psychoanalysis would have it) or families (as family systems would have it). Instead, they believe that problems arise because people are indoctrinated into narrow and self-defeating views of themselves.

To counter the way society convinces people that they are their problems, narrative therapists **externalize** problems. Instead of *having* a problem or *being* a problem, clients are encouraged to think of themselves as *struggling against* their problems. Neither the patient nor the family is the problem; the *problem* is the problem. Accordingly, narrative therapists aren't interested in problem-maintaining interactions or structural flaws. They aren't interested in the family's impact on the problem but rather in the problem's impact on the family.

As narrative therapists shifted their attention from families as the source of problems and toward cultural beliefs and practices, they turned to the writings of Michel Foucault (1965, 1980), a French social philosopher who devoted his life to exposing how social discourses objectified and dehumanized marginalized groups. Foucault not only believed that those constructing the dominant narratives in a society (those deemed to have expert knowledge) had the power to subjugate but that the narratives themselves became internalized truths, such that people judged their bodies, achievements, and personalities on the basis of standards set by society's judges (doctors, educators, clergy, psychotherapists, politicians, celebrities). Thus, Foucault influenced White to take the social constructionist axiom that there are no absolute truths in a political direction, toward deconstructing the established truths that oppress people's lives.

Narrative therapists applied Foucault's political analysis to understand how individuals and families are dominated by oppressive narratives from which they need liberation. They drew from the work of Jerome Bruner (1986, 1991) to understand how personal narratives are constructed and can be deconstructed.[1]

NORMAL FAMILY DEVELOPMENT

Narrative therapists not only avoid judgments about what is normal, they reject the very idea of categorizing people. Recall how Foucault criticized the way theories of normality were used to perpetuate patterns of privilege and oppression. Too often in human history, the judgments made by people in power regarding normality and abnormality have been used to subjugate those with no voice in the matter.

While it's easy to see the dangers of reducing people to DSM-IV diagnoses, family therapists may have trouble seeing their own concepts—such as *rigid boundaries*, *cross-generational coalitions*, and *enmeshment*—as dehumanizing. But becoming a postmodern narrative therapist means giving up all such categories. Narrative therapists avoid pigeonholing people

as normal or abnormal and reject general principles about what causes problems or what resolves them. They try not to stand over people in judgment—in any way—but instead strive to help them make sense of their own experience.

In the spirit of collaboration, narrative therapists endeavor to *situate* themselves with clients; that is, to disclose the beliefs that inform their therapy so that clients can know what they're getting into. Clients are also encouraged to educate therapists regarding their cultural predicaments and to correct them when they make assumptions that don't fit the client's experience (Freedman & Combs, 1996).

Although narrative therapists try not to make judgments, it may be impossible not to have some assumptions about people and how they change. From the ideas described in the previous section, we can distill certain basic assumptions narrative therapists make about normal families. People (1) have good intentions (they don't need or want problems); (2) are profoundly influenced by the discourses around them; (3) are not their problems; and (4) can develop alternative, empowering stories once separated from their problems and from the cultural myths they have internalized.

DEVELOPMENT OF BEHAVIOR DISORDERS

When the stories people take on lead them to construe their experience in unhelpful ways, they tend to get bogged down with problems. Such problems are likely to persist as long as these unhelpful stories remain fixed, obscuring other, more preferred, versions of events.

A single mother struggles to be everything she can be as a parent of her teenage daughter, believing that as a single mother she can never do enough. Thus, when her daughter violates her curfew, she tends to

---

[1]The term *deconstruction* is most closely associated with Jacques Derrida (1992), who analyzed literary texts to show they had no one true meaning. Narrative therapists use the term in a political way to mean subverting dominant discourses, whereas Derrida's intent was more relativistic.

react furiously. The cultural narrative about being a perfect parent makes the mother notice all the times her daughter stays out late or leaves cigarette butts on the porch and not notice the times when she gets her homework done or volunteers to wash the dishes. Each of the daughter's transgressions confirms the mother's story line that she isn't doing a good job.

The daughter, in turn, dwells on how often her mother criticizes her friends or explodes over small mistakes but doesn't remember the times her mother showed respect for her opinions or praised her achievements. The daughter gradually develops a narrative around never being able to satisfy people and becomes increasingly controlled by "rebelliousness." This makes her not care what her mother thinks and instead prompts her to indulge in whatever makes her feel better, like partying late into the night.

In short, both sides remain stuck, not simply in a pattern of control and rebellion but more specifically of noticing only incidents of control and rebellion.

This analysis might not sound all that different from one which other schools of family therapy might make for an escalating cycle of antagonism between a mother and a daughter. The difference is that the narrative approach doesn't focus on their behavior. Narrative therapists reject the cybernetic notion that the mother and daughter are stuck in a dysfunctional feedback loop—acting and reacting to each other in unhelpful ways. Instead, they concentrate on the way mother and daughter narrate their exchange. It's their *stories* (needing to be the perfect mother, being picked on) that affect not only what they notice (lateness, scolding) but also how they interpret it.

Narrative therapists refer to these patterns of tunnel vision as **problem-saturated stories**, which once they take hold, encourage people to respond to each other in ways that perpetuate the problem story. As long as parents focus on their children's misbehavior, they will concentrate on criticizing and controlling them. As long as children think of their parents as hassling them, they will likely remain reactive and rebellious. Their responses to each other become invitations to more of the same and lead to further hardening of problem stories.

Such closed and rigid narratives make people vulnerable to being overtaken by destructive emotional states that narrative therapists like to portray as alien invaders. Narrative therapists don't really see problematic feelings or beliefs as external entities, but they do believe that such emotional responses *are* external in the sense that they are socially constructed. Externalizing problems cuts down on guilt and blame. The daughter isn't the problem; "rebelliousness" is. The mother isn't the problem; "oversensitivity" is. Mother and daughter can unite to combat rebelliousness and oversensitivity rather than each other.

Instead of looking inside families for the source of their problems, narrative therapists look outside to the toxic effects of cultural narratives that govern people's lives. In Michael White's (1995) words:

> The discourses of pathology make it possible for us to ignore the extent to which the problems for which people seek therapy are the outcome of certain practices of relationship and practices of the self, many of which are actually informed by modern notions of "individualism" . . . [and] are so often mired in the structures of inequality of our culture, including those pertaining to gender, race, ethnicity, class, economics, age, and so on. (p. 115)

Anorexia nervosa, for example, can be viewed as an internalization of our culture's obsession with slenderness. By seeing women who starve themselves as having a disease or belonging to a dysfunctional family, we not only ignore the bigger picture but also avoid having to confront our own participation in cultural stereotypes.

Family arguments are fueled by negative story lines about other family members.

GOALS OF THERAPY

Narrative therapists aren't problem solvers. Instead, they help people separate themselves from problem-saturated stories and destructive cultural assumptions to open space for new and more constructive views of themselves. Narrative therapy transforms identities from flawed to preferred, not by getting family members to confront their conflicts but by separating persons from problems and then uniting the family to fight a common enemy. This is facilitated by combing the family's history for **unique outcomes,** or "sparkling events"; times when they resisted the problem or behaved in ways that contradicted the problem story.

*I*f Alice sees herself as codependent because of the way she relates to men, a narrative therapist wouldn't explore the reasons for this condition, nor would he or she give Alice suggestions for altering this pattern. Instead, the therapist would ask questions about what codependency means to Alice and come up with a name for the negative effects of these ideas on her.

If, for example, Alice says that her codependency gets her to blame herself, the therapist might ask about the effect of *Self-blame* on her life, ask family members to help her defeat *Self-blame*, and highlight times in Alice's life when she related to men in ways she prefers. The therapist might also invite Alice to consider how our society's view of women contributed to *Self-blame*'s grip on her life.

Thus, narrative therapists see their work as a political enterprise, freeing people from oppressive cultural assumptions and empowering them to become active authors of their own lives. Once liberated from problem-saturated stories, family members can unite with one another and with communities of support to deal with their problems with more optimism and persistence.

 CONDITIONS FOR BEHAVIOR CHANGE

Narrative therapists help clients *deconstruct* unproductive stories in order to *reconstruct* new and more productive ones. As noted earlier, **deconstruction**, a term borrowed from literary criticism, means questioning assumptions.

Reconstruction involves creating new and more optimistic accounts of experience. Narrative therapists use externalizing conversations to help separate persons from problems. This is one way to deconstruct disempowering assumptions. Rather than talk of "Sally's laziness," for example, they'll inquire about times when "*Procrastination* takes hold of her." Once a problem has been externalized and redefined in more experience near terms, a person can begin to resist it. By viewing the problem as an external entity, narrative therapists free families to challenge its influence on their lives.

In externalizing conversations, therapists ask "effects" questions—for instance: How does the problem affect you? Your attitudes? Your ideas about yourself? Your relationships? Through this process, the problem's field of influence is broadened so that clients can begin to notice areas of their lives where the problem has been less powerful. It is in these areas that clients can notice *unique outcomes*—experiences that would not be predicted by a telling of the problem story, times when they resisted the problem's influence. Identifying unique outcomes creates room for *counterplots*, new and more empowering ways of construing events. A man who identifies himself as depressed sees life through a glass darkly. Depression becomes a career, a lifestyle. But if the man begins to think of, say, "*Self-doubt* getting the best of him," then he may be able to remember times when he didn't let *Self-doubt* get him down. These newly recognized times of effectiveness provide openings around which to weave a new and more optimistic story.

Just as narrative therapists use externalizing conversations to shift clients' perceptions of themselves, they also endeavor to shift family members' perceptions of each other from *totalizing views* (reducing them to one set of frustrating responses) that lead to antagonism and polarization. Thus, parents who see their teenagers as "irresponsible," as though that were the sum total of their being, are likely to be seen in return as "unfair." Likewise, parents who totalize their children as "lazy" may be seen as "bossy" or "demanding." As long as both sides remain fixed in such polarized perspectives, they may be too busy to think about their own preferences. In unhappy families, people may be so busy *not* being what others expect that they have no time to figure out what they want for themselves.

Michael White set an inspiring example of seeing the best in people even when they've lost faith in themselves. He was famous for his persistence in questioning negative stories. He just wouldn't allow people to slip away into their misery. The tenacious confidence in people that narrative therapists convey with genuine respect is contagious. As clients come to trust their therapist, they can borrow that confidence and use it in dealing with their problems.

THERAPY

Assessment

A narrative assessment begins with getting the family's story, including not only their experience with their problems but also their presuppositions about those problems. Getting the family's story isn't just information gathering; it's a deconstructive inquiry, designed to move clients from passivity and defeatism toward a sense that they already have some power over the problems that plague them.

The narrative therapist approaches assessment as both an anthropologist and a hypnotist. As an anthropologist, the therapist asks, "Tell me this story. Let us see what we can make of it together." Always, the therapist conveys respect:

"What would you have preferred to happen?" "What were you hoping to accomplish here?" This anthropological investigation slides imperceptibly into a hypnotic process of asking questions to empower clients.

Once problems have been personified as alien entities, the therapist first maps the influence of the problem on the family and then maps the influence of the family on the problem. In *mapping the influence of the problem on the family*, the therapist explores the distressing impact of the problem on their lives. Clients' responses to this line of inquiry usually highlight their own sense of inadequacy.

Case Study

Alesha Jackson, a single mother of four with a live-in boyfriend, sought therapy because her four-year-old was getting into trouble at preschool. Two or three times a week Jermaine got into arguments that resulted in his hitting and biting other children. Jermaine was also a problem at home. Although he got along reasonably well with his brothers and sisters, he frequently threw tantrums when his mother tried to make him do something. Alesha sheepishly admitted that she was probably too easy on Jermaine, but she had gotten to the point where she felt helpless.

"I don't know what to do," she said. "I've tried everything. Nothing I do makes any difference. Luke, that's my boyfriend, he can make Jermaine behave, but he can get mean about it. He thinks I spoil Jermaine. Lately, Luke's been getting mad and going out after supper by himself, which leaves me all alone with the kids."

The therapist listens not just to get Alesha's story of the problem (what Jerome Bruner [1991] called "the landscape of action") but also to explore the conclusions ("the landscape of consciousness") she has drawn from her experience. The therapist asks questions like these:

"What conclusions about yourself as a mother have you drawn because of your problems with Jermaine?"

"What conclusions have you drawn about your relationship with Luke because of this problem?" (Note that it is the problem affecting the relationship, rather than the relationship causing the problem.)

This line of questioning allows Alesha to tell her unhappy story but also tries to make her aware that the problem is burdening her. Alesha begins to realize that rather than she and her family being somehow dysfunctional, they're struggling against an enemy.

In *mapping the family members' influence on the problem*, the therapist explores the extent to which they have been able to stand up to the problem's oppression. To supply this information, family members are encouraged to recognize their own competence. Questions of the following form are useful:

"How have you been able to avoid making mistakes that most people with similar problems usually make?"
"Were there times in the recent past when this problem may have tried to get the better of you and you didn't let it?"
"How did you do that?"

This mapping process not only creates a sense of empathy and understanding between the therapist and the family, but it is also an empowering experience for the family.

Case Study

Although Alesha continued to disparage her abilities as a mother, she was able to describe times when she had been firm with Jermaine and insisted that he do what he was told—"even though that boy pitched one heck of a fit!"

In this phase of the assessment, the therapist did not try to coax Alesha to be more optimistic. Rather, the therapist confined herself to helping her client remember incidents of effectiveness that didn't fit her idea of herself as being at the mercy of her problems.

We tend to think of memory as a recorder or a camera, where the past is filed and can be called up at will, but memory is none of these things. Memory is a storyteller. It creates shape and meaning by emphasizing some things and leaving others out. The narrative therapist's assessment explores two sides of the clients' memory, beginning with the problem narrative, a story of affliction (not pathology). The problem story is understood not as a personal failing but as an account of domination, alienation, and frustration. Then the therapist helps clients search their memories for the other side of the story—the side that honors their courage and persistence, the side that offers hope.

Therapeutic Techniques

Narrative interventions take the form of questions. These therapists almost never assert anything or make interpretations. They just ask question after question, following the clients' lead, often repeating the answers and writing them down.

In the first session, the therapist begins by finding out how clients spend their time. This gives the therapist a chance to appreciate how clients see themselves without getting into a lengthy history and the attributions of blame that so frequently accompany such histories. The therapist pays special attention to talents and competencies. As a further means of establishing a collaborative atmosphere, Zimmerman and Dickerson (1996) encourage clients to ask any questions they might have about the therapist: "Okay. Is there anything you would like to know about me, either professionally or as a person?"

Therapists also invite clients to read their notes if they wish. And, they often take notes as each person talks, which not only helps them retain important points but also gives clients the sense that their points of view are being respected.

Externalizing Conversations. Narrative therapists begin by asking clients to tell their problem-saturated story and listen long enough to convey their appreciation for what the family has been going through. By using externalizing language, the therapist separates the client from the problem, making its destructive effects apparent and also establishing a sense of trust with the client.

Each person is asked for his or her own perspective on the problem. The therapist asks about the problem's effects rather than its causes (causative questions usually lead to attributions of blame), mapping the influence of the problem:

"How does *Guilt* affect you?"
"What other effects does it have?"
"What does *Guilt* 'tell' you?"

The therapist's questions about the identified problem imply that it isn't possessed by the clients but instead is trying to possess them. For example, in a case where parents describe the problem as a lack of trust in their daughter because of her sneakiness, the therapist doesn't reflect back "So your daughter's sneakiness bothers you." Instead the therapist might say, "So *Sneakiness* made your daughter act in ways that caused a rift between you. Is that right?"

Sometimes patterns of interaction are externalized. For example, in a case in which a teenager's parents were responding to her sneakiness with increasing control, Vicki Dickerson chose to highlight the rift that was encouraging this pattern. One thing they could all agree on was that they didn't like the breach that was splitting them apart. Thus, instead of identifying the daughter's sneakiness or the parents' distrust as the problem, the *Rift* became the enemy. The *Rift* told the parents that their daughter couldn't be trusted; the *Rift* made the daughter more secretive and told her to pull away from her parents. The *Rift* was something they could join forces against (Zimmerman & Dickerson, 1996).

Problems are almost always personified—portrayed as unwelcome invaders that try to dominate people's lives. For example, while discussing her eating problems, a woman is asked how *Anorexia* convinces her to starve herself. A phobic child is asked how often *Fear* is able to make him do what it wants and how often he is able to stand up to it. A guilt-ridden mother is asked how *Self-hate* is making her feel bad about her parenting.

This line of questioning can be disconcerting, unaccustomed as most people are to talking about imaginary entities in their households. Therapists who treat externalization as a gimmick may lack the conviction necessary to overcome the initial awkwardness of talking this way. On the other hand, therapists will find that externalizing questions flow naturally if they actually learn to think of problems as enemies that feed on polarizations and misunderstandings. One way to get more comfortable with this way of thinking is to start using externalization as a way to think about problems in your own life. (Maybe it isn't just our clients who could benefit from a little more compassion.)

While externalization may initially be a difficult concept to embrace, it can be profoundly helpful in minimizing self-blame. For example, a woman who thinks of herself as *being* insecure or *having* insecurity has internalized the problem and come to see it as who she is. Over time, people become identified with their problems. They believe that the problem's existence is proof of their flawed character.

This way of thinking poisons confidence. When a problem is externalized, it's as if the person can peek out from behind it, and family members can see the healthier person that the problem has been hiding from them. Helping an "insecure woman" shift to seeing herself as *struggling with* Self-Criticism frees her from identifying with this problem and encourages her to discover her ability to do something about it. Michael White suggested that problems are dependent on their effects for their survival, so by standing up to a problem and not allowing it to affect them, clients cut off the problem's "life-support system."

Externalizing helps clinicians develop a more sympathetic view of clients who engage in "inappropriate behavior." For example, thinking of a woman as being captured by emotions such as fear of abandonment or rage, rather than as being histrionic or ill-tempered or having a borderline personality, makes it easier to empathize with her. You can dislike the emotional reaction rather than the client. From there, you can look for times when she was able to avoid being captured by those emotions or was able to respond differently, despite the emotions' pressure.

In the course of shifting from having a problem to having a struggle with a problem, it's important to note that problems don't exist in isolation; they are embedded in a network of support that includes polarizations in the family and assumptions from the culture. When families are in conflict over the definition of a problem—"*He's* the problem." "No, *they're* the problem!"—you can externalize the conflict. Instead of seeing themselves as struggling against each other, they can begin to see themselves as struggling against *Arguments*.

Externalizing problems that are linked to cultural expectations helps to separate problems from people and expose taken-for-granted beliefs that support those problems.

Case Study

William Madsen (2007) describes how a young woman who came to therapy complaining of depression began to talk about Self-Doubt. As she examined her experience with Self-Doubt, "Marie" described her fear of not living up to expectations: "I'm not thin enough, I'm not attractive enough, I'm not making enough money to suit my middle-class parents, and I'm not sexually satisfying to my boyfriend."

Madsen's inquiring about the *Expectations* that encouraged self-doubt helped Marie consider the pernicious effects of gender stereotypes. When asked where her life would be headed if *Expectations* were to set the direction, Marie said that *Expectations* would encourage her to "starve myself, get plastic surgery, get a job I hated to satisfy my parents, and become a sexual slave to my boyfriend." From there, she began to consider what direction she would prefer to set for her own life.

Placing *Expectations* in a larger cultural context only helped Marie escape the burden of self-loathing. In addition, doing so helped her to develop a more sympathetic view of her parents and boyfriend as also falling under the influence of *Expectations*. As Marie put it, "They're just caught up in that middle-class success thing, and he's just worried that he's not gonna be a real man without some Barbie Doll on his arm."

Sallyann Roth and David Epston (1996) developed an exercise to help therapists grasp what it's like to think of problems as external. They have a group of trainees take turns being a problem—such as *Self-hatred*—while others interview them. The interviewers might ask the person playing *Self-hatred* such questions as "Under what circumstances do you manage to get into X's world?" and "How are you intervening in the lives of X's family and friends?"

Who's in Charge, the Person or the Problem? Over many sessions, therapists ask a multitude of questions that explore how the problem has managed to disrupt or dominate the family versus how much they have been able to control it. These are called **relative influence questions**. By including all family members in the discussion, it usually becomes clear that the problem has succeeded in disturbing their relationships with each other—dividing and conquering them:

> "How much has the *Bulimia* that's taken over Jenny kept you from being the way you want to be with her?"
> "When *Depression* gets the better of Dad, how does that affect family life?"
> "When *Tantrums* convince Joey to yell and scream, do you think your response gives *Tantrums* more or less fuel?"

In explaining how he explores the relative influence of problems, John Neal (Neal, Zimmerman, & Dickerson, 1999) said:

When a man, for instance, says his wife's behavior is the problem and that its effects on him are to make him angry, we are interested in how this anger affects him and the relationship. We do not wonder what it is about him, his wife, or their respective backgrounds that gets him angry or gets her to behave in whatever way she does. We do not wonder whether his anger is "justified." Nor do we pursue whether he gets angry because of some "deeper" hurt. Instead, we explore how this anger affects his experience of himself, of his partner, and of the relationship. (p. 370)

The following vignette, showing how Neal explores the relative influence of a problem, is adapted from a case study in James Donovan's *Short-Term Couple Therapy* (Neal, Zimmerman, & Dickerson, 1999).

Case Study

John: So what's the problem you would like some help with?

Larry: Well, we have more than one problem. Let's see, certainly money is a problem, and that aggravates other problems. Communication is a problem. Sex is a problem.

John: So money is a problem, and it aggravates communication and sex?

Larry: Yes.

John: I'll want to come back and ask you more about this, but if it's okay, first I'm going to ask Elizabeth the same question. Okay? (He nods.) Elizabeth, what's your experience?

Elizabeth: All that's true. We went through some counseling before, and we made some progress. The anger got less, and we started talking. Then we just slid back into our old ways.

John: So there was a time when you were experiencing the anger as decreasing and felt some progress. Then it slid back into the way it was before?

Elizabeth: We had been given some things to focus our energy on. Given the opportunity to not focus on each other, we don't. We just get distant.

John: So together these things create *distance* between the two of you?

Elizabeth: Yes.

John: And when you notice that *distance*, how do you find it affects you?

Elizabeth: I think it's sad, and I'm not quite sure what to do. And if I know that we have to go to counseling, then I put it on the back burner and wait to bring it up here. We don't really talk to each other, unless we're going to counseling.

John: So the *distance* makes you sad and not sure what to do about it, and it gets you to put things on the back burner? Do you mean you put communication on the back burner?

Elizabeth: I put the relationship on the back burner. We can do the day-to-day stuff in a habitual way, but I don't want our relationship to be like that. It's bad, but it's better than not getting along. (She starts to cry.)

John: When the *distance* or the *arguing* take over, do they encourage you to see Larry in a certain way?

Elizabeth: Yes, I get real judgmental. He finds it insulting, but that's not what I'm trying to do. I feel real judgmental and critical. I'm wanting more from him, and I'm not getting it.

John: So you find yourself wanting more, and these feelings encourage you to see Larry in judgmental and critical ways. Do these feelings also get you to view the relationship in certain ways?

The therapist returns to the husband and continues posing "effects" questions for several more minutes. Finally, after diligently exploring the effects of the couple's problems, Neal is able to summarize their experience using externalizing language.

John: Okay, let me summarize my understanding to make sure I've got it right. Certain things are difficult to talk about that create trouble between the two of you, money being the most difficult. And the way it works is that the trouble about this creates distance—that this distance gets Larry to withdraw rather than bring things up, to kind of "check out," as Elizabeth says. And the distance puts Elizabeth in the position of not being able to bring things up, of putting the relationship on the "back burner" out of concern that if she does bring it up, she will say the wrong thing. In spite of the ways this trouble has created distance, there have been some times when the two of you have found ways to talk. Elizabeth, in spite of this, has found a way over the past few years to open up about how dealing with money is difficult. And Elizabeth, you noticed that Larry is more present at those times, right? (Both partners nod their agreement.)

Reading Between the Lines of the Problem Story. While asking relative influence questions, the therapist listens for sparkling events or unique outcomes when clients were able to avoid the problem's effects and then asks for elaboration on how that was done:

> "Can you remember a time when *Anger* tried to take you over, but you didn't let it? How did you do that?"
> "Have there been times when your daughter didn't believe the lies *Anorexia* tells her about her body?"
> "When Jenny has withstood the tremendous pressure she feels from *Alcoholism*, have you appreciated the magnitude of that accomplishment?"

These unique outcomes become the building blocks of new, more preferred stories.

In *Collaborative Therapy with Multi-stressed Families*, Bill Madsen (2007) describes his work with a

Case Study

secretary referred by her employee assistance plan after a run-in with her boss in which she became distraught and angry. Fran described herself as depressed, disorganized, and intimidated by her boss. She had trouble sleeping and couldn't focus at work.

In the first session, Fran said that she felt worthless and unlikable, an accusation supported by an abusive father and a painful history of being teased at school. Depression's hold on Fran was strong, and the few exceptions to its influence that she noticed were quickly dismissed by her as inconsequential.

In the second session, Fran came in looking tired after attending a science fiction movie marathon. She was an avid fan who read voraciously and was familiar with almost every science fiction movie made. Even though she was exhausted, there was a sparkle in her eyes, which contrasted sharply with how she looked in the first session. In that session, when Fran described coping with the teasing she experienced as a child by watching endless hours of science fiction movies on TV, Madsen had thought of this as an escape from painful reality. Now he began to wonder what science fiction might be an entry into rather than an escape from.

When Fran spoke enthusiastically about an upcoming science fiction conference, Madsen asked her to describe the Fran one would see at this conference.

"A big kid," she replied, "a nut who has fun, wears outrageous costumes, and enjoys herself; a girl who is confident and not afraid of people, someone who is friendly and open." They agreed that the conference was like a depression-free zone, and the following conversation ensued.

Fran: You know, it's like I live in a Sea of Depression and there are these Islands of Sanctuary where it can't get me. Some, like the conference, are bigger islands and some are very small. Some aren't even islands. They're like coral reefs where I can just keep my head above water.

Bill: What is it that you like about the islands?
Fran: I'll drown out in the sea. The seas will kill me. The islands sustain me.

They talked further about Fran's struggle with teasing and taunting in grade school and then eventually returned to her metaphor of islands and coral reefs.

Bill: You talked about wanting to get more solid places to stand like islands. What do you think would need to happen to build some of those coral reefs into islands?
Fran: I need to do what always happens to coral reefs: add sediment. The sediment is the people around me who will help me remember who I am and not get washed away by depression.

In the sessions that followed, Fran and her therapist fleshed out what she felt was the solid foundation in her life and the people who made her happy and brought out the best in her. In looking back on this successful treatment, Madsen observed:

All too often in our work as therapists, we focus on the sea of problems, rather than the islands of client abilities, skills, and know-how. It is an ironic and tragic paradox that our attempts to help often result in therapists and clients learning more about problems' influence and less about clients' resistance and coping. Again, it is important to not ignore the influence of problems but to juxtapose the dominant tragic story of the problem's influence with a heroic counter-story of client agency.

Reauthoring. Evidence of competence relative to the problem, gathered from sifting through the clients' history, can serve as the start of new narratives regarding what kind of people they are. To make this connection, the therapist begins by asking about what the series of past and present victories over the problem says about the client:

"What does it say about you as a person that you were able to defeat *Depression* on those occasions?"

"What qualities of character must your son possess to be able to do that?"

The therapist can also expand the historical purview beyond episodes relating to the problem to find more evidence to bolster the new self-narrative:

"What else can you tell me about your past that helps me understand how you were able to handle *Anger* so well?"

"Who knew you as a child who wouldn't be surprised that you have been able to stand up to *Fear* on these occasions?"

As the new self-narrative begins to take shape, the therapist can shift the focus to the future, inviting clients to envision upcoming changes that will fit the new story:

"Now that you've discovered these things about yourself, how do you think these discoveries will affect your relationship with *Self-hate*?"

The self-story now has a past, present, and future. It's a complete narrative.

Here's how John Neal moved into the reauthoring process with the couple whose trouble communicating resulting in distancing from each other.

Case Study

John: So (turning to Larry), feelings of inadequacy and (turning to Elizabeth) overresponsibility have been interfering in your relationship. But you (Elizabeth) said sometimes you've been feeling it's not you?

Elizabeth: Yes, the two times I thought about it I didn't feel defensive . . . and I didn't feel angry. And things have been better in general.

John: During those two times, you were feeling better about yourself?

Elizabeth: Yes, I could understand that Larry was struggling and let him know I understood. So we've been communicating better.

John: Did this cause problems for the *distance*?

Elizabeth: (laughing) Yes, you could say that.

Larry: (also laughing) I would agree.

John: (to Elizabeth) In the moments when you felt better about yourself—can you tell me a little more about that?

Elizabeth: Well, maybe because I wasn't defensive, he was more like he used to be, really listening to me.

John: And how did that affect you?

Elizabeth: Well, it was *really* great (smiling). That's what gave *distance* the trouble.

John: So (later turning to Larry) you noticed a difference between the two of you also? What was your experience?

Larry: Things have been better, and I've been feeling better, too.

John: When you were aware of that, what was going on?

Larry: Elizabeth has been different, and I thought about what you said, that the *feelings of inadequacy* are there for everybody. It's not true that I'm inadequate. I've always known that's true, but I've never really thought about it in terms of feeling badly about myself.

John: And that helped give *distance* a run for it?

Larry: (again laughing) Sometimes.

John: Are you surprised that Elizabeth is seeing you differently at these times?

Larry: Not really. I think I have been different.

And then because preferred developments usually have a history, even if it is often forgotten in the face of current problems, the therapist invited the couple to reflect back on the strengths that drew them to each other in the first place.

John: Is this closeness something that used to be much more a part of the relationship?

Larry: Yes, things used to be like this a lot more.

John: If you think back to that time, was that before the kids?

Larry: Yes.

John: If back then, you could have looked into the future and seen the last few weeks, would either you or Elizabeth have been surprised that the two of you have been giving distance a run for it?

Larry: No, not at all.

John: So it speaks to something that was true of you back then?

Larry: Yes. I've always felt, or I used to feel, that we wanted to understand each other. She made the effort to understand me, and I think I was good at being present for her.

Elizabeth: That's definitely true. It was one of the things that attracted me to Larry. I felt respected, and we were real partners.

Reinforcing the New Story. Because they believe that the self is constituted in social interaction, narrative therapists make a point of helping clients find audiences to support their progress in constructing new stories for themselves.

Clients might be asked to contact people from their past who can authenticate their new story—who can confirm and add to examples of their acting capably. Clients are also encouraged to recruit people in their lives who can serve as supportive witnesses, or "allies" (Dickerson, 2004a) to their new story. Sometimes leagues are formed, support groups of people with similar problems, to reinforce one another's efforts to resist the problem. For example, the Vancouver Anti-Anorexia/Anti-Bulimia League (Madigan, 1994) has a newsletter and monitors the media, writing letters to company presidents, newspapers, and magazines that portray an emaciated ideal for women and encourage them to diet.

David Epston (1994) has pioneered the use of letter writing to extend the therapeutic conversation beyond the session. These letters often convey a deep appreciation of what the client endured, the outline of a new story, and the therapist's confidence in the client's ability to continue to progress. The advantage of this technique is that the words in a letter don't vanish the way words do after a conversation. Clients have reported to Epston that they reread letters he sent them years earlier to remind themselves what they went through and how far they have come.

All of these efforts—recruiting authenticators and audiences, forming teams and leagues, writing letters and making certificates—are in keeping with the social constructionist emphasis on interaction in creating and maintaining change. For people to solidify new identities, they need communities that confirm and reinforce revisioned narratives and that counter cultural and familial messages to the contrary. What happens in a session is just a beginning, because the goal isn't just to solve a problem; it's to change the whole way of performing one's life.

At the end of each session, narrative therapists summarize what happened, being sure to use externalizing language and emphasizing any unique outcomes that were mentioned. These summaries are what Epston often puts into his letters to clients. The effect of these reviews is to convey to clients that the therapist is with them and celebrates their blossoming new identity. This sense of being cheered on by the therapist can be extremely encouraging.

Deconstructing Destructive Cultural Assumptions. At times, narrative therapists make the connection to cultural narratives more explicit. For example, an anorexic woman might be asked how she was recruited into the belief that her worth depended on her appearance. This would lead to other questions regarding the position of women in American society. Similarly, a violent man might be asked how he came to believe that men should never be weak or tender, and a deconstructing of the messages men receive would ensue.

of his efforts to remain gentle and loving in spite of his socialization.

A Case of Sneaky Poo. White's therapy comes to life in his case descriptions, as in the following excerpt from his description of a family with an encopretic child (White, 1989).

To clarify what this deconstructing of cultural attitudes might look like, we will present one of White's cases, as described by Mary Sikes Wylie (1994):

> John . . . came to see White because, says White, "he was a man who never cried"—he had never been able to express his emotions— and he felt isolated and cut off from his own family. As a child, John had been taught, both at home and at his Australian grammar school, that any show of gentleness or "softness" was unmanly and would be met with harsh punishment and brutal public humiliation. White asks John a series of questions that are at once political and personal, eliciting information about the man's "private" psychological suffering and linking it to the "public" cultural practices, rigidly sexist and aggressively macho, that dominated his youth. "How were you recruited into these thoughts and habits [of feeling inadequate, not sufficiently masculine, etc.]? What was the training ground for these feelings? Do you think the rituals of humiliation [public caning by school authorities, ridicule by teachers and students for not being good at sports or sufficiently hard and tough] alienated you from your own life? Were they disqualifications of you? Did these practices help or hinder you in recognizing a different way of being a male?" (p. 43)

After deconstructing the masculine image in this way, White helped John to remember times when he resisted it and to recognize the nobility

When mapping the influence of family members in the life of what we came to call "Sneaky Poo," we discovered that:

1. Although Sneaky Poo always tried to trick Nick into being his playmate, Nick could recall a number of occasions during which he had not allowed Sneaky Poo to "outsmart" him. These were occasions during which Nick could have cooperated by "smearing," "streaking," or "plastering," but he declined to do so. He had not allowed himself to be tricked into this.

2. There was a recent occasion during which Sneaky Poo could have driven Sue into a heightened sense of misery, but she resisted and turned on the stereo instead. Also, on this occasion, she refused to question her competence as a parent and as a person.

3. Ron could not recall an occasion during which he had not allowed the embarrassment caused by Sneaky Poo to isolate him from others. However, after Sneaky Poo's requirements of him were identified, he did seem interested in the idea of defying these requirements. . . .

4. It was established that there was an aspect to Sue's relationship with Nick that she thought she could still enjoy, that Ron was still making some attempts to persevere in his relationship with Nick, and that Nick had an idea that Sneaky Poo had not destroyed all of the love in his relationship with his parents.

After identifying Nick's, Sue's, and Ron's influence in the life of Sneaky Poo, I introduced questions that encouraged them to perform meaning in relation to these examples, so that they might "re-author" their lives and relationships.

How had they managed to be effective against the problem in this way? How did this reflect on them as people and on their relationships? . . . Did this success give them any ideas about further steps that they might take to reclaim their lives from the problem? . . . In response to these questions, Nick thought that he was ready to stop Sneaky Poo from outsmarting him so much, and decided that he would not be tricked into being its playmate anymore. (pp. 10–11)

Two weeks later, White found that Nick had fought Sneaky Poo valiantly, having only one minor episode, and he seemed happier and stronger. Sue and Ron had also done their parts in the battle. In her effort not to cooperate with Sneaky Poo's requirements for her to feel guilty, Sue had begun to "treat herself" when Sneaky Poo was getting her down, and Ron had fought Sneaky Poo's attempts to keep him isolated by talking to friends about the problem. As White explains:

I encouraged the family to reflect on and to speculate about what this success said about the qualities that they possessed as people and about the attributes of their relationships. I also encouraged them to review what these facts suggested about their current relationship with Sneaky Poo. In this discussion, family members identified further measures that they could take to decline Sneaky Poo's invitations to them to support it. (p. 11)

White reports that the family expanded these efforts in the interim, and by the third session they felt confident that Sneaky Poo had been defeated. At a six-month follow-up, they were still doing well.

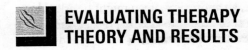

EVALUATING THERAPY THEORY AND RESULTS

The narrative model captured the imagination of the field in the 1990s, only to suffer the inevitable backlash to new ideas. The approach was too convoluted or too simplistic, it was just another form of cognitive therapy, or it was just about stories.

The fallout from the backlash was twofold. The first had to do with a watering down of the political aspect of the model, attending to the story aspect only and reducing externalizing to a linguistic sleight-of-hand. Some incorporated the techniques into other models (e.g., Eron & Lund, 1996); others found much to criticize from a family systems perspective (Minuchin, 1998). Little has been written that successfully distinguishes between a narrative metaphor and a systems approach, although Levy (2006) recently addressed this issue. What adherents of this approach maintain is that the narrative metaphor is applicable to either an intrapsychic *or* a systemic approach (Dickerson, 2007).

The second effect of the backlash was a rejection of social constructionism. This was the "too convoluted" argument. Also, because evidence-based therapies, along with more multidimensional approaches, are being promoted in the twenty-first century, theorists have moved away from conversations about ways of knowing.

The two most powerful ingredients in narrative therapy are the narrative metaphor itself and the practice of externalizing conversations. The strength and weakness of this approach is its cognitive focus. In rejecting the cybernetic model (families stuck in dysfunctional feedback loops), narrative therapists repudiated the idea that families with problems have something wrong with them. Unfortunately, at least early on, narrative therapists seem to have turned their backs on the three defining innovations of family therapy: (1) recognizing that psychological symptoms are often related to family conflict; (2) thinking about human problems as interactional, which means thinking in terms of twos (complementarity, reciprocity) and threes (triangles); and (3) treating the family as a unit.

Viewing problems as stories to be deconstructed overlooks the fact that some families have real conflicts that don't disappear because they team up to fight an externalized problem. For example, parents whose lives are empty may have trouble letting their children grow up. Does that emptiness evaporate after they help their children battle *Rebelliousness*?

In the process of helping people restory their experience, narrative therapists often subscribe to a view of unhappy emotions (anger, fear, anxiety, depression) as annoyances to avoid rather than explore. They ask how anger or fear "defeats" clients but rarely why clients are angry or what they are afraid of.

Early versions of family therapy *did* cast families in a bad light and blame them for maintaining problems. The narrative movement helped shift the field toward a more collaborative stance. In the process of rejecting the patronizing consciousness of that earlier age, however, narrative therapists have often neglected systems thinking, emphasizing its mechanistic elements while ignoring its more humanistic aspects. One of family therapy's greatest contributions was to bring a contextual understanding of people and their problems into the consulting room. Nonsystemic therapists, influenced by the disease model, had encouraged people to fight problems (with medication, support groups, education) rather than explore the network of relationships in which their problems were embedded. Although opposed to the disease model, narrative therapists return to a similarly acontextual view of problems as things to be fought and eschew efforts to understand their interpersonal roots.

Most narrative therapists would agree with Vicki Dickerson's statement that narrative therapy is "primarily about situating problems in their cultural context" (Freedman, 1996). That is, it's about helping clients identify and challenge the ubiquitous but commonly unexamined prejudices that permeate society and make self-worth and harmonious relating difficult at best. But how does one do that without imposing one's own political biases?

Although some therapists still make a case for strict therapeutic neutrality, many now agree that it is sometimes necessary to question cultural assumptions. It's true that popular culture promotes many unhealthy values. The question is: What is the best way to help people free themselves from those influences without imposing one's own values? This is a complex problem, and narrative therapy answers it one way. We hope their example inspires all family therapists to grapple with this issue.

Finally, as with all models, the narrative approach continues to evolve. Kaethe Weingarten, for example, in her book *Common Shock: Witnessing Violence Every Day* (2003), offers a framework for understanding human psychology and behavior that is social constructionist in spirit but goes beyond a narrative therapy approach. Bill Madsen, in the second edition of his *Collaborative Therapy with Multistressed Families* (2007), applies a narrative approach to community work in difficult circumstances. Helen Gremillion, who teaches gender studies at Indiana University, looks at the connections between contemporary anthropology and a narrative approach to young women with eating disorders in her ethnography *Feeding Anorexia* (2003). Vicki Dickerson (2004b) extends narrative thinking to show that you sometimes have to break the rules to get what you want in life in a self-help book for young women called *Who Cares What You're Supposed to Do?* Art Fisher, from Nova Scotia, travels extensively showing how he has adapted narrative ideas to his approach for working with men who are violent.

SUMMARY

The narrative approach is built around two organizing metaphors: personal narrative and social construction. When memory speaks, it tells a narrative truth, which comes to have more influence than historical truth. The "facts" presented to a therapist are partly historical and partly constructions. The constructions that make up the shared reality of a family represent mutual understandings and shared prejudices, some of which are useful and some of which are not.

Narrative therapists seek to break the grip of unhelpful stories by *externalizing* problems. By challenging pessimistic versions of events, therapists make room for hope. Locating *unique outcomes* provides an opening through which new and more optimistic stories can be envisioned. Finally, clients are helped to create audiences of support to encourage their progress in restorying their lives along preferred lines.

The strategies of narrative therapy fall into three stages: (1) recasting the problem as an affliction (externalizing) and focusing on its effects, rather than its causes; (2) finding exceptions, or partial triumphs over the problem and instances of effective action; and (3) recruiting support. Encouraging some kind of public ritual to reinforce new and preferred interpretations moves cognitive constructions past private insight into socially supported action.

Putting these strategies into practice involves an elaborate series of questions:

- *Deconstruction questions:* To externalize the problem. "What does Depression whisper in your ear?" "What conclusions about your relationship have you drawn because of this problem?"

- *Opening space questions:* To discover unique outcomes. "Has there ever been a time when Arguing could have taken control of your relationship but didn't?"
- *Preference questions:* To make sure unique outcomes represent preferred experiences. "Was this way of handling things better or worse?" "Was that a positive or a negative development?"
- *Story development questions:* To develop a new story from the seeds of (preferred) unique outcomes. "How is this different from what you would have done before?" "Who played a part in this way of doing things?" "Who will be the first to notice these positive changes in you?"
- *Meaning questions:* To challenge negative images of self and emphasize positive agency. "What does it say about you that you were able to do that?"
- *Questions to extend the story into the future:* To support changes and reinforce positive developments. "What do you predict for the coming year?"

The social constructionist underpinnings of narrative therapy give the approach its political cast and deemphasizes family dynamics and conflict. Instead of looking within families for dysfunctional interactions, narrative therapists look outside for destructive influences of cultural values and institutions. These therapists invite family members to pull together to oppose these values and practices. Instead of neutrality, they offer advocacy.

[handwritten note: narrative can be about family narrative as well!]

RECOMMENDED READINGS

Bruner, J. S. 1986. *Actual minds, possible worlds.* Cambridge, MA: Harvard University Press.

Diamond, J. 2000. *Narrative means to sober ends: Treating addiction and its aftermath.* New York: Guilford Press.

*[handwritten note: * rainbow of discourses !]*

Dickerson, V. C., and Zimmerman, J. 1992. Families with adolescents: Escaping problem lifestyles. *Family Process. 31*:341–353.

Eron, J., and Lund, T. 1996. *Narrative solutions in brief therapy.* New York: Guilford Press.

Freedman, J., and Combs, G. 1996. *Narrative therapy: The social construction of preferred realities.* New York: Norton.

Gilligan, S., and Price, R. 1993. *Therapeutic conversations.* New York: Norton.

Minuchin, S. 1998. Where is the family in narrative family therapy? *Journal of Marital and Family Therapy. 24*:397–403.

White, M. 1989. *Selected papers.* Adelaide, Australia: Dulwich Centre Publications.

White, M. 1995. *Re-authoring lives: Interviews and essays.* Adelaide, Australia: Dulwich Centre Publications.

White, M., and Epston, D. 1990. *Narrative means to therapeutic ends.* New York: Norton.

Zimmerman, J., and Dickerson, V. 1996. *If problems talked: Narrative therapy in action.* New York: Guilford Press.

REFERENCES

Bruner, J. S. 1986. *Actual minds, possible worlds.* Cambridge, MA: Harvard University Press.

Bruner, J. S. 1991. The narrative construction of reality. *Critical Inquiry. 18*:1–21.

Derrida, J. 1992. *Derrida: A critical reader*, D. Wood, ed. Oxford, UK: Blackwell.

Dickerson, V. 2004a. Allies against self-doubt. *Journal of Brief Therapy* (Special Edition):83–95.

Dickerson, V. 2004b. *Who cares what you're supposed to do? Breaking the rules to get what you want in love, life, and work.* New York: Perigree.

Dickerson, V. 2007. Remembering the future: Situating oneself in a constantly evolving field. *Journal of Systemic Therapy. 26*: 23–37.

Dickerson, V., and Zimmerman, J. 1992. Families with adolescents: Escaping problem lifestyles. *Family Process. 31*:341–353.

Epston, D. 1994. Extending the conversation. *Family Therapy Networker. 18*:30–37, 62.

Eron, J., and Lund, T. 1996. *Narrative solutions in brief therapy.* New York: Guilford Press.

Foucault, M. 1965. *Madness and civilization: A history of insanity in the age of reason.* New York: Random House.

Foucault, M. 1980. *Power/knowledge: Selected interviews and other writings.* New York: Pantheon.

Freedman, J. 1996. AFTA voices on the annual meeting. *American Family Therapy Academy Newsletter.* Fall:30–32.

Freedman, J., and Combs, G. 1996. *Narrative therapy: The social construction of preferred realities.* New York: Norton.

Freeman, J., Epston, D., and Lobovits, D. 1997. *Playful approaches to serious problems.* New York: Norton.

Gremillion, H. 2003. *Feeding anorexia.* Chapel Hill, NC: Duke University Press.

Held, B. 1995. *Back to reality: A critique of postmodern theory in psychotherapy.* New York: Norton.

Levy, J. 2006. Using a metaperspective to clarify the structural-narrative debate in family therapy. *Family Process, 45*:55–74.

Madigan, S. 1994. Body politics. *Family Therapy Networker. 18*:27.

Madigan, S., and Epston, D. 1995. From "spy-chiatric gaze" to communities of concern: From professional monologue to dialogue. In *The reflecting team in action*, S. Friedman, ed. New York: Guilford Press.

Madsen, W. C. 2007. *Collaborative therapy with multi-stressed families*, 2nd ed. New York: Guilford Press.

Maisel, R., Epston, D., and Borden, A. 2004. *Biting the hand that starves you.* New York: Norton.

Minuchin, S. 1998. Where is the family in narrative family therapy? *Journal of Marital and Family Therapy. 24*:397–403.

Neal, J., Zimmerman, J., and Dickerson, V. 1999. Couples, culture and discourse. In *Short-term couple therapy*, J. Donovan, ed. New York: Guilford Press.

Roth, S. A., and Epston, D. 1996. Developing externalizing conversations: An introductory exercise. *Journal of Systemic Therapies. 15*:5–12.

Weingarten, K. 2003. *Common shock: Witnessing violence every day.* New York: Dutton.

White, M. 1989. *Selected papers*. Adelaide, Australia: Dulwich Centre Publications.

White, M. 1995. *Re-authoring lives: Interviews and essays*. Adelaide, South Australia: Dulwich Centre Publications.

White, M., and Epston, D. 1990. *Narrative means to therapeutic ends*. New York: Norton.

Wylie, M. S. 1994. Panning for gold. *Family Therapy Networker*. 18:40–48.

Zimmerman, J., and Dickerson, V. 1993. Bringing forth the restraining influence of pattern in couples therapy. In *Therapeutic conversations*, S. Gilligan and R. Price, eds. New York: Norton.

Zimmerman, J., and Dickerson, V. 1996. *If problems talked: Narrative therapy in action*. New York: Guilford Press.

Integrative Models

14

A More Flexible Approach to Treatment

In breaking with the dominant paradigm of the time, family therapists defined themselves in opposition to all things psychoanalytic. Did psychoanalysis maintain that behavior was an artifact of unconscious forces, that family relationships were a function of individual psychodynamics, and that only insight brought about lasting change? Then family therapists would insist that behavior could be understood without reference to "the ghost in the machine," that an individual's behavior was dictated by the structure of the family, and that insight was unnecessary to problem solving.

Similarly, as they worked out the implications of their own insights, the various schools of family therapy emphasized not only their own strengths but also their differences from each other. Bowen sought to reason with family members one at a time; Minuchin insisted that the way to get at relationships was to have people talk directly to each other. Nor are the new schools immune from this us-against-them mentality; both solution-focused and narrative therapists have made a point of rejecting some of the defining features of the traditional schools. They are antimechanistic, decidedly not behavioral, and they pretty much ignore conflict as a source of family problems.

For this very reason, radical revisionists often remain trapped within old categories. They represent an antithesis, not a synthesis, and they are condemned to the dispensibility of all merely partial and polemical views. Just as it took systems therapists years to get over their denigration of psychodynamics, it will probably take time for these postmodernists to bring back what we've learned about family dynamics into their work.

In any field of endeavor, it seems that integration is only possible after a period of differentiation. It's no surprise then that in the early years of family therapy, when the emerging schools were devoted to differentiating themselves, the idea of *integration* had a negative connotation. It was seen as a watering down, rather than an enrichment, of the classic models.

During the past decade, however, there has been a growing awareness that no single approach has a monopoly on clinical effectiveness. The time of distinct and competitive schools of family therapy has passed. As family therapy moves ahead in the twenty-first century, the dominant trend is integration.

When it's described as respect for the multiplicity of truth, integration seems like an unassailably good idea. The obvious argument for incorporating elements from different approaches is that human beings are complicated creatures—thinking, feeling, and acting—who exist in a complex system of biological, psychological, and social influences. No therapy can succeed without having an impact on all of these dimensions. There is, however, an equally valid argument that eclecticism can rob therapy of the intensity made possible by focusing on one or two elements of experience. There may be many ways to skin a cat, but it might not be advisable to try all of them at once.

As we will see in this chapter, *integration* refers to three very different kinds of approaches. First there is *eclecticism*, which draws from a variety of models and methods. Second is *selective borrowing*, in which relative purists use a few techniques from other approaches. Third are *specially designed integrative models*.

ECLECTICISM

One of the advantages of graduate education is that students are exposed to a variety of approaches and taught to think critically about them. On the other hand, graduate schools often produce better critics than clinicians.

What do you do in the first session? Try to make sure that everyone shows up, greet each of

them, and try to make them comfortable. Ask about the presenting problem, of course. But then what?

Suppose a mother says that her fourteen-year-old has become rude and disrespectful. Do you focus on her feelings? Ask what her husband thinks? Set up an enactment in which she talks to her teenager? Inquire about exceptions? Any of these options might be useful. But trying to do all of them may lead to a lack of focus.

Effective integration involves more than taking a little of this and a little of that from various models. In creating a workable integration, there are two things to avoid. The first is sampling techniques without conceptual focus. The problem here isn't so much theoretical inelegance as clinical inconsistency.

A student who was being supervised in a psychodynamic approach asked to present at a case conference when, after some good initial progress, the therapy bogged down. Most of the people at the case conference weren't familiar with the psychodynamic model, and they were impressed by what the student had accomplished. But when it came time for discussion, several of those present suggested that the way to get the case moving again might be to try a different approach—cognitive-behavioral, structural, narrative, or what have you, depending on who was doing the suggesting.

The second thing to avoid is switching horses in midstream. Almost every treatment runs into difficulty at some point. When this happens, beginners may be tempted to shift to a different model. If a structural approach isn't working, maybe a narrative one will. The problem here is that almost any strategy will work for a while— and then stall. Getting stuck isn't a reason to change models; rather, it should be a signal that you and your clients are getting to what may be the heart of their problems. This is the time to sharpen your tools, not discard them.

Postgraduate training programs once provided an antidote to unfocused eclecticism through intensive instruction in one consistent approach. Unfortunately, fewer therapists these days take the time and expense to seek out advanced training. Many recent graduates would like to get more training, but they have loans to pay off, they want to settle down, or they feel they already know enough to get started. Those who do make the sacrifice to get postdoctoral training are likely to consider it the best decision they ever made.

 ## SELECTIVE BORROWING

When family therapy's elders were asked to discuss their careers in an issue of the *American Family Therapy Academy Newsletter* (Winter, 1999), many said that over the years they'd become less doctrinaire and had adopted ideas from other models—but they had held onto the core of their original theory as a base. For example, feminist family therapist Betty Carter was trained in Bowen's model and believed it to be substantial enough to evolve with her. "I never felt I had to trash the whole theory and start over again. Though, of course, Bowen theory had the same blind spot that all the early theories had about power, so that all had to be added" (Mac Kune-Karrer, 1999, p. 24). Today there are few purists among seasoned therapists. Most, like Carter, become selective borrowers.

To borrow selectively, you need a solid foundation in one paradigm. Which one you choose will depend in part on what is available in your training program. It's a good idea to take advantage of what's offered by learning as much as you can from whomever you happen to be supervised by. However, the approach you eventually specialize in should also make sense to you. At some point, you will be free to seek out training and supervision, and the approach you choose

should be consistent with how you think about people and how you like to interact with them. If narrative therapy inspires you, seek out training in this approach. In graduate school, you may not have a lot of choice about what your instructors offer. But after that, it can be a mistake to settle for a particular kind of training merely because it's convenient.

Therapists who eventually manage to combine approaches or successfully master more than one usually don't try to learn them all at once. Using techniques from here and there without conceptual focus produces a muddled form of eclecticism. Effective borrowing doesn't mean a hodgepodge of techniques, and it doesn't mean switching from one approach to another whenever therapy reaches a temporary impasse. Borrowing techniques from other approaches is more likely to be effective if you do so in a way that fits into the basic paradigm within which you are operating.

*C*onsider, for example, a structural therapist treating a mother and daughter who are locked in a battle in which the mother constantly criticizes the daughter for being irresponsible, and the daughter constantly acts irresponsibly. If the mother would back off and stop criticizing, the girl might feel less browbeaten and begin to take more responsibility for herself—or if the daughter would start to take more responsibility, maybe the mother would back off. But as long as each of them remains preoccupied with the other one, and the awful things she's doing, neither is likely to break this cycle.

Suppose the therapist were to try the narrative technique of externalizing the problem. Instead of "nagging" and "irresponsibility" polarizing the mother and daughter, perhaps they could be convinced to start thinking in terms of a "breach" that's come between them. This shift in thinking might open space for them to recapture a more cooperative way of relating. But if the mother and daughter's quarrelling was a product of enmeshment, attempting to bring them together in a more harmonious way might not solve the problem.

In fact, the case we've just described isn't hypothetical. Here's how the therapist actually did introduce the technique of externalizing in this situation.

Case Study

Because he saw the mother and daughter's quarrelling as a result of their enmeshment, the therapist concentrated first on helping the mother address with her husband some of the conflicts that were keeping them distant. As they started to get closer, the mother began to spend less time worrying about what her daughter was or wasn't doing.

Then in separate sessions with the daughter, the therapist found a useful way to introduce the externalizing technique. As a result of her mother's nagging, the daughter had gotten into the habit of actively shirking responsibility, and as a result, her school performance had plummeted. It was as though when she had a homework assignment, she felt the same kind of oppression she felt from her mother's nagging.

The therapist pointed this out, but found that the girl had begun to internalize her mother's harsh characterizations. "I guess I'm just lazy," she'd say, in what was becoming a self-fulfilling prophesy. The therapist responded by asking her about times when *Procrastination* got the better of her, and times when It didn't. This device proved effective in helping the girl separate herself from the negative introject she'd adopted, and thus energized, she was able to start getting back on track with her school work.

SPECIALLY DESIGNED INTEGRATIVE MODELS

While most practitioners eventually become selective borrowers, grafting ideas and practices onto their basic model, some therapists create a new synthesis out of complementary aspects of existing models. Some of these integrative efforts are comprehensive systems that include a whole range of approaches under one umbrella, while others simply combine elements of one approach with another, forming a hybrid model.

Comprehensive, Theoretically Inclusive Models

The maturing of the field has seen an erosion of sectarianism and a more pragmatic approach to practice. For some, this has meant not limiting one's practice to any one model but drawing on a variety of existing approaches.

The advantage of these comprehensive approaches is that they bring a wider range of human experience into focus. They also offer more options for intervention. For example, rather than simply try to pry apart an enmeshed mother and child, a therapist whose purview includes cultural issues might help the mother reexamine the assumptions keeping her from getting more satisfaction out of her own life.

The disadvantage of comprehensive approaches is that they require a great deal of therapists. Therapists can't just specialize in, say, untangling family triangles; they have to consider a variety of other issues—intrapsychic, transgenerational, even political—and a greater range of interventions. In addition, therapists who adopt a more comprehensive framework must guard against the tendency to switch haphazardly from one strategy to another.

Here we will present two examples of models designed to increase comprehensiveness. The first, *metaframeworks*, selects key ideas that run through the different schools of family therapy and connects them with superordinate principles. The second, *integrative problem-centered therapy*, links several different approaches in sequence and provides a decision tree for shifting from one to another when therapists get stuck.

The Metaframeworks Model. Metaframeworks grew out of the collaboration among three family therapy teachers who worked at the Institute for Juvenile Research in Chicago: Douglas Breunlin, Richard Schwartz, and Betty Mac Kune-Karrer. This approach offers a unifying theoretical framework operationalized with six core domains of human functioning, or metaframeworks: intrapsychic process, family organization, sequences of family interaction, development, culture, and gender (Breunlin, Schwartz, & Mac Kune-Karrer, 1992).

The application of metaframeworks is conceived in terms of releasing the constraints, at whatever level, that are keeping a family from solving its problems.

*F*or example, a depressed woman may be constrained on many fronts simultaneously. At the level of internal process, she may be burdened by guilt over wanting a little time for herself or because her children complain that they have no friends. (If children are unhappy, it must be their mother's fault, right?) At the level of family organization, she may be stuck in a stale second marriage to a man obsessed with his career while she's left to run the house and raise the kids. In addition, she may be preoccupied with her hyperactive son and polarized with her own mother over how to deal with him. This pattern may be part of a sequence in which her son's behavior gets worse after monthly visits with her ex-husband. Finally, the woman's situation may be part of a transgenerational pattern maintained by the family and cultural belief that women should be devoted to their families and never be selfish.

As the therapist considers the network of constraints impeding this woman and her family, one framework often emerges as a point of departure, but the therapist is always aware of the others and can shift when necessary. Thus, therapy may start in the gender metaframework by reexamining the woman's beliefs about selfishness and her husband's unbalanced expectations about the proper roles of men and women. At some point, the focus might shift to the internal framework when the therapist asks about the parts of each partner that hold these beliefs and what they are related to from their pasts. This exploration might make the woman want to reorganize the family responsibilities and the shift is to the organizational metaframework. At another point, the couple might discuss their son's oscillating between acting younger and older than his age, and they're in the developmental framework, and so on.

The metaframeworks model isn't simple. In an age when therapists often seek to fall back on formulaic techniques, it challenges clinicians to consider a wide range of possibilities. Yet for therapists who've felt boxed in by the narrow scope of the original models, the metaframeworks approach offers a more comprehensive view and a broader range of options.

Integrative Problem-Centered Therapy. Whereas metaframeworks distills elements from different theories into a new synthesis, integrative problem-centered therapy incorporates a variety of family and individual approaches in sequence, without trying to combine them. Integrative problem-centered therapy has been developed over the past twenty years by William

Pinsof (1995, 1999) and his colleagues at the Family Institute at Northwestern University.

Like many therapists, Pinsof began his career convinced that the model he was trained in (strategic family therapy) could be effective with any and every sort of problem. Unlike selective borrowers, however, when he ran up against his theory's limitations, he didn't just add new techniques; he added whole new approaches. For example, if his strategic model didn't seem to be working, he might help family members explore their emotions à la Virginia Satir. In other cases, if problems persisted, he might recommend a psychopharmacological assessment. With continued failure, he might bring in grandparents or even offer individual therapy to some family members.

This sequencing made sense to Pinsof (1999) partly because it reflected his own personal development—but it also makes sense that some problems are deep seated while others are not. Some families will respond to behavioral interventions while others may need more of an in-depth focus. Why not consider the whole spectrum of psychotherapies if necessary rather than assume that all troubles should be treated with just one approach?

*T*o illustrate Pinsof's approach, consider a couple in their sixties who have been caught up in picky but intense fights for the past year. They relate the fighting to the husband's increasing impotence. In exploring the meaning each attaches to these events, the therapist finds that the wife sees her husband's lack of sexual response as a reflection of her diminished attractiveness, while he considers it a sign of waning virility. These conclusions are painful to each of them, and so they avoid discussing, much less having, sex.

The therapist forms an alliance with each of them so they feel safe enough to disclose their private pain and clear up their misconceptions about the other's feelings. If at that point they respond well—fewer fights and more satisfactory sex—therapy can stop. If not, the therapist would explore possible physiological causes of the impotence—fatigue, depression, incipient diabetes. If improvements don't follow the exploration at that level, the therapist might discuss with each partner the unexamined assumptions that they have about the aging process. If the problem still remains unsolved, the focus would shift to intrapsychic blocks, and either or both of them might be engaged in individual therapy.

By now you may be daunted at the prospect of having to master so many different therapeutic models. But Pinsof doesn't expect therapists to be competent in all these approaches. Integrative therapy often involves teamwork among a number of therapists, particularly when key family members are vulnerable and need their own therapists. Although separate therapists with differing orientations can be a nightmare, the integrative framework provides common ground for collaboration.

The metaframeworks and integrative approaches represent two possible reactions to the realization that all models have their limitations. One solution (metaframeworks) is alchemical—taking pieces from here and there to forge a new synthesis. The other (integrative) is additive—linking whole models together without trying to revise them or connect them theoretically.

Models That Combine Two Distinct Approaches

Some theorists who found one approach too limiting were satisfied to improve their model by combining it with just one other, believing that two heads were better than one—and probably also better than five or six.

The Narrative Solutions Approach. One of the things that troubles some seasoned practitioners is the tendency for solution-focused and narrative therapists to turn their backs on valuable elements of the older models. That's why Joseph Eron and Thomas Lund's narrative solutions model (Eron & Lund, 1993, 1996), which combines the MRI model with narrative techniques, is a welcome addition.

Among the reasons strategic therapy fell into disfavor were its mechanistic assumptions and manipulative techniques. The way some strategists applied the cybernetic model, families were seen as stubborn and not to be reasoned with. You can't talk sense to a machine. Family histories were dismissed as irrelevant. Therapy was ideological and therefore often impersonal. The meretriciousness of this kind of thinking, however, wasn't essential to the insight that families often get stuck applying solutions that don't work. Eron and Lund resuscitated that insight and incorporated it into a blend of strategic and narrative therapy.

Eron and Lund began collaborating in the early 1980s as brief strategic therapists. Although they were attracted to the narrative model, there were aspects of the strategic approach they didn't want to give up, so they combined the two. The resulting narrative solutions approach revolves around the concept of the **preferred view**:

- Preferred views include the qualities people would like to possess and have noticed by others; for example, "determined," "caring," "responsible."
- Preferred views shape the attributions one makes about behavior. "I did that (got into that fight) because I am cool, independent, able to manage my own affairs."
- Preferred views also include people's hopes, dreams, and intentions for living their lives. "I want to be different from my mother who was a self-sacrificing martyr."
- Preferred views may or may not have anything to do with one's actual behavior. "I may not have done well in school, but I like to think of myself as a hard-working and self-disciplined person. I expect to go to a good graduate school, even though, given how I'm doing now, it isn't likely."

Eron and Lund believe that problems arise when people aren't living according to their preferred views. To address this discrepancy, they use a combination of reframing from the MRI model and restorying from the narrative approach. They subscribe to the basic premise of the MRI model that problems develop from the

Eron and Lund's narrative solutions therapy combines narrative techniques with the MRI insight that people often perpetuate their problems with misguided attempted solutions.

mishandling of life transitions. However, Eron and Lund are more specific. They propose that people begin to think and act in problematic ways when they experience a discrepancy between their preferred view of themselves and their perception of their actions or their impression of how others regard them.

Note that while Eron and Lund follow the MRI model in looking for more-of-the-same cycles, they differ in focusing not just on behavior, but also on what people think about their problems. Conflict, according to this model, is driven by disjunctions between individuals' preferred views of themselves and how they perceive others as responding to them.

Eron and Lund (1996) offer the following guidelines to therapists for managing helpful conversations.

Maintain an Interest in Clients' Preferences and Hopes. The therapist must pay attention to stories that reflect how clients prefer to see themselves and how they want to be seen by significant others. The following questions may be asked to help clients get in touch with their preferred views:

- When are you at your best—at home, work, school, with friends?
- Who notices—family, colleagues, teachers, friends?
- What do they notice about you at these times?
- Who are your favorite relatives, friends, teachers, other adults?
- What do they like about you?
- What do they see in you?
- When you think back on your life, are there other times when you felt at your best?
- When you look to the future and you are the person you would like to be, what do you envision?

In *Narrative Solutions in Brief Therapy*, Eron and Lund (1996) offer the example of Al, who became depressed in the wake of retirement and the onset of emphysema.

Case Study

Al preferred to think of himself as productive and useful, yet he worried that he might not be able to remain as active as in the past and that his family would no longer view him as someone to rely on.

The disjunction between Al's preferences and his perceptions led to his feeling sad and listless. The more depressed Al seemed, the more family members began to do for him, finishing projects he started and trying to cheer him up, which only deepened his despondency. The negative *frame* through which Al viewed his current circumstances affected the *stories* he recalled from the past. He pictured himself following in the footsteps of his own father, who had deteriorated rapidly after retiring. According to Eron and Lund, negative frames of the present shape the stories people recall from the past, which in turn influence their perspectives on the future.

When Al was asked when he had felt he was the person he wanted to be, he recalled several stories. These stories revealed a man who felt close to his family and liked being helpful. Al also recalled times when he had taken control of his life under challenging circumstances. For example, he decided to stop drinking because it was having a bad effect on his family relationships. When Al recounted these occasions in which he had acted in line with his preferred attributes (e.g., being helpful, caring, in control, connected with family members), he became more hopeful. He also noticed the gap between the person he wanted to be and how he was currently acting.

In describing their approach to working with couples, Eron and Lund (1996) offer the following example.

Case Study

Jim came to counseling after his wife consulted an attorney about a separation. Rita told Jim that she had hoped that their relationship would improve after he got sober, but his violent outbursts continued.

When the therapist asked Jim when he felt at his best, he said it was when he made the decision to seek sobriety. He felt he was finally taking control of his life and taking a stand to separate himself from his brothers and father who remained raging alcoholics. When asked how this action fit with his wife's account of his temper, her fear, and her decision to seek a separation, Jim became thoughtful and began talking of his experience growing up in an alcoholic household. The therapist's questions reoriented Jim to the person he wanted to be, creating a motivational spark rather than defensiveness and resistance.

Explore the Effects of Behavior. The therapist helps clients examine the effects of their behavior on themselves and others. The following are typical questions:

- What happened when you did *X*, or didn't do *Y*?
- How was that for you? A good thing? A bad thing?
- How do others (parents, teachers, friends, relatives) react? What do they think? What do they say?
- How is that for you? Does anything feel good about it? Bad about it? What do you do?
- Has *X* happened in the past?
- How was that for you?

With Jim, the violent husband, the therapist asked, "How is it for you when your temper gets the best of you?"

Jim, looking perplexed, responded, "What do you mean?"

The therapist elaborated, "How do you feel about yourself when you wind up banging the door down, getting in your wife's face and threatening to hurt her?"

"Not very good," Jim said.

The therapist then asked, "What effect does this have on Rita?"

Jim hesitated. "She gets scared. She doesn't want to talk with me."

"How is that for you?"

"I hate it when Rita doesn't talk to me."

The therapist asked about the effects of Jim's rage on his children. Jim looked down and said that his kids feared and avoided him.

The therapist then highlighted Jim's preferences: "You'd like to be in control, and you said you felt best about yourself when you made the decision to get sober—and you stuck to it."

He reminded Jim of how Rita regarded him when he took control of his drinking. "Rita said that she was proud of you for taking charge of your life."

The therapist also highlighted the effects of Jim's current behavior. "You don't like it when Rita pulls away from you. You said that you'd like to talk with her and understand her."

Case Study

When Al was asked about the effects of his current behavior on his family, he said that they were avoiding him. He also told a story about a recent incident in which he tried shoveling the snow in his driveway. He went at it full tilt, as usual, but five minutes into the task, he started having trouble breathing. In disgust, he threw down the shovel and retreated to the house, where he collapsed on the couch for the rest of the afternoon. When asked what happened to the driveway, a pained look came over Al's face. "My son had to finish it."

Effects questions externalize problems; they separate the person from the problem. This allows clients to talk about problematic behavior without feeling ashamed.

Effects questions also hold people accountable for the discrepancy between who they would like to be and the impact of their actions. When therapists confront negative behavior without taking into account this discrepancy, clients are apt to become resistant, to deny or minimize their responsibility. However, when therapists help clients confront this gap in the context of noticing their preferred selves, clients are more likely to think of creative ways to bridge the gap. They come up with solutions.

Use Past and Present Stories. The therapist helps clients find past and present stories that are in line with their preferences and that contradict problem-maintaining behavior.

When the therapist asked Jim about what motivated his decision to get sober, Jim told a story about riding in a car with his brothers who were drinking. Jim was in the passenger seat and his younger brother was driving recklessly while his older brothers were fighting in the back seat. Jim managed to quiet his brothers, convince them to stop the car, and turn over the driving to him.

After this incident, Jim vowed to get sober. While telling this story, Jim appeared calm and in control, a contrast to his current aggressive behavior at home. As therapy progressed, the therapist often reminded Jim of this story and of his capacity to be in control.

Discuss the Future. The therapist asks clients to imagine what the future will look like when the problem is resolved.

When the therapist asked Al to envision a future without his problems, he pictured being less depressed and more involved with his family. He imagined himself coping with the emphysema while remaining useful to others and not following in the footsteps of his father who deteriorated with retirement and illness.

Jim imagined a future in which he was more in control of his temper. He also pictured himself having more positive conversations with Rita, in which he didn't criticize her or get angry and in which she didn't run away from him.

Pose Mystery Questions. The therapist asks clients **mystery questions**—for example, how did a person with X preferred attributes (hardworking, productive) wind up in Y situation (acting listless, feeling depressed) and being seen by people in Z ways (uncaring, lazy)?

Mystery questions invite clients to reconcile the discrepancy between who they would like to be and the facts of their problematic behavior. Mystery questions inspire reflection in a nonthreatening way. People often begin to rethink their predicaments; how it is they came to act out of line with their preferred views and what they can do about it. Eron and Lund recommend asking these questions in a puzzled, rather than confrontive, way.

Al was asked how it was that someone who had always been there for his family would find himself so withdrawn. How could someone who had faced previous challenges by taking control and setting realistic limits (as with quitting drinking) wind up acting out of character in the wake of emphysema?

Al seemed curious to find an explanation, and he asked the therapist to meet with his family to explore how his behavior had affected them. He reflected on his father's deterioration and on how he was following in his footsteps, even though he didn't want to. Al realized that his family was floundering and needed his guidance about how to be helpful. He began to rethink his approach to emphysema and to his family.

Coauthor Alternative Explanations. The therapist works with clients to develop new explanations for the evolution of the problem that fit with how they prefer to be seen, and inspire new actions.

Jim was asked how it was that a man who had taken a stand against violence and taken control of his drinking would wind up losing control of his temper and being seen by his wife as untrustworthy. Jim grew thoughtful. He talked about growing up in an alcoholic family, where violence and loss of control were the norm. Jim hated it when his mother and father fought. He felt protective of his mother and brothers, but he was afraid.

Remembering these scenes from his past helped Jim see the effect of his temper on Rita's withdrawal. Perhaps she was doing what he had done as a boy. Perhaps his own aggressive behavior was the reason for her withholding love and affection, not his unlovablity. Armed with this alternative explanation, Jim became more motivated to alter his approach to Rita.

Encourage Discussion. The therapist prompts clients to talk to significant others about their preferences, hopes, and intentions.

Al felt empowered to talk to his doctor about his illness after he was able to recall preferred experiences indicating that he was a take-charge kind of guy. He also began reframing the motives of family members away from the belief that they saw him as useless to viewing them as bewil-

dered, not knowing how to help him. Al's depression lifted after he met with his family and told them what was and wasn't helpful.

Jim sat down and talked with Rita about what he'd like in their relationship. He said that he missed their closeness and wanted to be able to talk with her without becoming angry. Rita said she admired Jim for staying sober but no longer wanted rage or violence in her marriage. What she wanted was understanding and support.

This preference-focused, nonblaming conversation between Rita and Jim set the stage for other helpful conversations in which Jim demonstrated control of his temper and a willingness to support Rita in her dreams and aspirations. Rita chose to stay with Jim, and their relationship improved.

Integrative Couples Therapy. Neil Jacobson of the University of Washington, one of the preeminent behavioral family therapists, teamed with Andrew Christensen of UCLA to figure out how to improve the limited success rates they were finding with traditional behavioral couples therapy. They discovered that their results improved when they added a humanistic element to the standard behavioral mix of communication training, conflict resolution, and problem solving. The approach they developed is described in *Integrative Couple Therapy* (Jacobson & Christensen, 1996).

Traditional behavioral couples therapy is based on the behavior exchange model. After a *functional analysis* showing how partners in a relationship influence one another, they're taught to reinforce changes they wish to bring about in each other.

Anyone who's been married for a long time can tell you what's missing from this approach.

Therapy may be about change, but a successful relationship also involves a certain amount of acceptance of differences and disappointments. Some things in an unhappy marriage may need to change for the relationship to improve, but some things about partners are part of the package, and couples who survive the break-in period learn to accept these things. It's this element, *acceptance*, that Jacobson and Christensen added in their new approach.

In contrast to the teaching and preaching of traditional behavioral therapy, integrative couples therapy emphasizes support and empathy, the same qualities that therapists want couples to learn to show each other. To create a conducive atmosphere, this approach begins with a phase called the *formulation*, which is aimed at helping couples let go of blaming and open themselves to acceptance and personal change. The formulation consists of three components: a *theme* that defines the primary conflict; a *polarization process* that describes their destructive pattern of interaction; and the *mutual trap*, which is the impasse that prevents the couple from breaking the polarization cycle once it's triggered.

Common themes in couples' problems include conflicts around closeness and distance, a desire for control but unwillingness to take responsibility, and disagreements about sex. Whereas partners view these differences as indicating deficiencies in the other person and as problems to be solved, Jacobson and Christensen encourage couples to see that some differences are inevitable. This kind of acceptance can break the cycles that build up when each is constantly trying to change the other. Also, as the formulation phase continues, the partners begin to see that they aren't victims of each other but of the *pattern* they've both been trapped in. As with Michael White's externalizing, the couple can unite to fight a mutual enemy, the pattern. For example, when Jacobson asked a couple to describe their pattern,

the husband replied, "We fight over whether or not to be close. When she is not as close to

me as she wants to be, she pressures me into being close, and I withdraw, which leads to more pressure. Of course, sometimes I withdraw before she has a chance to pressure me. In fact, that's how it usually starts." (Jacobson & Christensen, 1996, p. 100)

Notice how the formulation process helps this couple describe their fight as a pattern to which they both contribute, rather than in the accusatory language typical of distressed couples.

Strategies to produce change include the two basic ingredients of behavioral couples therapy: behavior exchange and communication skills training. Behavior exchange interventions involve *quid pro quo* and *good faith* contracts, by which couples learn to exchange favors or to initiate pleasing behavior in the hope of getting the same in return. For example, each partner might be asked to generate a list of things he or she could do that would lead to greater satisfaction for the other. (Ask not what your partner can do for you; ask what you can do for your partner.) After each compiles a list, he or she is instructed to start doing some of the things that will please his or her partner—and to observe the effect of this benevolence on the relationship.

The second ingredient—communication training—involves teaching couples to listen and to express themselves in direct but nonblaming ways. Learning to use active listening and to make "I-statements" is taught by assigned reading, instruction, and practice. As they learn to communicate less defensively, couples not only are better able to resolve conflicts, but they are also more accepting of each other.

It's too soon to evaluate the effectiveness of integrative couples therapy, but it seems to be an improvement over traditional behavioral therapy. Its significance isn't only in improving a model but also in the shift it represents toward the humanizing of behavioral technology. In emphasizing acceptance and compassion, integrative couples therapy joins other family therapies of the twenty-first century—from solution-focused to strategic to narrative—in recognizing the importance of nurturing relationships. Carl Rogers would be proud.

✍

The narrative solutions model illustrates a principle that every good matchmaker knows: Make sure the partners aren't incompatible before pushing them together. Because MRI techniques are similar to narrative ones and because both traditions emphasize changing cognitions rather than emotions and downplay psychic conflict and developmental history, these two approaches are fairly compatible. Had they tried to combine either with, say, psychoanalytic therapy, it might be like trying to mix oil and water.

Jacobson and Christensen's amalgamation also involved compatible marriage candidates: behavioral and experiential. Both models are concerned with communication; they just have different emphases. Behaviorists focus on contracts and reinforcement, while experientialists are interested in emotions and empathy. Blending some of the latter into the former is not a huge stretch. Encouraging partners to show more compassion needn't interfere with helping them learn to be better problem solvers.

Other Integrative Models. Although we've singled out some of the most innovative examples, there are in fact so many integrative approaches that it's impossible to list them all. While many of these are new, some of them have been around so long they don't always get the attention they deserve.

Carol Anderson and Susan Stewart wrote one of the most useful integrative guides to family therapy back in 1983. Two other integrative approaches that have been around for a while are those designed by Larry Feldman (1990) and William Nichols (1995). The tradition of offering practical advice that transcends schools of family therapy is upheld in a splendid book by Robert Taibbi (2007) called *Doing Family Therapy*. Others have attempted to integrate struc-

tural and strategic therapies (Liddle, 1984; Stanton, 1981), strategic and behavioral (Alexander & Parsons, 1982), psychodynamic and systems theory (Kirschner & Kirschner, 1986; Nichols, 1987; Sander, 1979; Scharff, 1989; Slipp, 1988), and experiential and systems theory (Duhl & Duhl, 1981; Greenberg & Johnson, 1988).

One particularly elegant model that's been around for a while (first described in 1981) is Alan Gurman's *brief integrative marital therapy*, which combines social learning theory and psychodynamics. As in behavior therapy, marital problems are seen as due to poor communication and problem solving, but as in object relations theory, these deficits are understood as having roots in unconscious conflicts. What might seem like simply a deficit—poor relationships skills—may turn out to serve a protective function of limiting intimacy to a level that a couple can tolerate without undue anxiety.

Gurman's assessment begins with problematic themes in a couple's relationship. In a recent chapter on brief integrative marital therapy, Gurman (2002) describes a case in which Sue is angry and critical of Karl's emotional unavailability. This familiar demand-and-withdraw pattern is assumed to reflect not only the couple's interaction but also the intrapsychic conflicts that motivate this interaction.

Case Study

Like an analyst, Gurman sees Sue's attacking as serving the defensive function of avoiding dealing with her own fears of abandonment. Meanwhile, Karl's distance helps him avoid his conflicts about intimacy. The partners' complaints about each other ("nagging," "withdrawing") allow them to maintain a consistent and tolerable sense of themselves, even if it limits the satisfaction they share in their relationship.

Like a behaviorist, Gurman also looks at the *consequences* of the couple's problematic interaction, noting what (positive and negative) reinforcements or punishments may be maintaining these patterns. Karl negatively reinforced Sue's criticism by apologizing and coming closer to her after her complaints reached the shouting stage. Sue inadvertently punished Karl's closeness by venting her pent-up anger and frustration whenever the couple did spend time together—thus violating the first law of social learning theory.[1]

In order to explore the impact of one or both partners' personal conflicts on the couple's relationship, Gurman may talk at some length to each partner individually while the other just listens. Talking separately to the partners (à la Murray Bowen) helps minimize anxiety and thus makes therapy a safer "holding environment."

Gurman's blocking of Sue's criticism allowed Karl to explore how he felt about trying to balance his commitments to career and family. As Karl opened up about his fears of failure, Sue softened enough to empathize with his struggles—and to share her own fears of being alone.

In addition to addressing couples' problematic interactions and the conflicts underlying them, Gurman's brief integrative marital therapy also includes practical problem-solving discussions, advice, teaching of self-control techniques, exploration of the past, modeling, coaching, bibliotherapy—in short, the wide and flexible variety of interventions that characterize the best kinds of integration.

Other integrative approaches haven't received as much attention in mainstream family therapy as they have by federal funding agencies. These include Scott Henggeler's *multisystemic model* (Henggeler & Borduin, 1990) and Howard Liddle's *multidimensional family therapy* (Liddle, Dakoff, & Diamond, 1991). These approaches both evolved out of research projects with difficult adolescents, a population that challenges

theorists to expand their views beyond the limits of one school of therapy or one level of system.

Liddle developed his integrative approach while working with drug-abusing, inner-city adolescents. His multidimensional family therapy brings together the risk factor models of drug and problem behavior, developmental psychopathology, family systems theory, social support theory, peer cluster theory, and social learning theory. In practice, the model applies a combination of structural family therapy, parent training, skills training for adolescents, and cognitive-behavioral techniques.

One of the most useful aspects of Liddle's approach is the way he integrates individual and systems interventions. While he makes liberal use of the structural technique of enactment, he frequently meets with individual family members to coach them to participate more effectively in these family dialogues. Liddle also uses these individual sessions to focus on teenagers' experiences outside the home. Here, sensitive subjects like drug use and sexual behavior can be explored more safely in private. The need to meet with teenagers to focus on their lives outside the family reflects a growing recognition of the limited influence families have in comparison to peers and culture.

Scott Henggeler of the University of South Carolina and a number of research-oriented colleagues who work with difficult-to-treat children tried to improve on their systems-oriented family therapy by (1) more actively considering and intervening into the extra-familial systems in which families are embedded, in particular their school and peer contexts; (2) including individual developmental issues in assessments; and (3) incorporating cognitive-behavioral interventions (Henggeler & Borduin, 1990). This multisystemic model has shown promising results in several well-designed outcome studies of juvenile offenders and families referred for abuse or neglect. For that reason, it is highly regarded among governmental funding agencies, and Henggeler has received a number of large grants.

---

[1]You catch more flies with honey than with vinegar.

Models Designed for Specific Clinical Problems

One sign that family therapy was maturing was when therapists began focusing on specific clinical problems rather than generic families. Some groups applied preexisting models to the problems they were wrestling with; for example, structural family therapy was used with anorexia nervosa and brittle diabetes (Minuchin, Rosman, & Baker, 1978). Other groups had to be more creative because they decided to tackle problems that weren't typically seen in the practice of family therapy. Such problems often require more than any single approach offers.

Working with Family Violence. One of the most impressive integrative efforts is the approach to treating spousal abuse developed by Virginia Goldner, Peggy Penn, Marcia Sheinberg, and Gillian Walker at the Ackerman Institute in New York (Goldner, 1998; Goldner, Penn, Sheinberg, & Walker, 1990; Walker & Goldner, 1995). When Goldner and Walker began studying violence in couples, the standard approach involved separating the partners and treating the man in a group with other offenders and the abused woman in a support group. This treatment was informed by the feminist critique of systems-based therapies that implied that both partners were responsible for the violence and consequently could be treated together like any other couple.

Goldner and Walker share the feminist conviction that a man is responsible for his violent behavior, no matter what provocation he might feel. However, they also believe that there is value to treating couples together and attending to the woman's part in these couples' dangerous dramas. Instead of taking sides in the systems theory versus feminism battles, they bridged the polarized thinking that pervaded the field of family violence. Could it be possible to take both positions simultaneously? Yes, the man is responsible for controlling his violence, but both partners participate in a process of interaction that must change. As Goldner says, "A battered woman is not equally responsible for her broken nose, even if she acknowledges having been angry or 'provocative'; just as the victim of sexual abuse is not equally responsible for what happened in the middle of the night, even if she felt aroused" (Goldner, 1998, p. 266). With this more nuanced position, it became possible to examine both partners' roles in their escalations of conflict without blaming the victim.

Goldner and Walker work with couples together, but they make violence *the* problem, no matter how many other issues the couple may present, and they make each partner responsible for creating a safe relationship. They show the man how rage and violence may feel like something overwhelming him but that it is actually comprised of many small choices he makes (not leaving the room when he starts to get too angry, brooding over injustices large and small, insisting on dealing with contentious issues when he is overwrought, and so on). They also challenge the woman to be responsible for putting her safety above all other considerations (protecting the man from shame or arrest, keeping the family together, arguing when it is unsafe to do so, and so on).

Goldner points out that separating violent couples rarely promotes safety because they are often so symbiotically attached that they quickly reunite, and those women who do leave are the

Virginia Goldner's work with violent couples combines a sophisticated clinical approach with a passionate feminist sensitivity.

most likely to be attacked. On the other hand, if they are together in treatment, the victim can explain to the abuser how damaging his aggression is in the presence of a therapist who can emphasize the imperative to stop.

Goldner and Walker use the language of "parts" to help partners detach from global labels like *abuser* and *victim* and to bring intrapsychic insights into the conversation. He can talk about the angry part of himself and she the part that needs to protect him rather than look after herself. As they inquire into the origin of these parts, Goldner and Walker find themselves listening to painful stories from each partner's past. "Here we typically find ourselves back in a time when the man was a boy, subject to sadistic acts of violence, power and control" (Goldner, 1998, p. 275). This compassionate witnessing helps reduce the partners' antagonism toward each other.

Goldner and Walker also incorporate an active listening format so that not only are past traumas witnessed, but the man must listen to the woman describe the pain and terror she suffered from his attacks. Here again there's a both/and message to the man: Yes, you suffered as a boy, and that's

related to your violent behavior, but you are still choosing to be violent, and that's unacceptable. Similarly, regardless of how passive the woman has been in the past, she can choose to protect herself without feeling disloyal.

This nondichotomous position is an advance over the either/or positions of both the feminist and psychoanalytic models. Feminist therapists believe that to explore a man's troubled childhood would imply excusing his violence, while psychoanalysts too often see violence as a symptom of underlying pathology for which they don't hold anyone accountable. Goldner (1998) writes, "From a both/and perspective, violence is best conceptualized as simultaneously willful and impulse-ridden, as both instrumental and dissociative" (p. 279).

Although Goldner and Walker's approach was designed for violent couples, it offers important lessons for the integration of therapy models in general. It illustrates the value of stepping out of the dichotomies that dominate clinical work (especially around volatile issues like domestic violence) to see that more than one perspective has validity and can coexist with oth-

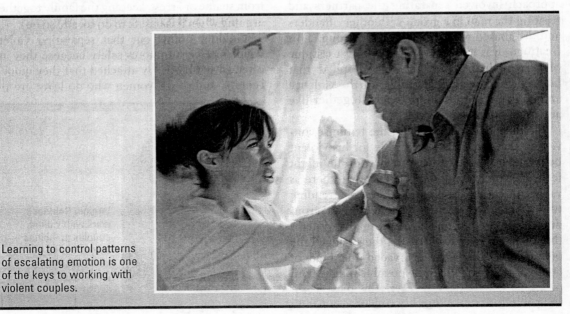

Learning to control patterns of escalating emotion is one of the keys to working with violent couples.

ers. Too often, "ideas that could mutually enrich one another have instead been set up as oppositional positions, creating a polarizing context of forced choices between adequate alternatives" (Goldner, 1998, p. 264). The depolarizing effect is a major virtue of integration.

Community Family Therapy

Many family therapists start out working in agencies with poor families, but as they realize how powerless therapy alone is to deal with many of the problems impoverished families face, they get discouraged and opt for private practice with middle-class clients. This recognition of family therapy's limits had the opposite effect on Ramon Rojano.

According to Rojano, the greatest obstacle poor people face is the sense of powerlessness that comes with being controlled by a multitude of dehumanizing bureaucracies and the futility of having no hope of achieving the dream of a decent job and a comfortable home. Rojano uses his knowledge of and personal connections with the helping systems to make clients feel reconnected to their communities and empowered to advocate for what they need. Not only does he help families find the resources to survive—child care, jobs, food stamps, housing—which is the essence of traditional casework, but he also begins encouraging aspirations beyond mere survival.

Laura Markowitz (1997) describes Rojano's work this way.

Ramon Rojano is a professional nudge. Let's say you're a single mother on welfare who goes to him because your teenage son is skipping school and on the verge of being expelled. Leaning forward in his chair, the stocky, energetic Rojano will start prodding and poking with his questions in his Spanish accent, zeroing in on your son like he's herding a stray lamb back into the fold. After some minutes of this interrogation, you actually hear your boy admit what's going on with him and promise in a small, sincere voice you haven't heard come

out of him in a long time, that he will go to school regularly if he can graduate. As your mouth opens in surprise, Rojano won't even pause. Now he'll urge the 15-year-old boy to apply for an after-school job he just heard about from someone who runs a program. . . . Rojano will write the phone number down and put it directly into the boy's hand, look him in the eye and use his name a few times to make sure he knows Rojano actually cares whether or not this kid ends up on the streets or in a gang. . . . You think the session is over, right? Not quite. He has plans for you too. Be prepared—he might ask you something outrageous, like whether you've thought about owning your own house. You may be a single mother barely getting by, but as he leans toward you it's like the force of his confidence in you pulls you in, and now he's pressing a piece of paper into your hand with the number of a woman he knows who runs a program that helps people with no money buy a home of their own. (pp. 25–26)

Rojano will ask clients about things that they, in their state of hopelessness and disconnection, never considered—running for the school board, going to college, starting a business or an advocacy program—in such a way that these things seem possible. This is partly because Rojano can see strengths that disheartened clients have forgotten and partly because he has the connections to get the ball rolling. Rojano also recognizes that community empowerment is not enough. Without ongoing family therapy, it wouldn't be long before the single parent in the previous scenario might start being late for work because of renewed conflicts with her son, and that dream of a house would evaporate.

So this is the integration: family therapy with community psychology and social work. Rojano has taken a version of structural family therapy and bolstered it with hands-on advocacy. Structural family therapy was developed in the Wiltwyck agency in Harlem in the late 1950s. Retrospectively, Braulio Montalvo, one of its developers, said, "We couldn't get the resources around the family to uphold the changes they were able to make in family therapy" (quoted in Markowitz, 1997, p. 28). Forty years later, someone has taken the next step by incorporating those resources.

Once again we see that integration requires a new way of thinking. Rojano had to step out of the mind-set that said therapy takes place in an office, even though clients are often constrained by forces untouched in the office. Why not take it to the street so the whole system is addressed? It seems like an obvious question—but maybe not so obvious when you're trapped in your circumstances.

SUMMARY

In the founding decades of family therapy, a number of clearly articulated models were developed, and most family therapists became disciples of one of these approaches. Each of the major schools concentrated on a particular aspect of family life. Experientialists opened people up to feeling, behaviorists helped them reinforce more functional behavior, and Bowenians taught them to think for themselves. By concentrating their attention this way, practitioners of the classic models focused their power for change. If in the process they got a little parochial and competitive, what was the harm?

The harm was that by ignoring the insights of other approaches, orthodox disciples of the various schools limited their impact and applicability. But maybe this parochialism should be understood from a developmental perspective— as a necessary stage in the consolidation of the original insights of the founding models. Perhaps it was useful for the schools to pursue the truth as they knew it in order to mine the full potential of their ideas. If so, that time has passed.

Most of the schools of family therapy have been around long enough to have solidified their approach and proven their worth. That's why the time is ripe for integration.

Valuable as integrative efforts are, however, there remains a serious pitfall in mixing ingredients from different approaches. You don't want to end up with what happens when you blend too many colors from a set of poster paints. The trick is to find a unifying conceptual thread. A successful integration draws on existing therapies in such a way that they can be practiced coherently within one consistent framework. Adding techniques willy-nilly from here and there just doesn't work.

A successful synthesizing effort must strike a balance between breadth and focus. Breadth may be particularly important when it comes to conceptualization. Contemporary family therapists are wisely adopting a broad, biopsychosocial perspective in which biological, psychological, relational, community, and even societal processes are viewed as relevant to understanding people's problems. When it comes to techniques, on the other hand, the most effective approaches don't overload therapists with scores of interventions.

Finally, an effective integration must have clear direction. The trouble with being too flexible is that families have a way of inducting therapists into their habits of avoidance. Good family therapy creates an environment where conversations that should happen at home, but don't, can take place. These dialogues won't happen, however, if therapists abruptly shift from one type of intervention to another in the face of resistance.

Family therapy is ultimately a clinical enterprise, its worth measured in results. The real reason to combine elements from various approaches is to maximize their usefulness, not merely their theoretical inclusiveness. To contradict Billy Crystal, it's better to be effective than to look marvelous.

RECOMMENDED READINGS

Anderson, C., and Stewart, S. 1983. *Mastering resistance: A practical guide to family therapy.* New York: Guilford Press.

Breunlin, D. C., Schwartz, R. C., and Mac Kune-Karrer, B. 1992. *Metaframeworks: Transcending the models of family therapy.* San Francisco: Jossey-Bass.

Eron, J., and Lund, T. 1996. *Narrative solutions in brief therapy.* New York: Guilford Press.

Goldner, V. 1998. The treatment of violence and victimization in intimate relationships. *Family Process.* 37:263–286.

Jacobson, N. S., and Christensen, A. 1996. *Integrative couple therapy.* New York: Norton.

Pinsof, W. M. 1995. *Integrative problem-centered therapy.* New York: Basic Books.

Taibbi, R. 2007. *Doing family therapy*, 2nd ed. New York: Guilford Press.

REFERENCES

Alexander, J., and Parsons, B. 1982. *Functional family therapy.* Pacific Grove, CA: Brooks/Cole.

American Family Therapy Academy Newsletter, Winter 1999, Washington, DC.

Anderson, C., and Stewart, S. 1983. *Mastering resistance: A practical guide to family therapy.* New York: Guilford Press.

Breunlin, D., Schwartz, R., and Mac Kune-Karrer, B. 1992. *Metaframeworks: Transcending the models of family therapy.* San Francisco: Jossey-Bass.

Duhl, B., and Duhl, F. 1981. Integrative family therapy. In *Handbook of family therapy*, A. Gurman and D. Kniskern, eds. New York: Brunner/Mazel.

Eron, J., and Lund, T. 1993. An approach to how problems evolve and dissolve: Integrating narrative and strategic concepts. *Family Process.* 32:291–309.

Eron, J., and Lund, T. 1996. *Narrative solutions in brief therapy.* New York: Guilford Press.

Feldman, L. 1990. *Multi-dimensional family therapy.* New York: Guilford Press.

Goldner, V. 1998. The treatment of violence and victimization in intimate relationships. *Family Process.* 37:263–286.

Goldner, V., Penn, P., Sheinberg, M., and Walker, G. 1990. Love and violence: Gender paradoxes in volatile attachments. *Family Process.* 29:343–364.

Greenberg, L. S., and Johnson, S. M. 1988. *Emotionally focused therapy for couples.* New York: Guilford Press.

Gurman, A. S. 1981. Integrative marital therapy: Toward the development of an interpersonal approach. In *Forms of brief therapy*, S. H. Budman, ed. New York: Guilford Press.

Gurman, A. S. 2002. Brief integrative marital therapy: A depth-behavioral approach. In *Clinical handbook of couple therapy*, 3rd ed., A. S. Gurman and N. S. Jacobson, eds. New York: Guilford Press.

Henggeler, S., and Borduin, C. 1990. *Family therapy and beyond: A multisystemic approach to treating the behavior problems of children and adolescents.* Pacific Grove, CA: Brooks/Cole.

Jacobson, N., and Christensen, A. 1996. *Integrative couple therapy.* New York: Norton.

Kirschner, D., and Kirschner, S. 1986. *Comprehensive family therapy.* New York: Brunner/Mazel.

Liddle, H. A. 1984. Toward a dialectical-contextual-coevolutionary translation of structural-strategic family therapy. *Journal of Strategic and Systemic Family Therapies.* 3:66–79.

Liddle, H. A., Dakoff, G. A., and Diamond, G. 1991. Adolescent substance abuse: Multidimensional family therapy in action. In *Family therapy with drug and alcohol abuse*, 2nd ed., E. Kaufman and P. Kaufman, eds. Boston: Allyn & Bacon.

Mac Kune-Karrer, B. 1999. A conversation with Betty Carter. *American Family Therapy Academy Newsletter*, Winter, Washington, DC.

Markowitz, L. 1997. Ramon Rojano won't take no for an answer. *Family Therapy Networker.* 21:24–35.

Minuchin, S., Rosman, B., and Baker, L. 1978. *Psychosomatic families: Anorexia in context.* Cambridge, MA: Harvard University Press.

Nichols, M. P. 1987. *The self in the system.* New York: Brunner/Mazel.

Nichols, W. C. 1995. *Treating people in families: An integrative framework.* New York: Guilford Press.

Pinsof, W. 1995. *Integrative problem-centered therapy.* New York: Basic Books.

Pinsof, W. 1999. Choosing the right door. *Family Therapy Networker.* 23:48–55.

Sander, F. M. 1979. *Individual and family therapy: Toward an integration.* New York: Jason Aronson.

Scharff, J., ed. 1989. *The foundations of object relations family therapy.* New York: Jason Aronson.

Slipp, S. 1988. *Technique and practice of object relations family therapy.* New York: Jason Aronson.

Stanton, M. D. 1981. An integrated structural/strategic approach to family and marital therapy. *Journal of Marital and Family Therapy.* 7:427–440.

Taibbi, R. 2007. *Doing family therapy*, 2nd ed. New York: Guilford Press.

Walker, G., and Goldner, V. 1995. The wounded prince and the women who love him. In *Gender and power in relationships*, C. Burcke, and B. Speed, eds. London: Routledge, Chapman and Hall.

Comparative Analysis

15

The Essential Differences Among Models

The exponential growth of family therapy crowded the field with competing models, each of which made important contributions. This diversification produced a rich and varied literature, bearing witness to the vitality of the profession, while at the same time creating a confusing array of concepts and techniques. See Table 15.1 for a summary of these models. In this chapter, we offer a comparative analysis of the various models. Each school proclaims a set of truths, yet despite some overlap there are notable conflicts among these truths.

 ## THEORETICAL FORMULATIONS

Theories bring order out of chaos. They organize our awareness and help us make sense of what families are doing. Instead of seeing a "blooming, buzzing confusion," we begin to see patterns of pursuit and distance, enmeshment and disengagement, and problem-saturated stories. The minute you begin to see ineffectual attempts to settle arguments between children as enmeshment, your goal shifts from intervening more effectively to backing off and letting the children settle their own disputes. Here, we evaluate theories in terms of their pragmatic function: understanding families in order to better help them.

Families as Systems

Communications therapists introduced the idea that families are systems. More than the sum of their parts, **systems** are the parts *plus* the way they function together.

Table **15.1** Models of Family Therapy

	Bowenian	Strategic	Structural
Founder(s)	Murray Bowen	Don Jackson Jay Haley	Salvador Minuchin
Key Theoretical Constructs	Differentiation of self	Homeostasis Feedback loops	Subsystems Boundaries
Core Problem Dynamic	Triangles Emotional reactivity	More-of-the-same solutions	Enmeshment/ Disengagement
Key Techniques	Genogram Process questions	Reframing Directives	Enactments Boundary making

	Experiential	Psychodynamic	Cognitive-Behavioral
Founder(s)	Virginia Satir Carl Whitaker	Nathan Ackerman Henry Dicks Ivan Boszormenyi–Nagy	Gerald Patterson Robert Liberman Richard Stuart
Key Theoretical Constructs	Authenticity Self-actualization	Drives Self objects Internal objects	Reinforcement Extinction Schemas

Core Problem Dynamic	Emotional
	  suppression
	Mystification
		Conflict
		Projective identification
		Fixation and regression
			Inadvertent
			  reinforcement
			Aversive control

Key Techniques	Confrontation Structured exercises	Silence Interpretation	Functional analysis Teaching positive control

	Solution-Focused	Narrative
Founder(s)	Steve de Shazer Insoo Kim Berg	Michael White David Epston
Key Theoretical Contructs	Language creates reality	Narrative theory Social constructionism
Core Problem Dynamic	Problem talk	Problem-saturated stories
Key Techniques	Focusing on solutions Identifying exceptions	Externalization Identifying unique outcomes Creating audiences of support

Once, not accepting systems theory was like not believing in apple pie and motherhood. Now the postmodern movement has challenged systems thinking as just another modernist framework, a metaphor taken too literally, and has shifted emphasis from action to meaning and from the organization of the family to the thinking of its members.

It's easy to say that a good therapist takes into account both the self *and* the system. In practice, however, deciding when to delve into individual experience or focus on interactional patterns presents a host of hard choices.

Stability and Change

Communications theorists described families as rule-governed systems with a tendency toward stability or homeostasis (Jackson, 1965), but in order to adjust to changing circumstances, families must also be capable of revising their rules and modifying their structure.

The dual nature of families—*homeostatic* and *changing*—is best appreciated by the communications, structural, and strategic models. They don't presume that symptomatic families are inherently dysfunctional but rather that they have failed to adapt to changing circumstances.

Anyone who ignores this developmental principle runs the risk of placing undue emphasis on pathology. A therapist who sees a family having trouble but fails to consider that they may be stuck at a transitional impasse is apt to think they need an overhaul when a tune-up might do. Therapies that emphasize long-range goals are all susceptible to this therapeutic overkill. Psychoanalytic, experiential, and extended family practitioners are inclined to assume that families need fundamental reorganization. Because they have the equipment for major surgery—long-term therapy—they tend to see their clients as needing it.

The pioneers of family therapy (with the notable exception of Virginia Satir) tended to overestimate homeostatic forces in families and underestimate their flexibility and resourcefulness. This viewpoint encouraged therapists to act as provokers, controllers, and strategizers. The corollary of the family trapped by systemic forces they can't understand was the clever therapist who would do the understanding for them.

Many of the newer approaches are designed to elicit families' resources rather than battle with their resistance. These models encourage therapists to collaborate with families to work out solutions rather than assume that they won't change unless provoked, but when some of these collaborative approaches—like solution-focused therapy, for example—presume that change is easy, that seems as much naive as optimistic.

Process/Content

Most schools of family therapy emphasize the **process** of family interaction. Psychoanalysts and experientialists try to reduce defensiveness and foster open expression of thoughts and feelings; communications therapists increase the flow of interactions and help family members reduce the incongruence between levels of communication; Bowenians block triangulation and encourage "I-positions"; strategic therapists counter problem-maintaining interactions; behaviorists teach parents to use positive control and couples to eliminate coercive communication; structural therapists realign boundaries and strengthen hierarchical organization.

Despite their commitment to process, however, therapists often get caught up in **content** issues. Psychoanalysts lose sight of process when they concentrate on individual family members and their memories of the past. Experientialists often become overly central while working with individual family members to help them overcome emotional defensiveness. The danger is that by so doing, the therapist will neglect interactional processes that affect individual expression.

Behavior therapists neglect process in favor of content when they isolate behavior from its context and ignore the interactional patterns surrounding it. They often interfere with the process of family interaction by assuming a directive, teaching role. (As long as a teacher stands in front of the class lecturing, there's little opportunity to find out what the students can do on their own.)

Process concepts are so central to Bowen systems therapy that there's little danger of forgetting them. Only naive misunderstanding of Bowen's theory would lead someone to think merely of reestablishing family ties without also being aware of processes of triangulation, fusion, and differentiation. The same is true of structural family therapy and communications therapy; process issues are always at center stage.

The newer models, with their deemphasis on systems thinking, have moved away from process. Narrative constructivists are less interested in interactional patterns than in the ways family members understand their problems. They're less interested in changing behavior than in expanding stories. Similarly, because solution-focused therapists have no interest in how problems got started, they ignore the family processes that surround them. The only processes they do attend to are interactions that constitute "exceptions"; times when the problem wasn't a problem.

Monadic, Dyadic, or Triadic Model

Some therapists (e.g., psychoeducational) continue to think of the individual as the patient and include the rest of the family as an adjunct to that person's treatment. Keep in mind that psychoeducational therapists work primarily with serious mental illness (schizophrenia, bipolar disorder), where the family's influence is almost certainly less than in the majority of cases treated by family therapists.

The same cannot be said for narrative therapists, whose focus on cognition leads them to concentrate on individuals and largely ignore the defining characteristics of family therapy: (1) recognizing that psychological symptoms are often the result of family conflict; (2) thinking about human problems as interactional, which means thinking in twos and threes (complementarity, triangles); and (3) treating the family as a unit. Although narrative therapists disregard family conflict in their formulations, their efforts to redefine problems as alien invaders have the effect of uniting families to overcome the problem's influence. It would be interesting to speculate on whether ignoring family conflict but rallying family members to unite in concern would be more effective in cases like anorexia, where problems take on a life of their own, than in others, like school refusal or misbehavior, where the problem is more likely to be a result of family conflicts.

Psychoanalysts tend to think about personality dynamics, whether they meet with individuals or families. They see family life as a product of internalized relationships from the past, and they're often more concerned with these mental ghosts than with the flesh-and-blood family of the present. Behavior therapists use a **monadic model** when they accept a family's definition of a symptomatic child as the problem and set about teaching parents to modify the child's behavior. Experiential therapists focus on individuals to help them uncover and express their feelings.

Actually, no living thing can adequately be understood in terms of the monadic model. A bird's egg may be the closest thing in nature to a self-contained unit. The fetus is locked away inside its shell with all the nutrients it needs to survive. Even this view is incomplete, however, because there is an exchange of heat between the egg and the surrounding environment. Without its mother's warmth, a baby bird will die.

Dyadic concepts are necessary to explain the fact that people act in relation to one another. Even the psychoanalytic patient, free-associating on the couch, filters memories and dreams through reactions to the analyst. Most of the time family therapists operate with dyadic concepts. Even with a large family in treatment, the focus is usually on various pairs or units of the family.

Helping two people learn to relate better doesn't always mean that the therapist thinks in dyadic terms. Behavior therapists work with couples but treat them as individuals, each deficient in the art of communicating. A true **dyadic model** is based on the recognition that two people in a relationship aren't independent entities interacting with each other; they each define the other. Using this model, a wife's agoraphobia would be understood as a reaction to her husband and as a means of influencing him. Likewise, his decision to send her for behavior modification reflects his reluctance to accept his role in her life.

Family therapists of all schools use dyadic concepts: unconscious need complementarity, expressive/instrumental, projective identification, symbiosis, intimacy, quid pro quo, double bind, symmetrical/complementary, pursuer/distancer, and behavioral contract. Some terms are based on dyadic thinking even though they may involve more than two people: *compliant* (referring to a family's relationship to a therapist) and *defiant*. Some seem to involve only one: *countertransference*, *dominant*, and *supercompetent*. Still other concepts are capable of encompassing units of three or more but are often used to refer to units of two: *boundary*, *coalition*, *fusion*, and *disengagement*.

Too often family therapists neglect triadic complications. Murray Bowen did more than anyone to point out that human behavior is always a function of triangles. Structural therapists have consistently emphasized that enmeshment or disengagement between two people is a function of reciprocal relationships with third parties. Communications therapists wrote about triadic relationships but tended to think in units of two. The same is true of most strategic therapists, although Haley, Selvini Palazzoli, and Lynn Hoffman are consistently aware of triangles.

The advantage of the **triadic model** is that it permits a more complete understanding of behavior in context. If a child misbehaves when his mother doesn't use firm discipline, teaching her to be stricter won't work if her behavior reflects her relationship with her husband. Perhaps she allows her child to misbehave as a way of undermining her husband's authority, or she and her husband may have worked out a relationship where her ineffectiveness reassures him that he's the strong one.

The fact that triadic thinking permits a more complete understanding doesn't mean that family therapists must always include all parties in treatment. The issue isn't how many people are in the consulting room but whether the therapist considers problems in their full context.

The Nuclear Family in Context

Just as most family therapists endorse the idea of systems theory, most also describe families as **open systems**. The family is open in that its members interact not only with each other but also with extrafamilial systems. Indeed, a major emphasis in contemporary family therapy has been to expand the focus of attention to include how families are affected by race, gender, ethnicity, class, and sexual orientation. For today's therapist, talking about the social context of families is no longer an idle abstraction.

Members of the Palo Alto group introduced the concept of open systems but treated families as self-contained units. They paid little attention to stressors outside the family and rarely considered the impact of the community or extended family. The first to take the extrafamilial into account were Murray Bowen and Ross Speck. Bowen stressed the role of extended family relationships, and Speck mobilized networks of friends and neighbors to aid in treatment.

Bowen systems therapists and network therapists almost always include people outside the nuclear family in treatment; psychoanalytic, solution-focused, behavioral, and narrative therapists rarely do. Among experientialists, Whitaker routinely invite members of the extended family for one or two sessions.

Including extended family members or friends in treatment is often useful, sometimes essential. It is not, however, the same as thinking of the family as an open system. An open system isn't a larger system; it's a system that interacts with its environment.

Nowhere is the idea of families as open systems better articulated than in Minuchin's (1974) *Families and Family Therapy*. Writing about "Man in His Context," Minuchin contrasts family therapy with psychodynamic theory. The latter, he says, draws on the concept of man as a hero, remaining himself despite the circumstances.[1] On the other hand, "The theory of family therapy is predicated on the fact that man is not an isolate. He is an acting and reacting member of social groups" (p. 2). Minuchin credits Gregory Bateson with erasing the boundary between inner and outer space and goes on to say that just as the boundary separating the individual from the family is artificial, so is the boundary separating the family from the social environment.

One of the things that anyone who works with agency families quickly learns is that attempts to help them often get caught in a sticky web of competing influences from courts, probation departments, child protective agencies, family services, housing programs, group homes, domestic violence agencies, and so on. If middle-class families can be treated as organizationally closed units, with poor families that's impossible. Poor families live in homes without walls.

As services proliferate, fiefdoms multiply. The most obvious problem is lack of coordination. Take, for example, a recent case involving a fifteen-year-old boy who had sexually abused his two adolescent sisters and younger brother. There were agencies working with the female victims: one with the older girl and another with the younger one. One agency worked with the younger boy, one worked with the perpetrator, and one worked with the mother of the victims. There was an art therapist in the public school working with the sexually abused children, and the fifteen-year-old was in a residential school where he had individual and group therapy. Is it any wonder that these helpers were pulling in different directions?

A second, more invidious, problem is that most agencies are mandated to serve individuals: victims or victimizers, adults or children. By addressing themselves to the rights of persons in need of protection or correction, these agencies support individuals, not the family unit.

The usual reaction of therapists who run into these networks of unorganized altruism is to make an effort to coordinate the various inputs and then, when they discover their lack of leverage with all these agencies and helpers, to give up and do the best they can with the family in the office. Among those who aren't willing to give up, Evan Imber-Black (1988) and Richard Kagan and Shirley Schlosberg (1989) have written practical books about working with families in perpetual crisis. Patricia Minuchin, Jorge Colapinto, and Salvador Minuchin (1998) published an inspiring account of their efforts to bring a family focus to agency social work with families of the poor.

Under the influence of social constructionism, the newer models of family therapy have become acutely aware of the social context of the families they treat. This awareness is, however, less likely to take the form of including people outside the family in treatment than being sensitive to social and political influences on the modern family.

THE PERSONAL AS POLITICAL

At one time, it was axiomatic that therapists should maintain therapeutic neutrality: They

---

[1] Although we recognize that it was until recently the rule, use of the masculine pronoun here may be particularly apt. The model of the hero is of a man who keeps his moral integrity hard and intact. He is an isolate, stoic and enduring, cut off from family, community, and faith—that is, the trivial, suffocating world of women.

shouldn't make judgments, take sides, or tell people what to do. They should remain steadfastly objective, encouraging communication or making interpretations, but refrain from imposing their personal opinions and values. Today, however, many practitioners believe that therapists should stand for some things and against others.

Since feminist family therapists first challenged us to face up to gender inequality (e.g., Goldner, 1985; Hare-Mustin, 1978), a growing number of practitioners in the narrative tradition have begun to help family members identify the harmful influence of certain cultural values and practices on their lives and relationships (e.g., Freedman & Combs, 1996; White & Epston, 1990). Indeed, one of the most powerful ways they motivate people to become more active in their own destinies is to help them think of themselves as not flawed but oppressed. Once they start to make progress, the narrative therapist seeks to recruit other people as witnesses and a cheering squad to support the client's new and more positive sense of self.

There is certainly a case to be made for helping people question values that may be contributing to their problems. Who says women should be as thin as runway models? That adolescence must be a time of turmoil? That a man's first obligation is to his career? Moreover, by defining certain destructive assumptions as culturally imposed, narrative therapists invite family members to pull together in opposing those values. Questions can be raised, however, about how this political awareness is put into practice.

Sometimes a readiness to identify oppressive cultural attitudes can lead to ignoring a client's role in his or her own problems in favor of projecting blame outward. Take, for example, the case of a woman who starts to wonder if something about what she's doing might be responsible for her lack of success with men. What happens if the therapist redefines the woman's problem as "The Voice of Insecurity" and urges her to consider this doubt as part of a cultural pattern whereby women learn to conform to the expectations of men? It may be true that women

are more accommodating than men, but what about *this* woman? If her consideration of how she might be contributing to the pattern of unsuccessful relationships in her life is blamed on society, does this empower her?

It's fine to be sympathetic, even to be the client's champion, but when therapists start assuming that their patients are victims of patriarchy, men, racism, or heterosexism, they may fall into the kind of linear, blaming mentality that family therapy was designed to combat in the first place.

At times, the readiness to identify cultural influences as villains in the lives of clients seems like posturing, with the therapist as a knight in shining armor against the forces of oppression. On the other hand, ignoring racism, sexism, ethnocentrism, poverty, crime, and alienation—thinking of families as though they were living on a desert island—makes about as much sense as hiding your head in the sand.

It is impossible to understand relationships without taking into account the social and cultural forces impinging on the partners.

Given the impact of social conditions on families, do family therapists have a unique role to play in politics and society, or are they, at least in their professional capacity, primarily clinicians, trained to treat psychological problems but having no special authority or expertise to right social wrongs? These are important questions without easy answers.

Boundaries

The most useful concepts of interpersonal boundaries are found in the works of Murray Bowen and Salvador Minuchin. Bowen is best at describing the boundary between the self and the family; Minuchin is best at identifying boundaries among various subsystems. In Bowen's terms, individuals vary on a continuum from **fusion** to **differentiation**, while Minuchin describes boundaries as ranging from diffuse to rigid, with resultant **enmeshment** or **disengagement**.

Bowen's thinking reflects the psychoanalytic emphasis on *separation* and *individuation* (Mahler, Pine, & Bergman, 1975), with special attention to the resolution of oedipal attachments and leaving home. In this model, we become ourselves by learning to stand alone. Bowen paid less attention to the emotional isolation stemming from rigid boundaries, treating this as an artifact; a defense against a lack of psychological separateness. Bowen used a variety of terms—*togetherness*, *fusion*, *undifferentiation*, *emotional reactivity*—all referring to the danger of people losing themselves in relationships.

Minuchin offers a more balanced view, describing the problems that result when **boundaries** are either too weak *or* too strong. *Diffuse boundaries* allow too much interference into the functioning of a subsystem; *rigid boundaries* allow too little support. Bowen described only one boundary problem—fusion—and only one goal—differentiation. Fusion is like a disease; you can have a bad case or a mild one. Minuchin speaks of two possibilities—enmeshment or disengagement—and his therapy is designed to fit the specific case.

Bowen's *fusion* and Minuchin's *enmeshment* both deal with blurred boundaries, but they aren't synonymous. **Fusion** is a psychological quality of individuals, the opposite of individuation. The dynamics of fusion have an impact on relationships (especially in the form of reactivity and triangulation), but fusion is *within* the person. Enmeshment is *between* people.

These conceptual differences also lead to differences in treatment. Bowenian therapists encourage relationships but emphasize autonomy. Success is measured by **differentiation** of self. Structuralists encourage authenticity but strive to restructure family relationships either by strengthening *or* weakening boundaries. Success is measured by the harmonious functioning of the whole family.

NORMAL FAMILY DEVELOPMENT

As a rule, family therapists have had little to say about developmental issues.[2] One of the distinguishing characteristics of family therapy is its focus on here-and-now interactions. Normal family development, which involves the past and what's healthy, has therefore been underemphasized.

Most therapists have assumptions about what's normal, and these ideas influence their work. The problem is that as long as these implicit models remain unarticulated, they may reflect personal bias as much as anything else. When it comes to setting goals for family treatment, the choice isn't between having or not having a model of what's healthy but between using a model that's been spelled out and exam-

---

[2]This is true despite the current popularity of disavowing impositional models of normality. It's one thing to challenge universals in favor of the particular, but accusing traditional family therapists of operating with fixed views of normality is a straw-man argument.

ined or operating on the basis of ill-defined personal standards.

Family therapists concerned with the past, especially members of Bowenian and psychoanalytic schools, have had the most to say about normal development. Although most schools of family therapy aren't concerned with how families get started, Bowenians and psychoanalysts have a great deal to say about marital choice. Bowen talked about *differentiation*, *fusion*, and *triangles*, while psychoanalytic writers speak of *unconscious need complementarity*, *projective identification*, and *idealization*. However, they seem to be using different terms to describe similar phenomena. Psychoanalysts speak of marital choice as an object of *transference* from the family of origin and of people choosing partners to match their own level of maturity; Bowen said that people pick partners who replicate familiar patterns of family interaction and select mates at similar levels of differentiation.

These are descriptions of ways in which people marry their own alter egos. Both schools also discuss how people choose mates who appear to be different, at least on the surface, in ways that are exciting and seem to make up for deficiencies in the self. Obsessive individuals tend to marry hysterical individuals, and according to Bowen, togetherness-oriented people often marry distancers. This brings up another way in which the Bowenian and psychodynamic schools are similar to each other and different from others. Both recognize that personalities have layers. Both think that the success of a relationship depends not only on shared interests and values but also on the nature of the partners' internal object images.

Even if they don't emphasize the past, most of the other schools of family therapy have concepts for describing normal family development. For example, communications therapists speak of the *quid pro quos* (Jackson, 1965) exchanged in normal marriages, while behaviorists describe the same phenomenon in terms of *social exchange theory* (Thibaut & Kelley, 1959).

Virginia Satir described normal families as those in which communication is direct and honest, where differences are faced rather than hidden, and where emotions are openly expressed. Under these conditions, she believed, people develop healthy *self-esteem*, which enables them to take the risks necessary for authentic relationships.

According to Minuchin (1974), clinicians should have some appreciation of the facts of ordinary family life to become effective therapists. Therapists need to distinguish functional from dysfunctional structures, as well as pathological structures from structures that are simply transitional.

Because structural therapy begins by assessing the adequacy of a family's organization, it sometimes appears to impose a standard. In fact, however, normality is defined in terms of functionality, and structural therapists recognize that diverse patterns may be equally functional. The clarity of subsystem boundaries is more important than the composition of the subsystem. For example, a parental subsystem made up of a single parent and oldest child can function effectively if the lines of authority are clearly drawn. Patterns of enmeshment and disengagement are viewed as preferred styles, not necessarily as indications of abnormality.

Most therapists don't think in terms of remaking families and therefore believe they have little need for models of what a family should be like. Instead, they intervene around specific problems—problem-maintaining interactions, problem-saturated stories, forgotten solutions—conceptualized in terms of function, not structure. The patterns they observe are dysfunctional; therefore, by implication, what's functional must be just the opposite.

Although it may not be necessary to understand a family's past in order to help them, it is useful to have a way of understanding the family's organization in the present, using a model of normal behavior to set goals for treatment. Such a model should include a design for the present and for change over time. Among the ideas presented in this book, the most useful for a basic model of normal family functioning include *structural hierarchy*, *effective communication*, and *family life-cycle development*.

DEVELOPMENT OF BEHAVIOR DISORDERS

In the early days of family therapy, patients were seen as victims—**scapegoats**—whose symptoms maintained family stability. Much of the literature was about dysfunctional ways of keeping the peace: *scapegoating*, *pseudomutuality*, *family projection process*, *double bind*, *mystification*, and so on. These malignant mechanisms may have torn young people apart, but they helped keep families together. It was a simple and satisfying tale of malevolence. No one exactly blamed the parents—their coercions weren't really deliberate—but these explanations did rest on parental faults and failings and as such had mythic force. The idea that schizophrenia was a sacrifice children made for their families was absolutely riveting—and absolutely untrue.

Today, family therapists think less about what causes problems than how families unwittingly perpetuate them.

Inflexible Systems

Early observers of schizophrenic families emphasized their inflexibility. Wynne coined the term **rubber fence** to dramatize how psychotic families resist outside influence and **pseudomutuality** to describe their facade of harmony. R. D. Laing showed how parents, unable to tolerate their children's individuality, used **mystification** to deny their experience. Communication theorists thought that the most striking disturbance in schizophrenic families was that they lacked mechanisms for changing their rules. They were programmed for negative feedback, treating novelty and change as deviations to be resisted.

This tradition of viewing families of mentally ill patients as rigidly homeostatic was taken into the 1980s by Selvini Palazzoli in the form of her concept of "dirty games." Carol Anderson and Michael White countered this negative perspective by suggesting that rigidity might be the result of living with serious problems and of being blamed for them by mental health professionals.

Explaining family problems in terms of homeostatic inflexibility became one of the cornerstones of the strategic school. Dysfunctional families respond to problems with a limited range of solutions. Even when the solutions don't work, these families stubbornly keep trying. Behaviorists use a similar idea when they explain symptoms as resulting from faulty efforts to control behavior. Often, when parents think they're punishing misbehavior, they're actually reinforcing it with attention.

According to psychoanalytic and experiential theories, intrapsychic rigidities, in the form of *conflict*, *developmental arrest*, and *emotional suppression*, are the individual's contribution to family inflexibility. Psychoanalysts consider unhealthy families as **closed systems** that resist change. When stressed, inflexible families regress to earlier levels of development, where unresolved conflicts left them fixated.

Experientialists describe dysfunctional families as emotionally stagnant. If it's true that you sometimes have to try something different just to know you're alive, families afraid of rocking the boat become timid and lifeless. The symptom bearer is a victim of the family's opposition to the life force.

Structural therapists locate the inflexibility of families in the boundaries between subsystems, but structural problems are not necessarily the result of some flaw in the family. Normal families may develop problems if they are unable to modify a previously functional structure to cope with a crisis. Family therapists should be clear on this point: Symptomatic families are often basically sound; they simply may need help adjusting to changed circumstances.

Solution-focused and narrative therapists avoid implicating family members in the development of their problems. Both camps prefer to focus on the strengths of individuals in the family and on times when they used their resources to triumph over their troubles. What these models do identify as problematic are rigid habits of thought that lead people to consider themselves defeated. Solution-focused therapists leave it at that; they don't speculate about the origins of defeatist thinking. Narrative therapists point to what they consider toxic systems of belief in the culture that are internalized by family members. It's society, not the family, that's inflexible.

The Function of Symptoms

The first family therapists portrayed the identified patient as serving a function in disturbed families by detouring conflict and thus stabilizing the family. Vogel and Bell (1960) described emotionally disturbed children as "family scapegoats," singled out as objects of parental projection on the basis of traits that set them apart. Thereafter, the patient's deviance promotes cohesion in the family by uniting the parents in concern.

Today, most family therapists deny that symptoms have either meaning or function. Indeed, narrative, solution-focused, and psychoeducational therapists are so diametrically opposed to the idea that symptoms serve a purpose that these approaches can be seen as inspired to counter that idea. Narrative therapy is built around the metaphor of symptoms as alien oppressors, and the psychoeducation approach is devoted to exonerating families from responsibility for mental illness.

Behaviorists have always argued against the idea that symptoms are a sign of underlying pathology. Behavioral family therapists treat problems as skill deficits or as the result of faulty efforts to change behavior. Restricting their focus to symptoms is one reason they're successful in discovering the contingencies that reinforce them; it's also the reason they aren't very successful in cases where a child's behavior problems function to stabilize a conflicted marriage or where a couple's arguments protect them from dealing with deeper conflicts.

Some schools of family therapy continue to believe that symptoms signal deeper problems and may serve to maintain family stability. In families that can't tolerate open conflict, a symptomatic member may act as a smokescreen and a diversion. In psychoanalytic, Bowenian, and structural formulations, a couple's inability to form an intimate bond may be ascribed to the fact that one or both of them are still embroiled in their parents' relationship. In this way, symptomatic behavior is transmitted across generations and serves to stabilize the multigenerational family system.

Pathologic Triangles

Pathologic triangles are at the heart of several family therapy explanations of behavior disorder. Among these, Bowen's theory is the most elegant. Bowen explained how when two people are in conflict, the one who experiences the most anxiety will triangle in a third person. This model not only provides an explanation of systems pathology but also serves as a warning: As long as a therapist remains tied to one party in an emotional conflict, he or she is part of the problem.

In psychoanalytic theory, oedipal conflicts are considered the root of neurosis. Here the triangle is triggered by family interactions but lodged in the individual psyche. A mother's tenderness may be seductive and a father's jealousy threatening, but the wish to do away with the father and possess the mother is a product of fantasy. Pathological fixation of this conflict may be caused by developments in the outer space of the family, but the conflict is harbored in the inner space of the child's mind.

Structural family theory is based on triangular configurations in which a dysfunctional boundary between two subsystems is the reciprocal of a boundary with a third. A father and son's enmeshment reflects the father and mother's disengagement; a single mother's disengagement from her children is the counterpart of her over-involvement outside the family. Structural theory also uses the concept of pathological triangles to explain *conflict-detouring triads*, whereby parents divert their conflict onto their child. Minuchin, Rosman, and Baker (1978) have even demonstrated that physiological changes occur when parents in conflict transmit their stress to a psychosomatic child.

Strategic therapists typically work with a dyadic model, in which one person's symptoms are maintained by others' efforts to resolve them. Haley and Selvini Palazzoli, however, used a triangular model in the form of **cross-generational coalitions**. These "perverse triangles," as Haley (1977) called them, occur when a parent and child collude to form a bastion of covert opposition to the other parent.

Triangular functioning is less central to the newer models because they're not concerned with *how* families develop problems. It might even be argued that ignoring family dynamics is one of the strengths of narrative and solution-focused approaches, if doing so helps these therapists zero in on the constricting habits of thought they're interested in. It might also be said, however, that ignoring family dynamics is one of the weaknesses of these approaches, especially in cases in which conflict in a family isn't just going to disappear because family members work together to solve a common problem.

When things go wrong, it's tempting to look for someone to blame. Your partner never talks about his feelings? He must be from Mars. Families drop out after the first couple of sessions? They must be resistant.

Before we get too judgmental, let's recognize that it's perfectly natural to attribute our problems to other people's influence. Because we look at life from inside our own skins, we're most aware of other people's contributions to our problems—but therapists, we'd hope, aren't handicapped by this egocentric bias. No, they're handicapped by another bias.

Whenever you hear one side of an unhappy story, it's only natural to sympathize with the person doing the telling. If a friend tells you her boss is a jerk, your sympathy puts you automatically on her side. Experience suggests that most stories have two sides, but when your impulse is to show solidarity with someone who's telling you his or her troubles, the temptation is to look abroad for villains. Among professional helpers, this temptation is too often not resisted.

One reason for blaming family problems on easily vilified influences—men, racism, mothers—is that it's hard to see past individual personalities to the patterns of interaction that make them a family, unless you see the whole group and see them in action. That's why family therapy was invented in the first place.

GOALS OF THERAPY

The goal of psychotherapy is to help people change in order to relieve their distress. This is true of individual therapy, group therapy, and family therapy. Why, then, is so much written about the goals of various schools of therapy?

Some of it has to do with differing ideas about how people change, some of it merely with alternate vocabularies for describing that change. When Bowenians speak of *differentiation of self* and psychoanalysts speak of *increased ego strength*, they mean pretty much the same thing.

All therapists are interested in resolving problems, but they vary from concentrating exclusively on symptom resolution to being concerned with the health of the entire family system. Strategic, solution-focused, and behavioral therapists are least concerned with changing the whole system; psychoanalytic and Bowenian therapists are most concerned with systems change.

The goal of structural family therapy is both symptom resolution and structural change, but the structural change that is sought has the modest aim of reorganizing that part of the family that's failed to adjust to meet changing circumstances. Narrative, communications, and experiential therapists also aim midway between symptomatic improvement and family reorganization. Practitioners from these schools focus neither on presenting complaints nor on the overall family system. Instead they concentrate on processes they believe underlie symptoms: cognitive constructions, patterns of communication, and emotional expressivity. Improvements in these processes are thought to resolve symptoms and promote growth.

The focus of strategic therapy and its solution-focused offshoot is on problem solving. The goal is simply to resolve whatever complaints clients present. Narrative therapists, many of whom rebelled against the mechanistic aspects of their own strategic background (cf. Freedman & Combs, 1996), aim to help clients solve the problems they come in with, but also to leave with an enhanced sense of personal agency.

CONDITIONS FOR BEHAVIOR CHANGE

To establish family treatment as a distinct and innovative approach, family therapists began by emphasizing their differences with individual therapy. Later, they emphasized differences among themselves. Today, there is much cross-fertilization among the schools. But while most schools share a broad consensus about principles of change, they still differ on many specific issues.

Action or Insight?

Action and insight are the primary vehicles of change in family therapy. Most therapists use both mechanisms, but some schools emphasize either action (strategic, behavioral) or insight (psychoanalytic, narrative).

The case for action is based on the observation that people often don't change even though they understand that they should. The truth of this is familiar to anyone who's ever tried to lose weight, quit smoking, or spend more time with the kids.

Behaviorists make the case for action by pointing out that behavior is often reinforced unwittingly. Explanations, they say, don't change behavior; reinforcement does. Like behaviorists, strategic therapists focus on behavior and aren't concerned with insight. They don't believe in fostering understanding, and they don't believe in teaching; instead, they believe that the way to change behavior is through manipulation. They box stuck families into a corner from which the only way out is to become unstuck.

The case for insight is based on the belief that if people understand themselves better, they'll be free to act in their own best interests. Psychoanalysts believe that people are blind to their real motives. Without insight into hidden conflicts, action can be self-defeating, even dangerous.

What some people consider action may be regarded by psychoanalysts as acting out; diversions to mask the anxiety that signals underlying conflicts. Only by understanding their impulses and the dangers involved in expressing them can people achieve lasting change.

Discussions of insight are often divisive, because insight is a buzzword. Proponents extol it; opponents belittle it. Advocates of insight endow it with pseudomedical properties: Insight, like medicine, cures. Actually, insight doesn't cure anything; it's something through which cure occurs. To say that a family acquires insight means that family members learn what they intend by their actions and what their consequences are; how they act on that insight is up to them.

In contrast to the polar positions taken by some schools, others work with action *and* insight. In structural family therapy, change is initiated in action and then supported by understanding. According to Minuchin (Minuchin & Nichols, 1993), family structure and family beliefs support and reinforce each other; the only way to achieve lasting change is to challenge both. Action comes first because it leads to new experiences that make insight possible.

In Bowen systems theory, interventions also use both action and understanding, but the order of effect is reversed. Bowenians begin by calming people down so that they'll stop blaming each other and start reflecting on the relationship processes they're caught up in. Once they begin to see their role in triangles and polarizations (like the pursuer/distancer dynamic), family members are encouraged to carry out relationship experiments in which they alter their participation in these patterns.

The Milan model and the later work of Cecchin, Boscolo, and Hoffman elevated the importance of working with systems of meaning. Thus systems-oriented family therapists became less tied to behavioral analyses and action-oriented interventions. Taking into account the *externalizing* technique of Michael White and David Epston, the therapy as conversation model of the late Harry Goolishian and Harlene Anderson, the popularity of social construction-ism, and the reemergence of psychodynamic influence, the trend in the field is definitely away from action and toward, if not insight, at least cognition.[3]

Resistance

Families are notorious for **resistance** to change. In addition to the recalcitrance of individual family members, the system itself resists change—or to bring this abstraction down to earth, the structure that holds a family together is supported by the habits of every one of its members.

The same device that gives family therapy its greatest leverage—bringing all the players together—also carries with it the seeds of resistance. With all parties to a problem present, it's hard to resist the temptation to blame someone else—or at least to wait for someone else to change first.

It's popular these days to speak of "the death of resistance," and many of the newer schools claim that resistance isn't a problem in their nonhierarchical approaches. This is partly true, partly posturing. While it is true that resistance is more to be expected against the highly visible confrontations of a Minuchin or a Whitaker, resistance—or reluctance to change—is still an issue even for today's persuasive, cognitive approaches. Narrative therapists neither argue with nor confront clients about their contribution to family conflicts, but what they describe as externalizing and deconstructive conversations are part of an effort to impose their own narrative shape on clients' stories. Resistance may not be overt, but people do not as readily give up their "problem-saturated stories" as you might think.[4]

Behavior therapists ignore resistance and succeed only when their clients are willing to follow instructions. Other schools of family therapy consider resistance a major obstacle and have devised various ways to overcome it.

Psychoanalysts believe that resistance is motivated by unconscious defenses, which must be made manifest and then resolved through interpretation. This is an intrapsychic model, but it doesn't ignore conscious and interactional resistances. Instead, analytic therapists believe that interactional conflict—among family members or between the family and therapist—has its roots in unconscious resistance to basic drives. Experiential therapists have a similar model; they see resistance to emotional expression, and they

---

[3]The difference is that *insight* refers to an understanding of the true nature of things; in the context of psychotherapy, this means the underlying motivations behind one's thoughts and behavior. *Cognition*, on the other hand, refers more narrowly to one's point of view. In the context of therapy, cognitive change involves a shift to a more productive point of view—not necessarily one that is more true, only more useful.

---

[4]People come to therapy not just to solve problems but to complain and to talk about their troubles—and because they aren't at home, they expect someone to listen.

blast away at it using confrontation and emotive exercises. Experientialists believe that breaching defenses releases healthy strivings; change occurs from the inside out.

Minuchin's solution to the problem of resistance is straightforward: He wins families over by joining and accommodating them. This gives him the leverage to utilize powerful confrontations designed to restructure family interactions. Resistance is seen as a product of the interaction between therapist and family; change is accomplished by alternately challenging the family and then rejoining them to repair breaches in the therapeutic relationship.

Steve de Shazer denied the existence of resistance, saying that it's the family's way of cooperating. It's up to the therapist to learn to use it. Richard Schwartz sees resistance as a reasonable reaction of protective parts of family members whose job it is to not allow anyone into the family until it's clear that person won't harm them. Schwartz goes to great lengths to reassure those protective parts.

Finally, under the heading of resistance, we should consider the phenomenon of *induction*. Induction is what happens when a therapist is drawn into a family system and abides by its rules. Induction is so subtle that it's hard to see, so seductive that it's hard to resist. As helpers and healers, therapists are prone to take over for people, doing for them what they don't do for themselves. But taking over—being inducted—precludes real change. As long as families have someone to do for them, they won't learn to do for themselves.

One reason early family therapists encountered so much resistance was that they were eager to change people and slow to understand them. It turns out that families, like you and me, resist efforts to change them by people they feel don't understand them. Family therapists learned to see nagging and withdrawal as circular, but they were slow to see them as human. Only later did therapists come to see through the nagging to the pain behind it and to understand the anxiety that motivates withdrawal.

Rigidly stuck families are run by their fears, and therapists, eager to be liked, are vulnerable to those fears. Families quickly teach therapists what's threatening: "Don't ask *him* about *that*." The art of therapy is understanding and sympathizing with those fears but avoiding induction enough to be able to challenge them. As in so many things, progress sometimes means doing what you're afraid to do.

THERAPY

Comparing techniques by reading about them is difficult because clinicians often describe their interventions in abstract terms. When techniques are described in theoretical jargon—*restructuring, unbalancing, externalizing, differentiating*— it's not always clear precisely what's meant. In this section, we treat issues of technique as a series of practical questions about how to conduct therapy.

Assessment

Each school of family therapy has a theory about families that determines where they look for problems and what they see. Some consider the whole family (Milan, structural, Bowenian); some concentrate on individuals (psychoanalytic, experiential); some focus on sequences that maintain symptoms (strategic, behavioral); and some pay very little attention to what causes problems, preferring instead to mobilize people to work against them (solution-focused, narrative).

Behaviorists place the greatest emphasis on assessment and use the most formal procedures. The advantage of the behavioral emphasis on assessment is that it provides baseline data, definite goals, and a reliable way to determine whether therapy succeeds. The disadvantage is that by using standardized interviews and questionnaires, you don't see families in action. By looking at only part of the family (mother and child, or marital couple), you miss the total context; by relying on questionnaires, you learn only what the family reports.

Structural therapists also emphasize assessment, but their evaluations are based on observation. Enactments give the therapist a chance to observe enmeshment and disengagement. The strengths of this school's assessment procedure are that it uses the family's patterns of interaction among themselves, it includes the entire family, and it's organized in terms that point directly to desired changes.

The Bowenian school also does an excellent job of considering the whole family. Unlike structuralists, however, Bowenians rely on what they're told, and they're interested in the past as well as the present.

The breadth of psychoanalytic theory enables practitioners to speculate well ahead of their data; a little information suggests a great deal. The advantage is that the theory provides valuable leads to hidden meanings. The danger is that the theory may distort the data, leading clinicians to see only what they expect to see. Experientialists have neither these advantages nor disadvantages. Their evaluations are guided by a simple theory about feelings and how they are suppressed; they may not uncover much that's hidden, and they tend not to see things that aren't there.

Two of the newer schools, narrative and solution-focused, eschew any form of assessment. Solution-focused therapists believe that dwelling on problems undermines the positive thinking they hope to generate. They also believe that solutions aren't necessarily related to the ways problems come about. Narrative therapists believe that looking within families for problems perpetuates the therapist-as-expert stance they want to get away from. By personifying problems and talking about their effects rather than their causes, they circumvent the finger pointing that often accompanies discussions of how problems got started. The danger is that by disregarding how problems arise, they may overlook real conflicts—and conflict, as you may have noticed, doesn't necessarily go away just because you ignore it.

Decisive Interventions

Family therapists use a wide variety of techniques; some dictated by their model, others by the therapist's personality and experience. Even if we limited our attention to the techniques specific to each of the schools, the list would be long and confusing. Some techniques are used by virtually everyone—asking questions, reflecting feelings, clarifying communication—and this list has been growing as the field has become more integrated. Each school, however, relies on one or two techniques that are unique and decisive.

In psychoanalytic therapy there are two definitive techniques. The first of these, *interpretation*, is well known but not well understood. Properly used, interpretation refers to elucidating unconscious meaning. It does not mean statements of opinion ("You need to express your feelings before you can really be close"); advice ("As long as you continue writing to him, the affair isn't over"); theory ("Some of the reasons you were attracted to him were based on unconscious needs"); or confrontations ("You said you didn't care, but you were really angry"). Interpretations are statements about unconscious meaning: "You've been complaining about your son's arguing with you all the time. Based on what you've said previously, I think that some of your anger is deflected from your husband. He does the same thing, but you're afraid to tell him so, and that's why you get so mad at your son."

By refraining from asking questions or giving advice, psychoanalytic practitioners maintain a stance of listening and fostering understanding. By limiting interventions to interpretations, the therapist makes it clear that treatment is designed for learning; whether families take advantage of this atmosphere and change their behavior as a result of what they learn is up to them.

The second decisive technique in analytic treatment is *silence*. A therapist's silence permits him or her to discover what's on a patient's mind and to test a family's resources; it also lends force to the eventual interpretations. When a therapist is silent, family members talk, following their own thoughts rather than responding to the therapist's. When they learn that the therapist won't interrupt, they react and respond to each other. This produces a wealth of information that might not otherwise emerge. If a father begins by saying "The problem is my depression" and the therapist immediately asks "How long have you been depressed?," he or she may not discover what thoughts are associated in the man's mind with his depression or how the man's wife responds to his complaint.

The decisive technique in experiential therapy is *confrontation*. Confrontations are designed to provoke emotional reactions and are often blunt. It isn't unusual for experiential therapists to tell clients to shut up or to mock them for being insincere. Confrontations are often combined with *personal disclosure*, the second signature technique of this school. Experientialists use themselves as emotionally expressive models. Finally, most experiential therapists also use *structured exercises*. These include role-playing, psychodrama, sculpting, and family drawings. The rationale for these techniques is that they stimulate emotional experiencing; their drawback is that they're artificial. Family members may get something off their chests in a structured exercise but may not transfer this to their interactions at home.

Most people associate reinforcement with behavior therapy, but reinforcement isn't a technique used in cognitive-behavioral family therapy; *observation* and *teaching* are the vehicles of this approach. Behavioralists begin by observing the contingencies of reinforcement. Their aim is to discover the antecedents and consequences of problem behavior. Once they've completed a *functional analysis of behavior*, they become instructors, teaching families how they inadvertently reinforce undesirable behavior. As teachers, their most useful lesson is the use of positive control. They teach parents that it's more effective to reward good behavior than to punish bad behavior; they teach married couples to substitute being nice to each other for their usual bickering.

Positive control—rewarding desirable behavior—is one of the most useful principles in psychotherapy. It's a valuable lesson for families and for therapists. Therapists, like parents, tend to chide their charges for mistakes. Unfortunately, if you're told that you're suppressing your feelings, spoiling your children, or using coercive control, you're apt to feel picked on and put down. Although it may be necessary to point out people's mistakes, it's more effective to concentrate on praising the positive aspects of their behavior. Among practicing family therapists, this point seems best understood by structuralists, who speak of working with the family's strengths; by strategists and Milan therapists, who use reframing and positive connotation to support efforts to do the right thing; and of course by solution-focused and narrative therapists, who have raised the power of positive thinking to an art form.

As behavior therapists have paid increasing attention to cognition, they have endeavored to uncover and challenge assumptions that underlie unproductive behavior. That is, they do when they're using the cognitive-behavioral model effectively. We have observed a sharp difference between some practitioners of this approach who attribute clichéd assumptions to clients—assuming, for example, that anyone who is depressed must be pessimistic about themselves, the world, and the future—and those practitioners who don't make assumptions and don't preach. These cognitive-behaviorists use Socratic questioning to find out what their clients actually believe and then to help them test the validity of those assumptions for themselves.

Bowen systems therapists are also teachers, but they follow a different curriculum. They *teach people to be responsible for themselves* and how by doing so they can transform their entire families. Being responsible for yourself means getting clear about what you think and feel—not what your mother says or what you read in the *New York Times* but what you really believe—and then being true to your beliefs in dealings with other people. You don't take responsibility by changing others or wishing they were different; you do so by speaking for yourself and maintaining your own values. The power of this position is tremendous. If a client can accept who he or she is and that other people are different from him- or herself, then he or she no longer has to approach relationships with the idea that someone has to change. This enables the client to be in contact with people without becoming unduly upset or emotionally reactive.

In addition to teaching differentiation, Bowenian therapists promote two corollary lessons: *avoiding triangulation* and *reopening cut-off family relationships*. Taken together, these three lessons enable one person to transform the whole network of his or her family system. Even if her spouse nags, if his children are disobedient, if her mother never comes to visit, the *client* can create a change. Other schools of therapy gain leverage by including the entire family in treatment. Bowenians teach individuals to be themselves, to make contact with others, and to deal directly with the people they have conflicts with. This gives a person a tool for change that's portable and lasting.

Communications family clinicians contributed so much to the theoretical base of family therapy that it's difficult to single out their interventions. Perhaps their greatest achievement was pointing out that communication is multilayered and that often the most important things being said are said covertly. Therapy was designed to make the covert overt. Initially, this was done by *clarifying communication* and pointing out hidden messages. When this direct approach met with resistance, therapists began using directives to make the rules of family functioning explicit and to provoke changes in the rules.

Strategic therapy is an offshoot of communications theory, and the techniques used by strategists are refinements of those used by communicationists. Principal among these are *reframing*, *directives*, and *positive connotation*. Strategic practitioners begin by getting concrete descriptions of problems and then attempt to solve them. In the process, they pay particular attention to the family's language and expectations. They try to grasp the family's point of view and acknowledge it—in a positive connotation, then they use reframing to shift the family's point of view and directives to interrupt problem-maintaining behavior.

Directives are designed to interrupt homeostatic patterns, they are assigned to be carried out when the family is at home, and they are often paradoxical. Although strategic therapists emphasize fitting the treatment to the patient, they often assumed that indirect interventions are necessary to outwit resistance. This is sometimes but not always true. It's not so much that some families are resistant and others aren't, but that resistance isn't a property *in* families. It's a quality of interaction *between* therapist and family. A therapist who proceeds on the assumption that families are unable and unwilling to follow advice is likely to encounter the expected resistance.

Structural family therapy is also a therapy of action, but in this approach, the action occurs in the session. The decisive techniques are *enactments* and *boundary making*. Rigid boundaries are softened when the therapist gets people to talk with each other and blocks attempts to interrupt them. Diffuse boundaries are strengthened when the therapist works to support autonomy of individuals and subsystems.

Several promising techniques emerged in the 1980s around which whole models of therapy were built. Steve de Shazer and his colleagues expanded the technique of *focusing on successful solutions* that family members had tried but abandoned. The result was solution-focused therapy. Michael White did the same with the technique of *externalization*—personifying problems and attributing oppressive intentions to them, which is a powerful device for getting family members to unite against a common enemy.

Actually, externalization is a concept, not a technique. The decisive technique of narrative therapy is a persistent and forceful series of *questions*—whereby the therapist begins by trying to understand the client's experiences of suffering but then switches from understanding to prodding the clients to think about their problems as malevolent agents. Narrative therapists use a relentless series of questions to challenge negative images and convince clients that they have reason to be proud of themselves and that their fates are in their own hands.

In reaction to the sectarian techniquism that reached a peak in the early 1980s, family therapists today borrow freely from other approaches and deemphasize technique in favor of a less hierarchical and more respectful quality of therapist-family relationship. Both trends are healthy, but we would like to end this section with two questions: When is cross-fertilization enriching, and, when does eclecticism rob separate approaches of their muscle by watering down their distinctive elements? How best can family therapists get away from a formulaic emphasis on technique without losing leverage altogether by practicing a more congenial but less effective form of treatment?

SUMMARY

The theme of the early years in the development of family therapy was the proliferation of competing schools, each advertised as unique and uniquely effective. Today, in the twenty-first century, the theme is integration. So many talented therapists have been working for so long that the field has accumulated a number of useful ways of looking at and treating families. In what follows, we offer some very subjective comments about a few of the concepts and methods that have proven themselves classics of family therapy.

Theories of family functioning have both a scientific and a practical purpose. The most useful theories treat families as systems; have concepts to describe forces of stability and change; notice the process underlying the content of family discussions; recognize the triadic nature of human relationships; remember to consider the context of the nuclear family rather than viewing it as a closed system; and appreciate the function of boundaries in protecting the cohesiveness of individuals, subgroups, and families.

Clinicians are more concerned with pathology and change than with normality, but it's useful to have some ideas about normal family functioning—both to mold treatment goals and to distinguish what's problematic and needs changing

from what's normal and doesn't. Some of the most useful concepts of normal family functioning include the structural model of families as open systems in transformation; the communications model of direct, clear, and honest communication, with rules firm enough to ensure stability and flexible enough to allow change; the behavioral model of equitable exchange of interpersonal costs and benefits, the use of positive control instead of coercion, and mutual reinforcement between partners; the strategic model of systemic flexibility, which allows adjustment to changing circumstances and the ability to find new solutions when old ones don't work; and the Bowenian model, which explains how differentiation of self enables people to be independent at times, intimate at others.

Most family therapy concepts of behavior disorder focus on systems and interactions, but the psychoanalytic, Bowenian, narrative, and experiential models add psychological depth to the interactional view, bridging the gap between inner experience and outward behavior. The fact that many divorced people repeat the mistakes of their first marriages supports the idea that some of what goes on in families is a product of individual character. Some of the most valuable concepts of personal dysfunction in families are Bowen's concept of fusion; the experiential concepts of repressed affect and fear of taking risks; and the psychoanalytic concepts of developmental arrest, internal object relations, instinctual conflict, and hunger for appreciation.

These concepts of individual dynamics are useful adjuncts, but the major ideas in the field explain behavior disorder in terms of systems theory. The most influential of these are about inflexible systems, too rigid to accommodate individual strivings or adjust to changing circumstances; symptomatic family members promoting cohesion by stabilizing the nuclear and extended families; inadequate hierarchical structure; families too tightly or too loosely structured; and pathologic triangles.

Some of the goals of family therapy are universal—clarifying communication, solving problems, promoting autonomy—and some are unique. Some of the schools take presenting problems at face value, whereas others treat them as metaphors. In either case, goals shouldn't be so broad as to neglect symptom resolution or too narrow to ensure the stability of symptom resolution. Incidentally, values are seldom discussed in the family therapy literature, the notable exception being Boszormenyi-Nagy. Too little consideration has been given to practicing therapists' ethical responsibilities, including the possibility of conflicting responsibilities to individuals, families, and the larger community.

If narrative therapists have tended to ignore family dynamics in order to emphasize the ills of the culture, perhaps this will turn out to be one of those swings of the pendulum that eventually corrects itself. There's surely no need to neglect systems theory to introduce an ethical dimension to working with people in context.

Some of the major differences among family therapists about how behavior is changed are focused on the following issues: action or insight; change in the session or change at home; duration of treatment; resistance; family–therapist relationship; paradox; and the extent to which it's important to work with the whole family system, part of it, or just motivated individuals. Even though general consensus exists about some issues (for example, once most family therapists believed that action was primary and insight was secondary), there have always been divergent opinions on every one of these points. Strategic therapists, for example, flatly denied that insight is useful.

We've looked at some of the major methodological issues and tried to separate out the decisive techniques of the different schools. As is always the case when a number of variables are involved in a final result, it's not easy to know how much each variable contributes to that result or how important each one is. Furthermore, the more we talk about techniques, the greater the danger of seeing family therapy as a purely technological enterprise. Studying families is like solving a riddle; the art of treating them is to relieve suffering and anguish. The job of the theoretician is to decode and decipher, which requires theory and ingenuity. The job of the therapist is healing, which requires theory but also conviction, perseverance, and caring. Treating families isn't only a matter of theory and technique; it's also an act of love.

RECOMMENDED READINGS

Dattilio, F. M. 1998. *Case studies in couple and family therapy: Systemic and cognitive perspectives.* New York: Guilford Press.

Gurman, A. S. 1978. Contemporary marital therapies: A critique and comparative analysis of psychoanalytic, behavioral and systems theory approaches. In *Marriage and marital therapy*, T. J Paolino and B. S. McCrady, eds. New York: Brunner/Mazel.

Madanes, C., and Haley, J. 1977. Dimensions of family therapy. *Journal of Nervous and Mental Diseases.* *165*:88–98.

Piercy, F. P., Sprenkle, D. H., and Wetchler, J. L. 1996. *Family therapy sourcebook*, 2nd ed. New York: Guilford Press.

Sluzki, C. E. 1983. Process, structure and world views: Toward an integrated view of systemic models in family therapy. *Family Process. 22*:469–476.

Sluzki, C. E. 1987. Family process: Mapping the journey over 25 years. *Family Process. 26*:149–153.

REFERENCES

Freedman, J., and Combs, G. 1996. *Narrative therapy: The social construction of preferred realities*. New York: Norton.

Goldner, V. 1985. Feminism and family therapy. *Family Process. 24*:31–47.

Haley, J. 1977. Toward a theory of pathological systems. In *The interactional view*, P. Watzlawick and J. Weakland, eds. New York: Norton.

Hare-Mustin, R. T. 1978. A feminist approach to family therapy. *Family Process. 17*:181–194.

Imber-Black, E. 1988. *Families and larger systems: A family therapist's guide through the labyrinth*. New York: Guilford Press.

Jackson, D. D. 1965. Family rules: The marital quid pro quo. *Archives of General Psychiatry. 12*: 589–594.

Kagan, R., and Schlosberg, S. 1989. *Families in perpetual chaos*. New York: Norton.

Mahler, M. S., Pine, F., and Bergman, A. 1975. *The psychological birth of the human infant*. New York: Basic Books.

Minuchin, P., Colapinto, J., and Minuchin, S. 1998. *Working with families of the poor*. New York: Guilford Press.

Minuchin, S. 1974. *Families and family therapy*. Cambridge, MA: Harvard University Press.

Minuchin, S., and Nichols, M. P. 1993. *Family healing: Tales of hope and renewal from family therapy*. New York: Free Press.

Minuchin, S., Rosman, B., and Baker, L. 1978. *Psychosomatic families: Anorexia nervosa in context*. Cambridge, MA: Harvard University Press.

Thibaut, J. W., and Kelley, H. H. 1959. *The social psychology of groups*. New York: Wiley.

Vogel, E. F., and Bell, N. W. 1960. The emotionally disturbed child as the family scapegoat. In *The family*, N. W. Bell and E. F. Vogel, eds. Glencoe, IL: Free Press.

White, M., and Epston, D. 1990. *Narrative means to therapeutic ends*. New York: Norton.

Research on Family Intervention

FAMILY TREATMENT AND PREVENTION PROGRAMS

16

George W. Howe
Colleen M. Varga

George Washington University

 ## THE EVOLUTION OF FAMILY-FOCUSED INTERVENTIONS

As family therapy has matured in the twenty-first century, so too have attempts to study when and how it is effective. In this chapter, we describe how scientific methods have been used to test effectiveness. We use the somewhat cumbersome term *family-focused interventions* to encompass the wide range of methods developed to work with families. Some of these interventions involve traditional family therapy, while others work with families to prevent problems in the future; some focus on helping families adapt to new life challenges, and some are designed to enrich family life rather than to treat problems. Here we touch on four important contexts where family intervention has taken root.

Family Therapy for Patients with Diagnosable Psychopathology

Some of the earliest family therapists worked with the families of individuals with severe psychopathology such as schizophrenia, bipolar disorder, major depression, and substance abuse. Because severe psychopathology is typically treated pharmacologically, the emphasis for families has shifted to psychoeducational programs to provide guidance in managing these conditions as chronic illnesses. Most of the research on program effectiveness has been conducted on such psychoeducational programs, which integrate education about psychopathology, practical problem-solving during rehabilitation, and, in occasional family sessions, the reduction of hostile family interactions that can contribute to symptom recurrence. Given strong evidence that depression is associated with relationship distress, family interventions for adult depression have developed a focus on the marital relationship.

Children with Behavior and Conduct Problems

Aggressive, oppositional, and delinquent behavior are among the primary reasons children are referred for treatment, and early family therapists began to see parents and children together in an effort to change such behavior. More recent programs have integrated family sessions with a broader ecological focus that attends to other aspects of the child's life, including school functioning and peer relationships. Other clinicians developed parent-training programs to help parents learn new ways to respond to such behavior, working with parents individually and in group settings.

More recently, parent-focused programs have been designed to prevent problem behavior and have been used with parents who have physically abused their children. These include prevention programs designed for high-risk families such as single-parent families, low-income families, families of children with subclinical problem behavior, and families going through major life changes and other stressful challenges.

Troubled Marriages

Marriage counseling is one of the earliest forms of conjoint therapy. The development of behavioral marital therapy and more recent emotion-focused techniques have been accompanied by substantial research on their effectiveness. This work has also expanded into the field of prevention, as clinicians have developed programs for premarital couples that build on intervention techniques from therapy and integrate them with education about how marriages develop and change over time.

Families Facing Stressful Transitions

Both clinical experience and a growing body of research have found that exposure to major stressful events increases the likelihood of emo-

tional and behavioral disorder and can disrupt normal development. This is particularly true of transitions involving major disruptions in relationships, such as separation and divorce. Family-oriented clinicians have developed a number of programs to support families during such challenging times. These include family life education programs, first developed over twenty years ago, as well as more recent programs designed to help families weather specific types of transitions, such as the birth of a child, divorce, or remarriage.

Characterizing Family-Focused Interventions

This brief sample of family interventions illustrates the burgeoning growth of intervention methods focusing on family relationships. Such programs have become increasingly common for a wide range of goals across a number of service delivery systems, both public and private. We provide a summary of this diversity in Table 16.1.

Such programs can be characterized in terms of their emphasis on prevention, treatment of acute conditions, or care for chronic conditions. Programs can also be characterized in terms of participants. Some models, though designed to improve family relationships, work only with individual family members. These include parent training programs and programs for reducing the burden of those who care for disabled or infirm family members. Other programs work directly with dyads, including couples or parents and children, or larger groups of family members, including everyone in the household. Lastly, programs can be characterized in terms of the outcomes they are designed to achieve. These include programs to treat or prevent diagnosable emotional or behavioral problems, programs to treat or prevent relationship distress, and programs designed to assist families in adapting to major life challenges.

Table 16.1 Types of Effectiveness Research for Each Target of Intervention

Target of Intervention	Type of Review		Types of Findings Available			
	Box Score Review of Trials	Meta-Analytic Review	Comparing Program Components	Comparing Different Programs	Comparing to Treatment as Usual	Testing Mediators of Efficacy
Interventions for Individual Disorders						
Child or adolescent depression					X	X
Child or adolescent anxiety	X	X				
Child or adolescent conduct disorder	X	X			X	
Child or adolescent ADHD	X	X			X	
Adolescent substance abuse	X			X		
Adult depression	X					
Adult substance abuse	X			X		
Adult schizophrenia	X		X	X		
Interventions for Relational Disorders						
Attachment disorders	X		X			X
Child maltreatment	X	X	X			
Marital conflict	X	X	X	X	X	X
Domestic violence		X		X		
Interventions for Transition or Adversity						
Transition to marriage	X	X				X
Transition to parenthood						
Transition to school	X					
Divorce and post-divorce parenting	X				X	
Remarriage and step-parenting						
Later life burden of care	X	X				
Palliative and end-of-life care	X	X			X	

THE EMERGENCE OF SCIENTIFIC METHODS FOR STUDYING PROGRAM EFFECTIVENESS

The scientific study of program effectiveness has also evolved over the past few decades, driven by several factors. During this time, the field of clinical medicine came to rely heavily on *randomized clinical trials* for testing the effectiveness of medical treatments, and psychiatrists began to apply this method to study the effects of drug therapies for emotional and behavioral disorders. Around the same time clinical psychologists began to apply methods from experimental psychology to study the effects of behavioral treatments, researchers began to use these methods to study interventions that targeted family relationships.

This period also saw the emergence of *program evaluation research*. Program evaluation methods, including field experiments, were developed to study the effectiveness of government-sponsored social programs, such as Head Start. In addition to studying the effects of particular types of interventions, program evaluation researchers came to realize that those interventions were usually provided within larger social institutions, such as schools, clinics, or community programs. Those programs could be applied to treat specific problems, but they were often designed for a variety of other purposes, including the prevention of new problems. Many federal agencies supporting programs working with families came to view program evaluation research as an essential means of testing the effects of those projects.

Finally, this period saw the growth of medical insurance, including reimbursement for treatment of psychiatric disorders. As insurance costs grew, insurers began to search for ways to contain costs by identifying the most effective and efficient practices. This process stimulated interest in developing scientific evidence to support the use of specific treatment methods. Terms such as *evidence-based practice* and *empirically supported therapy* reflect this growing emphasis on the use of scientific methods to test intervention effectiveness.

SCIENTIFIC METHODS FOR TESTING THE EFFECTIVENESS OF FAMILY-FOCUSED INTERVENTIONS

In its most basic form, a *scientific experiment* is designed to test whether some condition causes some outcome even after all other plausible causes have been accounted for or ruled out. This process requires a scientist to eliminate the effects of other possible causes. *Isolation* is one method for eliminating such effects. For example, a social psychologist might bring all participants into the same laboratory room, isolated from outside sights or sounds, and ask them to view pictures of facial expressions of anger on a computer screen to test whether such expressions affect their thoughts. Isolation techniques are not possible when studying the effects of complex social interactions, such as a course of family therapy extending over weeks or months, so family researchers must use other methods to rule out potential extraneous causes of change.

Random assignment is another method for ruling out the effects of alternate causes. For example, the social psychologist might create two sets of pictures, one involving expressions of anger and one involving neutral expressions, and then randomly assign a sample of participants to view one of the two sets. If the sample is large enough, this random assignment leads to groups that are approximately equal on a wide range of characteristics, such as age, gender, and personality, effectively eliminating these factors as possible causes of group differences in outcome.

Although the logic of random assignment is frequently used to study the effects of family-focused interventions, many adaptations have been required because of the complex nature of the intervention process. Here we discuss several methods and how they can help us understand intervention outcomes.

Specifying the Intervention

Family-focused interventions are far more complex than a simple presentation of faces expressing anger. They involve multiple sessions, each lasting an hour or more, spread over weeks or months. They can involve a multitude of activities, including discussion of family history, guided interactions among family members, and homework assignments. They can also involve meetings with groups of families.

To conduct an adequate test of a particular family intervention, researchers need to be certain that all intervention activities are carried out in similar ways for all families. For example, it would be difficult to claim that a program involving family communication training was responsible for reduced conflict if some of the families in the study did not actually receive training in most of the communication exercises. Researchers have developed two methods for ensuring that interventions are delivered as planned. First, they develop *program manuals* that provide specific guidelines for how the intervention should be carried out. Second, they use *fidelity checks*, observing or recording intervention sessions and rating them on how well they followed the guidelines.

Choosing the Sample

Randomized clinical trials in medical research are usually designed to test the effects of a medical treatment on a specific medical condition. Such trials usually screen out people who have other co-occurring medical conditions. Some experimental tests of family interventions have selected families based on the presence of a condition diagnosed in one family member. This approach can be overly restrictive, particularly because many diagnosable conditions, such as depression, are often comorbid with other disorders. In addition, such disorders may "cluster" in families. As a result, family researchers often use the presence of a single disorder as the criterion for including families but will not eliminate families based on the presence of other disorders in the target person or other family members. Although this approach may seem less rigorous than medical research trials, it allows family researchers to find out if a treatment works in the "real world" and not just in a controlled laboratory environment.

Other sampling approaches are used for family interventions designed to prevent future problems or to help families adapt to life challenges. A common approach involves using findings from prior research to identify factors known to put family members at risk for future problems and identifying families with high levels of those risk factors.

Choosing the Comparison Condition

Some researchers have conducted *clinical case series*, which involve following a series of family intervention cases over time to see whether changes occur during and after treatment. Campbell and Stanley (1963) pointed out that such studies cannot rule out changes that would have occurred even in the absence of treatment. For example, Waite and Luo (2002) found that nearly two-thirds of unhappily married spouses who remained married reported that they were happy with their marriages when recontacted five years later. This suggests that marital dissatisfaction is sometimes resolved over time without treatment.

To take such spontaneous resolution into account, family researchers use *comparison groups* who do not participate in the program being tested. If families in the experimental group do better than the comparison group, these differences are not likely due to such resolution. In some cases, researchers are interested in whether one type of program is more effective than another or if a program with a particular component is more effective than the program without that component. In those situations, the comparison group participates in the other type of program.

Sometimes a comparison group will receive no intervention. However, this approach is not ethically acceptable when other forms of treatment have already been found to be effective. In that situation, a *treatment-as-usual* condition can be used to compare a new program to the usual range of treatments families would receive. Such studies usually allow families in the intervention program to participate in any other form of treatment they would normally pursue to test whether the program adds value above and beyond that of usual care.

Assignment to Condition

Family researchers have conducted studies in which families are allowed to choose whether they participate in the experimental condition or the comparison condition. However, such designs cannot rule out *selection effects*, or the possibility that differences in outcomes are due to different types of families being included in the two different conditions. For example, families with more resources may be more likely to seek out or be able to participate in the intervention and thus make more progress regardless of treatment.

Random assignment to the experimental or comparison group is a powerful means of eliminating selection effects, because each family has an equal chance of being in either condition. Random assignment can break down, however, if people decide to drop out of the program before the end of the study and are not included in data analysis. Such attrition can reintroduce selection effects because different groups of families may be more likely to drop out of one group than the other. For example, families with more severe problems who are assigned to the intervention condition may become discouraged by a lack of progress and drop out more frequently than such families in the control condition. If this is

the case, group differences at the end of treatment may be due to the fact that the treatment group contains fewer families who began with more severe problems, rather than being due to the effects of treatment.

To eliminate this problem, researchers have developed the *intent-to-treat* design. In this design, all families assigned to either condition are assessed after the program is over, regardless of how much they participate in the intervention, and data from all families are included in the test of group differences. This design eliminates such selection effects, although it can dilute the effects of the intervention on the treatment group, given that some proportion of that group did not actually receive the treatment.

Measurement of Outcomes

The goal of many research interventions is to reach a level at which a treatment can be declared efficacious and effective. *Efficacy* studies demonstrate which treatments work under carefully controlled conditions, while *effectiveness* studies answer questions about which treatments work in actual clinical and community settings. Studies of program efficacy or effectiveness always include measures of targeted outcomes. Outcome measures include aspects of individual functioning, such as depression and aggressive behavior, as well as features of family functioning, such as marital conflict and parental sensitivity with children. Studies may also include measures of factors not considered primary outcomes, because these factors may be in areas of family functioning that will be changed by the intervention and will, in turn, lead to changes in primary outcomes. Such factors are called *mediating variables*, or *mediators*. Some early studies of family therapy only assessed individual outcomes such as substance abuse, even though the proposed mechanism for reducing substance abuse involved changes in family interaction. By including measures of both, investigators can test whether the program brought about change in the primary outcome through changing other important targets using *mediation analysis*.

In recent years, researchers have become more interested in the economic cost of interventions, motivated in part by the concerns of government agencies and insurance companies who pay for such programs. This has led to *cost–benefit analyses*, which compare the financial costs of treatment to the economic benefits to the family and society.

Assessing Change

All studies of program effectiveness measure outcomes soon after the program is over. However, unlike treatments for acute medical conditions, most family-focused interventions are designed to bring about lasting change. This is particularly true of prevention programs. *Long-term follow-ups* are necessary to study whether the effects of a program last over time or consolidate and expand. Some studies continue to conduct follow-up interviews for twenty years or more after the original intervention, yielding valuable information about long-term maintenance and change. Some programs even demonstrate *sleeper effects* that emerge months or years later, even when the initial effects are weak.

 **COMBINING RESULTS FROM MULTIPLE STUDIES**

No single study can provide incontrovertible evidence that an intervention program is effective. The more studies we have that show evidence of effects, the more confidence we can have in the general effectiveness of the intervention. This is because each study likely conducts the intervention in a slightly different way with different therapists and with families of different racial, ethnic and socioeconomic backgrounds. If the intervention effects are robust across these variations, we can be more confident that the effects are stable and replicable, and clinicians can have greater confidence in their usefulness.

Researchers have developed several ways to summarize findings from multiple studies. The *box score review* provides a simple count of how many studies report significant effects, while a *narrative review* discusses the various results from a set of studies. A *meta-analytic review* uses more sophisticated statistical methods for combining results across studies to reach conclusions about intervention effects. Meta-analysis has two important advantages. First, it creates a common metric for determining the size of the effect attributable to treatment, regardless of the actual measures employed. This allows investigators to combine findings from studies using different measurement methods. Second, meta-analysis uses statistical methods that combine treatment effects from all studies to form an overall estimate of *treatment effect size*, with each study contributing to this effect size in proportion to the number of participants in that study. This allows the investigator to test for treatment effects using a much larger combined sample, leading to more stable estimates of effect size than are possible for any single study and increasing the ability to detect effects that might not reach significance for single studies with smaller samples. Meta-analyses can also be applied to more complex questions, such as whether there is evidence of different effects for different treatment components and whether evidence concerning mediators is found with consistency.

Research in some areas is more advanced than in others, with only a few types of family-focused interventions currently classified as "evidence-based treatments." Evidence-based treatments are those for which there is systematic evidence that the treatment helps to resolve the clinical problems it is designed to treat. Sexton, Kinser and Hanes (2008) noted that, even for treatments classified as evidence-based, there may be substantial differences in the amount of evidence available. Treatments range from those that are efficacious within specific populations treated for specific clinical problems to those that are broadly effective, achieving successful outcomes with a range of clients, clinical problems, and service delivery contexts. We found that in some areas of research, only box score and narrative reviews have been published. Some areas have reported only one or two randomized trials, while other areas have conducted enough trials to support meta-analytic reviews. The most advanced areas have studies comparing different programs or program components, meta-analyses of program mediation, and in a few cases, even cost-benefit analyses. We therefore provide a summary of the state of research in each area, as illustrated in Table 16.2.

RESEARCH FINDINGS ON THE EFFECTIVENESS OF FAMILY-FOCUSED INTERVENTION

We covered three broad areas of outcome: individual clinical outcomes, relationships themselves, and adaptation to stressful transitions. We believe this to be a relatively comprehensive "review of reviews." However, particularly in the case of box score reviews and in situations where there are as yet very few trials, we do not assume that our coverage is exhaustive. Even so, we feel it provides a reasonable overview of the state of research on family intervention outcomes from this broad perspective.

This chapter also includes in-depth descriptions of three exemplary trials. These exemplary trials represent the state of the art in terms of family therapy research and are provided to illustrate more fully the types of interventions and research methods in current use.

FAMILY INTERVENTIONS FOR INDIVIDUAL DISORDERS

Childhood and Adolescent Disorders

Family interventions have been used to treat various mental health problems and to target different family members. For child disorders, some interventions use parents as cotherapists, while others address the family system as a whole, attempting to alter underlying patterns that contribute to child symptoms.

Child and adolescent problems are often described in terms of externalizing or internalizing disorders. *Externalizing disorders* involve oppositional, defiant, or aggressive behavior, as well as problems with attention and hyperactivity. They also include conduct problems involving rule breaking, as well as delinquency and substance abuse. *Internalizing disorders* involve anxiety and depression. All of these problems are of concern because they frequently lead to other academic, emotional, and relationship problems, as well as to adult adjustment difficulties (Burke, Loeber, & Birmaher, 2002).

Externalizing Disorders. Chamberlain and Rosicky (1995) summarized the results of eighteen trials in a meta-analysis of programs for child conduct disorders. They concluded that family interventions were significantly more effective than comparison treatments. Five of these studies found that family interventions, including structural family therapy (see Chapter 7), were effective in reducing aggression and other conduct problems. A more recent review by Kazdin and Weisz (1998) reinforced this conclusion, finding that family therapy led to significant improvements in both parent and teacher reports of child externalizing behavior, as well as in independent indicators based on records of school suspensions and police reports.

Behavioral parent training (see Chapter 10) is one particular form of family therapy that has garnered substantial support for reducing younger children's externalizing problems. Parent training helps parents develop skills for increasing the frequency of children's prosocial behavior and decreasing the frequency of conduct-disordered behavior (Patterson, 1976). A significant research base exists for the effectiveness of such studies (Carr, 2009). For example, in a recent meta-analysis of thirty behavioral parenting training

Table 16.2 Program Focus and Outcomes

Target of Intervention	Focus of Intervention Program			Intervention Targets Found to Change
	Individuals	Dyads or Greater	Triads Specific	
Interventions for Individual Disorders				
Child or adolescent depression			X	Family conflict; Parent–child relationship problems; Suicidality; Functional impairment; Depressive symptoms
Child or adolescent anxiety			X	Decrease in parental psychological control of the adolescent; Depressive symptoms; Anxiety
Child or adolescent conduct disorder		X	X	Decreased externalizing behavior; Decreased school suspensions and arrests; Improved familial communication
Child or adolescent ADHD	X	X	X	Decreased ADHD-related symptoms; Decreased parental ratings of negative child behavior; Decreased observed negative parent–child interactions; Decreased child internalizing symptoms; Decreased school-related problems
Adolescent substance abuse	X	X	X	Decreased drug use; Improved family functioning; Reduced family conflict; Increased grade-point average; Prevention of substance abuse problems in younger siblings
Adult depression		X		Decreased depression for maritally distressed couples; Increased marital satisfaction
Adult substance abuse	X	X		Increased initiation of treatment among substance-abusing partners whose spouses participated in unilateral treatment; Decreased spousal enabling behavior; Increased sobriety
Adult schizophrenia	X	X		Decreased patient relapse, and psychiatric symptoms; Improved family member well-being; Increased patient participation in vocational rehabilitation; Improved patient social functioning

continued

Table 16.2 (continued)

Interventions for Relational Disorders

Attachment disorders	X	X		Increased maternal sensitivity and security of attachment
Child maltreatment	X	X	X	Reduced risk of physical maltreatment; Improved child-friendly attitudes and beliefs; Changed beliefs about corporal punishment
Marital conflict		X		Decreased marital distress
Domestic violence	X			Decreased recidivism (slight)

Interventions for Transition or Adversity

Transition to marriage		X		Improved couples communication; Improved couples conflict management; Increased satisfaction with relationship
Transition to parenthood	X	X		Improved couples communication; Increased general satisfaction with relationship; Increased satisfaction with sexual relationship
Transition to school	X			Improved child school functioning; Improved child emotional functioning; Decreased child problem behavior; Improved positive parenting
Divorce and postdivorce parenting	X	X		Improved positive parenting; Improved diagnosable psychopathology in children; Decreased maternal depression; Increased son externalizing
Remarriage and step-parenting	X		X	Improved parenting; Decreased child problem behavior
Later-life burden of care	X			Decreased caretaker feelings of burden; Decreased caretaker depression; Improved caretaking skills; Decreased symptoms of care recipient
Palliative and end-of-life care	X			Decreased family member depression
Loss and bereavement	X	X		Decreased child internalizing and externalizing symptoms

studies and forty-one individual therapy studies, behavioral parent training was found to be significantly more effective than individual therapy in reducing childhood problem behaviors (McCart, Priester, Davies, & Azen, 2006).

The literature frequently differentiates between childhood externalizing behaviors and those that are more commonly diagnosed in adolescence, such as conduct disorder. A number of meta-analyses and systematic reviews of the effects of family therapy for adolescent conduct disorder have been conducted, with increased attention in the last decade. In a meta-analysis of eight family therapy studies, Woolfenden, Williams, and Peat (2002) found that functional family therapy (FFT) and multisystemic therapy (MST) were more effective than usual care in reducing jail time, risk of re-arrest, and recidivism. Another review of four studies investigated the effectiveness of family therapy with low socioeconomic-status delinquent adolescents and found that treatment involving eight to thirty-six sessions of behavioral or functional family therapy led to improved family communication, decreased externalizing behavior, and lower recidivism rates (Brosnan & Carr, 2000). Curtis, Ronan, and Borduin (2004) conducted a meta-analysis of eleven studies of MST and found that in comparison to those receiving usual care, adolescents receiving MST maintained lower levels of negative outcomes for up to four years after treatment had been concluded.

Because of concerns that family therapy is a more expensive form of treatment than individual intervention, the results of a study by Crane, Hillin, and Jakubowski (2005) were particularly noteworthy. This study found that in-office family therapy treatment was more effective and therefore more cost effective than individual therapy treatment and reduced costs for care by 32 percent over the next thirty months. As a result, it seems that any additional resources required to manage the logistics of including family members in treatment for adolescent conduct disorders may be offset by decreased need for follow-up care.

Another externalizing problem often treated with family intervention is attention deficit hyperactivity disorder (ADHD). Nevertheless, pharmacotherapy remains the most frequent treatment for ADHD. Up to 85 percent of diagnosed children take stimulant medication and the disorder is currently thought to be congenital rather than extrinsic (Barkley, 2005; Olfson, Gameroff, Marcus, & Jensen, 2003). However, because ADHD has been associated with problematic family relationships (Johnston & Mash, 2001), family therapy has been viewed as a promising intervention that can alter maladaptive relationship patterns associated with this condition. A large-scale randomized controlled trial recently found that during the first two years of treatment, a combination of medication management and multimodal behavioral therapy (parent, school, and child components, with therapist involvement gradually reduced over time) was more effective than either component alone or usual community care (Jensen et al., 2007). However, this difference was not found at thirty-six months, suggesting that the research on medication and multimodal treatment for ADHD is still inconclusive.

In terms of specific symptoms, a recent box score review of twenty-eight published studies concluded that manualized family treatments for children with ADHD led to a decrease in parental rating of negative child behavior and a decrease of observed negative parent–child interactions (Chronis, Chacko, Fabiano, & Pelham 2004). Results of a meta-analysis of programs involving parents in ADHD treatment indicated that parent training and family therapy were in the low-to-moderate effectiveness range in decreasing ADHD-related behavior and had a moderate effect on decreasing child internalizing symptoms and school-related problems (Corcoran & Dattalo, 2006). Several factors were found to moderate the effectiveness of treatment. Older children received greater benefit from parent training than younger children. Children in single-parent families did not improve as much as children in two-parent families. In sum, research indicates that parental involvement in child ADHD treatment can be effective in treating both core symptoms and comorbid difficulties.

Finally, results of recent research have shown that family therapy can serve as an effective treatment for adolescent substance abuse. The family system appears to play an important role in adolescent substance abuse problems, due to both heritability and negative relationship patterns (Muck et al., 2001). Williams and Chang (2000) reviewed fifty-three studies and concluded that family therapy was more effective than individual therapy, therapeutic communities, outward-bound programs, and twelve-step programs. Armed with the knowledge of its efficacy, researchers are currently exploring the utility of family-oriented treatment for preventing adolescent substance use. A randomized controlled study of Hispanic youth found that a parent-centered prevention program focused on improved family functioning and increased HIV awareness reduced smoking and unsafe sexual behavior as well as illicit drug use by strengthening the family system (Prado et al., 2007). Such results were found above and beyond those achieved by an HIV awareness intervention alone or in combination with an intervention targeting specific health behavior, substantiating claims that improving family functioning is an important path for treating adolescent substance abuse.

Two recent meta-analyses indicate that family-based treatments should now be considered well-established interventions for substance abuse (Becker & Curry, 2008; Waldron & Turner, 2008). FFT, brief strategic family therapy (BSFT), and *multidimensional family therapy (MDFT)* are all manualized treatments whose effects have been replicated by independent investigators across multiple sites, and Becker and Curry (2008) indicate that the quality of evidence for MDFT is particularly strong for its effects on both substance abuse and conduct problems.

One randomized controlled trial of MDFT compared with two other treatment approaches (one involving groups of families and one consisting of group treatment of adolescents) found that those adolescents treated with MDFT showed the greatest improvement at the end of treatment, as well as significant changes in academic performance and family functioning at one-year follow-up (Liddle et al., 2001). We have included a detailed description of this trial as one of our exemplary trials of family intervention.

Exemplary Trial

MDFT for Adolescent Drug Abuse

Based on research suggesting that adolescent drug abuse is influenced by a variety of social contexts, Howard Liddle and his colleagues developed MDFT as a means of treating adolescents who are abusing drugs (Liddle et al., 2001). MDFT targets several aspects of an adolescent's life, including individual, emotional, and cognitive functioning, family and peer relationships, and social behavior in general. Moreover, MDFT works with parents to help them develop more positive relationships with their children. MDFT consists of three phases in which adolescents and parents receive both individual therapy and sessions as a family. The first phase of treatment seeks to build therapeutic alliances among the adolescent, family members, and other individuals who play a significant role in the adolescent's life. The therapist personalizes the therapeutic program by helping the adolescent and family identify specific goals while also integrating more general goals, such as reducing drug use and becoming involved with healthier activities.

The second phase of MDFT helps adolescents build concrete skills, such as effective communication of thoughts, feelings, and experiences, and healthy ways of handling stress. The therapist helps parents reflect on their relationship with their children and enact scenarios in which they practice parenting techniques. This phase also aids adolescents and parents in working through obstacles in their relationships.

The third phase of the treatment helps families apply newly learned skills to the outside world. Therapists facilitate maintenance of the skills and interaction patterns established in therapy and help the adolescent and family predict how these new skills might be employed in future situations.

Liddle and his colleagues (2001) used a randomized trial to test the effectiveness of the MDFT program, comparing it to two other treatment approaches. The first, a multifamily educational intervention (MEI), differs from MDFT in that it is conducted as a group treatment. A group of three to four families met weekly to receive lectures and homework assignments, participate in structured group discussions and skill-building exercises, and confer with the other families in family problem solving. In general, the treatment emphasized stress reduction, risk and protective factors for individuals and families, family organization and rules, and family communication and problem solving. The therapist encouraged families to support each other and act as a supportive community. MEI has a more psychoeducational focus than MDFT.

The second comparison condition involved adolescent group therapy (AGT). AGT focuses on building individual social skills including communication, self-control, self-acceptance, problem solving, and solidarity among members of the group. This intervention had four phases. Phase 1 involved two family sessions and one individual session with the adolescent and focused on information gathering, promoting family support, and motivating participants. Phases 2 and 3 were conducted with groups of six to eight adolescents and paired activities designed to encourage self-disclosure and increase group cohesiveness with skill-building exercises and homework focusing on how to refuse offers of drugs, conflict resolution, anger management, development of healthy activities, and communication skills. The last phase emphasized maintenance and application of newly acquired skills.

This trial used referrals from juvenile justice services, schools, and other health and mental health agencies to identify 182 youth aged thirteen to eighteen who were currently using illegal substances other than alcohol. They and their families were randomly assigned to either MDFT or one of the two comparison groups. The investigators developed detailed treatment manuals for training and supervising clinicians in all three interventions to maintain program fidelity. They collected data on drug use through adolescent and parent reports, as well as through urinalysis. They also videotaped families during discussion tasks and trained raters to assess family interactions. These measures were taken before the intervention began, immediately after it ended, and again twelve months later to study whether the effects of the intervention were lasting.

All three treatments resulted in improvement for participants, but MDFT showed the greatest gains in terms of improved academic performance, healthier family functioning, and reduced problem behavior and drug use. These improvements remained stable over a twelve-month period. The investigators concluded that MDFT's focus on the specific issues faced by individual families and adolescents led to its increased effectiveness compared to the group approaches of AGT and MEI.

Internalizing Disorders. Internalizing problems such as anxiety and depression often coexist with externalizing problems, and as noted earlier, some interventions for externalizing also have a positive effect on these problems. The results of several randomized trials in this area provide mixed support for the effectiveness of family interventions for childhood internalizing disorders. Birmaher and his colleagues (Birmaher et al., 2000) compared individual cognitive-behavioral therapy (CBT), systematic behavioral family therapy (SBFT), and nondirective supportive therapy for adolescent depression. SBFT is an approach that draws from functional family therapy (Sexton & Alexander, 2005) and promotes family problem-solving skills, communication, and positive interaction between family members. No significant differences were found in long-term reduction of depressive symptoms. More recently, Trowell and colleagues (Trowell et al., 2007) found integrative family therapy was as effective as psychodynamic therapy in reducing depressive symptoms. Integrative family therapy utilizes techniques from several family therapy models, focusing on the links between the child's depression, problematic family scripts, and insecure family attachment patterns (Byng-Hall, 1995). Both family therapy and psychodynamic therapy led to a significant reduction in double depression (major depression and dysthymia) and rates of other comorbid disorders, but family therapy achieved these effects in less than one-third the number of sessions required by psychodynamic therapy (Trowell et al., 2007). Overall, a recent review by Carr (2009) suggests that family-focused interventions for depression are as effective as individual cognitive behavioral interventions.

Siqueland, Rynn, and Diamond (2005) reported mixed success with a family-focused intervention for adolescent anxiety disorders. Based on research showing associations between such disorders and excessive parental control, conflict, and overprotection as well as reduced cohesion and support (McClure, Brennan, Hammen, & Le Broque, 2001; Stark, Humphrey, Laurent, Livingston, & Christopher, 1993), they developed a family therapy intervention designed to change these family interaction patterns. This program combined individual CBT sessions for the adolescent with family-focused sessions designed to coach parents to provide appropriate support for their children and to help them overcome feelings of anxiety. In addition, restructuring techniques were used to alter family interaction patterns, encourage parents to be open to and respectful of their adolescents' wishes, and increase the children's level of freedom in expressing their emotions and seeking age-appropriate autonomy. Families were randomly assigned to this sixteen-session program or to a sixteen-session program of individual CBT for the adolescent.

Results indicated no differences between the two treatments in reducing adolescent anxiety or increasing adolescent-reported acceptance by parents (Siqueland et al., 2005). However, adolescents in the family intervention rated their parents as less psychologically and emotionally restrictive and more tolerant of their autonomy. One recent meta-analysis that reviewed nine studies of individual CBT versus CBT accompanied by varying amounts of parent involvement suggests that although family-focused programs may be more effective in improving the quality of family functioning, the evidence for the superiority of either model in decreasing anxiety symptoms is lacking at the present time (Barmish & Kendall, 2005). Overall, these findings suggest that family interventions may lead to changes in family interactions that perpetuate adolescent anxiety disorders, but to date no conclusive evidence exists that such interventions increase effectiveness in treating anxiety.

Summary. The results supporting the effectiveness of family therapy for a host of child and adolescent externalizing disorders are robust. For some disorders, including substance abuse and conduct disorder, family treatment is more effective than other approaches, suggesting that family approaches are the treatment of choice for children and adolescents with these diagnoses. For other areas, including ADHD, more research is needed to determine how child and family factors (e.g., child age and two-parent versus one-parent family) influence the effectiveness of family treatments in order to best identify the subset of children and adolescents with ADHD who would most benefit from family intervention.

Evidence concerning the utility of family interventions for internalizing disorders of childhood and adolescence is less strong, particularly in regards to anxiety. There is only weak evidence that family-focused anxiety interventions may add to the effectiveness of individual cognitive-behavioral forms of intervention. However, there is growing evidence for the effectiveness of family therapy in the treatment of childhood depression (Carr, 2008).

Adult Disorders

Clinical trials of family interventions to treat emotional and behavioral disorders of adulthood have focused on three areas: depression, substance abuse, and severe mental illness.

Depression. Substantial research has documented associations between marital conflict and depression. As a result, a number of clinicians have developed couples treatments for depression. A recent meta-analysis of eight randomized or quasi-randomized controlled trials involving over 500 subjects compared couples therapy to individual psychotherapy, drug therapy, or a wait list condition (Barbato & D'Avanzo, 2008). Therapies included emotionally focused couples therapy, behavioral marital therapy, cognitive marital therapy, interpersonal marital therapy, and systemic marital therapy. The results indicate that couples therapy is as effective as individual treatment in reducing depressive symptoms. Couples therapy was found to be significantly more effective than no treatment, and the results concurred with previous literature suggesting that couples treatment is more effective in reducing relationship distress, a common risk factor for adult depression (Barbato & D'Avanzo, 2008; Gilliam & Cottone, 2005). In one randomized study of hospitalized depressed patients, both multifamily group and single-family systemic family interventions were found to be more effective than treatment as usual, with higher rates of treatment responders and fewer individuals using antidepressant medication 15 months later (Lemmens, Eisler, Buysse, Heene, & Demyttenaere, 2009).

However, the effects of couples therapy may depend on whether the depression occurs in the presence of marital distress. For example, Jacobson and colleagues (Jacobson, Dobson, Fruzzetti, Schmaling, & Salusky, 1991) con-ducted a randomized controlled trial of behavioral marital therapy (BMT) (see Chapter 10), individual cognitive therapy (CT), and combined therapy (including elements of both). Each group received twenty sessions of treatment. BMT focused on behavioral exchange, communication, and problem-solving training, and included such techniques as behavior rehearsal and contingency management supplemented with cognitive techniques such as reframing. CT focused on the assessment and modification of maladaptive cognitions and behavioral aspects of depressive symptoms. The combined therapy included at least eight sessions of BMT and six sessions of individual CT. Results indicated that BMT was as effective as CT for individuals who reported marital distress but was less effective for individuals who did not report marital distress. This suggests that marital therapy for depression may be most effective in treating depressed individuals who also report marital distress.

Epidemiologic studies have shown that major depressive episodes are likely to recur, even after successful treatment. More research is needed to determine whether long-term effects of improved marital satisfaction decrease the likelihood of recurrence and whether different models of couples interventions and individual interventions show differences in their ability to prevent recurrence.

Substance Abuse. Research indicates that involving family members in the treatment of adult substance abusers plays a key role in influencing the course of chronic alcoholism. O'Farrell and Fals-Stewart (2003), in a review of thirty-eight controlled studies of marital and family therapy (MFT), concluded that several MFT approaches are effective in encouraging alcoholics to enter treatment and in helping family members cope if the alcoholic does not enter treatment. Effective approaches include Barber and Crisp's (1995) pressure-to-change approach (PCA), the community reinforcement and family change (CRAFT) approach, and the twelve-step family disease approach with Al-Anon participation. O'Farrell and Fals-Stewart (2003) also concluded that in the acute treatment phase, MFT is clearly more effective than individual treatment at increasing rates of abstinence and improving family functioning, particularly in the case of behavioral couples therapy (BCT). BCT involves two primary facets of treatment: alcohol-focused interventions focused on abstinence, and relationship-focused interventions aimed at improving the alliance with the nonalcoholic spouse. One recent study indicates that brief family treatment patients in inpatient detoxification were more likely than treatment-as-usual patients to enter a continuing care program after detoxification (O'Farrell, Murphy, Alter, & Fals-Stewart, 2008). Moreover, twelve to twenty-four sessions of couples-focused therapy focusing on improving marital communication also had a significant effect on sobriety at six-month follow-up. Results of one meta-analysis indicate that family therapy is more effective than nonfamily therapy in reducing the substance abusing partner's drug and alcohol use (Stanton & Shadish, 1997). In addition, the use of family intervention is a cost-effective addition to methadone maintenance treatment for heroin-addicted individuals.

Results are less promising, in the aftercare phase of treatment, with no treatment demonstrating effectiveness in the long term (two or more years following primary treatment). Thus, while many programs have proven effective in short-term decreases of substance abuse, a high proportion of substance abusers relapse regardless of the use of these family-focused treatments (Edwards and Steinglass, 1995). In addition, several factors appear to influence the effectiveness of all levels of treatment, including level of spousal investment in the relationship and family commitment to abstinence.

Research on the cost effectiveness of MFT has yielded inconclusive results. Two studies found that the reduction in jail and hospital stays after behavioral couples therapy saved over five times the cost of delivering BCT (O'Farrell et

al., 1996a, 1996b). For drug-abuse patients, BCT was equally cost effective when compared with individual treatment (Fals-Stewart, O'Farrell, & Birchler, 1997). In summary, MFT demonstrates a clear advantage over individual treatment in active treatment focused on abstinence and in improving family functioning during treatment. However, more research is needed on the cost effectiveness of marital and family therapy, as well as on the comparative effectiveness of MFT in getting alcoholics to enter treatment.

Major Mental Illness. Some of the earliest applications of family therapy were designed to treat schizophrenia (see Chapter 1). As research on the etiology of schizophrenia and bipolar disorder progressed, attention turned to biological factors with an emerging consensus that vulnerability for major mental illness is influenced by genetics and neurobiology. This paralleled the development of pharmacotherapies that helped to reduce many of the more extreme symptoms of schizophrenia. However, these drug therapies had less impact on certain symptoms of schizophrenia, and research on the emotional climate of families with schizophrenic members found that factors such as *expressed emotion* (reflecting a critical, hostile, and overinvolved family climate) had a profound impact on relapse and on the general functioning of the family member with schizophrenia (Miklowitz, 2004). This led to the development of psychoeducational family programs for schizophrenia and their adaptation for families with members who have bipolar disorder (see Chapter 11).

These programs are designed to reduce symptom relapse and to facilitate return to independent functioning. Family psychoeducation has two main goals: (1) to obtain the best possible treatment and outcome for the individual with mental illness, and (2) to support family members in their efforts to aid in that individual's recovery. This often includes an explicit focus on how family climate can trigger symptoms and how families can reduce expressed emotion to prevent this. The term "psychoeducation" can be misleading, because it includes many elements of cognitive, behavioral, and supportive therapeutic models.

Family psychoeducation is a well-established model; multiple meta-analyses over the past twenty-five years have supported the conclusion that family psychoeducation consistently results in a lower relapse rate than medication with or without individual therapy. Several elements appear common to most successful psychoeducation programs. Working with the World Schizophrenia Fellowship, Leff, Falloon, and McFarlane (described in McFarlane, Dixon, Lukens, & Luckstead, 2003) developed a consensus report regarding the central tenets of treatment included in the most effective family interventions. To support the patient, family psychoeducation leaders assist families in coordinating treatment and rehabilitation, obtaining optimal medication management, meeting the social needs of the patient, and providing relevant support and ongoing consultation. To support family members so they can most effectively support the patient in recovery efforts and also to improve family well-being, clinicians work to provide problem-solving training, resolve family conflicts and feelings of loss, improve communication, and assist families in widening and strengthening their social support systems. Evidence suggests that these programs are most effective when they last at least nine to twelve months.

Pfammatter, Junghan, and Brenner (2006) recently conducted a meta-analysis of the thirty-one most methodologically sound randomized controlled trials of family psychoeducation, while simultaneously providing a review of the three prior meta-analyses of psychoeducational family therapy (Pharaoh, Mari, Rahbone, & Wong, 2006; Pilling et al., 2002; Pitschel-Walz, Leucht, Bäuml, Kissling, & Engel, 2001). All four meta-analyses found that compared to medication alone, family psychoeducation in combination with antipsychotic medication consistently led to fewer relapses, fewer hospitalizations, and increased adherence to medication regimes. Long-term family interventions were found to be more effective than short-term relatives' groups. Pfammetter's new meta-analysis further found that compared with medication alone, family psychoeducation increased knowledge of the disorder among family members, reduced expressed emotion, improved patients' social adjustment, and resulted in lower rates of symptoms up to two years postintervention. In sum, the evidence is robust for the effectiveness of family therapy for patients with schizophrenia, particularly when offered within a multimodal program including antipsychotic medication.

Summary. Family-focused interventions for adult disorders appear to be most useful when they target specific aspects of family functioning associated with onset or maintenance of the disorder or when they help family members support independent functioning of the person experiencing the disorder. For depression, data suggest that marital therapy is a strong treatment option when clients report high levels of relationship distress. In treating substance abuse, spouse involvement is related to gains in treatment engagement and decreases in substance use in the short term, but no treatment has been shown to maintain these gains in the long term. Finally, involving family members of patients who suffer from major mental illness in psychoeducation programs can provide those family members the resources to provide long-term care and support to the client, while maximizing the possibility that family members will feel adequately supported in that task.

 FAMILY INTERVENTIONS FOR RELATIONSHIP DISORDERS

Beach and Kaslow (2006) suggest that understanding relationship processes is imperative to better comprehend various mental health outcomes. The programs we reviewed earlier all assumed that individual disorders are influenced by family relationships. However, it is also possible to view some relationship patterns as problematic or disordered in their own right. The *DSM-IV-TR* (American Psychiatric Association, 2000) includes V codes that address this issue, and there have been suggestions that relational disorders should be included more completely in revisions of this diagnostic system (Beach, Wamboldt, Kaslow, Heyman, & Reiss, 2006). We were able to identify empirical studies of family interventions for three types of relational problems: disorders of attachment, child maltreatment, and marital conflict.

Disorders of Attachment

Attachment involves the development of a set of emotional responses that determine how a child will respond to stressful contexts (see Chapter 4). Attachment theory, supported by substantial research, indicates that the majority of children form secure attachments with one or more adults, seeking proximity and comfort when under stress (Bowlby, 1977; Zilberstein, 2006). However, some children develop anxious-avoidant or resistant attachment styles and are less able to use a parent as a source of comfort and safety. The most disturbed form of attachment involves disorganized attachment, often occurring in response to physical abuse or a caretaker who is frightening or unpredictable (Main & Solomon, 1990). While all insecure attachments are risk factors for later emotional problems, a disorganized attachment style places a child at highest risk for a variety of negative developmental outcomes (AACAP, 2005).

Severe problems of attachment have also been incorporated into *DSM-IV-TR*. *Reactive attachment disorder* is defined as resulting from pathogenic care and is associated with abnormal social interactions across multiple contexts (*DSM-IV-TR*, 2000). There are two types of reactive attachment disorders: inhibited and disinhibited. The *inhibited* type involves social withdrawal and emotional constriction. A child diagnosed with the *disinhibited* type does not discriminate among attachment figures, which signifies that the child has poor boundaries that can put him or her at risk for being taken advantage of by adults. Reactive attachment disorder is a relatively recent addition to the diagnostic system, and little research is available on treatment effectiveness. Further research is needed to better understand its etiology and treatment (AACAP, 2005; Chaffin et al., 2006; Hanson & Spratt, 2000).

A number of programs have been developed to treat children with insecure attachment. These programs work directly with parents, and many involve dyadic work with the child and the primary caretaker. A few programs have included both mothers and fathers. Some attachment therapies have been proposed that use coercive strategies, such as holding and rebirthing. These interventions are controversial, and a number of professional organizations warn against using them, based on reports that children have died as a result of their application (AACAP, 2005; Chaffin et al., 2006).

Two recent meta-analyses have examined the effectiveness of various interventions for insecure attachment. Bakersman-Kranenburg, van Izjendoorn, and Juffer (2003) reviewed seventy studies testing the impact of early preventive interventions on the child's attachment security and maternal sensitivity to the child, with the majority of programs attempting to influence child attachment through changing maternal sensitivity. The authors concluded that these interventions were generally effective in improving both maternal sensitivity and child attachment and that interventions focusing on increasing parental sensitivity led to the most improvement in attachment. These programs taught mothers to carry infants close to their chests for extended periods of time and to recognize and respond to infants' signals in order to preclude and minimize distress. The most effective interventions used sixteen or fewer sessions and had a behavioral focus. In addition, this meta-analysis concluded that interventions were most effective with both children and mothers who initially exhibit more highly reactive and insecure attachment (Bakersman-Kranenburg, van Izjendoorn, & Juffer, 2003; Klein Velderman, Bakersman-Kranenburg, Juffer, & van Izjendoorn, 2006).

These programs were also effective with multiproblem families. Although shorter inventions were more effective overall, adding long-term and broadly focused support to the targeted intervention appeared better able to help multiproblem families cope with the multitude of stressors they face. Although only a few programs included fathers, doing so was associated with increased effectiveness. Recently, Van Zeijl et al. (2006) developed a home-based intervention program that focuses not only on promoting sensitive parenting but also on parental discipline. A randomized, controlled trial found this program effective on multiple levels, improving maternal sensitivity and sensitive discipline as well as reducing externalizing behaviors in children. This program was particularly effective for children of multiproblem families with higher levels of daily hassles and higher levels of marital discord (Van Zeijl et al., 2006).

In a more recent meta-analysis, Bakersman-Kranenburg, van Izjendoorn, and Juffer (2005) examined fifteen studies that included disorganized attachment as an outcome measure. The results indicate that the most effective interventions began after children were more than six months old. Interventions that focused on parental sensitivity were more effective than interventions that focused on support or parents' mental representations of their children. Interventions that focused on at-risk children were more effective than interventions that focused on at-risk parents. The studies that included more children with disorganized attachment in the control group were more effective than those with fewer children with disorganized attachment in the control group, perhaps because having a more representative control group highlighted the effectiveness of the treatment. Although it appears that increasing parental sensitivity can improve disorganization, the authors concluded that more interventions are needed that focus specifically on disorganized attachment itself.

Child Maltreatment

Over 3.2 million cases of child maltreatment were reported in the United States in 2007, with over 794,000 confirmed incidences of abuse (U.S. Department of Health and Human Services, 2007). Approximately 60 percent of these incidences involve neglect. The actual number of cases is almost certainly higher, because many cases of abuse go unreported. *Child maltreatment* is the umbrella term used to describe neglect as well as physical, emotional, or sexual abuse (Cicchetti & Toth, 2005). Exposure to abuse is strongly associated with emotional and behavioral problems in both childhood and adulthood. Furthermore, a recent meta-analysis demonstrated that maltreated infants were significantly more likely than children in comparison families to have insecure or disorganized attachment, suggesting a strong link between maltreatment and attachment disorders (Baer & Martinez, 2006).

Child maltreatment raises a host of difficulties for treatment (Cicchetti & Toth, 2005). The various definitions of child maltreatment represent legal definitions and do not describe specific parenting practices. There are no clear standards of acceptable discipline and parenting, and to further complicate matters, different cultures have different ideas about childrearing and what is considered appropriate. Nevertheless, many studies have been conducted on the variety of programs used to treat victims of child maltreatment.

These programs are frequently family oriented and often include dyadic therapy, home visitation, school-based programs, and parent education. A number of recent reviews concur that for child maltreatment, effective therapy is family-based, structured, and extended over at least six months. Effective programs address multiple aspects of child maltreatment, including children's post-traumatic adjustment problems, parenting skills, and the supportiveness of the family environment (Lundahl, Nimer & Parsons, 2006; MacLeod & Nelson, 2000; Skowron & Reinemann, 2005). In a meta-analysis of twenty-one studies of child maltreatment therapies, Skowron and Reinemann (2005) found that all types of treatment, including family, individual parent, individual child, and parent training programs including both parent and child, led to approximately equal improvements compared to placebo, wait list, or community case management control groups.

Other controlled studies have focused on physical abuse, framing positive outcomes as reduction in the risk of further abuse. One study of both conjoint and concurrent cognitive-behavioral family therapy found that these treatments were more effective than standard care in reducing the risk of further physical abuse (Kolko & Swenson, 2002). MST, discussed earlier as a treatment for adolescent externalizing disorders, has also been found effective for child abuse and neglect. Brunk, Henggeler, and Whelan (1987) found that both MST and parent training were effective in decreasing parental psychiatric symptomology, reducing family stress and the severity of identified problems. MST was more effective than parent training at restructuring parent-child relations, while parent training was more effective than MST at reducing identified social problems.

Lundahl, Nimer, and Parsons (2006) conducted a meta-analysis to examine the effects of twenty-three parent training programs. The results indicate that parent training was effective in reducing the risk of further physical or emotional abuse, although it did not influence the risk for sexual abuse. Through parent training, parents developed more child-friendly beliefs and attitudes and changed their attitudes about corporal punishment. Behavioral programs resulted in better parenting, while nonbehavioral programs were more effective in changing attitudes. Greater attitude change occurred with a greater number of sessions and when the format included both group and individual work (Lundahl et al., 2006).

Treatment for sexual abuse has received increasing attention. A recent meta-analysis of seven studies found that in comparison to child-only treatment, treatment involving the non-offending parent is more effective at reducing multiple outcomes including internalizing behaviors, externalizing behaviors, sexualized behaviors, and posttraumatic stress symptoms in children (Corcoran & Pillai, 2008).

A number of family-focused programs have also been developed to *prevent* child maltreatment in at-risk families. Geerart, Van den Noortgate, Grietens, and Onghena (2004) conducted a meta-analysis of early family prevention programs that found that these programs are highly effective in decreasing abusive and neglectful acts as well as improving child functioning, parent-child interaction, and overall family functioning. MacLeod and Nelson (2000) conducted a meta-analysis of fifty-six programs designed to promote family wellness and prevent child maltreatment. Proactive interventions showed increasing effectiveness over time, with stronger effects found at follow-up than immediately after the end of the program. On the other hand, reactive interventions demonstrated a greater effect at the end of the program, and these effects diminished somewhat by the time of follow-up.

Programs using home visits to work with parents on preventing child maltreatment have also shown positive effects (Geerart et al., 2004; MacLeod & Nelson, 2000). These programs were more effective if they included more than twelve visits and lasted six months or longer. Programs that included a strengths-based approach, social support components, or had a high participation rate were more effective than programs that did not.

Other reviews have examined the effectiveness of existing programs. Abuse-focused cognitive behavioral therapy and parent–child interaction therapy both include a family component and were identified as "best practices" by the Kauffman Best Practices Project (Herschell & McNeil, 2005). In addition, because child maltreatment often creates an insecure attachment, treatments that are effective in treating attachment disorders also work well for child maltreatment (Hanson & Spratt, 2000). Because many cases of maltreatment go unreported, Peterson, Tremblay, Ewigman, and Saldana (2003) have suggested that programs designed to prevent child maltreatment are likely to be more cost effective and may have wider impact. Recently, Prinz and colleagues (Prinz, Sanders, Shapiro, Whitaker, & Lutzker, 2009) implemented a randomized trial of the "Triple P" Positive Parenting Program in eighteen counties with over 600 service providers. The program resulted in large effect sizes indicating fewer substantiated child maltreatment reports, child out-of-home placements, and child maltreatment injuries. The results of this study point to the feasibility and cost benefits of implementing a large-scale parenting intervention to prevent child maltreatment.

Exemplary **Trial**

Parent–Child Therapy with Physically Abusive Parents

Mark Chaffin and his colleagues developed parent–child interaction therapy (PCIT) as a means of reducing instances of child abuse in families where parents had been reported for such behavior (Chaffin et al., 2006). PCIT is a two-part program. The first six sessions focus on orientation of the participants and seek to motivate participants to actively involve themselves in the program and homework assignments. The second component, lasting between twelve and fourteen sessions,

entails instruction on healthy parent–child interactions and live coaching as parents interact with their children. Instructors focus on helping parents practice basic parenting skills, such as praising good behavior, eliminating sarcasm and criticism, and ignoring minor misbehavior.

Chaffin and colleagues (2006) conducted a randomized trial to investigate the effectiveness of PCIT, guided by several questions. First, does PCIT reduce future abuse more effectively than standard group parent training? Second, does PCIT improve interaction between parents and children and decrease parental behaviors that characterize the coercive cycle of abuse? More exactly, does PCIT treat these behaviors specifically and not other untargeted factors, such as parent distress, attitudes, and perceptions of children's behavior that might show changes with more standard interventions? Finally, can PCIT alone reduce future abuse without supplemental treatments for parents, and will supplemental treatments augment the effectiveness of PCIT?

To investigate these questions, 112 parent–child pairs, consisting of an abusive parent and his or her physically abused child, were recruited from the child welfare system. The children ranged in age from four to twelve. Sixty-four percent of the families fell below the poverty line, 65 percent received public assistance, and 48 percent were of ethnic minority status.

The researchers randomly assigned each parent–child pair to one of three groups: PCIT, PCIT with supplemental services (enhanced PCIT or EPCIT), or a standard community group. The PCIT group completed the standard program and also participated in four added sessions, during which participants had the opportunity to discuss issues of concern. This was added so that the PCIT program would last as long as the six-month standard community parenting group intervention.

The participants in EPCIT received the same basic regimen of PCIT but with the addition of home visits to help with application of PCIT skills in the home, cognitive therapy and antidepressant medication for parental depression, and psychotherapy for family, marital, and domestic violence issues. Participants received supplemental services depending on the individual issues identified as problem areas.

The standard community group provided a three-part intervention that focused on improving parenting practices. The first six sessions served as an orientation during which parents learned about the agency's services as well as basic information on listening skills, the influence of parenting practices on child development, and the influence of parents' own upbringing on their discipline and parenting. The second twelve sessions emphasized child development, appropriate praise and discipline, behavior management, communication skills, stress management, and how the problems of parents can affect children. Finally, the third twelve sessions focused on anger management, self-awareness, self-control, and the cultivation of compassion and empathy. The main difference between PCIT and this intervention entailed the emphasis that PCIT placed on detailed, live coaching of positive parenting practices as the parents interacted with their children.

The results of this study indicated that PCIT alone effectively reduced future abuse among abusive parents. Compared to the standard group intervention, PCIT was significantly more effective. Only 19 percent of PCIT participants had additional reports of abuse after 850 days, whereas 49 percent of participants in the standard community group had additional reports of abuse. The study also showed that PCIT specifically targets parent behaviors that lead to abuse, rather than untargeted factors such as parent distress, attitudes, and perceptions of children's behavior. Although these factors may be related to abuse, the researchers concluded that more standard interventions can treat these issues, while PCIT offers a particularly effective means of preventing parental abuse. Additionally, the researchers found that therapists implementing PCIT need not have high levels of expertise in PCIT but only a basic level of competence. This

suggests that therapists with brief training in PCIT can achieve positive results. Finally, supplemental services (EPCIT) did not increase the effectiveness of PCIT.

One limitation of this study is that therapists conducted the treatments at different facilities and under different conditions, suggesting the possibility that interventions were administered inconsistently. Such variations in treatment delivery could have influenced the study's results, highlighting a need for future studies to investigate these treatments while controlling for changes caused by individual therapists and varied settings.

Couples Conflict

Relationship distress and conflict are extremely common problems, particularly in Western industrialized societies where nearly half of all marriages end in divorce. Dissatisfied couples seek treatment primarily because of concerns about conflict, poor communication, and lack of affection (Doss, Simpson, & Christensen, 2004). Couples often worry about the effects of their conflict on their children, and evidence is strong that couples' conflict can have a deleterious impact on parent–child relationships and on child development (Gerard, Krishnakumar, & Buehler, 2006).

Research on couples therapy has a longer history than other areas of family therapy research, and more reviews have compared the efficacy of different treatments. Early reviews comparing the various methods found evidence of the "dodo bird effect," whereby all treatments were effective and none were found to be superior (Luborsky, Singer, & Luborsky, 1975). (In Lewis Carroll's *Alice in Wonderland*, it was the dodo bird who declared, "Everyone has won, and all must have prizes!") Three more recent reviews and meta-analyses provide a more nuanced picture.

Behavioral approaches to couples therapy have received the most attention to date. Behavioral couples therapy (see Chapter 10) focuses on helping partners develop communication and problem-solving skills to negotiate a more equitable relationship. Shadish and Baldwin (2005) conducted a meta-analysis of thirty randomized controlled trials of BMT. Consistent with earlier reviews, they concluded that BMT is more effective than no treatment. However, they also found that the overall level of effectiveness was lower than had been reported in earlier reviews. The authors suggested that this finding could be due in part to publication bias, which is the tendency for studies to be published only if they have significant findings. Shadish and Baldwin searched for and included clinical trials reported in dissertations and other studies that were unpublished. Their conclusions were therefore based on a larger number of studies, reducing the effects of publication bias.

Trials of other approaches to couples therapy are becoming more frequent. This is particularly true of emotionally focused couples therapy (EFT), which uses attachment theory to focus on developing ways of adjusting emotional responses so as to meet each other's attachment needs and build attachment security within the relationship (see Chapter 8). Wood, Cran, Schaalje, and Law (2005) used a meta-analysis to compare the effectiveness of EFT and BMT based on results of twenty-three studies. They also included trials of programs that used specific components of BMT, as well as a few trials of programs that did not fit easily into either category. For couples experiencing mild levels of distress, both of these approaches were equally effective. Moderately distressed couples appeared to experience more improvement with EFT. The authors could find only one trial of BMT for couples who were seriously distressed, and this approach was found to be highly effective for that group. The authors concluded that EFT was significantly more effective than treatments using isolated components of BMT. Overall, using a full treatment model provided more consistent results than using isolated components of a treatment.

Byrne, Carr, and Clark (2004) also conducted a review of trials to compare the efficacy of different forms of marital therapy. Consistent with Wood et al. (2005), they found that BMT leads to both short- and long-term gains for moderate to severely distressed couples and that EFT leads to both short- and long-term gains for mild to moderately distressed couples. Adding a cognitive component did not increase the effectiveness of either BMT or EFT. The authors also reviewed the results of a small set of trials of integrated systemic therapy and insight-oriented therapy for couples. There were some indications that these approaches were effective, as well as indications that integrated systemic therapy may lead to more rapid and sustained improvement in couples who stay together (Christensen, Atkins, Yi, Baucom, & George, 2006). However, the small number of trials precluded any general conclusions concerning their comparative effectiveness.

Couples-based sex therapy has also been found to be effective for sexual problems including hypoactive sexual desire, female orgasmic disorder, female sexual pain disorders, and premature ejaculation. Although there have been no meta-analyses conducted on couples-based treatments for these disorders, a number of narrative reviews have found that couples-based cognitive behavioral therapy is effective in challenging the beliefs, attitudes and expectations that interfere with sexual desire and psychological intimacy (Duterte, Segraves, & Althof, 2007; Meston, 2006; Meston & Bradford, 2007). However, there is also some evidence that these improvements are not always well sustained, particularly in regards to treatment for hypoactive sexual desire and premature ejaculation (Duterte et al., 2007). Overall, Carr (2009) suggests that services for couples with psychosexual difficulties should be multi-modal, including both couples sex therapy and medication. Further, sexual problems are often accompanied by relationship distress, highlighting the importance of the couples therapy component of treatment.

Domestic violence can be seen as the most extreme type of couples' conflict. The research on treatment for domestic violence is still sparse, with little evidence concerning empirically supported treatments (O'Leary & Vega, 2005). Research on the treatment of male perpetrators suggests that some interventions may be effective, but the evidence is not strong (Edleson & Tolman, 1992; Rosenfield, 1992). A meta-analysis conducted by Babcock, Green, and Robie (2004) found a small effect of treatment, but the research studies used in the meta-analysis were not all rigorous. Some research exists on the use of couples therapy to treat domestic violence, although Stith and Rosen (2003) suggest that this research has been hampered by a prejudice against doing therapeutic relationship work with couples when violence has occurred (see Chapters 3 and 11). In a narrative review of six studies, Stith and Rosen (2003) found that careful and appropriately delivered couples therapy can be as effective as individual treatment if couples are committed to staying together and the violent partner can agree to a no-harm contract. Stith, Rosen, McCollum, and Thomsen (2004) found in one randomized trial that group couples therapy may be more effective than single-couple therapy. Multi-couple therapy was found to reduce male violence, decrease marital aggression and acceptance of spousal battering, and increase marital satisfaction. Single-couple therapy did not demonstrate the same results. However, this sample of couples was small, and researchers in this area continue to call for a greater focus on family and couples treatments for domestic violence (Murray, 2006; Sartin, Hansen, & Huss, 2006).

INTERVENTIONS TO HELP FAMILIES WEATHER NORMATIVE CHANGE, ADVERSITY, AND HIGH-RISK TRANSITIONS

Times of change and adversity pose significant risks for families. This is true for changes that are unforeseen as well as those that are expected.

There is substantial evidence, for example, that stressful life events, such as losing a job, going through a separation or divorce, or being a victim of violent crime, increases the risk for depression (Kendler, Hettema, Butera, Gardner, & Prescott, 2003). Exposure to more enduring periods of adversity also contributes to emotional distress (Brown & Harris, 1978). In addition, exposure to severe stressors or ongoing adversity can disrupt family life, in part through increasing conflict and reducing support among family members (Howe, Levy, & Caplan, 2004). Such events and adversities can also disrupt parenting and interfere with the support and socialization of children (Conger & Elder, 1994).

Predictable events and life transitions also pose threats to the emotional functioning of individuals and to the quality of family relationships. Normative life transitions, such as marriage or the birth of a child, place new demands on families. Many families successfully adapt, but others fail to make these transitions without distress.

Family therapists have paid close attention to both expected and unexpected transitions and life challenges, because they increase the risk for emotional, behavioral, and interpersonal problems and because they can usher in periods of pain and discomfort worthy of intervention in their own right. Many programs have been developed to help families make transitions more smoothly or to cope with and resolve stressful life challenges. Some of these programs were designed as educational interventions, including family life education workshops, which were developed almost fifty years ago. A number of training programs for Family Life Educators still thrive, and the National Council on Family Relations has an active certification program. In addition, many efforts have been made to develop programs that work with individuals and families to address the interpersonal patterns that increase support and decrease conflict within the family during such times and to develop new ways to adapt to and resolve the challenges attendant on such transitions or stressful events (see Chapter 11). These programs usually include education around the transition or stressful context but integrate that component with family therapy techniques, such as communications training and structural re-alignment.

Programs to Help Families Make Normative Developmental Transitions

Our search of the empirical literature identified studies on three sets of programs designed to help families make normative transitions. These include programs for couples planning to marry, programs for parents in the process of having a child, and programs for couples with a child about to begin school or with a teenager about to begin high school.

Preparation for Marriage or Long-Term Commitment. Carroll and Doherty (2003) were able to identify thirteen studies testing the effects of programs working to help couples develop and maintain more satisfying and less conflictual relationships as they moved toward marriage. These studies, conducted between 1970 and 2001, involved slightly over 1,000 couples who were mostly young, middle class, and of European descent. All programs used a couples group format and often included practice in communication skills. The theoretical orientations guiding these programs were predominantly family development theory, social learning theory, and communications theory. Groups met for three to eight sessions, across a total of twelve to twenty-four hours.

Using a meta-analysis to assess the effectiveness of these programs, Carroll and Doherty concluded that as a group, the programs were effective in improving how couples communicated, how they managed conflict, and how they felt about the overall quality of their relationship. There was also evidence that these gains lasted for at least six months to three years. Few studies followed couples long enough to assess whether these programs prevented divorce. A study of the premarital enrichment program (PREP; Mark-man, Renick, Floyd, Stanley, & Clements, 1993) followed couples for longer periods of time and found somewhat reduced rates of divorce, though not at a level that reached statistical significance.

Carroll and Doherty also noted one cautionary finding: In one of the very few tests of program effects for couples with different risk profiles, Halford, Sanders, and Behrens (2001) found that high-risk couples in the program—where the woman's parents had divorced or the man reported that his father had been violent toward his mother—were interacting less negatively one year later and were less likely to be dissatisfied with their relationship four years later. However, low-risk couples who participated in the program actually showed less satisfaction than control couples four years later. These findings need replication, but they point to the importance of studying how such programs work for different types of couples.

Maintaining Relationship Quality. A substantial number of trials have been conducted to test the effects of marriage and relationship education (MRE) programs for couples. Recent meta-analyses (Blanchard, Hawkins, Baldwin, & Fawcett, 2009; Hawkins, Blanchard, Baldwin, & Fawcett, 2008) identified 117 studies, with 41 using randomized trial designs. Most of the programs in these studies involved couples group psychoeducational programs ranging from nine to twenty hours in length. The meta-analyses found moderate effects on both relationship quality and communication skills lasting for at least six months. This was true of both universal interventions open to any couple and indicated interventions for couples reporting significant distress at the beginning of the program. Findings were stronger for directly observed couple interactions than for self-reported descriptions of relationship quality, raising the question of whether couples were able to integrate new communication skills into their everyday lives. There was also evidence that effects were maintained for at least six months and possibly longer, although there have not been enough long-term follow-ups to determine whether the effects were maintained for longer periods.

Birth of a Child. The birth of a child increases stress for many couples and can be associated with growing dissatisfaction with the relationship if a couple does not adapt well to the transition to parenthood (Glade, Bean, & Vira, 2005). Glade and colleagues were able to find only three trials of programs designed to help couples make this adaptation.

The best documented trial to date involves an experimental test of Cowan and Cowan's (1992) Becoming a Parent program. This program employed a couples support group that met for three months before and three months after the birth. Although the content of group discussion was structured around concrete topics related to how couples make this transition, group leaders allowed group members to discuss any issues emerging over this period. A two-year follow-up indicated that participating couples reported higher continuing satisfaction and better communication and were more likely to stay together than control couples.

Kermeen (1995) tested a less intensive program that integrated relationship enhancement strategies with prenatal childbirth classes, finding increased satisfaction with sexual aspects of the relationship postpartum but no differences in overall marital satisfaction. Glade et al. (2005) noted that several trials of such programs are currently under way, including a recently completed trial by Feinberg and Kan (2008) who tested a couples group intervention for first-time parents that focused on coparenting. Post-test data collected when infants were six months old found significant positive effects on coparenting support, the parent–child relationship, and infant self-regulation, as well as reductions in maternal depression. Overall, these studies suggest that programs helping couples with the transition to parenthood hold promise but need further testing.

Transition to School. Families can face significant challenges in helping children make a successful transition into school or when moving from middle school to high school. Although school readiness has become an important topic of study, there are as yet few reports of trials testing programs to help families deal with these transitions.

Cowan, Cowan, and Heming (2005) provide a comprehensive report of their test of a couples-based program. Using a family development and family systems framework, they designed and compared two types of sixteen-week couples group interventions, one targeting relationship issues and one targeting parenting skills, for couples with a young child soon to begin school. Using a randomized trial design, they found that both programs had a positive impact on child school and emotional functioning during and after the transition, although each affected somewhat different aspects of child adjustment. In addition, the relationship-based intervention had a positive impact on parenting, but the parenting intervention had no impact on the quality of the couples' relationship.

Australian researchers have recently tested the efficacy of applying a parent training program named Triple P (Positive Parenting Program) as part of an intervention available to all parents of young children beginning school (McTaggart & Sanders, 2003). This behaviorally oriented program involved four parenting group sessions with video presentations on positive parenting and homework, as well as weekly follow-up calls to each family by a program facilitator. Teachers were asked to rate children's problem behavior, and their reports indicated the program was successful both in improving child behavior and in maintaining that improvement over six months.

Children's transition to high school can also be a challenging time for families, and direct parent involvement is associated with better adolescent adjustment (Falbo, Lein, & Amador,

2001). However, we were able to identify only one preliminary report of a program to help families during this time (Ralph & Sanders, 2003). This program, an extension of the Triple P program for families of adolescents, showed initial evidence of positive effects on parent behavior, attitudes, and experience of stress in an uncontrolled study of Australian families.

Effectiveness of Programs Helping Families Cope with Stress

We have identified five sets of programs designed to help families cope with stressful events or ongoing adversity that have been subjected to some empirical test of efficacy. These include programs for families facing divorce and postdivorce parenting, remarriage and stepparenting, providing later-life care for impaired family members, palliative and end-of-life care, and loss and bereavement.

Divorce. Divorce is a risk factor for adult depression (Kendler et al., 2003) and reduced well-being (Amato & Keith, 1991). Parental divorce also increases the risk for problems in children's academic achievement, conduct, psychological adjustment, self-concept, and social relations (Amato, 2001). Family therapists have developed interventions for helping families weather the stress and conflicts that arise as couples go through a breakup and divorce (Kaslow, 1995), but we were unable to identify any rigorous tests of such interventions, with the exception of divorce mediation programs.

Divorce mediation programs have been developed largely within family court systems for the purpose of reducing conflict and supporting the establishment of custody and visitation rules to benefit children and as an attempt to reduce litigation. Although earlier research on the efficacy of these programs suggested that they were effective in helping divorcing couples in conflict (Benjamin & Irving, 1995), recent reviews have suggested a more complex picture (Beck & Sales, 2001; Beck, Sales, & Emery, 2004).

In one of the few randomized trials, Emery and Wyer (1987) found that families assigned to mediation reported greater satisfaction with dispute settlement and with its effects on the family when compared to couples who used traditional legal services. However, there is little evidence that mediation, compared to adversarial litigation, has an impact on the emotional functioning of the divorcing adults in terms of reducing depression, frustration, worry, or anger.

A subset of programs involving private fee-for-service mediation did show increases in positive couples interaction. Such programs are quite different from most court-mandated mediation in that they offer many sessions, address a wide range of issues, and include referral for therapy when necessary. Even with this level of intervention, the effects disappeared after two years, although Emery and colleagues (Emery, Laumann-Billings, Waldron, Sbarra, & Dillon, 2001) found that nonresidential parents who had gone through mediation remained more involved with their children twelve years later. Cost-comparison research in general failed to find that mediation leads to reduced court costs, and in some cases it actually increased those costs (Beck et al., 2004). However, little work has been done to study overall cost-benefit patterns of mediation.

Postdivorce Parenting. Substantial evidence shows that the postdivorce adjustment of children is strongly influenced by the quality of their relationships with their parents in the first year or two after divorce and by how much they are exposed to continuing conflict between the divorced parents (Whiteside & Becker, 2000). A number of programs have been developed to help children during this period. Most programs subjected to rigorous evaluation have focused only on the children (Stathakos & Roehrle, 2003), but a handful have tested more family-focused interventions.

A number of education programs have been developed for parents following divorce, and some communities have mandated participation in such programs (Deutsch, 2008). There appear to be no randomized trials of such programs as yet. Non-experimental evaluations of several programs do suggest that they can help parents focus on children's needs, reduce interparental conflict, and reduce litigation, although these findings await more rigorous testing.

We were able to locate three randomized trials of programs that work with families facing divorce. The New Beginnings Program (Wolchik, West, Westover, & Sandler, 1993), which integrated both parent and child group sessions, has received one of the most rigorous long-term evaluations, and we describe it in detail as an exemplary trial. Notably, this trial included a six-year follow-up that demonstrated reductions in psychopathology for children whose families were involved in the intervention (Wolchik et al., 2002).

Exemplary Trial

The New Beginnings Program

The New Beginnings Program, developed by Sharlene Wolchik, Irwin Sandler, and their colleagues at Arizona State University, was designed to reduce the negative impact of parental divorce on children (Wolchik et al., 2002). The program consists of two components.

The first is a structured program for mothers, involving eleven ninety-minute group sessions and two individual sessions. Group sessions, conducted by two group leaders, involve structured activities, including review of videotape models and role-playing practice, as well as regular homework assignments. The groups focus on four aspects of family relationships associated with positive adjustment following divorce: the use of effective discipline, ways of maintaining a positive and supportive relationship with the child, ways of supporting the child's relationship with the father, and methods for handling conflict between parents.

The second program component involves eleven ninety-minute child groups. These groups also focus on factors associated with positive adjustment to divorce, including the use of active as opposed to avoidant coping, ways of appraising divorce-related stressors, and positive communication with the child's mother. The groups teach such skills as recognizing and labeling feelings, deep-breathing relaxation, and problem-solving approaches. The group leaders use videotape models and modeled skills directly, and the children practice applying the skills to divorce-related situations. This component also includes a conjoint session in which children practice communication skills with their mothers. Program activities were documented in a detailed manual, and group leaders were trained to carry out the program following this manual.

The research team employed a number of methods to test the efficacy of this program. To engage a broad range of divorced families, they used computerized court records and media advertisements to identify potential families and were able to enroll 240 families from a wide range of economic backgrounds in their study. Families were randomly assigned to experimental or comparison conditions. To test whether the child component was important, some families participated only in the mother program, while another group of families participated in both the mother and the child programs. The remaining families were given a set of readings about adjustment to divorce to use as a self-study guide. The investigators also used several methods to be sure the programs were conducted with fidelity. Sessions were videotaped and viewed by raters who assessed whether each intervention segment was completed. Attendance data were kept to gauge levels of participation. Mothers were asked to keep diaries about homework to assess completion of homework assignments.

The primary goals of the program were to reduce emotional and behavioral problems in children who had experienced divorce and to prevent such problems in the future. The investigators measured both externalizing and internalizing symptoms before and after the program. They also collected data on more proximal targets that they felt would influence child symptoms, including quality of parent–child relationships, mothers' use of effective discipline, conflict between parents, and children's contact with fathers. They recontacted families six months and again six years after the end of the program to study whether changes had been maintained and whether the program had a long-term protective effect.

These results demonstrated that the mother program had positive effects on mother–child relationship quality, mothers' use of effective discipline, mothers' attitudes toward father–child contact, and on child externalizing problems, particularly for those children who were showing higher levels of such problems before the program started. The six-year follow-up indicated that the program had a strong preventive effect. Children whose families participated in the program were only half as likely as those in the comparison group to have diagnosed mental disorders at that time. In addition, those children who had higher levels of problems before the program were even less likely to be using alcohol or drugs at the six-year follow-up.

The Parenting Through Change Program, developed at the Oregon Social Learning Center (see Chapter 10), has also been subjected to rigorous evaluation in a study of single mothers with sons between the ages of six and ten (Forgatch & DeGarmo, 1999). This program included both weekly parenting groups and weekly telephone support of homework assignments over fourteen weeks. Follow-ups over the next three years found a moderately positive effect on parenting that waned somewhat but still remained significant

after thirty months. The program also demonstrated "sleeper effects," leading to reductions in maternal depression and child externalizing that appeared at the end of the follow-up period (Bullock & Forgatch, 2005).

Research has also pointed to the importance of postdivorce relationships with fathers as a factor in children's adjustment, but we were only able to identify one program that has been tested for efficacy, the Dads for Life program (Braver et al., 2005). This program developed dramatic videotape material used in eight group sessions and included two individual sessions with fathers. Preliminary results indicated that the program reduced child internalizing problems for those children who were initially more troubled and reduced interparental conflict for families that were initially more highly conflicted.

Remarriage and Stepparenting. Remarriage and adaptation to stepfamily life have also been the target of family interventions (Bray, 1995), given the evidence that poor adaptation to this transition increases risk for emotional and behavioral problems in both children and parents (Bray & Easling, 2005). We were only able to identify two randomized trials of programs for stepfamilies.

Nicholson and Sanders (1999) compared therapist-directed and self-directed behavioral family interventions to a control condition and found no differences between the two methods; both methods reduced child behavior problems and couples' conflict regarding parenting at the end of the intervention. Forgatch, DeGarmo, and Beldav (2005) extended the Parenting Through Change Program described earlier to stepfamilies, finding evidence for strong benefits to effective parenting practices and resultant decreases in child noncompliance in both home and school behavior.

Later-Life Burden of Care. Increasing life expectancy has greatly increased the number of families faced with caring for elderly members with physical ailments and dementia. Sorensen, Pinquart, and Duberstein (2002) recently conducted a meta-analysis of seventy-eight studies testing the effects of programs to help caregivers of elderly family members. These programs focused on the caregiver and employed psychoeducational programs, support groups, skills training, respite care, and psychotherapy.

None of the programs appeared to include multiple caregivers within the immediate or extended family. Findings suggested that these programs had an immediate positive impact on the caretaker's feelings of burden, depression, and well-being, as well as on caretaking skills and symptoms of the care recipients. Effects on the caretaker were maintained at follow-ups from six to twelve months, but effects on care recipient symptoms were not. However, these effects varied across caretakers and situations and were stronger for adult children than for spouse caretakers, for younger caretakers, and for caretakers of family members who did not have dementia. Shorter programs of seven to nine sessions appear adequate for increasing caretaking skills, but more extended programs appear necessary to reduce caretaker depression.

Palliative and End-of-Life Care. Families are also faced with the emotional and practical burdens of caring for dying family members. Although a number of palliative care team programs have been studied, few have focused on the family as a unit.

Higginson and colleagues (Higginson et al., 2003) reported a meta-analytic review of twenty-six programs with palliative care teams, finding modest positive effects on patient quality of life, particularly when care was provided in the home. However, there was little evidence of positive effects on family caregivers (although very few studies tested for such effects). Higginson et al. also suggested that measures of quality of life may not as yet adequately assess the deeper personal meanings around death and dying that could be affected by such programs.

Although a number of family therapists have developed approaches to working with families with dying members, a study by Kissane and colleagues (Kissane et al., 2006) appears to be the only randomized trial to date of a family-focused grief therapy. Families having a member dying of cancer received standard palliative care, including counseling and medication as necessary. In addition, half of these families were randomly assigned to brief family-focused grief therapy. Family therapy was associated with modest reductions in depression for all family members and had the strongest effects for family members reporting the highest level of depression before the intervention. The program did not, however, appear to be beneficial for families with high levels of hostility.

Loss and Bereavement. Families must also deal with the grief and readjustment that follows the death of a family member. Particular effort has focused on developing programs for children who have lost a parent (Tremblay & Israel, 1998). However, only a handful of these programs have been evaluated for effectiveness.

The Family Bereavement Program (Sandler et al., 2003), developed to work with children and surviving parents, is one of the only programs to be studied using a randomized trial. Results indicated that the program led to improved parenting, coping, and caregiver mental health. One year later, children in the program had fewer problems, but this was true only for girls and those who had more problems at the beginning of the program.

A recent meta-analysis of interventions for bereavement, mostly involving individuals or peer groups, may have important implications for future work on family interventions. Currier, Neimeier, and Berman (2008) found that such interventions had small and vanishing effects on adjustment for those experiencing normal course of bereavement, but could be very effective when targeting grievers showing marked difficulties in adapting to loss.

Summary

Programs designed to help families weather a wide range of transitions and adversities have demonstrated some success in strengthening and stabilizing family relationships as well as reducing emotional difficulties. However, not all of these efforts have proven successful, and in many instances, the effects have dissipated over time.

Most of the programs subjected to empirical testing have tried to integrate relationship skills training with education around transitions or ways of coping with adversity and have been based on a combination of family development and social learning frameworks. Few attempts have been made to focus on broader systemic characterizations of family process (with the work of Cowan and Cowan being an important exception). As a result, many of these programs have worked only with individual family members, even when the target of the intervention was to change patterns of family interaction. In addition, long-term follow-ups are uncommon but clearly needed to study whether program effects are lasting. This is particularly important for programs designed to prevent future problems.

Finally, very little work has been done to test whether family and individual characteristics might influence the effectiveness of these programs. Studies in several different areas suggest that such programs may be most helpful for people who are experiencing stronger emotional reactions to these challenges. However, it also seems that the most challenging situations, such as those involving separation, divorce, or death of a family member, may require longer and more intensive interventions. In addition, such programs may be less effective for families already caught up in high levels of hostile conflict.

FAMILY INTERVENTION PROCESS RESEARCH

The clinical trials described thus far have been concerned with the *outcome* of family interventions, but they have said little about the specific mechanisms responsible for therapeutic effects. Family researchers have also developed a variety of scientific techniques for studying the *process* of family intervention to understand which intervention activities, styles, and techniques are most effective.

Process Research Methods

Process researchers often employ direct observation or recording of family therapy sessions to describe therapists' activities and their effects. For example, Michael Robbins and his colleagues studied the effects of therapist *reframing*, or noncritical statements that frame adolescent behavior as normal, by recording and rating each statement by the therapist and by family members during the initial sessions of functional family therapy with families having delinquent adolescents (Robbins, Alexander, Newell, & Turner, 1996). Robbins and colleagues found that adolescents were less likely to respond negatively to reframing than to any other type of therapist statement.

Observational systems have been developed to capture a variety of family therapy processes, including specific strategies such as enactment (Allen-Eckert, Fong, Nichols, Watson, & Liddle, 2001) and general therapist styles such as supportiveness and defensiveness (Waldron, Turner, Barton, Alexander, & Cline, 1997). Methods of discourse analysis have also been imported from linguistics to study meaning formation and change during family therapy sessions (Burck, Frosh, Lisa, & Morgan, 1998). More recently, researchers have begun studying the degree to which therapists adhere to specific manualized therapies for family interventions. For example, Hogue and colleagues (Hogue et al., 2008) developed the Therapist Behavior Rating Scale–Competence (TBRS–C) to capture how closely therapists adhere to evidence-based practices for adolescent substance abuse treatment.

Process researchers have typically employed correlational designs to study the associations between various aspects of the intervention process and later outcomes. Such designs can be compromised by potential confounds, however, and need to be interpreted with caution. For example, characteristics of the family and the therapist—such as problem severity, family rigidity, and the individual personality style of the therapist—can often shape both the processes observed in therapy and the functioning of the family at the end of treatment. Statistical and sampling methods for reducing or eliminating plausible confounds can be used to increase confidence in study findings. Randomized experiments are a more powerful means of eliminating such confounds, although they have been used infrequently.

Butler and Wampler (1999) used a randomized design to study the effects of couples therapist strategies described as "couples-responsible," including enactment and use of accommodation, when compared to strategies labeled "therapist-responsible," such as therapist–couple interaction, therapist interpretation, and direct instruction. Couples therapists were randomly assigned to use one of the two methods in a therapy session. Couples ratings indicated that perceived responsibility was higher and conflict lower when therapists employed couple-responsible strategies. These types of studies help family intervention researchers understand not only *if* certain types and aspects of therapy are effective, but *how* and *by what means* these therapies create change.

The Therapeutic Alliance

Process research has been applied most consistently to the study of *therapeutic alliance*. A *positive alliance*, often defined in terms of a client's willingness to talk openly and freely with a therapist and to work jointly with the therapist to address the client's problems (Robbins et al., 2006), is considered essential in keeping clients engaged in therapeutic activity and reducing the likelihood of premature termination. Process research in this area asks the question "What makes for good alliances with couples and families?" (Alexander, Robbins & Sexton, 2000). In a review of the past forty years of family research, Friedlander, Escudero, and Heatherington (2006) conclude that a large body of both large-sample, quantitative studies and intensive qualitative studies supports the importance of the therapeutic alliance in leading to both therapy continuation and positive outcomes. Another recent narrative review of nineteen studies of therapeutic alliance concluded that the therapeutic alliance is an integral aspect of family counseling (Mahaffey & Granello, 2007). However, this review also noted that many studies lacked diversity in participant demographics and treatment sources, and none of the studies reviewed addressed the role of therapist experience and setting as they affect the formation of alliances.

In an attempt to address these criticisms, a number of researchers have developed methods for tracking the formation and outcome of therapeutic alliances across diverse family groups, while others have focused on analyzing the mechanisms by which a positive alliance leads to positive outcomes. Process researchers have studied the effects of specific therapist strategies on improving alliance in family therapy. Diamond, Liddle, Hogue, and Dakoff (1999) found that significant gains in working alliance were more evident when the therapist attended to the adolescent's experience, formulated personally meaningful goals, and acted as the adolescent's ally. Lack of improvement or deterioration in alliance was associated with the therapist spending too much time explaining the nature of therapy and waiting too long to discuss how the therapy could be personally meaningful for the teenager.

The alliance between therapist and client can also be affected by cultural and demographic concerns. Jackson-Gilfort, Liddle, Tejeda, and Dakof (2001) found that the discussion of culturally specific themes enhanced treatment engagement of African American male substance-abusing youth. Exploration of particular themes in one session, including anger and rage, alienation, and the meaning of the journey from boyhood to manhood as an African American man, were associated with both increased participation and decreased negativity by adolescents in the next treatment session.

The therapeutic alliance is more complicated in family therapy than in individual therapy because of the need to form multiple alliances. For example, working with family psychoeducation interventions for relatives of individuals with schizophrenia, Smerud and Rosenfarb (2008) found that the development of a positive alliance with the therapist was correlated with fewer signs of relapse and lower likelihood of rehospitalization for the patient. Further, relatives who developed a positive alliance with the therapist were less rejecting and less likely to feel burdened. In another study, Heatherington and Friedlander (1990) explored relational control communication patterns and their impact on the development of the therapeutic alliance. They found that therapists and family members tended to interact in complementary ways, rather than having symmetrical or competitive exchanges. However, neither pattern was related to family members' perceptions of the quality of the therapeutic relationship.

Garfield's (2004) review of research on alliance in couples therapy corroborated the findings of previous reviews, noting that the alliance is predictive of treatment outcomes across a variety of individual therapeutic approaches. Further, Garfield provided a number of helpful recommendations for working with couples with a variety of problems. He identified three dimensions affecting the therapeutic alliance—the "loyalty dimension," the impact of couples' early family-of-origin experiences, and the impact of couples' gender concerns—and presented empirical rationales and clinical considerations related to each dimension.

However, conceptualizing the alliance as an aspect of the relationship between clients and therapists overlooks crucial aspects of clients' experience of the alliance. Recent research on integrative psychotherapy alliance models (see Chapter 14) highlights the importance of considering and measuring the systemic alliances within couples and families (Pinsof, Zinbarg, & Knobloch-Fedders, 2008). In other words, the alliances and coalitions or the "splits" that can form within families have a significant effect on treatment outcome. In many cases, these outcomes are negative, as when angry adolescents refuse to cooperate with therapists because they see the therapist as "on their parents' side." However, Friedlander, Escudero, and Heatherington (2006) note that the multiple alliances of family therapy can also be beneficial, as when strong therapist-parent alliances lead to improvements in parenting skills.

Recently, Escudero, Friedlander, Varela, and Abascal (2008) found that families' sense of having a Shared Sense of Purpose (one aspect of Friedlander et al.'s 2006 System for Observing Family Therapy Alliances, or SOFTA) was consistently associated with perceptions of progress in therapy. In another study utilizing SOFTA, Friedlander, Lambert, and de la Pena (2008) found in a sample of low-income, multiproblem families that feeling safe in the therapeutic environment with other family members led to productive family collaboration, which, in turn, resulted in symptom improvement and perceived progress in therapy.

An examination of the alliance building process in MDFT found that adolescents were more likely to complete treatment when therapists had stronger relationships with their parents. Additionally, stronger therapeutic relationships with adolescents were associated with greater decreases in their drug use but only when the therapeutic alliance with the parent was also strong (Shelef, Diamond, Diamond, & Liddle, 2005).

Robbins, Turner, Alexander, and Perez (2003) used observational ratings of functional family therapy sessions with adolescent substance abusers and their parents to measure alliances with both parents and adolescents. They found that dropout cases had significantly higher levels of unbalanced alliances, characterized by discrepancies between adolescent and parent alliance with the therapist, than did completer cases. In a second study with a predominantly African American sample, Robbins and colleagues (Robbins et al., 2006) found that stronger alliances with both adolescents and mothers in the second session were associated with a lower likelihood of dropout. A third study by Robbins and colleagues (Robbins et al., 2008) found that families with adolescents involved in drug use who completed brief strategic family therapy had higher levels of inter-family alliances than did dropout cases. The findings of Robbins and colleagues' studies, combined with evidence from other researchers, suggest that while individual alliances in the first session are not predictive of therapy dropout, both the strength of the individual alliance and the balance of alliances within the family system may be important in family interventions.

These and other studies of the alliance in family therapy have yielded clinically important findings. Currently, researchers are attempting to use observational tools to examine the links between the therapeutic relationship and outcomes in family therapy, but much more work needs to be done in this area of family intervention.

Critical Events and Change Points

Process research has also focused on focal events during therapy that appear to usher in significant changes in family interaction or resolution of problems. *Change event analysis* (Woolley, Butler, & Wampler, 2000) requires researchers to identify likely critical events to study whether they differ in important ways from other episodes of therapy and to determine whether these events do, in fact, lead to important changes in interaction or problem resolution.

For example, Friedlander, Heatherington, Johnson, and Skowron (1994) identified structural family therapy cases in which families had been able to move successfully from disengagement to engagement (for a review of structural family therapy, see Chapter 7). Using an exploratory inductive approach, they identified events in which engagement was successfully sustained during the sessions. Although no consistent pattern characterized the resolution of each family's impasse, periods of sustained engagement generally involved active solicitation by the therapist of each family member's thoughts and feelings about the impasse and the benefits of reengagement and therapist strategies aimed at helping family members hear each other's point of view. Similarly, Greenberg, Ford, Alden, and Johnson (1993) compared peak to poor session events during emotion-focused couples therapy. Peak events were more frequently characterized by affiliative, self-disclosing statements and accepting statements by partners. Therapist facilitation of self-disclosure in one partner led to increased likelihood that the other partner would respond with an affiliative statement.

Michael Nichols and his students have studied highly trained and experienced family therapists (Nichols & Fellenberg, 2000), focusing on the use of enactments. Their findings indicate that breaking through family conflict and helping families shift their relational stance is a complex process that requires active, directive facilitation by the therapist. Essential ingredients of successful enactments include preparing the family prior to the enactment, specifying an agenda and explaining the need for dialogue, giving directions about how the discussion should go, avoiding unnecessary interruption, pushing family members to work harder during the enactment, and closing by providing clients with clear direction on how to communicate with each other.

Additional studies by this group have demonstrated that the most effective sessions of family therapy appear to be those in which therapists establish a clear and focused systemic goal (e.g., helping to overcome parental disengagement, rather than working on general problem solving) while intensely pushing for change to occur within the session (Favero, 2002; Fellenberg, 2003; Miles, 2004). However, Hammond and Nichols (2008) found that an empathic therapeutic alliance was a prerequisite to making these focused and forceful interventions effective; that is, focused and forceful intervening seems to be important in producing change in family therapy, but family members appear more willing to accept such forceful challenges when the therapist has established an empathic bond with them.

Diamond and Liddle (1996, 1999) used task analysis of MDFT sessions to identify interventions likely to resolve in-session impasses involving negative exchange, emotional disengagement, and poor problem solving. Successful interventions included actively blocking or addressing and working through negative affect and evoking thoughts and feelings that promote constructive dialogue. A kind of "shuttle diplomacy" also proved fruitful, where therapists created emotional treaties among family members by working in alternate sessions with parents alone and adolescents alone. In cases with a successful resolution of the impasse, the therapist was able to transform the nature and tone of the interaction, shifting the parent from blaming to feelings of regret and loss and eliciting the adolescent's thoughts and feelings about relationship roadblocks with parents and others.

Summary

Process studies have clarified a number of therapeutic strategies that contribute to effective family therapy. Approaches that emphasize building of alliances through understanding and supporting the goals of family members are likely to increase engagement and reduce dropout. The alliance between therapists and clients is an important contributor to positive outcomes, but recent research has also highlighted the importance of focusing on the alliances among members of a family. Lastly, the results of critical event studies suggest that change events are facilitated when the therapist moves family members to a more vulnerable, self-disclosing, affective level and helps other family members to listen and respond.

CONCLUSIONS AND FUTURE DIRECTIONS

Our review of family-focused interventions strongly supports the basic underlying principle of family therapy: that family relationships are important targets for clinical interventions designed to treat and prevent a range of emotional and behavioral problems. The application of this principle has evolved and differentiated over the past few decades, as therapists and program developers have attempted to apply it in a growing number of contexts and with an expanding set of clinical objectives. The parallel growth of new scientific methods for testing the effects of interventions and studying intervention process has led to a large and growing body of research on the effectiveness of these efforts.

Some areas of intervention have been studied longer and in greater detail allowing more confidence in findings and more attention to how and when particular forms of intervention will likely be most effective. These areas include family therapy, parent therapy, and family-focused prevention programs for childhood externalizing.

They also include family psychoeducational programs for major mental illness, parent-focused programs for insecure attachment and reduction of child maltreatment, behavioral marital therapy and emotion-focused marital therapy for marital conflict, and communication training programs in preparation for marriage or long-term commitment. Research supports the effectiveness of family-focused interventions in each of these areas but also raises important concerns about the limits of current interventions. For example, some family-focused interventions for child maltreatment may be more successful at changing parental attitudes than in changing parent behavior, and reactive interventions demonstrate initial effects that tend to fade over time. Fading effectiveness may also be a concern with marital therapy. These findings are limited by the absence of long-term follow-ups in the majority of studies covered in this review and point to the importance of such follow-ups in future work.

Empirical tests of other areas of family-focused intervention are less advanced, but the findings are often promising. These include marital therapy for depression in individuals who are also experiencing marital distress, family engagement in treatment of alcohol abuse, and programs to support families weathering adversity and high-risk transitions such as divorce, remarriage, and later-life or end-of-life palliative care. Findings from these programs suggest that family-focused interventions hold particular promise for supporting emotional development and preventing the destructive effects of major life stressors on emotional functioning, including severe emotional disorders. Nonetheless, insufficient rigorous trials have been conducted of such programs to provide full confidence in their effectiveness and to clarify which individuals and families are most likely to benefit.

Research has also advanced in studying the specific strategies and techniques that lead to effective intervention, although this work is still at a relatively early stage and no meta-analytic reviews were found in this area. Alliance building through sensitivity to the goals of family members and facilitation of change during family sessions are areas that have received the most attention. Heatherington, Friedlander, and Greenberg (2005) note that this area would benefit in particular from more integration with theories of family-change process.

We end by noting two issues that will be important in the next stage of this work. First, it is becoming clear that our understanding of emotional and behavioral problems must be placed in developmental perspective. The consideration of developmental psychopathology as a framework for understanding how disorders emerge, are maintained, and are resolved or recur over the lifespan has become a central guide for those interested in preventing or treating them (Howe, Reiss, & Yuh, 2004). Families play a central role in both normal and problematic development. Family-focused interventions informed by developmental research and theory are an increasingly central part of our intervention toolkit and already inform many of the programs reviewed here.

Second, many of the family-focused interventions we reviewed here have attempted to influence family relationships through working with individual family members or with dyads. This approach has borne some fruit but leaves open the questions of when and how we need to work with larger groupings, including family households and extended family groups, to effect change. A few trials have given hints that systemic and multisystemic approaches may be essential to bring about long-term change, but other trials have failed to find much added value in more intensive interventions. It is clear that many families benefit from more limited problem-focused interventions with individuals or dyads, but we suspect that other families will require more in-depth systemic approaches to bring about lasting benefit.

RECOMMENDED READINGS

Alexander, J. F., Holtzworth-Munroe, A., and Jameson, P. B. 1994. Research on the process and outcome of marriage and family therapy. In *Handbook of psychotherapy and behavior change*, 4th ed., A. E. Bergin & S. L. Garfield, eds. New York: John Wiley & Sons.

Barbato, A., and D'Avanzo, B. 2008. Efficacy of couples therapy as a treatment for depression: A meta-analysis. *Psychiatric Quarterly. 79*(2):121–132.

Blanchard, V. L., Hawkins, A. J., Baldwin, S. A., and Fawcett, E. B. 2009. Investigating the effects of marriage and relationship education on couples' communication skills: A meta-analytic study. *Journal of Family Psychology. 23*(2):203–214.

Carr, A. 2009. The effectiveness of family therapy and systemic interventions for child-focused problems. *Journal of Family Therapy. 31*:3–45.

Carr, A. 2009. The effectiveness of family therapy and systemic interventions for adult-focused problems. *Journal of Family Therapy. 31*:46–74.

The Cochrane Collaboration: Cochrane Reviews. www.cochrane.org/index.htm.

Friedlander, M. L., Escudero, V., and Heatherington, L. 2006. *Therapeutic alliances in couple and family therapy: An empirically informed guide to practice*. Washington, DC: American Psychological Association.

O'Farrell, T. J., and Fals-Stewart, W. 1999. Treatment models and methods: Family models. In *Addictions: A comprehensive guidebook* (pp. 287–305), B. S. McCrady and E. E. Epstein, eds. New York: Oxford University Press.

Pinsof, W. M., and Lebow, J. L., eds. 2005. *Family psychology: The art of the science*. New York: Oxford University Press.

Pitschel-Walz, G., Leucht, S., Bäuml, J., Kissling, W., and Engel, R. 2001. The effect of family interventions on relapse and rehospitalization in schizophrenia—A meta-analysis. *Schizophrenia Bulletin. 27*:73–92.

Sexton, T. L., Kinser, J. C., and Hanes, C. W. 2008. Beyond a single standard: levels of evidence approach for evaluating marriage and family therapy research and practice. *Journal of Family Therapy. 30*:386–398.

Stith, S., and Rosen, K. 2003. Effectiveness of couples treatment for spouse abuse. *Journal of Marital and Family Therapy. 29*(3):407–426.

REFERENCES

AACAP. 2005. Practice parameters for the assessment and treatment of children and adolescents with reactive attachment disorder of infancy and early childhood. *Journal of the American Academy of Child and Adolescent Psychiatry. 44*(11):1206–1219.

Alexander, J. F., Robbins, M. S., & Sexton, T. L. 2000. Family-based interventions with older, at-risk youth: From promise to proof to practice. *Journal of Primary Prevention. 21*:185–205.

Allen-Eckert, H., Fong, E., Nichols, M. P., Watson, N., and Liddle, H. A. 2001. Development of the Family Therapy Enactment Scale. *Family Process. 40*(4):469–478.

Amato, P. R. 2001. Children of divorce in the 1990s: An update of the Amato and Keith (1991) meta-analysis. *Journal of Family Psychology. 15*(3):355–370.

Amato, P. R., and Keith, B. 1991. Parental divorce and adult well-being: A meta-analysis. *Journal of Marriage & the Family. 53*(1):43–58.

American Psychiatric Association. 2000. *Diagnostic and statistical manual of mental disorders* (text revision). Washington, DC: Author.

Atkins, D. C., Berns, S. B., George, W. H., Doss, B. D., Gattis, K., and Christensen, A. 2005. Prediction of response to treatment in a randomized clinical trial of marital therapy. *Journal of Consulting and Clinical Psychology. 73*(5):893–903.

Babcock, J. C., Green, C. E., and Robie, C. 2004. Does batterers' treatment work? A meta-analytic review of domestic violence treatment. *Clinical Psychology Review*. 23(8):1023.

Baer, J. C., & Martinez, C. D. 2006. Child maltreatment and insecure attachment: A meta-analysis. *Journal of Reproductive and Infant Psychology*. 24(3):187–197.

Bakermans-Kranenburg, M. J., van Ijzendoorn, M. H., and Juffer, F. 2003. Less is more: Meta-analyses of sensitivity and attachment interventions in early childhood. *Psychological Bulletin*. 129(2):195–215.

Bakermans-Kranenburg, M. J., van Ijzendoorn, M. H., and Juffer, F. 2005. Disorganized infant attachment and preventive interventions: A review and meta-analysis. *Infant Mental Health Journal*. 26:191–216.

Barbato, A., and D'Avanzo, B. 2008. Efficacy of couples therapy as a treatment for depression: A meta-analysis. *Psychiatric Quarterly*. 79(2):121–132.

Barkley, R. 2005. *Attention deficit hyperactivity disorder: A handbook for diagnosis and treatment*, 3rd ed. New York: Guilford Press.

Barmish, A., and Kendall, P. 2005. Should parents be co-clients in cognitive-behavioral therapy for anxious youth? *Journal of Clinical Child and Adolescent Psychology*. 34:569–581.

Beach, S. R. H., and Kaslow, N. J. 2006. Relational disorders and relational processes in diagnostic practice: Introduction to the special section. *Journal of Family Psychology*. 20(3):353–355.

Beach, S. R. H., Wamboldt, M. Z., Kaslow, N. J., Heyman, R. R., and Reiss, D. 2006. Describing relationship problems in DSM-V: Toward better guidance for research and clinical practice. *Journal of Family Psychology*. 20:353–355.

Beck, C. J., and Sales, B. D. 2001. Future mediation theory. In *Family mediation: Facts, myths, and future prospects* (pp. 181–204). Washington, DC: American Psychological Association.

Beck, C. J., Sales, B. D., and Emery, R. E. 2004. Research on the impact of family mediation. In *Divorce and family mediation: Models, techniques, and applications* (pp. 447–482), J. Folberg, A. L. Milne, and P. Salem, eds. New York: Guilford Press.

Becker, S. J., and Curry, J. F. 2008. Outpatient interventions for adolescent substance abuse: A quality of evidence review. *Journal of Consulting and Clinical Psychology*. 76(4):531–543.

Benjamin, M., and Irving, H. H. 1995. Research in family mediation: Review and implications. *Mediation Quarterly*. 13(1):53–82.

Birmaher, B., Brent, D., Kolko, D., Baugher, M., Bridge, J., Holder, D., Iyengar, S., and Ulloa, R. 2000. Clinical outcome after short-term psychotherapy for adolescents with Major Depressive Disorder. *Archives of General Psychiatry*. 57(1):29–36.

Blanchard, V. L., Hawkins, A. J., Baldwin, S. A., & Fawcett, E. B. 2009. Investigating the effects of marriage and relationship education on couples' communication skills: A meta-analytic study. *Journal of Family Psychology*. 23(2):203–214.

Bowlby, J. 1977. The making and breaking of affectional bonds: I. Aetiology and psychopathology in the light of attachment theory. *British Journal of Psychiatry*. 130:201–210.

Braver, S. L., Griffin, W. A., Cookston, J. T., Sandler, I. N., Williams, J., Wolchik, S. A., Winslow, E., and Smith-Daniels, V. 2005. Programs for promoting parenting of residential parents: Moving from efficacy to effectiveness. In *Family psychology: The art of the science* (pp. 295–324). New York: Oxford University Press.

Bray, J. H. 1995. Systems-oriented therapy with stepfamilies. In *Integrating family therapy: Handbook of family psychology and systems theory* (pp. 125–140), R. H. Mikesell, D.-D. Lusterman, and S. H. McDaniel, eds. Washington, DC: American Psychological Association.

Bray, J. H., and Easling, I. 2005. Remarriage and step-families. In *Family psychology: The art of the science* (pp. 267–294), W. Pinsoff and J. L. Lebow, eds. New York: Oxford University Press.

Brent, D. A., Holder, D., Kolko, D., Birmaher, B., Baugher, M., Roth, C., Iyengar, S., and Johnson, B. A. 1997. A clinical psychotherapy trial for adolescent depression comparing cognitive, family, and supportive therapy. *Archives of General Psychiatry*. 54(9):877–885.

Brosnan, R., and Carr, A. 2000. Adolescent conduct problems. In *What works with children and adolescents?: A critical review of psychological interventions with children, adolescents, and their families* (pp. 131–154), A. Carr, ed. Florence, KY: Taylor & Francis/Routledge.

Brown, G. W., and Harris, T. O., eds. 1978. *Social origins of depression: A study of psychiatric disorder in women*. London: Tavistock.

Brunk, M., Hengeller, S., and Whelan, J. 1987. Comparison of multi-systemic therapy and parent training in the brief treatment of child abuse and neglect. *Journal of Consulting and Clinical Psychology*. 55(2):171–178.

Bullock, B. M., and Forgatch, M. S. 2005. Mothers in transition: Model-based strategies for effective parenting. In *Family psychology: The art of the science* (pp. 349–371). New York: Oxford University Press.

Burck, C., Frosh, S., Lisa, S.-C., and Morgan, K. 1998. The process of enabling change: A study of therapist interventions in family therapy. *Journal of Family Therapy*. 20(3):253–267.

Burke, J., Loeber, R., and Birmaher, B. 2002. Oppositional defiant disorder and conduct disorder: A review of the past 10 years, part II. *Journal of the American Academy of Child and Adolescent Psychiatry*. 41:1275–1293.

Butler, M. H., and Wampler, K. S. 1999. Couple-responsible therapy process: Positive proximal outcomes. *Family Process*. 38(1):27–54.

Byng-Hall, J. 1995. *Rewriting family scripts. Improvisation and change*. New York: Guilford.

Byrne, M., Carr, A., and Clark, M. 2004. The efficacy of behavioral couples therapy and emotionally focused therapy for couple distress. *Contemporary Family Therapy: An International Journal*. 26(4):361–387.

Campbell, D. T., and Stanley, J. C. 1963. *Experimental and quasi-experimental designs for research*. Chicago: Rand McNally.

Capaldi, D. M., Shortt, J. W., and Kim, H. K. 2005. A life span developmental systems perspective on aggression toward a partner. In *Family psychology: The art of the science*. (vol. 18, pp. 141–167), W. M. Pinsof and J. L. Lebow, eds. New York: Oxford University Press.

Carr, A. 2009. The effectiveness of family therapy and systemic interventions for child-focused problems. *Journal of Family Therapy*. 31:3–45.

Carr, A. 2009. The effectiveness of family therapy and systemic interventions for adult-focused problems. *Journal of Family Therapy*. 31:46–74.

Carroll, J. S., and Doherty, W. J. 2003. Evaluating the effectiveness of premarital prevention programs: A meta-analytic review of outcome research. *Family Relations: Interdisciplinary Journal of Applied Family Studies*. 52(2):105–118.

Chaffin, M., Hanson, R., Saunders, B. E., Nichols, T., Barnett, D., Zeanah, C., Berliner, L., Egeland, B., Newman, E., Lyon, T., LeTourneau, E., and Miller-Perrin, C. 2006. Report of the APSAC Task Force on attachment therapy, Reactive Attachment Disorder, and attachment problems. *Child Maltreatment*. 11(1):76–89.

Chamberlain, P., and Rosicky, J. G. 1995. The effectiveness of family therapy in the treatment of adolescents with conduct disorders and delinquency. *Journal of Marital and Family Therapy*. 21(4):441–459.

Chambless, D. L. 1996. In defense of dissemination of empirically supported psychological interventions. *Clinical Psychology: Science and Practice*. 3:230–235.

Christensen, A., Atkins, D., Yi, J., Baucom, D., and George, W. 2006. Couple and individual adjustment for 2 years following a randomized clinical trial comparing traditional versus integrative behavioral couple therapy. *Journal of Consulting and Clinical Psychology*. 74(4):1180–1191.

Christensen, A., Baucom, D. H., Vu, C. T.-A., and Stanton, S. 2005. Methodologically sound, cost-effective research on the outcome of couple therapy. *Journal of Family Psychology*. 19(1):6–17.

Chronis, A. M., Chacko, A., Fabiano, G. A., Wymbs, B. T., and Pelham Jr., W. E. 2004. Enhancements to the behavioral parent training paradigm for families of children with ADHD: Review and future directions. *Clinical Child and Family Psychology Review*. 7:1–27.

Chronis, A. M., Jones, H. A., and Raggi, V. L. 2006. Evidence-based psychosocial treatments for children and adolescents with attention-deficit/hyperactivity disorder. *Clinical Psychology Review*. 26(4):486–502.

Cicchetti, D., and Toth, S. L. 2005. Child maltreatment. *Annual Review of Clinical Psychology*. 1(1):409–438.

Conger, R. D., and Elder, G. H. 1994. *Families in troubled times: Adapting to change in rural America*. New York: Aldine de Gruyter.

Corcoran, J., and Dattalo, P. 2006. Parent involvement in treatment for ADHD: A meta-analysis of the published studies. *Research on Social Work Practice.* 16(6):561–570.

Corcoran, J., & Pillai, V. 2008. A meta-analysis for parent-involved treatment for child sexual abuse. *Research on Social Work Practice.* 18(5):453–464.

Cowan, C. P., and Cowan, P. A. 1992. *When partners become parents: The big life change for couples.* New York: Basic Books.

Cowan, C. P., Cowan, P. A., and Heming, G. 2005. Two variations of a preventive intervention for couples: Effects on parents and children during the transition to school. In *The family context of parenting in children's adaptation to elementary school* (pp. 277–312), P. A. Cowan, C. P. Cowan, J. C. Ablow, V. K. Johnson, and J. R. Measelle, eds. Mahwah, NJ: Erlbaum.

Crane, D., Hillin, H., and Jakubowski, S. 2005. Costs of treating conduct disordered Medicaid youth with and without family therapy. *American Journal of Family Therapy.* 33(5):403–413.

Currier, J. M., Neimeyer, R. A., & Berman, J. S. 2008. The effectiveness of psychotherapeutic interventions for bereaved persons: A comprehensive quantitative review. *Psychological Bulletin.* 134(5):648–661.

Curtis, N., Ronan, K., and Borduin, C. 2004. Multisystemic treatment: A meta-analysis of outcome studies. *Journal of Family Psychology.* 18(3):411–419.

Deutsch, R. M. 2008. Divorce in the 21st century: Multidisciplinary family interventions. *The Journal of Psychiatry & Law.* 36:41–66.

Diamond, G., and Liddle, H. A. 1996. Resolving a therapeutic impasse between parents and adolescents in multidimensional family therapy. *Journal of Consulting and Clinical Psychology.* 64(3):481–488.

Diamond, G., and Liddle, H. A. 1999. Transforming negative parent–adolescent interactions: From impasse to dialogue. *Family Process.* 38(1):5–26.

Diamond, G., Liddle, H. A., Hogue, A., and Dakof, G. A. 1999. Alliance-building interventions with adolescents in family therapy: A process study. *Psychotherapy: Theory, Research, Practice, Training.* 36(4):355–368.

Dodge, K. A. 2000. Conduct disorder. In *Handbook of developmental psychopathology*, 2nd ed., A. J. Sameroff, M. Lewis, and S. M. Miller, eds. Dordrecht, The Netherlands: Kluwer.

Doss, B. D., Simpson, L. E., and Christensen, A. 2004. Why do couples seek marital therapy? *Professional Psychology: Research and Practice.* 35(6):608–614.

Duterte, E., Segraves, T., and Althof, S. 2007. Psychotherapy and pharmacotherapy for sexual dysfunctions. In *A guide to treatments that work*, 3rd ed. P. Nathan and J. Gorman, eds. (pp. 447–474). New York: Oxford University Press.

Dutton, M. A., El-Khoury, M., Murphy, M., Somberg, R., and Bell, M. E. 2005. Women in intimate partner violence: Major advances and new directions. In *Family psychology: The art of the science* (vol. 18, pp. 191–221), W. M. Pinsof and J. L. Lebow, eds. New York: Oxford University Press.

Edleson, J. L., and Tolman, R. M. 1992. *Intervention for men who batter: An ecological approach.* Thousand Oaks, CA: Sage.

Edwards, M. E., and Steinglass, P. 1995. Family therapy treatment outcomes for alcoholism. *Journal of Marital and Family Therapy.* 21(4):475–509.

Emery, R. E., Laumann-Billings, L., Waldron, M. C., Sbarra, D. A., and Dillon, P. 2001. Child custody mediation and litigation: Custody, contact, and coparenting 12 years after initial dispute resolution. *Journal of Consulting and Clinical Psychology.* 69(2):323–332.

Emery, R. E., and Wyer, M. M. 1987. Child custody mediation and litigation: An experimental evaluation of the experience of parents. *Journal of Consulting and Clinical Psychology.* 55:179–186.

Escudero, V., Friedlander, M. L., Varela, N., & Abascal, A. 2008. Observing the therapeutic alliance in family therapy: Associations with participants' perceptions and therapeutic outcomes. *Journal of Family Therapy.* 30(2):194–214.

Falbo, T., Lein, L., and Amador, N. A. 2001. Parental involvement during the transition to high school. *Journal of Adolescent Research.* 16(5):511–529.

Fals-Stewart, W., O'Farrell, T. J., and Birchler, G. R. 1997. Behavioral couples therapy for male substance abusing patients: A cost outcomes analysis. *Journal of Consulting and Clinical Psychology.* 65:789–802.

Fals-Stewart, W., Yates, B. T., and Klostermann, K. 2005. Assessing the costs, benefits, cost-benefit ratio, and cost-effectiveness of marital and family treatments: Why we should and how we can. *Journal of Family Psychology.* 19(1):28–39.

Favero, D. 2002. Structural enactments as methods of change in family therapy. Unpublished doctoral dissertation, Virginia Consortium Program in Clinical Psychology, Virginia Beach, Virginia.

Feinberg, M. E., and Kan, M. L. 2008. Establishing family foundations: Intervention effects on coparenting, parent/infant well-being, and parent-child relations. *Journal of Family Psychology.* 22(2):253–263.

Fellenberg, S. 2003. The contribution of enactments to structural family therapy: A process study. Unpublished doctoral dissertation, Virginia Consortium Program in Clinical Psychology, Virginia Beach, Virginia.

Forgatch, M. S., and DeGarmo, D. S. 1999. Parenting through change: An effective prevention program for single mothers. *Journal of Consulting & Clinical Psychology.* 67(5):711–724.

Forgatch, M. S., DeGarmo, D. S., and Beldavs, Z. G. 2005. An efficacious theory-based intervention for stepfamilies. *Behavior Therapy.* 36(4):357–365.

Friedlander, M. L., Escudero, V., and Heatherington, L. 2006. Therapeutic alliances in couple and family therapy: An empirically informed guide to practice. Washington, DC: American Psychological Association.

Friedlander, M. L., Heatherington, L., Johnson, B., and Skowron, E. A. 1994. Sustaining engagement: A change event in family therapy. *Journal of Counseling Psychology.* 41(4):438–448.

Friedlander, M. L., Lambert, J. E., and de la Pena, C. M. 2008. A step toward disentangling the alliance/improvement cycle in family therapy. *Journal of Counseling Psychology.* 55(1):118–124.

Garfield, R. 2004. The therapeutic alliance in couples therapy: Clinical considerations. *Family Process.* 43(4):457–465.

Geerart, L., Van den Noortgate, W., Grietens, H., and Onghena, P. 2004. The effects of early prevention programs for families with young children at risk for physical child abuse and neglect: A meta-analysis. *Child Maltreatment,* 9(3):277–291.

Gerard, J. M., Krishnakumar, A., and Buehler, C. 2006. Marital conflict, parent–child relations, and youth maladjustment: A longitudinal investigation of spillover effects. *Journal of Family Issues.* 27(7):951–975.

Gilliam, C., and Cottone, R. 2005. Couple or individual therapy for the treatment of depression?: An update of the empirical literature. *American Journal of Family Therapy.* 33(3):265–272.

Glade, A. C., Bean, R. A., and Vira, R. 2005. A prime time for marital/relational intervention: A review of the transition to parenthood literature with treatment recommendations. *American Journal of Family Therapy.* 33(4):319–336.

Greenberg, L. S., Ford, C. L., Alden, L. S., and Johnson, S. M. 1993. In-session change in emotionally focused therapy. *Journal of Consulting and Clinical Psychology.* 61(1):78–84.

Halford, W., Sanders, M. R., and Behrens, B. C. 2001. Can skills training prevent relationship problems in at-risk couples? Four-year effects of a behavioral relationship education program. *Journal of Family Psychology.* 15(4):750–768.

Hammond, R., and Nichols, M. P. 2008. How collaborative is structural family therapy? *The Family Journal: Counseling and Therapy for Couples and Family.* 16(2):118–124.

Hanson, R. F., and Spratt, E. G. 2000. Reactive attachment disorder: What we know about the disorder and implications for treatment. *Child Maltreatment.* 5(2):137–145.

Hawkins, A. J., Blanchard, V. L., Baldwin, S. A., Fawcett, E. B. 2008. Does marriage and relationship education work? A meta-analytic study. *Journal of Consulting and Clinical Psychology.* 76(5):723–734.

Heatherington, L., and Friedlander, M. L. 1990. Complementarity and symmetry in family therapy communication. *Journal of Counseling Psychology.* 37(3):261–268.

Heatherington, L., Friedlander, M. L., and Greenberg, L. 2005. Change process research in couple and family therapy: Methodological challenges and opportunities. *Journal of Family Psychology.* 19(1):18–27.

Henggeler, S. W., Melton, G. B., and Smith, L. A. 1992. Family preservation using multisystemic therapy: An effective alternative to incarcerating serious juvenile offenders. *Journal of Consulting and Clinical Psychology.* 60(6):953–961.

Herschell, A. D., and McNeil, C. B. 2005. Theoretical and empirical underpinnings of parent–child interaction therapy with child physical abuse populations. *Education and Treatment of Children.* 28(2):142–162.

Higginson, I. J., Finlay, I. G., Goodwin, D. M., Hood, K., Edwards, A. G., Cook, A., Douglas, H.-R., and Normand, C. E. 2003. Is there evidence that palliative care teams alter end-of-life experiences of patients and their caregivers? *Journal of Pain and Symptom Management.* 25(2):150–168.

Hogue, A., Dauber, S., Chinchilla, P., Fried, A., Henderson, C., Inclan, J., et al. 2008. Assessing fidelity in individual and family therapy for adolescent substance abuse. *Journal of Substance Abuse Treatment.* 35(2):137–147.

Holtzworth-Munroe, A., and Meehan, J. C. 2005. Partner violence and men: A focus on the male perpetrator. In *Family psychology: The art of the science* (vol. 18, pp. 169–190), W. M. Pinsof and J. L. Lebow, eds. New York: Oxford University Press.

Howe, G. W., Levy, M. L., and Caplan, R. D. 2004. Job loss and depressive symptoms in couples: Common stressors, stress transmission, or relationship disruption? *Journal of Family Psychology.* 18:639–650.

Howe, G. W., Reiss, D., and Yuh, J. 2002. Can prevention trials test theories of etiology? *Development & Psychopathology.* 14(4):673–694.

Jackson-Gilfort, A., Liddle, H. A., Tejeda, M. J., and Dakof, G. A. 2001. Facilitating engagement of African American male adolescents in family therapy: A cultural theme process study. *Journal of Black Psychology.* 27(3):321–340.

Jacobson, N. S., Dobson, K., Fruzzetti, A. E., Schmailing, K. B., and Salusky, S. 1991. Marital therapy as a treatment for depression. *Journal of Consulting & Clinical Psychology.* 59(4):547.

Jensen, P., Arnold, L., Swanson, J., Vitiello, B., Abikoff, H., and Greenhill, L., 2007. 3-year follow-up of the NIMH MTA study. *Journal of the American Academy of Child and Adolescent Psychiatry.* 46:989–1002.

Johnston, C., and Mash, E. J. 2001. Families of children with attention-deficit/hyperactivity disorder: Review and recommendations for future research. *Clinical Child and Family Psychology Review.* 4(3):183–207.

Kaslow, F. 1995. The dynamics of divorce therapy. In *Integrating family therapy. Handbook of family psychology and systems theory* (pp. 271–284), R. H. Mikesell, D.-D. Lusterman, and S. H. McDaniel, eds. Washington, DC: American Psychological Association.

Kazdin, A. E., and Weisz, J. R. 1998. Identifying and developing empirically supported child and adolescent treatments. *Journal of Consulting & Clinical Psychology.* 66(1):19.

Kendler, K. S., Hettema, J. M., Butera, F., Gardner, C. O., and Prescott, C. A. 2003. Life event dimensions of loss, humiliation, entrapment, and danger in the prediction of onsets of major depression and generalized anxiety. *Archives of General Psychiatry.* 60(8):789–796.

Kermeen, P. 1995. Improving postpartum marital relationships. *Psychological Reports.* 76(3, Pt. 1): 831–834.

Kissane, D. W., McKenzie, M., Block, S., Moskowitz, C., McKenzie, D. P., and O'Neill, I. 2006. Family focused grief therapy: A randomized, controlled trial in palliative care and bereavement. *American Journal of Psychiatry.* 163(7):1208–1218.

Klein Velderman, M., Bakersman-Kranenburg, M. J., Juffer, F., and van Izjendoorn, M. H. 2006. Effects of attachment-based interventions on maternal sensitivity and infant attachment: Differential susceptibility of highly reactive infants. *Journal of Family Psychology.* 20(2):266–274.

Knobloch-Fedders, L. M., Pinsof, W. M., and Mann, B. J. 2004. The formation of the therapeutic alliance in couple therapy. *Family Process.* 43(4):425–442.

Lemmens, G. M. D., Eisler, E., Buysse, A., Heene, E., and Demyttenaere, K. 2009. The effects on mood of adjunctive single-family and multi-family group therapy in the treatment of hospitalized patients with major depression. *Psychotherapy and Psychosomatics.* 78:98–105.

Liddle, H. A., Dakof, G. A., Parker, K., Diamond, G. S., Barrett, K., and Tejeda, M. 2001. Multidimensional family therapy for adolescent drug abuse: Results of a randomized clinical trial. *American Journal of Drug and Alcohol Abuse.* 27(4):651.

Luborsky, L., Singer, B., and Luborsky, L. (1975). Comparative studies of psychotherapies: Is it true that "everyone has won and all must have prizes?" *Clinical Psychology: Science and Practice.* 2:106–109.

Lundahl, B. W., Nimer, J., and Parsons, B. 2006. Preventing child abuse: A meta-analysis of parent training programs. *Research on Social Work Practice.* 16(3):251–262.

Macleod, J., and Nelson, G. 2000. Programs for the promotion of family wellness and the prevention of child maltreatment: A meta-analytic review. *Child Abuse and Neglect.* 24(9):1127–1149.

Mahaffey, B. A., and Granello, P. F. 2007. Therapeutic alliance: A review of sampling strategies reported in marital and family therapy studies. *The Family Journal.* 15(3):207–216.

Main, M., and Solomon, J. 1990. Procedures for identifying infants as disorganized/disoriented during the Ainsworth Strange Situation. In *Attachment in the preschool years: Theory, research, and intervention* (pp. 121–160), M. T. Greenberg, D. Cicchetti, and M. E. Cummings, eds. Chicago: University of Chicago Press.

Markman, H. J., Renick, M. J., Floyd, F. J., Stanley, S. M., and Clements, M. 1993. Preventing marital distress through communication and conflict management training: A 4- and 5-year follow-up. *Journal of Consulting and Clinical Psychology.* 61(1):70–77.

McCart, M., Priester, P., Davies, W., and Azen, R. 2006. Differential effectiveness of cognitive-behavioral therapy and behavioral parent-training for antisocial youth: A meta-analysis. *Journal of Abnormal Child Psychology.* 34:527–543.

McClure, E. B., Brennan, P. A., Hammen, C., and Le Brocque, R. M. 2001. Parental anxiety disorders, child anxiety disorders, and the perceived parent-child relationship. *Journal of Abnormal Child Psychology.* 29(1):1.

McFarlane, W. R., Dixon, L., Lukens, E., and Luckstead, A. 2003. Family psychoeducation and schizophrenia: A review of the literature. *Journal of Marital and Family Therapy.* 29(2):223–245.

McTaggart, P., and Sanders, M. R. 2003. The Transition to School Project: Results from the classroom. *Australian e-Journal for the Advancement of Mental Health.* 2(3):n.p.

Meston, C. 2006. Female orgasmic disorder: treatment strategies and outcome results. In *Women's sexual function and dysfunction: Study, diagnosis, & treatment.* I. Goldstein, C. Meston, S. Davis, and A. Traish, eds. (pp. 449–461). London: Taylor & Francis.

Meston, C., and Bradford, A. 2007. Sexual dysfunctions in women. *Annual Review of Clinical Psychology.* 3:233–256.

Miklowitz, D. J. 2004. The role of family systems in severe and recurrent psychiatric disorders: A developmental psychopathology view. *Development and Psychopathology.* 16(3):667–688.

Miles, D. 2004. The effectiveness of therapist interventions in structural family therapy: A process study. Unpublished doctoral dissertation, Virginia Consortium Program in Clinical Psychology, Virginia Beach, Virginia.

Muck, R., Zempolich, K. A., Titus, J. C., Fishman, M., Godley, M. D., and Schwebel, R. 2001. An overview of the effectiveness of adolescent substance abuse treatment models. *Youth and Society.* 33:143–168.

Murray, C. E. 2006. Controversy, constraints, and context: Understanding family violence through family systems theory. *Family Journal: Counseling and Therapy for Couples and Families.* 14(3): 234–239.

Nichols, M. P., and Fellenberg, S. (2000). The effective use of enactments in family therapy: A discovery-oriented process study. *Journal of Marital & Family Therapy.* 26(2):143–152.

Nicholson, J. M., and Sanders, M. R. 1999. Randomized controlled trial of behavioral family intervention for the treatment of child behavior problems in stepfamilies. *Journal of Divorce & Remarriage.* 30(3–4):1–23.

O'Farrell, T. J., Choquette, K. A., Cutter, H. S. G., Brown, E. D., Bayog, R., McCourt, W., et al. 1996a. Cost-benefit and cost-effectiveness analyses of behavioral marital therapy with and without relapse prevention sessions for alcoholics and their spouses. *Behavior Therapy.* 27:7–24.

O'Farrell, T. J., Choquette, K. A., Cutter, H. S. G., Floyd, F. J., Bayog, R. D., Brown, E. D., et al. 1996b. Cost-benefit and cost-effectiveness analyses of behavioral marital therapy as an addition to outpatient alcoholism treatment. *Journal of Substance Abuse.* 8:145–166.

O'Farrell, T. J., and Fals-Stewart, W. 2003. Alcohol abuse. *Journal of Marital and Family Therapy.* 29(1):121–146.

O'Farrell, T. J., Murphy, M., Alter, J., and Fals-Stewart, W. 2008. Brief family treatment intervention to promote continuing care among alcohol-dependent patients in inpatient detoxification: A randomized pilot study. *Journal of Substance Abuse Treatment.* 34:363–369.

O'Leary, K., and Vega, E. M. 2005. Can partner aggression be stopped with psychosocial interventions? In *Family psychology: The art of the science.* (vol. 18, pp. 243–263), W. M. Pinsof and J. L. Lebow, eds. New York: Oxford University Press.

Olfson, M., Gameroff, M. J., Marcus, S. C., and Jensen, P. S. 2003. National trends in the treatment of attention deficit hyperactivity disorder. *American Journal of Psychiatry.* 160(6):1071.

Patterson, G. 1976. *Living with children.* Champaign, IL: Research Press.

Peterson, L., Tremblay, G., Ewigman, B., and Saldana, L. 2003. Multilevel selected primary prevention of child maltreatment. *Journal of Consulting and Clinical Psychology.* 71:601–612.

Pfammatter, M., Junghan, U., and Brenner, H. 2006. Efficacy of psychological therapy in schizophrenia: Conclusions from meta-analyses. *Schizophrenia Bulletin.* 32(Suppl. 1):S64–S80.

Pharoah, F., Mari., J., Rahbone, J., and Wong, W. 2006. Family intervention for schizophrenia. *Cochrane Database of Systematic Reviews*, Issue 2. Art. No.: CD000088. DOI: 10.1002/14651858 .CD000088.pub2.

Pilling, S., Bebbington, P., Kuipers, E., Farety, P., Geddes, J., Orbach, G., and Morgan, C. 2002. Psychological treatments in schizophrenia: I. Meta-analysis of family intervention and cognitive behavior therapy. *Psychological Medicine.* 32:763–782.

Pinsof, W. M., and Lebow, J. L., eds. 2005. *Family psychology: The art of the science.* New York: Oxford University Press.

Pinsof, W. M., Zinbarg, R., and Knobloch-Fedders, L. M. 2008. Factorial and construct validity of the revised short form Integrative Psychotherapy Alliance Scales for family, couple, and individual therapy. *Family Process.* 47(3):281–301.

Pitschel-Walz, G., Leucht, S., Bäuml, J., Kissling, W., and Engel, R. 2001. The effect of family interventions on relapse and rehospitalization in schizophrenia—A meta-analysis. *Schizophrenia Bulletin.* 27:73–92.

Prado, G., Pantin, H., Briones, E., Schwartz, S. J., Feaster, D., Huang, S., Sullivan, S., Tapia, M. I., Sabillon, E., Lopez, B., and Szapocsnik, J. 2007. A randomized controlled trial of a parent-centered intervention in preventing substance use and HIV risk behaviors in Hispanic adolescents. *Journal of Consulting and Clinical Psychology.* 75:914–926.

Prinz, R. J., Sanders, M. R., Shapiro, C. J., Whitaker, D. J., and Lutzker, J. R. 2009. Population-based prevention of child maltreatment: The U.S. Triple P System Population Trial. *Prevention Science.* 10:1–12.

Ralph, A., and Sanders, M. R. 2003. Preliminary evaluation of the Group Teen Triple P program for parents of teenagers making the transition to high school. *Australian e-Journal for the Advancement of Mental Health.* 2(3):1–10.

Robbins, M. S., Alexander, J. F., Newell, R. M., and Turner, C. W. 1996. The immediate effect of reframing on client attitude in family therapy. *Journal of Family Psychology.* 10(1):28–34.

Robbins, M. S., Liddle, H. A., Turner, C. W., Dakof, G. A., Alexander, J. F., and Kogan, S. M. 2006. Adolescent and parent therapeutic alliances as predictors of dropout in multidimensional family therapy. *Journal of Family Psychology.* 20(1):108–116.

Robbins, M. S., Mayorga, C. C., Mitrani, V. B., Szapocznik, J., Turner, C. W., and Alexander, J. F. 2008. Adolescent and parent alliances with therapists in brief strategic family therapy with drug-using Hispanic adolescents. *Journal of Marital and Family Therapy.* 34(3):316–328.

Robbins, M. S., Turner, C. W., Alexander, J. F., and Perez, G. A. 2003. Alliance and dropout in family therapy for adolescents with behavior problems: Individual and systemic effects. *Journal of Family Psychology.* 17(4):534–544.

Rosenfield, B. D. (1992). Court-ordered treatment of spouse abuse. *Clinical Psychology Review.* 12:205–226.

Sameroff, A. J., Lewis, M., and Miller, S. M. 2000. *Handbook of developmental psychopathology*, 2nd ed. CITY: The Netherlands: Kluwer.

Sandler, I. N., Ayers, T. S., Wolchik, S. A., Tein, J.-Y., Kwok, O.-M., Haine, R. A., Twohey-Jacobs, J., Suter, J., Lin, K., Padgett-Jones, S., Weyer, J. L., Cole, E., Kriege, G., and Griffin, W. A. 2003. The Family Bereavement Program: Efficacy evaluation of a theory-based prevention program for parentally bereaved children and adolescents. *Journal of Consulting and Clinical Psychology.* 71(3):587–600.

Sartin, R. M., Hansen, D. J., and Huss, M. T. 2006. Domestic violence treatment response and recidivism: A review and implications for the study of family violence. *Aggression and Violent Behavior.* 11(5):425–440.

Sexton, T. L., and Alexander, J. F. 2005. Functional family therapy for externalizing disorders in adolescents. In *Handbook of clinical family therapy* (pp. 164–191), J. L. Lebow, ed. Hoboken, N.J.: John Wiley & Sons.

Sexton, T. L., Kinser, J. C., and Hanes, C. W. 2008. Beyond a single standard: Levels of evidence approach for evaluating marriage and family therapy research and practice. *Journal of Family Therapy.* 30:386–398.

Shadish, W. R., and Baldwin, S. A. 2005. Effects of behavioral marital therapy: A meta-analysis of randomized controlled trials. *Journal of Consulting and Clinical Psychology.* 73(1):6–14.

Shelef, K., Diamond, G. M., Diamond, G. S., and Liddle, H. A. 2005. Adolescent and parent alliance and treatment outcome in multidimensional family therapy. *Journal of Consulting and Clinical Psychology.* 73(4):689–698.

Siqueland, L., Rynn, M., and Diamond, G. S. 2005. Cognitive behavioral and attachment based family therapy for anxious adolescents: Phase I and II studies. *Journal of Anxiety Disorders.* 19(4): 361–381.

Skowron, E., and Reinemann, D. 2005. Effectiveness of psychological interventions for child maltreatment: A meta-analysis. *Psychotherapy: Theory, Research, Practice, Training.* 42(1):52–71.

Smerud, P. E., and Rosenfarb, I. S. 2008. The therapeutic alliance and family psychoeducation in the treatment of schizophrenia: An exploratory prospective change study. *Journal of Consulting and Clinical Psychology.* 76(3):505–510.

Sorensen, S., Pinquart, M., and Duberstein, P. 2002. How effective are interventions with caregivers? An updated meta-analysis. *Gerontologist.* 42(3): 356–372.

Stanton, M. D., and Shadish, W. R. 1997. Outcome, attrition, and family-couples treatment for drug abuse: A meta-analysis and review of the controlled, comparative studies. *Psychological Bulletin.* 122(2):170–191.

Stark, K. D., Humphrey, L. L., Laurent, J., Livingston, R., and Christopher, J. 1993. Cognitive, behavioral, and family factors in the differentiation of depressive and anxiety disorders during childhood. *Journal of Consulting and Clinical Psychology.* 61(5):878.

Stathakos, P., and Roehrle, B. 2003. The effectiveness of intervention programmes for children of divorce—A meta-analysis. *International Journal of Mental Health Promotion.* 5(1):31–37.

Stith, S., and Rosen, K. 2003. Effectiveness of couples treatment for spouse abuse. *Journal of Marital and Family Therapy,* 29(3):407–426.

Stith, S., Rosen, K., McCollum, E., and Thomsen, C. 2004. Treating intimate partner violence within intact couple relationships: Outcomes of multi-couple versus individual couple therapy. *Journal of Marital and Family Therapy.* 30(3):305–318.

Symonds, D., and Horvath, A. O. 2004. Optimizing the alliance in couples therapy. *Family Process.* 43:443–455.

Tremblay, G. C., and Israel, A. C. 1998. Children's adjustment to parental death. *Clinical Psychology: Science and Practice.* 5(4):424–438.

Trowell, R., Joffe, I., Campbell, J., Clemente, C., Almqvist, F., Soininen M., Koskenranta-Aalto, U., Weintraub, S., Kolaitis, G., Tomaras, G., et al. 2007. Childhood depression: A place for psychotherapy. An outcome study comparing individual psychodynamic psychotherapy and family therapy. *European and Adolescent Psychiatry.* 16(3):157–167.

U.S. Department of Health and Human Services, Administration on Children, Youth, and Families. 2007. *Child maltreatment.* Washington, DC: Author.

Van Zeijl, J., Mesman, J., Marinus, H., Van Ijzendoorn, M., Bakermans-Kranenburg, F. J., Stolk, M. N., et al. 2006. Attachment-based intervention for enhancing sensitive discipline in mothers of 1- to 3-year-old children at risk for externalizing behavior problems: A randomized controlled trial. *Journal of Consulting and Clinical Psychology.* 74(6):994–1005.

Waite, L. J., and Luo, Y. 2002, August. *Marital quality and marital stability: Consequences for psychological well-being.* Paper presented at the meetings of the American Sociological Association, Chicago, Illinois.

Waldron, H. B., Turner, C. W., Barton, C., Alexander, J. F., and Cline, V. B. 1997. Therapist defensiveness and marital therapy process and outcome. *American Journal of Family Therapy.* *25*(3):233–243.

Waldron, H. B., and Turner, C. W. 2008. Evidence-based psychosocial treatments for adolescent substance abuse. *Journal of Clinical Child and Adolescent Psychology.* *37*(1):238–261.

Whiteside, M. F., and Becker, B. J. 2000. Parental factors and the young child's postdivorce adjustment: A meta-analysis with implications for parenting arrangements. *Journal of Family Psychology.* *14*(1):5–26.

Williams, R., and Chang, S. 2000. A comprehensive and comparative review of adolescent substance abuse treatment outcome. *Clinical Psychology: Science and Practice.* 7:138–166.

Wolchik, S. A., Sandler, I. N., Millsap, R. E., Plummer, B. A., Greene, S. M., Anderson, E. R., Dawson-McClure, S. R., Hipke, K., and Haine, R. A. 2002. Six-year follow-up of preventive interventions for children of divorce. A randomized controlled trial. *Journal of the American Medical Association.* *288*(15):1874–1881.

Wolchik, S. A., West, S. G., Westover, S., and Sandler, I. N. 1993. The children of divorce parenting intervention: Outcome evaluation of an empirically based program. *American Journal of Community Psychology.* *21*(3):293–331.

Wood, N. D., Crane, D., Schaalje, G., and Law, D. D. 2005. What works for whom: A meta-analytic review of marital and couples therapy in reference to marital distress. *American Journal of Family Therapy.* *33*(4):273–287.

Woolfenden, S., Williams, K., and Peat, J. 2002. Family and parenting interventions for conduct disorder and delinquency a meta-analysis of randomized controlled trials. *Archives of Diseases in Childhood.* *86*(4):251–256.

Woolley, S. R., Butler, M. H., and Wampler, K. S. 2000. Unraveling change in therapy: Three different process research methodologies. *American Journal of Family Therapy.* *28*(4):311–327.

Zilberstein, K. 2006. Clarifying core characteristics of attachment disorders: A review of current research and theory. *American Journal of Orthopsychiatry.* *76*(1):55–64.

Appendix A
RECOMMENDED READINGS

General Principles of Family Systems

Carter, B., and McGoldrick, M. 1999. *The expanded family life cycle: A framework for family therapy*, 3rd ed. Boston: Allyn & Bacon.

Guerin, P. J., Fogarty, T. F., Fay, L. F., and Kautto, J. G. 1996. *Working with relationship triangles: The one-two-three of psychotherapy*. New York: Guilford Press.

Hoffman, L. 1981. *The foundations of family therapy*. New York: Basic Books.

Kerr, M. E., and Bowen, M. 1988. *Family evaluation*. New York: Norton.

Minuchin, S. 1974. *Families and family therapy*. Cambridge, MA: Harvard University Press.

Nichols, M. P. 2008. *Inside family therapy*, 2nd ed. Boston: Allyn & Bacon.

Paolino, T. J., and McCrady, B. S., eds. 1978. *Marriage and marital therapy*. New York: Brunner/Mazel.

Watzlawick, P., Beavin, J., and Jackson, D. 1967. *Pragmatics of human communication*. New York: Norton.

Culture and Family Therapy

Boyd-Franklin, N. 1989. *Black families in therapy: A multisystems approach*. New York: Guilford Press.

Davis, L., and Proctor, E. 1989. *Race, gender, and class: Guidelines for practice with individuals, families and groups*. Upper Saddle River, NJ: Prentice Hall.

Fontes, L. A. 2008. *Interviewing clients across cultures*. New York: Guilford Press.

Pedersen, P. 1987. The frequent assumptions of cultural bias in counseling. *Journal of Multicultural Counseling and Development*. 15:16–24.

Pinderhughes, E. 1989. *Understanding race, ethnicity, power: The key to efficacy in clinical practice*. New York: Free Press.

Sue, D. W., and Sue, D. 1990. *Counseling the culturally different: Theory and practice*, 2nd ed. New York: Wiley.

Walsh, F. 1998. *Re-visioning family therapy*. New York: Guilford Press.

Marriage

Dicks, H. V. 1967. *Marital tensions*. New York: Basic Books.

Guerin, P. J., Fay, L., Burden, S., and Kautto, J. 1987. *The evaluation and treatment of marital conflict: A four-stage approach*. New York: Basic Books.

Lederer, W., and Jackson, D. 1968. *The mirages of marriage*. New York: Norton.

Lerner, H. G. 1985. *The dance of anger: A woman's guide to changing patterns of intimate relationships*. New York: Harper & Row.

Scarf, M. 1987. *Intimate partners: Patterns in love and marriage*. New York: Random House.

Solot, D., and Miller, M. 2002. *Unmarried to each other*. New York: Marlowe & Company.

In-Laws and the Extended Family

Guerin, P. J., ed. 1976. *Family therapy: Theory and practice*. New York: Gardner Press.

Lerner, H. G. 1989. *The dance of intimacy: A woman's guide to courageous acts of change in key relationships*. New York: Harper & Row.

McGoldrick, M., and Gerson, R. 1985. *Genograms in family assessment*. New York: Norton.

Families with Babies and Small Children

Brazelton, T. B. 1983. *Infants and mothers: Differences in development*, rev. ed. New York: Dell.

Combrinck-Graham, L., ed. 1988. *Children in family contexts: Perspectives on treatment*. New York: Guilford Press.

Faber, A., and Mazlish, E. 1974. *Liberated parents, liberated children*. New York: Grosset & Dunlap.

Ginott, H. 1969. *Between parent and child*. New York: Macmillan.

Nichols, M. P. 2004. *Stop arguing with your kids*. New York: Guilford Press.

Patterson, G. 1975. *Families: Application of social learning theory to family life*. Champaign, IL: Research Press.

Families with Older Children

Bank, S., and Kahn, M. 1982. *The sibling bond*. New York: Basic Books.

Blos, P. 1979. *The adolescent passage: Developmental issues*. New York: International Universities Press.

Faber, A., and Mazlish, E. 1987. *Siblings without rivalry*. New York: Norton.

Fishel, E. 1979. *Sisters: Love and rivalry inside the family and beyond*. New York: Quill/William Morrow.

Micucci, J. 1998. *The adolescent in family therapy*. New York: Guilford Press.

Schlaadt, R., and Shannon, P. 1986. *Drugs of choice*, 2nd ed. Upper Saddle River, NJ: Prentice Hall.

Sells, S. 1998. *Treating the tough adolescent*. New York: Guilford Press.

Divorce, Remarriage, and Stepparenting

Ahrons, C., and Rodgers, R. 1987. *Divorced families: A multidisciplinary developmental view*. New York: Norton.

Isaacs, M. B., Montalvo, B., and Abelsohn, D. 1986. *The difficult divorce*. New York: Basic Books.

Vaughan, D. 1986. *Uncoupling: Turning points in intimate relationships*. New York: Oxford University Press.

Visher, E., and Visher, J. 1988. *Old loyalties, new ties: Therapeutic strategies with stepfamilies*. New York: Brunner/Mazel.

Leaving Home and the Postchildrearing Years

Levinson, D. 1978. *The seasons of a man's life*. New York: Ballantine.

Nichols, M. P. 1987. *Turning forty in the eighties*. New York: Fireside/Simon & Schuster.

Viorst, J. 1986. *Necessary losses*. New York: Simon & Schuster.

Family Therapy Technique

Anderson, C., and Stewart, S. 1983. *Mastering resistance: A practical guide to family therapy*. New York: Guilford Press.

Dattilio, F., ed. 1998. *Case studies in couple and family therapy: Systemic and cognitive perspectives*. New York: Guilford Press.

Donovan, J. M. 1999. *Short-term couple therapy*. New York: Guilford Press.

Fisch, R., Weakland, J., and Segal, L., 1982. *The tactics of change*. San Francisco: Jossey-Bass.

Gerson, M-J. 1996. *The embedded self: A psychoanalytic guide to family therapy*. New York: Analytic Press.

Guerin, P. J., Fay, L., Burden, S., and Kautto, J. 1987. *The evaluation and treatment of marital conflict: A four-stage approach*. New York: Basic Books.

Minuchin, S., and Fishman, H. C. 1981. *Family therapy techniques*. Cambridge, MA: Harvard University Press.

Minuchin, S., and Nichols, M. P. 1993. *Family healing: Tales of hope and renewal from family therapy*. New York: Free Press.

Minuchin, S., Nichols, M. P., and Lee, W-Y. 2006. *Assessing families and couples: From symptom to system*. Boston: Allyn & Bacon.

Taibbi, R. 2007. *Doing family therapy: Craft and creativity in clinical practice*, 2nd ed. New York: Guilford Press.

White, M., and Epston, D. 1990. *Narrative means to therapeutic ends*. New York: Norton.

Appendix B

GLOSSARY

accommodation Elements of a system automatically adjust to coordinate their functioning; people may have to work at it.

attachment The innate tendency to seek out closeness to caretakers in the face of stress.

aversive control Using punishment and criticism to eliminate undesirable responses; commonly used in dysfunctional families.

basic assumption theory Bion's concept that group members become diverted from the group task to pursue unconscious patterns of *fight–flight*, *dependency*, or *pairing*.

behavior exchange theory Explanation of behavior in relationships as maintained by a ratio of costs to benefits.

black box concept The idea that because the mind is so complex, it's better to study people's input and output (behavior, communication) than to speculate about what goes on in their minds.

blended families Separate families united by marriage; stepfamilies.

boundary Emotional and physical barriers that protect and enhance the integrity of individuals, subsystems, and families.

boundary making Negotiating the boundaries between members of a relationship and between the relationship and the outside world.

circular causality The idea that actions are related through a series of recursive loops or repeating cycles.

circular questioning A method of interviewing developed by the Milan Associates in which questions are asked that highlight differences among family members.

classical conditioning A form of respondent learning in which an unconditioned stimulus (UCS), such as food, which leads to an unconditioned response (UCR), such as salivation, is paired with a conditioned stimulus (CS), such as a bell, the result of which is that the CS begins to evoke the same response; used in the behavioral treatment of anxiety disorders.

closed system A functionally related group of elements regarded as forming a collective entity that does not interact with the surrounding environment.

coalition An alliance between two persons or social units against a third.

cognitive-behavioral therapy Treatment that emphasizes attitude change as well as reinforcement of behavior.

collaborative model A more egalitarian view of the therapist's role; advocated by critics of what is viewed as authoritarianism in traditional approaches to family therapy.

communications theory The study of relationships in terms of the exchange of verbal and nonverbal messages.

complainant De Shazer's term for a relationship with a client who describes a complaint but is at present unwilling to work on solving it.

complementarity The reciprocity that is the defining feature of every relationship.

complementary relationship Based on differences that fit together, where qualities of one make up for lacks in the other; one is one-up while the other is one-down.

concurrent therapy Treatment of two or more persons, seen separately, usually by different therapists.

conjoint therapy Treatment of two or more persons in sessions together.

constructivism A relativistic point of view that emphasizes the subjective construction of reality.

Implies that what we see in families may be based as much on our preconceptions as on what's actually going on.

content What families talk about.

context In family therapy, the interpersonal context, including the family but also other social influences.

contextual therapy Boszormenyi-Nagy's model that includes relational ethics.

contingency contracting A behavior therapy technique whereby agreements are made between family members to exchange rewards for desired behavior.

contingency management Shaping behavior by giving and taking away rewards.

countertransference Emotional reactivity on the part of the therapist.

cross-generational coalition An inappropriate alliance between a parent and child, who side together against a third member of the family.

culture Shared patterns of behavior and experience derived from settings in which people live.

cultural competence Familiarity with and, more important, sensitivity to other peoples' ways of doing things.

customer De Shazer's term for a client who not only complains about a problem ("complainant") but is motivated to resolve it.

cybernetics The science of feedback; how information, especially positive and negative feedback loops, can help self-regulate a system.

deconstruction A postmodern approach to exploring meaning by taking apart and examining taken-for-granted categories and assumptions, making possible newer and sounder constructions of meaning.

detriangulation The process by which individuals remove themselves from the emotional field of two others.

differentiation of self Bowen's term for psychological separation of intellect and emotions and independence of self from others; opposite of fusion.

directives Homework assignments designed to help families interrupt homeostatic patterns of problem-maintaining behavior.

disengagement Psychological isolation that results from overly rigid boundaries around individuals and subsystems in a family.

double bind A conflict created when a person receives contradictory messages on different levels of abstraction in an important relationship and cannot leave or comment.

dyadic model Explanations based on the interactions between two persons or objects: Johnny shoplifts to get his mother's attention.

emotional cutoff Bowen's term for flight from an unresolved emotional attachment.

emotional reactivity The tendency to respond in a knee-jerk emotional fashion, rather than calmly and objectively.

emotionally focused couples therapy A model of therapy based on attachment theory, in which the emotional longings beneath a couple's defensive reactions are uncovered as they are taught to see the reactive nature of their struggles with each other, developed by Leslie Greenberg and Susan Johnson.

empathy understanding someone else's beliefs and feelings.

enactment An interaction stimulated in structural family therapy in order to observe and then change transactions that make up family structure.

enmeshment Loss of autonomy due to a blurring of psychological boundaries.

entitlement Boszormenyi-Nagy's term for the amount of merit a person accrues for behaving in an ethical manner toward others.

epistemology The branch of philosophy concerned with the study of knowledge. Used by Bateson to mean worldview or belief system.

equifinality The ability of complex systems to reach a given final goal in a variety of different ways.

ethnicity The common ancestry through which groups of people evolve shared values and customs.

exception De Shazer's term for times when clients are temporarily free of their problems. Solution-focused therapists focus on exceptions to help clients build on successful problem-solving skills.

expressive leader Serving social and emotional functions; in traditional families, the wife's role.

extended family The network of kin relationships across several generations.

externalization Michael White's technique of personifying problems as external to persons.

extinction Eliminating behavior by not reinforcing it.

family drawing An experiential therapy technique in which family members are asked to draw their ideas about how the family is organized.

family group therapy Family treatment based on the group therapy model.

family homeostasis Tendency of families to resist change in order to maintain a steady state.

family life cycle Stages of family life from separation from one's parents to marriage, having children, growing older, retirement, and finally death.

family myths A set of beliefs based on a distortion of historical reality and shared by all family members that help shape the rules governing family functioning.

family of origin A person's parents and siblings; usually refers to the original nuclear family of an adult.

family projection process In Bowenian theory, the mechanism by which parental conflicts are projected onto the children or a spouse.

family ritual Technique used by Selvini Palazzoli and her Milan Associates that prescribes a specific act for family members to perform, which is designed to change the family system's rules.

family rules A descriptive term for redundant behavioral patterns.

family sculpting A nonverbal experiential technique in which family members position themselves in a tableau that reveals significant aspects of their perceptions and feelings.

family structure The functional organization of families that determines how family members interact.

family system The family conceived as a collective whole entity made up of individual parts plus the way they function together.

feedback loop The return of a portion of the output of a system, especially when used to maintain the output within predetermined limits (negative feedback), or to signal a need to modify the system (positive feedback).

first-order change Temporary or superficial changes within a system that do not alter the basic organization of the system itself.

first-order cybernetics The idea that an outside observer can study and make changes in a system while remaining separate and independent of that system.

fixation Partial arrest of attachment or mode of behavior from an early stage of development.

formula first-session task Solution-focused therapists routinely ask clients at the end of the first session to think about what they *do not* want to change as a result of therapy. This focuses them on strengths in their lives and begins the solution-generating process.

function of the symptom The idea that symptoms are often ways to distract or otherwise protect family members from threatening conflicts.

functional analysis of behavior In operant behavior therapy, a study of a particular behavior, what elicits it, and what reinforces it.

fusion A blurring of psychological boundaries between self and others and a contamination of emotional and intellectual functioning; opposite of differentiation.

general systems theory A biological model of living systems as whole entities that maintain themselves through continuous input and output from the environment; developed by Ludwig von Bertalanffy.

genogram A schematic diagram of the family system, using squares to represent males, circles to indicate females, horizontal lines for marriages, and vertical lines to indicate children.

group dynamics Interactions among group members that emerge as a result of properties of the group rather than merely their individual personalities.

here-and-now experience Immediate experience, what is felt in the present as opposed to descriptions of what has happened, prized by experiential therapists.

hermeneutics   The art of analyzing literary texts or human experience, understood as fundamentally ambiguous, by interpreting levels of meaning.

hierarchical structure   Family functioning based on clear generational boundaries, where the parents maintain control and authority.

homeostasis   A balanced steady state of equilibrium.

idealization   A tendency to exaggerate the virtues of someone, part of the normal developmental process in children's relationships to their parents and in intimate partnerships.

identification   From psychoanalytic theory, not merely imitation, but appropriation of traits of an admired other.

identified patient (IP)   The symptom-bearer or official patient as identified by the family.

instrumental leader   Decision-making and task functions; in traditional families, the husband's role.

intensity   Minuchin's term for changing maladaptive transactions by using strong affect, repeated intervention, or prolonged pressure.

internal family systems model   A model of the mind that uses systemic principles and techniques to understand and change intrapsychic processes, developed by Richard Schwartz.

internal objects   Mental images and fantasies of oneself and others, formed by early interactions with caregivers.

introjection   A primitive form of identification; taking in aspects of other people, which then become part of the self-image.

invariant prescription   A technique developed by Mara Selvini Palazzoli in which parents are directed to mysteriously sneak away together.

invisible loyalties   Boszormenyi-Nagy's term for unconscious commitments that children take on to help their families.

joining   A structural family therapy term for accepting and accommodating to families to win their confidence and circumvent resistance.

linear causality   The idea that one event is the cause and another is the effect; in behavior, the idea that one behavior is a stimulus, the other a response.

live supervision   Technique of teaching therapy whereby the supervisor observes sessions in progress and contacts the therapist to suggest different strategies and techniques.

managed care   A system in which third-party companies manage insurance costs by regulating the terms of treatment. Managed care companies select providers, set fees, and control who receives treatment and how many sessions they are entitled to.

marital schism   Lidz's term for pathological overt marital conflict.

marital skew   Lidz's term for a pathological marriage in which one spouse dominates the other.

medical family therapy   A form of psychoeducational family therapy involving collaboration with physicians and other health care professionals in the treatment of people with medical problems.

metacommunication   Every message has two levels: report and command; metacommunication is the implied command or qualifying message.

miracle question   Asking clients to imagine how things would be if they woke up tomorrow and their problem was solved. Solution-focused therapists use the miracle question to help clients identify goals and potential solutions.

mirroring   Expression of understanding and acceptance of another's feelings.

modeling   Observational learning.

monadic model   Explanations based on properties of a single person or object: Johnny shoplifts because he is rebellious.

morphogenesis   The process by which a system changes its structure to adapt to new contexts.

multigenerational transmission process   Bowen's concept for the process, occurring over several generations, in which poorly differentiated persons marry equally immature partners, ultimately resulting in children suffering from severe psychological problems.

multiple family group therapy   Treatment of several families at once in a group therapy format; pioneered by Peter Laqueur and Murray Bowen.

multiple impact therapy   An intensive, crisis-oriented form of family therapy developed by Robert MacGregor in which family members are treated in various subgroups by a team of therapists.

mystery questions Questions designed to get clients wondering how their problems got the best of them, which helps to externalize the problems.

mystification Laing's concept that many families distort their children's experience by denying or relabeling it.

narcissism Self-regard. The exaggerated self-regard most people equate with narcissism is pathological narcissism.

narrative therapy An approach to treatment that emphasizes the role of the stories people construct about their experience.

negative feedback Information that signals a system to correct a deviation and restore the status quo.

network therapy A treatment devised by Ross Speck in which a large number of family and friends are assembled to help resolve a patient's problems.

neutrality Selvini Palazzoli's term for balanced acceptance of family members.

nuclear family Parents and their children.

object relations Internalized images of self and others based on early parent–child interactions that determine a person's mode of relationship to other people.

object relations theory Psychoanalytic theory derived from Melanie Klein and developed by the British School (Bion, Fairbairn, Guntrip, Winnicott) that emphasizes relationships and attachment, rather than libidinal and aggressive drives, as the key issues of human concern.

open system A set of interrelated elements that exchange information, energy, and material with the surrounding environment.

operant conditioning A form of learning whereby a person or animal is rewarded for performing certain behaviors; the major approach in most forms of behavior therapy.

ordeals A type of paradoxical intervention in which the client is directed to do something that is more of a hardship than the symptom.

paradox A self-contradictory statement based on a valid deduction from acceptable premises.

paradoxical injunction A technique used in strategic therapy whereby the therapist directs family members to continue their symptomatic behavior. If they conform, they admit control and expose secondary gain; if they rebel, they give up their symptoms.

parental child A child who has been allocated power to take care of younger siblings; adaptive when done deliberately in large or single-parent families, maladaptive when it results from unplanned abdication of parental responsibility.

positive connotation Selvini Palazzoli's technique of ascribing positive motives to family behavior in order to promote family cohesion and avoid resistance to therapy.

positive feedback Information that confirms and reinforces the direction a system is taking.

postmodernism Contemporary antipositivism, viewing knowledge as relative and context-dependent; questions assumptions of objectivity that characterize modern science. In family therapy, challenging the idea of scientific certainty and linked to the method of deconstruction.

preferred view Eron and Lund's term for the way people would like to think of themselves and be seen by others.

Premack principle Using high-probability behavior (preferred activities) to reinforce low-probability behavior (nonpreferred activities).

prescribing the symptom A paradoxical technique that forces a patient to either give up a symptom or admit that it is under voluntary control.

pretend techniques Madanes's playful paradoxical intervention in which family members are asked to pretend to engage in symptomatic behavior. The paradox is if they are pretending to have a symptom, the symptom cannot be real.

problem-saturated stories The usual pessimistic and blaming accounts that clients bring to therapy, which are seen as helping keep them stuck.

process How members of a family or group relate.

projective identification A defense mechanism that operates unconsciously, whereby unwanted aspects of the self are attributed to another person and that person is induced to behave in accordance with these projected attitudes and feelings.

pseudohostility Wynne's term for superficial bickering that masks pathological alignments in schizophrenic families.

pseudomutuality Wynne's term for the facade of family harmony that characterizes many schizophrenic families.

psychoeducational family therapy A type of therapy developed in work with schizophrenics, which emphasizes educating family members to help them understand and cope with a seriously disturbed family member.

quid pro quo Literally, "something for something," an equal exchange or substitution.

reconstruction Reweaving narrative accounts into more palatable and coherent histories.

reflecting team Tom Andersen's technique of having the observing team share their reactions with the family following a session.

reframing Relabeling a family's description of behavior to make it more amenable to therapeutic change; for example, describing someone as "lazy" rather than "depressed."

regression Return to a less-mature level of functioning in the face of stress.

reinforcement An event, behavior, or object that increases the rate of a particular response. A positive reinforcer is an event whose contingent presentation increases the rate of responding; a negative reinforcer is an event whose contingent withdrawal increases the rate of responding.

reinforcement reciprocity Exchanging rewarding behaviors between family members.

relative influence questions Questions designed to explore the extent to which the problem has dominated the client versus how much he or she has been able to control it.

resistance Anything that patients or families do to oppose or retard the progress of therapy.

restraining A strategic technique for overcoming resistance by suggesting that a family not change.

rituals In strategic therapy, a set of prescribed actions designed to change a family system's rules.

role-playing Acting out the parts of important characters to dramatize feelings and practice new ways of relating.

role rehearsal Role-playing desired ways of behaving, especially in couples therapy.

rubber fence Wynne's term for the rigid boundary surrounding many schizophrenic families, which allows only minimal contact with the surrounding community.

scaling questions Solution-focused clients are asked to rate on a 10-point scale how much they want to resolve their problems, how bad the problem is, how much better it is than the last time, and so on. Designed to break change up into small steps.

scapegoat A member of the family, usually the identified patient, who is the object of displaced conflict or criticism.

schemas Underlying core beliefs that an individual has developed about the world and how it functions.

schizophrenogenic mother Frieda Fromm Reichmann's term for aggressive, domineering mothers thought to precipitate schizophrenia in their offspring.

second-order change Basic change in the structure and functioning of a system.

second-order cybernetics The idea that anyone attempting to observe and change a system is therefore part of that system.

self psychology Heinz Kohut's version of psychoanalysis that emphasizes the need for attachment and appreciation.

self object Kohut's term for a person related to not as a separate individual, but as an extension of the self rather than sex and aggression.

separation–individuation Process whereby the infant begins, at about two months, to draw apart from the symbiotic bond with mother and develop his or her autonomous functioning.

shaping Reinforcing change in small steps.

social constructionism Like constructivism, challenges the notion of an objective basis for knowledge. Knowledge and meaning are shaped by culturally shared assumptions.

social learning theory Understanding and treating behavior using principles from social and developmental psychology as well as from learning theory.

solution-focused therapy Steve de Shazer's term for a style of therapy that emphasizes the solutions that families have already developed for their problems.

structure Recurrent patterns of interaction that define and stabilize the shape of relationships.

subsystem Smaller units in families, determined by generation, sex, or function.

symmetrical relationship In relationships, equality or parallel form.

system A group of interrelated elements *plus* the way they function together.

systems theory A generic term for studying a group of related elements that interact as a whole entity; encompasses general systems theory and cybernetics.

theory of social exchange Thibaut and Kelley's theory according to which people strive to maximize rewards and minimize costs in a relationship.

three-generational hypothesis of schizophrenia Bowen's concept that schizophrenia is the end result of low levels of differentiation passed on and amplified across three succeeding generations.

time-out A behavioral technique for extinguishing undesirable behavior by removing the reinforcing consequences of that behavior; typically, making the child sit in a corner or go to his or her room.

token economy A system of rewards using points, which can be accumulated and exchanged for reinforcing items or behaviors.

transference Distorted emotional reactions to present relationships based on unresolved, early family relations.

triadic model Explanations based on the interactions among three people or objects: Johnny shoplifts because his father covertly encourages him to defy his mother.

triangle A three-person system; according to Bowen, the smallest stable unit of human relations.

triangulation Detouring conflict between two people by involving a third person, stabilizing the relationship between the original pair.

unconscious Memories, feelings, and impulses of which a person is unaware. Often used as a noun, but more appropriately limited to use as an adjective.

undifferentiated family ego mass Bowen's early term for emotional "stuck-togetherness" or fusion in the family, especially prominent in schizophrenic families.

unique outcome Michael White's term for times when clients acted free of their problems, even if they were unaware of doing so. Narrative therapists identify unique outcomes as a way to help clients challenge negative views of themselves.

visitor De Shazer's term for a client who does not wish to be part of therapy, does not have a complaint, and does not wish to work on anything.

Appendix C

CAREERS AND TRAINING

Becoming a Family Therapist

There are many paths to becoming a family therapist. Not all of them involve going through an academic program in marital and family therapy, although that's the most direct path. Many people who have a state marital and family therapy (MFT) license or certificate graduated with a more traditional degree—a master's or Ph.D. in clinical psychology, an M.S.W. from a social work program, or a master's in counseling or nursing. Depending on their state's requirements, these therapists, after completing their non-MFT degree, have to take some additional MFT coursework and receive extensive supervision in order to be able to call themselves marital and family therapists. (See the section on licensing that follows.)

Which path you choose should depend on what you want to do in your career. For example, if you hope to teach or do research in family therapy, you would do well to go through a Ph.D. program. If, on the other hand, you primarily want to do clinical practice, either in an agency or in private practice, you may not need a Ph.D. and could go to one of the many master's programs in MFT. (For a list of approved MFT academic programs, contact the American Association for Marriage and Family Therapy, described later.)

If you're interested in studying an aspect of mental health not thoroughly covered in MFT programs, for example, psychological testing, social policy, individual psychotherapy, or psychopharmacology, you could get a non-MFT degree and then pick up the required courses and supervision from one of the many nonacademic family therapy institutes described in the last section of this appendix.

Professional Organizations

The *American Association for Marriage and Family Therapy* (AAMFT), located in Alexandria, Virginia, was organized in 1942 by Lester Dearborn and Ernest Graves as a professional organization to set standards for marriage counselors. In 1970, it was expanded to include family therapists and has become the major credentialing body for the field. Through its requirements for membership, standards have been set for becoming a family therapist that are used by the various states that regulate the profession. AAMFT also lobbies state and federal governments for the interests of family therapists, such as state licensing.

AAMFT's membership has grown enormously, reflecting the growth of the field. The organization has more than doubled since 1982 and now represents more than 24,000 marriage and family therapists. This kind of membership and the money generated from it has made AAMFT a powerful player in mental health politics and has aided in public and governmental recognition of family therapy as a distinct field.

AAMFT has a code of ethics that covers the following issues: responsibility to clients; confidentiality; professional competence and integrity; responsibility to students, employees, supervisees, and research subjects; financial arrangements; and advertising. AAMFT is located at

112 South Alfred Street, Alexandria, VA 22314; telephone: 703-838-9808; website: www.aamft. org.

Although the AAMFT has a presence in California, the dominant organization for MFTs there is the California Association of Marriage and Family Therapists (CAMFT). With twenty-nine regional chapters and 29,000 members, CAMFT's size has given it a strong voice in the state legislature. CAMFT sponsors an annual conference and publishes *The Therapist*. For further information, contact CAMFT, 7901 Raytheon Road, San Diego, CA 92111; telephone: 858-292-2638; website: www.camft.org.

The *American Family Therapy Academy* (AFTA) was organized in 1977 to serve the needs of the field's senior researchers, clinicians, and trainers who wanted a smaller, more intimate context for sharing ideas and developing common interests. Despite high standards for membership regarding years of teaching and clinical experience and an interest in remaining small, AFTA's membership has doubled since 1983, from 500 to over 1,000. AFTA is a high-level think tank focused around its annual conference and its newsletter. For more information, contact the AFTA, 1608 20th Street, NW, 4th Floor, Washington, DC 20009; telephone: 202-483-8001; website: www.afta.org.

The *International Family Therapy Association* (IFTA) was begun in 1987 as a way for family therapists around the globe to connect. Each year, IFTA sponsors the World Family Therapy Congress in a different country. So far the countries that have hosted the congress include Finland, Greece, Holland, Ireland, Israel, Hungary, Mexico, Poland, Germany, the United States, Norway, Brazil, and Slovenia. In addition, IFTA biannually publishes *The International Connection*. The official journal of IFTA is the *Journal of Family Psychotherapy*. IFTA can be reached through: William Hiebert, General Secretary, IFTA, Marriage and Family Counseling Services, 1800 3rd Avenue, Suite 512, Rock Island, IL 61201; telephone: 309-786-4491; website: www.ifta-familytherapy.org.

Conferences

Besides the multitude of workshops or conferences privately sponsored and put on by local chapters of AAMFT, there are four main national meetings. The largest is AAMFT's annual conference each October. With over 200 presentations on various family therapy topics to select from, there is usually something for everyone.

The second largest (over 3,600) is the Psychotherapy Network Symposium held each March in Washington, DC. Sponsored by the *Psychotherapy Networker* magazine (described later), all presenters are invited so that quality throughout the eighty workshops is ensured. Each year, the symposium has a theme, and invited plenary speakers are often famous for work done outside the field of family therapy. For information, telephone 202-537-8950.

AFTA's annual meeting deliberately has a flavor different from that of other conferences. Because of its small size (usually around 300—it's not open to nonmembers), it's the one place where leaders of the field can gather in a relatively informal setting to discuss ideas. Rather than conduct workshops, the meeting is organized around interest groups and brief presentations designed to promote dialogue and debate.

The other conference where many family therapists can be found isn't devoted exclusively to family therapy. The American Orthopsychiatric Association is a multidisciplinary organization whose annual conference usually contains a sizable percentage of presentations devoted to family therapy and issues of interest to systems-oriented clinicians.

Publications

The first book devoted entirely to the diagnosis and treatment of families was Nathan Ackerman's the *Psychodynamics of Family Life*, published in 1958. The field's first journal, *Family Process*, was founded in 1961. Since these early publications, the family therapy literature has proliferated to the point where it is virtually impossible to stay on top of it. Over twenty journals or newsletters are devoted to some aspect of family therapy published in the United States, with many other countries publishing their own journals. The number of books is equally overwhelming, so refer to Appendix A for a selective guide to some of the most useful books and articles in the field. Some of the major periodicals are described in the following discussion.

Family Process continues to exert a powerful influence on the field. Many of the debates and developments described in earlier chapters of this book appeared first in its pages. Founded in 1961 by Don Jackson and Nathan Ackerman, its editors have included Jay Haley, Don Bloch, Carlos Sluzki, Peter Steinglass, and Carol Anderson. The *Journal of Marital and Family Therapy* is also quite influential and, as the official journal of AAMFT, has a large readership. Under the editorship of Alan Gurman during the 1980s and Douglas Sprenkle and Froma Walsh in the 1990s, it increased its focus on research and improved its standards. Current editor, Ronald J. Chenail, is balancing the research and clinical foci.

The *Psychotherapy Networker*, a magazine devoted to issues related to family therapy and psychotherapy in general, also has a strong influence. Its large readership (over 70,000) has been won through tackling provocative issues with high-quality writing. Rich Simon turned what began as a small newsletter into the most widely read publication on psychotherapy and, in so doing, introduced many of family therapy's ideas to therapists throughout the country.

There are a number of other well-established journals that, like *Family Process* and *Journal of Marital and Family Therapy*, are devoted to general issues in the field. These include the *American Journal of Family Therapy*, *Journal of Family Psychotherapy*, *International Journal of Family Therapy*, *Contemporary Family Therapy*, and *Family Therapy Collections*. In addition, a number of specialized journals have emerged. For example, the *Journal of Systemic Therapies* (formerly the *Journal of Strategic and Systemic Therapies*) is widely read by therapists who use

those adjectives to describe themselves, while Bowen systems therapists read *Family Systems* and those interested in Michael White's work subscribe to the *Dulwich Centre Review* and *Family Therapy Case Studies*.

The cross-fertilization of family therapy with other fields is represented by *Families, Systems, and Health*, a journal devoted to the collaboration between medicine and family therapy; by the *Journal of Family Psychology*, published by a division of the American Psychological Association; and by *Feminism and Family Therapy*, which reflects the growing influence of feminist thought on the field.

News within the field and digests of important developments are conveyed through AAMFT's newsletter, *Family Therapy News*, and through the *Brown University Family Therapy Newsletter*. Those interested in the branch of sociology called family studies have much in common with family therapists and read *Family Relations* and the *Journal of Marriage and the Family*.

Licensing

Forty-eight states currently regulate MFTs, and many other states are currently considering licensing bills. Most state requirements for licensure are comparable to the standards for clinical membership in AAMFT. Common requirements include graduation from an accredited marital and family therapy program, two years of postdegree supervised clinical experience, and passing the state exam or the national exam for MFTs, which is conducted by the Association of Marital and Family Therapy Regulatory Board.

Training Centers

As discussed earlier, family therapy developed primarily outside academia. There are, however, a handful of doctoral programs and a larger number of master's degree programs specializing in marital and family therapy in universities around the country. The American Association for Marriage and Family Therapy accredits 105 graduate and postgraduate programs. Because we are aware of no comparable list of the major nonacademic training centers, some of the best-known centers in the United States are described here. Although other major centers exist throughout the world, the space is too limited to list them. The reader may notice that the majority of the centers described are clustered in the Northeast where family therapy is most strongly rooted.

The *Family-Centered Services Project* in the Boston area was founded by William Madsen in 2000 as an attempt to move from simply training family therapists to developing family-centered agencies. This organizational change project offers a mix of clinical and organizational training and consultation as well as ongoing coaching and support. For more information, contact William Madsen, Director, or Philip Decter, Associate Director, The Family-Centered Services Project, 51 Kondazian Street, Watertown, MA 02472; telephone: 617-868-9044.

The *Family Solutions Institute*, originally the *Kantor Institute*, was founded by David Kantor and then reestablished as Family Solutions by Rob Guise and Jackie Gagliardi and Michael Vickers in 1993. The institute is informed by David Kantor's structural/analytic model of therapy, as well as by psychodynamic and other family therapy influences. This institute offers a sequence of three one-year training programs that build on each other but can be taken independently. They also offer a specialized program in couples treatment and in organizational consultation, as well as a variety of apprenticeships, internships, and courses. For more information, contact Rob Guise, 19 Peter Parley Road, Jamaica Plain, MA 02130.

The *Minuchin Center for the Family* is a nonprofit training and consultation institute in New York City, founded in 1981 by Salvador Minuchin. The faculty also includes Amy Bagel, Ema Genijovich, David Greenan, Richard Holm, Wai-Yung Lee, and George Simon. Special programs are designed for onsite training and consultation with agencies that work with poor families, foster care, substance abuse, the homeless, and children in psychiatric facilities. The extern training program is at three levels: beginning family therapists, more experienced therapists, and supervision for supervisors. The orientation emphasizes structural family therapy but has been influenced by feminism and multiculturalism. A summer intensive and one-day workshops offer clinicians with limited time opportunities to study at the center. Inquiries may be directed to Patricia Dowds, Executive Director, 303 Fifth Avenue, Suite 603, New York, NY 10016; website: www. minuchincenter.org.

The *Ackerman Institute for the Family* in New York City was founded as the Family Institute by Nathan Ackerman in 1960. Following Ackerman's death in 1971, the center was renamed in his honor and the directorship was assumed by Donald Bloch, who was followed by Peter Steinglass and now Lois Braverman. The institute's faculty includes noted family therapists Peggy Papp, Jorge Colapinto, Marcia Sheinberg, Peter Fraenkel, Constance Scarf, Marcia Stern, and Evan ImberBlack. The institute offers training in systemic family therapy. It offers a two-year clinical externship program for more experienced family therapists and weekend workshops throughout the year. For further information, contact Marcia Sheinberg, Director of Training and Clinical Services, 149 East 78th Street, New York, NY 10021.

The *Family Institute of Westchester* in Harrison, New York, is directed by Elliott Rosen. The institute teaches the multicontextual approach, which includes aspects of structural and strategic techniques, and is based on the Bowenian model. The institute has been in operation since 1977 and is primarily known for its training program, which usually takes three years to complete. There is also a two-year advanced program that meets weekly. Specialized training programs are offered in multicultural family therapy and therapy with gay and lesbian couples and families.

Additional information is available from Pat Colucci-Coritt, Director of Training, Family Institute of Westchester, 600 Mamaroneck Ave., Suite 303, Harrison, NY 10528.

The *Center for Family Learning* in Rye Brook, New York, was founded in 1973 by Philip Guerin, who was trained by Murray Bowen. The center has maintained a threefold mission for thirty years: the development of family systems models of clinical intervention; postgraduate education in these models; and community education through the mechanism of public meetings and cable television. Postgraduate training is tailored to the specific educational needs of individuals, groups, or organizations. For additional information, contact Patricia Schmolling, Administrator, at 14 Rye Ridge Plaza, Suite 228, Rye Brook, NY 10573; telephone: 914-253-9190; e-mail: PJGuerinM.D.@aol.com.

The *Family Therapy Training Program at the University of Rochester* was established in 1983 by Judith Landau-Stanton and M. Duncan Stanton. This program teaches the Rochester model, an integration of structural, strategic, transgenerational, experiential, and ecosystemic approaches in a series of externships and seminars. Special areas of interest are cultural transition and medical family therapy. Cases are provided for trainees. The faculty includes Lyman Wynne, Susan McDaniel, David Seaburn, and the founders. For more information, contact Pieter le Roux, Director, Family Therapy Training Program, Department of Psychiatry, University of Rochester, 300 Crittenden Boulevard, Rochester, NY 14642-8409.

The *Multicultural Family Institute* was founded in 1991 by its directors, Monica McGoldrick and Nydia Garcia Preto. The institute is committed to training, research, and service in support of cultural diversity and the empowerment of those voices U.S. society silences. In addition to a two-year certificate program and an annual cultural conference, the institute offers a variety of workshops, lectures to the community, and consultation to schools and other organizations.

Minority scholarships are available. Other notable therapists participating on the faculty include Eliana Gil, Paulette Moore Hines, Ken Hardy, Joanne Krestan, and CharlesEtta Sutton. For further information, contact Monica McGoldrick, 328 Denison St., Highland Park, NJ 08904; telephone: 732-565-9010; website: www.MulticulturalFamily.org.

The *International Institute of Object Relations Therapy* is led by codirectors David and Jill Scharff and is located in the suburbs of Washington, DC. Formerly at the Washington School of Psychiatry, the Scharffs are the leading exponents of object relations family therapy. The institute has a variety of training programs, speakers, and workshops, including two-year courses in object relations theory and couple, child, and family therapy. Both programs consist of weekly seminars and two-week summer institutes. In addition to the Scharffs, the faculty includes many distinguished clinicians from throughout the world (notably from the Tavistock Center). In addition to its headquarters in Washington, DC, the institute has satellite programs in Burlington, VT; Charlottesville, VA; Long Island, NY; Manhattan, NY; New Orleans, LA; Omaha, NE; Philadelphia, PA; Salt Lake City, UT; San Diego, CA; and Panama City, the Republic of Panama. For more information, write David Scharff, M.D., and Jill Savege Scharff, M.D., Codirectors, International Institute of Object Relations Therapy, 6612 Kennedy Drive, Chevy Chase, MD 20815-6504; telephone: 301-215-7377; e-mail: iiort@mindspring.com; website: www.iiort.org.

The *Bowen Center for the Study of the Family* (formally *Georgetown Family Center*), founded by Murray Bowen and located in Washington, DC, exists to refine, test, and extend Bowen systems theory. Michael Kerr, Daniel V. Papero, and Ruth Sagar comprise the current board of directors. Training programs include a biweekly postgraduate program and a special program for out-of-towners that meets for three consecutive days, four times a year. Other learning opportunities include the monthly clinical conference, the main symposium in the fall, and the annual spring conference, usually in April. Descriptions of these programs can be found on the center's website: www.thebowencenter.org.

The *Family Therapy Practice Center of Washington, DC*, was founded in 1980 by Marianne Walters after she left the Philadelphia Child Guidance Clinic. The center has a structural family therapy base and offers a postgraduate externship. In addition, the center develops programs for dealing with at-risk populations and changing family structures, such as their adolescent foster care project, family violence assistance project, and runaway youth/multiple family group project. For more information, contact Director of Training, 2153 Newport Place NW, Washington, DC 20037.

The *Philadelphia Child and Family Training Center, Inc.*, was created in the late 1990s to continue the training programs previously conducted at the famous Philadelphia Child Guidance Center. Most of the center's faculty taught at the former institution and worked there with Salvador Minuchin as he developed structural family therapy. The faculty includes notable structural therapists: Marion Lindblad-Goldberg, Edward A. Igle, Ann Itzkowitz, C. Wayne Jones, and Steve Simms. The center runs a two-year, COAMFTE-accredited postgraduate program, a three-week summer practicum, AAMFT-approved correspondence courses, and an AAMFT-approved supervision mentoring course. Traveling faculty conduct training in agencies and institutions nationally and abroad. The center is known for its development of an updated clinical model, ecosystemic structural family therapy, and its use in mental health home-based services and training. For more information, contact Marion Lindblad-Goldberg, Director, Philadelphia Child and Family Therapy Training Center, Inc., P.O. Box 4092, Philadelphia, PA 19118-8092; website: www.philafamily.com.

The *Brief Family Therapy Center* (BFTC) of Milwaukee is known for its specialization in the research, training, and clinical practice of brief, solution-focused therapy. BFTC provides short- and long-term training in solution-focused therapy that attracts practitioners from across North America, Europe, and Asia. The leading figure is Insoo Kim Berg, who presented workshops and seminars in more than thirty countries and wrote extensively on solution-focused therapy. For further information, contact Brief Family Therapy Center, P.O. Box 13736, Milwaukee, WI 53213.

The *Family Institute at Northwestern University* (formerly of Chicago) was founded in 1968 by Charles Kramer to provide training, research, and clinical services. William Pinsof is the president of the institute, which probably has the largest full-time faculty in the country, including notable family therapists Douglas Breunlin, Cheryl Rampage, and Jay Lebow. They offer a variety of training programs grounded in a multilevel, integrative approach. Elements of the approach include integrative problem-centered therapy, the metaframeworks perspective, feminism, and multiculturalism. They offer a two-year certificate program that is accredited by AAMFT, a master's program in family therapy in affiliation with Northwestern University, a one-year clinical training practicum, a psychology internship, a postgraduate fellowship, and a variety of courses, consultation, continuing education workshops, and conferences. In 1994, the institute opened a spacious new facility in Evanston, Illinois. For more information, contact the Family Institute, Bette D. Harris Center, 618 Library Place, Evanston, IL 60201; telephone: 847-733-4300.

The *Chicago Center for Family Health* (CCFH) was begun in 1991 by codirectors John Rolland and Froma Walsh. Affiliated with the University of Chicago, the center's strengths-based family resilience orientation integrates systems theory with a multigenerational family life-cycle framework. In addition to general training in family therapy, CCFH offers specialized training in couples therapy, school-based partnerships, divorce mediation, and family-oriented health care. Training programs include a two-year certificate program, workshops and courses, and consultation groups. Faculty also includes other notable family therapists such as Gene Combs, Jill Freedman, and Tom Todd. For more information, contact CCFH, Suite 1442, 20 North Wacker Drive, Chicago, IL 60606; telephone: 312-372-4731.

The *Mental Research Institute* (MRI) in Palo Alto, California, was founded in 1959 by the late Don Jackson and is considered one of the birthplaces of family therapy. The MRI is best known for its brief therapy approach to families. It offers a wide variety of training programs, including workshops, continuing seminars, and programs in brief therapy and strategic therapy. For further information, contact MRI, 555 Middlefield Road, Palo Alto, CA 94301.

Name Index

Subject Index

Photo Credits

p. 11, Michael Newman/PhotoEdit; p. 21, Ken Whitmore/Getty Images; p. 26, photo courtesy of Wndal Ray. Used with permission of the Jackson Estate and the Don D. Jackson archive; p. 58, Pixland/JupiterImages; p. 60, Bruce Ayres/Getty Images; p. 78, Roy Mahon/Corbis; p. 104, photo courtesy of the Psychotherapy Networker. Used by permission of Monica McGoldrick; p. 109, Tony Freeman/PhotoEdit; p. 114, photo courtesy of and copyright Andrea Maloney Schara, and used with her permission; p. 114, photo courtesy of the Psychotherapy Networker. Used with the permission of Philip J. Geurin; p. 118, photo courtesy of Betty Carter and used with her permission; p. 130, Gary Conner/Phototake; p. 142, photo provided courtesy of the Erikson Fdtn., Inc., and reprinted with their permission; p. 152, photo provided courtesy of the Erikson Fdtn., Inc. Reprinted with permission of Jay Haley; p. 166, photo courtesy of Cloe Madanes and used with her permission; p. 168, photo courtesy of the Psychotherapy Networker. Used with permission of Salvador Minuchin; p. 178, Comstock/Getty Images; p. 194, photo courtesy of the Psychotherapy Networker. Used with permission of Muriel V. Whitaker; p. 201, photo courtesy of the Psychotherapy Networker. Used with permission of Avanta, The Virginia Satir Network, 2104 SW 152nd Street, #2, Burien, WA 98166. All rights reserved; p. 204, Greg Ceo/Getty Images; p. 208, photo courtesy of the Psychotherapy Networker. Used with permission of Susan Johnson; p. 219, photo courtesy of the Psychotherapy Networker. Used with permission of Jill and David Scharff; p. 222, Creatas /JupiterImages; p. 247, Image Source/Corbis; p. 251, Liz Banfield/Getty Images; p. 253, Roy McMahon/CORBIS; p. 278, photo courtesy of the Psychotherapy Networker. Used with permission of Peggy Papp, Olga Silverstein, Marianne Walters, and Betty Carter; p. 284 left, photo courtesy of the Psychotherapy Networker. Used with permission of Nancy Boyd-Franklin; p. 284 right, photo courtesy of the Psychotherapy Networker. Used with permission of Ken Hardy; p. 286, Michael Newman/PhotoEdit; p. 320, photo courtesy of Steve deShazer and used with his permission; p. 320, photo courtesy of Insoo Kim Berg and used with her permission; p. 348, photo courtesy of Michael White and used with his permission; p. 353, Ellen Senisi / The Image Works; p. 375, photo courtesy of the Psychotherapy Networker. Used with permission of Joe Eron; p. 383, photo courtesy of the Psychotherapy Networker. Used with permission of Virginia Goldner; p. 384, Banana Stock/AGE Fotostock; p. 395, Stockbyte/Getty Images.